# THE ILLUSTRATED
# BIBLE

EDITOR-IN-CHIEF **FATHER MICHAEL COLLINS**

# THE ILLUSTRATED
# BIBLE

## RETOLD AND EXPLAINED

FROM THE CREATION TO THE RESURRECTION

## LONDON, NEW YORK, MELBOURNE, MUNICH, AND DELHI

### DORLING KINDERSLEY LONDON

**Project Art Editors**
Francis Wong, Duncan Turner

**Project Editor**
Ruth O'Rourke-Jones

**Senior Art Editor**
Ina Stradins

**Senior Editor**
Angeles Gavira

**Designer**
Fiona Macdonald

**Editor**
Gill Pitts

**Production Editors**
Joanna Byrne, Ben Marcus

**Senior Production Controller**
Erika Pepe

**Creative Technical Support**
Adam Brackenbury

**Jacket Designer**
Mark Cavanagh

**Jacket Editor**
Manisha Majithia

**Jacket Design Development Manager**
Sophia MT Turner

**Cartographer**
Ed Merritt

**Picture Researcher**
Liz Moore

**Managing Art Editor**
Michelle Baxter

**Managing Editor**
Camilla Hallinan

**Publisher**
Sarah Larter

**Art Director**
Phil Ormerod

**Associate Publishing Director**
Liz Wheeler

**Publishing Director**
Jonathan Metcalf

### DORLING KINDERSLEY INDIA

**Designers**
Anuj Sharma, Amit Malhotra, Parul Gambhir, Arijit Ganguly, Shreya Anand Virmani, Arushi Nayyar

**Editors**
Dharini Ganesh, Parameshwari Sircar

**Project Designer**
Devika Dwarkadas

**Senior Editor**
Alka Ranjan

**Deputy Managing Art Editor**
Mitun Banerjee

**Managing Editor**
Rohan Sinha

**Consultant Art Director**
Shefali Upadhyay

**Senior DTP Designer**
Harish Aggarwal

**DTP Designers**
Neeraj Bhatia, Vishal Bhatia, Jagtar Singh

**DTP Manager/CTS**
Balwant Singh

**Production Manager**
Pankaj Sharma

### cobaltid

The Stables, Wood Farm, Deopham Road,
Attleborough, Norfolk NR17 1AJ
www.cobaltid.co.uk

**Art Editors**
Paul Reid, Darren Bland

**Picture Research**
Louise Thomas

**Editors**
Marek Walisiewicz, Richard Gilbert,
Christopher Westhorpe, Sarah Tomley,
Susan Malyan, Kati Dye, Moire Lennox,
Jemima Dunne

First published in Great Britain in 2012
by Dorling Kindersley Limited
80 Strand, London WC2R 0RL

Penguin Group (UK)
6 8 10 9 7

012-180670-Mar/2012

A CIP catalogue record for this book is available from the
British Library.

ISBN: 978-1-4053-9138-2

Reproduction by Colourscan, Singapore
Printed and bound in Hong Kong

Discover more at
**www.dk.com**

## EDITOR-IN-CHIEF

### Father Michael Collins

Studied Philosophy, Greek, and Roman Civilization at University College Dublin and graduated from the Pontifical Institute of Christian Archeology. Among his publications is DK's *Vatican*.

## CONSULTANTS

### Dr Debra Reid

Director of Online Learning and Tutor in Old Testament, Spurgeon's College, London, UK, which specializes in training for service within the Baptist denomination.

### Revd Dr Michael Thompson

Vice-Principal, Ridley Hall, an Anglican theological college, Lecturer in New Testament Studies in the Cambridge Theological Federation, UK, and an Episcopal priest.

## PRINCIPAL CONTRIBUTORS AND EDITORIAL ADVISERS

### Rev Mike Beaumont

Lecturer in Theology and Pastor, Oxfordshire Community Churches

### Nick Page

Writer and historian

## CONTRIBUTORS

### Dr Derek Tidball

Former Principal, London School of Theology, UK

### Rev Dr Andrew Stobart

Minister, Darlington Methodist Circuit, UK

### David Perry, M.Div.

Dean of Theology, King's Theological College, Oxford, UK

### Martin Manser

Writer and Editorial Consultant

## SPECIALIST CONSULTANTS

### Dr Richard Harvey

Lecturer in the Hebrew Bible, Hebrew language, and Jewish studies at All Nations
Chri

### Dal Schindell

Director of Publications, Instructor in Christianity and Art, Regent College,
Vancouver, British Columbia, Canada

### Dr Rupert Chapman

Honorary Secretary of the Palestine Exploration Fund, UK

### Dr Jonathan Stökl

Research Associate, Department of History, University College London, UK

# CONTENTS

## THE HISTORY OF THE BIBLE

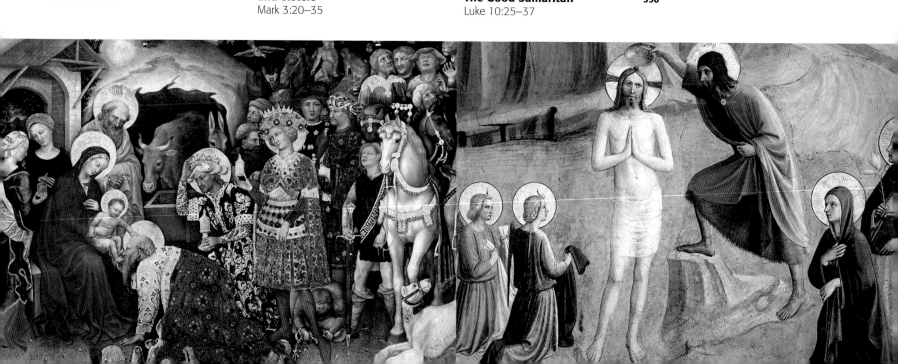

# 4

# Foreword

**T**he Bible is the most famous book in the world. The very name comes from *biblos*, the Greek word for "book". Composed over a period of more than a thousand years, no other work of literature – apart from the Qur'an – has had such impact on human history, or such a lasting hold on our imagination. Its pages are full of poetry, mythical tales, historical accounts, and hymns. Tales of deceit, murder, and war rub shoulders with sublime love stories. Kingdoms are stolen and regained. Treachery and hatred are intertwined with extraordinary feats of forgiveness and redemption.

For many, the Bible is far more than a collection of the greatest stories ever told. More than a third of the world's population believe that the Bible is the word of God or in its origin came from God. Jews, Christians, and Muslims trace their spiritual ancestry to one man, Abraham of Ur, the first great figure of the Old Testament. The central themes of the Bible, although uniquely Judeo-Christian, have much in common with other great religions of the world – including the golden rule of *do unto others as you would have them do to you* as a guide for living, and a belief in an afterlife.

At the heart of human lives for much of history and across many parts of the world, the Bible has also inspired magnificent works of art and sublime music. The sumptuously illustrated manuscripts of medieval monasteries were invariably texts from the Bible. The glorious fresco cycle by Michelangelo in the Vatican's Sistine Chapel in Rome is a spectacularly visual version of the Bible from the creation of the world to the Last Judgment. Composers have drawn from the Bible for oratorios, Passions, Masses, operas, and spirituals. Even our everyday language is peppered with expressions which come from the Bible – *to turn the other cheek, a sign of the times, to the ends of the Earth.*

In the 15th century, the Bible became one of the very first books ever printed and, in whole or in part, it has now been translated into more than 2,000 languages. Over two millennia, belief in the Bible's message has impelled hundreds of thousands of Christians to travel to far lands to spread their faith. The main message of the Bible is about the love which God and his people have for each other. As such, it has inspired countless generations.

Yet for many, the Bible in its traditional form remains a closed book. In *The Illustrated Bible*, our aim has been to bring to life its extraordinary stories, characters, and teachings for the widest possible readership. We consulted with a team of expert scholars and writers, from a variety of denominations and disciplines. We wrote for people from many differing faith backgrounds or none, for those already familiar with the Bible, and for those who know little of it. We sought out the most beautiful and informative illustrations, from maps to old masters, historical artefacts to photographs of the Bible lands today. This is, we hope, a book for everyone and for all time.

*Michael Collins*

**EDITOR-IN-CHIEF**

**SCENES FROM GENESIS**
Michelangelo's fresco on the ceiling of the Sistine Chapel in the Vatican, Rome, was painted between 1508–12. It depicts the creation of man and the expulsion of Adam and Eve from Eden.

IN THE BEGINNING GOD CREATED THE HEAVENS AND THE

WAS OVER THE SURFACE OF THE DEEP, AND THE SPIRIT OF

THERE BE LIGHT", AND THERE WAS LIGHT. GOD SAW THAT

DARKNESS. GOD CALLED THE LIGHT "DAY", AND THE DARK

WAS MORNING – THE FIRST DAY. AND GOD SAID, "LET THER

# 1

# THE HISTORY
# OF THE BIBLE

KTH. NOW THE EARTH WAS FORMLESS

WAS HOVERING OVER THE WATERS

LIGHT WAS GOOD, AND HE SEPARAT

HE CALLED "NIGHT". AND THERE

A VAULT BETWEEN THE WATERS

# From Tablets of Stone

*When examining the history of the Bible, one clue to its origins can be found in its name. The word "Bible" is derived from the Greek "biblia", meaning "books".*

THE BIBLE IS NOT ONE work but a series of books, all of Jewish origin, which were written by many authors over the course of some 1,400 years. The Bibles of Judaism and Christianity differ considerably, but even within the Christian religion, the number and order of books that make up a Bible vary greatly, depending upon whether the version in question is Protestant, Eastern Orthodox, or Roman Catholic.

All Christian Bibles, however, are divided into two parts: the Old and New Testaments. Within each are many types of literature, including history, laws, poetry, prophecy, proverbs, stories, and letters. The first section, which Christians call the Old Testament, contains many sacred writings of Judaism, which are also known as the Hebrew Bible. Jews term this collection the *Tanakh*, which in Judaic tradition is generally divided into three main sections: the five books of the *Torah* (the Pentateuch, also known as the "Law"); the *Nevi'im* ("Prophets"); and the *Ketuvim* ("Writings", or "Hagiographa").

The second section of the Christian Bible consists of the collected scriptures known to Christians as the New Testament. The word "testament" is derived from the late Latin *testamentum*, itself taken from the earlier Greek *diatheke*, which has two meanings: "a covenant or dispensation" and "a testament" or "will". Most Christians associate the word with the former meaning – a covenant – in this instance, one that was granted by God to his chosen people.

This idea of a covenant with God is in fact central to both the Hebrew Bible and the Christian New Testament. It is in the very first book of the Old Testament, the book of Genesis, that God makes a covenant with Abraham, granting him and his descendants the land of Canaan. It is this covenant that Moses renews with God in the book of Exodus following the exile of the Israelites in Egypt, and which Christians believe is finally fulfilled by the death and resurrection of Jesus Christ.

### Languages and subject matter

In addition to having over 40 authors (and some historians think this is a conservative estimate), the books of both Testaments were created in different languages. Initially passed down through generations as a series of oral tales, most books of the Old Testament were written down in Hebrew, with some sections first recorded in Aramaic.

In contrast, the New Testament was written almost entirely in Greek (athough it contains some Aramaic and Latin), which was brought to the region by Alexander the Great in 332 BC.

In broad terms, the "action" described in the books of the Bible presents a history of mankind, from the Earth's creation as recorded in Genesis, the first book of the Old Testament, to a prophetic vision of the end of the world in the final book of the New Testament, known as Revelation. It is a mixture of history, prophecy, and folklore, and contains tales that may have circulated by word of mouth for many centuries before being set down in writing.

Dating biblical tales is therefore a twofold process; dating the text the tale is written in, and looking for evidence within the tale that links it to other known historical facts. For example, the oldest existing fragments of the Hebrew

**THE BOOKS OF MOSES**
According to the Old Testament, God appointed Moses as the deliverer of the Israelites. He also gave him laws written on two stone tablets which, tradition has it, contained the Ten Commandments.

**ARAMAIC BIBLE**
This page of a gospel written in Aramaic was found in the Church of St Thomas, Mosul, Iraq. Aramaic, a Semitic language, is thought to date from the 11th century BC.

**FIRST WRITTEN RECORDS**
The first Bible stories were recorded on many different materials: pottery shards, papyrus, parchment, and clay tablets, such as the one above. This tablet, written in cuneiform script, dates from the 2nd millennium BC.

## EARLIEST BIBLE TALES

Assessing the age of the earliest biblical texts is extremely difficult. The best scholars can do is try to date individual stories and passages, and one way of doing this is by analyzing any artefacts found alongside the text fragments. Another key to a text's age are the historical references within the text itself. For example, Deuteronomy 26:5 begins with the phrase "My father was a wandering Aramean…", which suggests that this section must be very old indeed, given the fact that, in more recent Jewish history, the Arameans were sworn enemies of the Jews.

Another way of assessing the age of a text is to compare its grammar and vocabulary with other ancient, non-biblical sources. A good example of this can be seen in the victory song of Deborah (Judges 5:2–31). Based on its style and language, scholars believe that this could have been written as early as the 12th century BC.

**ST DEBORAH**

Bible, the Dead Sea Scrolls, are understood mainly to date from between 150 BC and 70 AD. However, scholars believe that some of the tales could date to 1200 BC.

## Forms of transmission

The Bible begins with stories: tales of ancestors and heroes, encounters with deities, different accounts preserved by tribes, all of which were passed down through many generations, as part of an oral tradition. The Bible itself reinforces this fact. In Genesis, for example, nothing is mentioned as being written. God speaks and the world is created; verbal promises are given to Abraham, Isaac, and Jacob; all law is conveyed via speech.

Record-keeping is first mentioned in Exodus, the second book of the Old Testament. Here, according to verse 17:14, Moses is instructed to write God's words on a scroll "to be remembered". The most famous account of record-keeping occurs on Mount Sinai, where the laws most Christians know today as the Ten Commandments are described as being engraved on two "tablets of stone inscribed by the finger of God" (Exodus 31:18).

The Bible claims these words came from God. For Christians, this is what makes the Bible different from other religious works. To believers, it is much more than a collection of ancient books: no matter what its exact origins, its words are considered to have been divinely inspired, originating from God.

### BIBLE OF BORSO D'ESTE
Handwritten on vellum (animal skin) between 1455 and 1461, this sumptuous Vulgate Bible was commissioned by Borso d'Este, a 15th-century Italian duke. The book's 1,000 illuminations were painted by five artists, including Taddeo Crivelli and Franco dei Russi, and cost 5,000 lire to produce. A page from the book of Exodus is displayed here.

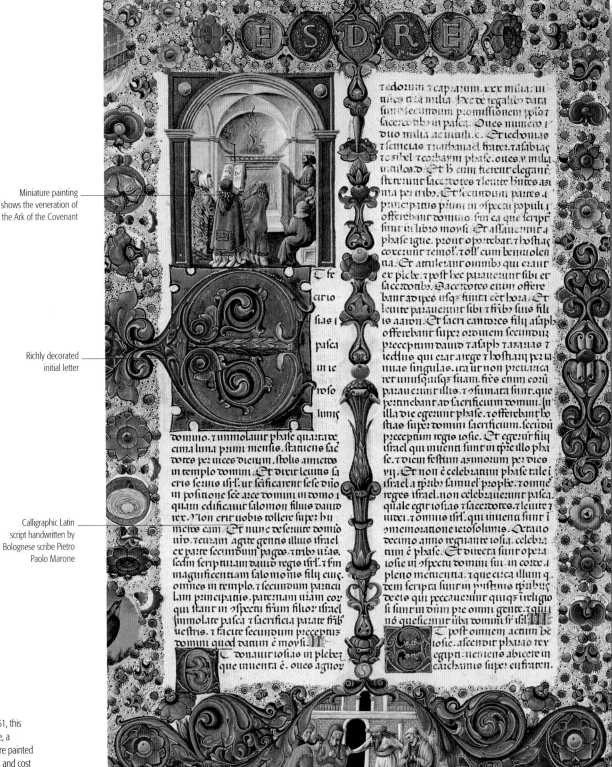

Border decorated with colourful rosettes

Miniature painting shows the veneration of the Ark of the Covenant

Richly decorated initial letter

Calligraphic Latin script handwritten by Bolognese scribe Pietro Paolo Marone

" … Moses went and told the people all the LORD's words and laws… **Moses then wrote down everything the LORD had said.**"

EXODUS 24:3,4

# The Hebrew Scriptures

*The 24 Jewish scriptures known as the Hebrew Bible – called the Old Testament by Christians – consist of sacred works, the majority of which are thought to have been written by various authors between c.1200 and 100 BC.*

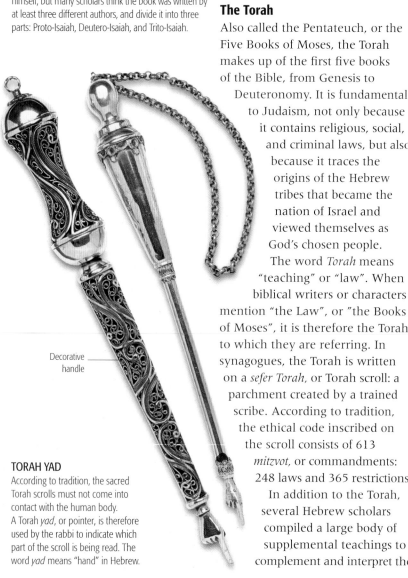

**THE PROPHET ISAIAH**
The Book of Isaiah in the Hebrew Bible and Christian Old Testament is commonly attributed to the prophet himself, but many scholars think the book was written by at least three different authors, and divide it into three parts: Proto-Isaiah, Deutero-Isaiah, and Trito-Isaiah.

**T**RADITIONALLY, THESE works are ordered into three sections: the five books of the Torah, followed by the Nevi'im and the Ketuvim. Modern Jews know this collection as the *Tanakh,* a word derived from the first letters of the names of each of these sections, and each section is further subdivided into various "books" or groups of books. The Hebrew Bible forms a large part of the Christian Bible, and most probably reached its present form during the 2nd century AD.

## The Torah

Also called the Pentateuch, or the Five Books of Moses, the Torah makes up of the first five books of the Bible, from Genesis to Deuteronomy. It is fundamental to Judaism, not only because it contains religious, social, and criminal laws, but also because it traces the origins of the Hebrew tribes that became the nation of Israel and viewed themselves as God's chosen people. The word *Torah* means "teaching" or "law". When biblical writers or characters mention "the Law", or "the Books of Moses", it is therefore the Torah to which they are referring. In synagogues, the Torah is written on a *sefer Torah,* or Torah scroll: a parchment created by a trained scribe. According to tradition, the ethical code inscribed on the scroll consists of 613 *mitzvot,* or commandments: 248 laws and 365 restrictions. In addition to the Torah, several Hebrew scholars compiled a large body of supplemental teachings to complement and interpret the

**TORAH YAD**
According to tradition, the sacred Torah scrolls must not come into contact with the human body. A Torah *yad,* or pointer, is therefore used by the rabbi to indicate which part of the scroll is being read. The word *yad* means "hand" in Hebrew.

Decorative handle

Mythological unicorn

Text set out in diamond shape

Figure of a winged grotesque

> " … I gain understanding from your precepts… **Your word is a lamp for my feet, a light on my path.**"

**PSALMS** 119: 103–105

Floral design

Parchment (or "vellum") made from animal skin

Page design inspires the Christian Kennicott Bible in 1476

**ILLUSTRATION OF HEBREW MANUSCIPTS**
Like Christian Bibles, medieval Jewish religious works were also highly illuminated. This page from the Jewish Cervera Bible, produced in 1299, is decorated in a Gothic style, with animals, grotesques, and floral designs.

laws set down in the Torah. This supplement, the *Mishna* ("repeated study"), was put into its final form in the 3rd century AD, but contains material dating from earlier centuries. Traditionally it is attributed to a rabbi (or eminent teacher) named Judah ha-Nasi (AD 135–220).

From the 3rd to 6th centuries AD, the Mishna itself was studied by two groups of scholars in Babylonia and Israel, and their subsequent analyses and commentaries in turn make up two separate works, each known as the *Gemara* (meaning "completion"). The Mishna and Gemara together form the *Talmud*, the core text of modern Judaism, but because there are two Gemaras, there are also two Talmuds: the Jerusalem (or Palestinian) Talmud and the Babylonian Talmud. Unlike the Torah, which is believed to be a work of divine inspiration, the Gemara is held by both schools to be open to interpretation.

### The Nevi'im

The second section of the Tanakh is the Nevi'im, or "Prophets", which was put into its current form by a rabbinic council in Jamnia (in present-day Israel) in around AD 100. It is divided into two sections.

The "Former Prophets" contains the books of Joshua, Judges, Samuel, and Kings. These relate the history of the Israelites before their exile to Babylon in 586 BC, including the appointment of Joshua as the one who led the Hebrews to the Promised Land.

The books of the "Latter Prophets" include Isaiah, Jeremiah, and Ezekiel, followed by the 12 "Minor Prophets" Hosea, Joel, Amos, Obadiah, Jonah, Micah, Nahum, Habakkuk, Haggai, Zephaniah, Zechariah, and Malachi. The "minor" prophets are so called because of the brevity of their texts, not because they are less important.

### The Ketuvim

The final set of works, called the the Ketuvim, or "Writings", is a diverse collection of material that includes histories (Chronicles, Ezra, and Nehemiah), stories (Ruth, Esther, and Job), poetry (The Song of Songs and Lamentations), and the "Wisdom Books" of Ecclesiastes and Proverbs. There is also Daniel (part history, part prophecy), and the book of Psalms, made up of 150 sacred songs, or poems meant to be sung. The psalms range from meditations on the nature of suffering to expressions of awe at God's creation; many are used in public celebrations at the Temple.

**ANCIENT CITY OF BABYLON**
Many parts of the Old Testament were written or compiled during the time of the Jewish exile in Babylon, c.586–538 BC. Jewish scribes were particularly active in this period, questioning the causes of their captivity, and calling on God to return them to Israel.

## PAPYRUS AND SCROLLS

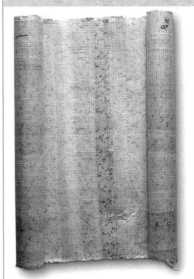

**PAPYRUS SCROLL**

Although official records were often recorded on metal or stone tablets, literary and religious works in the ancient world were often recorded on scrolls. These were created by gluing together strips of papyrus, made from the pith of a particular type of reed, or by stitching together sections of parchment, created from animal skins. Scrolls usually contained more than one column of text per page, and were rarely more than 9m (30ft) in length; any longer and they became too cumbersome to use. Most Old Testament books, as well as some early New Testament works, were written on such scrolls, but parchment *codices*, or collections of pages, gradually replaced these scrolls for ease of use.

HOME OF HIDDEN TEXTS
In the mid-19th century, Konstantine von Tischendorf found the Greek texts known as the *Codex Sinaiticus* here at St Catherine's Monastery, in the Sinai Peninsula, Egypt. Some had been kept in a rubbish bin.

# The Christian Scriptures

*The first followers of Jesus did not possess the writings today's Christians call the New Testament.*
*Their original "Bible" was a Greek translation of the Hebrew books of the Old Testament. It was only*
*in the latter half of the 1st century AD that new, specifically Christian, texts began to appear.*

THE WORKS THAT make up the Christian New Testament seem to have developed in much the same way as those of the Old Testament: as oral traditions that were gradually brought together and set down in writing. Unlike the Old Testament, however, these new scriptures are understood to have been written not over the course of hundreds of years, but in just over a century: between the late 40s AD (within 20 years of the death of Jesus) through to approximately the middle of the 2nd century.

Another difference between the Old and New Testaments is the languages in which they were written. By the time of Jesus, Hebrew, the language of the Old Testament, had given way to Aramaic as the day-to-day language of Israel (although Hebrew was still spoken in synagogues). And yet, in spite of this, most of the New Testament scriptures were written in Greek. The explanation for this lies in the fact that the Mediterranean region had been increasingly "Hellenized", or shaped by Greek culture, since the time of Alexander

the Great (356–323 BC) and his empire. Although the Romans invaded in 63 BC, Greece remained the primary cultural influence in the region in the 1st and 2nd centuries AD, and Greek remained widely spoken. As a result, while the narratives recorded in the New Testament (particularly those claiming knowledge of Jesus' life and teachings) were originally circulated verbally among Christians in Aramaic, they were first set down in writing in Greek. And the type of Greek they were written in was *koiné* or common

Greek, which had become the language of trade throughout the eastern Mediterranean.

## New Testament structure

In modern Christian Bibles, the 27 books of the New Testament are grouped into three categories. First, there are the Gospels and Acts, which claim to provide biographical and historical accounts of the life and teachings of Jesus and the first years of the Church. Then there are the letters, or epistles, attributed variously to apostles, or followers of Jesus,

The New Testament letters, or epistles, make up a third of the New Testament. They were written by various apostles and were addressed to fledgling Christian communities, whether in cities (Corinth) or regions (Galatia), offering advice on matters of faith and conduct. Of the 14 letters attributed to the apostle Paul, four are known as the Prison Epistles, since they were written during his imprisonment in Rome (AD 60–62), and three are called his Pastoral Epistles, since they concern the pastoral oversight of churches. Other letters are ascribed to the apostles Peter, James, Jude, and John, though the authorship of some has been disputed. The absorption of Christianity into society is one of the main themes running through the letters of the New Testament.

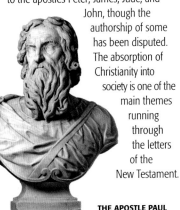

**THE APOSTLE PAUL**

such as Paul, John, and Peter. Finally, there is the book of Revelation, or Apocalypse, with its visionary language.

The arrangement of some of these works has turned out to be unchronological (the Gospel of Mark, for example, is the oldest gospel, although it is inserted after Matthew), and it was many years before they were all collected into the canon, or officially approved selection, that formed a new testament. Indeed, the New Testament canon was not agreed until the late 4th century, but controversy and debate raged among various church leaders surrounding the inclusion of some works until the mid-16th century.

### Chronology of the works

The earliest datable documents do not belong to the first four books (the gospels), but to the 14 letters thought to have been written by the apostle Paul (c.AD 5–67). The earliest is probably 1 Thessalonians, believed to have been written between AD 48 and 52.

**SAINT ATHANASIUS**
Bishop of Alexandria, c.296–373, the Egyptian Athanasius identified the 27 books of the New Testament included in modern Bibles, and promoted the orthodox belief that Christ was divine but possessed a human soul.

Although letters attributed to the apostles circulated among early Christians, the extent to which they were "divinely inspired" has always been hotly debated. Around AD 150, the early Christian apologist St Justin mentioned the importance of the "memoirs of the apostles". Later, Irenaeus, Bishop of Lyons (writing c.170–180) became the first church official to advocate accepting the four gospels as canonical, arguing they alone were "true and reliable". It was also at this time that the Scriptures were divided into Old and New Testaments.

The New Testament took shape gradually; the criteria for inclusion stated scripture should be the work of apostles, or of those associated with them. In AD 367, Bishop Athanasius of Alexandria distributed a list of what he considered acceptable books. Although it was centuries before all branches of Christianity gave it their approval, the content of the New Testament had been established.

Columns indicate text may have been copied from single-column scrolls

Vellum, or scraped animal skin

> "**When you come, bring the cloak** that I left with Carpus at Troas, **and my scrolls, especially the parchments.**"
> **2 TIMOTHY** 4:13

**CODEX VATICANUS**
*Codex Vaticanus* vies with *Codex Sinaiticus* as the oldest complete Bible in the world. Both were produced some time in the fourth century AD. It gets its name from its present home – the Vatican Library – where it has been since at least 1481.

# The Gospel Writers

*The New Testament books of Matthew, Mark, Luke, and John are called the Gospels. Each gives an account of the life, works, death, and resurrection of Jesus, but while three share a similar framework, John stands apart.*

**T**HE WORD GOSPEL is derived from the Old English *gōd spel* or *gōdspell*, which is a translation of the Koine Greek *euangélion*, meaning "good news". To the authors of the New Testament, Jesus was the bringer of the good news of salvation as promised in the Old Testament book of Isaiah (52:7). Indeed, Paul's letters, such as 1 Corinthians (15:1–7), suggest that such a use of *euangélion* had been common for some time. By the 2nd century AD, however, the word was also being used as we use it today: to name a genre of writing devoted to the life and teachings of Jesus.

The four gospels were not the only documents about Jesus to be circulated within the early Church.

Scholars have suggested that there were others, which may have been incorporated into the gospels, including an Aramaic collection of Jesus' sayings and an earlier gospel in Aramaic. The books of Matthew, Mark, Luke, and John are officially recognized as canonical by the Church, not least because each seems to contain memories of the first followers of Jesus, and each relates the Passion – or suffering, crucifixion, and subsequent resurrection – of Christ. For this reason, these four books are also classed as "Passion narratives".

## Dates and authorship

The dating of the gospels, and the order and method of their composition, are still fiercely debated. Many scholars place Mark, Matthew, and Luke's gospels in the 70s AD, with John's significantly later. Others argue for Mark and Luke in the early 60s, Matthew shortly after, and John in the 80s. A further complication is the fact that none of the books' authors are attributed within their respective texts, although John describes himself as "the beloved disciple" (13:1). However, the early Church accepted that two of the gospels' authors were friends of Jesus: Matthew the tax collector, and John (although whether this was John the Apostle or another John is unclear). The other two evangelists were "apostlic men" who did not know Jesus: Mark, a friend of Peter, and Luke, a friend of Paul. Luke was also the author of the Acts of the Apostles; the two books (Luke and Acts) were possibly intended as two volumes of a single work.

**SAINT MATTHEW**
The Gospel of Matthew was once thought to have been the earliest gospel written. Its author was said to have been one of Jesus' original 12 disciples, but many now think Matthew lived later in the 1st century AD.

> **"** Jesus performed many other signs… which are not recorded in this book. But **these are written that you may believe that Jesus is the Messiah**, the Son of God…**"**
>
> **JOHN** 20:30–31

**ROME**
With its emphasis on Jesus' defiance of Roman authority, it is widely believed that the Gospel according to Mark was written in Rome. Mark is generally thought to have been a disciple of Peter and an associate of Paul.

**EPHESUS**
One theory is that the Gospel according to John was written in Ephesus, in Asia Minor, in the latter half of the 1st century AD. Paul is also said to have visited in the 50s AD, accompanied by Luke the Evangelist.

Matthew is portrayed as a winged man, capable of transcendence

Luke is a winged ox, a symbol of duty, sacrifices and strength

Mark's symbol is a winged lion, thought to represent courage

An eagle, a bird once believed to be capable of staring into the sun, represents John

## OTHER GOSPELS

At least 24 other gospels, usually classed as apocryphal, circulated among early Christians, but most of these date from the 2nd century AD onwards, with some believed to have been written as late as the 9th century. While some, such as the Gospel of the Nazoreans (an expanded version of Matthew) and the Gospel of the Ebionites, probably followed the same format as the Synoptic Gospels, most do not. Among the most controversial is the Gospel of Thomas, one of the "sayings gospels", which dates from the mid-2nd century. It includes 114 sayings attributed to Jesus, some of which were classed as "secret" (these include private revelations received in visions), but without a supporting narrative. Fourth-century documents relate a story of finding a Hebrew "Gospel according to Matthew" in India, supposedly left behind by St Bartholomew, one of Jesus' 12 apostles.

**SAINT BARTHOLOMEW**

## The Synoptic Gospels

Matthew, Mark, and Luke are often grouped together by biblical scholars as the Synoptic Gospels, from the Greek *syn* meaning "together" and *optikos* meaning "view". Broadly speaking, they see events from a similar perspective and follow the same format. In fact, in some places, they share verses word for word.

Most scholars agree that Mark is the oldest gospel and the main source for Matthew and Luke. However, as well as having unique verses of their own, Matthew and Luke also share other material – about 230 sayings of Jesus – that is not present in Mark. Scholars suggest this information comes from an unknown source, dubbed "Q"

**ST JOHN'S GOSPEL**
This papyrus fragment of the Gospel of John dates from around AD 200. Although John's is the youngest Gospel, another fragment exists that is the oldest surviving New Testament manuscript.

(from German *Quelle*: "source"). To date, however, no copy of Q has been discovered.

## John's Gospel

The Gospel according to John is different from the Synoptics, in both the order and nature of its material. The author omits much of what is contained in the Synoptics, confining the narrative mainly to Judea. The Synoptic parables are missing, and few miracles are chronicled. Instead, the events John describes are settings for the discourses of Jesus, which are mainly of a mystical nature. The focus of the entire gospel is on the person of the Redeemer; his divinity, and the union of God with his people.

One theory suggests that John's Gospel was written in Ephesus, in what is now Turkey. It is likely that it was written to counter those who were denying the divinity of Christ. Such doubts are known to have spread among Christians towards the end of the 1st century AD.

## THE GOSPEL WRITERS' SYMBOLS
The evangelists are often depicted by symbols, based on a passage in Ezekiel where four "living creatures" draw the throne-chariot of God. This page from the Book of Kells (c.800) is from the Gospel of Matthew.

# Dead Sea Scrolls Rediscovered

*In 1947, in caves on the north-western shore of the Dead Sea, a shepherd boy discovered some ancient manuscripts and text fragments, written mainly in Hebrew. These Dead Sea Scrolls, as they are known, have revolutionized scholars' understanding of the Bible.*

**T**HE 1947 DISCOVERIES, together with subsequent finds near the ruins of the ancient city of Qumran, about 16km (10 miles) south of Jericho, are collectively referred to as the Dead Sea Scrolls. They were written variously on papyrus, vellum, and copper, and some were stored in terracotta jars, lamps, and other pottery items. Dating from the 3rd century BC to the 2nd century AD, the core works are a series of scrolls found in 11 caves near Qumran, thought by many scholars to have been the location of the community that produced them.

The Dead Sea documents contain a range of Jewish literature which, because it was not subject to later editing or censorship, offers an invaluable insight into Jewish society and its beliefs, both before and during the time of Jesus. In addition to secular works, apocryphal texts, and previously unknown psalms, these scrolls include about 100 biblical texts which cover all of the Hebrew Bible (apart from the book of Esther), as well as a 1st-century Greek translation of the Minor Prophets and a version of Leviticus that dates to the 3rd century BC. One of the longest items discovered was a manuscript now known as the "Temple Scroll". This provides detailed instructions for the building of the Temple of Jerusalem, and extensive regulations about temple practice.

While some of the texts are nearly identical to those of the traditional Hebrew Bible, others differ both in language and content. This shows that the Old Testament was a much more varied body of material than had previously been imagined.

## Other discoveries

Fifty years before the discovery of the Dead Sea Scrolls, archaeology had begun to shed light on the worlds of both the Old and New Testaments. One of the most

### NAG HAMMADI

**COVER OF CODEX II**

In 1945, in Upper Egypt, two peasants went hunting for *sabakh*, a soft soil used as a fertilizer, and found a red earthenware jar containing 13 leather-bound papyri made up of 52 texts. These included a substantial number of heretical books dating from AD 350–400, such as gospels attributed to Philip, Thomas, and Mary, and apocalyptic visions attributed to John, Paul, and James. Fragments of Gnostic gospels were recorded in the works of other writers; but until Nag Hammadi, no complete versions had ever been discovered. The Nag Hammadi Library, as the find became known, gives a unique insight into Gnostic belief. The books probably belonged to the nearby monastery of St Pachomius and were buried during a purge of heretical books.

**PUZZLE PIECES**
These fragments, part of the "Community Rule" scroll, deal with laws governing community life. This was one of the first scrolls to be found.

**QUMRAN CAVES**
Many scholars claim that these caves at Qumran, Israel, were the dwelling place of the Essenes (see p.271), a sect of ascetic Jewish scribes who are believed to have written some of the Dead Sea Scrolls. However, the authorship of the scrolls has yet to be conclusively proven, and fierce debate still rages about it today.

Caption: Most of the Dead Sea Scrolls were written on vellum

## SCHOLARSHIP

Although only a handful of the Dead Sea Scrolls were found intact, scholars have managed to reconstruct around 850 different manuscripts of various lengths from the fragments found in the caves of Qumran. The discovery of the Dead Sea Scrolls pushed the date of the earliest Bible copies back by almost a thousand years. By studying them, scholars can determine how the Bible was recorded, and in what forms it was transmitted through the centuries. For example, parts of the Dead Sea Scrolls texts are similar to those of modern Hebrew Bibles, but differences between the two can help resolve problems in translations; in fact, many modern Bibles now incorporate some of the information derived from the scrolls. The scrolls also shed light on the Judaism of Jesus' day, showing that it was more diverse and complex than previously thought.

**ANALYZING THE DEAD SEA SCROLLS**

important finds occurred in Egypt, at Oxyrhynchus, where, beginning in 1897, archaeologists unearthed an ancient rubbish dump. In it they found thousands of papyrus fragments: wills, shopping lists, letters, and other everyday writings, all recorded in Koine Greek. Alongside them, and written in the same everyday Greek, was an astounding number of Old and New Testament fragments, as well as other early Christian literature, including material from non-canonical gospels and early hymns, dating variously from the 1st to the 6th centuries AD. The Oxyrhynchus finds contained fragments from an unparalleled number of different copies of the New Testament books. They also provided vital information about the development of early Christian churches – particularly the unorthodox branches.

Before the 1900s, information about supposed heretical Christian groups was limited mainly to the works of Irenaeus, 2nd-century bishop of Lyon, and other heresiologists (Christian authors describing unorthodox groups). In 1945, however, this changed dramatically with the discovery of 12 codices and parts of a 13th near the town of Nag Hammadi in Egypt (see box, left). Dating mainly from the 4th century, the Nag Hammadi texts contain Coptic (late Egyptian) translations of more than 48 manuscripts, including supposed "secret sayings" of Jesus, theological treatises, and Gnostic myths (see p.461). Many of these works were known to have been condemned by Irenaeus (see p.19) and others. Gnostic and other unorthodox writers were one of the factors which led to the gradual formation of the canonical New Testament. Their beliefs forced Church leaders to decide which books were reliable, authentic, and therefore canonical. Bishop Marcion of Sinope (c.85–160), for example, on studying Jewish Scriptures and early Christian teachings, concluded that Judaism and Christianity were incompatible. It was he who proposed the first canon of the New Testament – but this consisted of only 11 books, from which all references to Judaism and Jesus' childhood had been removed. It was St Athanasius, Bishop of Alexandria, who first listed today's New Testament canon, in 367.

> ❝ I warn everyone who hears the words of… this scroll: **if anyone adds anything to them, God will add to that person the plagues** described in this scroll. ❞
> **REVELATION** 22:18

### SHRINE OF THE BOOK
Part of the Israel Museum in Jerusalem, the Shrine of the Book houses most of the Dead Sea Scrolls. Some of the least fragile texts are on display to the public.

# The Bible in the World

*Although no one knows exactly how many copies have been printed, sold, or distributed, the Bible is generally considered to be the bestselling book of all time. Until the Reformation, however, it was the preserve of an educated elite.*

**ST JEROME**

A priest, theologian, and historian, St Jerome translated the Bible into Latin. His text – known as the Vulgate – became the official Latin version of the Roman Catholic Church, and formed the basis for all subsequent translations in the West for over 1,000 years.

## THE BIBLE AS INSPIRATION

**ORIGINAL SCORE OF HANDEL'S *MESSIAH* (1741)**

The Bible has probably influenced the Western world more than any other book throughout history. Images and ideas from its pages fill Western culture. Much of the world's fine art was commissioned by the Church: nearly one-third of the paintings in the National Gallery, London, are of biblical scenes. Musical notation was developed in European monasteries for Gregorian chant, which includes the singing of psalms, and classical music is full of chorales, oratorios, and requiems that draw on scriptural verses and stories – Handel's *Messiah* is just one example. Literature, too, is full of references to the Bible, from Dante's *Inferno* to Blake's *Songs of Innocence and of Experience*. Even modern pop songs boast titles such as *Hallelujah*, while films such as *The Ten Commandments* and *The Seventh Seal* take both their names and themes from the Bible.

FOR CENTURIES THE Bible was transcribed by hand. In 382 AD, for example, Eusebius Hieronymus, usually known as St Jerome, was commissioned by Pope Damasus to produce a Latin version of the Bible from various translations. Jerome's revised Latin Gospels appeared around 383, followed by Latin translations of parts of the Greek Septuagint version of the Old Testament, including the Psalms and the book of Job.

Eventually, disatisfied with his efforts, Jerome translated the entire Old Testament from the original Hebrew, completing the project around 405. This became the official version of the Western church, and was known as the Vulgate – the *versio vulgata*, or "common version". It became the standard translation used by Western Christianity for the next thousand years.

As the Eastern, Byzantine Empire weakened in the 13th century, scholars moved west, taking with them ancient manuscripts that included texts of the Greek and Hebrew Bible. Any translations that were made from these, however, remained in the official Latin Vulgate sanctioned by the Church.

### Accessibility and printings

From the mid-1370s, John Wycliffe, a lay preacher and doctor of divinity at Oxford University, England, began to attack what he saw as the corruption of the Roman Catholic

**GUTENBERG BIBLE**

The Gutenberg Bible is the earliest known book printed on Johannes Gutenberg's mechanical movable-type printing press. It is also known as the 42-Line Bible, due to the fact that most pages were set out in 42 lines of type.

Church. He also believed that the Bible should be accessible to the common man in the language of the people, as opposed to Latin Vulgate, the language of scholarship. To that end, Wycliffe and his followers created the first complete translation of the Bible into English.

However, Wycliffe's views were considered seditious by the Church, and the Wycliffe Bible was banned in England in 1407. In Europe, meanwhile, other vernacular (native-language) Bibles were discouraged by church authorities, but were never declared illegal.

Pages were made of vellum or paper

Oil-based ink was developed to suit Gutenberg's metal typefaces

## Printing and translations

In the 1450s, the world changed dramatically when, in Mainz, Germany, Johannes Gutenberg invented the printing press. The edition of the Bible he produced c.1455 was the first to be printed with movable type. Printing made the Bible more accessible (if still expensive at first), but Latin Vulgate was still the only language sanctioned by the Church.

In 1516, Dutch humanist and scholar Desiderius Erasmus published an edition of the Greek New Testament with an accompanying Latin translation. Drawn from a variety of manuscripts, rather than from a single text, it marked the beginning of the ongoing quest by scholars to provide the most accurate edition of the Bible possible.

Accuracy, however, wasn't the only concern of biblical scholars. Learned theologians such as Martin Luther (1483–1546) came to believe that the Bible alone was the source of Christian truth, and as such it deserved to be understood by everyone. The result of his conviction was not only a split with the Roman Catholic Church that gave rise to Protestantism, but also a translation of the New Testament into vernacular

**" … go and make disciples of all nations, baptizing them in the name of the Father and of the Son and of the Holy Spirit…"**

MATTHEW 28:19–20

German. This, combined with the advent of the printing press, paved the way for the creation of Bible translations in many languages.

### King James and beyond

In England, however, translation of the Bible into the vernacular remained illegal. In 1524, scholar William Tyndale went to Germany to create a translation of the New Testament in English, and the book was smuggled into England from 1525. Tyndale was executed for heresy before completing his English Old Testament, but the movement he had begun could not be stopped: his English Bible was officially approved by Henry VIII, and became the model for the 1611 King James Version.

Since then, the Bible has become one of the world's most influential books – as well as one of its most translated. When Luther translated the Bible into German, only around 15 other translations had been made. That figure had risen to 40 by 1600, and to 52 by 1700. By 1800, due to the creation of various national Bible societies, parts of the Bible were available in more then 500 languages. By 1950, that number had risen to more than 1,100, and by the 21st century it was more than 2,000.

Today, the Bible has also moved from standard book form into other media, including online, ebook, and audio versions. Altogether, it is estimated that some 50 Bibles are now sold every minute.

Illumination was still done by hand

Spacious margin allowed for decoration to be added

gen esis

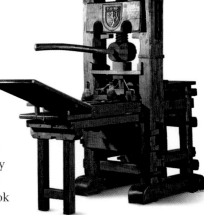

**GUTENBERG PRESS**
The invention of the printing press played a crucial role in shaping not just the history of books and printing in general, but the history of the Bible as well.

### LANGUAGE AND THE BIBLE

Translation into other languages must also take cultural differences into account. When Bishop Ulfilas (c.311–382) translated the Bible for the Germanic Goths, he had to invent the Gothic alphabet. Because crosses were unknown in Gothic culture, he used the word "pole" to suggest a suitable image. Similarly, St Cyril (827–869) invented an alphabet to bring Christian verses to the Slavs, and this became the basis for the Cyrillic alphabet.

**CYRILLIC BIBLE**

GENESIS · EXODUS · LEVITICUS · NUMBERS · DEUTERONOMY

SAMUEL · 1 KINGS · 2 KINGS · 1 CHRONICLES · 2 CHRONICLES

PSALMS · PROVERBS · ECCLESIASTES · SONG OF SONGS · ISAI

EZEKIEL · DANIEL · HOSEA · JOEL · AMOS · OBADIAH · JONAI

ZEPHANIAH · HAGGAI · ZECHARIAH · MALACHI

# 2

# THE OLD
# TESTAMENT

# Old Testament Lands

*The drama of the Old Testament takes place in a region known as the Fertile Crescent. This is an arc of relatively well-watered land stretching from Egypt in the south, northwards through Canaan and Phoenicia, and eastwards through Mesopotamia.*

**T**HE FERTILE CRESCENT is often called the Cradle of Civilization, for it was here, at around 9000 BC, that the first Neolithic farming settlements were established. As agriculture flourished, so did towns and cities, and trade routes became vital arteries connecting communities. One such artery passed through Canaan, a land that stood at the crossroads between Asia, Africa, and Europe. Due to its economic and strategic importance, this area was fought over by numerous powers during the Old Testament period, the most dominant being Egypt, Assyria, and Babylon.

In the Bible, this was the Promised Land awarded by God to Abraham and his descendants. God revealed his intentions for the Israelites in the form of the Law, after they had fled famine in Canaan, endured slavery in Egypt, and were being led back to Canaan by Moses, the prophet to whom the Law was given when he received the Ten Commandments.

After the rule of David and Solomon, the land of Canaan was divided into two: the northern kingdom, called Israel, and the southern kindom, called Judah. Israel eventually fell to the Assyrians in 722 BC, and Judah to the Babylonians in c.587 BC. By the end of the Old Testament period, the Israelites were in disarray. Though the Temple of Jerusalem was rebuilt by 516 BC, many questioned their covenant with God; the New Testament would see its affirmation.

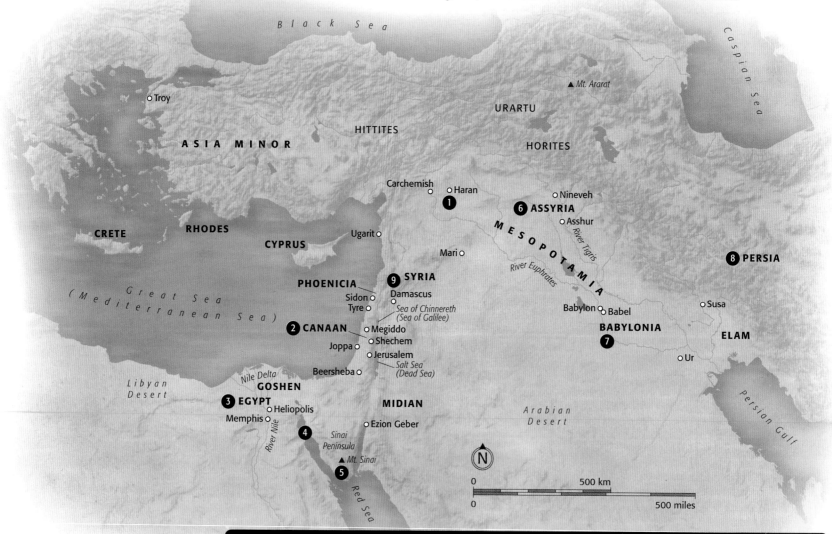

## CROSSROADS OF THE ANCIENT WORLD
The lands of the Old Testament stretch from Asia Minor (present-day Turkey) to the Red Sea, and from Persia (present-day Iran) to Egypt. The events described in the Bible unfold against the backdrop of the struggle between Egypt, Assyria, and Babylon, for control of territory and lucrative trade routes through Canaan.

**KEY**

**1** Haran is the Assyrian city in which God promised the land of Canaan to Abraham (see p.48).

**2** Jacob's family travelled from Canaan to Egypt to escape famine (see pp.88–91).

**3** Moses led the Israelites from slavery in Egypt back to Canaan (see pp.96–115).

**4** The Red Sea divided to allow the Israelites to escape from Egypt to Canaan (see pp.102–03).

**5** Moses received the Ten Commandments on Mount Sinai (see pp106–07).

**6** Assyria defeated Israel in 722 BC, taking thousands of Israelites into captivity (see p.220).

**7** The Babylonians supplanted the Assyrian Empire, taking control of Judah in c.612 BC (see pp.236–39).

**8** The Persian defeat of the Babylonians freed the Israelites from captivity in 538 BC (see pp.252–53).

**9** The Syrian-based Seleucid dynasty took control of Judea in 198 BC (see pp.266–67).

## THE PROMISED LAND

The book of Exodus defines the land promised to Abraham and his descendants as stretching from Egypt and the Red Sea to the River Euphrates in Mesopotamia. It was called Canaan. The Israelites never conquered the northern part of this territory; at their fullest extent, the kingdoms of Israel and Judah occupied a narrow belt of land between the desert on the east and the Mediterranean on the west.

Sidon

Damascus

P H O E N I C I A

Mt. Hermon ▲

Tyre

Dan
(Laish)

A R A M

Kedesh

Lake Huleh
(Lake Merom)

Merom

Hazor

B A S H A N

Acco

Aphek

Sea of Chinnereth
(Sea of Galilee)

Ashtaroth

**1** Mt. Carmel

Golan

▲ Mt. Tabor

Endor

River Yarmuk

Dor

▲ Mt. Moreh

Megiddo

**3** Jezreel

G I L E A D

**2**

Beth-shan

Ramoth
Gilead

Mt. Gilboa ▲

River Jordan

Dothan

S A M A R I A

Samaria **4**

Tirzah

**5**

Mt. Ebal ▲

**6**

Shechem **7**

Mt. Gerizim ▲

Penuel

River Jabbok

Mahanaim

Joppa

I S R A E L

Plain of Sharon

**8** Shiloh

Jogbehah

**9**

Bethel

Ai

**10**

Rabbah
(Amman)

Gezer

Gilgal

A M M O N

Gibeon

Jericho

Ekron

**12**

**11**

Ashdod

Beth-shemesh

Jerusalem

Heshbon

Gath

Bethlehem

Beth Jeshimoth

Ashkelon

Shephelah

J U D A H

▲ Mt. Nebo

Gaza

Eglon

Hebron

Plain of Philistia

Lachish

**13**

Salt Sea
(Dead Sea)

Makkedah

River Arnon

Aroer

P H I L I S T I A

Debir

En-gedi

M O A B

Beersheba

**14**

I D U M A E A

Kir-hareseth

The  N e g e v

(  M e d i t e r r a n e a n   S e a  )

( G r e a t   S e a )

### KEY

**1** Elijah demonstrated the power of Yahweh over Baal on Mount Carmel (see pp.198–99).

**2** Megiddo is where Josiah died fighting the armies of the Egyptian Pharoah Neco (see pp.232–33).

**3** Jezreel was the location of one of the palaces of King Ahab of Israel (see pp.194–205).

**4** Samaria was the capital of the northern kingdom of Israel (see pp.208–09).

**5** Joshua built an altar on Mount Ebal. Here he gave his people the choice either to obey God or to be punished (see p.122).

**6** Jacob wrestled with the angel of God at Penuel, near the River Jabbok (see pp.76–77).

**7** Shechem is where Joshua gathered the tribes of Israel to renew their promise to worship God (see p.125).

**8** Shiloh is where the Tabernacle was erected (see pp.112–13).

**9** At Bethel, Jacob dreamed of a ladder leading from Earth to Heaven (see pp.70–71).

**10** Joshua led the Israelites across the River Jordan into the Promised Land (see p.121).

**11** Jericho was the first city to be taken by the Israelites on reaching the Promised Land (see pp.122–23).

**12** Jerusalem was the capital of the southern kingdom of Judah and the site of the Temple (see pp.162–63).

**13** King David ruled from Hebron until he took Jerusalem, which he made his capital (see pp.78–79).

**14** Beersheba is where Abraham, Isaac, Jacob, and Elijah all had encounters with God.

**CANAAN VIEWED FROM MOUNT NEBO**

N

0   25 km

0   25 miles

# BEGINNINGS

"**In the beginning God created the heavens and the earth.** Now the earth was
formless and empty, darkness was over the surface of the deep, **and the Spirit of God
was hovering over the waters.**"

**THE CREATION OF ADAM**
This panel, painted in c1510, from Michelangelo's fresco on the ceiling of the Sistine Chapel, depicts man made in God's likeness. Adam reaches out to God, who leans towards him; their outstretched fingers suggest vital energy passing into the created.

 HE BIBLE BEGINS WITH THE BOOK OF GENESIS, the name of which derives from the Greek *gignesthai* ("origin", from the Hebrew *Bereishit*, "in the beginning"), setting the stage on which the story of God and his people will be played out. The great questions of life are introduced – the origin of creation, of humanity, and of sin – as well as God's desire to put things right once the perfect world was spoiled. The story opens not with human beings, but with God. His existence is taken for granted; he brings all creation into being by merely speaking a command.

This creation, or coming into being through the divine word, is described as not a chance affair, but an orderly process that climaxes in the creation of human beings. Humans differ from animals in one key aspect – they are made following the likeness of God, who breathed his own life into them: "… in the image of God he created them; male and female he created them" (Genesis 1:27).

**THE FALL**
According to the story told in Genesis, Adam, the first man, and Eve, the first woman, enjoyed a close relationship with God in the idyllic Garden of Eden. But before long, in response to the enticement of Satan in the guise of an evil serpent, they chose to contravene the one restriction that God had given them. After their sin, or transgression of God's law, Adam and Eve's relationship with God was fractured, their interaction with creation changed, they could no longer live in the garden where they had been placed, and their relationship with one another was marred.

**OUT OF EDEN**
Adam and Eve's family grew after leaving Eden, but sin continued to blight their lives. Cain, the oldest son of Adam and Eve, killed his brother Abel. Although there were positive developments, such as music and metalwork, God lost patience with human beings because of their wickedness and violence. Despite grieving over his creation, God decided to wipe out humanity by means of a flood, but he spared one family on whom the future of the world would depend. Noah, chosen because he was "a righteous man" (6:9), obeyed God's command to build an ark, or boat, in the desert. Here he preserved his family, along with the Earth's animals, securing a future for God's creation.

**AFTER THE FLOOD**
The flood receded, marking a new beginning for humanity, but sin continued to corrupt the goodness of God's creation. Noah's three sons were to give rise to the nations and territories of the region. However, they were not always faithful to God or their father.

The challenge made to divine authority by the sons' descendants was typified by the building of a tower at Babel in an attempt to reach heaven. God intervened, worried by what a homogenous group of people were accomplishing. To thwart such co-operation in the future, he caused people to speak in different languages and then he scattered them over the Earth.

**NOAH'S ARK**
This illustration from a 12th-century Bible depicts Noah's family and the ark, which God had commanded Noah to build to save himself, his family, and the animals of the world.

## BEFORE

God is the starting point for all of time and creation, but according to Genesis, he himself is without beginning.

### ETERNAL CREATOR

In Genesis God's existence is assumed, and **no attempt is made to explain him or his origins**. God brings the world into being, not by manufacturing something out of existing raw materials, but by creating it from nothing. "Creates" is a verb the Bible **only ever uses to describe God's activity**.

### ORIGINS OF GENESIS

The **earliest sources for Genesis** are thought to date from the 1st millennium BC. While traditions dating to the 6th century BC **attributed authorship to Moses**, modern scholarship argues that Genesis was **compiled from several sources and authors** at different periods of Israel's history, from the early **divided monarchy 192–93 ❯❯** to the **post-exile period 252–53 ❯❯**. The clues lie in Hebrew words and expressions that are identifiable to distinct historical periods. Genesis as we know it is **thought to have taken its current form** in the 5th century BC.

**HEBREW BOOK OF GENESIS, 14TH CENTURY AD**

# Creation

*The majestic opening chapter of the Bible tells the story of God's creation of the world in six days, culminating in the creation of the first man and woman. On the seventh day God rested, satisfied that all he had made was good.*

THE BIBLE begins with a creation narrative that sets out God's authorship of an ordered and coherent world, but also hints at the mysterious nature of the creator. There is no way to go further back than "In the beginning God…" (Genesis 1:1). No reference is made to him having an origin: he just is (see panel, left). Everything else started from him – God is a creator by nature so did not choose a solitary existence – and he brought the world to life.

God's first act of creation was to bring into being the cosmos and the Earth, but it was a dark, watery, shapeless, and uninhabited place: "the earth was formless and empty, darkness was over the surface of the deep, and the Spirit of God was hovering over the waters" (1:2). God's Spirit stirred, setting in motion the events by which the creation that we recognize would spring into being.

### A good creation

Genesis tells us that God's act of creation occurred in an orderly fashion. On the first day he spoke the words "Let there be light" (1:3), which separated the light from the darkness to form day and night. The events of the day then drew to a close with a phrase that recurs throughout the creation story: "And there was evening, and there was morning – the first day" (1:5).

On the second day, God separated the waters on the surface of the Earth from the waters above it. He spoke the command "Let there be a vault between the waters to separate water from water" (1:6), creating an expanse that he named "sky".

On the third day, God said "Let the water under the sky be gathered to one place, and let dry ground appear" (1:9). He separated dry land from the water to form continents and oceans, and also planted trees, fruit, vegetables, and

> " God saw **all that he had made**, and it was **very good**. "
>
> GENESIS 1:31

## SYMBOLS

### THE NUMBER SEVEN

In the Bible, the number seven – *zayin* in Hebrew – is more than just the digit that comes after six.

God rested on the seventh day because creation was complete (Genesis 2:3), and from then on, the number seven in Judaism came to signify completion, fullness, or perfection.

Israel organized aspects of its religious celebrations (see pp.318–19), such as the seven-day long Feast of Tabernacles, and designed some of its artefacts – such as the Menorah, a seven-branched candlestick (see pp.113) – based on the number seven.

**JEWISH MENORAH**

other plants. The empty land was transformed into a vibrant, flourishing world.

God's words alone were enough to bring creation into being. All he had to do was say, "Let there be…", and it happened. At the end of the third day, God declared that what he had made was "good".

### Heavens and earth

On the fourth day, God fixed the stars in the sky and created the Sun and Moon, "to govern the day and the night, and to separate light from darkness" (1:18). On the fifth day, he returned to the sea and sky and populated them with fishes and birds, commanding "Let the water teem with living creatures, and let birds fly above

## HISTORY AND CULTURE
### CREATION STORIES IN THE ANCIENT WORLD

EGYPTIAN PAPYRUS DEPICTING THE SKY GODDESS, NUT, RISING OVER THE EARTH GOD, GEB.

Stories of creation are found in a number of different cultures in the ancient world, such as Egyptian myths involving multiple deities. The *Enuma Elish* creation story from 12th-century BC Babylon also bears similarities to Genesis – such as creation bringing order out of chaos – but the nature of God differs markedly. The gods fight in *Enuma Elish*, resulting in the death of the goddess Tiamat. Marduk – the

chief god – creates the heavens and Earth out of the two halves of her corpse. He creates human beings, with assistance, from clay and the blood of one of Tiamat's allies. In this story, humans are created as slaves without any dignity. In Genesis, God creates alone and from scratch – simply by the power of his word – giving humanity a significant and dignified role in the maintenance of creation.

> # "Thus the heavens and the earth were completed in all their vast array."
>
> GENESIS 2:1

the earth across the vault of the sky" (1:20). God blessed them, saying "Be fruitful and increase in number, and fill the water in the seas, and let the birds increase on the earth" (1:22).

On the sixth day, God created animals to live on the Earth. From his imagination he created a vast array of different animals, but the best of all was left till last. None of these animals adequately reflected him, "So God created mankind in his own image, in the image of God he created them; male and female he created them" (1:26). Here, finally, was a creature capable of enjoying a close,

#### CREATION OF THE WORLD
This 12th-century French illustration depicts the phases of creation described in Genesis, from the creation of the Earth and the heavens, to plants, animals, and human beings.

special relationship with the creator, and worthy of the responsibility that God bestowed upon them: "Rule over the fish in the sea and the birds in the sky and over every living creature that moves on the ground"(1:28). God also imparted fertility to his creation, implanting in it the power to regenerate itself.

### A day of rest

When God reviewed his creation, he pronounced himself satisfied: "God saw all that he had made, and it was very good" (1:31). On the seventh day, he rested, and "blessed the seventh day and made it holy, because on it he rested from all the work of creating that he had done" (2:3). Creating the world had been less than a week's work for God (see panel, right) – the formless Earth had been transformed into a fruitful planet.

AFTER ≫

In the Genesis story, creation took six days, but is "day" a literal 24 hours?

#### LITERAL OR LITERARY
The reference to evening and morning in the creation story **suggests a literal seven-day period**. However, the Hebrew word used in Genesis for day – *yom* – can mean a longer or even ill-defined period (see Psalm 90:4, 95:8), and the **carefully arranged poetic scheme** supports a non-literal interpretation.

#### THE SABBATH
God's example of resting introduced the idea of the **Sabbath 320–21 ≫**, a weekly rest day enabling people to be "recreated". The Jewish Sabbath begins with a family meal on Friday evening. Christians in the early Church changed the Sabbath to Sunday to mark the **resurrection of Jesus 404–05 ≫**.

JEWISH SABBATH MEAL

**BEFORE**

God brought life and order to primal chaos, and everything in creation was "very good" (Genesis 1:31).

### HUMANITY'S DISTINCTIVENESS

Once the water cycle had been set into motion, **the created Earth ‹‹ 32–33** teemed with life, variety, and colour. Aside from this fertile and sustainable system, the high point of creation had been God **making human beings in his own image**. Whatever else that image entailed, it meant that humans were created to relate and communicate with God in a superior way to other creatures. They also acted as his representatives on Earth, caring for – and marvelling at – creation.

### EARTHLY PARADISE

Rich plantlife along the River Duden in Turkey hints at what Eden might have looked like. The Bible describes a river watering the garden and many kinds of trees growing there that were "pleasing to the eye" (Genesis 2:9).

# The Garden of Eden

*After creating and populating the Earth, God established a fertile garden and commissioned the first man, Adam, to look after it. No suitable helper could be found for Adam, so God created the woman, Eve, who became his wife.*

**W**HILE THE first chapter of Genesis sets out the general themes and sequence of events of creation – including the creation of men and women – the second chapter focuses on one specific place – the Garden of Eden – and one specific species – human beings.

The book of Genesis implies that God's new creation had taken time to develop: "no shrub had yet appeared on the earth and no plant had yet sprung up, for the LORD God had not sent rain on the earth and there was no one to work the ground" (Genesis 2:5). Although full of potential, the roots and seeds in the ground were lying there dormant until God provided water, whereupon the vegetation sprang into life.

God was to appoint the man to look after the garden. The man – named in the book of Genesis as Adam, after he had given names to the animals and birds – was the crown of God's creation, even though he had been made from the dust, indicating both his fragile nature and his continuity with the earth. God breathed his own breath into this dusty shell, and the man came alive: "the LORD God formed a man from the dust of the

> **" Now the LORD God had planted a garden in the east, in Eden."**
> GENESIS 2:8

ground and breathed into his nostrils the breath of life, and the man became a living being" (2:7). This living creature, unlike all the others, uniquely bore the image of God.

## Man's responsibility

The first man's primary responsibility was to care for the garden God had planted in Eden, a place that shares much with the notion of paradise in the ancient world.

## Eden's geography

Scholars have proposed several theories for the location of Eden, but the story of Genesis implies that it lay somewhere to the east of Israel in the Arabian Peninsula. A river that provided water to the garden divided into four as it left Eden, forming the rivers Pishon, Gihon, Tigris, and Euphrates. This would have made the garden a lush oasis in the midst of a dry landscape.

## Forbidden fruits

God had created all sorts of trees in Eden – some were simply beautiful, while others provided delicious fruit to eat. He gave Adam the freedom to pick fruit from any of the luxuriant trees, except for one. In the centre there were two trees: one of life, and one of the knowledge of good and evil. The man was told to leave the latter alone: "You are free to eat from any tree in the garden; but you must not eat from the tree of the knowledge of good and evil, for when you eat from it you will certainly die" (2:16,17).

## A helper for Adam

Only one problem marred Adam's idyllic existence. As the crown of creation, and with no equal to whom he could relate, he was lonely. God overcame this by creating a companion for him: "So the LORD God caused the man to fall into a deep sleep; and while he was sleeping, he took one of the man's ribs and then closed up the place with flesh" (2:21). God used part of the man's own body: "Then the LORD God made a woman from the rib he had taken out of the man, and he brought her to the man" (2:22).

When the man saw God's creation, he immediately recognized her resemblance to himself, and composed a poem to celebrate that she was made of the very same stuff as he. He said, "This is now bone of my bones and flesh of my flesh; she shall be called 'woman', for she was taken out of man" (2:23). The Christian idea of marriage has its roots in this early example of relationship.

In the idyllic Eden, the man and the woman enjoyed complete innocence, which was symbolized by their nakedness, for which they felt no shame. This intimacy would be lost because of their disobedience to God (see pp.36–37).

### CREATION OF EVE

In this 1483 woodcut from the Nuremberg Bible, God creates woman from the man as he sleeps, while angels watch on from the heavens. The stylized motif also shows the Earth – lush and verdant with greenery – inhabited by animals on the land and fish beneath the sea, clouds, stars, and the Sun and Moon.

> ## "The LORD God said 'It is **not good** for the **man** to be **alone.** I will make a **helper** suitable for him.'"
>
> GENESIS 2:18

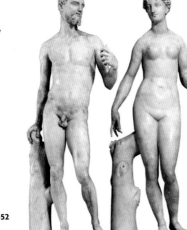
### AFTER

From beginning to end, gardens play an important role in the Bible's story.

**GARDENS IN THE BIBLE**
The Garden of Eden served as Adam and Eve's original home. Although they were soon **expelled from it because of their sin 36–37 》** the story of the Bible traces how

**12TH-CENTURY DEPICTION OF NEW JERUSALEM**

Eden will be restored in the future. For Christians, the decisive change in human fortunes occurred through Christ, who was betrayed in the **garden of Gethsemane 390–91 》**. Revelation 22 describes the **New Jerusalem 464–65 》 and paradise restored**. God will live among his people again in a garden where there is a life-giving river, and a tree that brings healing (Revelation 22:2).

## « BEFORE

Satan appears as a serpent in Genesis without introduction, but a few hints are given elsewhere in the Bible.

### ORIGINS OF SATAN

Satan's origin is not clearly explained. Job 1, which may date from the period in which Genesis was written, describes him as a **fallen member of God's heavenly court** who tried to undermine God. Isaiah 14:12–15 and Ezekiel 28:12–17 may support this. Jesus says he "saw Satan fall like lightning from heaven" (Luke 10:18). A minority view is that he was one of **the Nephilim**, the "heroes of old" (Genesis 6:4).

**SERPENTS FEATURE IN MANY WORLD MYTHS**

### SYMBOLS

## THE FORBIDDEN FRUIT

The depiction of the forbidden fruit as an apple does not come from Genesis. The creation story bears similarities to examples of Mesopotamian mythology, so the fruit could have been one of any number of luscious Middle Eastern varieties, such as the pomegranate. Artists have painted the fruit as an apple down the centuries, perhaps because the Latin *malus* means both "apple" and "evil", from which the English words "malicious", "malign", and "malevolent" are derived.

**SAMPLING THE FORBIDDEN FRUIT**

### THE FALL OF MAN

Lucas Cranach the Elder's 1526 painting shows Adam and Eve, surrounded by animals in the luscious paradise of Eden, considering their first bite into the forbidden fruit. Above them in the tree is the insidious serpent.

# Tempted by the Serpent

*The pure delight of Eden was ruptured when Satan – represented by the serpent – questioned God's command. Adam and Eve foolishly ate from the forbidden tree, resulting in the loss of the innocence they had once enjoyed.*

**T**HE BIBLE gives no suggestion of where it came from, but suddenly a serpent slithered up to Eve and whispered a question in her ear that was to have lasting consequences. The serpent is often understood as a symbol of evil, or of Satan – Hebrew for "accuser" – whose ambition was to destroy what God had created. Its very movement has come to epitomize a sly, cunning nature.

### Temptation

At first the serpent did not attack God outright. Satan's first words to Eve were instead intended to plant a seed of doubt in her ear. "Did God really say, 'You must not eat from any tree in the garden'?" (Genesis 3:1). Satan knew he had captured Eve's attention when she replied with an ambiguous version of God's command: "We may eat fruit from the garden, but God did say, 'You must not eat fruit from the tree that is in the middle of the garden'" (3:3).

The serpent grew bolder, claiming that God had only commanded Adam and Eve not to eat from the tree in the centre of the garden so that he could keep humans in their place, as inferior beings dependent on him. Satan said that eating the forbidden fruit would not lead to death, as God had claimed, but would simply put them on a level with God.

The combination of the persuasive words, delicious-looking fruit, and the prospect of being as wise as God proved too much, and Eve took a bite. Although the serpent spoke to Eve first, Adam was also complicit. He did not stand up to the serpent or stop Eve from eating the fruit, but disobeyed God by taking a bite.

Catastrophe was to follow on every level – in their relationship with God, and with each other. Adam and Eve lost the naked innocence of their relationship, making coverings from fig leaves to hide their shame. This primitive clothing placed a small but significant barrier between them.

### The Fall

When God was walking in the garden later that day, Adam and Eve dared not face him. Fear displaced the trusting friendship that they had enjoyed with God. When they finally responded to his call, they tried to shift the blame for what had happened, first onto each other, then onto the serpent, but God apportioned blame where it was due. The serpent was cursed and warned that human beings would bear him hostility from that moment on. God said that although the serpent – Satan – would cause much damage in the world, in the future the offspring of a woman – whom Christians believe to be Jesus – would crush him.

Adam and Eve were punished for their disobedience too. God declared that the woman would suffer pain in childbirth, and that "Your desire will be for your husband, and he will rule over you" (3:16). Then he told Adam

**THE TREE OF LIFE**
Adam and Eve's disobeyance of God in eating the forbidden fruit led to them being banished from Eden, never to sample the fruit of another tree – the Tree of Life – which would offer them eternal life.

that he would find the ground cursed, producing thorns and thistles, and work that had once been a delight would become a back-breaking chore.

Genesis tells us that Adam and Eve did not die physically when they ate the fruit, as God had warned they would. Instead they died inwardly, and were no longer fit for the paradise of Eden. They were exiled from the garden – strangers to God, each other, and the world over which they had been created to rule.

> **"** …when you **eat** from it your **eyes** will be **opened**, and you will be like **God**, knowing good and evil. **"**
>
> GENESIS 3:5

**AFTER** »

Locked out of Eden, which was now guarded by the cherubim, Adam's status – and that of all humankind – had changed forever.

### FALLEN HUMANITY

God's image in Adam and his descendants was marred by sin. The **human race was now fallen** – as Paul wrote in the New Testament, "sin entered the world through one man, and death through sin" (Romans 5:12). The remedy for Adam's failure lay in **a second Adam**, who had not sinned, and in whom God's image was not tarnished. This Adam, who the New Testament calls "the firstborn over all creation" (Colossians 1:15) would be Jesus, who made God's grace available to all and **offered humanity a new start** through his perfect obedience, both in life and **death 398–99** ».

---

### PEOPLE

## HEAVENLY CREATURES

After Adam and Eve's banishment, cherubim mounted a guard at the gates of Eden to prevent them returning. These mysterious, heavenly creatures are not the cherubic babies portrayed in art, but are God's security guards. The Ark of the Covenant was adorned with golden cherubim (Exodus 25:18–22). The prophet Ezekiel described them as God's attendants, each with four wings and four faces – that of a man, bull, eagle, and lion (Ezekiel 1:4–24; 10:3–22). Other heavenly beings are mentioned in the Bible, such as the winged seraphim of Isaiah 6:1–7, and angels acting as messengers from God, who appear in various guises.

**FOUR-FACED CHERUBIM OF EZEKIEL'S VISION**

# The Fall

*Adam and Eve's decision to defy God's command affected not just them, but the whole of humanity. The rest of the Bible illustrates the consequences of this first sin, known as "the Fall", and the New Testament explains God's plan to redeem humanity's sin through his son Jesus, and restore his creation and his image in human beings.*

**A**DAM AND EVE were created as responsible human beings, free to make choices. God did not create them to mechanically follow orders, which would have made them less than human. But their freedom to choose carried an inherent risk – namely, that they might make wrong choices.

The outcome of Adam and Eve's action would be neither trivial nor temporary. After they had eaten from the tree of the knowledge of good and evil, God's judgment fell upon them, and Adam and Eve were banished from the Garden of Eden (see pp.36–37).

Due to Adam and Eve's actions, all of humanity fell from the state of grace – or perfection – in which they were created. Their original goodness was corrupted and God's image was marred. The "life" of intimacy and friendship with God gave way to the "death" of sin and a fear and suspicion of God; even the Earth's environment suffered (see p.37) because of Adam's sin.

Ever afterwards, people were born to sin, and biblical history provides plenty of evidence of humankind's propensity to sin. Even the most godly and noble of characters – such as Abraham, Moses, David, and Paul – did wrong.

God did not leave sin unchecked, however, but provided the Torah – "instructions" in Hebrew – to the people of Israel. The Torah provided them with a way of handling sin in their community, so that it would not destroy them. Yet God was also concerned with the restoration of humanity, not just the restraint of sin. Ultimately, the Law would prove insufficient for either purpose, so God provided another answer through his son, Jesus.

Adam and Eve had to live with the consequences of their actions, and sin continued to plague their family (see pp.40–41). However, in the New Testament, Paul wrote that although all humanity fell due to Adam's sin, a second Adam could be the means of humanity's restoration (Romans 5:12–19). This second man needed – like the first – to be made in God's image and face temptation, but, unlike the first, to live a sinless life. Jesus lived without sin and did not deserve to die, but paid the debt for humanity's sin by dying as a sacrifice. Those who had faith in him could be restored to God's favour, and a new humanity could begin.

> "So the LORD God **banished him** from the **Garden of Eden**."
>
> GENESIS 3:23

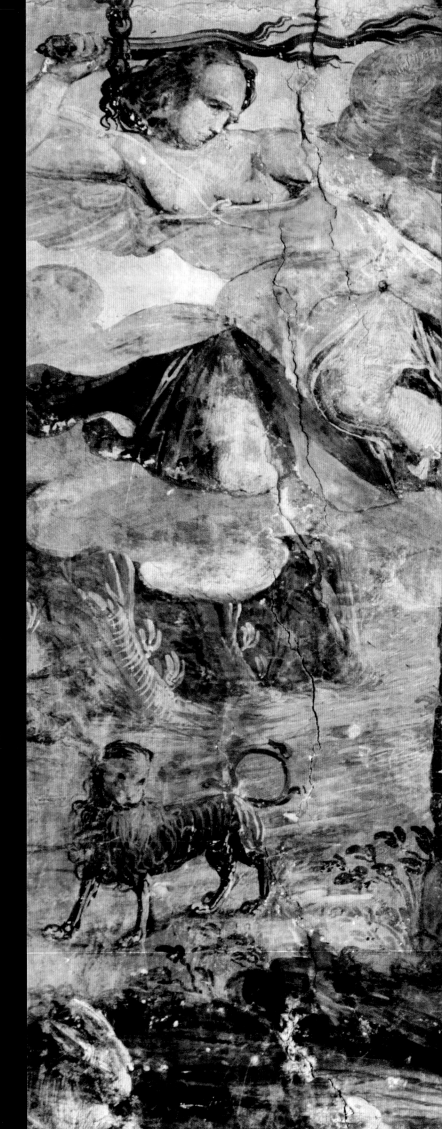

**OUT OF EDEN**
In the 17th-century Italian fresco *Expulsion of Adam and Eve from Paradise*, the Cherubim wields a sword to bar Adam and Eve from Eden, while death – symbolized by a skeleton – hangs over them.

**BEFORE**

After their expulsion from the Garden of Eden, God continued to care for Adam and Eve.

**CLOTHING AND CHILDREN**
In spite of his judgment on them, forcing Adam to work the ground, God continued to provide for both Adam and Eve, as seen in the replacement of their fig leaves with "garments of skin" (Genesis 3:21).

Eve's role as **"the mother of all the living"** (3:20) had not changed. She produced several children.

# Cain and Abel

*Sin continued in the generation after Adam and Eve, when Cain murdered his brother Abel and invoked God's judgment. But God had not withdrawn from creation, and was still responsible for giving and preserving life.*

F OLLOWING THEIR expulsion from the Garden of Eden, Adam and Eve started a family. Eve recognized God's help in this – "With the help of the LORD I have brought forth a man" (Genesis 4:1).

### Like father like son
Adam and Eve named their first son Cain, a word similar to the Hebrew for "brought forth" or "acquired", echoing Eve's earlier statement. Cain grew crops, while their next son, Abel, looked after animals. The two were also different from one another in character.

The brothers brought offerings to God from their labours. Cain brought some "fruits of the soil"

**OFFERINGS OF CAIN AND ABEL**
Master Bertram of Minden's *The Offerings of Cain and Abel*, 1383, from the Grabower Altar of St Peter's church, Hamburg, shows the sons of Adam and Eve. Cain presents God with a sheaf of wheat, while Abel offers an animal sacrifice.

❝ But if you do not do what is right, **sin is crouching at your door**; it desires to have you, but **you must rule over it.** ❞
GENESIS 4:7

**ANALYSIS**

## THE SANCTITY OF LIFE

Murder is the taking of human life, and in biblical terms, a killer usurps God's authority to bestow and end life. Cain's punishment for this crime was severe. God placed him under a curse, but it was tempered with mercy because Cain also experienced God's protection. In this way, God sought to avert a cycle of violence and retaliation.

In Israel, "Anyone who takes the life of a human being is to be put to death" (Leviticus 24:17), although places of refuge were designated for anyone "who kills accidentally and unintentionally" (Joshua 20:3).

**THE STONING OF JEREMIAH DEPICTED IN A 13TH-CENTURY ILLUMINATED LETTER V**

(4:3) and Abel brought "fat portions" (the choicest part) from the firstborn of his flock. God accepted Abel's offering, but rejected Cain's.

Cain brooded on this and became angry and depressed. God warned him that unless he mastered his emotions, they would prove destructive and sinful. As with his parents, Cain's undisciplined desire proved to have catastrophic consequences. Ignoring God's warning, Cain plotted against his brother, lured him into a field, and murdered him there.

### Cain cursed
When God questioned Cain as to his brother's whereabouts, he responded angrily: "I don't know… am I my brother's keeper?" (4:9). God knew what Cain had done, and told Cain that he could hear Abel's blood crying out to him from the ground. He placed Cain under a curse: since the earth had received Abel's blood from Cain's hands, it would no longer yield up its crops to those same hands. Instead, Cain would become a nomad, "a restless wanderer on the earth" (4:12).

God realized that others might take the law into their own hands and kill Cain, so he promised vengeance seven times over on any who killed him, and placed a mark upon him. Cain then left for the land of Nod, "east of Eden" (4:16).

After this, Cain was married and had a son, Enoch. He then began "building a city" (4:17) – the first mention of a city in the Bible – an organized community of permanent dwellings rather than the less formal arrangements of nomadic life. The Bible says that the sixth generation of Cain's family was responsible for progress in several fields: Jabal was the founder of

tent-dwellers and herders, his brother Jubal "was the father of all who play stringed instruments and pipes" (4:21), while their step-brother Tubal-Cain "forged all kinds of tools out of bronze and iron" (4:22).

❝ **Am I my brother's keeper?** ❞
GENESIS 4:9

**AFTER**

Following Cain's banishment from God's presence, humanity veered from faithfulness to sinful disobedience.

**THE BEGINNING OF PRAYER**
Another son, Seth (meaning "granted"), was born to Adam and Eve. The blessings and struggles experienced in life meant that **humanity began to pray and seek God's help**: "At that time people began to call on the name of the LORD" (Genesis 4:23).

**SIN RETURNS**
Despite the achievements of Cain's descendants, sin persisted. **Five generations later, Lamech committed the second murder** (Genesis 4:26), although the Bible does not disclose the victim's identity.

**THE ENGLISH *EGERTON GENESIS PICTURE BOOK*, c.1360, ILLUSTRATES ADAM AND HIS DESCENDANTS: (FROM LEFT): ADAM, SETH, ENOSH, KENAN, MAHALALEL, JARED, ENOCH, METHUSELAH**

THE FIRST MURDER
Cain's killing of his brother – the first murder
recorded in the Bible – is the subject of
*The Death of Abel* by Andrea Schiavone
(c.1510–63). Cain was jealous because God
chose Abel's offerings instead of his own.

« BEFORE

From Adam to Noah, people lived for a long time, but were increasingly distant from God. Although there were righteous exceptions – such as Enoch (Genesis 4:17) and Noah – humanity as a whole increasingly ignored God.

### HOW OLD?

Before the flood, the Bible attests that people lived **extraordinarily long lives**. The longest living person recorded in the Bible is Methuselah, who died just short of a millennium at the age of 969 years old (Genesis 5:27). Various explanations have been offered about these figures. Did those who first recorded the story of Genesis use a different system of calculation? Are the age spans symbolic? Was a year shorter than the 365-day period we now know to be the duration of a complete orbit of the Sun by the Earth? Or do the ancient ages simply convey that the events described all happened far back in the mists of prehistory? Possibly it is a symbolic way of conveying that **life before the flood was very different from life afterwards**.

### EPIC OF GILGAMESH

Several ancient accounts of a flood myth exist outside the Bible, most notably the Babylonian text *The Epic of Gilgamesh*, the earliest elements of which can be traced to the late 3rd millenium BC. Gilgamesh and Genesis both feature a hero and a boat as humanity faced judgment, birds dispatched to check if the flood was over, and a memorial sign once the waters receded.

The accounts differ in their view of God, why the flood happened, and its extent. While Noah's family and animals were saved in the ark, only powerful people were saved in Gilgamesh. In Genesis, the flood rises over a long period, but in Gilgamesh the flood is sudden, frightening even the gods. Gilgamesh lacks the promise of God's grace, which is the climax of the Genesis account.

**STATUE OF GILGAMESH, 8TH CENTURY BC**

# The Great Flood

*Human disobedience led God to take action to restore his creation. He sent a flood as punishment for sin, which almost wiped out humanity. The future of the Earth was safeguarded through the obedience of one man – Noah – and his family.*

**W**ITHIN TEN generations of Adam, the world that God had made was unrecognizable. Evil of all kinds abounded and the Earth was "full of violence" (Genesis 6:11). People were corrupt in their hearts and in their deeds – it was a tragedy, and God grieved that he had ever created human beings. After exercising patience for generations, God decided to start again by wiping out the population of the world through a great flood: "I will wipe from the face of the earth the human race I have created – and with them the animals, the birds and the creatures that move along the ground" (6:7).

### One righteous man

The new start would not be a start from scratch, however. God identified one family who did not join in the sinful ways of others, and devised a plan to use them as the means of restoring creation. The future hung by a thread – that of Noah's obedience.

Noah was already 600 years old when he received a command from God: "Make yourself an ark of cypress wood; make rooms in it and coat it with pitch inside and out" (6:14). God gave Noah the precise dimensions of the ship – it was to be a very large vessel – and specified that it should have three decks and a door in its side.

**TWO BY TWO**
This 13th-century French illustration depicts "every kind of bird, every kind of animal, and every kind of creature that moves along the ground" (Genesis 6:20) entering the ark in pairs.

Noah obeyed God's command, taking care to follow the precise instructions exactly.

Seven days before the flood, Noah and his family boarded the ship and stocked it with food. He

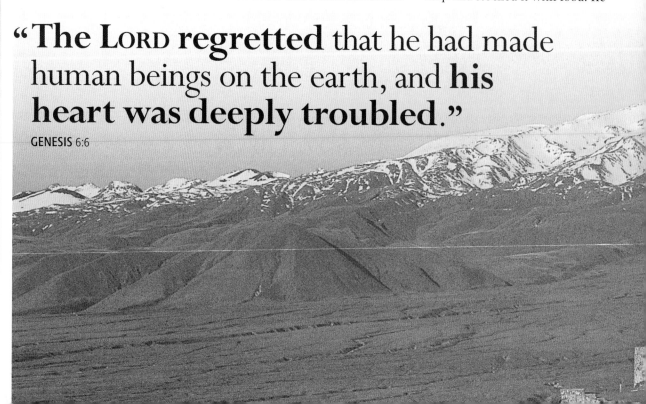

> "**The LORD regretted** that he had made human beings on the earth, and **his heart was deeply troubled**."
>
> GENESIS 6:6

also took one male and one female of every species, and seven – the number of completion (see p.32) – of those animals classified by God as ceremonially clean, since they would be needed for sacrifices and food. They would continue to procreate, ensuring the future of the animal kingdom.

## The deluge

Once Noah and his companions were safely on board the ark, God released floodwaters from the springs below the Earth, and rain above it. The water kept coming for 40 days until everything except for the ark was immersed. The floodwaters remained for almost six months, guaranteeing that everything on the Earth was destroyed. However, God had not forgotten his faithful servant: "God remembered Noah and all the wild animals and the livestock that were with him in the ark, and he sent a wind over the earth" (8:1). Finally, the waters began to recede.

The ark came to rest on the mountains of Ararat, and after a further 40 days, Noah began to send birds as scouts to look for dry land elsewhere. At first, the raven

## THE DOVE

Noah tested whether the flood was over by releasing a dove from the ark. The olive branch it carried in its beak on its second return has become an international symbol of peace. Elsewhere in the Bible the dove was used in sacrifice, and named as a metaphor for moaning in distress due to sin (Ezekiel 7:16), or one who is easily deceived or senseless (Hosea 7:11). In the New Testament, at Jesus' baptism the Holy Spirit descended "like a dove" (Matthew 3:16).

**NOAH AND DOVE, ST MARK'S CATHEDRAL, VENICE**

he sent kept returning because the waters had not fully receded. Then he sent a dove. On its second mission it returned with an olive branch, signalling that vegetation was appearing on the Earth once again. The dove did not return from its third mission, presumably because it had found dry land in which to live. Noah realized that it was now safe to disembark.

## Covenant confirmed

God had given words of promise to Noah as part of a covenant agreement (6:18), guaranteeing

him protection and blessing. When he left the ark, the first thing Noah did was to build an altar and offer to God a sacrifice of clean animals. God then gave Noah the same command to be fruitful that he had given to Adam (1:28). God confirmed the covenant he had made with Noah: "I establish my covenant with you: Never again will all life be destroyed by the waters of a flood; never again will there be a flood to destroy the earth" (9:11). Finally, God placed a rainbow in the sky as a perpetual reminder of his covenant.

**Noah had three sons – Shem, Japheth, and Ham – who behaved differently towards their father.**

### HAM'S ERROR

Despite the new start, the world still felt the effects of **the Fall ‹‹ 38–39**. When Noah lay naked on his bed, drunk, Ham dishonoured his father by looking at his nakedness and telling his older brothers, who respectfully covered Noah without looking at him (Genesis 9:22,23). Noah cursed Ham – whose son Canaan founded **the Canaanites 118–19 ››** – and **a rift emerged** between him and his brothers that was echoed in the relationship between their descendants.

**NOAH'S SHAME, MONREALE CATHEDRAL, SICILY**

### MOUNT ARARAT

The monastery at Khor Virap, Armenia, is dwarfed by the bulk of Mount Ararat, which lies in neighbouring Turkey. Ararat was known as Mount Masis until the Middle Ages, when it became one of several sites associated with the setting down of the ark.

**BEFORE** «

Noah's family dispersed after the flood. He lived to be 950, and the world was fruitful, just as God had promised.

### NOAH'S SONS

Noah's sons became the founders of **large and complex nations**, who developed their own cultures (Genesis 10). The descendants of Japheth settled in northern Mesopotamia, Ham's descendants settled in the regions of Canaan and Ethiopia, while Shem's descendants settled in the east.

### CONFUSED CHRONOLOGY

Genesis 10 describes the **initial dispersal of Noah's sons**, along with a genealogy for each, which cover the family's expansion after the events of Babel (Genesis 11).

# The Tower of Babel

*The people of the world displayed their arrogance in building a tower, at Babel, to reach up to heaven. As a result, God shattered their unity and brought confusion to the common language they had enjoyed.*

**A**FTER THE FLOOD, Noah's expanding family was not tied to the land around Mount Ararat, where the ark came to rest. They migrated to the East to a land known as Shinar, near the future city of Babylon. Their journey east echoes the judgment on Adam, Eve, and Cain, who settled "east of Eden" (Genesis 4:16). In spite of their growing numbers, they still enjoyed great unity, partly because they all spoke the same language.

### Proud builders

Cain had built a city before the birth of his son Enoch (4:17), but unlike this earlier settlement made from stone and mortar, in their new location Noah's descendants learned the art of brick-making. The bricks were hard-baked to give them strength, and were held together by bitumen. The people were proud

> **"** Come, let us build… **a tower that reaches to the heavens,** so that we may **make a name for ourselves…"**
> GENESIS 11:4

## ZIGGURATS

The tower of Babel may have been inspired by ziggurats, the raised temples built in Mesopotamia from the 3rd millennium BC. Several examples have been uncovered and restored, and their religious purpose is well documented. Ziggurats had a wide base on which a number of staggered platforms were built, each storey decreasing in size to give the impression of a man-made mountain. Access to each storey was gained via a sloping ramp or steps. The top storey was seen as the abode of the gods, where they would receive homage and talk with humans.

**RESTORED ZIGGURAT OF UR, IRAQ**

# "That is why it was called Babel – because **there the LORD confused** the **language of the whole world.**"

GENESIS 11:9

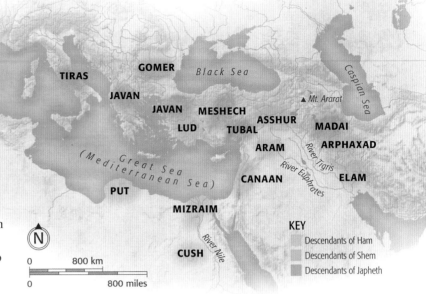

NOAH'S DESCENDANTS
The descendants of Noah's three sons – Shem, Ham, and Japheth – repopulated the world after the flood. These descendants and the areas they settled, according to Genesis 10, are shown here.

of the quality of their bricks, but "pride goes before destruction", as Proverbs 16:18 would later warn.

## Towering ambitions

With an ambition verging on arrogance – human beings were attempting to reach the realm of God – the people joined together to build a city, the centrepiece of which would be a tower high enough to reach to the heavens.

### SPRAWLING FOLLY
In *Tower of Babel* (1563) Pieter Brueghel the Elder depicts humankind's efforts to reach the heavens as a chaotic, ill-engineered folly. The leader in the foreground is thought to be Nimrod, whose "first centres of... kingdom were in Shinar" (Genesis 10:10).

This was a monument motivated in part by a desire for fame and renown, but was also a response to their fear of dispersal: "otherwise we will be scattered over the face of the whole earth" (11:4). The people felt that the tower would provide security and unity. In reality, they were repeating the same sin that Adam and Eve had committed: attempting to become like God himself.

In a move reminiscent of Eden, God "came down" (11:5) to the people. The tower had failed to approach heaven, but he was still concerned about the spiritual implications of the building. God feared that humans were going to withdraw from their role in creation – to be fruitful and multiply across the whole world, and to be stewards of the Earth and the creatures of air, land, and sea (see pp.34–35) – and he was displeased at their vanity and pride. If they succeeded with building the tower, they would think they could do anything: "The LORD said, 'If as one people speaking the same language they have begun to do this, then nothing they plan to do will be impossible for them'" (11:6).

## Babbling confusion

God devised a plan to stop the people in their tracks. The building project's success had hinged on their ability to communicate with one another. God's simple strategy was to confuse the peoples of the Earth by making them speak different languages.

The name of the city in which the tower was built was Babel,

meaning "gate of the gods" to the Babylonians, but sounding like the Hebrew word for "confusion". The people babbled to each other incomprehensibly from then on, and "the LORD scattered them from there over all the earth, and they stopped building the city" (11:8). Those who had once pulled together now drew apart from one another; unity gave way to division.

### ARTISTIC INSPIRATION
The minaret of Samarra in Iraq – completed in AD 851 – may have been influenced by Mesopotamian ziggurats. At 52m (170ft) in height, it has inspired many artistic depictions of the tower of Babel.

**AFTER** »

The New Testament gives a glimpse of how God's Holy Spirit would restore that which was corrupted.

### FROM NOAH TO ABRAHAM
After Babel, the Bible narrows from Noah's diverse family to the **one family of Abraham 48–49** ». The genealogy of Noah's descendants at the end of Genesis 11 focuses on a single branch of the family of Shem, whose great-grandson was Eber, from whom the word "Hebrew" derives. This genealogy emphasized the thread that connected Shem – and so Noah, and through him, Adam – through Eber to Abraham, who was to become **the father of the Hebrew people**.

### LANGUAGE NO BARRIER
The ethnic divisions that would follow God's introduction of different languages at Babel were to continue throughout the Bible. Even so, a significant step to reverse the confusion took place on the **day of Pentecost 416–17** », when people from many nations heard the gospel – the good news of Jesus – in their own language due to **the Holy Spirit** (Acts 2:1–11).

DAY OF PENTECOST

# THE PATRIARCHS

"**I will make you into a great nation, and I will bless you**; I will make
your name great, and you will be a blessing. **I will bless those who bless you,** and
whoever curses you I will curse; and all peoples on earth will be blessed through you."
GENESIS 12:2,3

ENESIS 1–11 IS THE BIBLICAL ACCOUNT OF how everything was created, what went wrong, and a description of "the table of nations" (Genesis 10). Genesis 12 begins the story of God's plan to put things right – a plan that involved building up a family through which everyone on Earth would be blessed. The start of this story is set in the late third millennium BC, when great civilizations had emerged along the banks of the Tigris and Euphrates rivers in Mesopotamia and the Nile in Egypt. Yet it was not through mighty nations that God unfolded his plan, but through a nomadic childless couple.

**THE THREE PATRIARCHS**
This detail from a panel of the Grabower Altar of St. Peter's Church, Hamburg, painted by Master Bertram of Minden in the 14th century, shows episodes in the lives of the three biblical patriarchs (from left to right): Abraham, Isaac, and Jacob.

The story begins with three heads of the family, known as the patriarchs ("father-rulers"). The family's founding father was Abraham, originally from Chaldea in Mesopotamia, who was the descendant of one of Noah's sons, Shem, and had been raised as a pagan.

### ABRAHAM'S FAMILY

God revealed himself to Abraham – or Abram as he was called – and commanded him to go to the land of Canaan. God pledged that Abraham's people would possess this place and there become a great nation. Abraham went to Canaan, travelling through it as a pastoral nomad and erecting altars to God each time he pitched his tent.

Having followed God's instructions obediently, it was in Canaan that the childless, and now elderly, Abraham started a family. The firstborn was Ishmael, from whom the Arab nations descended, and then came Isaac – the son God had promised would be born to Abraham's wife, Sarah. Isaac, the second patriarch, had two sons: Esau and Jacob.

### RIGHT PEOPLE, WRONG PLACE

It was through Isaac's son Jacob, the third of the patriarchs, that God's plan unfolded. Jacob produced 12 sons, who became the founders of the 12 tribes of Israel.

It would be from the ranks of these tribes that the Messiah would one day emerge, and this Messiah would be a saviour not just for Israel, but for the whole world.

A major development in the story came through Joseph, one of Jacob's sons, who was sold into slavery by his brothers and was taken by his captors into Egypt. There, he became highly valued for his ability to interpret dreams and rose to become a powerful courtier to the pharaoh. Among his many accomplishments, Joseph directed plans to avoid a famine that God had warned was coming.

Joseph eventually brought his whole family to Egypt, where they continued to grow and prosper, just as God had promised his great-grandfather Abraham. The family was now safe, but in the wrong place, for God had promised that Canaan would be their home.

### THE NATURE OF GOD

This section of Genesis tells us many things about the nature and purposes of Israel's God. He is a God who has a plan to save the world, who wants a relationship with people, who makes a covenant, or binding contract, with those who trust him, and who takes the bad things of life and works them into good. As this family grew in number, so it also grew in its understanding of God.

**ABRAHAM'S PAST**
This 3rd-century BC cuneiform tablet from Mesopotamia is a tally of goats and sheep. Abraham (the forefather of the Israelites) had become wealthy with flocks of livestock before he received his calling.

# God Calls Abram

### AN ANCIENT CITY

The Sumerian city of Ur, a cradle of civilization, dated back to at least the 4th millennium BC. Ur was **one of several city-states situated along the Tigris and Euphrates rivers** and was at the height of its power in Abram's time. Archaeological finds show that, by 3200 BC, Ur was a large city with 10,000 inhabitants. Many different types of building have been uncovered, including a huge temple known as the Great Ziggurat, several royal tombs, and large numbers of ordinary houses.

### A CIVILIZED SOCIETY

The Sumerians' gifts to humanity included writing, art, new styles of architecture, fine craftsmanship, and advances such as the plough and wheel. **They worshipped many gods**: Ur's city god was Sin – a moon deity, represented by the crescent moon.

**A GOLDEN RAM, c.2550 BC, FROM A ROYAL TOMB IN UR**

*The Bible's story of God's rescue plan for humanity began with the establishment of a nation from whom all the nations on the Earth would be blessed. It all started with a barren couple: Abram and Sarai.*

**A**BRAM'S father, Terah, set out from the family's home in Ur for the land of Canaan. He took his family with him, including his son Abram and Abram's wife, Sarai. However, when they reached Haran in northern Mesopotamia, the family settled there for many years.

In Haran, God spoke to Abram, telling him to leave his country, his people, and his father's household, and travel to a land that God would show him.

### God blesses Abram

God's call contained a surprising promise. Although Sarai was barren, God told Abram that "I will make you into a great nation and I will bless you" (Genesis 12:2). He promised to make the name of Abram great, and said that "you will be a blessing" (12:2). Everyone who blessed Abram would be blessed themselves, while those who cursed him would be cursed. Then he added an extraordinary promise: "all peoples on earth will be blessed through

> **" Go from your country... to the land I will show you. "**
> GENESIS 12:1

you" (12:3). This was no less than a restoring of God's blessing on humankind that had been lost in the Garden of Eden (see pp.34–35).

Abram left Haran, even though by then he was 75 years old, and God had not told him where he was going. He packed up his possessions and set out with Sarai, his nephew Lot, and his servants, leaving behind everything familiar. The group set out towards the south, and after a while reached the town of Shechem in the central region of Canaan.

### The promised land

The group camped by the great tree of Moreh, a notable landmark with sacred associations (see Genesis 35:4). Here God appeared to Abram, promising, "To your offspring I will give this land" (12:7). Abram immediately set about building an altar to God in that place.

The group moved on, heading south, and then pitched their tents in the hills east of Bethel. Abram

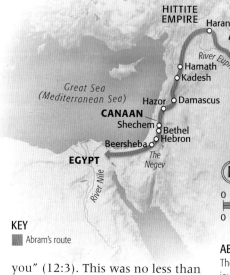

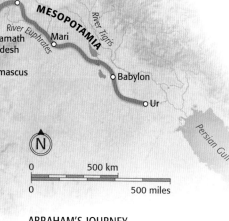

**KEY**
■ Abram's route

**ABRAHAM'S JOURNEY**
The Bible (Genesis 11:27–12:14) charts Abraham's journey from his ancestral home in Ur, in modern Iraq, via trade routes to Haran (in modern Turkey) and Canaan and then into Egypt.

again built an altar, thereby claiming the land for God, whom he now began to call on by name: the LORD (*Yahweh* in Hebrew). Later Abram moved further south again, towards the Negev, a semi-desert region with little rainfall, which would provide little sustenance for him and his family during the forthcoming famine.

**A famine in Canaan caused Abram to relocate temporarily to Egypt.**

### DESPERATE MEASURES

Abram feared that the Egyptians might kill him to take his beautiful wife Sarai. For this reason, **he told Sarai to pretend she was his sister**. Sarai nevertheless caught Pharaoh's eye and he took her into his palace, treating Abram well "for her sake" (Genesis 12:16). Displeased with the relationship, God **inflicted disease on Pharaoh's household**. Pharaoh summoned Abram, confronted him about his deceit, and then sent both him and Sarai away.

---

### GOD'S PROMISES TO ABRAM

**1** To make him into a great nation.

**2** To bless him.

**3** To make his name great.

**4** To make him a blessing to others.

**5** To bless those who blessed him.

**6** To curse those who cursed him.

**7** To bless all peoples on Earth through him.

### SITE OF HARAN

A tower and an arch are among the archaeological remains of the Temple of Sin, the Sumerian moon god, at the site of Haran in what is now Turkey. Haran was an important centre of the moon god cult and was located on an established trade route to Ur.

**THE JOURNEY OF ABRAM AND LOT**
A fresco in San Gimignano, Tuscany, by the Italian artist Bartolo di Fredi (1330–1410), depicts Abram, Sarai, and Lot setting out from Haran towards Canaan, in obedience to God's command.

« **BEFORE**

When expanding herds put pressure on pasture and water supplies, Abram and his nephew Lot agreed to separate.

### FAMILY DISPUTES

God's blessing was starting to have its challenges. Growing flocks meant it was not long before Abram's and Lot's herdsmen were **arguing over access to pasture** and watering places (Genesis 13). Abram did not want a family dispute, so he suggested that he and Lot go their separate ways, even giving Lot first choice of where he wanted to go. From Bethel's lofty position, the land by the **Jordan Valley** looked ideal, so Lot chose it and set off. Abram continued living in Canaan, while Lot moved south towards the notorious cities of **Sodom and Gomorrah 56–57** ».

JORDAN VALLEY

### HISTORY AND CULTURE

### COVENANTS

In the ancient world, a covenant was a binding contract between two parties. Breaking a covenant could mean death. The participants would often perform a ritual, described in this story, of walking between the two halves of bisected animals. This symbolized the pledge: "May this happen to me if I break the covenant."

COVENANT TREATY BETWEEN EGYPTIANS AND HITTITES, 13TH CENTURY BC

### ABRAHAM'S CHILDREN

God promised Abraham and Sarah that they would have a child. Abraham would be the father of countless generations, with his descendants numbering as many as the stars in the heavens.

# God Makes a Covenant

*To be called by God to a task is one thing; to have God make a binding contract with you to ensure it happens is incredible. Yet this was exactly what God was about to do for Abram.*

**W**HEN GOD CALLED Abram to go to Canaan, he had promised to make a great nation from him. As time passed, however, and still Sarai had no child, Abram's frustration grew. When God appeared in a vision, telling him not to be afraid and promising that he would protect and reward him, that frustration poured out. What sort of a reward was it if he had no son, and a mere servant would be his heir?

God answered: "This man will not be your heir, but a son who is your own flesh and blood will be your heir" (Genesis 15:4). Taking Abram outside, God told him to count the stars in the heavens, telling him that his offspring would come to number just as many. Displaying strong faith, and despite the fact that it did not seem likely that he would have a son given his age,

# "Look up at the sky and **count the stars** – if indeed you can count them… **So shall your offspring be.**"

GENESIS 15:5

### THE VOCATION OF ABRAM
God appeared to Abram, pictured here in a 16th-century tapestry by Bernard van Orley, to make a covenant with him, promising that if Abram kept faith in him, he would be greatly rewarded.

Abram trusted that God would keep his promise to him. In response to this demonstration of faith, God declared Abram to be righteous, reaffirming that the land of Canaan would be his.

### God's covenant
Abram asked God for a sign of all that he had said; so God told him to get a cow, goat, and ram, each three years old, and two birds – a dove and a pigeon. Following a covenant ritual that would have been familiar to him (see Covenants panel, left), Abram cut the larger animals in half, laying the halves opposite each other. At sunset, he fell into deep sleep, and God spoke to him again, reassuring him that his descendants would indeed possess the land of Canaan, though not for some time. To confirm what he had said, God made a binding contract, or covenant, with Abram. Appearing as a smoking firepot and blazing torch, God passed between the separated pieces of the animals. He did not require Abram to also pass between the animals, however, underlining there was nothing Abram could bring to the promise and the commitment to give Abram's descendants the land.

### A name and a sign
Fourteen years passed and God's promise of a child still had not come to pass. On his wife Sarai's suggestion, Abram decided to try to help God by having a child – Ishmael – with Sarai's Egyptian slave Hagar (see pp.54–55).

Another 13 years passed before God appeared again to Abram, to reconfirm his covenant through two enduring signs. First, God changed his name from Abram (meaning "exalted father" in Hebrew) to Abraham (meaning "father of many"), to underline the promise that Abraham would indeed become the father of kings and nations, and reaffirming that Canaan would belong to his descendants for ever. Then, God instituted a new sign of his covenant: every male in Abraham's household and all their male descendants were to be circumcised when they were eight days old. Anyone who did not do this would be excluded from the covenant.

### A promise to Sarah
God changed Abraham's wife Sarai's name too, to Sarah, and said: "I will bless her and will surely give you a son by her. I will bless her so that she will be the mother of nations; kings of peoples will come from her" (17:16). Abraham burst out laughing at this point – after all he was now 99, and Sarah was 90. However, God stressed that Sarah would indeed have a son, within the year, and that it would be through this child and his descendants that God would uphold his promise.

AFTER »

God's righteousness meant that his promise to Abraham about the land of Canaan would take many years to come to pass.

### FUTURE SLAVERY IN EGYPT
Although God had promised **Canaan 118–19 »** to Abraham, his inherent nature of acting justly meant that his promise would not be fulfilled immediately. The sin of the present occupants of Canaan, whose pagan religious practices would eventually include child sacrifice and ritual prostitution, had not yet reached the point where it would be clear to the surrounding nations that God's judgment – the removal of the inhabitants of Canaan – was just. So Abraham's descendants would have to wait several generations. During that waiting, they would end up as **slaves in a foreign land 90–91 »** – a prediction of the years to be spent in Egypt.

# "Your name will be **Abraham**, for I have made you a **father of many nations.**"

GENESIS 17:5

### CIRCUMCISION IN ANCIENT EGYPT
This relief in the tomb of a doctor called Ankhamaor, in the burial ground of Saqqara in Egypt, shows scenes of circumcision. This ritual was an accepted practice in Ancient Egypt, and was a central part of the covenant God made with Abraham.

EGYPTIAN SLAVE BEATEN BY HIS MASTER

## HISTORY AND CULTURE

# Gods and Goddesses

"You were **shown these things** so that you might know that the LORD **is God**; besides him **there is no other**."

DEUTERONOMY 4:35

**SACRIFICIAL CALF**
This model calf and shrine from the Middle Canaanite period were found in Tel Ashkelon in Israel. Sacrifice was a part of all cultures in the ancient Near East.

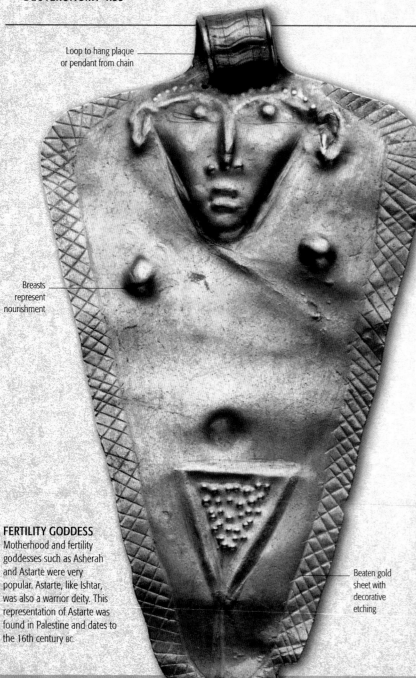

Loop to hang plaque or pendant from chain

Breasts represent nourishment

**FERTILITY GODDESS**
Motherhood and fertility goddesses such as Asherah and Astarte were very popular. Astarte, like Ishtar, was also a warrior deity. This representation of Astarte was found in Palestine and dates to the 16th century BC.

Beaten gold sheet with decorative etching

The ancient world was a place full of gods and goddesses, who were thought to dominate every aspect of life. In Old Testament times there were gods such as Dagon (Assyro-Babylonian), Chemosh (Moabite), Baal (widespread), and Molech (widespread). The Mesopotamian, Canaanite, and Egyptian religions were polytheistic, with a hierarchy of deities – a handful of widely worshipped major gods were supplemented by a large number of local cults. The Israelites also worshipped several deities until the monotheistic concept of "One God" became widely accepted.

Things were little different in New Testament times: in the Graeco-Roman world the pantheon of gods and goddesses ran into the thousands.

## SHRINES AND IDOLS

Much religious worship took the form of worshipping statues or sacred poles erected in temples and shrines. Canaan, for example, was a region with many gods and with shrines on sacred high places. The presence of these multiple shrines contrasted with the Israelites' worship of Yahweh, their one, true god. The Bible is full of reminders to the Israelites about leaving such things behind: "Long ago your ancestors, including Terah the father of Abraham and Nahor, lived beyond the River Euphrates and worshipped other gods" (Joshua 24:2). The tension is summed up in the battle between Elijah and the prophets of Baal on Mount Carmel (see pp.198–99).

Indeed, Elijah's name acts as a reminder, for it means "the Lord is my God".

**HIGH PLACE**
This unique sanctuary at Tel Gezer, west of Jerusalem, has a row of ten monolithic stones, or steles, and a square stone basin.

Emperor Augustus (reigned 27 BC – AD 14) was sole ruler of the Roman Empire and was deified after his death. The cult of emperor-worship was designed to promote the benefits of Roman rule to the world. There were temples to successive emperors in Rome and in most provincial capitals. Jews and Christians could have nothing to do with this. When Caligula threatened to put a statue of himself in the Temple in Jerusalem, there were huge protests and Jews were prepared to sacrifice their lives. Many Christians also preferred to face death rather than swear an oath and make a sacrifice to an emperor.

**AUGUSTUS**

## GREEK AND ROMAN GODS

The Greek poet Hesiod, who was writing around 700 BC, claimed that there were more than 30,000 different gods. By the time of Christ, just as in the Old Testament period, there were major and minor gods. Most cities had temples and shrines to the major gods such as Zeus (king of the Greek gods), Artemis, Apollo, and Hermes, but they also had their own local favourites. Many of the Roman gods were similar to the ancient Greek gods; for example, the king of the Roman gods was Jupiter, who was very similar to Zeus, while Venus, the Roman goddess of love, beauty, and fertility, is the equivalent of the Greek goddess Aphrodite, who in turn is linked with the Egyptian goddess Isis.

### GREEK GODS
Many of the ancient gods multi-tasked. Poseidon, Athena, Apollo, and Artemis were gods of the sea, wisdom, the Sun, and the hunt respectively, but they each had many other attributes.

## FOREIGN INFLUENCE

Gods crossed borders. In the bigger cities, travellers would find temples to various foreign gods: Greek, Roman, Egyptian, Syrian. The places of worship reflected the cities' diverse ethnic and cultural nature, and it was perfectly normal for Roman worshippers to join in celebrations in honour of Egyptian gods. Local priests saw no difficulty in allowing worshippers to make a vow or put up an altar to the Greek goddess Aphrodite in a temple dedicated to Egyptian Isis.

Herod the Great, the Jewish king at the time of Jesus' birth, sponsored temples to pagan gods in Roman and Greek territories, most notably in Sebaste and Caesarea Philippi.

## DAILY WORSHIP

Many Roman households had domestic shrines to the *lares*: the protective spirits of the family. A shrine, or *lararium*, could come in different forms, from a simple wall painting or wooden cupboard to a large, elaborate marble shrine. A snake, which represented the guardian spirit, was often depicted beneath the lararium. Prayers and offerings such as incense and food were made to these household gods every day. Similarly, out on the roads and in the countryside there were spirits at work who would protect travellers if asked.

Everyone was expected to offer sacrifices to the important gods of the Roman state and to the guardian spirit of the emperor (see panel, above), although not on a daily basis. People would also make offerings to the relevant god for a specific blessing relating to any aspect of life. For example, a graffito to the merchant god Hermes in the Roman seaport of Ostia pleads: "Hermes, good fellow, bring me a profit!".

### HOUSEHOLD SHRINE
This *lararium* from the 1st century AD is in the form of a temple. It frames a fresco of Minerva, the Roman goddess or war, wisdom, and handicrafts.

## PEOPLE OF ONE GOD

Judaism and Christianity ran counter to the Roman and Greek forms of worship – they were monotheistic religions, recognizing only one god. When Jesus asked his disciples "Who do you say I am?" (Matthew 16:15) he was in Caesarea Philippi – a city that contained shrines to Roma and Augustus and had once been a place where Baal was worshipped. The setting makes Jesus' question even more pointed.

The monotheistic Jews, and their descendants the Christians, turned their backs on the lure of other gods. They refused to join in with festivals and ritual banquets, and had qualms about eating meat that had previously been offered to idols. For this reason "pagans" viewed Jews as prickly and exclusive. In his *Histories*, the Roman historian Tacitus wrote: "They look after their own, but hate everyone else." This is also why Christians were viewed as atheists, because they preached against the worshipping of Roman and other gods.

### THE LORD IS ONE
The Jewish prayer called the *Shema* is written on parchment (below) and placed in the *Mezuzah* (left). Its first line is: "Hear, O Israel: The Lord is our God, the Lord is one."

שְׁמַע יִשְׂרָאֵל יְהוָה אֱלֹהֵינוּ יְהוָה אֶחָד וְאָהַבְתָּ אֵת יְהוָה אֱלֹהֶיךָ בְּכָל לְבָבְךָ וּבְכָל נַפְשְׁךָ וּבְכָל מְאֹדֶךָ וְהָיוּ הַדְּבָרִים הָאֵלֶּה אֲשֶׁר אָנֹכִי מְצַוְּךָ הַיּוֹם עַל לְבָבֶךָ וְשִׁנַּנְתָּם לְבָנֶיךָ וְדִבַּרְתָּ בָּם בְּשִׁבְתְּךָ בְּבֵיתֶךָ וּבְלֶכְתְּךָ בַדֶּרֶךְ וּבְשָׁכְבְּךָ וּבְקוּמֶךָ וּקְשַׁרְתָּם לְאוֹת עַל יָדֶךָ וְהָיוּ לְטֹטָפֹת בֵּין עֵינֶיךָ וּכְתַבְתָּם עַל מְזוּזֹת בֵּיתֶךָ וּבִשְׁעָרֶיךָ

## BEFORE

When Lot's decision to move south led to his being captured by invaders, Abraham was quick to rescue him.

### INTO BATTLE

Lot moved south to **Sodom and Gomorrah 56–57 »**, a corrupt and unstable region, as he soon discovered. A coalition of four Mesopotamian kings attacked five kings of the region (Genesis 14). The local kings were routed and Lot and his family were captured, along with their possessions. Upon hearing that his relative was in trouble, **Abraham gathered his 318 fighting men** (reflecting the now considerable size of his household) and caught the invaders as they were returning home. Attacking by night, he defeated them, recovering all of the goods taken and **rescuing Lot and his family**. Abraham not only refused a reward from the local kings, but also gave one-tenth of the spoils of the battle to Melchizedek, priest of God Most High, who blessed him.

**MELCHIZEDEK AND ABRAHAM WITH ISAAC**

> **"** So **Hagar** bore Abram a son, and Abram gave the name **Ishmael** to the **son she had borne."**
>
> GENESIS 16:15

# Abraham, Hagar, and Ishmael

*When Sarah still bore no child for Abraham, despite God's promise, she suggested that he should have a child with her slave. The birth of this child would be the beginning of many difficulties for the family.*

**W**ITH NO CHILD forthcoming, Sarah became more and more desperate. Barrenness was seen as a great misfortune at that time; some even believed that God must have cursed a barren woman for some great sin. The stigma was therefore enormous, increasing Sarah's desperation to give her husband a child. She finally suggested to Abraham that they should use Hagar, her Egyptian slave, as a surrogate mother. This was common practice in those

### SARAH PRESENTS HAGAR

Louis-Joseph Le Lorrain's 1743 painting shows Sarah, childless and desperate, presenting her Egyptian slave Hagar to Abraham, in the hope that he will agree to father a child for them with her.

days, and, as a slave, Hagar was Sarah's property to do with as she willed. Since God had kept her and Abraham from having children of their own, Sarah reasoned, maybe he would give them a child through Hagar instead. She said to Abraham: "The LORD has kept me from having children. Go, sleep with my slave; perhaps I can build a family through her" (Genesis: 16:2).

### Hagar becomes pregnant

Abraham agreed with Sarah and, at the age of 85, he fathered a child through Hagar. The plan soon went wrong, for when Hagar knew she was pregnant, she began to despise Sarah. Sarah in turn became angry with Abraham, whom she blamed for the present situation. Abraham said that Hagar was Sarah's slave, to do with as she saw fit. Sarah began to ill-treat her and, finally, Hagar fled.

### A meeting with an angel

Hagar headed south and stopped one day by a spring in the desert. Here she met the angel of the LORD. The angel already knew her name, and he also knew that she was the slave of Sarah. He asked her where she had come from and where she was going. Hagar explained that she was fleeing from her mistress, but she did not give an answer as to where she was going. The angel then spoke to Hagar, telling her

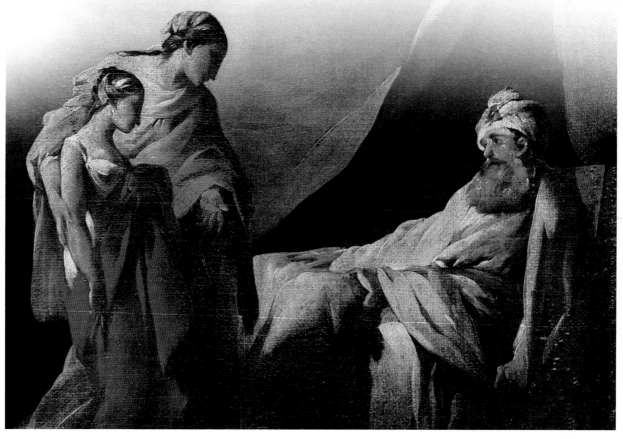

DESERT EXILE
Sarah's slave Hagar, pregnant with Abraham's child, fled into the bleak and inhospitable landscape of the wilderness of Shur, where she was visited by the angel of God near a spring of water.

## ISHMAEL

Abraham loved Ishmael, and grieved when Sarah later insisted that he and Hagar should be sent away (Genesis 21:8–20). God earmarked Ishmael for blessing, promising he would father 12 rulers (fulfilled in Genesis 25:12–16). Ishmael was included among those circumcised, showing that, even if he was not part of the covenant community, he and his descendants would be blessed, and God was clearly with him as he grew up (21:20). Some Arab peoples trace their line to the descendants of Abraham through Ishmael. The holy book of Islam, the Qu'ran, says that the Ka'aba – a monument in Mecca that is the most sacred site for Muslims – was built by Abraham and Ishmael.

THE KA'ABA AT MECCA

that she should return to Sarah and submit to her, but also making her a promise: "I will increase your descendants so much that they will be too numerous to count" (16:10).

### Ishmael's destiny

The angel then confirmed to Hagar that she was pregnant with a son, and told her that she was to call him Ishmael, meaning "God hears", as a reminder that God had heard her desperate cry for help in the desert. He also prophesied that Ishmael would be like a wild desert donkey, loving freedom and unable to be trained, and would constantly live in hostility towards his brothers. The angel told Hagar that her son's "hand will be against everyone and everyone's hand

against him" (16:12). This was a reference to Ishmael's desendants, who would later have uneasy relationships with other tribes.

### The God who sees

Hagar responded by giving a name to God – "the God who sees me", saying "I have now seen the One who sees me" (16:13). After her encounter, the spring by which she had met the angel became known as Beer Lahai Roi ("Well of the Living One who sees me").

Encouraged by her experience in the desert, Hagar returned home to Sarah and Abraham, and in due course gave birth to Abraham's son, who he named Ishmael. Abraham was now 86 years old.

AFTER ❯❯

**Hagar, with her son Ishmael, was once again sent away by Abraham.**

#### INTO EXILE

God's prophecy to Abraham was fulfilled at the age of 100, when Sarah gave birth to Isaac. Some two years later, Sarah saw Ishmael mocking Isaac and urged her husband to **send Ishmael away 58 ❯❯**. Abraham was distressed because Ishmael was his son, but God promised that Ishmael too would **become a great nation 67 ❯❯**. Abraham complied with Sarah's wishes, and God miraculously provided for Hagar and Ishmael on their journey (Genesis 21:8–20).

THE ANGEL RESCUES HAGAR AND HER SON, BY EUSTACHE LE SUEUR, c.1648

**TALE OF TWO CITIES**
John Martin's 1852 painting *The Destruction of Sodom and Gomorrah* illustrates the annihilation of Sodom and Gomorrah, after their inhabitants descended into sinful ways.

**« BEFORE**

**A meeting with three travellers would change Abraham's life when he discovered they were not mortal men, but God and two angels.**

**AN UNLIKELY PROMISE**
One day, Abraham was sitting by his tent when he noticed **three men** nearby (Genesis 18:1,2). With traditional hospitality, Abraham invited the mysterious visitors to stay and eat. While the meal was being prepared, they suddenly asked, "Where is your wife Sarah?" If Abraham was surprised these strangers knew her name, he did not show it, but simply pointed to the tent. It was then that one of them, now revealed as God himself, promised that **Sarah would have a son** (Genesis 18:10), reaffirming **his earlier covenant « 51**. Sarah, listening from inside the tent, laughed aloud. After all, they were both very old now. But God said, "Is anything too hard for the LORD?" (18:14), promising that within the year Sarah would have her son.

# Sodom and Gomorrah

*When God told Abraham about the judgment coming on the cities of Sodom and Gomorrah, Abraham pleaded for mercy. However, a visit by angels revealed that judgment was inevitable. Although Abraham's nephew, Lot, escaped, Lot's wife's hesitation was to cost her dearly.*

**A**FTER ABRAHAM and his wife Sarah were visited by God and two angels, and Sarah was given the prophecy that she would bear Abraham a child within a year, God and his angels prepared to leave. God spoke to Abraham, telling him that the cities of Sodom and Gomorrah – where

Abraham's nephew Lot lived – were so sinful that the news had reached heaven itself, and that the cities would be destroyed.

**Bargaining with God**
Mixing faith with the custom of bartering, Abraham appealed to God's justice. Surely God would not destroy a whole city, both

righteous people and sinners together? What if there were 50 righteous people in Sodom – surely then God would spare the city? God agreed, saying: "If I find fifty righteous people in the city of Sodom, I will spare the whole place for their sake" (Genesis 18:26). However, Abraham was not satisfied with this, asking what if there were not 50, but 45 righteous people, what would God do then? He kept pressing his point, and argued for 45, 40, 30, 20, and then ten people. And God agreed with him at each stage,

> **"** Then the **LORD rained** down burning sulphur on Sodom and Gomorrah.**"**
>
> **GENESIS** 19:24

# "But Lot's wife looked back, and she became a pillar of salt."

GENESIS 19:26

**LOT'S WIFE LOOKS BACK**
Lot and his family, depicted in this 13th-century stained glass panel, are urged on by two angels to flee from Sodom while the city burns behind them. Lot's wife is unable to resist looking back and becomes a pillar of salt.

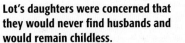

**ANALYSIS**

## JUDGMENT IN THE BIBLE

This is one of many Bible stories about God's judgment. It features the precise timing of a natural event – an earthquake. The region around Sodom and Gomorrah was rich in bitumen, sulphur, and petroleum, so the ingredients for destruction on a massive scale were already there. Earthquakes are common in this area, and could have set off a chain reaction, resulting in explosions and falling burning sulphur (which is described as

"brimstone and fire" in older translations). Whenever the Bible speaks of judgment, however, it also speaks of God's provision for escape, through repentance and faith. The people of Sodom and Gomorrah were not prepared to change, and so reaped the inevitable consequences of their behaviour. Jesus later used the fate of Lot's wife as a warning not to look back but to be ready for judgment day (Luke 17:32).

**SYMBOLS**

## PROVERBIAL CITIES OF SIN

After the dramatic demonstration of God's judgment on Sodom and Gomorrah, the names of these cities became bywords for gross wickedness, particularly of a sexual kind, and a dramatic warning of God's judgment. The book of Revelation, describing Babylon's destruction at the end-time, notes that "the smoke from her goes up for ever and ever" (Revelation 19:3), which is a reference to the smoke that rose up from Sodom and Gomorrah and that would never be forgotten.

finally telling Abraham that if just ten righteous people could be found in Sodom, his judgment would be withheld.

### A mixed reception

God sent his two angels to Sodom, and when they arrived there, they found Abraham's nephew, Lot, at the city gate. He invited the strangers into his home, and offered them food and a place to stay for the night. The angels agreed, but before they went to their beds that evening, men from across the city surrounded the house, demanding that Lot should bring out his guests so they could have sex with them. Lot was horrified, but the men were determined and even tried to break down the door. Lot was pulled inside his house by the angels, who

blinded those outside. The angels told Lot to gather his family quickly and get them out of Sodom, explaining that God was about to destroy the city. But Lot's sons-in-law thought he was joking and would not leave. With dawn fast approaching, the angels said to Lot: "Hurry! Take your wife and your two daughters who are here, or you will be swept away when the city is punished" (19:15). Lot still hesitated, so the visitors grabbed hold of him, his wife, and his two daughters and rushed them out of the city, urging them to keep running until they reached the mountains and not to look back. Lot begged the angels to let him go to nearby Zoar, and they agreed that this small town could be spared.

### A disastrous ending

At sunrise, burning sulphur began to fall on Sodom and Gomorrah, destroying all of the inhabitants of the cities and the surrounding

**NATURAL MONUMENT**
This column of rock, known as "Lot's wife", overlooks the salt-rich waters of the Dead Sea at Mount Sodom in southern Israel. It is claimed by some to be where Lot's wife turned back to look at the city of Sodom.

region, and also all of the plants growing on the land. And then personal tragedy struck for Lot: his wife failed to follow the angels' instructions, but looked back at Sodom and Gomorrah, and was turned into a pillar of salt.

### Raised to the ground

The following morning, Abraham returned to the place where he had walked with God and had pleaded for mercy for the righteous of Sodom and Gomorrah. When he looked towards the two cities, all he

saw was dense smoke, resembling the smoke from a furnace, rising up into the sky. Lot had been saved and Abraham knew that God's judgment had been fulfilled.

**AFTER** ›››

Lot's daughters were concerned that they would never find husbands and would remain childless.

**THE DAUGHTERS OF LOT**
Lot was afraid to stay in Zoar, so he moved into the mountains. Living with him in a cave, Lot's two daughters worried they would never have children. So they got Lot drunk and, on consecutive nights, went to bed with him, without his even knowing it. Both became pregnant by their father. The elder daughter's son, Moab, became the ancestor of the **Moabites 136–37** ››; the younger daughter's son, Ben-Ammi, became the ancestor of the **Ammonites 131** ››.

**LOT'S CAVE, NEAR SAFI, JORDAN**

**BEFORE** «

When Abraham resorted to half-truth about Sarah, only God's intervention prevented disaster.

### SOUTH TO GERAR

Abraham moved to Gerar, which was ruled by the Philistine king, Abimelech (Genesis 20). Repeating **the ploy he had used in Egypt << 49**, he pretended that Sarah was his sister. Abimelech took Sarah into his harem, but **God showed the king in a dream that Sarah was married**. Abimelech was outraged that he had been lied to and protested that he had not touched Sarah.

**TEL HAROR IN ISRAEL, SITE OF ANCIENT GERAR**

### ABRAHAM'S PRAYER

After explaining that he had been afraid for his life, and that Sarah really was his half-sister, Abraham was **reunited with his wife and given gifts by Abimelech**. He then prayed for Abimelech's household, which was under a curse of barrenness because the king had taken Sarah into his harem. **The curse was lifted** and the women were able to have children – in contrast to Abraham and Sarah, who were still childless.

# Abraham and Isaac

*When at last Sarah miraculously bore Abraham a son in their old age, as God had promised, their joy was unimaginable. Yet God's promise that he would make a great nation from Abraham seemed doubtful when he told him to sacrifice his son, Isaac.*

A BRAHAM'S THREE mysterious visitors had told him that he and Sarah would have their promised son within a year (see p.56). Despite Sarah's earlier disbelief, she did become pregnant and bore Abraham a son. Abraham was 100 and she was 90 – but God's promise was fulfilled despite their old age. Having previously laughed in disbelief, Sarah now laughed with sheer delight.

### The birth of Isaac

God had already told Abraham that the boy was to be named Isaac, meaning "he laughs", and he was circumcised on the eighth day, just as God had commanded (Genesis 17:12). As Isaac grew up, he faced mockery from his step-brother, Ishmael. This so maddened Sarah

### FAITH CONFIRMED

Giovanni Battista Tiepolo's 1715 fresco *Sacrifice of Isaac* portrays Abraham's trust in God at the moment the angel intervenes. Abraham's faith confirmed, God renews his promise to bless him, and all the nations, through his son Isaac.

that she had Ishmael and his mother Hagar, her Egyptian slave, banished from the household.

### Abraham tested

Some years later, Abraham received a command from God that he could hardly believe. God asked him to sacrifice his "only son" (22:2) – emphasizing that he really did mean Isaac, through whom God's promise to make Abraham's

descendants a great nation would be fulfilled, not the banished Ishmael. He was to take Isaac to a mountain in the region of Moriah that God would reveal to him. Not only was Abraham to sacrifice Isaac, but he was to make him a burnt offering (see panel, far right), thereby sealing his fate.

Despite any misgivings that he had, Abraham obediently set off the next morning, accompanied by

> "Now I know that you **fear God**, for you have not **withheld** from me your son, **your only son**."
>
> **GENESIS** 22:12

### FOUNDATION STONE

The Dome of the Rock mosque in Jerusalem is built over a rocky outcrop known as the Foundation Stone. According to Jewish tradition, this is the site in Moriah where Abraham took Isaac to sacrifice him.

Isaac, two servants, and a donkey loaded with wood. Approaching Moriah on the third day, Abraham told his servants to wait while he and Isaac went ahead – Isaac carrying the wood and Abraham carrying the fire and the knife.

Perplexed by the absence of an animal to be sacrificed, Isaac asked his father where it was. Still trusting in God's command, Abraham simply replied, "God himself will provide the lamb for the burnt offering, my son" (22:8). With that, they pressed on.

### God's intervention

Having arrived at Moriah, Abraham built a stone altar and arranged the wood on it. He then tied up Isaac, laid him on the altar, and quickly took his knife. It was just at that moment – the last possible minute – that the angel of the Lord called out to him to stop: "Abraham, Abraham!" (22:11).

Abraham's commitment to God had passed the ultimate test – he was willing to sacrifice Isaac if God commanded it, trusting in him and not withholding the very child that God had promised him. When Abraham looked up, he suddenly saw a ram caught by its horns in a thicket. He quickly went over, took the ram, and sacrificed it as a burnt offering instead of Isaac.

### A promise renewed

To commemorate the incident, Abraham gave Moriah a new name: *Yahweh Yireh*, which means "the Lord will provide" in Hebrew. However, God had not finished.

His angel told Abraham that because he had been ready to make this incredible sacrifice, God was now reaffirming his promise – Abraham's descendants would indeed become as numerous as the stars in the sky and the grains of sand on the seashore. Through his offspring, all the nations on Earth would be blessed.

## BURNT OFFERINGS

When God tested Abraham's faith, he told him not just to sacrifice Isaac, but to make him a "burnt offering" (Genesis 22:2). According to Jewish law, in some cases animals could be eaten after being ceremonially sacrificed. However, for a burnt offering, the animal was killed then burned until nothing was left but ashes.

Burnt offerings were seen as an expression of total commitment to God, symbolically holding nothing back for oneself. When God challenged Abraham to offer this sort of sacrifice, he wanted to see how far his commitment would go, for nothing would have been left of God's promise or Abraham's hope if God had not intervened at the end.

**ISRAELITE ALTAR FOR BURNT OFFERINGS**

## AFTER

**God's chosen people would be descended through Isaac.**

### FATHER OF NATIONS

Ishmael was Abraham's firstborn son, but it was through Isaac that the Judaic line would be traced. Isaac became one of Israel's **three great patriarchs** (Abraham, Isaac, and Jacob), while Ishmael **founded the Arab nations 67 >>**. The New Testament compares Isaac – the child of God's promise rather than human effort – to Christians, who are saved by grace alone (Galatians 4:21–23).

**MUSLIMS AND JEWS TRACE LINE TO ABRAHAM**

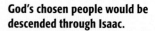

# Abraham

> " …**Abraham** in hope believed and so became **the father of many nations**…"
>
> ROMANS 4:18

**T**HE BIBLE IS full of stories of God doing things with unpromising material or people, and Abraham is a classic example. When God wanted to build a family of faith, he began with a man whose wife, Sarai (Sarah), was childless, but God promised him that his descendants would be numerous: "Look up at the sky and count the stars – if indeed you can count them… So shall your offspring be" (Genesis 15:5).

Abraham (originally named Abram) came from Ur in Mesopotamia, where he would have grown up believing in many gods. Nonetheless, God chose to reveal himself to Abraham, calling him to go to Canaan (see pp.48–49). With that call came God's promise to make him into a great nation that would bless many other nations. So, aged 75, Abraham set off.

Abraham was a wealthy man, with servants, livestock, and many possessions. He quickly established himself as a respected leader in the region, and his rescue of his nephew Lot from invading kings showed that he was a fighter too. However, he still had no son, and it was difficult to see how God would fulfil his promise.

### God's covenant

It was at this point that God made a covenant (see p.50) with Abraham, which had two aspects. The first was concerned with the land, "from the Wadi [river] of Egypt to… the Euphrates" (15:18), which God promised to Abraham and his descendants. Over the years, Abraham travelled through this land, from Dan in the north (14:14) to Beersheba in the south (21:33).

(see pp.48–49)

## HISTORY AND CULTURE

### BETHEL

Bethel (meaning "House of God") is where Abraham built an altar when he first arrived in Canaan (Genesis 12:8). Jacob had two special experiences there (see pp.70–71 and pp.76–77). In later biblical history, the Ark of the Covenant was at Bethel for some time (Judges 20:26–28), and, after the kingdom divided, Jeroboam placed a golden calf there for people to worship (1 Kings 12:26–30). This became a popular shrine, but Amos and Hosea denounced it as idolatrous and prophesied its overthrow. The godly King Josiah finally destroyed the altar (2 Kings 23:15).

**AN IMAGE OF THE VILLAGE OF BEITIN, *c.*1900, BELIEVED TO BE THE BIBLICAL BETHEL**

### THE FATHER OF ISRAEL
This stained glass depiction of Abraham, the first patriarch, is by the English church designer Charles Eamer Kempe (1837–1907), who designed and installed windows, wall paintings, and embroideries. This depiction of Abraham is taken from the east window of St Editha's Church, Staffordshire, UK.

Yet at his death, all Abraham owned was a field with a cave, bought as a burial plot.

The second aspect concerned family. God had already promised Abraham a large family, so when Sarai remained barren, Abraham took her Egyptian slave, Hagar, as a surrogate mother, trying to further God's plan.

When Sarai heard that Hagar was pregnant she began to mistreat her. Hagar ran away, and was then visited by the angel of the LORD who told her: "You are now pregnant and you will give birth to a son. You shall name him Ishmael, for the Lord has heard of your misery" (16:11; "Ishmael" means "God hears"). The angel said that Ishmael would "live in hostility" (16:12) towards his brothers.

Thirteen years passed before God reaffirmed his promises and changed Abraham's name, from the original Abram ("Exalted Father") to Abraham ("Father of Many"), in a sign of what was to come (17:5). God also changed his wife's name, from Sarai (meaning "quarrelsome") to Sarah (meaning "princess"), because "kings of peoples will come from her" (17:16). There was to be a symbol of this covenant too: circumcision. Every male was to be immediately circumcised, and every subsequent baby boy at eight days old. Three heaven-sent visitors, appearing as ordinary men, told Abraham that within the year, he and Sarah would hold a son of their own in their arms (18:10–15).

## A son at last

Abraham named his son Isaac, meaning "he laughs", because the happy sound of laughter now filled their home. Some years later this joy was shattered, when God told Abraham to sacrifice this longed-for son (22:1–18). Abraham was obedient, trusting God would do something. His faith was rewarded,

as an angel stopped the sacrifice at the last moment and God provided a substitute sacrifice of a ram.

When Sarah died, at the age of 127, Abraham immediately set about arranging a wife for Isaac and a new matriarch for the family. So he sent his chief servant to Mesopotamia to find a wife from among his own people there. God guided the servant and he came back with the beautiful Rebekah,

### ABRAHAM'S VISITORS
A Macedonian icon, c.1700, *Abraham and the Three Angels*, depicts the "three visitors" (Genesis 18) who came to Abraham's tent at Mamre and promised a son to him and Sarah within a year.

whom Isaac married. In his will, Abraham named Isaac as his heir. When Abraham died he was 175, having spent 100 of his years on Earth following the God who had revealed himself to him. It would be left to his descendants – his son Isaac, Isaac's son Jacob, and Jacob's 12 sons, who founded the 12 tribes of Israel – to fulfil God's promise to Abraham.

## A man of faith
Abraham is one of the Old Testament figures often mentioned in the New Testament, as an example of faith. Abraham was by no means perfect, but the New Testament uses him to show how faith is the key element in having a relationship with God, rather than through being good, trying hard, or getting everything right. God's promise to Abraham, that every nation would be blessed, was to come to fruition some 2,000 years later, through Abraham's descendant, Jesus.

### HISTORY AND CULTURE
## ABRAHAM AND THE ABRAHAMIC FAITHS

No other figure in the Bible – apart from Jesus – has dominated the sphere of religion more than Abraham. He is significant for the world's three great monotheistic (believing in one god) faiths: Judaism, Christianity, and Islam.

Jews see Abraham as Israel's founding father, and the first patriarch of the Jewish people. He was an inspiration through his obedience and faith, and the first to teach the idea that there is only one god. Christians see Abraham as an example of relationship through faith. It is through Abraham's descendent, Jesus, that God's promises are fulfilled. Muslims see Abraham (Ibrahim) as a great prophet whose son Ishmael was "the father of Arab peoples" and ancestor of Muhammad, the founder of Islam.

**18TH-CENTURY ISLAMIC DEPICTION OF IBRAHIM PREPARING TO SACRIFICE ISAAC**

« BEFORE

**When Abraham's wife Sarah died, he buried her in a cave.**

### A FINAL RESTING PLACE

Sarah died at the age of 127 (Genesis 23:1,2). As a nomad, **Abraham owned no land**, so he approached local Hittites in Hebron to buy some land where he could bury Sarah. After much negotiating at the city gates, a price – and an exorbitant one at that – was finally agreed. The field and cave of **Machpelah** were sold to Abraham and he buried Sarah in the cave, a common practice in ancient times.

ANCIENT BURIAL CAVE IN THE KIDRON VALLEY

# A Wife for Isaac

*Abraham sent a servant to find a wife for his son Isaac. In a classic romance story, the servant was led to the beautiful Rebekah, who gladly returned home with him to marry Isaac.*

A S THE YEARS passed and Abraham grew older, he became acutely aware of the need to find Isaac a wife. He therefore called his chief servant and made him swear an oath that he would not look among the Canaanites, but would go to Abraham's homeland and find a woman there among his relatives. The servant asked what to do if the woman would not come back with him – could he take Isaac there? Abraham was clear,

however: God had promised the land of Canaan to him and his offspring, so God would ensure the task was fulfilled.

Armed with gifts of "all kinds of good things from his master" (Genesis 24:10), the servant set off. Arriving at a well outside Nahor in northwest Mesopotamia, the servant stopped to water his camels. It was evening, the time when women drew water from the well, so he prayed, asking God for the

following sign: if he said to a woman, "Please give me a drink," and she replied, "Drink, while I give some water to your camels

> **" Go to my country** and my own relatives and **get a wife for my son Isaac."**
>
> GENESIS 24:4

too", then he would know that this was the one God had chosen.

### The prayer is answered

Before the servant had finished praying, a young woman called Rebekah appeared and he asked her for some water. She offered him a drink from a jar she had just filled from the well, and also returned to the well to bring water for his camels. The servant gave her gifts and asked who her father was and whether there was room in her father's house for him to spend the night. When she replied, he realized that God had led him

### A TOKEN OF GOLD

Abraham's servant lavished gifts of valuable gold and silver jewellery on Rebekah and her family, as well as clothing and costly gifts, to fulfil the custom of paying a bride-price (see pp.64–65).

to part of Abraham's extended family and that his prayer was indeed being answered.

### At Rebekah's home

When Rebekah arrived home with expensive gifts, her brother Laban invited the servant into their home. There, the servant explained how Abraham had sent him to find a wife for Isaac, and how he had prayed earlier that day and his request for a sign had been granted. Laban and his father, Bethuel, said they could see this was God's doing and offered Rebekah in marriage to Isaac. The servant then lavished costly gifts on them all as the bride-price – an amount commonly paid by the groom's family to the bride's family – and spent the night there.

### The journey home

Although the servant was eager to leave, the family asked to spend another ten days with Rebekah, perhaps to ensure that everything was in order before she left. However, the servant underlined the urgency of his task and, having checked with Rebekah that she was ready to go, her family blessed them on their way.

### MEETING PLACE

Abraham's servant waited at a well where the women of the town would come to draw water. Wells are highly valued in places where water sources are scarce and in desert regions, such as the Ténéré in Niger, pictured here, women still gather to use them.

### LABAN

Laban was the grandson of Nahor, Abraham's brother. His branch of the family had remained in Haran when Abraham left for Canaan, so he grew up as an Aramean (Genesis 28:5), with Aramaic practices and gods. In both the Isaac and Jacob marriage stories, Laban appears as a self-interested opportunist, happy to deceive others to make money, as Jacob – himself a trickster – discovered when Laban tricked him into working 14 years for his bride (see pp.72–73). Laban even tricked his own daughters, Leah and Rachel, saving nothing for them from the bride-price Jacob paid through his labour, and prompting Rachel's theft of the household gods *in lieu* (Genesis 31:14–19).

**GENEALOGICAL TREE OF LABAN**

## "So she became his wife, and he loved her…"

GENESIS 24:67

Isaac was sitting out in the fields, praying, when he looked up and saw camels approaching. When Rebekah saw him, she got down from her camel and asked the servant who this was. When she heard it was Isaac, she put on her veil, to indicate she was his bride, and the servant told Isaac all that had happened. So Isaac took her into the tent of his mother Sarah – who had died before Abraham had despatched his servant – as a sign not only that he was marrying her but that she was taking his mother's place as matriarch of the family. And so it was that he married Rebekah.

AFTER »

One hundred years after God had called him to Canaan, Abraham died (Genesis 25:7–10).

#### A PROPHECY FULFILLED

As his death drew closer, Abraham assigned all of his wealth to Isaac. He died at the age of 175, having lived the long life God had promised (Genesis 15:15). He was **buried alongside his wife Sarah** in the cave of Machpelah. While Abraham had been promised a nation, all he actually possessed by his death was a burial plot. It would be through his descendants that God's promise to him would be realized.

**CAVE OF THE PATRIARCHS, MACHPELAH**

### CLOSE FAMILY MARRIAGES

Marrying someone from the same tribe, clan, or family (known as endogamy) was common in the ancient world (see pp.64–65), and remains so in many cultures, usually for ethnic, religious, or social concerns. Since there is no suggestion that Laban's family shared Abraham's faith, his desire to find a wife for his son Isaac from his own country and relatives was perhaps more ethnic than anything else. It may have been that he wanted to perpetuate family traditions, or because he was surrounded by Canaanites, who were descended from Canaan, whose father Ham had angered his father Noah, and had been put under a curse (Genesis 9:20–27). Abraham may have been directing his son towards a Semite, descended from Noah's son Shem, who had received his father's blessing.

HISTORY AND CULTURE

# Marriage and Family Life

"He who **finds a wife** finds what is **good** and **receives favour** from the LORD."

PROVERBS 18:22

**PASSING ON TRADITIONS**
A mother leads her daughter in the ceremonial lighting of candles at sunset on Friday to mark the start of *Shabbat*, the Sabbath.

L ife and society in ancient Israel was centred on the importance of family. Life was far less individualistic than in the West today, with people having a sense of belonging to something bigger than themselves. The first level of belonging was to the family or household. The head, or patriarch, of the household supported his wife or wives, his sons and their wives, his grandchildren, and other family members who were dependent on him. When a patriarch died, his place was taken by his eldest son, who inherited twice as much as any other sons, because he now needed the resources to support the wider family.

All levels of society were seen as extensions of the core family. The clan consisted of a group of families who were linked by kinship or territory (kinship was usually created for those linked by territory alone), and clan elders were considered the first point of authority in matters such as marriage, inheritance, and war.

The clans joined to form a tribe, of which there were 12 in ancient Israel, each descended from one of the 12 sons of Jacob (see pp.74–75). These 12 tribes made up the nation of Israel. However, increasing centralization of power from around 1020 BC reduced the importance of the clans and tribes.

Important training and religious teaching occurred within the family. Mothers taught their daughters domestic and possibly farming skills, while fathers taught their sons their trade. Though a father's authority was absolute, his wife and daughters were not altogether subservient, as in some ancient civilizations.

**TWELVE TRIBES OF ISRAEL**
The 12 tribes are the descendants of the 12 sons of Jacob, whose name was changed to Israel. Around the central *menorah* are the symbols of the tribes: the lion represents Judah, for example.

## FINDING A BRIDE

Single women remained at home under their patriarch's care and authority until a marriage was arranged, and then they joined their husband's family. Marriages were arranged by parents, and were normally kept within the clan, ideally with a close relative, although occasionally people would marry into different cultures. However, arranged marriages did not always mean the couple had no say in the matter, as the story of Jacob and Rachel shows (see p.72).

The first step was betrothal, a legal commitment to marry. This period could last up to a year. During this time, the couple lived apart and, in the earliest times, the man prepared the bride price –

**SHEKELS**
Wealthy men who were required to pay the bride price would offer an agreed sum of money or a piece of property.

payment, either in money or its equivalent, such as cattle, land, woven goods, or work, to compensate the bride's family for losing a daughter. The bride price was also a sort of insurance, which would be given to the woman if her husband died.

From the Second Temple period (c.516 BC– AD 70), however, this practice was abandoned in favour of the dowry system, whereby the bride's family would pay the husband to take their daughter as his wife.

**PRIZED POSSESSION**
Prospective grooms who were not rich enough to pay money provided a bride price of raw materials or other goods, such as textiles, or even offered to work for the bride's family.

## THE WEDDING

Accompanied by friends, the groom went to the bride's home, where she was waiting, veiled and in her finest apparel. In a simple ceremony, he declared that she was his wife and he was her husband, and the marriage was complete. The wedding banquet could last up to a week for wealthier families, with the whole village invited.

**MARRIAGE CONTRACT**
The *ketubah* replaced the biblical bride price and dowry systems with a promise for the groom to pay the widow a certain sum in case of death or divorce. It is still in use today.

**WEDDING CANOPY**
Today, the main part of the service is conducted beneath a cloth canopy called a *huppah*, symbolizing the home in which the newly wed couple begin their married life. In biblical times the huppah was a room or tent.

---

## SWADDLING

Giving birth was not always straightforward, so a safe delivery was marked with special ceremonies, such as naming, circumcision, and redemption (see p.319), as an expression of gratitude to God.

After the birth, midwives washed the baby, rubbed its skin with salt and oil to cleanse and toughen it, then wrapped the infant tightly in swaddling cloths, coarsely woven linen strips, in the belief that this helped strengthen the bones. The cloths were loosened periodically so that the mother could rub the baby's skin with olive oil and dust it with powdered myrtle leaves.

## HAVING CHILDREN

In biblical times, having many children was seen as God's blessing and, by contrast, childlessness was viewed as a great misfortune, or even as God's judgment. If it was the wife who was deemed to be infertile and the man had no other wives, one way around the problem was for the wife to give her maidservant to her husband so that he could have a child through her, as Sarah did with Hagar (see pp.54–55). But the Bible contains many stories of people who simply trusted God for a solution to their infertility – as did Hannah, Samuel's mother (see pp.142–43).

Sons were considered to be especially important. The family line was thought to live on through its sons and grandsons, and sons also provided for their parents in old age.

Education was higly valued. After the exile, religious education became particularly important to preserve identity, and education became compulsory for boys.

In the New Testament Jesus taught the value of children. He refused to exclude them and told people they could learn from them (Matthew 19:13–15; 21:14–16).

**BOYS LEARNING THE TALMUD**
In contrast to today, in ancient times children did most of their learning at home and it was the duty of the head of the family to teach them the commandments (Deuteronomy 6:7).

**ESAU CEDES HIS BIRTHRIGHT**
Pictured left by Guarino da Solofra (1611–54),
Esau gave up his birthright – entitling him to a
larger inheritance as the eldest son – to his
brother Jacob for a plate of stew.

**BEFORE**

Although God's plan would be continued through Abraham and Sarah's son, Isaac, God also blessed Abraham's other son Ishmael, just as he had promised to do.

### ISHMAEL'S LINE

God told Abraham that his son Ishmael – whose mother was not Sarah, but **Hagar ‹‹ 54–55**, Sarah's slave – would also be fruitful and that he would have many descendants (Genesis 17:18–22). Ishmael had 12 sons (as did Nahor, Esau, and Jacob), and his sons became the **founders and rulers of 12 tribes** who lived as wandering nomads across the Arabian desert and who dominated the trade routes from the coast to **Egypt, Syria, and Mesopotamia**. Ishmael himself lived to the age of 137 (Genesis 25:12–18).

**DESERT-DWELLING NOMADS**

## PEOPLE

### REBEKAH

Rebekah was clearly a woman of strong character, reflected in her prompt decision to leave her family in Mesopotamia and go with the servant to marry Isaac, and her bold questioning of God about her uncomfortable pregnancy (Genesis 25:22). Rebekah's strength also had its bad side, however, shown in the way she schemed to get Isaac's blessing for Jacob, her favourite (see pp.68–69). She paid the price for this, promising Jacob that any curse provoked by what they were doing would fall on her alone (27:12–13). This was perhaps fulfilled in her never seeing Jacob again after their trickery.

> **"Isaac prayed to the Lord** on behalf of his wife, because she was childless. The Lord answered his prayer, and **his wife Rebekah became pregnant."**

GENESIS 25:21

# Esau and Jacob

*Like his mother, Sarah, Isaac's wife Rebekah was barren; but after Isaac prayed for her, she became pregnant with twins. However, a rivalry that began in her womb would continue through life, with far-reaching consequences.*

A BRAHAM HAD brought Rebekah from his family in northwest Mesopotamia to be a wife for his son Isaac so that God's promise, made many years earlier, of a great family that would become a great nation might be fulfilled. Twenty years of marriage passed by, however, and the couple remained childless. Isaac prayed for Rebekah and at last she became pregnant – with twins.

### A prophetic sign

Rebekah's pregnancy was not comfortable; the two babies were constantly jostling one another in her womb, so much so that she asked God what was happening. God told her that two nations were in her womb; one would be stronger than the other, and the older would serve the younger.

When the time came for her delivery, two baby boys were born. The first to appear was red, with a body covered in hair, and so they named him Esau ("Hairy"). His brother was born immediately afterwards, so close that he was grasping Esau's heel, and so they called him Jacob ("He grasps the heel"). This beginning would symbolize the lifelong strife between the two brothers.

### A birthright lost

As the boys grew up, Esau became a skilful hunter who loved the outdoors, while Jacob was a quieter character who preferred to stay at home. Their different natures meant that favouritism crept into the family; Isaac, who loved wild game, preferred Esau, while Rebekah preferred Jacob.

One day, Jacob was cooking some stew when Esau came in from the country, clearly having had no

success at hunting that day. He asked Jacob for some of his meal because he was famished. Jacob quickly seized this opportunity to take advantage of his brother, and demanded that Esau should first sell him his birthright – the privileges of the firstborn son. Esau was so hungry, and the stew smelled so good, that he wondered what good the birthright was if he was about to starve to death. Jacob pressed his advantage, making Esau swear an oath to give the birthright to him. Without thinking of the implications of his actions, Esau swore the oath, and Jacob gave him some bread and stew. Esau ate quickly and then left, having given up his birthright to merely satisfy his hunger.

### FAVOURED SON

Isaac was closest to his eldest son Esau, who was a skilful hunter and could provide for the family. They are pictured here in a detail from Lorenzo Ghiberti's spectacular 15th-century bronze *Gates of Paradise*.

**AFTER ››**

From precarious beginnings, Isaac gradually established himself in Canaan, eventually settling in the region of Beersheba.

### GROWING SUCCESS

As had happened to Abraham before him, Isaac faced a **severe famine** in Canaan, causing him to go to the territory of Abimelech, the Philistine king, where he repeated his father's deception of **pretending that his wife was his sister ‹‹ 49**. Here God reaffirmed that his promises to Abraham were promises to Isaac too and that he should therefore stay in Canaan (Genesis 26:1–6). Isaac was a successful farmer – his livestock increased and he grew wealthy. This provoked **the Philistines**, who blocked his wells and quarrelled with him over watering rights (26:12–22).

Isaac eventually moved to Beersheba, where God again appeared to him and confirmed the **blessing promised to Abraham ‹‹ 50–51**. Abimelech realized that it was better to have Isaac as an ally than a foe, and so he proposed a treaty, which Isaac agreed to.

**A SHEPHERD TENDING HIS FLOCKS**

**BEFORE**

Isaac's failing sight was symbolic of
the effects of the Fall.

**PHYSICAL AILMENTS**

When Adam and Eve **rebelled against God
≪ 36–37**, the world began to lose the
perfection in which God had created it.
Humankind experienced the consequences
of that, including the **appearance of
suffering, physical ailments, and death**
(see Genesis 3:16–19). Many cultures in
the ancient world saw disease as a reflection
of the displeasure of God or the gods.
Although the Bible sometimes portrays
disease as God's judgment – for example
the "**serious diseases**" that occurred in
Pharaoh's household when he **took
Abram's wife Sarai into his harem ≪ 49**
(Genesis 12:17) – it also describes it as the
consequence of life in a now imperfect
world. Isaac's failing sight is one of the **first
examples in the Bible of physical ailments**.

# A Father's Blessing

*The favouritism that Isaac and Rebekah each had for one of their sons
culminated in Rebekah helping Jacob to trick Isaac into giving him the
blessing that would make Jacob the future leader of the tribe.*

**A** **WARE THAT HE WAS**
getting older and that his
eyesight was now failing,
Isaac sent for his favourite son,
Esau. He asked Esau to go out and
hunt some wild game and then
make him a meal from it, after
which he would give Esau his
blessing as the firstborn son.

*A scheming mother*

As Esau left, Rebekah, who had
overheard the conversation, told
Jacob – whom she favoured over

Esau – to get some goats from the
flock so that she could prepare one
of Isaac's favourite meals. Jacob
could then take it to him in place
of Esau, and get Isaac's blessing
before Esau returned.

Jacob was doubtful about the
plan; after all, Isaac's sight might
be poor, but what if he
touched him? Esau
was hairy, but
Jacob had
smooth skin. If
the trickery

were uncovered, Jacob worried
that he might end up with a curse
rather than a blessing. His mother
replied that she would let any
curse fall on her not him, and
urged him to do as she had said.
She took Esau's best clothes and
put them on Jacob, and covered
his hands and neck with
goatskins to make

> "May God give you **heaven's
> dew** and **earth's richness**…
> May **nations serve you**
> and **peoples bow down
> to you**."
> GENESIS 27:28,29

them feel hairy. Then she sent him to Isaac with the meal of meat and bread, prepared in just the way that Isaac liked it.

## A deceived father

As Jacob entered, Isaac's failing sight meant he had to ask who was there. Jacob said "I am Esau your firstborn" (Genesis 27:19). This was at best half truth and half lie, for while he was not Esau, he was the son who had the birthright of the firstborn, because Jacob had bought this from Esau (25:29–34). Isaac was suspicious, and asked how he had found the game so quickly. Jacob replied piously that God had helped him. Doubting it

### MOMENT OF DECEPTION
Blind and confused, Isaac – depicted here by Dutch painter Govaert Flinck (c.1638) – was tricked by his younger son Jacob into giving him the blessing he had intended for his first son Esau.

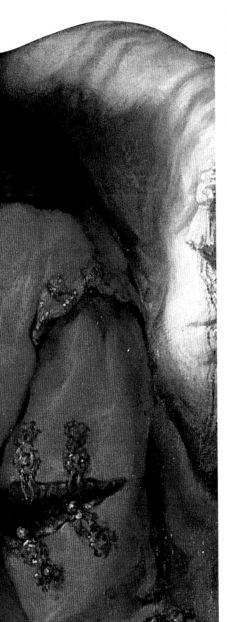

was Esau's voice, Isaac told him to come closer so he could touch him. However, this made him even more confused: the voice sounded like Jacob, but the hands felt like Esau. He asked again if he was Esau, and Jacob said he was. So Isaac ate the food, then called his son closer to bless him. As Jacob approached, the smell of Esau's clothes finally convinced Isaac. He pronounced his blessing, praying that this son's land would be fertile, nations might serve him, and his brothers would recognize him as leader. Isaac had unwittingly made possible God's earlier revelation to Rebekah that the older twin would serve the younger (25:23).

## A devastated brother

Jacob had scarcely left when Esau came in with his food, ready for his blessing. Isaac asked who it was, and when Esau told him, Isaac knew that something terrible had happened. Whom had he already blessed? Esau sobbed, his dream

### WILD GAME
Isaac asked Esau to go hunting in the open country for wild game, such as gazelle; this would not have been an everyday meat for the family, so he was asking Esau to prepare a very special meal before he gave his blessing.

of the future shattered, and implored his father to bless him too.

At last Isaac realized that Jacob had deceived him. Esau was furious: not only had Jacob gained his birthright, but he had now received their father's blessing too. Was nothing left for him? However, Isaac had already given Jacob his patriarchal blessing, and it could not be revoked (see panel, below). Despite his son's desperate pleas, all he could do was to tell Esau that his life would be hard and his land infertile, and that he would be ruled by his brother; but that a day would come when his descendants would throw off that rule – although it would not be for hundreds of years (2 Kings 8:20–22).

# "Haven't you reserved any blessing for me?"

GENESIS 27:36

## ANALYSIS

### BLESSINGS

Blessings – and their opposites, curses – were taken seriously in biblical times, not as mere words but as something that had real power to bring about what was declared. Once spoken, it was believed that a blessing could not be "unsaid" or revoked, such was the power of its words. It was recognized that God himself was the source of blessing, but people believed they could pray that blessing on to others, conferring God's presence, or his favour or help. Feasts commonly accompanied the giving of a blessing, so it was not unusual for Isaac to have asked Esau to prepare food for him. Deathbed blessings were particularly solemn and were considered binding, especially if delivered by a patriarch. The New Testament sees Jesus as God's ultimate blessing. In Christian art, Jesus is often depicted with his right hand raised – a sign of blessing.

JESUS WITH HIS RIGHT HAND RAISED

## SYMBOLS

### LAYING-ON OF HANDS

Blessings were often conferred on one person by another by the laying-on of hands on the recipient's head – a symbol of conveying God's presence, blessing, or power. The laying-on of hands could also symbolize God's commissioning of someone for service (see Numbers 27:18–23; Acts 13:1–3). Jesus laid his hands on children to bless them (Mark 10:16). The Holy Spirit was often received through the laying-on of hands (see Acts 8:17; 9:17; 19:6).

GESTURE OF BLESSING

## AFTER ≫

Esau was so angry that he planned to kill Jacob once Isaac was dead (Genesis 27:41), so Rebekah sent Jacob away.

### REBEKAH PROTECTS JACOB
Rebekah came up with a plan to send Jacob to her brother Laban, who lived in Haran. She told Isaac that she was disgusted with Esau's Hittite wives – who were "foreigners"

SETTLEMENT IN HARAN, MESOPOTAMIA

descended from Canaan – and that if Jacob also married a Hittite, her life would be unbearable. Isaac agreed to send him to find a wife from among their own people. When Esau heard the news, he took another wife, from Abraham's line – in the hope of gaining his father's approval (28:6–9). The struggle between the brothers would be mirrored in the future in the struggle between their descendants, Edom and Israel 78 ≫.

# Jacob's Ladder

*With Isaac deceived and Esau angry, Rebekah had arranged to send Jacob to her family in Mesopotamia. Jacob did not know whether God's promises to Abraham would be his, after all he had done. An encounter with God on his journey provided the answer.*

**J**ACOB'S JOURNEY was long – some 725 km (450 miles) – and many overnight stops were needed. One such stop changed his life for ever. Jacob had settled down for the night, using a stone as a pillow. As he slept, he dreamed about a stairway: its base was on the Earth and its top touched heaven, and angels were climbing up and down it. At the top stood God, who declared, "I am the LORD, the God of your father Abraham and the God of Isaac" (Genesis 28:13). God then promised to give Jacob the land where he was now lying, to make his descendants as widespread as the dust of the Earth, and through them to bless everyone on Earth – a reaffirmation of his promise to Abraham. God then added something that probably surprised Jacob after all he had done: he said, "I am with you and will watch over you wherever you go, and I will bring you back to this land. I will not leave you until I have done what I have promised you" (28:15).

Jacob awoke and was afraid, because he realized that God was there and that he had not been aware of it, and that this was a holy place, God's house, the very gate of heaven. Early the next morning, he took the stone that had been his pillow and erected it as a pillar, consecrating it with oil. He changed the place's name from Luz to Bethel, which means "House of God". Then he made a vow, saying that if God would be with him and watch over him on this journey, and would allow him to return home safely, then the LORD would be his God, this would be a holy spot for ever, and he would give God a tenth of all he received. He then went on his way.

This event was a key moment for Jacob, firstly because he realized that the God of his fathers could be his God too, and secondly, because he now understood that God could be encountered anywhere. His dream had revealed to him the connection between God in heaven and the people on Earth. It had shown Jacob that the God who had said he was with him and would not leave him, who would watch over him wherever he went, and would bring him back to Canaan, was no mere territorial God. He could be found anywhere and could go with his people anywhere – a crucial revelation.

> "**This is** none other than the **house of God;** this is the **gate of heaven**."
>
> GENESIS 28:17

## STAIRWAY TO HEAVEN
*Jacob's Ladder*, a watercolour by William Blake (1757–1827), depicts Jacob asleep on a rock. Above him, an ethereal golden ladder winds into the sky, with angels along its length, making their way to and from heaven and Earth.

**BEFORE** «

When Jacob reached Paddan Aram (the "Plain of Aram"), he met Rachel, seemingly by accident.

## A CHANCE ENCOUNTER?

After arriving in Paddan Aram, Jacob asked some shepherds at a well if they knew Laban. Just at that moment Rachel, Laban's daughter, arrived with his sheep to water them. Jacob, **immediately smitten**, removed the stone from the well's mouth so she could water her sheep, kissed her (highly unusual in those days), cried, and told her that he was her close relative. She ran and told Laban, who came to the well and **brought Jacob to his home in Haran**.

**JACOB MEETS RACHEL**

**THE GROOM AT A FEAST**

# Jacob is Cheated

*Jacob had found Rachel, the woman he wanted as a wife, and was living in the home of her father, Laban. But Jacob – who had previously cheated his own father – was about to fall victim to Laban's tricks.*

**J**ACOB HAD BEEN staying at the home of Laban for one month, during which time he had busied himself tending his flocks. He was deeply in love with Rachel, the younger of Laban's two daughters, and wished to marry her.

Laban said to Jacob, "Just because you are a relative of mine, should you work for me for nothing?" (Genesis 29:15). He offered to reward Jacob for looking after his livestock, and asked him how much he would like to be paid. Jacob replied with a proposal – he would work for Laban for seven years in return for Rachel's hand in marriage. Laban saw that he could turn this offer to his own advantage; he agreed to Jacob's terms but carefully avoided naming Rachel in the bargain.

### Laban's trick

Jacob loved Rachel very much, so the seven years of labour passed quickly. At the end of the period, he asked Laban for his wife. Laban agreed and invited everyone to a feast. Wedding feasts lasted a week, and the Hebrew word for "feast" used in the biblical account reveals that this was a drinking feast. This helped Laban to pull off the next stage of his plan to trick Jacob.

In a darkened tent and with his daughter mostly hidden under a veil, he substituted his elder daughter Leah for Rachel without Jacob noticing. (Perhaps Jacob had drunk too much wine at the drinking feast.) It was Leah that Jacob slept with that night, and it was only the next morning that Jacob discovered that Laban had tricked him.

### A new proposal

Jacob was furious, and stormed off to see Laban. He said "I served you for Rachel, didn't I?" (Genesis 29:25) and demanded to know why he had been deceived. Laban calmly explained that it was not the custom in those parts to let the younger daughter marry before the firstborn (see pp.64–65) – a defiant statement that recalls Jacob's own blatant trickery of his firstborn brother. Laban, turning the situation to his own benefit again, offered Rachel as a wife too – providing that Jacob worked for him for another seven years. Jacob had little choice but to agree to Laban's terms. He finished the

**LEAH'S WOE**

Less beautiful than her sister, married by trickery, and less loved by her husband, Leah's life appears to have been a sad one. However, she was also blessed, bearing seven children with Jacob.

> "Now **Laban had two daughters**… the elder one was Leah, and… the younger was Rachel."
>
> GENESIS 29:16

# "What is this you have done to me? **I served you for Rachel,** didn't I? **Why have you deceived me?**"

GENESIS 29:25

traditional bridal week (see panel, left) with Leah, after which Laban gave him Rachel as his second wife, but denied him a wedding feast. Of his two wives, Rachel always

remained the one that Jacob truly loved. And so began the next seven years of Jacob's life, working for Laban to pay for the wife he thought he had already bought.

**When God saw that Jacob did not love Leah, he showed her special kindness.**

### JACOB'S CHILDREN

God blessed Leah by **enabling her to become pregnant** – not just once, but seven times. Genesis attributes this as God's response to Jacob's lack of love for his first wife: "When the LORD saw that Leah was not loved, he enabled her to conceive" (Genesis 29:31). She gave birth to Jacob's **first four sons 74 ≫** – **Reuben, Simeon, Levi, and Judah**. Meanwhile Rachel, Jacob's favourite, remained childless, which made her jealous of her sister.

**LEAH AND HER CHILDREN**

**« BEFORE**

Jacob went looking for one wife, but ended up with four "wives" who became the mothers of his children.

### JACOB'S WIVES

Laban **tricked Jacob** into marrying his elder daughter, Leah, before he could marry Rachel, **the one he loved « 72–73**. Each wife was given a slave: Zilpah and Bilhah. These women would later become **Jacob's concubines** – slaves taken as secondary wives to produce heirs. Polygamy was a common practice at that time, ensuring that a family had enough children to provide for the parents in their old age. In Jacob's case, taking multiple wives would enable the **rapid expansion of God's people**.

### LISTS

#### SONS OF JACOB

**1** Reuben ("See, a son"), Jacob's first son with Leah

**2** Simeon ("He who hears"), second son with Leah

**3** Levi ("Attached"), third son with Leah

**4** Judah ("Praise"), fourth son with Leah

**5** Dan ("He has vindicated"), with Rachel's slave Bilhah

**6** Naphtali ("My struggle"), with Rachel's slave Bilhah

**7** Gad ("Good fortune"), with Leah's slave Zilpah

**8** Asher ("Happy"), with Leah's slave Zilpah

**9** Issachar ("Hired"), fifth son with Leah

**10** Zebulun ("Honoured"), sixth son with Leah

**11** Joseph ("May he [God] add"), first son with Rachel

**12** Benjamin ("Son of my right hand"), second son with Rachel

BUILDING A NATION
Jacob's 12 sons are pictured here in stained glass in the Great West Window at Westminster Abbey in London, created by Joshua Price and James Thornhill (1735). Jacob is also known as Israel, after being given that name by an angel; the Bible lists his sons as the founders of the 12 tribes of Israel.

# A Nation Begins

*God had reaffirmed to Jacob his earlier promise to Abraham of a growing family. Over the coming years, Jacob fathered 12 sons, who would become the founders of the 12 tribes of Israel.*

**W**HEN GOD SAW that Jacob did not love his wife Leah as he loved Rachel, he enabled Leah to conceive and she became the mother of Jacob's first four sons. The first she called Reuben, for it meant "See, a son" but sounded in Hebrew like the expression "He has seen my misery" – a recognition of God's kindness to her. Surely Jacob's attitude to her would change now, she thought; but it did not. Three more sons followed – Simeon, Levi, and Judah – but still Jacob favoured Rachel over Leah.

### Jealous responses

Rachel, in contrast, did not get pregnant. She became jealous of Leah, demanding of Jacob that he give her children too, or she would die. Jacob angrily replied that it did not depend on him: "Am I in the place of God, who has kept you from having children?" (Genesis 30:2). So Rachel offered him her servant to act as a surrogate mother, saying, "Here is Bilhah, my servant. Sleep with her so that she can bear children for me and I too can build a family through her" (Genesis 30:3). Bilhah bore Jacob two further sons: Dan and Naphtali. This in turn prompted jealousy in Leah, who at this point had stopped having children. So she presented Jacob with her servant Zilpah, who bore him two further sons: first Gad, then Asher.

### More sons for Leah

The rivalry between the two sisters continued, for Rachel still longed to have children of her own, while

## "Then God remembered Rachel..."

GENESIS 30:22

Leah hoped for Jacob's favour. One day, when Leah's son Reuben returned from the fields with some mandrake plants, which were believed to help fertility, Rachel begged Leah to give her some. Leah replied, "Wasn't it enough that you took away my husband? Will you take my son's mandrakes too?" (30:15).

However, Leah decided to use the mandrakes as a bargaining tool, and told Rachel that she could have the mandrakes if Rachel would let her sleep with Jacob. Rachel agreed, and that night Leah became pregnant, and soon bore Jacob a fifth son. She named him Issachar, meaning "Hired" – a

REUBEN          SIMEON          LEVI          JUDAH          ZEBULUN          ISSACHAR

## DIVINATION

Laban told Jacob that he knew by "divination" that God's blessing on him had been due to Jacob. Laban lived in a polytheistic society that worshipped many gods, and shared the popular belief that the will or activities of the gods could be discovered by observing various indicators. These included abnormalities in the entrails of sacrificed animals, the way arrows fell when thrown into the air, the unusual flight patterns of birds, or unpredictable events. Divination would later be prohibited in the Jewish Law.

DIVINATION ARTEFACT REPRESENTING ANIMAL LIVER, MESOPOTAMIA, 19TH CENTURY BC

painful reminder that she had been driven to hire her own husband that night. She then conceived again, giving Jacob his sixth son with her. She said, "God has presented me with a precious gift. This time my husband will treat me with honour, because I have borne him six sons" (30:20). She named her son Zebulun, which means "honoured". Some time later she also had a daughter with Jacob, who she named Dinah.

### Children for Rachel

After many years of waiting, Rachel at last conceived and became pregnant, giving Jacob another son – his eleventh – whom she named Joseph, meaning "May he [that is, God] add", which was an expression of her longing for one more son.

Rachel's prayer was answered, though at a heavy price. When they were finally back in the Promised Land, she gave Jacob another son, who he named Benjamin, but she died during childbirth (Genesis 35:16–19z).

And so Jacob had 12 sons.

### THE 12 TRIBES

Jacob's 12 sons founded the 12 tribes of Israel, who would eventually settle in Canaan, as promised by God. The map shows the areas in which they settled, based on the biblical text of Joshua 13–22.

AFTER

**After 14 years working for Laban, Jacob decided to return home.**

### INCREASING FLOCKS

God had brought Laban prosperity through Jacob's work; now Jacob told Laban it was **time for his own family to prosper**. He asked to build up his own flock by taking the dark lambs and speckled sheep and goats as his wages – a relatively small number of animals, as sheep were normally white and goats black or brown. Laban agreed but tried to trick Jacob again by first moving any such animals away from the flock. However, through a mixture of breeding insights and folklore, Jacob got the flock to produce lots of speckled offspring, all of which, as agreed, belonged to him. Over the next six years (Genesis 31:41) Jacob became **very wealthy**, with large flocks and many servants. He was now **ready to return home**.

Laban's hostile attitude and a message from God combined to persuade Jacob that it was time to return home.

### A HASTY DEPARTURE

Jacob's growing wealth **« 75** meant that the **attitude of Laban and his sons** towards him "was not what it had been" (Genesis 31:2). God now told Jacob to return to Canaan. Jacob explained this to Rachel and Leah, who were happy to leave, feeling that **their father had treated them badly « 72**. They left immediately, but unknown to Jacob, Rachel stole Laban's precious heirloom *teraphim*, or household gods. Three days later, Laban heard they had fled, and set out to pursue them. He caught up with them in Gilead, east of the Jordan, and **rebuked Jacob for leaving as he had**. Strong words followed, but finally Jacob and Laban made a covenant, **piling up stones as a testimony** and to mark the boundary between their territories. And with that, they went their separate ways.

*TERAPHIM* FROM SYRIA, 3RD MILLENNIUM BC

> " So Jacob was left alone, and **a man wrestled** with **him** till daybreak."
>
> GENESIS 32:24

### WRESTLING WITH GOD

Giuseppe Vermiglio's *Fight between Jacob and the Angel* (1625) shows Jacob as he wrestles all night with a stranger who is actually God (here represented as an angel).

# Jacob Wrestles with God

*After his earlier deception of Esau, Jacob was anxious about their reunion, so he prepared the way by sending gifts ahead. God was also preparing, and a wrestling match was to change Jacob's life.*

**E**NCOURAGED BY the appearance of angels, Jacob sent messengers to Esau in Edom, the desert country southeast of the Dead Sea, hoping to win his twin brother's favour. They returned with the news that Esau was coming with 400 men, which only increased Jacob's fears.

Jacob divided his travelling companions and herds into two groups, thinking that at least one group might escape if there were to be an attack. Then he prayed. He asked the God of Abraham and Isaac for protection on the basis that he was in this situation only because of his obedience to the Lord. He recalled God's promises to prosper him and multiply his descendants, despite his own unworthiness of God's kindness to him.

### A gift for Esau

Jacob spent the night there at the site he had called Mahanaim, near the Jabbok River, preparing an enormous gift of livestock for his brother in recognition of the damage he had done to Esau by robbing him of his birthright and paternal blessing. Then Jacob sent his servants ahead, each with part of the gift, keeping space between them so that the accumulated gifts would "pacify" Esau (Genesis 32:20). Each servant was to say this was a gift from Jacob, who was following behind.

### Jacob's wrestling match

Jacob then sent his wives Rachel and Leah, their maidservants, his 11 sons, and his possessions across the ford of the river, while he spent a second night at the camp.

When he was alone, a stranger suddenly appeared and wrestled with him until daybreak. Jacob would not yield, so the stranger dislocated his hip; but Jacob fought on. At daybreak, the stranger told Jacob to let him go, but Jacob would not – not until the man had blessed him. The man asked his name, and Jacob told him. The stranger now said that his name would no longer

**BROTHERS REUNITING**
*The Meeting of Esau and Jacob*, after the painting by Peter Paul Rubens (1577–1640), illustrates the moment when Jacob makes peace with his twin brother many years after having robbed him of his birthright.

> ## "Your name will no longer be Jacob, but Israel, because you have struggled with God…"
> **GENESIS** 32:28

be Jacob, but Israel (meaning "He struggles with God"), for he had struggled with God and men and had overcome. Jacob now realized that he had been wrestling with none other than God himself. Avoiding Jacob's request to know his name, the stranger blessed him and disappeared. So Jacob named the place Peniel (meaning "Face of God"), for he had been in God's presence, and yet had lived.

As the sun rose, Jacob – limping from his hip injury – was powerless before Esau, whom he saw coming with his men. He bowed to the ground, but Esau threw his arms around him, and they burst into tears, reconciled at last.

**JABBOK RIVER**
At Peniel, to the north of the Jabbok River, Jacob both struggled with God and was reunited with Esau. Jacob named it Peniel "because I saw God face to face, and yet my life was spared" (Genesis 32:30). It was thought that no-one could see God and live (Exodus 33:20).

### AFTER ⟫

The reconciliation with Esau went better than Jacob had anticipated.

**MIGHTY IS THE GOD OF ISRAEL**
Esau wanted Jacob to live with him, but Jacob was resolved to return to Canaan. He **finally arrived at Shechem**, north of Bethel, where he bought a field for "a hundred pieces of silver" (Genesis 33:19), pitched his tents, and built an altar called *El Elohe Israel* ("God, the God of Israel"). **His ancestors' God was now firmly his own.**

**JACOB BUILT A SMALL ALTAR SIMILAR TO THIS 3RD MILLENNIUM BC EXAMPLE AT MEGIDDO**

**RESTING PLACE OF THE PATRIARCHS** Origins 4th millenium BC

# Hebron

> "So **Abram went to live** near the great trees of Mamre **at Hebron**, where he ...**built an altar to the Lord.**"

GENESIS 13:18

Map showing: Shechem, Gezer, Bethel, Gibeon, Jerusalem, Gath, Gaza, Hebron, Beersheba, Rabbah, Heshbon; Great Sea (Mediterranean Sea), River Jordan, Salt Sea (Dead Sea), River Arnon.

N

0 — 50 km
0 — 50 miles

**E**VERY NATION HAS places that acquire special affection, because of their past associations, in the hearts of its people. The town of Hebron was such a place for Israelites, rooted as it was in their faith and history.

Hebron (possibly from Semitic root words that mean "place of alliance") is situated on top of the Judean Hills, 927m (3,041ft) above sea-level – making it the highest city in Canaan. Its location meant that Hebron was cooler than Jerusalem, and rain carried by clouds coming in from the Mediterranean fell on the surrounding hills, which made the area good for agriculture. Archaeological discoveries show that Hebron was inhabited from at least the middle of the 4th millennium BC. It was originally named Kiriath Arba, meaning "Town of Arba", which might refer to a leader of the Anakites (Joshua 14:15) or to the four clans that lived there (*arba* is Hebrew for "four").

## Hebron and the patriarchs

Hebron became one of Israel's most holy places because of its association with the patriarchs. After a period of wandering, Abraham settled there, near the "great trees of Mamre" (Genesis 13:18), which may have been oaks offering welcome shade. Great

### CITY OF HEBRON

One of the most ancient cities of the Near East, Hebron lies just 32km (20 miles) from Jerusalem. It is situated in a well-watered valley; its fertile soil supports fruit and nut production.

oaks often marked Canaanite shrines, and Abraham quickly built an altar to God there – making it absolutely clear whom he was worshipping. It was here that "three men" (18:2) reaffirmed God's promise of a son to be born to his wife, Sarah, even though

---

### THE EDOMITES

Located between the Dead Sea and the Gulf of Aqaba, Edom's position enabled it to control the major north–south trade route, The King's Highway. The Edomites were said to be descended from Esau, Jacob's twin brother, and so related to Israel, though there was constant rivalry between them. They denied Israel passage on the journey to the Promised Land (Numbers 20:14–21), and there were ongoing conflicts throughout Old Testament times (1 Samuel 14:47). Edom was eventually overrun by Arab tribes, then settled by the Nabataeans, who for a while made Hebron their capital. Rome imposed Idumeans (as Edomites were now called) as rulers on Judea – Antipater and his son Herod the Great.

**7TH-CENTURY BC EDOMITE GODDESS IDOL**

### SITE OF SIGNIFICANCE

An important biblical location, Hebron – the existing old town is seen here – is associated with Abraham, Isaac, Jacob, Joseph, Caleb, Ruth, Jesse, David, Absalom, Abner, Rehoboam, Othniel, and other figures in Israel's history.

she was past child-bearing age. This promise was fulfilled within the year (Genesis 21:1–7).

Later, Abraham bought the cave of Machpelah at Hebron as a burial site for Sarah (Genesis 23). All the patriarchs would eventually be buried in this cave – Abraham himself and Sarah, Isaac and Rebekah, and Jacob and Leah (Genesis 49:31; 50:13). According to the 1st-century historian Josephus, all of Jacob's sons except Joseph were also buried there.

## Hebron and the conquest

After this, Hebron is not mentioned in the Bible until Israel's conquest of Canaan. Joshua's spies brought back a vine branch, heavy with grapes, from the Valley of Eshcol near Hebron as proof of the land's fertility (Numbers 13:22–25). When the Israelites finally reached Canaan, they were opposed by a coalition of five kings, including the king of Hebron, but Joshua routed them. Hebron was conquered by Caleb (Joshua 14:13–15). The land around it was given to him and his descendants, while Hebron was

designated as a town for Levites and a city of refuge, to which people could flee to ensure a fair trial (Joshua 21:11–13).

## Hebron and Israel's kings

By King David's time, Hebron was an important city in Judah. It was therefore a natural place for God to send David to be acknowledged as Judah's new king, after Saul had died in battle (2 Samuel 2:1–4). Two years later, David was acclaimed king of a united Judah and Israel, again in Hebron (2 Samuel 5), and the city became his

**TOMB OF THE PATRIARCHS**
Tradition holds that Hebron is the burial place of three biblical patriarchs and their wives: Abraham and Sarah, Isaac and Rebekah, and Jacob and Leah. Known as the Machpelah, the tomb is beneath the Ibrahimi mosque.

capital for seven-and-a-half years, until he relocated to Jerusalem. It was perhaps these associations with David that prompted his son, Absalom, to launch his coup d'état in Hebron (2 Samuel 15:1–12).

## Hebron in later history

After Judah's defeat by Babylon, Hebron was occupied by Idumeans (Edomites), though Jews returned there after the exile (Nehemiah 11:25). The rebel leader Judas Maccabeus reclaimed Hebron from Edom and it became part of the Hasmonean kingdom in the late 2nd century BC. When Judea's independence was ended by Rome in 63 BC, Herod the Great was installed as the country's puppet king (40–4 BC). In one of many attempts to win the Jews' favour, he built a shrine over the site of the patriarchs' tomb in Hebron. During the Jewish Revolt (AD 66–70, see pp.466–67), Hebron was the site of fierce fighting, until it was stormed by the Romans.

Nevertheless, Jews continued to live in Hebron in the Byzantine period and after its conquest by Muslim Arabs in AD 638. The Byzantines had built a church at the patriarchs' tomb, which the Muslims converted into a mosque. Today, the Ibrahimi mosque is one of Islam's four most sacred sites, known locally as *El Khalil* ("The Friend") in a reference to Ibrahim (Abraham) as the friend of God.

**A PANEL IN THE 12TH-CENTURY VERDUN ALTAR, KLOSTERNEUBURG, AUSTRIA, DEPICTS SAMSON CARRYING THE GATES OF GAZA**

# Joseph and his Brothers

*Favouritism from his father and a gift for interpreting dreams made Joseph the target of his brothers' hatred. Deciding to get rid of Joseph, they sold him to traders, who took him to Egypt.*

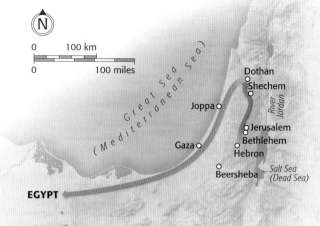

## BEFORE

After the reconciliation with his brother Esau, Jacob headed home with his family and his household.

### TRAVELLING HOME
In Bethel, Jacob buried his family's foreign idols and built an altar to the Lord. God appeared to him, reconfirming his covenant with Jacob and telling him that he would be known as "Israel" (Genesis 35). Jacob continued south, but **his wife Rachel died** on the journey, **during the birth of Benjamin** in Ephrath (Bethlehem). Jacob buried her there and set up a pillar over her tomb. He then continued on his way and joined his father, Isaac, in **Hebron ≪ 78–79**. The 12 sons of Israel, from whom the 12 tribes of Israel would descend, were **in the Promised Land at last**.

J ACOB HAD 12 SONS, but Joseph was his favourite, born as he was in Jacob's old age and to his beloved wife, Rachel. Jacob's preference for Joseph, his second-youngest son, was underlined when he gave Joseph a richly ornamented robe, while his brothers had to wear everyday clothes. Such blatant favouritism angered his brothers.

### Joseph's dreams
The brothers' unhappiness with Joseph came to a head when he started having dreams that belittled them. In one dream, he saw them all binding sheaves of grain; then his sheaf suddenly rose up, while theirs bowed down to it. In another dream, he saw the sun, the moon, and 11 stars all bowing down to him, which angered not only his brothers, but his father too.

### The brothers make a plan
Some time later, his brothers had taken the flocks north to find fresh pasture, and Jacob sent Joseph to find out if all was well with them and bring word back to him. He set off for Shechem, as directed by his father, but his brothers had already moved on. A man found him wandering aimlessly and told him that his brothers had moved on to Dothan, on the main north–south trade route. As Joseph approached, dressed in his fine robe, his brothers easily spotted him from

a distance, and decided to kill him. A plan was quickly hatched: they would kill Joseph, throw him into a nearby water cistern, and then tell Jacob that his son had been savaged by a wild animal. But Reuben, the eldest of the brothers, suggested that they should instead simply throw Joseph into the empty cistern and leave him there; Reuben secretly planned to return and rescue him later. The plan was agreed, and when Joseph arrived, they stripped off his robe and threw him into the cistern.

### Sold as a slave
Later that day, a caravan of Midianite traders passed by, their camels loaded with spices, balm, and myrrh from Gilead, on their way to Egypt. So Judah suggested that, rather than killing Joseph and getting nothing out of it, they should sell him to the traders and make some money. Everyone agreed, and they sold him for 20 shekels of silver – the price of a slave – and the traders took him with them.

Reuben had not been with his other brothers at the time and was unaware of what had taken place. When he returned to the cistern later to free Joseph and found that he was not there, he tore his

### KEY
- Joseph follows his brothers
- Joseph taken into Egypt

### JOSEPH'S JOURNEY
Sent by Jacob to find his brothers, Joseph's route north to Dothan is given in Genesis 37:14–17. From there, he was taken by the Midianite traders to an unspecified location in Egypt.

> **"Here comes that dreamer…** Come now, let's kill him and throw him into one of these cisterns…**"**
>
> GENESIS 37:19,20

**JOSEPH IS SOLD AS A SLAVE**
This fresco by Raphael (1483–1520), in St Peter's Basilica in Rome, shows Joseph's brothers, enraged with jealousy over their father's favouritism for Joseph, negotiating a price for him with Midianite traders.

**A SUCCESSFUL DECEPTION**
Jacob's sons show their father Joseph's ornate coat, covered in blood – depicted here in a *c.*1490 illustrated manuscript – convincing him that his beloved son had been killed by a wild animal.

**PEOPLE**

## THE MIDIANITES

The Midianites were descendants of Midian, one of Abraham's sons with his second wife, Keturah (Genesis 25:1–4). Occasionally referred to as Ishmaelites (Genesis 37:28), the Midianites settled in the deserts of Moab and Edom, and along the Red Sea, living by trading – as in this story – and by raiding. Despite links with Abraham and Moses (Moses married a Midianite), they resisted the Israelites as they travelled to Canaan (Numbers 22; 25), for which they became Israel's enemy (Numbers 25:16–18).

**MIDIANITE POTTERY**

## "**Examine it** to see whether it is **your son's robe**."

GENESIS 37:32

clothes in anguish. Returning to his brothers, he exclaimed, "The boy isn't there! Where can I turn now?" (Genesis 37:30).

### *Jacob is deceived*

Meanwhile Joseph's other brothers had covered up what they had done. Taking Joseph's special robe, they dipped it in the blood of a slaughtered goat, and took it to Jacob, claiming they had found it and asking if it was Joseph's. It was unmistakable, and Jacob exclaimed, "It is my son's robe! Some ferocious animal has devoured him" (37:33). Jacob was devastated, and began to grieve, tearing his clothes and putting on sackcloth, and saying that he would mourn for Joseph till his dying day. All his children tried to console him, but he could not be comforted.

**AFTER** »»

**While his brothers had abandoned him, Joseph's experiences in Egypt showed that God had not.**

### NEW RESPONSIBILITIES

The traders **took Joseph to Egypt**, where they sold him as a slave to Potiphar, one of Pharaoh's officials. When Potiphar noticed that everything Joseph did seemed to be blessed, he made him his administrator, **putting him in charge of the household** and its affairs. From that moment on, Potiphar too was successful, so much so that he **entrusted everything he had to Joseph's care**, while he focused his attentions simply on eating well.

**JOSEPH IS SOLD INTO EGYPT**

**« BEFORE**

**Joseph's favour in Potiphar's household soon ended when Potiphar's wife took a liking to him.**

**POTIPHAR'S WIFE**

Joseph's success in managing his master's household affairs brought him to the notice of not just Potiphar, but **also of Potiphar's wife**. While Potiphar's interest lay in Joseph's management skills, his wife's lay in his good looks and fine build. Every day she pestered him to go to bed with her, but Joseph refused, saying that such a thing would dishonour his master. One day, when the servants were outside, Potiphar's wife grabbed hold of Joseph, but he wriggled free, **leaving his cloak behind**. Infuriated at being spurned, she concocted a story for Potiphar, saying Joseph had tried to molest her and she had fought him off. She had the proof in her hands – his cloak. Potiphar was livid, and immediately had Joseph **thrown into Pharaoh's prison**.

**POTIPHAR'S WIFE TRYING TO SEDUCE JOSEPH**

**CATTLE BY THE NILE**
In Pharaoh's first dream, seven healthy, fat cows emerged from the Nile and grazed on reeds by the banks of the river. Seven thin, ugly cows then emerged from the water and stood beside them, and then the gaunt cows ate the healthy ones.

# Pharaoh's Dreams

*Joseph had been unfairly thrown into jail, but this setback would bring him to Pharaoh's attention, as an interpreter of dreams. Through this he would not only save Egypt, but ultimately save his own family.*

I N THE PRISON, the warder quickly saw Joseph's abilities and realized he could useful. He put him in charge of the prisoners, which is how Joseph came to meet two of Pharaoh's officials – his cupbearer and his chief baker – who had also been imprisoned. One night, both officials had dreams that they could not understand, and, next morning, Joseph saw that they were dejected. He told them that God could interpret their dreams, and asked them to recount them. The cupbearer said he had dreamed of three vine branches; he had squeezed the grapes into Pharaoh's cup and put the cup in Pharaoh's hand. Joseph interpreted the dream:

within three days the cupbearer would be restored and would serve Pharaoh again. He asked the cupbearer to remember him when this happened and get him out of prison.

When the baker heard this favourable interpretation, he shared his dream too. He had been carrying three baskets of bread on his head, and birds had eaten the bread from the top basket. Joseph explained that, within three days, Pharaoh would hang him and leave his body for the birds to eat. Both of Joseph's interpretations

were borne out, when, three days later, Pharaoh restored his cupbearer, and hanged his baker. But the cupbearer forgot Joseph's request.

### A troubling dream

Two years passed, and still Joseph was in prison, but his fortunes were about to change. One night, Pharaoh dreamed that he was standing by the Nile when out came seven fat cows, followed by seven thin cows. The thin cows swallowed the fat ones. Later that night, he had a similar dream, but this time seven heads of scorched and withered grain swallowed up seven heads of healthy grain.

The next morning, Pharaoh was troubled, so he sent for both his magicians and his wise men, but none of them could interpret his dreams. At that moment, the cupbearer remembered the young Hebrew man he had met in prison. He told Pharaoh how Joseph had interpreted their dreams and how things had turned out exactly as he said. So Pharaoh sent for Joseph.

### Joseph before Pharaoh

Pharaoh said he had heard that Joseph could interpret dreams, but Joseph replied that it was not him who did this; it was God. Pharaoh recounted his two dreams and Joseph said that they both had the same meaning. The seven fat cows and the seven good heads of grain

**DROUGHT RECORDS**
The inscription on the Famine Stele, found on Sehel Island in the Nile, records the details of a seven-year period of extreme drought and severe famine that ravaged Egypt during the reign of pharaoh Djoser of the third dynasty (c.2686–2613 BC).

represented seven years; the seven lean cows and the seven poor heads of grain were seven more years. God was telling Pharaoh that seven years of abundance were coming to Egypt, followed by seven years of famine – and the two dreams underlined the certainty that this would happen.

### Taking charge of Egypt

Joseph advised Pharaoh to appoint someone wise to take charge of the situation. He should set aside a fifth of Egypt's harvest over the next seven years and store it up for the seven years of famine to follow. Who better for the job, asked Pharaoh, than the wise man before him? So he put Joseph in charge of all Egypt, and showered him with gifts. Thirteen years had now passed since Joseph's brothers had sold him into slavery.

## NUMBERS IN THE BIBLE

In the Bible, numbers – including seven – often carry symbolic significance:

 **1** Uniqueness "The LORD is one" (Deuteronomy 6:4).

**2** Unity Jesus sent his disciples out in twos to deliver his word (Mark 6:7).

 **3** God's power Jesus' resurrection was on the third day, underlining that it was God's doing (Acts 10:40).

**4** The world "The four corners of the Earth" (Revelation 7:1) means the whole world.

 **5** Half-complete Jesus' parable of five wise and five foolish virgins (Matthew 25:1–13).

 **6** Man's number Man was created on the sixth day (Genesis 1:26–31). The Antichrist's number is 666, emphasizing that he is human not divine (Revelation 13:18).

**7** God's number God rested on the seventh day of creation (Genesis 2:1–3); seven signifies his perfection, planning, or timing.

 **10** Complete The ten virgins signify complete humanity (Matthew 25:1–13). 1000=10x10x10, which is a Hebrew way of saying absolutely complete.

**12** God's people From the 12 tribes of Israel (Genesis 49:1–28; Revelation 21:12).

**AFTER** ≫

> " So, Pharaoh said to Joseph, 'I hereby put you in charge of the whole land of Egypt."
>
> GENESIS 41:41

**THE INTERPRETATION OF DREAMS**
In Raphael's magnificent fresco cycle (c.1515), painted on the arches of the Loggia at the Vatican, Joseph has been brought before a troubled Pharaoh, who asks him for help in understanding the meaning of his two disturbing dreams.

**Joseph experienced good fortune, not only in his public life as a ruler of Egypt, but also in his private life.**

**MANY BLESSINGS**
Over the next seven years, Joseph collected so much grain that it **could not be measured**. So when the start of the famine came, Egypt was well prepared.

By then, **Joseph had two sons** by his wife, Asenath, who had been given to him by Pharaoh. He called his first son Manasseh, meaning "Forget", for God had now made him **forget all his troubles**. The second he named Ephraim, meaning "Fruitful", for God had made him **fruitful in the land of his suffering**.

**FARMING GRAIN IN EGYPT**

## ANCIENT EMPIRE Founded c.3100 BC

# Egypt

## "But the Egyptians are mere mortals and not God…"

ISAIAH 31:3

**T**HE LAND OF EGYPT plays a significant role in the Bible, but its fortunes varied greatly through the biblical period. When Abraham went there, in around 2090 BC, the Egyptian civilization was already a thousand years old and was becoming a mighty nation. Within another millennium, Egypt's greatness was past and it would soon be swallowed up by other empires.

At the heart of Egypt's life lay the River Nile. Beginning at Lake Victoria in Uganda, the Nile flows north for 6,670km (4,145 miles) ending in a delta of swampy marshland, just north of modern Cairo, before entering the Mediterranean Sea.

### Egypt's artery

The Nile was ancient Egypt's main travel artery, carrying boats up and down, as well as its lifeblood, bringing fertility to an otherwise arid desert. The Nile flooded annually between June and September – the result of melting snows and monsoons – and the floodwaters deposited millions of tons of rich sediment on the river's banks. For the Egyptians, the season of *akhet* ("inundation") was the coming of the god Hapi, who brought life to the land. Crops were planted, and when the flood subsided in March or April, the harvest was ready. This reliable food supply was the most significant contributor to Egypt's wealth and power. Genesis describes how Joseph's brothers went to Egypt for grain in a time of famine (Genesis 42; see pp.86–87).

### Egypt's religion

The ancient Egyptians were polytheists (believing in multiple gods) apart from a brief period of monotheism (worship of one god) under Akhenaten. Among their many gods were Amun (creator deity), Osiris (the ruler of the dead), Ra (the sun god), Khonsu (moon god), and Hapi (god of the

Nile). The Egyptian ruler, Pharaoh, was seen as the intermediary between the gods and people. He made offerings to the gods on behalf of his people in return for the gods' blessings, and he represented the gods on Earth by building great temples to them. Priests were the gods' servants, bringing offerings of food and drink to their temples three times a day. Ordinary people could not enter the temples; they worshipped at small local shrines, only ever seeing the gods when statues were

carried in processions at festivals. Egyptians were superstitious, and wore protective amulets (charms), notably the scarab-beetle. Dreams were seen as predictions of the future, which is why Pharaoh was so interested in Joseph's ability to interpret dreams (see pp.82–83).

According to the Book of Exodus, Moses was raised in Pharaoh's household (see pp.92–93), so this was the background of his religious experience for his first 40 years.

### Death and eternal life

The Egyptians believed that, at death, the soul left the body and began a journey to the next life. Personal possessions were buried with the deceased for that journey, including food, clothes, jewellery, chariots, and even beds. Some tombs, like that of the Pharaoh Tutankhamun, were crammed with

**INTO THE AFTERLIFE**
The mortuary temple of Queen Hatshepsut – meaning "foremost of noble ladies" – is located in Luxor (Thebes). Hatshepsut reigned c.1479–c.1458 BC and was the principal queen of Thutmose II.

Great Sea
(Mediterranean Sea)

Buto
Alexandria — Nile Delta — Tanis
Rameses
LOWER — GOSHEN — Succoth
EGYPT — Pithom
— Heliopolis
Pyramids — — SINAI
at Giza — Memphis

Red Sea

River Nile

Valley of — Karnak
the Kings — Thebes (Luxor)

N

UPPER
EGYPT
— Aswan

0 — 200 km
0 — 200 miles

### EGYPT AND THE NILE
The River Nile was the central feature of Egypt – all of the nation's major settlements were located along its banks, while its waters irrigated agricultural land.

riches. The poor were buried in sand, where the sun's heat dried out their bodies, whereas the rich were mummified. This process involved removing the brain and large organs, packing the body in salt, and filling the cavities with resin. The body was then covered with resin, wrapped in bandages, and placed in a coffin. Genesis states that both Jacob and Joseph were mummified (50:2,3,26).

Spells were cast to help the dead to pass through judgment. Kings were believed to spend the afterlife with Ra, the sun god, riding his boat across the sky by day and visiting Osiris in the underworld by night. In the New Kingdom period (c.1540–1070 BC), pharaohs were buried in the Valley of the

## HISTORY AND CULTURE
### THE ROSETTA STONE

Discovered in 1799, this stone was significant in aiding the understanding of hieroglyphics – the system of pictograms (word-signs) used in Egypt from c.3000 BC. The triple inscription, carved in 196 BC, bore the same text in hieroglyphics, Egyptian demotic script – a later form of hieroglyphs – and Greek.

**ROSETTA STONE**

French historian Jean-François Champollion used the Greek to decipher the hieroglyphs, realizing that they represented not just letters, but sounds. It enabled scholars to decipher inscriptions on temples and tombs, and aided biblical studies by revealing Egyptian references to rulers and locations in Canaan.

Kings, on the west bank of the Nile, opposite Thebes. The west, where the sun set, symbolized the ending of the old and the beginning of the new. It was this belief that death could be controlled that made the biblical tenth plague on

Egypt so significant – death swept through the land and the Egyptians could do nothing about it (see pp.98–99). The God of the Bible's Israelites was shown to be more powerful than the greatest of Egypt's gods (Exodus 12:29,30).

**BEFORE** ≪

Jacob heard there was grain in Egypt, and sent his sons there to buy some.

### EXTREME DROUGHT

The Bible describes a **severe famine** that affected every country except Egypt. Through a combination of irrigating crops from the Nile and Joseph's wise planning, Egypt had enough grain to feed its people and to sell too. So **Jacob despatched his sons to Egypt** to buy grain for the family, but kept Benjamin, the youngest, with him.

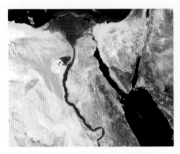

**SATELLITE IMAGE OF THE RIVER NILE**

# Brothers Reconciled

*The famine that Joseph had prophesied arrived, and his brothers travelled to Egypt to buy food. Joseph recognized them immediately, and initiated a plan that would result in reconciliation and his family coming to Egypt.*

I**T WAS JOSEPH'S JOB** to sell grain to all the people. When his brothers arrived, they went to see him, but they did not recognize him. As soon as he saw his brothers, Joseph recognized them but, not revealing who he was, he said to them, "You are spies! You have come to see where our land is unprotected" (Genesis 42:9). They protested that they had simply come to buy food. They were ten of 12 brothers, they explained, one of whom was back home with their father, and one of whom was dead. Joseph said he would not believe them unless the youngest brother was brought to him as proof of their story, and then he threw them in jail.

### The return home

Three days later, Joseph said that one brother, Simeon, must stay as a hostage while the rest went to get their youngest brother to prove that they were telling the truth. The brothers said to one another that this was happening to them because of how they had treated Joseph many years before – not realizing that he understood every word, for he had been using an interpreter. Joseph had their bags filled with grain, and their silver returned to their sacks, and then sent them off. Arriving home, they told Jacob what had happened,

### TIME OF PLENTY

Workers carry bundles of sugar cane as they harvest their crops in Luxor, Egypt. The fertile region of the Nile Delta yielded enough food for Joseph to stockpile provisions for the time of famine ahead, "so that the country may not be ruined" (41:36).

# "I have heard that **there is grain in Egypt**. Go down there and **buy some** for us, so that we may live and not die."

GENESIS 42:2

and explained that they had to take Benjamin back. However, fearing that he would lose another son, Jacob refused to let them go.

### The second journey to Egypt

The famine continued, and Jacob had no choice but to send his sons back for more grain. Reluctantly, he agreed that Benjamin should go with them. When they arrived, and Joseph saw that they had brought Benjamin with them, he ordered a banquet to be arranged. He accepted the gifts they had brought, and enquired after their father. As Joseph looked at his brothers, his eyes rested upon Benjamin. He asked, "Is this your youngest brother, the one you told me about?" (43:29). He was overcome with emotion, and rushed out and wept. Once Joseph had regained his composure, he ordered the meal to begin. To the brothers' surprise, they found that they were seated in age order, and Benjamin was served with bigger portions.

The next morning, before they left, Joseph had his silver cup hidden in one of their bags. The brothers had not gone far when his servants rushed after them and accused them of theft. They protested their innocence, and we re horrified when the silver cup was discovered in Benjamin's sack. The brothers

were brought before Joseph, who said that Benjamin must become his slave and the rest of them could go home. Judah pleaded with Joseph, saying that their father was aged and the shock of seeing them without Benjamin might kill him.

### Joseph reveals himself

At this point, Joseph was unable to keep his identity secret any longer. Clearing the room, he revealed

who he really was. His brothers were dumbstruck, and suddenly fearful for their lives. Joseph said to them, "Do not be distressed and do not be angry with yourselves for selling me here, because it was to save lives that God sent me ahead of you" (45:5). He threw his arms around Benjamin, kissed all of his brothers, and wept.

When Pharaoh heard what had happened, he ordered Joseph's brothers to fetch their father from Canaan, so that the whole family could live safely in Egypt.

### PEOPLE
#### BENJAMIN

Jacob's 12th son was special to him, born as he was to Rachel, who died during his birth (Genesis 35:16–18). After the loss of Joseph, Rachel's only other son, Benjamin enjoyed even more of Jacob's favour, not being allowed to go to Egypt, for example, to ensure his safety (Genesis 42:3,4). Jacob prophesied that Benjamin's descendants would be like a ravenous wolf – bold, even ruthless (Genesis 49:27). His famous descendants include King Saul in the Old Testament (see pp.146–47) and Paul in the New Testament (see pp.448–49).

**JOSEPH EMBRACES BENJAMIN AFTER REVEALING HIS OWN IDENTITY**

The brothers went back and told Jacob what had happened, saying "Joseph is still alive! In fact, he is ruler of all Egypt"(45:26). Jacob was shocked, but agreed that the extended family would set off back to Egypt. On the way there, God spoke again to Jacob, reassuring him not to be afraid of going to Egypt, for he would be with him, and would make him into a great nation there. As they arrived in Goshen, in the eastern Nile delta, Joseph went to meet them, and wept when he saw his father. Pharaoh gave permission for them to stay in Goshen, and over the coming years they prospered and increased in numbers.

### BENJAMIN'S CUP

This 13th-century relief – one of a series in San Gennaro Cathedral in Naples, Italy depicting the life of Joseph – portrays Joseph's servants discovering their master's cup in Benjamin's possessions, and apprehending him along with his brothers.

# "I am your brother Joseph, the one you sold into Egypt!"

GENESIS 45:4

### AFTER

After 17 years in Egypt, the time came for Jacob to prepare for his death.

#### FINAL WORDS
With his death approaching, Jacob **blessed Joseph's two sons**, giving them equality with his own sons. Joseph wanted the greater blessing for Manasseh, his firstborn, but Jacob gave it to Ephraim instead, saying that he would be the greater of the two. He then gathered his own sons and **foretold their destinies** (Genesis 49). After his death, Joseph buried Jacob with his ancestors in the cave of Machpelah in Canaan, as he had promised. Joseph's brothers were anxious about how he might now treat them after Jacob's death, but they had nothing to fear, as Joseph recognized that **God had been at work**. When Joseph's own death approached, he reminded his brothers that they would one day **return to Canaan 118–19 ≫**, and asked that his bones be taken there too.

**BURIAL OF JACOB IN CANAAN**

# THE EXODUS

"**I am the Lord, and I will bring you** out from under the yoke of the Egyptians. **I will free you…** and I will redeem you with an outstretched arm and with **mighty acts of judgment.** I will take you as my own people, **and I will be your God."**

**CROSSING THE RED SEA**
A 16th-century illustration from a translation of the Bible by Martin Luther depicts Moses by the Red Sea. The book of Exodus describes how Moses stretched out his hand so the divided sea returned, drowning the Egyptians.

I SRAEL'S FLIGHT FROM EGYPT IS ONE OF THE greatest and most dramatic stories in the Bible. This story is not just about God freeing the Israelites from slavery, and then watching over them protectively as they made their way safely to liberty. It is about them becoming God's own people. The Israelites were given God's laws in order to live according to his will and to serve as an example to other nations of his kingdom on Earth. They were his chosen people. When his people failed, however, God never gave up on them. He is presented as holy and righteous, compassionate and just.

As the book of Exodus (meaning "way out") opens, it is the 15th century BC – more than 300 years after Joseph's death at the end of Genesis. The dynasty of pharaohs who had been grateful to Joseph for saving Egypt was long gone.

All that the reigning dynasty knew about the Israelites was that Joseph's descendants, living in the Nile Delta region, had multiplied prolifically. Wary of their growing numbers and the potential threat from within, the Egyptian regime pursued a policy of slavery and genocide to control them. It was against this background that the Israelites cried out for their freedom.

### THE STORY

Exodus recounts Moses' encounter with God, Moses and Aaron being sent to Pharaoh, the Israelites' escape from Egypt, and the people being led by God to Mount Sinai. Here, God made a covenant with them, giving them his laws to live by, and a mobile sanctuary where they could worship and offer sacrifices, as recorded in Exodus and Leviticus.

God then led the Israelites through the wilderness of the desert; and the book of Numbers describes the hardships of this nomadic period, as well as the lack of belief that led to a whole generation being told they would never enter the Promised Land. Only when that generation had died did God take the Israelites to the edge of Canaan, where the covenant was renewed, as described in the book of Deuteronomy. The Exodus is thus understood to be the turning point in Israel's history, and the story of its birth as a nation.

### THE BOOKS

Jews call the first five books of the Bible – Genesis, Exodus, Leviticus, Numbers, and Deuteronomy – the Torah, often translated as "The Law". For Jews, the Torah is the heart of their Scriptures because of its association with Moses, traditionally believed to have been its author. These first five books of the Bible are also known by Christians as the Pentateuch, meaning "five books".

### KEY THEMES

There are several key themes in this section of the Bible, notably revelation, recollection, and redemption. God reveals himself to people who are not necessarily looking for him; for example, he appears to Moses in a burning bush. The importance of remembering what God has done is stressed, and is demonstrated by the institution of annual festivals, such as the Passover. God frees his people as a sign that they are forgiven; he redeems.

**EGYPTIAN WEALTH**
This is an ancient Egyptian mirror case, made out of gold and inlaid with precious stones. It is in the shape of the *ankh*, the Egyptian hieroglyph meaning "life", which was a powerful sacred symbol. As they left Egypt, the Israelites were given gifts of gold, silver, and clothing.

« BEFORE

**In the centuries between the books of Genesis and Exodus, life changed dramatically for Israel.**

### DYNASTIC CHANGE

When **Jacob moved his family to Egypt to avoid Canaan's famine «  86**, he could not have known that his descendants would stay there for 430 years, according to the Bible (Exodus 12:40). During that period "the Israelites were exceedingly fruitful; they multiplied greatly, increased in numbers and became so numerous that the land was filled with them" (Exodus 1:7).

With the passage of time, there were not just changes of ruler but changes of dynasty, meaning that all that Joseph, Jacob's son, had **done for Egypt «  83, 86–87** was forgotten.

**EGYPTIAN OFFICIAL WEARING GOLD ADORNMENTS FOR LOYAL SERVICE**

# Hebrews Enslaved in Egypt

*Over the centuries, the descendants of Jacob's 12 sons – the founders of Israel's 12 tribes – had so proliferated that Egypt's Pharaoh began to consider them a threat.*

**J**ACOB'S FAMILY had numbered just 70 people when they first went to Egypt, but over the years the family grew and grew, just as God had promised to Abraham (Genesis 17:2; 22:17).

The Israelites spread across Goshen in the eastern Nile delta, where Joseph had settled his family. The Pharaoh of the dynasty that was now ruling Egypt knew nothing of what Joseph had done for Egypt in the past. He became anxious about the growing numbers of Israelites, and fearful that they might ally themselves with his kingdom's enemies.

### Slavery in Egypt

Pharaoh therefore decided to make the Israelites slaves and force them to help with the construction of Pithom and Rameses "as store cities for Pharaoh" (Exodus 1:11). In ancient Egypt, the Egyptians themselves were often required to supply labour for state projects as a form of taxation, but it was not unusual for less privileged groups to be forcibly enslaved as well, as Pharaoh did here.

### A bitter experience

Even though Pharaoh "put slave masters over them to oppress them with forced labour" (1:11), the more the Israelites were subject to oppression, the more they multiplied and spread. This only made the Egyptians more fearful, so that "they came to dread the Israelites and worked them ruthlessly" (1:12,13).

The Israelites were forced to perform a range of manual tasks, from "harsh labour in brick and mortar" to "all kinds of work in the fields" (1:14). This was demanding work, and made the lives of the Israelites "bitter", a fact commemorated as one of the aspects of the Passover "Seder" meal (see pp.100–01), when the Jews eat two types of bitter-tasting "herbs" – commonly horseradish and romaine lettuce root – to symbolize the bitterness and harshness of the slavery they endured in Egypt.

### Infanticide

When the numbers of Israelites still did not decrease as Pharaoh had hoped (1:10), he tried another approach and ordered two Hebrew midwives, Shiphrah and Puah, to intervene. If an Israelite mother gave birth to a daughter, they could let her live; but if it was a son, they were to kill him.

### HISTORY AND CULTURE

## WHO WAS THE PHARAOH?

**THUTMOSE III, FROM THE MORTUARY TEMPLE OF HATSHEPSUT, DEIR EL-BAHARI, EGYPT**

According to one system of dating, the story of Exodus could be placed in 1446 BC, when the pharaoh would have been Thutmose III (reigned *c.*1479–1425 BC). But the mention of the northeastern Nile Delta city of Rameses (former Avaris, near modern-day Tell el-Dab'a), built by the Hebrew slaves, leads some biblical scholars to identify Seti I (reigned *c.*1294–1279 BC) and Rameses II (reigned *c.*1279–1213 BC) as the pharaohs of the Hebrews' slavery and the Exodus respectively.

### HEBREW LABOUR

An illustration from the medieval Hebrew manuscript known as the Barcelona Haggadah (*c.*1350) – the traditional Jewish text that describes the order of the Passover Seder meal – depicts Jewish slaves building cities for Pharaoh.

**BONDED WORKERS**
This relief from the Great Temple of Ramses II at Abu Simbel in Egypt shows slaves roped together. Slaves formed a conscripted workforce used for large building projects. They may have been prisoners of war, people working to repay a debt, or traded by slave merchants.

This abominable instruction was the first – though not the last – attempt at the genocide of God's people. But the midwives respected God too much to do this, and they let the boys live. When Pharaoh summoned them to explain why the boys were still alive, they told the king that Hebrew women gave birth so quickly that the babies were born before they got there – there was nothing they could do. This action of the midwives was viewed favourably by God, who increased the population of Israelites further still. In an act of desperation, Pharaoh now issued this order: "Every Hebrew boy that is born you must throw into the Nile, but let every girl live" (1:22).

Around this time, a baby boy was born who would not only escape this childhood death sentence but change the history of Israel (see pp.94–95).

> ❝ So they **put slave masters over them to oppress them** with forced labour, **and they built Pithom and Rameses** as store cities for Pharaoh. ❞
>
> EXODUS 1:11

## ANALYSIS
## THE BIBLE AND SLAVERY

God's response to the abuses of slavery is reflected in his intervention to rescue Israel (Exodus 3:7–10). Slavery was permitted in Israel, but with restrictions. For example, a person could clear a debt by entering a period of voluntary servitude, but it could only last six years, and then the slave was freed (Exodus 21:2–4; Deuteronomy 15: 12–15,18). Upon release, the master was urged to "give to them as the LORD your god has blessed you" (Deuteronomy 15:14).

**CHRIST WITH FREED SLAVES (c.1218), CHURCH OF SAN TOMMASO IN FORMIS, ROME**

By Roman times, slavery was so entrenched in society that opposing it would have been treasonous. However, in the New Testament Paul undermined slavery by calling for mutual respect between slaves and masters, and urging Philemon to free his runaway slave, Onesimus, "as a fellow man and as a brother" (Philemon 16). He urged all Christians, slave or free, to live as "one in Christ Jesus" (Galatians 3:28).

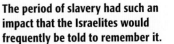

**AFTER**

**The period of slavery had such an impact that the Israelites would frequently be told to remember it.**

**RECALLING SLAVERY**
The rescue from slavery in Egypt was so important to Israel that it appears at the very beginning of the **Ten Commandments 106–07 »**. God reminded his people he had called them "out of Egypt, out of the land of slavery" (Exodus 20:2). This rescue would be recalled annually in **the festival of Passover 100–01 »**, commemorating the night those in bondage escaped. At the **Seder** table, the Jewish family would gather for a ritual reading of the **Haggadah**, retelling the story of the liberation of the Israelites.

**PROPHET AND LAWGIVER** Born *c.*1526 BC  Died *c.*1406 BC

# Moses

> "...no prophet has risen in Israel like Moses, whom the LORD knew face to face, **who did all those signs and wonders** the LORD sent him to do in Egypt..."

DEUTERONOMY 34:10,11

**THE CHOSEN ONE**
The horns on Moses' head in this 16th-century sculpture by Pietro Francavilla were inspired by the Latin Vulgate Bible translation, which says that when Moses came down from Mount Sinai "he knew not that his face was horned from the conversation of the LORD" (Exodus 34:29).

**B**ORN AS an Israelite slave, raised in an Egyptian palace, a killer who was forced to flee – Moses may not seem to be the obvious candidate for a great leader. Yet this was the man God chose to lead his people out of slavery. Moses was born into a family descended from Levi, Jacob's third son, at the time when Pharaoh was ordering that every Hebrew baby boy be killed because of his concern about growing Hebrew numbers (see pp.94–95). Moses was hidden: first at home, then by his mother among the Nile reeds. He was discovered by Pharaoh's daughter, who adopted him (Exodus 2:1–10).

### The life of Moses
According to Jewish tradition (see Acts 7:23), Moses spent 40 years in Pharaoh's household. However, after killing an Egyptian slave-master for mistreating an Israelite, Moses fled to Midian, where he spent the next 40 years in the desert. It was then that God appeared to him, calling Moses to return to Pharaoh and demand that he free the Israelites. After a series of dramatic plagues (see pp.98–99), Pharaoh finally yielded and set them free.

The final 40 years of Moses' life were spent leading the Israelites through the wilderness to the Promised Land – a ten-day journey by the usual trade route but the Israelites wandered for 40 years through the desert because God was angry with them for their lack of faith

PEOPLE

### THE KENITES

**5TH-CENTURY MOSAIC IN ROME DEPICTS MOSES' MARRIAGE TO ZIPPORAH**

The Kenites were a nomadic people who made a living, in part, from metalworking. The tribe lived mainly in the Negev, Sinai, and around the Gulf of Aqaba, but they also travelled. After Moses had killed an Egyptian, he fled to Midian, where he married a Kenite named Zipporah, who was the daughter of a priest called both Ruel (meaning "Friend of God") and Jethro. Israel generally maintained good relations with the Kenites (1 Samuel 15:6).

(Deuteronomy 1:34,35). The key moment in this journey took place at Mount Sinai. Here, God made a covenant with the Israelites, giving Moses his laws for them to live by (see pp.108–09).

Moses finally reached the edge of the Promised Land. His final words, recorded in Deuteronomy 32 and 33, bear witness to God's faithfulness to his people and bring words of blessing to each of the 12 tribes in turn. Moses died at the age of 120 on Mount Nebo, in full view of the Promised Land, but never having entered it.

### The character of Moses

The stories suggest that Moses was a mixture of opposing characteristics. He is shown as often tempestuous, as demonstrated when he killed the Egyptian slave-master (Exodus 2:11,12), or when his future father-in-law's daughters were harassed (Exodus 2:16,17), or when he got angry with the Israelites for complaining (Numbers 20:2–12). Moses also could be timid, telling God that he could not lead the Israelites or go to Pharaoh because he was not a good speaker (Exodus 4:10) – which was when God appointed his brother Aaron to act as his spokesman.

Yet Moses was eventually courageous, seeking an audience with Pharaoh and making demands for the release of his slaves. He was also genuinely humble, for although he was the only man with whom God spoke face to face, he never abused this

**WATER OUT OF A ROCK**
Moses miraculously made water flow from a rock to satisfy the thirsty Israelites in the desert. This episode is shown in the painting *Moses Strikes the Rock* by Raphael (1483–1520) in St. Peter's Basilica, Rome.

privilege, trusting his cause to God when others opposed or attacked him (Numbers 12).

### The significance of Moses

Scholars agree that no man towers over the Old Testament, or over Jewish life even today, like Moses; he was a civil leader and judge, a prophet, priest, and intercessor for the people. He was both a friend of God ("the Lord would speak to Moses face to face, as one speaks to a friend", Exodus 33:11) and a mediator between God and his people. Through Moses, God revealed his laws – these showed what God himself was like and shaped the way his people lived. It was Moses who led Israel and formed it into God's community.

Moses was so associated with the Covenant and the Law that people came to speak simply of "Moses" when referring to the first five books of the Old Testament. In

the New Testament, Moses is highly honoured as the one who prepared the way for Jesus through his preparation of God's people (Hebrews 3:1–6). It was he who first pointed towards the coming of the Messiah, telling the people of Israel that God would one day, "raise up for you a prophet like me from among you, from your fellow Israelites. You must listen to him" (Deuteronomy 18:15).

- **c.1526 BC,** Moses is born, into a family descended from Levi. He is hidden among the bulrushes to escape Pharaoh's infanticide.
- **Brought up** in Pharaoh's palace.
- **c.1486 BC,** flees to Midian after killing an Egyptian.
- **c.1446 BC,** sees God at the burning bush; is sent to Pharaoh to demand the Israelites' freedom.
- **c.1446 BC,** Moses leads Israel out of Egypt and across the Red Sea.
- **c.1444 BC,** receives God's law on Mount Sinai.
- **Receives the Covenant** that God makes with Israel.
- **Goes back up** Mount Sinai; receives plans for the Ark of the Covenant, the Tabernacle, and the priests' duties.
- **Destroys the Ten Commandments** when he discovers that the Israelites have made a golden calf.

**MOSES DESTROYS THE COMMANDMENTS, 12TH-CENTURY INGEBORG PSALTER**

- **Intercedes when** God says he will not accompany the Israelites, and encounters the presence of God (Exodus 33:18–23).
- **Makes a copy** of the Ten Commandments.
- **Leaves Sinai** and leads Israel towards Canaan.
- **Sends spies** into Canaan. They return with a good report, but spread fear about its inhabitants. As judgment, God says no-one over 20 will enter Canaan. Spends the next 38 years leading Israel through the desert.
- **c.1406 BC,** Moses prepares the Israelites to enter Canaan, renews the Covenant, and appoints Joshua as his successor.
- **c.1406 BC,** dies on Mount Nebo, "from the plains of Moab to the top of Pisgah, opposite Jericho" (Deuteronomy 34:1) within sight of the Promised Land, where he is buried by God.
- **c.AD 32,** appears alongside Elijah and Jesus at the Transfiguration, during Jesus' ministry (see pp.354–55).

> " Moses was **a hundred and twenty years old** when he died, **yet his eyes were not weak nor his strength gone.** "
>
> **DEUTERONOMY** 34:7

**LOOKING AT THE PROMISED LAND**
Mount Nebo in modern-day Jordan is thought by many to be Moses' last resting place. Mentioned in the Bible (Deuteronomy 34:1), the mountain was a pilgrimage site for early Christians, who built a basilica there.

**THE RIVER NILE**
Moses was hidden in the dense rushes that grew along the River Nile – its banks are still lined with lush vegetation today. The Greek historian Herodotus described Egypt as "the gift of the Nile", the great river that endowed the kingdom with fertility and abundance.

## BEFORE

When Pharaoh's plans for curbing the Israelite numbers failed, he resorted to more drastic measures.

**PHARAOH'S DESPERATION**
Pharaoh's concern at **the growing number of Israelites within his kingdom ≪ 90–91** only worsened when his plans to have their baby boys killed at birth failed. He therefore increased the genocide, ordering all his people to throw any Israelite baby boys they found into the Nile, where they would drown or be eaten by crocodiles.

## HISTORY AND CULTURE
### PAPYRUS BASKETS AND BOATS

**HUNTING FOWL FROM A PAPYRUS BOAT**

Images of Moses being hidden in a baby basket are charming but inaccurate. In the Bible, the Hebrew word for "basket" is used only in the story about the birth of Moses and to describe Noah's ark. In other words, the "basket" would likely have been a miniature version of the papyrus boats, made out of bundles of reeds, that sailed up and down the Nile, mentioned in Isaiah 18:2. These were used for all manner of activities on the mighty waterway, from transporting cargo to bird-hunting trips.

> **" ... she got a papyrus basket** for him and coated it with tar and pitch. Then she placed the child in it and **put it among the reeds** along the bank of the Nile. **"**
>
> EXODUS 2:3

# The Baby in the Bulrushes

*Moses was born at a time when Pharaoh had ordered that every Israelite baby boy must die. However, God thwarted Pharaoh, not only saving Moses' life but putting him into the household of his would-be killer.*

**M**OSES' PARENTS were Israelites, descendants of Jacob's third son, Levi. The couple already had a daughter, Miriam, but when their son was born, they had to hide him to save him from Pharaoh's cruel edict.

The couple "saw that he was a fine child" (Exodus 2:1) and did their best to conceal the boy, which they managed to do for the first three months of his life. When they could not continue to hide him any longer, his mother made a papyrus basket and coated it with waterproofing tar and pitch. Then she placed her son tenderly in the basket and secreted it among the reeds along the riverbank.

### A royal discovery
The boy's mother returned home, but his sister, Miriam, stayed by the banks of the Nile, watching to see what happened.

Her anxious wait ended when Pharaoh's daughter came to the river to bathe, accompanied by her attendants. As she and her retinue walked along the riverbank, the princess spotted the basket among the reeds and sent her slave girl to get it. The princess opened the basket and saw the young boy lying inside. He was crying, and she felt sorry for him, a mere infant abandoned to his fate. "This is one of the Hebrew babies," she said to her attendants (2:6).

### A royal command
Miriam rushed out and asked the princess if she would like her to find a Hebrew woman to nurse the baby. When she agreed, the girl fetched her own mother. She took her to Pharaoh's daughter, who told her to take the baby home and nurse him, and said that she would pay her. So the baby's own mother took him home and cared for him, under royal protection, safe from Pharaoh's edict that Hebrew baby boys should be thrown into the Nile.

The time came to take the boy to Pharaoh's daughter, who then raised him as her own. The princess named him Moses. In Egyptian this meant "Begotten" or "Born", and was a word that formed a component of Egyptian royal names, such as Thutmose and Rameses. In Hebrew, it was likely to have been a play on words; "Mosheh" sounded like the Hebrew word *mashah* ("drawn out"). Indeed, after choosing the name for the boy, Pharaoh's daughter said "I drew him out of the water" (2:10).

The boy, now named Moses, who would grow up to defeat a future Pharaoh, was safely positioned within the Egyptian royal household.

**THE DISCOVERY OF MOSES**
*The Finding of Moses*, painted by Eduard Ihlee (1812–85), portrays the moment when Pharaoh's daughter finds a Hebrew baby boy, Moses, in a basket among the reeds along the River Nile, while the baby's sister Miriam watches in the background.

> **" When the child** grew older, she took him to **Pharaoh's daughter** and he became her son. **She named him Moses,** saying, 'I drew him out of the water.' **"**
>
> EXODUS 2:10

## AFTER

The years that Moses spent in Pharaoh's household would prove invaluable to him.

**MOSES' KNOWLEDGE**
In Acts, **Stephen quotes the Jewish tradition 424–25 ≫** of how "Moses was educated in all the wisdom of the Egyptians and was powerful in speech and action" (Acts 7:22). This would have involved wide-ranging skills, all useful during **the wanderings of the Israelites 114–15 ≫**: reading and writing, essential for writing **God's Laws 108–09 ≫**; languages and diplomacy, for communicating; administration and government, for organizing and leading Israel; and warfare, for overcoming any enemies who were encountered along the way.

**AN EGYPTIAN SCRIBE,** *c.*2475 BC

## EXODUS 3
# God Calls Moses

*One of the Bible's recurring themes is that God often reveals himself to people who are not looking for him, or who do not seem to deserve him – Moses fulfilled both these criteria. His unexpected encounter with God changed his life, and that of Israel, as the God of the Israelites' history became the God of their future, acting through Moses to determine the nation's character for all time.*

**M**OSES SPENT 40 years in a position of privilege in Pharaoh's palace, and was "powerful in speech and action" (Acts 7:22). But his circumstances changed when he had to flee the kingdom after killing an Egyptian for ill-treating one of his own people, an Israelite. He went to Midian, where he met and married the daughter of a priest, had a son, and spent 40 years (Acts 7:30). However, he was about to discover that God had a significant part for him to play in his plan for Israel.

One day, Moses was tending the flock on Mount Horeb (or Sinai) when he saw a bush suddenly on fire. This was not unusual in hot, arid places, but although this bush flared, it did not burn up. Moses went to look more closely. As he did, God called him by name from within the bush, then said: "Take off your sandals, for the place where you are standing is holy ground... I am the God of your father, the God of Abraham, the God of Isaac and the God of Jacob" (Exodus 3:5,6). Moses hid his face, terrified.

God said that he had seen the Israelites' misery in Egypt, was concerned at their suffering, and had come to rescue them and take

them to their own land. Then he commanded Moses: "So now, go. I am sending you to Pharaoh to bring my people the Israelites out of Egypt" (3:10).

Moses protested that he could not possibly do this, but God said he would be with him and that one day Moses would stand on this mountain again and know the truth of what God said.

Moses felt utterly inadequate: "Who am I that I should... bring the Israelites out of Egypt?" (3:11). God showed him that this was not about Moses; it was about God. Moses replied that the Israelites would ask him the name of the god in whom he spoke, for if he had truly met God, they would expect Moses to know his name.

The name that God now revealed showed his very character: "I AM WHO I AM" – *Yahweh* in Hebrew, which is related to the verb "to be" – adding that Moses could say, "The LORD... has sent me to you".

What God had said to Moses was: "My name is 'I am' but you can call me 'He is'". God was underlining that there is never a moment when he *is not*. He always *is* – always there, always working, always powerful, always providing what is needed.

## "God said to Moses, 'I AM WHO I AM.'"
EXODUS 3:14

**GOD REVEALS HIMSELF TO MOSES**
In this painting by Raphael (1483–1520), Moses is shown with his sandals off, as instructed by God, who is depicted in person speaking from within the burning bush. Moses hides his face because he is "afraid to look at God" (Exodus 3:6).

## BEFORE

**Following his encounter with God at the burning bush, Moses returned to Egypt.**

### A RELUCTANT MOSES

Even after **God's revelation ‹‹ 96–97**, Moses was hesitant to assume leadership of his people and made excuses not to act as God instructed. At first God responded gently, giving him miraculous signs to convince him, such as transforming his staff into a writhing snake. **Eventually, God grew angry**: he said Moses' brother, Aaron, would be his spokesman (Exodus 4:14–17). So, finally, Moses succumbed. God repeated his call to go to Pharaoh and **demand that he free the Israelites**; but God also warned Moses that he intended to harden Pharaoh's heart so that he would not let the people go (4:21).

# The Ten Plagues

*Moses demanded that Pharaoh should free the Israelites, but he would not listen. God inflicted a series of plagues on Egypt, but Pharaoh continued to resist – until the tenth and most devastating plague.*

**W**HEN MOSES arrived back in Egypt, he and Aaron gathered the elders of the Israelites. Aaron told them the message that God had given Moses, and demonstrated the miraculous signs that God had promised (Exodus 4:1–8). The people believed them, and bowed down in worship when they heard that God had remembered them in their need.

Then Moses went to Pharaoh, and said: "This is what the LORD, the God of Israel, says: 'Let my people go, so that they may hold a festival to me in the wilderness'" (5:1). Pharaoh said he did not know this God and would not release his slaves. In fact, Pharaoh made them work harder, and the Israelites complained to Moses and Aaron that they had made things worse.

God therefore reaffirmed to Moses that he was about to take his people to the Promised Land, though he warned that Pharaoh still would not listen and God would respond with "mighty acts of judgment" (7:4).

### *A sign for Pharaoh*

Moses and Aaron returned to Pharaoh with God's demand, this time backing it up with a sign.

### PLAGUE OF LOCUSTS

When conditions are right, locusts may form vast swarms that devastate crops, as seen here in North Africa. Exodus states that after the plague "nothing green remained on tree or plant in all the land of Egypt" (10:15).

Aaron threw his staff on the ground and it became a snake (the cobra was Pharaoh's symbol of power). Pharaoh's magicians repeated the miracle through their dark magic, and Pharaoh was unmoved.

### The plagues begin

Following God's instructions, the next morning Moses and Aaron waited for Pharaoh on the banks of the River Nile, the source of Egypt's economic power. Moses repeated God's demand for the Israelites to be freed, warning that the river would turn to blood as a sign that the Lord alone was God. Then Aaron raised his staff and the Nile flowed with blood. Immediately, all the fish died and the drinking water was fouled – the first plague. Despite this demonstration of God's power, Pharaoh still would not listen to Moses and Aaron.

Over the coming months, a further nine plagues followed. Some biblical scholars interpret the plagues as a challenge to Egypt's gods, revealing their powerlessness (see panel, right). Each plague can also be seen as a natural consequence of the previous one. With the Nile turned

to blood, frogs abandoned it and invaded people's homes; gnats and then flies bred prolifically in the flooded fields and on the bodies of dead frogs; a plague on livestock was next (possibly anthrax carried by the flies), though the animals belonging to Israelites survived; boils erupted on Egyptians and their remaining animals (perhaps skin anthrax caused by the flies). The seasonal winds brought three further plagues, blowing in abnormally heavy hail that killed people and animals; then locusts that destroyed the remaining crops; and finally sandstorms that brought darkness in daytime.

### Pharaoh's hard-heartedness

Although each plague may have followed on from another, it is clear that they happened only at Moses' command and by God's will, increasing in intensity, from mild irritation to outright

#### MOSES BEFORE THE PHARAOH
A folio illustration from a Syriac bible, dating from the 8th century AD or earlier, portrays Moses, acting on God's command, asking Pharaoh to release the Israelites in order to worship God in the desert.

#### THE FINAL PLAGUE
A coloured woodcut from the 15th-century *Nuremberg Bible* depicts the 10th plague to afflict Pharaoh's Egypt, when the Lord passed over the homes of the Israelites, but killed the firstborn of the Egyptians.

destruction. Pharaoh was given ample opportunity to respond to God. After each plague, Moses repeated God's demand to Pharaoh, but Pharaoh became ever more obstinate. So God told Moses that a tenth plague (the number of completion in the ancient world; see p.83) was to come, more devastating than all the previous ones: every Egyptian firstborn son, including Pharaoh's own son and heir, would die, but Israel's firstborn sons would not be harmed. Then, at last, Pharaoh would have had enough and would tell the Israelites to leave his land.

**LISTS**

## PLAGUES AND EGYPT'S GODS

**1** Nile became blood
Khnum was guardian of the Nile; Hapi was god of the Nile flood.

**2** Frogs
Heket was the Egyptian frog goddess of fertility.

**3** Gnats
The gnats come from the dust of the Earth, which was ruled by Geb.

**4** Flies or beetles
Khepri was the scarab-headed god of creation and rebirth.

**5** Livestock killed
Hathor, "mistress of heaven", was a cow-headed goddess.

**6** Boils
Imhotep, god of healing; Isis, goddess of protection.

**7** Hail
Nut was the Egyptian goddess of the sky.

**8** Locusts
Nepri, god of grain; Senehem, locust-headed god of protection.

**9** Darkness
Amun-Ra, sun god and chief deity of the Egyptian gods.

**10** Death of the firstborn
Horus, protector of Pharaoh, whose son dies.

**AFTER**

> " But **Pharaoh's heart was hard** and he would not listen, **just as the Lord had said**."

EXODUS 8:19

The Bible contains other examples of God using plague as a means of inflicting divine retribution.

#### THE WRATH OF GOD
When **Samuel had reached adulthood 142–43 ›** the Israelites were defeated by the Philistines, who **captured the Ark of the Covenant 144 ›** and took it to the temple of their god, Dagon, in Ashdod. When they did so the citizens were **struck down by tumours** by God. The Philistines moved the Ark to Gath, but the tumours appeared there too, then to Ekron, where the same thing happened. Finally, they **returned the Ark to the Israelites 145 ›**, together with reparations of gold (1 Samuel 6:4,5).

*THE PLAGUE OF ASHDOD* (1630), BY NICOLAS POUSSIN

## EXODUS 12

# The Passover

*Central to Jewish identity is Passover (**Pesach** in Hebrew), an annual festival when Jews relive the events of the night that God "passed over" their homes, sparing their firstborn from the tenth plague, which prompted the Pharaoh to free them from slavery.*

**M**OSES WENT TO SEE Pharaoh for the final time. He warned him that God was about to send one last plague: at midnight, every Egyptian firstborn son would die and, after that, Pharaoh would release the Israelites. Pharaoh still refused to listen, so Moses walked out.

God then gave Moses instructions that were to be re-enacted each year, to recall how God freed Israel from slavery in Egypt. For generations to come, every family was to take a year-old, perfect lamb, or share one with their neighbours. Three days later, the lamb was to be slaughtered at twilight, leaving time to cook the meat and to daub the lamb's blood on the doorframe of the house before midnight. For seven days the Israelites were to make bread without yeast, for there would be no time to wait for bread to rise. Everything spoke of haste: the lamb was to be roasted whole, the bread left unleavened, the meal eaten quickly.

Then God explained what would happen that night: at midnight, death would sweep through Egypt, taking the firstborn of both humans and livestock. Wherever God saw blood on the doorposts, that house would be "passed over" and its inhabitants spared.

Moses summoned Israel's elders and told them what God had said, instructing them to "Go at once and select the animals for your families and slaughter the Passover lamb" (Exodus 12:21). Then, at midnight, Egypt's firstborn, from the highest to the lowest, were struck down just as God had said: "...there was... not a house without someone dead" (12:30).

Pharaoh, broken at last, summoned Moses and Aaron and told them to leave before every Egyptian died. So the Israelites departed, with much Egyptian wealth given to them as they went, just as God had said (3:21). They had started life in Egypt as a family of just 70; they left, 430 years later, as a nation.

To this day, at Passover, Jews recall the formation of their community through God's act of deliverance. In the New Testament, Jesus reinterpreted the Passover meal around his own act of deliverance: his death on the cross to free people from sin (see pp.388–89).

"**Commemorate this day,** the day you came out of Egypt… because the LORD brought you out of it…"
EXODUS 13:3

**THE PASSOVER MEAL**
A German illuminated folio (c.1375) shows a Jewish family gathered round the table to celebrate *Pesach*, as God commanded: "for the generations to come you shall celebrate it as a festival" (Exodus 12:14).

# Escape from Egypt

*Realizing that he had lost his slaves, Pharaoh changed his mind and sent his army after them. God miraculously parted the waters of the sea to allow Israel to pass, but drowned the pursuing Egyptians.*

**G**OD WENT AHEAD of the Israelites in a pillar of cloud by day, and a pillar of fire by night. He guided them south – avoiding the easterly route that led towards the Philistines – then he took them north again, to make Pharaoh think they were wandering around in confusion.

## BEFORE

To ensure that Israel never forgot the events in Egypt, their first-born sons had to undergo a special ritual.

### THE COST OF REDEMPTION
God had protected Israel's first-born **while Egypt's first-born had died ‹‹ 100–01**, so they now belonged to him. God declared a price for this redemption. In the past, first-born sons became sanctuary priests. In the future, a first-born son would have to be redeemed (bought back) by the payment of five silver shekels, which went to Aaron and the priests (Numbers 18:16; 3:48). Known as the Pidyon Haben, parents still perform this ceremony because God redeemed Israel from slavery in Egypt.

Pharaoh mustered his army – 600 of his best chariots, along with horsemen and troops – and pursued the Israelites, reaching them as they camped by the sea near Pi Hahiroth.

### Pharaoh's pursuit
When the Israelites saw the Egyptians, they cried out to God and accused Moses of bringing them into the desert to die. Moses told them not to fear; to stand firm. He promised them that they would see God's deliverance: "The Egyptians you see today, you will never see again (Exodus 14:13).

> **"**'What have we done? We have **let the Israelites go** and have lost their services!' **So he had his chariot** made ready…**"**
>
> EXODUS 14:5–6

God then told Moses to do something strange: he was to tell the Israelites to advance, even though the sea was straight ahead of them. Then he should raise his staff and stretch out his hand to divide the water, so that the Israelites could pass through on dry ground. Pharaoh's army, chariots, and horsemen would follow, but God would demonstrate his greatness.

**STELE OF ANI**
This stele, named for the 19th-dynasty royal scribe Ani, shows an Egyptian chariot of the kind used to pursue the Israelites. The wheels of the chariots became bogged down in the mud, trapped when Moses closed the sea.

The angel of God, who had been at the head of Israel's army, moved to its rear along with the pillar of cloud. The two came between the Egyptian army and the Israelites for the night. All night the cloud

## THE RED SEA

**THE NILE DELTA**

Despite popular tradition, perpetuated in paintings and many Bible translations, the Israelites did not cross the Red Sea, but rather the "Reed Sea" (*Yam Suph* in Hebrew, meaning "Sea of Reeds"). This was a marshy area in the Nile delta, where a strong east wind blowing all night (Exodus 14:21) could drive back the waters. People on foot could then cross, while heavy chariots would get stuck.

Some scholars believe the parting of the sea may have been linked to a volcanic eruption on the Greek island of Santorini. A tsunami would then have caused a rapid withdrawal of water, followed by a violent inrush, which was devastating for Pharaoh and his army.

**WAVE POWER**
Exodus describes the sea dividing before Moses and being driven back to form a "wall of water" (14:22), then crashing back and swamping the Egyptian army.

brought darkness to one side and light to the other, so that neither side went near the other (14:20).

### God's miracle

Then Moses stretched out his hand, and God drove back the waters with a strong east wind, exposing dry land. The waters piled up to form a wall on either side, leaving the Israelites to pass through on dry ground. The Egyptian army quickly followed them into the sea.

And then, at first light, God jammed the wheels of the Egyptians' heavy chariots, and they realized that God was fighting for Israel. They wanted to get out, but it was too late. As Moses stretched out his hand at daybreak, the waters swept back, drowning the entire Egyptian army – the end result of Pharaoh's obstinacy.

As for the Israelites, when they saw this display of power, they feared God and put their trust in him and Moses.

> " Raise your staff and… **divide the water so that the Israelites can go through** the sea on dry ground."
>
> EXODUS 14:16

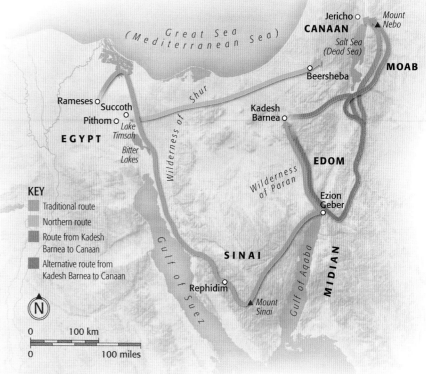

**KEY**

- Traditional route
- Northern route
- Route from Kadesh Barnea to Canaan
- Alternative route from Kadesh Barnea to Canaan

0   100 km
0   100 miles

**FROM EGYPT TO ISRAEL**
The Bible includes few clues as to the route taken by the Israelites from Egypt, though sites such as Rameses, Pithom, Mt Sinai, and Kadesh Barnea are mentioned in its text. Several alternative routes for the Exodus are shown above.

## AFTER ≫

**God deliberately avoided the shortest way to Canaan, but the Israelites' lack of faith made the journey even longer.**

### AN EXTENDED JOURNEY

God did not lead the freed Israelites along the quickest route to Canaan because it went through Philistine territory and they might have been attacked, changed their minds, and returned to Egypt (Exodus 13:17). Instead, he took them along the desert road through Sinai, for there were many things he needed to teach them on the way. Sadly, **the journey became even longer through Israel's unfaithfulness 114–15 ≫**, and they were to spend 40 years here, wandering in the wilderness of the Sinai peninsula, under God's judgment (Numbers 14:26–35).

**MOUNT SINAI, EDWARD LEAR, 19TH CENTURY**

**MANNA FROM HEAVEN**
The hungry and despondent Israelites are showered
by God with food in the form of manna. The
painting, c.1470, is by the French Renaissance
artist known as the Master of the Manna.

**BEFORE**

After the escape through the Red Sea, Moses led his people in a victory song.

### ISRAEL CELEBRATES

After the traumas of life in Egypt, and the destruction of Pharaoh's army in the Red Sea, Moses led the Israelites in a **song of gratitude to God**. The first verses recalled the events at the Red Sea, and the final verse anticipated God bringing the Israelites into the Promised Land. **Moses' sister Miriam** << **90–91** then led the women in dancing and singing.

**OASIS OF MARAH**
During the Exodus the Israelites rested at the Oasis of Marah (Exodus 15:22–26), where they could not drink the bitter water. Following God's instruction, Moses turned the water sweet. The oasis today is nearly dry.

# In the Desert

*The euphoria of escape from slavery passed quickly when the Israelites ran out of food and water in the desert. However, God miraculously provided both, then and for the coming 40-year journey.*

**A**FTER CROSSING THE Red Sea, Moses led the Israelites south into the Desert of Shur. They travelled for three days without finding water.

When the Israelites arrived at Marah (which means "bitter"), they found water, but it was not drinkable. Unaware that God was testing them, they grumbled to Moses. He turned to God, who told him to throw a piece of wood into the water, and the water became sweet. Then God told the Israelites that, if they obeyed him, the blights that befell the Egyptians would not come upon them.

### Sustenance

A month after leaving Egypt, the people arrived in the Desert of Zin. Here they complained about the lack of food. The Israelites forgot they had been slaves, saying, "If only we had died by the LORD's hand in Egypt! There we… ate all the food we wanted, but you have brought us out into this desert to starve…" (Exodus 16:3). So, as another test, God told Moses to assure the people that it would rain food from heaven. They should collect only what they needed each day, although on the sixth day they could collect twice as much – this is the first biblical reference to the Sabbath.

Moses and Aaron told the people they were grumbling not against them, but against God. Suddenly God's glory appeared to them in a cloud, to reassure them that he would provide meat and bread. That evening "quail came and covered the camp" (16:13). The next morning the ground was covered with thin flakes that tasted like sweet wafers. The people had never seen anything like it, and called the bread-like food *manna* (Hebrew for "what is it?"). Some people did as God instructed, but others took more than they needed, although the extra food always rotted.

The Israelites continued to receive manna for 40 years (Joshua 5:12). God told Moses to keep some for future generations, so he put it in a jar that Aaron later placed in the Ark of the Covenant (see pp.112–13) with the Ten Commandments.

### Water from rock

When they ran out of water again at Rephidim, the Israelites were ready to stone Moses to death. But God told him to strike the rock with his staff and water flowed. Moses called the place Massah ("testing") and Meribah ("quarrelling"); both had happened as the Israelites questioned whether God was truly with them.

> " **Strike the rock, and water will come out** of it for the people to drink."
>
> **EXODUS** 17:6

**AFTER**

**God provided for his people by protecting them from their enemies.**

### VICTORY OVER THE ENEMY

The Amalekites attacked the Israelites at Rephidim. **Moses asked Joshua 128–29** >> to fight while he stood on a hill, with hands raised in prayer. When his hands were aloft, the Israelites were winning; but if they were lowered, the enemy advanced. Aaron and Hur stood next to Moses, **supporting his hands** until Joshua was victorious. God told Moses to record the victory on a scroll.

**MOSES WITH AARON AND HUR AT REPHIDIM**

**PEOPLE**

## MIRIAM

Sister to Moses and Aaron, Miriam watched Moses' mother hide him in the bulrushes (see pp.94–95). When the pharaoh's daughter found Moses, it was Miriam who offered her mother as a nurse (Exodus 2:1–10). Miriam is not mentioned again until, with a tambourine, she leads the women in dance to celebrate the crossing of the Red Sea (Exodus 15:20,21), where she is described as a prophetess. Her prophetic gift got her into trouble when she complained to Aaron that Moses had married a Cushite wife and was acting as if he were the only person to whom God spoke. God rebuked her, and she was temporarily sick with leprosy (Numbers 12). She died at Kadesh in the Desert of Zin.

**STAINED GLASS WINDOW DEPICTING MIRIAM WITH HER TAMBOURINE**

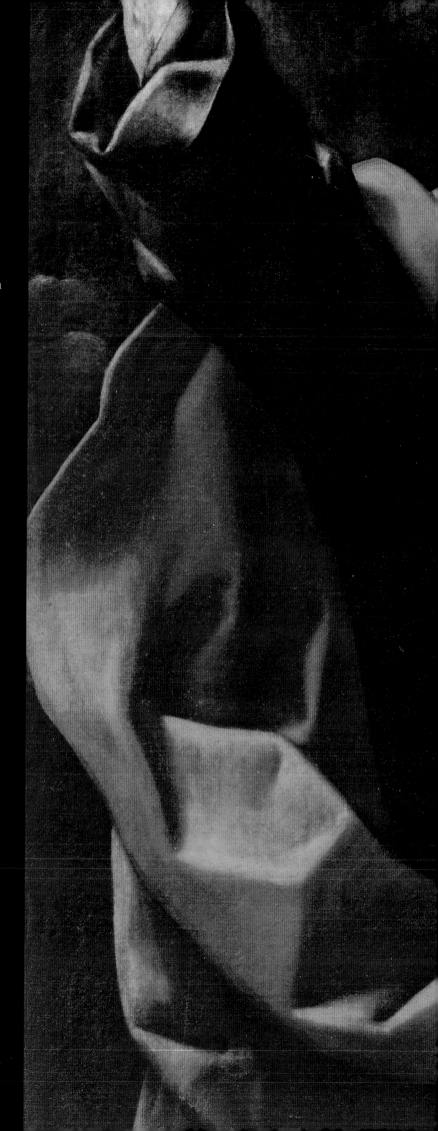

# The Ten Commandments

*Since their rescue from Egypt, the Israelites had experienced God's provision and protection; now they would encounter his presence, which would change them forever. God was about to reveal himself, making them his own nation and giving his people laws to live by.*

**T**HREE MONTHS after they had left Egypt, the Israelites arrived at Mount Sinai, where God had first revealed himself to Moses (see pp.92–93). In the first of several ascents over the coming days, Moses climbed the mountain to meet with God.

God told Moses that if the Israelites obeyed God and kept his covenant, they would become his "treasured possession… a kingdom of priests and a holy nation" (Exodus 19:5,6). Moses took God's message down to the people, returning with the leaders' agreement to obey. God then promised to reveal himself to Moses in a powerful way (a "theophany") on the third day. The people purified themselves for what was to occur.

On the third day, thunder, lightning, thick cloud, and a trumpet blast came from nowhere. The people trembled, but Moses led them to the foot of the mountain, which was covered in smoke as God came down in fire. God called Moses to the summit once again, but sent him down to say that no one must follow, apart from Aaron. Moses returned to the mountain and God gave him the commands that would help his redeemed people live in freedom:

"You shall have no other gods before me."

"You shall not make for yourself an image in the form of anything in heaven above or on the earth beneath or in the waters below…"

"You shall not misuse the name of the LORD your God…"

"Remember the Sabbath day by keeping it holy…"

"Honour your father and your mother…"

"You shall not murder."

"You shall not commit adultery."

"You shall not steal."

"You shall not give false testimony against your neighbour."

"You shall not covet… anything that belongs to your neighbour." (Exodus 20:3–17)

Known in Hebrew as "The Ten Words", the ten commandments are the only commands spoken directly to the people by God. They are the basis of the Jewish law and have formed the backbone of Judaeo-Christian civilization ever since.

## "I am the LORD your God… You shall have no other gods before me."
EXODUS 20:2,3

**RECEIVING THE LAW**
In *Moses with the Tablets of the Law* (c.1600–10) by Guido Reni, Moses receives the written tablets of stone the day after the commandments and laws had been first spoken to him by God (Exodus 24).

# God's Laws for Israel

*Having given the Ten Commandments, God applied the commands to Israel's daily life. He promised that his angel would prepare the way ahead of the Israelites, and made a covenant with them to seal their agreement to the laws that he had sent.*

**A**FTER GOD revealed the Ten Commandments on Mount Sinai, the Israelites realized that he was different from any other so-called god they knew. God told them that this should be reflected in how they worshipped. In particular, there should be no elaborate altars or idols, just simple altars of earth or uncut stones. God gave Moses instructions for Israel about how the people should live. The instructions were a mixture of commands and prohibitions, covering social, moral, and religious matters.

### Laws for Israel

Slavery was to be permitted, but only to pay off debt, and only for seven years (21:2–11). Personal injuries were to be dealt with in a proper, legal way (21:12–35), and property was to be protected from theft or negligence – restitution must be made for loss (22:1–15). The vulnerable were not to be abused, and special penalties would be imposed on anyone who harmed widows, orphans, refugees, or the poor (22:21–24). Justice was to be exercised with impartiality and integrity (23:1–9). Everyone, including slaves and animals, had the right to rest on the Sabbath; even the land was to be rested, by being unused every seventh year (23:10–13). Three festivals were to be celebrated (23:14–19): the feast of Unleavened Bread (later called Passover or *Pesach*), Harvest (later called Weeks or *Shavuot*, and Pentecost), and Ingathering (later called Tabernacles or *Sukkoth*). Each was an opportunity for every man to stand before God.

### The angel's protection

God then told Moses that he would send an angel to guard and guide the Israelites on their journey into the Promised Land. He told Moses

## BEFORE

**God's appearance on Mount Sinai had a powerful effect on the Israelites.**

#### MOSES TALKS FOR THE PEOPLE

While Moses and his brother Aaron received the words of God's Ten Commandments on the third day (Exodus 19:16–25), the people stayed down below. They could **see and hear the manifestation of God's presence** in the thunder, lightning, smoke, and loud trumpet blasts coming from the mountain.

That experience made the people afraid and they trembled. Keeping their distance, they begged, "Speak to us yourself and we will listen. But **do not let God speak to us or we will die**" (20:19).

Moses told them, "**Do not be afraid**. God has come to test you, so that the fear of God will be with you to keep you from sinning" (20:20). He returned to the mountain, where God told him the laws that Israel was to follow (see main text).

**MOSES RECEIVES THE TEN COMMANDMENTS, 15TH-CENTURY TAPESTRY**

**PLACE OF GOD**
The 2,300m (7,500 ft) granite peak of Mount Sinai, also known as Jebel Musa, is traditionally held to be the place that God gave the Ten Commandments to Moses, and later his detailed laws for living.

that if the people obeyed him and his angel, and continued to worship only God, he would bring them into the land of the Amorites, Hittites, Perizzites, Canaanites, and Jebusites, and "wipe them out" (23:23), so that the Israelites could possess the land that had been promised to Abraham.

God then told Moses to return to the mountain later, with his brother Aaron, Aaron's sons Nadab and Abihu, and Israel's 70 elders.

Moses went down the mountain and told the people everything that God had said, and they agreed that

> " Then **he took the Book of the Covenant and read it to the people**. They responded, '… **we will obey**.' "
>
> EXODUS 24:7

### HISTORY AND CULTURE

#### THE LAW CODE OF HAMMURABI

By the mid-15th century BC, the use of law codes was well established. The Stele of Hammurabi is a 2.4m (8ft) stone monolith inscribed with the ancient Babylonian code of law, dating back to the 18th century BC. Its upper part bears a relief of a king receiving his investiture from Shamash, the Babylonian sun god, who was also the god of law and justice. There are many parallels with Jewish laws, particularly on the wrongs of stealing and adultery, and the idea of "an eye for an eye" (Exodus 21:24), but Jewish law is intimately tied up with God's relationship with his people.

**THE BASALT STELE OF BABYLONIAN KING HAMMURABI**

# "The Lord ... called Moses to the top of the mountain."

**EXODUS** 19:20

"everything the Lord has said we will do" (24:3). He wrote down all God's words, and the next morning he built an altar at the foot of the mountain. There he led the people in a covenant-making ceremony. He took what he had written, now called "The Book of the Covenant" (24:7), and read it to the people; they again agreed to its laws. Covenants were always sealed with blood (see pp.58–59), so Moses took that of a sacrificed bull and sprinkled it over the book, saying "This is the blood of the covenant that the Lord has made with you ..." (24:8).

Then Moses returned to the mountain with his brother, sons, and the 70 elders, where they "saw the God of Israel" (24:10) and ate a meal in his presence, further sealing the covenant.

God then called Moses to walk further up the mountain, to collect tablets of stone on which God had set down the commandments and the law. As Moses climbed, the glory of the Lord settled on Mount Sinai in the form of a cloud. On the seventh day, God called to Moses from within the cloud, which now looked to the people below Mount Sinai as a consuming fire. Moses entered the cloud and went on up the mountain, where he stayed for 40 days and 40 nights (see pp.110–11).

## THE CODE OF LAW
This handwritten Torah scroll, known as a Sefer Torah, is from the Heichel Shlomo, the main synagogue in Jerusalem, where it is used in the ritual of Torah reading. The parchment is mounted inside a wooden box and its ends sewn on to two wooden rollers, so the scroll can be read.

Silver *rimmonim* or pomegranates that decorate the top ends of the wooden rollers, known as the Trees of Life.

The "Crown of the Law" signifies the majestic sovereignty of the law.

A Sefer Torah is made from specially prepared and Kosher parchment and thread, and written with a hand-carved, Kosher quill.

## LISTS
### SOCIAL CONCERNS IN TORAH

**1** The right to personal security (Exodus 21:12–36)

**2** Women are not to be exploited (Exodus 21:7–11, 22–32)

**3** Personal property can be defended (Exodus 22:1–15)

**4** Labourers should be paid (Deuteronomy 24:14,15)

**5** The powerless must not be exploited (Exodus 22:21–27)

**6** Judges must carry out fair trials (Deuteronomy 19:15–19)

**7** Punishment must be appropriate (Deuteronomy 25:1–3)

**8** Marriage must be honoured (Exodus 20:14)

**9** Sabbath rest should be available to all (Exodus 20:8–11)

**10** Leaders are not above the law (Deuteronomy 17:18–20)

**11** Animal welfare is important (Deuteronomy 22:4,6,7,10)

**12** Honesty is paramount (Deuteronomy 25:13–16)

## AFTER ≫

**Many Jews take God's instruction to bind his commands to their hands and foreheads literally.**

### THE TEFILLIN TEXTS
Deuteronomy records God as saying the people must remember his commands and **"tie them as symbols on your hands and bind them on your foreheads"** (6:8). Some Jews do this by strapping black leather cubes, or Tefillin, containing scrolls of parchment with texts from the Torah, to their left arms and foreheads for morning prayers. Four biblical texts mention God's instruction: two from Exodus (13:1–10, 11–16) and two from Deuteronomy (6:4–9; 11:13–21).

**RABBI WEARING TEFILLIN AND PRAYING**

## « BEFORE

Moses, now about 80 years old, had already made several ascents of Mount Sinai over the previous days.

### ASCENTS OF SINAI

On some of his ascents of Mount Sinai, Moses had mediated between God and the Israelites; on others he returned with specific laws for the people to follow. On one ascent, **God told Moses to remind the Israelites of all he had done for them** and to tell them that he would make them his own people if they obeyed him (Exodus 19:3–6). On another ascent, Moses received God's warning that the people should not force their way up the mountain (Exodus 19:21). On other visits he **received the Ten Commandments « 106–07** (Exodus 20:1–17) and **"the Book of the Covenant" « 108–09**. For the longest visit he took Aaron and his two eldest sons, Nadab and Abihu, and Israel's 70 elders (Exodus 24:9–18) **part way up the mountain to seal the covenant « 109**, then continued his journey on his own.

## LISTS

### ISRAEL'S MAIN SACRIFICES

The Book of Leviticus describes five offerings to be used in worship as a tribute to God.

**1** **Burnt offering:** to atone for unintentional sin (Leviticus 1; 6:8–13; 8:18–21; 16:24).

**2** **Grain offering:** to recognize God's goodness and provision (Leviticus 2; 6:14–23; Numbers 28:12–13).

**3** **Fellowship offering:** to re-establish friendship with God and others – this was the only sacrifice that could be eaten (Leviticus 3; 7:11–34).

**4** **Sin offering:** to atone for sin and ritual defilement, such as contact with a corpse or the unclean (Leviticus 4:1–5:13; 6:24–30; 8:14–17; 16:3–22; Numbers 15:22–29).

**5** **Guilt offering:** to atone for a sin that required restitution for damages (Leviticus 5:14–6:7; 7:1–6).

### THE FIRST HIGH PRIEST

This illumination from an 18th-century Hebrew Bible shows Aaron the High Priest. He was exclusively chosen by God, through the medium of Moses, to preside over the rituals of worship and sacrifices.

# Priests and Sacrifices

*On Mount Sinai, God gave Moses detailed instructions concerning Israel's worship, the consecration of priests, and the sacrifices that would be needed to maintain Israel's relationship with him.*

**M**OSES SPENT 40 days and nights with God on Mount Sinai. God gave Moses instructions for creating the Tabernacle, or tent of meeting – a portable dwelling place for the divine presence of God (see pp.112–13) – which could be carried with the Israelites on their journey through the wilderness. God also outlined the role of the priests who would regulate its use. He told Moses to appoint his brother Aaron as High Priest and Aaron's four sons – Nadab, Abihu, Eleazar, and Ithamar – as priests and gave detailed instructions about what they should wear. Craftsmen were to create a breastpiece, ephod (a vest-like outer garment), robe, tunic, turban, and sash, made from fine linen, gold, and yarn of blue, purple, and scarlet. Beneath, the priest would wear a simple

linen undergarment. On Aaron's robes, two onyx stones, each engraved with the names of six of Jacob's 12 sons were to be attached to the ephod's shoulders. The breastpiece, mounted with 12 precious stones (one for each tribe), was to be attached to the ephod. In this way, Aaron would symbolically bring the 12 tribes into God's presence. Into the breastpiece's pouch would be placed the Urim and Thummim, sacred stones for casting lots to discover God's will. Beneath the ephod, Aaron was to wear a blue robe, with bells on its hem that would ring when he entered the sanctuary of the Tabernacle. Finally, he was to wear a turban with a gold plate saying, "HOLY TO THE LORD" (Exodus 28:36), not because he himself was holy, but as a sign of what God had done for him and Israel.

### Consecration ceremony

God gave Moses instructions for ordaining the priests – a complex ceremony that would last seven days. It was to begin with ritual washing and dressing of Aaron and his sons. Then a bull and two rams were to be sacrificed in a prescribed manner.

After Moses descended from the mountain, Aaron and his sons were ordained

## "The life of a creature is in the blood, and I have given it to you to make atonement for yourselves on the altar."

LEVITICUS 17:11

exactly as God had instructed (Leviticus 8–9). On the eighth day they began their priestly ministry, and Aaron's first act was to bless God's people. As he and Moses did so, fire erupted from nowhere, consuming the sacrifice on the altar – confirmation that God had consecrated his priests.

### Sacrifices

Later, Moses ascended Mount Sinai for a final time. God told him how the priests were to perform their sacrifices in the Tabernacle. God explained that the sacrifices of the Israelites were different from those of other nations because they were not attempts to placate God; instead, they should be seen as God's gift to the

#### ALTAR OF INCENSE
Sacrifices were offered at altars, such as this horned limestone altar found at Megiddo. This altar, too small for animal sacrifice, was probably used for incense, grain offerings, and libations of wine.

#### PUNISHMENT OF NADAB AND ABIHU
This 14th-century French illumination depicts Nadab and Abihu, two of the sons of Aaron, who disobeyed God's explicit instructions by offering a sacrifice with unauthorized fire. They were burnt to death.

people. He detailed the various types of sacrifice (see panel, left) and the duties of the priests, including the monitoring of disease and sickness.

God also outlined the sacrifices to be made on one special day – the annual Day of Atonement (known as Yom Kippur). After many elaborate rituals (described in Leviticus 16) the High Priest was permitted to enter the most holy part of the Tabernacle – the only time he could do so – to offer sacrifice to atone for any sin that might have been overlooked. This ritual included using two goats: one was to be sacrificed together with a bull and a ram; the other was despatched into the desert, a "scapegoat" symbolizing the carrying away of Israel's sin, and the very heart of the sacrificial system that God gave his people.

## AFTER

The sacrifices instituted at Mount Sinai remained central to Israel's life for centuries to come.

### IMPORTANCE OF SACRIFICE
Sacrifice lay at the heart of Jewish faith as the means of maintaining or re-establishing a relationship with God. When the **Temple was destroyed 236–37 »** in c.587 BC by Babylon, the Jewish people had to rethink their religious practice without the ritual of priesthood and sacrifice: it was at this time that **synagogue worship developed**. The second Temple was finally destroyed by Rome in AD 70, ending sacrifice for Judaism. Jewish people still gather at **the Western Wall, the one remaining part of the Temple**, to plead for God to restore his favour and to come again with his blessing.

**PRAYER AT THE WAILING WALL**

## "I will consecrate the tent of meeting and the altar and will consecrate Aaron and his sons to serve me as priests."

EXODUS 29:44

**SYMBOLS**

### SCAPEGOAT

To make a person a scapegoat is to blame him for another's misdemeanour. The term comes from Leviticus 16 when, during the Day of Atonement ceremony, one goat was sacrificed while another was led off into the desert, as a symbol of Israel's sins being carried away. The term "scapegoat" was first used in William Tyndale's translation of English Bible of 1530.

**BEFORE**

**The Israelites' creation of a golden calf broke God's covenant.**

**THE GOLDEN CALF**

After Moses had been on Mount Sinai for 40 days, the Israelites assumed he must be dead. Aaron **made a golden calf** for the people to worship as their deliverer. Moses returned and in anger, broke the tablets inscribed with the **Ten Commandments** **<< 106–07** and destroyed the golden calf.

**NEW TABLETS, NEW REVELATION**

Moses made **two new stone tablets** and ascended Sinai again. God renewed the covenant, and revealed his character as never before (Exodus 34:6,7). When Moses came down, **his face was radiant**.

NICOLAS POUSSIN'S *THE ADORATION OF THE GOLDEN CALF*, 1634

**LISTS**

**THE ARK IN ISRAEL'S HISTORY**

1 Constructed at Mount Sinai (Exodus 37:1–9).

2 Led Israel through the wilderness (Numbers 10:33).

3 Led the march around Jericho (Joshua 6:6,7).

4 Captured by the Philistines (1 Samuel 4:1–11).

5 Held in Philistine cities where it caused plagues (1 Samuel 5–6).

6 Seventy men died after looking within it (1 Samuel 6:19–7:1).

7 Brought to Jerusalem by David (2 Samuel 6).

8 Placed in Solomon's temple (1 Kings 8:1–21).

9 Returned to the restored Temple by Josiah (2 Chronicles 35:3).

10 Disappears after Jerusalem's destruction in c.587 BC.

# The Tabernacle and the Ark

*During his 40-day stay on Mount Sinai, Moses received instructions from God to construct the Tabernacle, or tent of meeting, and its furnishings, including the Ark – a chest to hold the Tablets of the Law.*

**M**OSES TOLD the Israelites to make the Tabernacle, a portable sanctuary where they could meet with the God who would accompany them on their journey to the Promised Land. Moses told them God had said "Everyone who is willing is to bring to the LORD an offering of gold, silver and bronze; blue, purple, and scarlet yarn and fine linen; goat hair; ram skins dyed red and another type of durable leather; acacia wood; olive oil for the light; spices for the anointing oil and for the fragrant incense" (Exodus 35:5–8). Eager to redeem their mistake with the golden calf (see Before panel, left), the people brought offerings in abundance – so much that they had to be asked to stop. Moses told the people that God had chosen Bezalel and Oholiab as the master craftsmen. He had filled the two men

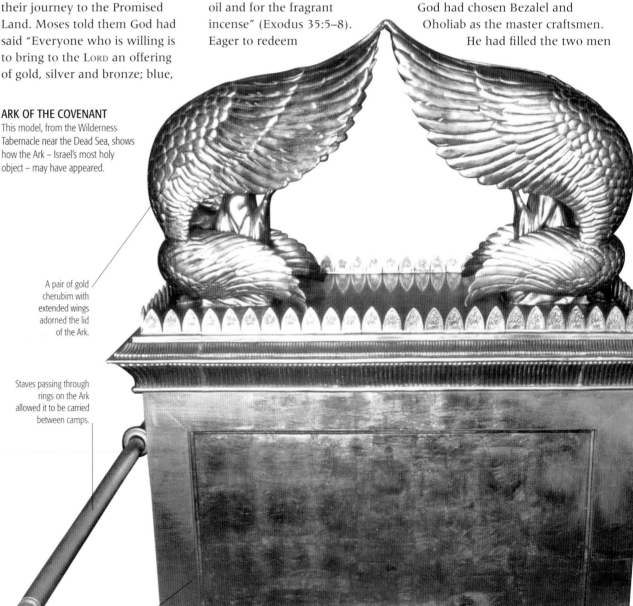

**ARK OF THE COVENANT**
This model, from the Wilderness Tabernacle near the Dead Sea, shows how the Ark – Israel's most holy object – may have appeared.

A pair of gold cherubim with extended wings adorned the lid of the Ark.

Staves passing through rings on the Ark allowed it to be carried between camps.

The Ark was built from acacia wood overlaid with gold.

**HOUSE OF GOD**
This life-size reconstruction of the Tabernacle in modern Israel is based on the biblical description. The horned altar in front of the tent held a fire that burned constantly.

> "Then he brought the **ark into the tabernacle** and hung the **shielding curtain** and shielded the ark of the covenant law as the LORD commanded him."
>
> **EXODUS** 40:21

**SYMBOLS**

### THE MENORAH

The lampstand used in the Tabernacle is one of Israel's oldest symbols. The design for the lamp, called the Menorah, was revealed to Moses directly by God. Its seven-branched structure, with six branches coming off one central stem, resembles a tree, which some think represents the Tree of Life in the Garden of Eden. The priests of the Tabernacle had to keep the lamp fuelled with olive oil and lit continually "from evening till morning" for generations to come (Leviticus 24:2–4).

**13TH-CENTURY ILLUSTRATION OF A MENORAH**

with his Holy Spirit and the skill and powers not only to make the Tabernacle, but also to teach their crafts to others.

### Making the tent of meeting

They began building the Tabernacle according to God's plans (Exodus 26): it was to be a tent measuring 30 cubits (13.8m/45ft) by 10 cubits (4.6m/15ft). First they made an inner linen tent, with blue, purple, and scarlet threads, joining its panels with gold clasps. This was covered by a second layer made from goat hair, joined by bronze clasps. For protection there were two more layers, one of leather and an outer one of hides of "sea cows". Then they made acacia frames that sat in silver bases and, finally, two curtains, one for the entrance and one to screen the Ark of the Covenant inside the tent.

### Furnishing the tent

Next the Israelites began to make the contents of the Tabernacle. They constructed the Ark of the Covenant, which was to hold the two stone tablets inscribed with the Ten Commandments (25:21). It was to be a gold-covered acacia-wood box with gold rings on either side, through which gold-covered carrying poles could be inserted. The lid, named the "atonement cover" (37:6), had a golden cherub at either end. The other furnishings included a gold-covered acacia-wood table, also with rings and carrying poles; a golden lampstand with three branches on either side (see The Menorah, right) to light the Tabernacle; gold- and bronze-covered acacia-wood altars, both with rings and carrying poles; and a bronze basin for washing. Finally, a great courtyard of linen curtains, 100 cubits (45m/150ft) long, enclosed everything.

### A place to meet and worship

Moses inspected the Tabernacle and blessed the people for their work. They had begun erecting it on the first day of the first month, almost a year after their escape from Egypt. Now everything was in place: the table, lampstand, and gold altar were in the Holy Place inside the Tabernacle; the Ark was in the Most Holy Place – an inner sanctum divided from the Holy Place by a thick curtain. The basin and bronze altar sat within the courtyard. Everything was anointed with oil and consecrated to God. Finally, Moses placed the Ten Commandments inside the Ark of the Covenant.

Nine months of hard work had come to an end and the Israelites finally had a place to meet with God. When they travelled, they carried the Ark at the front of their group; and when they rested, they placed it in the middle of their camp as a symbol that God was truly in their midst.

> "**There I will meet you and speak to you**; there also I will meet with the Israelites, and the place will be consecrated by my glory."
>
> **EXODUS** 29:42,43

**BUILDING MATERIAL**
The Tabernacle and the Ark were both constructed out of acacia wood. Acacia is one of the hardiest trees in the desert, and is indigenous to the area of southern Sinai, where the Tabernacle was constructed.

**AFTER »**

**With the work now finished, God's glory filled the Tabernacle.**

### GOD AMONG HIS PEOPLE

God appeared over the Tabernacle as a **pillar of cloud visible to all both by day and night**. Moses was so awe-struck by God's presence in the Tabernacle that he was afraid to enter it, but he heard God's commands issuing from within (Leviticus 1:1). The cloud was a sign that God had truly come to live among the Israelites, and was a powerful assurance of his presence. A cloud had led the people from Egypt, and it appeared again to lead them on **to the Promised Land 124–25 »**. The **apostle John 322–23 »** would later speak of how the eternal Christ came and **"made his dwelling among us"** (John 1:14). The Greek words he used literally meant "tabernacled among us", and referred back to this event.

# Wanderings in the Wilderness

*After 11 months at Sinai, the cloud lifted and the Israelites moved on towards the Promised Land. However, what should have been a journey of faith quickly deteriorated into grumbling and rebellion. As a result, a whole generation lost what they had been promised.*

**T**HE PEOPLE dismantled the Tabernacle and set off towards the Promised Land, but were soon complaining about the hardships of life in the desert. Moses told God he could not carry the burden of leadership on his own any longer, so God appointed 70 of Israel's elders to share it with him. Then he sent a strong wind to blow in quail for food (see pp.104–105). However, even though they had been provided with fresh meat to eat, the people still grumbled. Miriam and Aaron criticized Moses, saying that he was behaving as if God only spoke through him. God rebuked Miriam and Aaron, striking Miriam with leprosy for seven days.

Years later, the people's continued impatience resulted in a terrifying infestation of poisonous snakes in the camp, and many died. Moses made a bronze snake after God had said: "Make a snake and put it up on a pole; anyone who is bitten can look at it and live" (Numbers 21:8).

### BEFORE

After the plague, Moses acted on God's instruction to take a census of the whole Israelite community.

**THE CENSUS**
Thirteen months after the Exodus, there was a **census of men aged 20 and over** to identify how many could serve in Israel's army. There were 603,550 men, indicating a population of about **two million in 12 tribes**. The tribes were given their **positions around the Ark**, three on each side of the square. They were to advance in blocks of three behind it when on the march.

> **"** We are setting out for the place about which the LORD said, '**I will give it to you**.' **"**
>
> NUMBERS 10:29

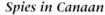

**A FERTILE LAND**
The spies sent by Moses to investigate the Promised Land, as pictured here in an illustration from a 15th-century printed book, returned with luscious fruit and described a fertile land.

### Spies in Canaan
When the Israelites reached Kadesh Barnea (see map, p.103), God told Moses to send 12 spies, one from each tribe, to explore Canaan. After 40 days the spies returned with a branch bearing an enormous cluster of grapes, as well as figs and pomegranates, as proof of the land's great fertility. However, they also reported that Canaan's people were powerful, its cities large, and its inhabitants "of great size" (13:32). As this information spread among the Israelites, they became fearful.

### *Judgment on a generation*
Once again the people started wishing they had died in Egypt or the desert, and even talked about returning. Moses and Aaron prayed, while Caleb and Joshua, two of the spies, tried to restore their faith. Exasperated with the Israelites, God threatened to wipe them out and work through Moses alone. Moses continued to pray, appealing to both God's reputation (asking what Egypt would think if he did not bring them to Canaan) and his character

**MOUNT SINAI**
The Israelites set off for Canaan from Mount Sinai, where Moses had received the Ten Commandments, but they would wander for 40 years in the wilderness before they finally reached the Promised Land.

(he was gracious and forgiving). God said he would forgive them, but said that no-one who was now over the age of 20 (apart from Caleb and Joshua) would enter Canaan. The Israelites would spend 40 years in the wilderness until a whole generation had died; only then would God bring their children into the Promised Land. To underline this, the spies who had spread the alarm were struck down. Suddenly the people wanted to go to Canaan after all – some tried to enter, but were defeated by its inhabitants.

### Wilderness years

The Israelites spent the next 38 years in the wilderness near Kadesh Barnea. Only after that did God lead them towards Canaan. Edom, south of the Dead Sea, refused them passage, so they bypassed it. They reached Moab, east of the Dead Sea, conquering the Amorite King Sihon before pressing north to Bashan, conquering King Og. They then returned to Moab's plains across the Jordan from Jericho.

There King Balak hired the prophet Balaam to curse Israel. God was angry, and sent the angel of the Lord to meet Balaam. At first only his donkey could see the angel, but Balaam soon recognized

**THE NATION OF ISRAEL**
This stele carries an inscription by the Egyptian king Merneptah, believed to be from the early 13th century BC. It is significant because contains the first written historical reference to the nation of Israel.

that God was with Israel, and blessed the people rather than cursing them (Numbers 22–24). Since this land east of the Jordan was good for livestock, the Reubenites, Gadites, and half of Manasseh asked for permission to settle. Moses agreed, but said they had to help the other tribes take their inheritance first. The wilderness wanderings were over and the Israelites were ready to take their Promised Land.

## THE BOOK OF DEUTERONOMY

The book of Deuteronomy, meaning "second law" or "repetition of the law" in Greek, records Moses' final words to the Israelites before they entered Canaan – words spoken on the plains of Moab. Looking back over their 40 years in the wilderness, he recalls the covenant that God made at Sinai, restating its requirements to the new generation of Israelites who face a new life in the Promised Land. Its warm tone is that of a father who knows he will not be with his family much longer.

Deuteronomy takes the form of a covenant renewal document, with its structure of prologue (Deuteronomy 1:1–4:43), covenant requirements (4:44–26:19), blessing and curses for keeping or breaking the covenant (27–28), and the covenant's renewal (29–30). Its key principle, that obedience leads to blessing and disobedience leads to curse, guided the writers of Israel's history in the books of 1 and 2 Kings.

### AFTER »

**Moses died without entering the Promised Land.**

#### DEATH OF MOSES

Moses **repeated God's law** to the new generation about to enter Canaan (Deuteronomy). Then, having appointed Joshua as his successor, he climbed Mount Nebo and **looked at the Promised Land**. God spoke to him, saying that he had brought Moses to see with his own eyes the land that would pass to his descendants. However, Moses was never to enter the Promised Land. He **died at the age of 120**, and, according to tradition, was buried by God on Mount Nebo itself.

**A VIEW TOWARDS CANAAN FROM MOUNT NEBO**

# INTO THE PROMISED LAND

"Then the LORD said to him [Moses], **'This is the land I promised** on oath to Abraham, Isaac and Jacob when I said, "I will give it to your descendants." I have let you see it with your eyes, **but you will not cross over into it.'**"

DEUTERONOMY 34:4

**T**HIS PART OF THE BIBLE COVERS THE STORY of the Israelites as they seek to conquer and settle in the Promised Land. The first book, Joshua, begins on the high note of Joshua's conquest, but God's chosen people soon went astray, as recorded in the next two books recounting the three centuries following Joshua's death, when many were left longing for a king who would provide strong leadership once again. The failure of the Israelites to listen to the words of Moses and obey God's commands sowed the seeds for external defeat by their enemies and internal destruction by their own people.

This section begins with the book of Joshua, the man who succeeded Moses, as he took the Israelites into the Promised Land. He was a courageous leader, who broke the power of the Canaanites. However, it fell to later generations to try to take full possession of the territories. Through a combination of harassment by their enemies and enticement to follow the Canaanite pagan religions, the Israelites failed to uphold the commands specified by Moses.

### BOOKS OF JUDGES AND RUTH

There was little national cohesion among the Israelites, for Joshua had failed to appoint a successor. Each tribe was largely left to itself in this period, as can be seen in the book of Judges which concludes with a reflection: "In those days Israel had no king; everyone did as they saw fit" (Judges 21:25). However, against this background of decline and decay there is a glimpse of hope in the story of Ruth, a reminder that, no matter how bad things get, there are always a few faithful people who will trust in God, do what is right, and see their situation redeemed.

The two books of Judges and Ruth are skilfully constructed. For example, the book of Ruth begins with an introduction of 71 Hebrew words and ends with a conclusion of 71 Hebrew words, with the key verse in the middle (Ruth 2:20) and the two parts of the story on either side.

Judges too is skilfully balanced. Its focal point is the contrast between a man reluctant to be king (Gideon) and a man who desired to be king (Abimelech). On either side come Deborah from the west and Jephthah from the east, both insignificant people in their culture – Deborah because she was a woman and Jephthah because he was a prostitute's son. Around these two stories come two loners: Ehud from the south and Samson from the north, which, according to scholars, is a literary technique to show the scale of Israel's impoverishment.

### UNDERLYING THEMES

There are key themes in each of the books: in Joshua, the importance of obeying God, and his faithfulness; in Judges, God's discipline and capacity for deliverance; and in Ruth, God's covenant of faithful love and redemption.

**REPORTS OF THE PROMISED LAND**
Nicolas Poussin's painting *Autumn*, *c.*1664, from a set of four called "The Four Seasons", depicts two of the spies sent by Moses into Canaan. They find a fertile land, and bring back a great cluster of grapes on a pole (Numbers 13:17–25).

**GIDEON AS GOD'S WARRIOR**
Gideon is painted in medieval armour on earthenware produced by the Della Robbia Pottery in Birkenhead, UK, *c.*1900. This famous pottery followed the ideas of the Arts and Crafts Movement in using subjects that symbolized moral strength.

Galilean ○ Hazor
Hills
Sea of
Chinnereth
(Sea of
Galilee)
▲ Mt. Carmel
Dor ○                    **GILEAD**
                         Beth-Shan
              Shechem ○
Joppa ○
                        ○ Bethel
Ashdod ○   Gezer ○      Jericho ○ ○ Gilgal
           Ekron ○      ○ Jerusalem
Ashkelon ○             Bethlehem
                        Salt Sea
                        (Dead Sea)
           ○ **JUDAH**
Gaza ○     ○ Hebron
                        River Arnon

(Mediterranean Sea)
Great Sea

Plain of Megiddo
River Jordan
River Jabbok
Central Highlands
C A N A A N

○ Beersheba

*The Negev*

## BIBLICAL HEARTLAND

# The Land of Canaan

## "It is a good land that the LORD our God is giving us."

DEUTERONOMY 1:25

**I**F THE BIBLE IS THE drama of God's plan for humankind, then the stage on which it unfolds is Canaan – a region between the Mediterranean Sea and the River Jordan, roughly corresponding to modern-day Lebanon, Palestine, and Israel. Canaan consisted of fortified towns, each of which dominated a hinterland.

According to the Bible, Canaan was named after the son of Ham, one of Noah's three sons. Ham dishonoured Noah, who said, "Cursed be Canaan! The lowest of slaves will he be to his brothers" (Genesis 9:25).

### Regional geography

According to the Bible, by the time Abraham arrived in the region Canaan's descendants were well-established. The region had six distinct geographical zones, each of which played their part in the Bible's story. First was the coastal

#### CANAANITE JEWELLERY

Canaanite necklaces often used Egyptian carnelian shaped into lotus pods. Canaan and Egypt had traded since at least 3,100 BC.

plain, bordering on the Mediterranean, which was fertile in the north but not in the south, causing the Philistines to constantly seek new territory. Second were the fertile foothills, between the coastal plains and the highlands, known as the Shephelah. This is the "hill country" often fought over by the Israelites and Philistines (Deuteronomy 1:7, Joshua 10:40, 11:16).

Third, at the heart of the region, were the central highlands, home to cities such as Jerusalem and Hebron. Sitting between the central highlands and the Galilean hills was the fourth region, the

#### BIBLICAL CANAAN

Corresponding to modern Israel, Palestine, Lebanon, and western Jordan, Canaan was the land promised to Abraham by God, who described its extent (Genesis 15:18–21). The map above shows its principal settlements in the time of Moses.

Plain of Megiddo. This was crossed by the main highway and so was strategically significant.

The area of Galilee formed the fifth region. This was the fertile lower hills around the Sea of Chinnereth (Sea of Galilee); it was rich in fish and contributed to the

#### HILL COUNTRY

This image of modern-day Upper Galilee, looking southwest from the city of Safed, Israel, is the "hill country" (Numbers 13:17) – a landscape typical of parts of biblical Canaan.

area's prosperity. Finally, the sixth region, the Jordan Valley, ran north to south from the Sea of Galilee to the Dead Sea – the lowest point on Earth at more than 400m (1,300ft) below sea level.

## Religious practices

The Bible denounces Canaanite religions as polytheistic (belief in multiple gods), idolatrous (worship of idols), and involving divination (witchcraft), child sacrifice, and sacred prostitution cults. Canaanites personified and worshipped the power of nature. The gods most

### THE CURSE OF HAM

In *The Curse of Ham* by Ivan Stepanovich Ksenofontov (1817–75), Noah curses his son Ham, and his children (the Canaanites), because Ham saw his father naked and dishonoured him by telling his brothers.

frequently mentioned in the Bible are Baal ("Lord"), the god of fertility and weather, who was often depicted standing on a bull (a symbol of strength), holding a lightning spear, and Ashtoreth (or Astarte), his consort. Ritual prostitution at their shrines was common as this was believed to stir the gods to send fertility to the land.

These Canaanite practices illustrate why God commanded Israel to destroy the Canaanites (Deuteronomy 7). However, God was patient in his judgment, telling Abraham he could not give Canaan to his descendants for 400 years, during which time Abraham's descendants would be strangers in a country not their own, where they would be ill-treated and enslaved. But God promised to "punish the nation they serve as slaves" (Genesis 15:14), and later give them great possessions.

## The Promised Land

Canaan's significance in the Bible comes from the fact that it is the "Promised Land" – God gave it to Abraham and his descendants "as an everlasting possession" (Genesis

When God spoke to Moses from the burning bush (see pp.96–97), he declared that he had come down to rescue his people and "bring them up out of that land into a good and spacious land, a land flowing with milk and honey – the home of the Canaanites" (Exodus 3:8).

This biblical description summarized Canaan's fruitfulness and God's provision of everything from staple (milk) to luxury (honey) aspects of diet – an image of total satisfaction. The region's fertility is confirmed in non-biblical records, such as the Ancient Egyptian *Story of Sinhue*.

17:8). In ancient times, Canaan lay surrounded by great nations: to its south lay Egypt and Arabia; to its east the nations of Mesopotamia; and to its north Syria and the Hittites. Whoever controlled this strip of land, through which all the great trade routes passed, could exert great influence over the nations in the surrounding region.

God's plan was that Abraham's descendants should influence all the nations, but the region was more often divided by conflict with the neighbouring nations. It would fall to Jesus, whose ministry also occurred within this small region, to send his followers from here into all the world.

> " You gave them this land you had sworn to give to their ancestors, **a land flowing with milk and honey**. "
>
> JEREMIAH 32:22

The first references to "Canaan" come from Mesopotamian and Egyptian sources in the 2nd millennium BC. The word is thought to mean "purple", deriving from the manufacture of purple dyes in the region. In the Bible, Joshua found Canaan inhabited by the Hittites, Jebusites, Amorites, Amalekites, and the Philistines, who dominated the southern coast.

**CAPTIVE PHILISTINES DEPICTED, c.1200 BC, AT THE TEMPLE OF RAMESES III AT MEDINET HABU, EGYPT**

**Descendants of Canaan** settle in the region. Canaan is one of the four sons of Ham and the grandson of Noah.

**c.2091 BC,** Abraham sent here by God; told by him that Canaan will belong to his descendants as "an everlasting possession to you and your descendants after you; and I will be their God" (Genesis 17:8).

**c.2000 BC,** inhabitants of Canaan invent the alphabet, from which all modern alphabets derive.

**c.1876 BC,** Jacob leaves Canaan for Egypt (Genesis 46).

**c.1440 BC,** Moses sends spies who return with reports of Canaan – "it does flow with milk and honey! … But the people who live there are powerful, and the cities are fortified and very large" (Numbers 13:27,28).

**c.1406 BC,** Joshua leads the Israelites into the Promised Land (Joshua 3–4), establishing the first permanent camp in Canaan at "Gilgal on the eastern border of Jericho" (Joshua 4:19).

**c.1375–1050 BC,** ruled by regional judges.

**c.1050–930 BC,** Israel established as a nation under Saul, David, and Solomon.

**c.930 BC,** land divided between Israel in the north and Judah in south (1 Kings 12).

**c.874–853 BC,** Ahab introduces Canaanite worship into Israel (1 Kings 16:29–33).

**c.875–848 BC,** Elijah challenges Canaanite religion; contest with Baal's prophets on Mount Carmel (1 Kings 18).

**c.724–722 BC,** Assyria invades; Samaria falls (721 BC); northern Canaan becomes an Assyrian province.

**c.697–642 BC,** Manasseh introduces Canaanite worship into Judah (2 Kings 21).

**c.587 BC,** Judah conquered by Babylon.

**c.538–432 BC,** Jews return to Canaan.

**333 BC,** absorbed into Alexander the Great's empire.

**301 BC,** absorbed into Egyptian Ptolemaic empire.

**200 BC,** absorbed into the Seleucid empire.

**167–147 BC,** Maccabean revolt to reclaim the land for Israel.

**147–37 BC,** autonomous rule by Hasmoneans.

**63 BC,** region conquered by Rome.

**37–4 BC,** ruled by the tetrarch Herod the Great, under the authority of Rome. His symbols (a helmet topped by a star and a tripod under a bowl) appear on coins.

**BRONZE COINS OF HEROD THE GREAT**

# Crossing the Jordan

*About 400 years after Joseph brought his family from Canaan to Egypt, his descendants were poised to return to Canaan. God miraculously blocked the flow of the River Jordan, enabling the Israelites to cross over and enter the land promised to Abraham some seven centuries earlier.*

**A**FTER MOSES' DEATH, God told Joshua to get ready to cross the River Jordan, reaffirming his promise about the land he would give the Israelites, and encouraging Joshua to be courageous and obedient.

Joshua told the leaders to prepare to cross three days later. Then he sent two spies on a reconnaissance of the land, in particular Jericho, the first fortress they would encounter. There they were hidden in the house of a woman called Rahab who, when questioned by Jericho's king, pleaded ignorance. That night she helped the two escape from the city, asking them to show kindness to her family when they attacked. The spies hid in the hills for three days, before returning to Joshua. They assured him that "all the people are melting in fear because of us" (Joshua 2:24).

The next morning the Israelites camped by the river. Joshua and the leaders explained God's strategy: 12 priests would carry the Ark of the Covenant, the symbol of his presence, into the river while the people crossed. However, this looked impossible as the Jordan, which only days earlier the spies had forded, was now in fierce flood. Joshua said to the Israelites, "…as soon as the priests who carry the ark of the LORD… set foot in the Jordan, its waters flowing downstream will be cut off and stand up in a heap" (3:13). Just as he promised, the moment the priests stepped into the river, the water stopped flowing.

The priests stood in the river until everyone had crossed. As soon as they came out of the water the river returned. The people camped at Gilgal, to the north-east of nearby Jericho, where Joshua set up 12 stones from the river where the priests had stood, as a memorial to what God had done. He then circumcised the men to indicate that they were truly God's covenant people. The next day the miraculous supply of manna (see pp.114–15) stopped. God's people were home at last; they had need of it no longer.

The River Jordan became significant in Israel's history and many would come to the river or cross it seeking to refresh their vision of God. Jesus himself would be baptized there. In Christian tradition, it became symbolic of any significant "crossing over" to a new stage, particularly the ultimate crossing over from life to death.

## "The LORD has surely given the whole land into our hands…"

JOSHUA 2:24

### FULFILMENT OF A PROMISE

In *The Ark of the Covenant*, by Flemish painter Frans Francken the Younger (1581–1642), the Israelites cross the River Jordan safely (as the waters are suspended) and finally enter the Promised Land, after 40 years. As directed by God, the priests carrying the Ark stand in the dry riverbed while the others pass.

**BEFORE**

With the circumcision ceremony completed and the Passover meal shared, the Israelites were now ready to continue to the Promised Land.

**GOD APPEARS TO JOSHUA**

As Joshua **approached Jericho**, he saw a stranger, his sword drawn. Joshua asked him whether he was **on the side of the Israelites or of their enemies**. Neither, the man replied, identifying himself as the commander of the LORD's army. Joshua recognized the holiness of the moment and fell to his face, realizing that **God was on nobody's side but his own**.

> **" When the trumpets sounded, the army shouted, and at the sound of the trumpet, when the men gave a loud shout, the wall collapsed."**
>
> JOSHUA 6:20

**LISTS**

### HISTORY OF JERICHO

1 **c.9000 BC** The area is first inhabited by people.

2 **c.8000 BC** Houses are first built on the site.

3 **c.1406 BC** Conquered and destroyed by Joshua and placed under a permanent curse.

4 **c.850 BC** Rebuilt by Hiel of Bethel at personal cost to his family (1 Kings 16:34).

5 **c.850 BC** Home to a school of prophets in the time of Elijah and Elisha (2 Kings 2:5).

6 **c.586 BC** King Zedekiah is captured here by the Babylonians as he tries to flee (Jeremiah 39:5–7).

7 **c.35 BC** Herod the Great builds a palace in Jericho.

8 **c.AD 33** Jesus heals blind Bartimaeus and eats with the city's tax-collector, Zacchaeus.

# The Capture of Jericho

*As the Israelites approached Jericho, its people closed the gates. However, as a result of a miraculous intervention by God, the city's massive walls and towers collapsed, and the Israelites were able to conquer the city.*

G OD TOLD JOSHUA that he would deliver the city of Jericho to him "along with its king and its fighting men" (Joshua 6:2). He gave instructions for the Israelite army to march around the city, behind the Ark of the Covenant, once a day for six days. On the seventh day, they were to march around the walls seven times, then give a loud shout at which, God said, the walls would collapse, allowing the Israelites to march straight into the city of Jericho.

### Six days of marching

Joshua explained the plan to the people and it was quickly put into action. An armed guard led the way, followed by seven priests blowing ram's horn trumpets. Then came the priests carrying the Ark of the Covenant, the symbol of God's presence, followed by a rear guard. Apart from the trumpets, there was not a sound to be heard; everyone marched in total silence. When they had completed the circuit of the city walls, they returned to their camp. The Israelites repeated the procession every day for the next five days. By now the people of Jericho must have been wondering what was happening.

### Day seven

On the seventh day, Joshua reminded the Israelites of what God had said: Jericho and everything in it was to be given to God through its total destruction. Apart from Rahab, the woman who had helped the two Israelite spies (see p.121), and her family,

no-one and nothing was to be spared. If any person took anything for himself, Joshua warned, it would bring disaster. All gold, silver, bronze, and iron were to be given to the LORD's treasury.

So, the Israelite army set out again, but this time, in accordance with God's instructions, they marched around the city walls seven times. Then, as the priests sounded a trumpet blast, Joshua told the people to "Shout! For the LORD has given you the city!" (6:16). As they did so, the huge city walls collapsed and the Israelites charged straight in.

### The city is taken

As Joshua had instructed, the Israelites "devoted the city to the LORD" (6:21). The two spies were sent to rescue Rahab and her family; all the other living creatures – "men and women,

**JEWISH SHOFAR**
The ram's horn trumpet, or *shofar*, was used by the priests besieging Jericho, and it is traditionally blown to mark the beginning of Rosh Hashanah, the Jewish New Year.

**FALL OF JERICHO**
This illustration from a 15th-century French work on Jewish antiquity shows the Ark of the Covenant being carried around the city of Jericho, as priests sound the seven trumpets.

young and old, cattle, sheep, and donkeys" (6:21) – were destroyed. The Israelites then burned the entire city and everything in it, but took the precious metals for the LORD's treasury. No warrior was to profit from God's victory. Then Joshua pronounced a curse on anyone who ever tried to rebuild Jericho. No reason is given for the city's total destruction, but Joshua's victory caused his reputation to spread rapidly through Canaan.

**AFTER**

Joshua solemnly renews Israel's covenant with God.

**JOSHUA ON THE MOUNTAIN**
Joshua **gathered together the leaders of all the tribes of Israel** before Mount Gerizim and Mount Ebal. Here, he **solemnly renewed the covenant**; this involved a rereading of the law to the people, reminding them of their responsibilities. and the construction of an altar made of " uncut stones" (Joshua 8:31).

**NABLUS, BETWEEN MT GERIZIM AND MT EBAL**

## JERICHO

Excavations have revealed at least 20 successive settlements at the site of Jericho, which at 250m (825ft) below sea level, is the lowest-lying town in the world. In biblical times Jericho was called "The City of Palms".

**BEFORE**

**While Canaanite kings joined forces to resist Israel, the Gibeonites tried to trick the Israelites into a peace treaty.**

### MAKING SERVANTS OF GIBEONITES

As news of **Israel's victories at Jericho and Ai ❮❮ 122–23** reached nearby Gibeon, its inhabitants resorted to a ruse. Wearing old clothes and carrying mouldy bread, they went to the Israelites and said: "We have come from a distant country; make a treaty with us" (Joshua 9:6). Without asking God, **Joshua made a treaty with them**, only to discover three days later they were actually neighbours. **Having taken an oath, the Israelites could not now attack them**, so they pressed them into service as woodcutters and water-carriers instead.

### JOSHUA FIGHTS THE AMORITES

This fresco, *Joshua Darkening the Sun* (c.1515) is part of a cycle of works by Raphael in the Vatican. Joshua is pictured commanding the Sun to stand still upon Gibeon so that he could attain total victory.

# Taking the Promised Land

*Having divided Canaan into two by defeating Jericho and Ai, Joshua and his people conquered the southern and then the northern regions. Some 30 years after entering the Promised Land, Canaanite power was broken.*

**A**FTER CONQUERING the city of Ai by means of a well-planned ambush, Joshua built an altar on Mount Ebal and renewed the covenant of the Israelites with God, "according to what is written in the Book of the Law of Moses" (Joshua 8:31). When Jerusalem's Amorite king, Adoni-Zedek, heard that Gibeon had made peace with the Israelites, he persuaded the Amorite kings of Hebron, Jarmuth, Lachish, and Eglon to join him in attacking Gibeon. The Gibeonites promptly appealed to Joshua for help. After an all-night march from his camp at Gilgal, Joshua launched a surprise attack. The army of the five kings, thrown into confusion by God, was routed. As the army

> " **Do not be afraid of them;** I have given them into your hand. **Not one of them will be able to withstand you.** "

JOSHUA 10:8

fled, God hurled huge hailstones that killed many of them, and the day seemed to lengthen: "So the sun stood still, and the moon stopped, till the nation avenged itself on its enemies… There has never been a day like it before or since…" (10:13,14).

### Southern victories

The Amorite kings fled to Makkedah and hid in a cave, where Joshua trapped them until his army had pursued and defeated their troops. Then Joshua had the kings brought out and executed. Their bodies were left exposed on poles until sunset, then thrown back into the cave, which was then blocked up with rocks.

Joshua pressed his advantage, conquering Makkedah, Libnah, and Lachish, and defeating Horam king of Gezer who had come to help Lachish. Supported by Caleb

**LITTLE RESISTANCE**
This modern-day image shows Egyptian houses in the Dakhla Oases, built using the same mud-brick techniques that would have been used in Canaan. In their quest to take over the Promised Land, the Israelites needed to conquer small towns like this.

(see panel, below) Joshua took the cities of Eglon, Hebron, and Debir. Having conquered this extensive swathe of southern land and "left no survivors" (10:40), the Israelites returned again to Gilgal.

### Northern victories

Joshua's army then turned north. Jabin, king of Hazor, had gathered a coalition of northern kings. Their vast army assembled at Merom. However, God told Joshua not to

be afraid: "… because by this time tomorrow I will hand all of them, slain, over to Israel" (11:6). At the Waters of Merom, Joshua and his army defeated the enemy and pursued them until there were no survivors; they hamstrung their horses and burned their chariots, before destroying Hazor. "So Joshua took this entire land" (11:16).

### Conquest complete

Some 30 years after it began, the conquest was almost complete. The Canaanites' power was broken, though their presence remained strong, hindering settlement by the Israelites.

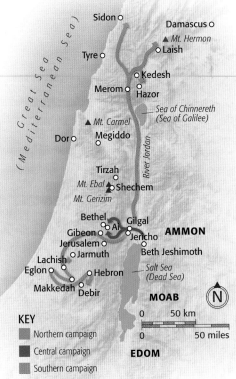

**CONQUEST OF CANAAN**
The locations of Joshua's campaigns, according to the Bible (Joshua 3–11), are mapped above. While the details of the conquests may not be historically accurate, they reinforce the role played by God in helping Joshua to take the Promised Land.

> " Then **Joshua dismissed the people,** each to their own inheritance. "

JOSHUA 24:28

**AMARNA TABLET**
This tablet is one of several hundred known as the Amarna letters. An example of Akkadian script, it dates from c.1350 BC and was correspondence from the Canaanite kings to the Pharaoh Akhenaten, mentioning attacks by Hebrew marauders.

### PEOPLE

#### CALEB

The Bible shows Caleb, "from the tribe of Judah… son of Jephunneh" (Numbers 13:6), to be an outsider who found a place among God's people. Not an Israelite but a Kennizite, his wholehearted following of God saved him and led him to play key roles in Israel's history.

Caleb was one of the 12 spies sent by Moses to explore Canaan, who bravely said, "We should go up and take possession of the land, for we can certainly do it" (13:30). He was one of the few Israelites over the age of 20 to enter Canaan (see pp.114–15), and he

was active in the campaigns against the Canaanites, even offering the hand of his daughter as an incentive to the man who could take the Canaanite city of Debir.

When Joshua was dividing up the land of Canaan between the tribes, Caleb, then 85 years of age, asked for, and was granted, the hill country around Hebron in return for his loyalty and in accordance with God's earlier promise to him. After Joshua's death, Caleb also helped Judah take up its inheritance (Judges 1).

### AFTER

Now in his late 90s, Joshua divided Canaan among Israel's 12 ancestral tribes, then later renewed the covenant with God.

**LAND ALLOTMENT**
While not every part of Canaan had been conquered, the key fortresses had been disabled, meaning that **settlement of the territory could begin**. Joshua 13–19 describes the area allotted to each tribe. This was important for **avoiding any future misunderstandings and conflicts**. Cities of refuge – where people could shelter from the threat of vengeance from others – were also designated at this time.

**REAFFIRMING GOD'S LAWS**
Some years later Joshua, now very old, summoned the tribal leaders together. He reminded them of all God had done and urged them to stay obedient to God. **Joshua led them in a covenant renewal ceremony at Shechem**, reaffirming the decrees and laws: "Now fear the LORD and serve him with all faithfulness" (Joshua 24:14). **He dismissed them to their territories, before dying at the age of 110**, his work complete.

HISTORY AND CULTURE

# Wildlife

"**Flowers appear** on the earth; the **season of singing** is come, the **cooing of doves** is heard in **our land**." SONG OF SONGS 2:12

**OPPORTUNISTIC FEEDERS**
Golden jackals lived in areas with plentiful food, often around humans, and scavenged at night to avoid the desert heat. They are still found in Israel today.

Canaan's landscape fell into six distinct zones (see pp.118–19), and this varied geography led to widely varying temperatures, especially

**MEADOW IN GALILEE**
Spring comes as early as February in Israel. The "flowers of the field" mentioned in the Bible probably include the common poppy, which grows profusely here.

during the winter – as it does in Israel today. January was the coldest month, and snow tended to fall at least once a year in the mountains. The coastal region had a typical Mediterranean climate, with cool, rainy winters and long, hot summers. Cooling breezes from the Mediterranean made the

summer heat more tolerable, but the *khamsin*, the hot, dry, dust-laden wind from the desert in the east, could make life unbearable – it could blow sporadically for up to 50 days. In the desert, the hot, dry summer days were followed by cold nights, and winters were mild with little rainfall.

As the summer drought was not always relieved by winter rain, famines are repeatedly mentioned in the Bible.

This range of habitats and climate meant the Bible lands supported a wide variety of wildlife. The Bible mentions more than 100 plants, but at least 2,500 species existed.

## MAMMALS

Some wild mammals were a welcome source of meat. Others, however, were at best a nuisance and at worst dangerous. Lions – common in Old Testament times, though rare by New Testament times and extinct in Israel today – lived in thickets in the Jordan Valley, preying on animals including livestock. They were a symbol of strength and power and were often hunted by kings and nobles. The leopard, which hunted at night in forests and rocky areas, was noted for its camouflage (Jeremiah 13:23), which helped it to creep up on its prey. The Syrian brown bear foraged in hills and woods for berries, roots, honey, and eggs, but would take lambs when particularly hungry. As a shepherd boy, King David had to fight off lions and bears (1 Samuel 17:34–37). Wolves hunted in packs, feeding on smaller animals,

**SYRIAN BROWN BEAR**
Common in biblical times, the Syrian brown bear is now extinct in Egypt, Israel, Lebanon, and, more recently, Syria too due to habitat loss and hunting.

though they sometimes attacked sheep and cattle. Foxes were a pest as they often damaged vines: "Catch for us the foxes, the little foxes that ruin the vineyards" (Song of Songs 2:15).

Other common wild mammals included roe and fallow deer, gazelle, and the Nubian ibex, which were all hunted for food.

## INSECTS

While some insects were disastrous for humans, others were a blessing. Bees, for example, made hives in rocks and trees and produced honey, which was highly valued as a delicacy and a sweetener. But other insects were less welcome, such as the moths whose larvae ate the woollen fabric of clothes and blankets (Isaiah 51:8).

**HONEY BEE**
Beekeeping has been practised in Israel for the last 3,000 years.

Locusts, unlike other insects, were a permitted food, but when they swarmed they would ruin a harvest (Joel 1:4). A plague of locusts could number hundreds of millions, even several billion, and would rapidly strip fields bare.

## PLANTS

Although the Bible lands were never densely forested, woodlands covered more areas than today. Many oaks have disappeared from the Plain of Sharon and Mount Carmel, and the Mount of Olives, once thick with olive trees, may have been stripped by the Romans during the siege of Jerusalem in AD 70. Oaks, firs, pines, and cypress grew on hills, while poplars, willows, and tamarisk formed dense thickets along the banks of the River Jordan.

Some trees were a source of food – for example figs and almonds – some had other everyday uses. Fir wood was used to make musical instruments, and cypress timber was excellent for boats. Oak was used for things that needed to last, such as oars or cult statues. The cedar of Lebanon's durable red wood carved well and was transported to Jerusalem in huge quantities for buildings such as palaces and the Temple.

## BIRDS

Among the many birds mentioned in the Bible, doves and pigeons are the most common. They were domesticated and used for food, carrying messages, and as sacrificial offerings (Genesis 8: 19–21). Quail, too, were a good source of food, as the Israelites experienced in the wilderness. Birds of prey included the eagle, which was a symbol of strength and power, the owl, which hunted at night, and the vulture, which scavenged off carcasses. All birds of prey were considered unclean.

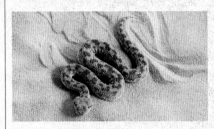

**FIRST OFF THE ARK**
The raven was the first bird sent from the Ark by Noah to see if the floodwaters had receded. The term "raven" also refers to crows and rooks.

Some trees, such as the oak, which can live for 300 years or more and grow to 24m (80ft), acquired symbolic significance, and the Canaanites established sanctuaries by them. One such was "the great tree of Moreh", where Abram worshipped (Genesis 12:6–7). Oaks were also seen as good places under which to bury the dead (Genesis 35:8).

## REPTILES

Many snakes lived in the Bible lands, some of them deadly – the Israelites were attacked by venomous snakes in the wilderness (Numbers 21:4–9). Common snakes included cobras, adders, and vipers such as the desert horned viper. Geckoes, skinks, and chameleons were all found in the region. All of them are unclean in Jewish Law and forbidden as food (Leviticus 11:29–38).

**DESERT HORNED VIPER**
Although humans are unlikely to die if bitten by this nocturnal snake, its venom can cause swelling, nausea, vomiting, and haemorrhaging.

**GREAT TREE**
The great trees of Mamre at Hebron, where Abram built an altar to the Lord, are likely to have been Kermes or Palestine oaks, such as this one.

Many shrubs had practical uses: broom made excellent charcoal; the seeds of the flax plant were crushed to produce linseed oil, while its fibres made nets, lamp-wicks, and, when steeped and combed, linen; "hyssop" (probably caper) sprigs were used for sprinkling blood in religious rituals. Other shrubs were used for making perfumes or incense: cassia bark, for example, was an ingredient of anointing oil; aloe resin and oil were used for perfume; and frankincense resin was burned as incense. Myrrh resin could be turned into a fragrant oil, but it also had medicinal properties – it was mixed with a drink and offered to Jesus as a painkiller when he was crucified (see pp. 398–99).

Flowers were prolific, but they are difficult to identify today from their biblical names.

# Joshua

**JOSHUA**
A stained glass window at the Church of All Saints, Norfolk, UK, depicts Joshua as a warrior and one of the most favoured leaders of Israel.

> "Be strong and courageous, because you will lead these people to inherit the land I swore to their ancestors to give them."
>
> JOSHUA 1:6

**J** OSHUA WAS A dominant figure in Israel's conquest of the Promised Land, yet little is known about his early years, other than that he was the Egypt-born son of Nun, who belonged to the tribe of Ephraim (part of the house of Joseph; see pp.80–81). At some point after the Exodus from Egypt, Moses chose Joshua to be his assistant.

## Hoshea becomes Joshua

Originally called Hoshea (which in Hebrew means "salvation"), Moses renamed him Joshua (meaning "The Lord saves"), perhaps to ensure there was no doubt about who would be responsible for the salvation that the Israelites would experience under his leadership.

**KADESH BARNEA**
It was from the oasis at Kadesh Barnea in the Sinai desert, on modern-day Israel's southern border, that Joshua was sent out into Canaan by Moses as one of the 12 spies. The Israelites camped here for many years before their entry into the Promised Land.

When the Jewish scriptures were rewritten in Greek, the name "Joshua" became "Jesus" (see pp.16–17). In the Greek translation, Joshua has "son of Nun" added to his name to distinguish him from Jesus Christ.

### The warrior Joshua

Joshua's first appearance in the Bible is as a military leader – a role that continues to feature strongly

### ANALYSIS

#### THE SUN STANDING STILL

In Joshua's battle with the Amorite kings (see pp.124–25), it is recorded that Joshua said to God:
"Sun, stand still over Gibeon,
  and you, moon, over the Valley of Aijalon.
 So the sun stood still,
  and the moon stopped,
   till the nation avenged itself on its
     enemies," (Joshua 10:12,13).
These verses, which are taken from the Book of Jashar – an early record of Israel's history written as poetry – can be seen as a poetic way of saying that the day was a long one and seemed to stretch incredibly. However, the text goes on to make it clear that the event was seen as a miracle: "There has never been a day like it before or since" (10:14). Clearly, something unusual was believed to have taken place, which may have been miraculous; or it may have been the sun ceasing to shine rather than move; or it may have been some other kind of natural phenomenon that was not understood at the time.

as his life progresses. No sooner had the Israelites begun to make their way through the desert after escaping from Egypt than the Amalekites attacked them. Moses said to Joshua, "Choose some of our men and go out to fight the Amalekites. Tomorrow I will stand on top of the hill with the staff of God in my hands" (Exodus 17:9).

 While Moses prayed on the hilltop, Joshua won a decisive victory, underlining the importance of faith and prayer for what lay ahead. In the coming years Joshua's military skills were hugely important. He led the battles that helped the Israelites take the Promised Land and he was an excellent strategist, as revealed in his plan to lure away and then ambush the defenders of Ai, before taking the city (Joshua 8).

### Faith and vision

From the beginning, Joshua is depicted as a man full of faith and vision. He was chosen as one of the 12 spies sent by Moses to explore Canaan, and while they all returned describing a good and fruitful land, ten of them said it would be too difficult to conquer (see pp.124–25). Only Joshua and Caleb believed that Israel could defeat the Canaanites, even though saying this almost cost the pair their lives, when in response "the whole assembly talked about stoning them" (Numbers 14:10).

In response to the people's grumbling, God had declared, "In this wilderness your bodies will fall – every one of you twenty years old or more who was counted in the census and who has grumbled against me" (Numbers 14:29). However, Joshua and Caleb's faith would be rewarded; they would be the only Israelites aged over 20 to enter the Promised Land.

Joshua promoted faith among the Israelites. He reminded them that they were God's chosen people through his renewing of the Covenant both on entering the Promised Land (Joshua 8:30–35) and once the conquest was completed (Joshua 24:1–28).

## Successor to Moses

From early on, Moses saw something special in Joshua. Although he appointed Joshua as his assistant, it was only on the plains of Moab that Moses – eager that his people would not be like sheep without a shepherd – formally appointed him as his successor, in obedience to God's instruction to do so: "Take Joshua son of Nun, a man in whom is the spirit of leadership, and lay your hand on him. Make him stand before Eleazar the priest and the entire assembly and commission him in their

**MOSES COMMANDS JOSHUA**
Moritz Daniel Oppenheim's 1841 painting, *Moses Gives Command to Joshua*, shows the appointment of Joshua as the leader – "he laid his hands on him and commissioned him, as the LORD instructed through Moses" (Numbers 27:23).

presence. Give him some of your authority so that the whole Israelite community will obey him" (Numbers 27:18–20). Joshua accompanied Moses in the tabernacle where God spoke to Moses "face to face" (Exodus 33:11), and remained in the tent afterwards – a sign of his devotion to God.

Joshua was present at several key moments as Israel entered the Promised Land. He heard God give Moses the plans for crossing the Jordan, defeating Jericho, exposing Achan's sin, conquering Canaan, dividing up the land, and designating cities of refuge.

After Moses' death, God spoke to Joshua and encouraged him to be courageous because God would be with him always: "I will never leave you nor forsake you" (Joshua 1:5). Joshua led the Israelites with enormous skill, bringing them into the land of their inheritance.

In many ways Joshua's ministry paralleled that of Moses: both were leaders who had sent spies to scout the Promised Land, led God's people across water that had miraculously parted for them, encountered the angel of the LORD, led Israel to victories, renewed the Covenant, called Israel to obedience to God's Law, and both men gave farewell addresses. Joshua was Moses' spiritual son and heir.

**TRADITIONAL SITE OF JOSHUA'S TOMB IN KIFL HARES, WEST BANK**

---

**HISTORY AND CULTURE**

## GILGAL

**MODERN-DAY GILGAL; "ON THE PLAINS OF JERICHO" (JOSHUA 5:10)**

Gilgal is described in the Bible as being located "on the eastern border of Jericho" (Joshua 4:19). After crossing the Jordan, the Israelites set up camp there, and Joshua erected a memorial of 12 stones from the river (4:19–24). All men born since the Exodus were circumcised and the Passover was celebrated for the first time in the Promised Land (Joshua 5). Gilgal was where the Israelites returned after each battle in the conquest of Canaan. For a time it was home to the Tabernacle, and became an important religious centre (1 Samuel 10:8; 11:14,15).

« BEFORE

When Joshua died, there was no-one to replace him as he had replaced Moses, and Israel quickly declined.

TOMB OF JOSHUA, NORTHERN GALILEE

## AFTER JOSHUA'S DEATH

The Book of Judges recalls Israel's conquest of Canaan and highlights why **Israel had not been successful in taking the land completely**. The reason was partly practical, for the **Canaanites had much better iron weapons**, and partly spiritual, for Israel had not been faithful to God. Following Joshua's death "another generation grew up who knew neither the LORD nor what he had done for Israel" (Judges 2:10) **and chose to follow Baal « 118–19**. This would lead to the repeated cycles of oppression and victory documented in Judges.

> "In those days **Israel had no king**; everyone did as they saw fit."
>
> JUDGES 21:25

## DEBORAH'S INTERVENTION

The medieval *Bible Moralisee*, France (c.1235) contains illustrations of tales from the Book of Judges, including the story of Deborah's reign as Judge. The Israelites are seen asking her for help, and later achieving victory over King Jabin through her intervention and command.

# The Judges

*The Book of Judges is not just about people who bring justice. The Hebrew word has a special use which means "deliverers"; these were people called by God to deliver Israel from their enemies at times of crisis.*

**J**OSHUA'S DEATH was followed by dark days for Israel – days of disunity and godlessness. The tribes formed a loose confederation with little central control and in times of crisis, it was the Judges who were called forward as temporary leaders to rescue God's people.

Each of the main stories in Judges follows a similar pattern: the Israelites transgress in the eyes of God; God punishes them through oppressors; the people repent and call to God for help; God sends a Judge to deliver them; the land returns to peace. This cycle was repeated many times over a period of 300 years, which scholars date to *c.*1375–1050 BC.

## The first Judges

The stories of the first three Judges, Othniel, Ehud, and Shamgar, are short, telling simply how these Judges disposed of the Israelites' enemies. They are followed by Deborah, the only female Judge. The Israelites had "done evil", so "the LORD sold them into the hands of Jabin king of Canaan" (Judges 4:1,2). After 20 years of oppression Israel called to God for help. In response, Deborah sent for a man named Barak, and told him of God's commands: he was to take 10,000 soldiers to Mount Tabor, where God would deliver Sisera, the leader of Jabin's army, and his troops. Barak agreed, on condition that Deborah would accompany him. She promised to do so, and also told him that "the LORD will deliver Sisera into the hands of a woman" (Judges 4:9). Barak successfully attacked and routed Sisera's army, but Sisera fled. He hid in the tent of Jael, wife of Heber the Kenite, and while he slept, she hammered a tent peg through his skull. When Barak arrived, she showed him the body. The glory had gone to a woman, Jabin's power was broken, and the Israelites at last had some respite.

The next Judge, Gideon (see p.132), was so popular that he was asked to become king, but he refused. In contrast, his son Abimelech murdered his 70 brothers to clear his path to becoming king. All we learn of Judges Tola and Jair is that each rose up to lead Israel for around 20 years.

## Jephthah's vow

Judge Jephthah was called upon to lead the Israelites against the Ammonites (see panel, above). On his way to battle, he rashly vowed to God that if he won, "whatever comes out of the door of my house to meet me when I return in triumph… I will sacrifice it as a burnt offering" (Judges 11:30,31). He returned victorious, but on reaching home was greeted by his only daughter, whom he then had to kill.

Three Judges are then dealt with in quick succession: Ibzan, Elon, and Abdon, before the book turns to Samson and his struggle against the Philistines (see pp.134–35).

> " They were unable to drive the **people from the plains,** because they **had chariots fitted with iron.** "
>
> JUDGES 1:19

**MOUNT TABOR**
Deborah and Barak defeated the army of King Jabin of Hazor at the Battle of Kishon on Mount Tabor. Some Christians believe that this is also the place of the Transfiguration of Jesus (see pp.354–55).

## AMMONITES

The Ammonites were a tribe descended from Lot's daughters (Genesis 19:36–38). Their land lay east of the River Jordan, between the Jabbok and Arnon rivers, and they controlled the trade on The King's Highway that passed through their territory. Although the Israelites were forbidden to conquer them because of family ties (Deuteronomy 2:19), the Ammonites still attacked them, especially during the period of the Judges and the early monarchy. They were defeated by King David (2 Samuel 11:1). In the 9th century BC they joined with the Moabites and Meunites to attack Judah again, but it experienced God's miraculous deliverance (2 Chronicles 20). The Ammonites were finally conquered by Babylon in 581 BC.

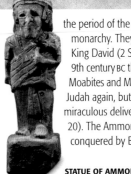

**STATUE OF AMMONITE KING YERAH AZAR**

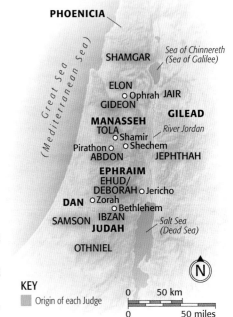

**THE LAND OF THE JUDGES**
The people of Israel rallied behind the Judges – leaders chosen for their political and military skills. The Book of Judges gives the region of origin of each Judge; this is shown on the map above.

KEY
Origin of each Judge

0     50 km
0     50 miles

**AFTER**

**Despite the Judges' best efforts, Israel remained fragmented, in turmoil, and unsure how to continue the fight against the Canaanites.**

### FIGHTING THE CANAANITES

Israel was never able to break Canaanite power completely. This was partly due to the Canaanites' superior technology, which allowed them to make strong iron weapons and magnificent chariots "fitted with iron" (Judges 1:19). The Israelites also **failed to extinguish the Canaanite religion, whose gods promised fertility**. When the Israelites became strong, "they pressed the Canaanites into forced labour but never drove them out completely" (1:28). Israel became increasingly fragmented. At the end of Judges, the Bible records that "The Israelites… went home to their tribes and clans, each to his own inheritance" (Judges 21:24). It was a lawless time when "everyone did as they saw fit" (24:25), that would continue until the **reign of King David 160–61 »**.

**CANAANITE TOOLS AND WEAPONS**

« BEFORE

**After 40 years of peace following Deborah's leadership, the Israelites once again "did evil in the eyes of the LORD" (Judges 6:1) and were attacked.**

### MIDIANITE AND AMALEKITE RAIDS

The Midianites (from along the Red Sea coast) and Amalekites (from the Negev and Sinai) raided southern Canaan, **destroying the Israelites' crops and killing livestock**. The raids were so fierce that the Israelites often had to **abandon their homes and hide in caves**. In despair, they finally cried out to the Lord for help (6:7).

## HISTORY AND CULTURE

### LOCAL SHRINES

**ASHERAH IDOL**

It was common for villages and towns to have their own shrines to gods, since only priests could enter the great temples, such as the temple that Ahab built for Baal (1 Kings 16:31–33). A shrine to Baal or Asherah, like the one on Gideon's father's land – which Gideon destroyed – provided a focus for worship. Baal was the Canaanite storm and fertility god, and in many areas his cult was synonymous with nature worship. Asherah was the Canaanite mother goddess; her name was also used to refer to the consecrated poles of a shrine, which might be living trees or carved poles. Remains of Asherah poles have been found at the Bronze Age settlement site of Shechem, where God said to Abraham, "To your offspring I will give this land" (Genesis 12:7).

### THE RIVER JORDAN

When Gideon and his army pursued the fleeing Midianites, he called upon the men of Ephraim to "seize the waters of the Jordan" (Judges 7:24). The boundary of the Promised Land was said to "go down along the Jordan" (Numbers 34:12).

# Gideon the Leader

*After seven years of oppression by the Midianites and Amalekites, Gideon was called by God to rescue Israel. Despite his initial reluctance, he was so successful that the Israelites pressed him to be their king.*

**T**HE ANGEL of the Lord appeared to Gideon saying, "The LORD is with you, mighty warrior" (Judges 6:12). Gideon asked the angel why Israel was suffering, but the angel ignored his questions and instead told him to go and save Israel from the Midianites (6:14).

Gideon found it hard to see how a man like him, insignificant and from Manasseh's weakest clan, could save Israel. So he asked the angel for a sign, but said first he would prepare an offering. The angel touched Gideon's offering of meat and bread with his staff, the offering burst into flames, and the angel disappeared. God then told Gideon to destroy his father's altar to Baal and cut down the wooden symbol of the goddess Asherah beside it. Gideon did this at night, so that no-one could see him. The next morning the town's people realized what he had done and wanted to kill him, but his father pointed out, "If Baal really is a god, he can defend himself" (6:31).

### Gideon's army

The Midianites, Amalekites, and some other tribes joined forces and set up camp in the Valley of Jezreel. Gideon felt God's Spirit come upon him, and he summoned his fellow tribesmen and the men of Zebulun, Manasseh, Asher, and Naphtali to follow him. However, he wanted another sign from God, so he said that if he truly was the one to save Israel, God should allow the morning dew to moisten a sheep's fleece he laid on the floor, but not the ground around it. The following morning this occurred, but still Gideon was not convinced. He asked God to do it again, but this time to make the ground moist and the fleece dry. When Gideon saw this had been done, he felt assured.

Gideon left for battle with 32,000 troops, but God said that the army was too large. He directed Gideon to take the men to water, and to separate them into those who lapped the water like a dog, and those who drank from cupped hands. He then told Gideon to send away all but the men who had lapped the water with their tongues, leaving him with an army of only 300. Gideon divided them into three groups and gave every man a trumpet, a torch, and an empty jar. That night, he and his men quietly surrounded the Midianite camp. Then, just after the changing of the guard, they blew their trumpets and smashed their jars. Startled by the noise and torchlights, the Midianites fled, while God confused them, causing them to "turn on each other with their swords" (Judges 7:22). Gideon's men chased the Midianites and captured their leaders. after this, Israel had peace for 40 years.

The Israelites wanted to reward Gideon by making him king, but he refused, saying Israel had no king apart from God. Gideon then made a disastrous mistake. He made an ephod (used by the high priests for discovering God's will) from the plundered gold, which was then worshipped by the townsfolk and "became a snare to Gideon and his family" (8:27).

## "Go in the strength you have and save Israel out of Midian's hand."

JUDGES 6:14

**GIDEON'S BATTLE**
A 17th-century fresco from the Cathedral of the Archangel, Moscow, depicts Gideon charging into battle, but makes clear that it is the angel of the Lord who bears the sword and kills Israel's enemies.

**GIDEON ASKS FOR A SIGN**
Gideon did not doubt that God would deliver the Israelites, but that God would achieve this through him. He asked for a sign, as illustrated in *The Miracle of Gideon's Fleece* (c.1490, French School).

### AFTER »

**When Gideon died, his son Abimelek was determined to become king.**

**CLEARING THE WAY**
Gideon had many wives and 70 legitimate sons; he also had an illegitimate son, named Abimelek, with his concubine. After Gideon died, Abimelek returned to Shechem, his mother's home town, and attempted to kill his 70 brothers. However, one survived, and shouted a parable about leadership to the townsfolk, to tell them how they would end up destroying one another. He fled and Abimelek became king, ruling for three years.

**ABIMELEK WAS KILLED BY A WOMAN DROPPING A MILLSTONE FROM A TOWER UNDER ATTACK**

« BEFORE

**The arrival of the Philistines on the coastal plain was to present many problems for Israel.**

### PATH OF DESTRUCTION

During the 13th and 12th centuries BC, the **Philistines migrated from Caphtor** (Amos 9:7; Jeremiah 47:4), which is thought to have been Crete. They made their way south along the Mediterranean coast, destroying everything before them. They reached Egypt but were defeated there in 1175 BC, so they retreated and **settled along Canaan's coastal strip in five city-states**: Gaza, Ashkelon, Ashdod, Gath, and Ekron. This gave them control of the Way of the Sea, the main coastal trade route. Their invasions caused devastation but also helped established a new culture.

# Samson's Story

*Samson was a Judge in Israel in the 11th century BC. Renowned for his enormous strength, he lead the Israelites for 20 years, fighting the Philistines who were dominating the land of Dan, his tribal territory.*

S AMSON'S BIRTH was miraculous. His mother, who was barren, was visited by an angel who told her she would soon be pregnant with a boy. The angel asked her to refrain from drinking wine or anything from the grapevine, and to shun unclean food; once the boy was born, she must ensure that his head was never touched by a razor, because he was to be a Nazirite. This meant that the boy himself must always shun wine and unclean food, never touch a corpse, and never cut his hair, as a sign of his dedication to God. The mother followed the angel's orders, and in time gave birth to a boy, whom she named Samson.

Some years later, Samson went to Timnah, where he saw a young Philistine woman whom he wanted for his wife. His parents were shocked that he would consider a Philistine, but Samson insisted. The three of them set out

### SAMSON AND THE LION
*Samson and the Lion*, from the Verduner Alter in the Klosterneuburg Convent, Vienna, Austria, is a 12th-century panel demonstrating Samson's strength. As God's Spirit comes upon him for the first time, he tears apart the lion with his bare hands.

" **The Spirit of the LORD came powerfully upon him…** he tore the lion apart. "

JUDGES 14:6

### THE PHILISTINES

Although today the word "Philistine" is synonymous with uncultured people, the Philistines had a highly developed culture, as their pottery reflects. But they were also warriors. When the coastal settlements in Canaan proved too small, they pressed inland, which led to clashes with the Israelites, especially during the period of the Judges when their presence caused many Danites to migrate north. One significant reason for their military success was their grasp of iron technology, which was then passed on to the regions they conquered. The Philistines never controlled much of Canaan, but their legacy was to leave a name for the region: Palestine.

**PHILISTINE BEER JUG**

+ SAMSO·CVLEONE ·

to see the woman at Timnah, and as they approached the town a lion came roaring towards Samson. The Spirit of the LORD came upon him "powerfully" (Judges 14:6) and he ripped the lion apart. On reaching the town, Samson met and liked the young woman. He later returned to marry her, and on his way he saw the lion's carcass, now swarming with bees. Violating his Nazirite vow, he touched the carcass to scoop out the honey.

### The first riddle

At the wedding Samson put a riddle to the guests, which the Philistines were unable to solve, so they asked his wife for the answer. After seven days of persistent pleading, Samson gave in to her, and she told the Philistines the meaning of the riddle. When Samson realized what had happened, God's Spirit came powerfully upon him. He killed 30 Philistines, and angrily returned to his parents' home.

Some time later, Samson returned to visit his wife, but her father said that he had given her to someone else, and offered Samson her sister instead. Samson was furious, saying: "This time I have a right to get even with the Philistines; I will really harm them" (15:3). He tied torches to the tails of 300 foxes, lit them, and let them loose, whereupon they burned down all the growing grain, vineyards, and olive groves. The Philistines then sought revenge, by burning to death Samson's wife and father-in-law.

Vowing now not "to stop until I get my revenge on you" (15:7), Samson slaughtered many of the Philistines, then took refuge in a cave. The Philistines threatened to fight the surrounding people of Judah unless they gave up Samson, and so Samson allowed the people of Judah to take him, bound, to the Philistines. But God's Spirit came on him; he snapped the

### DESTROYING THE PHILISTINE'S TEMPLE

When Samson was led to the Philistine's temple to entertain them, people crowded to watch – 3,000 men and women were said to be on the roof alone. They tumbled as the pillars cracked, shown here in *Samson's Revenge*, by Johan Georg Platzer (1704–61).

### SAMSON AND DELILAH

Delilah repeatedly asked Samson the secret of his strength, and three times he gave her false answers. After revealing the truth, he fell asleep in her lap, as painted by Lucas Cranach the Elder (1472–1553).

ropes, took up a donkey's jawbone as a makeshift weapon, and used it to slaughter 1,000 Philistines.

### Delilah's treachery

Samson led the people of Israel for 20 years. The Philistines never gave up their hunt for him, and he was once forced to rip Gaza's city gates off their hinges to flee the Philistine town. In the Valley of Sorek, he met and fell in love with a Philistine woman named Delilah. The Philistine leaders offered her money for the secret of Samson's strength, and she asked him to tell

her. Three times he gave her false answers, but finally he told her the truth: "if my head were shaved, my strength would leave me" (16:17). Delilah sent for the Philistines, who paid her, and while Samson was asleep, her servant cut off his hair. When the Philistines attacked he was helpless. They gouged out his eyes, took him to Gaza, and put him in jail.

Over time, his hair began to grow again and one day, the leaders sent for him to entertain them. Samson prayed to God to "strengthen me just once more" (16:28). Standing with a hand on the two main pillars of the Philistine's temple, the blind Samson pushed with all his might. The temple came crashing down, killing more than 3,000, including Samson.

> " After putting him to sleep on her lap, she called for someone to **shave off the seven braids of his hair** ... and his strength left him."
>
> JUDGES 16:19

## AFTER »

**The closing chapters of Judges reveal the disintegration of Israelite society at every level.**

### RELIGIOUS CHAOS

A man named Micah from Ephraim **stole a huge amount of silver** from his own mother (Judges 17). Thrilled when he confessed and returned it, she dedicated it to God, but then had an idol made from it, which was forbidden by the Ten Commandments. Micah then made a shrine and appointed his own priest, which was equally forbidden. The shrine later led some Dan Israelites astray.

### SOCIAL CHAOS

Judges 19–21 records the story of a **Levite's concubine** which involved sexual demands, rape, murder, and ultimately civil war as all the tribes "from Dan to Beersheba" (20:1) fought the Benjamites, their own brothers.

**FEMALE DEITY FROM TEL DAN**

# Ruth and Naomi

*The Book of Ruth tells the story of an outsider who found acceptance. After her husband died, Ruth's self-sacrifice led to not only her, but also her mother-in-law, Naomi, finding redemption.*

**W**HEN A FAMINE ravaged Israel, Elimelek of Bethlehem took his wife Naomi and their sons, Mahlon and Kilion, to Moab where there was food. Then tragedy struck: Elimelek died and, after marrying Moabite women, Naomi's sons died too.

### Back to Bethlehem

When news came that the LORD had ended Israel's famine, the three desolate women set out for Bethlehem. However, Naomi urged her daughters-in-law, Orpah and Ruth, to return to Moab, saying she was too old to provide for them. Orpah went, but Ruth clung to Naomi, "determined to go with her" (Ruth 1:18). So they continued their journey together.

In Bethlehem when someone asked, "Can this be Naomi?" (1:19), she said, "Don't call me Naomi… call me Mara [meaning "bitter"], because the Almighty has made my life very bitter. I went away full, but the LORD has brought me back empty" (1:20,21).

### Ruth meets Boaz

Ruth suggested to Naomi that she could go to gather the barley harvest. Ruth happened to choose a field that belonged to Boaz, a relative of Naomi's late husband, and as she started her work, Boaz appeared. The attractive stranger caught his eye and, discovering she was Naomi's daughter-in-law, Boaz told her to continue her work. He offered her food and water. When she asked why he helped a foreigner he said, "I've been told all about what you have done for your mother-in-law since the death of your husband… May the LORD repay you…" (2:11,12).

Later, Ruth mentioned Boaz to Naomi, who suddenly remembered that he was a relative and "one of our guardian-redeemers" (2:20), obliged to help them in their difficulty. She urged Ruth to stay with his workers.

### The threshing floor

One evening Naomi sent Ruth to the threshing floor where Boaz would be winnowing his grain.

> **"'Where you go I will go**, and where you stay I will stay. **Your people will be my people** and your God my God.'"**
>
> RUTH 1:16

« **BEFORE**

**In the centuries after Joshua's death, Israel's life had deteriorated.**

#### ISRAEL'S DARK DAYS
The period of **the Judges «  130–31** was one of dark days. Seduced by the Canaanites' religious practices, the Israelites' moral, spiritual, and social wellbeing worsened. Yet despite their repeated faithlessness, **God continued to send Judges to rescue them from enemies** – only for them to turn away again. It is against this background that Ruth's story is told.

#### IN BOAZ'S FIELD
In this c.1530 painting by Jan van Scorel, Naomi talks with her daughter-in-law, Ruth, in a field belonging to Boaz – a kinsman with an obligation to help them. Boaz is impressed by Ruth's loyalty to her mother-in-law, and shows her kindness.

**HAZOR CITY GATE**
In ancient times, town and city gates were used as meeting places. The gateway at Tell Hazor had two imposing towers, each with three chambers. In the Bible, Naomi's land was redeemed by Boaz before witnesses at the town gates.

When Boaz laid down next to his grain pile, Ruth laid down at his feet, as Naomi had told her. Boaz awoke during the night and, startled, asked who it was. "I am your servant Ruth", she replied. Then she made an appeal for him to marry her: "Spread the corner of your garment over me, since you are a guardian-redeemer of our family" (Ruth 3:9).

Boaz was delighted, but he knew there was a closer relative with the right of redemption who would need to be asked first. When Ruth returned to Naomi and told her what had happened, she knew the matter would be settled quickly.

### The marriage

Boaz called the other relative to meet with the elders at the town gate. He told him Naomi had land to sell, and the man was eager to buy it – until Boaz told him that with the land also came a widow, Ruth the Moabite. So the man ceded to Boaz the right to buy the land, which he did. Boaz then married Ruth to continue Naomi's family line. When Ruth bore a son named Obed, people were excited for Naomi, for whom God had provided a new guardian-redeemer. Obed was the father of Jesse, who would be the father of the great king, David.

## GLEANING IN THE FIELDS
Two women harvest ripe wheat in the hills of Judah. Ruth went to the fields to gather any grain that Boaz's barley harvesters had left behind, but when Boaz later instructed his men to leave "some stalks" (Ruth 2:16) for her, she managed to gather an *ephah*, around 13kg (29lb).

**ANALYSIS**

### REDEMPTION

The Hebrew text of Ruth reads: "he is one of our guardian-redeemers" (Ruth 2:20), which reveals that the key to this story is redemption. The meaning of redemption is buying back, and it is rooted in God redeeming the Israelites from slavery in Egypt. There the price paid was Egypt's firstborn sons, while Israel's firstborn escaped through the Passover sacrifice.

**1ST-CENTURY SANDALS FROM MASADA, ISRAEL**

Many reminders of this act of redemption were written into the Jewish Law (Leviticus 25:25,39–42,47–49). For example, Boaz legalized his transaction to redeem Naomi's land by taking off his sandal (Ruth 4:7). In the New Testament, redemption is one of the ways in which Jesus' death is described. He paid the price to free people from their sin (Matthew 20:28; Galatians 3:13,14; Colossians 1:14; 1 Peter 1:18,19).

**AFTER**

The story of Ruth ends with an epilogue noting her illustrious descendants, who include King David.

### FAMILY OF DAVID
**Underlining God's graciousness**, Ruth not only found acceptance, but became hugely significant – as the ancestor of **King David 152–53 >>** under whom Israel experienced the **peace, stability, and blessing** it could not find in the days of the Judges. David was an ancestor of Jesus, the redeemer for humankind.

**A BIBLE ILLUSTRATES RUTH'S DESCENDANTS**

## HISTORY AND CULTURE

# Villages, Towns, and Cities

" All these **cities** were **fortified with high walls**… and there were also a great many **unwalled villages**." DEUTERONOMY 3:5

**ANCIENT CITY**
Founded in around 4000 BC, Faiyum is the oldest city in Egypt. The flat roofs of the buildings are still used for drying vegetation, as they were in biblical times.

From early biblical times, people began to abandon nomadic existence in favour of village life. In Canaan, people lived in villages consisting of family groups living in houses made of mud-brick, sometimes with stone foundations, or, in later periods, made entirely from stone.

Towns, with different-sized houses, emerged later. They generally had defensive walls – Jericho is an early example of a walled settlement (see pp.122–23) – whereas villages did not, and were relatively small by today's standards, consisting of perhaps 150–200 homes. Even as larger towns were established,

many people remained in their villages, only retreating to the nearest town in times of danger.

Cities developed in Canaan in the mid-3rd millennium BC as a result of the ruling class's need for administrative centres. The ruins of great biblical cities such as Hazor may still be seen today.

## TENT COMMUNITIES

Portable and easy to erect, tents provided ideal shelter for nomadic communities. Some Israelites of the early Old Testament period, for example, lived in tents made from animal hides, usually from goats, cattle, or camels.

The tent consisted of a roof suspended from rows of poles, with "walls" of hide panels. It was divided into two sections: the rear for women and children and the front for men and their friends or other visitors. The floor was generally bare earth, although sometimes covered with matting.

Even after most people had settled in houses, tents continued to be used, especially by herdsmen (Genesis 4:20, 13:5) and soldiers (1 Samuel 4:10).

**MODEL HOME**
This clay model was made in the 3rd millennium BC in Mesopotamia. The same basic rectangular house design has been used across the Middle East for thousands of years.

Decorative moulding

Mud-brick wall

Flat roof used for sleeping on warm summer nights

Narrow window

**DESERT ABODE**
The tents of modern Bedouins are made to a design that is centuries old. Tents such as this would have been familiar to the Israelites.

## EARLY HOUSES

Formerly nomadic people gradually abandoned tents in favour of houses. Early Israelite dwellings were notable for being divided into four sections on two levels. The ground floor had three rooms, used for storage and stabling animals, while the family lived in a raised room at the rear.

The first villages consisted of little more than a group of mud-brick houses surrounded by strips of cultivated land. Later, houses were often built around a central courtyard. The walls were made of mud-brick or stone, while the roof was constructed by covering beams with brushwood, earth, and clay.

Access to the roof was via a ladder or outside staircase. In dry climates, the roof proved useful as a place for storage, or for drying food, as well as forming another room that often served as sleeping quarters.

Floors consisted of hardened, compacted earth, while "windows" were generally gaps in the walls, sometimes covered by lattice shutters or woollen curtains. Doors were made of woven twigs, although later wood or (rarely) metal was used. There were no toilet facilities, and little furniture. Beds were simple mats or thin mattresses, rolled out at night for the family to share.

### LIVING SPACE
This priest's family house in Old Jerusalem was more spacious than the usual houses of the period, reflecting his high status in the community.

## TOWNS AND CITIES

The inhabitants of early settlements were usually farmers. If the land could support it, a village's population expanded, giving rise to other occupations such as priests and craftsmen.

Life in ancient towns and cities was often cramped: houses were packed tightly together within protective city walls, and there were no real streets between them. City walls were generally "casemate": parallel stone walls with a gap between them that was often filled with rubble to absorb the shock of an enemy attack. It was not uncommon for dwellings, such as Rahab's house in Jericho, to form part of the city walls.

During the 9th and 8th centuries BC, a wealthy middle class developed, which built bigger and grander homes. By New Testament times, Jerusalem boasted a large quarter filled with the spacious homes of rich citizens, while the poor were squashed into the rest of the city. Because of the Temple, Jerusalem was the most important city – and therefore the most desirable place to live – for Jews.

## GRAECO-ROMAN INFLUENCES

By the New Testament period, Greek and Roman influences had led to highly sophisticated improvements in larger cities. In addition to the improved construction of the buildings themselves, these included

### 111
The number of aqueducts bringing water to the citizens of the city of Rome.

features such as planned streets and elaborate purpose-built water and sewage facilities.

Nomadic tribes dug latrines outside their camps, a practice later dictated by Jewish Law, but in towns sanitation practices varied considerably. During the New Testament period, however, the disposal of waste greatly improved within cities. This was due largely to the Romans, who introduced aqueducts that served cities as well as industrial sites with a reliable supply of clean water. Public baths were introduced, as well as

### PLUMB BOB
A weight, often made of lead but in this case brass, suspended from a piece of string will give a vertical reference line that can be used to ensure walls are built straight.

toilets with running water that drained into cesspools, from which waste was taken away in carts at night.

When Herod the Great rebuilt Samaria he renamed it Sebaste, in the Roman style. Its main street was lined with shops, baths, and a theatre; it also had an organized

Central pipe from which water is pumped out

Valve connecting pipe to cylinder housing piston

### ROMAN WATER PUMP
Elaborate systems of lead pipes used gravity to feed fountains and bath-houses. Pumps like this one were used to raise water to a higher level.

network of smaller streets and boasted a 15,000-seat arena.

Sepphoris, the capital of Galilee, was a city of 30,000 inhabitants that underwent major rebuilding during Jesus' time. Its limestone-paved streets were laid out in a grid pattern, a feature that remains characteristic of many modern cities in the Western world today.

## A CONSTANT WATER SUPPLY

Early settlements were located near sources of fresh water, such as rivers or springs. Water had to be fetched daily, a task that often fell to women, who carried it home in clay pots or wooden buckets, balanced on their heads. Around 1200 BC, the invention of cisterns meant that rainwater could be collected and stored. Cities had many cisterns; 50 have been discovered in Tell al-Nasbah on the West Bank, the probable site of Mizpah. The greatest innovation was the aqueduct – conduits perfected by the Romans that provided a constant water supply.

ROMAN AQUEDUCT AT CAESAREA, ISRAEL

# THE KINGDOM OF ISRAEL

"But the people refused to listen to Samuel. **'No!'** they said. **'We want a king over us. Then we shall be like all the other nations**, with a king to lead us and to go out before us and fight our battles.'"

1 SAMUEL 8:19,20

 HIS PART OF THE BIBLE TELLS THE STORY of Israel's dramatic transformation from a weak confederacy of 12 often divided and bickering tribes at the end of the dark days of the Judges, to a stable and strong nation under the leadership of King Solomon. Not only were the remaining Canaanite enclaves captured, but Israel's boundaries were pushed to their furthest limits and the surrounding nations responded by treating Israel with respect. However, the price of this transition was a move from theocracy (rule directly by God) to monarchy (rule by a king).

After years of rule by the judges, and in response to a continued threat from the Philistines, the people of Israel longed for a king. The judge Samuel, now an old man, reluctantly agreed to their request, but warned of the implications of monarchy, such as the power a king would have to compel subjects to serve him and to raise taxes in support of his armies and court (1 Samuel 8:10–18).

### FROM SAUL TO SOLOMON

God led Samuel to Saul, a young warrior of the kind Israel seemed to want, and Samuel reluctantly anointed him as king. However, Saul had weaknesses and was not always prepared to obey God, so he was replaced by the obedient David. According to the Bible, David drew the fragmented nation together and established a new capital in Jerusalem to which he brought the Ark of the Covenant, symbolizing his desire to bring his rule under God's rule. Yet despite his successes, David too had his own weaknesses (see 2 Samuel).

The Bible tells us that David was succeeded as king by his youngest son, Solomon. At this time the principle of hereditary monarchy was not firmly established in Israel, so to ensure stability in succession, Solomon was crowned king before David's death. Under his rule, Israel flourished: its borders were expanded and secured; trade developed; and intellectual pursuits flourished. Yet, as Samuel had warned, all this had a price – the imposition of taxes and compulsory labour, which were greatly resented.

The end of this period saw declining spiritual standards as Solomon married many wives from different countries, and the wives brought their foreign gods with them. By the end of his reign, a great dynasty had been built, but it had dangerous flaws.

### KEY THEMES

Several significant motifs emerge in this part of the Bible story. One is that although people may judge others based on attributes such as social class, looks, or stature, God accepts and approves by looking "at the heart" (1 Samuel 16:7), as he did when choosing David – an unpromising youngest child – to be king.

God's eternal covenant with David is made clear: his descendants would be on the throne "for ever" (2 Samuel 7:16). Out of this promise arises Israel's belief in a Messiah – a second David.

Another message is that obedience to God leads to his blessing; disobedience always brings disaster. Any sin can be forgiven, provided it is confessed to God – as David did over his sin with Bathsheba (see pp.166–67).

**JUDGE AND PROPHET** Born c.1105 BC Died c.1025 BC

# Samuel

## "The LORD came and stood there, calling…, 'Samuel! Samuel!' Then Samuel said, 'Speak, for your servant is listening.'"

1 SAMUEL 3:10

**S** AMUEL WAS BORN to Elkanah, a son of Jeroham, and his wife Hannah, who had been childless for many years. Hannah had prayed for a son, vowing that were she to have one, she would dedicate him to a lifetime in God's service. When Hannah eventually conceived, she believed it was through God's intervention, because she had been blessed by Eli the priest in the doorway of the sanctuary at Shiloh. Therefore, she named her son Samuel, which in Hebrew sounds like "heard by God", saying "Because I asked the LORD for him" (1 Samuel 1:20). Samuel became one of Israel's leading figures, serving as judge and prophet.

### Samuel the prophet

Hannah told Elkanah that she would keep her son with her until he was weaned and then take him to the sanctuary to fulfil her vow. Her husband encouraged her to do what she felt was best.

Once Samuel had reached about three years of age, Hannah took him to Shiloh and entrusted him to the priest Eli. She offered a prayer of praise, declaring "There is no one holy like the LORD; there is no one besides you; there is no Rock like our God" (2:2).

As Samuel grew up, he became aware that Eli's two sons were abusing their role as priests, by not behaving respectfully to those who came to sacrifice and "treating the

**THE PROPHET**
A 17th-century Russian Orthodox icon shows the prophet Samuel with an open scroll and a horn. Samuel used a horn to pour oil on to the head of David, anointing him as king.

LORD's offering with contempt" (2:17) – though he could not have imagined that God would call him to challenge their sinful behaviour.

According to the Jewish historian Josephus, Samuel was 12 years old when he first heard God speaking. Initially he thought Eli was calling him, but after he woke Eli three times, Eli realized it was God who was speaking to Samuel. Eli told Samuel that when he heard the voice again he should respond to God. So when God called again Samuel said, "Speak, LORD, for your servant is listening"(3:9). However, the message was not easy – God was about to judge Eli's family. Samuel was reluctant to tell Eli what had been said, but Eli recognized that it was the word of God. Over the coming years, the Israelites too began to see that God was speaking through Samuel.

### Samuel the king-maker

Later in life, a combination of Samuel's age, his own sons' corrupt behaviour as judges, and the danger represented by Philistine power, prompted the Israelites to ask Samuel to appoint a king as leader. Samuel was angry, but God said to him, "it is not you they have rejected, but they have rejected me as their king" (8:7).

Samuel solemnly warned the people about the many dangers of being ruled by a king (see p.141) but he granted their wish, anointing Saul as Israel's first king.

After Saul disobeyed God twice (see pp.148–49), Samuel was directed by God to anoint David as Israel's new king. Apart from an incident when Saul tried to

**TEL SHILOH**
These archeological remnants in Samaria are of Shiloh, which for centuries was the religious capital of Israel prior to Jerusalem. It was here that Samuel trained under Eli.

capture David during a visit to Samuel, little more is heard of Samuel in the Bible; his main work was completed. In his farewell speech, he warned Israel not to forsake God, criticized the people for asking for a king, and said that if they or their king failed to follow God "his hand will be against you, as it was against your ancestors" (12:15). His death, and Israel's mourning, is dealt with only briefly.

### A final appearance

Samuel returned once to Israel after his death. Terrified by the threat from the Philistines, a desperate Saul resorted to a medium to summon Samuel for advice. Samuel's sentiments in death were as they were in life, and he reiterated to Saul that God was now his enemy. Furthermore, he predicted that the Philistines would triumph over Israel, and that "you and your sons will be with me" (28:19). As predicted, Saul, his three sons, and his men later died fighting the Philistines (31:1–6).

### Inaugurator of monarchy

Samuel's significance was huge, reflected in the books of the Bible named after him. He managed Israel's transition from theocracy (rule by God) to monarchy (rule by a king) and is seen in Jewish tradition as not only the last of the judges, but also one of the great Old Testament prophets. He was a model of the importance of the prophet's role, bringing God's word to everyone, even kings. He made it clear that Israel's kings could not behave like those of surrounding nations. They were to be obedient to God, the King of Kings.

The two books of Samuel were not written by Samuel, but were named after him in honour of his significant role in Israel's history. Originally one book, it was compiled from earlier documents (1 Samuel 10:25; 2 Samuel 1:18) by an unknown author, probably after the kingdom's division in 930 BC. The work probably took its final shape during the Exile, along with Israel's other history books.

In medieval Europe, Old Testament scenes were often illustrated for the moral instruction of illiterate Christians. Known in one form as a *Bible moralisée*, a book such as Samuel, which evaluates kingship, may have had particular appeal for a commissioning monarch.

**A 13TH-CENTURY BIBLE MORALISÉE WITH ILLUSTRATIONS OF EPISODES FROM 2 SAMUEL**

- **c.1105 BC,** born to the barren Hannah, wife of the devout Elkanah.

- **Entrusted to Eli's care** at Shiloh around the age of three.

- **Aged about 12,** receives his first prophecy, a message from God of judgment on Eli and his wicked sons.

- **Begins to be recognized** by the people in Israel as a prophet.

- **Leads Israel** in a time of repentance and rededication at Mizpah after which God routs the Philistines. Erects a memorial stone, naming it Ebenezer ("Stone of Help").

**SAMUEL TAUGHT BY ELI, BY JOHN SINGLETON COPLEY (1738–1815)**

- **Establishes his home** at Ramah in the territory of Benjamin.

- **Becomes Israel's** last judge, following a circuit travelled each year through Bethel, Gilgal, Mizpah, and Ramah.

- **Angry when Israel** asks for a king, but is told by God to proceed.

- **c.1050 BC,** anoints Saul as God's chosen king.

- **Makes his farewell** speech, believing his life's work is done.

- **Rebukes Saul** when he offers a sacrifice without waiting for Samuel, and so disobeying the commands of God.

- **Tells Saul to destroy** the Amalekites because they had attacked and plundered the Israelites when they left Egypt. Saul obeys the order only partially, failing to "totally destroy all that belongs to them" (1 Samuel 15:3) by sparing some fattened livestock. As a result, Samuel confirms that Saul has been rejected as king.

- **Kills the king** of the Amalekites himself and abandons Saul, who is mentally tormented by his rejection.

- **c.1025 BC,** anoints David as Israel's new king, at first privately, then publically.

- **Dies and is buried** at Ramah.

- **Appears to Saul** at Endor, summoned at Saul's request by a medium after his death.

**BEFORE**

No longer content to remain in their five city-states along the coastal plain, the Philistines began to push inland.

**PHILISTINE WARRIORS' DISTINCTIVE HEADWEAR, EGYPTIAN TEMPLE RELIEF, c.1200 BC**

**PHILISTINE SUPERIORITY**

As **the Philistines, based in Gath, Ashdod, Askelon, Ekron, and Gaza ❰❰ 119**, looked to expand territorially, it inevitably brought them into conflict with the Israelites. Their superior weaponry, achieved through their mastery of **iron technology 149 ❱❱**, gave them a significant advantage over the poorly armed Israelites. The growing Philistine pressure made Israel increasingly desperate.

**LISTS**

**HISTORY OF THE ARK**

Made at Mount Sinai, to God's design; placed in the Tabernacle.

The Ten Commandments, Aaron's rod, and some manna put inside.

Led the Israelites through the wilderness, then across the River Jordan.

Led the Israelites' march around Jericho.

Located at Gilgal, Bethel, and Shiloh in the Judges period.

Captured by the Philistines, then placed in Kiriath Jearim when returned to Israel.

Brought to Jerusalem by King David; Uzzah is killed for touching it.

Placed in Solomon's Temple.

Taken from Jerusalem by David's supporters during Absalom's rebellion, but returned by David.

Disappears from history – probably destroyed after Babylon's destruction of Jerusalem in 587 BC.

# The Ark, Lost and Regained

*Remembering how the Ark of the Covenant had brought them victory on previous occasions, the Israelites took it into battle against the Philistines. However, God allowed the Philistines to capture the precious object.*

WHEN TENSION between the Israelites and the Philistines erupted again, Israel went to fight them at Aphek, 19km (12 miles) northeast of Joppa, the northern frontier of Philistine territory. The Israelites lost 4,000 men. Reflecting on their defeat, the elders resolved that they needed the Ark of the Covenant, the symbol of God's presence, to take into battle next time.

When Eli the priest's sons, Hophni and Phinehas, arrived carrying the Ark, a great shout erupted. The Philistines wondered what was happening – and when they heard that the Ark had arrived, they panicked, certain that they would now be defeated. Nevertheless, they launched an attack and the Israelites were routed – 30,000 Israelites were killed, among them Eli's two sons – and the Ark of the Covenant was captured. When Eli heard of the defeat, the death of his sons, and the capture of the Ark, he fell off his chair in shock, and broke his neck. When his pregnant daughter-in-law, who was near to term, heard that her husband and father-in-law were dead, she went into labour. She delivered her son but died during childbirth. Before she passed away, she named him Ichabod (meaning

> **"Let us bring the ark of the LORD'S covenant from Shiloh…'"**
>
> **1 SAMUEL** 4:3

**THE ARK IS CAPTURED**
Gerrit Bleker's painting *The Capture of the Ark* (1640) depicts the moment when the sons of Eli the priest, Hophni and Phinehas, are killed by the Philistines after having taken the Ark from Shiloh into the Israelite battle camp.

"no glory" in Hebrew), and said, "The Glory has departed from Israel, for the ark of God has been captured" (1 Samuel 4:22).

### From Ashod to Ekron

The Philistines took the Ark to Ashdod, and put it in the temple of their god Dagon alongside his statue. The next morning, they found the statue of Dagon lying face down on the ground before the Ark. The Philistines replaced the statue, but the next morning he was again on the ground, and this time his head and hands had broken off. Then the town became infested by rats, and the townsfolk began to break out in tumours (which some scholars interpret as the bubonic plague).

Fearful of Israel's god's power – "his hand is heavy on us and on Dagon our god" (5:7) – the Philistines decided to move the Ark to Gath, but similar events happened there. Next they sent the Ark to Ekron, where the story was repeated. After seven months, the Philistines had had enough and decided to send the Ark home.

### The Ark is returned to Israel

The Philistines' priests advised them not to send the Ark back to the god of Israel without a gift. However, the priests added: "by all means send a guilt offering to him. Then you will be healed..." (6:3), and, because of what had afflicted them, they chose to send models of five gold tumours and five gold rats. They prepared a new cart, hitched it to two cows that had never been yoked, and set the Ark upon it. The cows were sent on their way, and they headed for Beth Shemesh in Israelite territory. The people there were so happy when they saw the Ark that they made sacrifices to the Lord. The Philistines, who had been watching from a distance, returned home.

The Israelites' joy turned to sadness, however, when God struck down 70 men for daring to look inside the Ark. They were afraid, so invited the people of Kiriath Jearim to take the Ark, which is where it stayed for 20 years. The Ark was home, but was still not in its rightful place.

**RETURN OF THE ARK**
The Philistines returned the Ark to Israel after their cities were troubled by plagues. *The Ark Returned to Israel* is a 13th-century illumination from a Bible given to Alfonso X of Castile by Louis IX of France.

## DAGON WORSHIP

The Philistines' god Dagon, into whose temple the Ark of the Covenant was placed when it was captured, was worshipped throughout the region, with temples in Mesopotamia, Ugarit, and Canaan. The meaning of Dagon is uncertain – the word is similar to the Hebrew for "grain", but there is evidence that he personifies the wealth of fish in the ocean. Dagon was a significant god, and Israel named a town, Beth Dagon, after him (Joshua 15:41). He was still worshipped in Canaan in the 2nd century BC, but in the story told in 1 Samuel 5 Dagon was powerless before the Lord.

**ASSYRIAN RELIEF OF THE GOD DAGON**

**AFTER**

**The Ark stayed in Kiriath Jearim until the Israelites began to return to God.**

**THE ASSEMBLY AT MIZPAH**
Samuel wanted to know that the Israelites were sincere, and not just wanting God to remove the Philistines. He told them to **destroy their Baal and Ashtoreth idols**, and to serve the Lord alone. Then he asked them to assemble at **Mizpah 148 »**, where he would intercede with the Lord for them.

When the Philistines heard that Israel had assembled at Mizpah, **they suddenly attacked**. The Israelites were afraid, begging Samuel to ask God for help. As he offered a sacrifice and prayed, **God sent a thunderclap, throwing the Philistines into panic**. As they fled, the Israelites pursued and slaughtered them. Samuel then erected a standing stone as a reminder of God's help, calling it Ebenezer, meaning "stone of help", and said, "**Thus far the LORD has helped us**" (1 Samuel 7:12).

**Israel asked Samuel to give them a king, not out of faith, but out of fear.**

### THE NEED FOR A KING

Israel's **request for a king was founded on four needs** (1 Samuel 8). Firstly, Samuel was growing old. Secondly, his sons were corrupt and perverted justice; they did not follow Samuel's ways. Thirdly, other nations with kings were more prosperous. Fourthly, they needed a leader against the Philistines.

### WARNINGS ABOUT KINGSHIP

Samuel was initially angry at the people's request, but God assured him that it was not Samuel they had rejected, but him; **Samuel should give them what they wanted.** Samuel warned the people that a king would place huge demands on them – taking their food, their flocks and even their sons for his army – but the Israelites persisted. So **Samuel reluctantly agreed to appoint a king ‹‹ 142–43.**

**SAMUEL WITH HIS SONS JOEL AND ABIJAH**

### THEOCRACY TO MONARCHY

Since becoming a nation at Mount Sinai (Exodus 19:6), Israel had been a theocracy, a nation ruled directly by God. But with Saul's anointment, it became a monarchy: a nation ruled by a king.

### A WRONGFUL WISH

God told Samuel that Israel's wish for a king was an example of its unfaithfulness (1 Samuel 8:6–8), but the Law that God had given to Moses did make provision for kingship (Deuteronomy 17:14–20). Some theologians believe that it was not the request for a king that was unfaithful, but the timing and reasons that motivated it.

### ANOINTMENT

Anointing a king or priest (pouring oil on them) symbolized God's Spirit being poured out to equip them for their role.

**THE ANOINTING OF SAUL**
The prophet Samuel was already an old man when he anointed the young Saul "ruler over [God's] inheritance" (1 Samuel 10:1), as depicted in Franz Anton Maulbertsch's painting *Anointment of Saul* (1797).

# Saul, Israel's First King

*The meeting of Samuel and Saul seemed like a coincidence, but God was at work. Samuel told Saul what God planned for him and, the next day, anointed him as king. This was confirmed a few days later in a public ceremony.*

SAUL'S FATHER, Kish, had lost some donkeys and sent Saul to look for them. For three days Saul and his servant trekked through the hills, and Saul was ready to give up, but the servant said "Look, in this town there is a man of God… everything he says comes true. Let's go there now. Perhaps he will tell us what way to take" (1 Samuel 9:6).

The previous day, God had told Samuel that he would meet a man from the tribe of Benjamin who was to be Israel's first king. As Saul approached the gatehouse of the town, God told Samuel that this was the man. So Samuel greeted Saul, and told him, without being asked, to stop worrying about the lost donkeys because they had been found. Then he said,

> " This is the man I spoke to you about. **He will govern my people.**"
>
> 1 SAMUEL 9:17

somewhat cryptically, "To whom is all the desire of Israel turned, if not to you and your whole family line?" (9:20). Saul pointed out that he was from the smallest clan of the smallest tribe, and asked, "Why do you say such a thing to me?" (9:21). Undeterred, Samuel took Saul and his servant to a feast, where he sat them in the place of honour and told the cook to give them the meat that had been saved for them.

### Samuel anoints Saul

That night Samuel and Saul talked on the roof of Saul's house. In the morning, they walked together to the edge of town, but then Samuel asked Saul to send the servant on ahead, because he wished to give Saul a message from God. After the servant left, Samuel took a flask of oil, poured it over Saul's head, and pronounced him leader. Then he

**HAIL THE KING**
This 15th-century coloured woodcut from the Nuremberg Chronicle is a representation of Saul as King of Israel. He reigned from *c.*1050 BC, for around 40 years, until his defeat by the Philistines.

told him of a number of signs that would occur to confirm that God was with him, and told him to go to Gilgal and await further instructions. As Saul turned to leave, God's Spirit came upon him, and all the signs that Samuel had described were fulfilled.

### Saul crowned king

Samuel called a national assembly at Mizpah where, rather than announcing God's choice, he cast lots, working his way through tribes, clans, and families, until he came to Saul. But Saul had hidden among the supplies, so the people ran to get him. Samuel said that this man, who stood taller by a head than anyone around him, had been chosen by God.

Samuel then explained the rights and responsibilities of kingship to the people and sent them home. Not everyone was happy, however, and some despised Saul. But when Saul led the people to a resounding victory over the Ammonites, even the doubters were won over. Samuel said that they should all go to Gilgal, and reaffirm Saul's kingship in God's presence. This was duly done, with sacrifices and celebrations. The nation of Israel had its first king.

**THE FIRST KINGDOM**
Saul's Israel was more of a loose political confederation than a true kingdom. His battles against his hostile neighbours – Moab, Ammon, and Philistia – are recorded in 1 Samuel 14.

> " Then the people shouted, 'Long live the king!' "
>
> 1 SAMUEL 10:24

## AFTER

Recognizing that the appointment of a king meant a change in his own position, Samuel addressed the nation of Israel.

### THE ONLY SAVIOUR

Samuel told the Israelites that he was stepping down as Judge. He warned them that **a king would not save them**, because only continuing faithfulness to God could do that. He reminded them of his own service to Israel, the many times that God had saved them, and called on God to send a storm to confirm his words. The storm came and the people were afraid, but Samuel reassured them, and **called them to faithfulness**.

**HILL COUNTRY OF EPHRAIM**
Saul and his servant went hunting for the lost donkeys in the hill country of Ephraim; this is where Samuel was born and raised, and where Saul would be anointed.

**BEFORE**

«

The Philistines had been a threat since the days of the Judges, but they had significantly increased their attacks.

### BUILDING AN ARMY

Philistine attacks were one of the main reasons that Israel felt it needed a king. One of Saul's first acts was to **create a standing army**, instead of relying on ad-hoc militias from the tribes, which could muster impressive – but not always effective – numbers. When Saul **fought the Ammonites** « 147 with a temporary army, "the men of Israel numbered three hundred thousand and those of Judah thirty thousand" (1 Samuel 11:8). When **Saul became king** « 146–47, he chose 3,000 men from Israel; 2,000 stayed with him at Michmash (13:2), and 1,000 went with his son Jonathan to Gibeah, in Benjamin.

### SAMUEL REBUKES SAUL

Hans Holbein the Younger's drawing (1530) depicts Samuel expressing his disapproval of Saul for his treatment of the defeated Amalekites. Samuel told Saul that God had rejected him as king for his failure to follow God's orders.

# Saul Forsakes God

*The threat of attack by the Philistines that had resulted in Saul being crowned king, eventually cost him the throne. Panicking because of gathering Philistine forces, Saul disobeyed Samuel's instructions and later forfeited his kingship.*

**J**ONATHAN'S FORCES attacked a Philistine outpost at Geba, which provoked the Philistine army to gather in vast numbers just 16km (10 miles) away at Michmash – they had 3,000 chariots, 6,000 charioteers, and soldiers "as numerous as the sand on the seashore" (1 Samuel 13:5).

### Saul's first disobedience

Saul summoned the Israelite army to Gilgal, but they were afraid, and many soldiers fled, hiding in caves and thickets, in pits and cisterns – some went beyond the River Jordan and into the mountainous land of Gilead allocated by Moses to the tribes of Reuben, Gad, and Manasseh (Joshua 1:12–15).

Samuel had instructed Saul to wait at Gilgal with his army until he arrived. Saul waited for seven

**TEL MICHMASH**
In a great battle between Saul's forces and the Philistine army at Tel Michmash, the Israelites routed and pursued the Philistines to the valley of Aijalon (1 Samuel 14).

days, but still Samuel did not come. Saul's men began to scatter – so, feeling he had to do something, Saul offered a burnt offering himself, thinking this would bring God's blessing. Just as he finished, Samuel arrived. Saul rushed to greet him, but Samuel asked what

**❝'You have not kept the command the LORD your God gave you**; if you had, he would have **established your kingdom over Israel for all time.'❞**

1 SAMUEL 13:13

## ADVANCES IN METALWORK

Iron smithies in Ekron show that the Philistines arrived in Canaan at the beginning of the Iron Age, around 1200 BC, having acquired the ability to work with iron from the Hittites. The novelty of iron is evident in the description of Goliath's spear shaft as "like a weaver's rod" (1 Samuel 17:7), because there was no Hebrew word yet for "spear".

Israelites had to use the Philistine smiths to make and sharpen their implements (1 Samuel 13:19–21). It was not until the time of King David, who subdued Edom where there were rich iron deposits, that Israel began to develop the ability to forge iron weaponry.

**A BRONZE DAGGER WITH AN IRON SHEATH, c.1200 BC, FROM BETH-SHAN**

he had done. Saul explained that his men were starting to scatter and that because Samuel had not yet come and the Philistine army had gathered, he felt compelled to make the offering. "You have done a foolish thing", (1 Samuel 13:13) Samuel replied, and accused him of not keeping God's command. He told Saul that if he had obeyed God his kingdom would have been established forever, but now his kingdom would not last. Samuel told Saul that God had already chosen his successor, and with that he left Gilgal.

By now Saul had only 600 men, none of them properly armed because the Philistines had a monopoly on iron (see panel, above) – Saul and Jonathan were the only Israelites with swords. Yet, despite being ill-equipped and outnumbered, over the coming months and years the Israelites pushed the Philistines back to their own land.

### Saul's second disobedience

Some years later, God sent Samuel to Saul again. This time he was told to destroy the Amalekites and everything they had as punishment for attacking the Israelites when they fled Egypt (15:3–26). Saul summoned an enormous army – 200,000 foot soldiers and another 10,000 men from Judah – and attacked the Amalekites all the way from Havilah to Shur, near the eastern border of Egypt. However, instead of destroying everything, he spared Agag king of the Amalekites and kept their best livestock.

God revealed this sin to Samuel, who left the next morning to confront Saul. When they met, Saul welcomed Samuel and told him that he had carried out his instructions. However, Samuel asked about the bleating of sheep and lowing of cattle he could hear. Saul blamed his soldiers, saying they wanted to sacrifice the animals to God. But Samuel knew what had happened, and told Saul that God would far rather have obedience than offerings and sacrifices, and that rebellion and arrogance were as bad as divination and idolatry, "Because you have rejected the word of the LORD, he has rejected you as king" (15:23).

Saul begged for forgiveness but Samuel reaffirmed God's judgment. As Samuel turned to leave, Saul grabbed his robe and it tore. Samuel said to him, "The LORD has torn the kingdom of Israel from you today and has given it to one of your neighbours – to one better than you" (15:28). Samuel sent for King Agag and killed him there and then. Samuel never saw Saul again, though he mourned for him. The Lord grieved too that he had made Saul king.

ANALYSIS

## SAUL'S LEADERSHIP

Although he made a promising beginning as Israel's king, Saul soon showed his unsuitability for the role. His initial military successes won him popular support (1 Samuel 11). However, he soon proved to be a weak leader, unable to control his men under pressure (13:5–7) and unwilling to obey God's commands through the prophet Samuel (13:8-9; 15:1–23). His lack of wisdom was reflected when he instituted a fast, hoping to win God's favour, although his soldiers were desperately in need of sustenance. When he discovered his son Jonathan had eaten some honey, he was ready to kill him, and only the soldiers' pleading saved him (14:24–45). His growing mental instability made his leadership increasingly irrational and erratic.

**AFTER** »

Although God had rejected him, Saul was not about to abdicate. He clung on to power, becoming more desperate and depressed.

### SAUL'S DECLINE

In his desire to retain power, Saul's behaviour became erratic and dangerous. Threatened by the friendship that developed between **his son Jonathan and David 157** »
– as well as by David's later success in battle – Saul became increasingly jealous, causing David to flee. Saul hounded him for ten years, until ignominious **defeat on the battlefield brought things to an end 159** ».

**DAVID AND JONATHAN BY GIOVANNI BATTISTA (c.1505) SHOWS THE TWO FRIENDS (DAVID, LEFT)**

**« BEFORE**

Like most boys, David worked in the family business from an early age alongside his father Jesse and his many older brothers.

### DAVID THE SHEPHERD BOY

David had spent years on the hills tending the sheep. A shepherd's life was hard, dangerous, and demanded courage, such as David had shown by **confronting lions and bears that carried off sheep from the flock**: "Your servant has killed both the lion and the bear" (1 Samuel 17:36). The fact that Jesse did not bring David to Samuel when he asked to see his sons might suggest that he was **not yet 13 and therefore not yet deemed to be a man.**

**DAVID PROTECTING HIS FLOCK, WINCHESTER PSALTER, 12TH CENTURY**

**ANALYSIS**

### THE LORD SENDS THE EVIL SPIRIT

When the Bible says "an evil spirit from the LORD tormented" Saul (1 Samuel 16:14), the text is not suggesting that there is good and evil in God. It simply reflects the Hebrew perspective that absolutely everything in life – even evil spirits – is ultimately subject to God's control and that nothing can happen unless God permits it.

What befell Saul is a rare example of its kind in the Old Testament. Yet the idea of demonic possession and the exorcism of evil spirits – especially when illness is seen from the viewpoint of the time as being a result of sin – features several times during the brief ministry of Jesus. He was able to defeat the entities from the kingdom of evil, who were believed to inhabit a realm between heaven and Earth, because he embodied the kingdom of God. Luke summarized the meaning of this when he recorded Jesus saying, "...if I drive out demons by the finger of God, then the kingdom of God has come upon you" (Luke 11:20).

# God Calls David

*Having rejected Saul, God led Samuel to his chosen successor. Israel had wanted someone physically strong, but God wanted someone spiritually strong. In Bethlehem, Samuel found the unlikeliest of replacements.*

**A**FTER SAUL disobeyed God's command and kept the Amalekite king alive, Samuel was forced to intervene and kill the Amalekite. Saul and Samuel were never to meet again, but Samuel continued to mourn Saul's absence and fall from grace. God said that he had rejected Saul as king of Israel, and Samuel should stop mourning – there was a task at hand. He commanded Samuel,

### SHEEP AND THE SHEPHERD

A young shepherd tends his flock of sheep near Arbela or Irbil, in modern-day northern Iraq. At the time of his anointing by Samuel the prophet, David was a shepherd boy who looked after his father's sheep and safeguarded them from predators.

"Be on your way; I am sending you to Jesse of Bethlehem. I have chosen one of his sons to be king" (16:1).

### The search begins

Samuel was afraid, because he thought that if he went and Saul heard about this development, he would kill him.

So God instructed, "Take a heifer with you and say, 'I have come to sacrifice to the LORD.' Invite Jesse

to the sacrifice, and I will show you what to do. You are to anoint for me the one I indicate" (16:2,3).

### To Bethlehem in peace

When Samuel reached Bethlehem in Judah, the burial place of Rachel, the wife of Jacob (Genesis 35:19), the town elders were worried. They asked, "Do you come in peace?" (1 Samuel 16:4). Samuel confirmed that he had, and then, as instructed,

> **" People look at the outward appearance, but the LORD looks at the heart."**
> 1 SAMUEL 16:7

## BETHLEHEM IN THE BIBLE

Burial place of Rachel (Genesis 35:19).

Assigned to the tribe of Zebulun (Joshua 19:10–16).

Home of Ibzan the Judge (Judges 12:8–10).

Ruth settles in Bethlehem (Ruth 1:22).

David's hometown (1 Samuel 16:1).

Captured and garrisoned by Philistines (2 Samuel 23:14).

Fortified by Rehoboam (2 Chronicles 11:5,6).

Micah prophesies that a great ruler will come from Bethlehem (Micah 5:2).

Exiles return (Ezra 2:21).

Birthplace of Jesus (Luke 2:1–7).

### SAMUEL ANOINTING DAVID

This 3rd-century AD wall-painting depicts David and five of his brothers. It comes from the synagogue at Dura Europos in modern-day Syria, thought to have been home to an unusually liberal congregation, as the figures do not wear tassels on their garments as God commanded Moses (Numbers 15:38,39).

"Are these all the sons you have?" (16:11). Jesse said there was still the youngest, David, but he was tending the sheep. Samuel said that he should send for him, and that they would not sit down for the sacrificial feast until David arrived.

### God's chosen one

Jesse summoned David to appear before Samuel – "He was glowing with health and had a fine appearance and handsome features" (16:12). God then told Samuel that David was the chosen one. So Samuel took up a horn of oil and anointed David in the presence of his brothers, and afterwards returned home to Ramah.

From that day onwards God's Spirit "came powerfully upon David" (16:13). However, as God's Spirit filled David, so it drained from Saul, and an evil spirit tormented him instead. This would ultimately lead him to seek out David, an expert lyre player, to play music that soothed his troubled soul.

he said he had come to offer a sacrifice. He invited them, together with Jesse and his sons, to join him.

### Jesse's sons

When Jesse and his sons arrived at the place of sacrifice, Samuel saw Eliab, Jesse's eldest son, and was impressed by his appearance. He thought that surely this was God's anointed one standing before him. However, God said that he was not the one, and told Samuel not to consider the boy's appearance or his height – this was not as important as the boy's heart, which is what God always considered when judging someone.

Then Samuel met Abinadab, Jesse's second son. Samuel realised that he was not the one, and neither was the third son, Shammah. Jesse called seven of his sons before Samuel, but none of them were chosen by God. Samuel turned to Jesse and asked,

### FROM JESSE TO JESUS

An illustration from the 12th-century Ingeborg Psalter depicts the Tree of Jesse, a genealogy that shows David, Jesse's youngest son, anointed the king of Israel. Jesus belonged to the House of David.

AFTER ››

**Unwittingly, Saul brought to court the man who would one day replace him.**

### DAVID ENTERS ROYAL SERVICE

One thing that soothed Saul when he fell into dark moods was music. An attendant had heard that David could play the lyre well, so they sent for him. Saul immediately **took a liking to the young man** and asked Jesse to let David serve him. Every time a dark mood seemed imminent, **David would play his lyre 156–57 ››** and Saul's disposition improved.

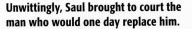

**SAUL WITH HIS SPEAR AND DAVID WITH HIS HARP, GERHARD VON KUEGELGEN, 1807**

> "Then the LORD said, 'Rise and anoint him; this is the one.' So **Samuel took the horn of oil and anointed him…**"
>
> 1 SAMUEL 16:12,13

**KING OF ISRAEL** Born *c.*1040 BC Died *c.*970 BC

# David

## "David reigned over all Israel, doing what was just and right for all his people."

2 SAMUEL 8:15

**D**AVID IS undoubtedly one of the towering figures of the Bible, and he reigned for 40 years. His is the classic story of a nobody who became a hero. His significance is reflected in the fact that no-one else in the Bible has the same name.

### David's life

The great-grandson of Ruth (see pp.136–37), David was the youngest of the eight sons of Jesse. He grew up in Bethlehem in the Judean hills, and tended the family's sheep. This was a hard job that demanded courage (see p.150), as he reminded King Saul when he wanted to face Goliath.

It was probably out on the hills, guarding his father's flocks, that he also learnt to play the lyre, and perhaps wrote some of his psalms, such as Psalm 23 – the Shepherd Psalm.

The course of David's life changed when Samuel anointed him as Israel's future king (1 Samuel 16), but it was Saul who first brought him to court, as a musician. Shortly after this, David became famous through his surprising victory over the Philistine giant Goliath. Saul made him a high-ranking officer in the

---

### ANALYSIS

#### KINGS AND CHRONICLES

The books of Kings and Chronicles give quite different, though not contradictory, pictures of David. While Kings tells every aspect of his story, Chronicles omits anything negative about him (his adultery, for example, is not recorded). This was partly because the authors had different aims. Kings was compiled while the Israelites were in exile, and questioned how they had ended up in this situation. The answer was that God's people, especially their kings, had been unfaithful, and even the best, like David, were not faultless. However, Chronicles was compiled after the return from exile, and questions whether God was still with Israel. The answer to this question was a clear "yes", based on God's promises to David. Each re-telling of the story of David has different priorities.

army, and took him into his household, where he formed a firm friendship with Saul's son, Jonathan. However, as David's subsequent military victories made him increasingly famous, Saul became jealous and made repeated attempts to kill him. David had to flee and spent the next ten years or so on the run, but by the time Saul died, he had a significant number of followers.

David finally became king, at first over Judah and then, seven years later, over the northern tribes of Israel as well. As ruler of the newly united kingdom, David was at last able to curb the Philistines' power and push them back to the coastal plain. He also subdued the Moabites, Arameans, Ammonites, and Edomites, Israel's ancient enemies, and conquered the Canaanite cities of Jerusalem, Beth Shan, and Megiddo. He turned Israel into an established nation and built a capital at Jerusalem, ending the quest that Joshua started and securing the land that God had promised to Abraham 1,000 years

## CITY OF DAVID
After taking Jerusalem from the Jebusites, David fortified the city and made it the capital of his newly united Israel. It came to be known as "the City of David" (2 Samuel 5:7; 1 Kings 2:10; Isaiah 22:9).

earlier. Yet David's reign was not entirely golden – 2 Samuel records his many weaknesses and wrong-doings, including adultery and conspiracy to murder.

### A new style of leader
David's life represented a new beginning for Israel, after the disastrous period of the Judges

## THE STAR OF DAVID

**SHIELD OF DAVID**

The "Magen David", also known as the Star or Shield of David, is Israel's most recognized symbol. Its origin has little to do with David, but such is his significance that it was named after him. It is not mentioned in the Bible – its earliest literary mention is in a 12th-century Jewish text, but it has been found on tombs dating back to the 3rd century AD. In 17th- and 18th-century Europe the star became a common symbol of Jewish communities, and the flag of the modern state of Israel features a blue Star of David.

and the badly managed monarchy under Saul. As king, David ruled in a different way over a newly united kingdom. He won victories over ancient enemies and received a new covenant from God, assuring him that one of his descendants would reign on the throne for ever. He led musicians and singers into joyful expressions of worship and honest prayer, like those expressed in many of the psalms, at least half of which are attributed to him.

David died in c.970 BC, but his line continued until the destruction of Jerusalem by the Babylonians in c.587 BC (see pp.236–37). Gradually, the people began to expect the coming of one of his descendants – the Messiah ("anointed one"), who would fulfil the promise God made to David of an everlasting kingdom (2 Samuel 7:11–16). This person, the prophets predicted, would be anointed with God's Spirit in a powerful way (Isaiah 11:1–11), set God's people truly free (Jeremiah 30:8,9), and shepherd God's people as God himself would do (Ezekiel 34:23,24). The New Testament depicts all this as fulfilled in Jesus, who is often referred to as "the Son of David", a title that Jesus himself freely accepted.

**MICHELANGELO'S STATUE OF DAVID**
Carved from 1501 to 1504, Michelangelo's statue shows David moments before killing Goliath. He gazes with concentration at the giant, his sling resting on his shoulder.

**DAVID CHOOSING SOLOMON AS HIS SUCCESSOR, FROM THE 13TH-CENTURY BIBLE OF GUYART-DES-MOULINS**

# David and Goliath

*When the Philistine champion, Goliath, taunted the Israelites, they fled from him in fear. One young armour-bearer stepped forward and offered to fight the giant single-handed, using only his sling and five smooth stones.*

## « BEFORE

The Philistines and the Israelites draw up battle lines on hills flanking the two sides of the Valley of Elah.

THE VALLEY OF ELAH, ISRAEL

### THE ARMIES GATHERED

The Philistines « 134 gathered their forces at Sokoh, some 24km (15 miles) west of Bethlehem, David's home town, further south than they had been during the whole campaign. The Israelites assembled in the Valley of Elah. The two armies then took up positions on facing hills either side of the Valley of Elah, and prepared for battle.

### DAVID THE BRAVE

After David was anointed « 150–51 he came to the attention of King Saul as a renowned lyre player. He was described as a "brave man and a warrior. He speaks well and is a fine-looking man. And the LORD is with him" (1 Samuel 16:18). David duly entered Saul's service as an armour-bearer.

**G**OLIATH OF GATH was enormous, standing over 3m (10ft) tall. He wore heavy bronze armour and carried an iron spear whose point alone weighed 7kg (15lb). The mere sight of him terrified the Israelites, whom he had challenged daily for 40 days: "Choose a man and let him come down to me. If he is able to fight and kill me, we will become your subjects; but if I overcome him and kill him, you will become our subjects" (1 Samuel 17:8,9). David heard these words as he was delivering food to his brothers in the ranks, and he asked the soldiers what the reward was for killing this uncircumcised Philistine. They told him that Saul had offered great wealth, tax exemptions, and his daughter in marriage. His questions were overheard and Saul sent for him. "Let no one lose heart on account of this Philistine," David said, "your servant will go and fight him" (1 Samuel 17:32). Saul asked how a young man could possibly fight a man like Goliath, but David replied that he had lots of experience fighting against lions and

### THE SLINGSHOT

David used his slingshot to handicap Goliath before beheading him. This stone carving depicts Assyrian soldiers carrying slingshots, which were whirled above the head and then released.

bears that had carried off his father's sheep. The God who had rescued him from them would also rescue him from this Philistine.

### Mortal combat

Saul agreed to let him fight, and dressed him in armour, but David immediately took it off again, saying he was not used to it. Instead he took up his staff, five stones from a stream, and his sling, and went to Goliath. The Philistine, seeing that David was a mere boy, snarled, "Am I a dog, that you come at me with sticks?… Come here and I'll give your flesh to the birds and the wild animals!" (17:43,44). David replied "You come against me with sword and spear… but I come against you in the name of the LORD Almighty… This day the LORD will deliver you into my hands" (17:45,46). He threatened to strike down Goliath, cut off his head, and feed him and his fellow soldiers to the birds instead, so everyone would know that there was a God in Israel. Goliath moved to attack him, and David ran towards him. Reaching into his bag, he took a stone from his pouch, slung it, and struck Goliath in the forehead. Goliath fell, and David ran to stand over him. Picking up the Philistine's sword, he killed him and cut off his head.

When the Philistines saw that Goliath was dead, they fled, and the Israelites pursued them all the way to Gath and Ekron. David put Goliath's weapons in his tent and took his head to Jerusalem.

> **"Who is this uncircumcised Philistine** that he should defy the armies of the living God?**"**
>
> 1 SAMUEL 17:26

## HISTORY AND CULTURE
### CLASH OF CHAMPIONS

ACHILLES DEFEATING HECTOR, BY RUBENS (1577–1640)

Many ancient cultures abound with myths extolling the glories of champions who determined wars through single combat. Achilles and Hector carried the fight between Greece and Troy in Homer's epic poem, *The Iliad*. In Celtic legend, the Irish hero Cúchulainn defended Ulster through a series of single combats against the queen of Connacht's army. Whichever champion won, his army was deemed to be victorious. Not only was single-handed combat more economical – only one life would be lost for an army to claim victory – it was also believed to reflect the judgment of the gods.

## AFTER »

With Goliath killed and the Philistines routed, Saul sent for David.

### DAVID IS PRESENTED TO SAUL

Abner, the commander of the Israelite army, brought David, still holding Goliath's head, to Saul. "Whose son are you, young man?" (1 Samuel 17:58) Saul asked. It seems strange that Saul did not recognize David, as David had earlier been taken into Saul's service. Some commentators have suggested there may have been two traditional stories about David's first appearance – one that states he played the lyre for Saul, and another that states he first came to Saul's attention through his fight with Goliath – and the Bible simply includes them both. Another interpretation is that Saul did not recognize David, who had grown up since he had played the lyre for Saul. Lastly, Saul does not ask for David's name, but his father's; he may only be seeking a reminder of his ancestry. When Saul speaks to David before the battle, no names are mentioned, so it is unclear whether he recognizes him.

## BEFORE

Saul's wrongdoing led Samuel to anoint David, who later became a hero when he defeated Goliath.

### DAVID BECOMES A HERO
After Saul sinned against God, Samuel was instructed to anoint David, son of Jesse, as the **future king of Israel «« 150–51**. David joined Saul's household as a lyre player and armour-bearer, but then defeated the giant Philistine Goliath, causing the **entire Philistine army to retreat «« 154–55**. After the combat, David spoke to Saul and met Jonathan for the first time; they immediately became good friends.

## HISTORY AND CULTURE
### THE BRIDE PRICE

**A KETUBAH, OR MARRIAGE CONTRACT**

A man wishing to marry in ancient Israel, would prepare a contract to present to the bride's family. An important part of this contract was the "bride price" – a payment from the bridegroom to the bride's family to compensate them for the loss of their daughter's labour when she moved to her husband's home. It also functioned as a kind of insurance policy to provide for the woman should the husband die or desert her. The bride price could be paid either in money or in kind. Jacob chose the latter to pay for his bride Rachel by working for her father Laban for seven years (Genesis 29:16–20). Saul knew that David did not have enough money to pay a bride price for a king's daughter.

### SAUL'S FURY
Incensed by David's growing popularity, Saul twice attempted – unsuccessfully – to kill David with a spear, as shown in *Saul attacking David* by Giovanni Guercino (1591–1666).

# Saul and Jonathan

*As David became increasingly popular, Saul tried to rid himself of the man he came to see as a threat. But Saul's eldest son, Jonathan, tried to save David, recognizing that God had chosen him as Israel's future king.*

**A**S THE ISRAELITES returned home after another successful raid on the Philistines, the women welcomed them with singing and dancing. The refrain of their song was: "Saul has slain his thousands, and David his tens of thousands" (1 Samuel 18:7). Saul became angry and jealous of David's popularity, wondering if there was anything more for David to gain, other than the throne itself.

### Saul's growing fear
The next day David was playing his lyre for Saul when suddenly the king experienced one of his dark moods. Twice he hurled his spear at David, but David eluded him both times. Saul had grown afraid, because he recognized that God had deserted him, but was with David. So he sent David away to fight, but he returned victorious. Everything he did was successful, and the people of Judah and Israel loved him. Seeing this, Saul became even more afraid.

The king resorted to scheming: his daughter Michal had fallen in love with David, and Saul decided to use this against him. He offered

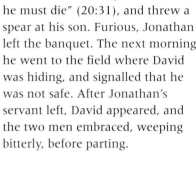

her to David, but David declined, saying he was too poor to pay the bride price (see panel, left). Saul assured him that the price was only 100 Philistine foreskins, thinking that David would surely be killed trying to fulfil such a demand. However, David returned from battle with 200 foreskins, so Saul was forced to give Michal to him. The people recognized David's prowess in war and Saul became even more afraid.

### Jonathan's friendship

Saul told his son Jonathan and his servants to kill David. However, Jonathan, who had formed a deep friendship with David, warned him and David fled. Jonathan reasoned with Saul, pointing out David's innocence and military usefulness to Israel, and Saul vowed that he would not harm David. Jonathan called David back and all was well until Saul became depressed again, and for a second time, he tried to kill David with his spear. Michal

warned David, "If you don't run for your life tonight, tomorrow you'll be killed" (19:11). She let him down through a window and he fled to Samuel's house at Ramah.

When Saul heard that David was with Samuel, he sent three groups of men to capture him, but God's Spirit fell on each group and all they could do was prophesy. Finally, Saul himself went to

Ramah, but the same thing happened to him, and he prophesied for 24 hours.

### Jonathan protects David

David went to Jonathan and asked why Saul wanted him dead. Jonathan said that he would do anything to help him. They devised a plan: David would hide in a field instead of attending the feast celebrating the new moon with the king. Jonathan would see how Saul responded to David's absence and would let David know whether or not it was safe to return, by shooting arrows close to David's hiding place, and using coded words. Then Jonathan "made a covenant with the house of David, saying, 'May the Lord call David's enemies to account" (20:16).

On the second day of David's absence, Saul became angry; he accused Jonathan of taking sides with David and pointed out that Jonathan would never be king if David lived. He ordered Jonathan

# "Saul had a spear in his hand and he hurled it, saying to himself, 'I'll pin David to the wall.'"

1 SAMUEL 18:10,11

### A LOYAL WIFE

David's wife Michal helped him escape through a window when Saul's men came to kill him, as depicted in this 13th-century stained glass window in Canterbury Cathedral, Kent. She also placed a dummy in his bed to further mislead the soldiers.

to send someone to get David, "for he must die" (20:31), and threw a spear at his son. Furious, Jonathan left the banquet. The next morning he went to the field where David was hiding, and signalled that he was not safe. After Jonathan's servant left, David appeared, and the two men embraced, weeping bitterly, before parting.

### THE PARTING OF FRIENDS
Rembrandt's painting, *David and Jonathan* (1642), captures the sorrow of their parting. Jonathan, the regally dressed older figure, stands in front of the stone of Ezel (20:19), where David had hidden.

## AFTER

**For ten years after his flight from Saul, David lived in hiding.**

### GOLIATH'S SWORD
David **fled first to Nob, where he asked Ahimelek, a priest, to feed him** and to give him any weapon that he might have. He explained that he was on an urgent mission, and had left without his own sword.

Ahimelek said that he had only the sword of Goliath, whom David had killed. David took the sword, saying "There is none like it" (21:9).

### DAVID IN HIDING
The next phase of David's life saw him **hiding in many places, including a Philistine city 158–59 ››**. God was **training him to be a courageous warrior and an inspiring leader**.

**BEFORE**

When David fled, he was in desperate need of supplies and called upon Ahimelek the priest.

**BREAD AND A SWORD**

David went to Nob and told Ahimelek that he was **on a secret mission for Saul** and needed "five loaves of bread, or whatever you can find" (1 Samuel 21:3). However, Ahimelek **only had consecrated unleavened bread from the sanctuary**, which he gave to David after being assured that the men's bodies were holy – they had been kept away from women, following Jewish law. Then David took **Goliath's sword** **«** 154, which had been kept there, and left. Jesus used this story (Matthew 12:1–8) to teach that **ceremonial rules can be broken in times of need.**

DAVID, A BRONZE BY VERROCCHIO, c.1475.

# David the Outlaw

*David spent the next ten years on the run. Twice he had Saul in his grasp, yet did not kill him because he was God's anointed king. Meanwhile, all sorts of people began to see David as their leader.*

**A**T FIRST DAVID FLED into the heart of enemy territory, to the Philistine city of Gath, and to its leader King Achish, whose servants reminded him that David was celebrated for killing Philistines, "Isn't this David, the king of the land? Isn't he the one they sing about in their dances" (1 Samuel 21:11). David pretended to be insane, and Achish decided he was not a threat.

### Seeking places of safety
David then moved to a cave at Adullam, 16km (10 miles) away. People began to join him, including his father's family and those who were in distress, in debt, or discontented. Soon there were 400 men with him, but the prophet Gad warned them not to stay there, so they left for the forest of Hereth. Meanwhile, Saul's paranoia worsened – he accused everyone of being bribed by David and conspiring against him. After hearing that the priest Ahimelek had given David supplies as well as Goliath's sword, he ordered Doeg the Edomite to kill Ahimelek and 85 other priests.

> **"**Those who were **in distress or in debt or discontented** gathered round him, and he became their **commander."**
>
> 1 SAMUEL 22:2

**KEILAH**
The city of Keilah, saved from the Philistines by David, has been identified with Khirbet Kila, Israel, a hill covered with ruins on the Judean side of the River Jordan. The people of Keilah betrayed David after he had saved them.

David always sought God's guidance. When the Philistines attacked Keilah, he asked God if he should rescue them, and God said yes. When Saul sent forces against David, he asked God whether Keilah would hand him over, and again God said yes. So David and his men, now numbering 600, escaped again to strongholds in the wilderness and the Desert of Ziph, where God continued to protect him.

Jonathan, David's closest friend, went to David and helped him find strength, saying, "'Don't be afraid... My father Saul will not lay a hand on you. You shall be king over Israel... Even my father Saul knows this'" (23:17). Jonathan and David "made a covenant before the Lord" (23:18) and then David fled to the Desert of Maon and hid in caves at En Gedi by the Dead Sea.

### David twice spares Saul's life

When Saul heard where David was, he pursued him with 3,000 men. At En Gedi Saul went into a cave to relieve himself, not knowing that David and his men lay deeper inside it. David crept up and cut off a corner of Saul's robe.

Afterwards, David felt guilty because Saul was still God's anointed king. He called down to Saul, showing him the corner of his robe and told him that he had spared him, though he could have killed him. He appealed to Saul to reconsider what he was doing. Saul was suddenly deeply moved: "You are more righteous than I... You have treated me well, but I have treated you badly... May the Lord reward you well for the way you treated me today" (24:17–19). For the first time, Saul knew David would be Israel's king. He simply asked that he would not kill his descendants when that happened. David gave his word.

#### DAVID AND ABIGAIL
Painted by Marten de Vos (1532–1603), *David and Abigail* depicts Abigail astutely taking food and wine to David to persuade him not to commit needless bloodshed against her husband Nabal.

#### DAVID AND SAUL
A 13th-century illumination (detail) from a French Bible depicts David cutting off a piece of Saul's robe. Saul was trying to kill David because he was afraid that his kingdom would be usurped, yet when David had a chance to strike at Saul, he spared him.

On another occasion when David was in the Desert of Ziph, David and Abishai, Joab's brother, crept to the edge of Saul's camp one night and, seeing him lying asleep, took his spear and water jug from near his head. The next morning David stood on the hilltop and taunted Abner, Saul's commander, for having failed to guard him, saying, "Look around you. Where are the king's spear and water jug...?" (26:16). Saul saw again how gracious David had been and promised never to harm him. David replied, "The Lord gave you into my hands today, but I would not lay a hand on the Lord's anointed." (26:23) Saul blessed him and they went their separate ways.

### David on the move

David had married Abigail, "an intelligent and beautiful woman" (25:3), during this time. Abigail's then-husband Nabal had died – "the Lord struck Nabal" (25:38) – after refusing David's request for supplies. After this, David moved to reside among the Philistines, whom he double-crossed by pretending to raid Israel (27:12). His scheming almost backfired when he was barely spared from going into full-scale battle against Israel at Aphek (29:4–11). The ensuing battle between Israel and the Philistines – as well as David's military success against the Amalekites (see panel, above) – confirmed Saul's enmity towards David once and for all.

> ## "Who can lay a hand on the Lord's **anointed and be guiltless?**"
> **1 SAMUEL** 26:9

#### PEOPLE
### THE AMALEKITES

The Amalekites were descended from Amalek, Esau's grandson, and lived in the Sinai and Negev regions. They had attacked the Israelites when they fled from slavery in Egypt and so were put under a curse (Exodus 17:14). They attacked again during the period of the Judges, but Gideon drove them back. Saul failed to wipe them out but David overcame them (1 Samuel 30). They declined over the coming years.

### AFTER

**Saul's life ended ignominiously in battle against the Philistines.**

#### SAUL'S DEATH
Faced with gathering enemy forces, Saul needed guidance, but Samuel was dead and Saul himself "had expelled the mediums and spiritists from the land" (1 Samuel 28:3). So **when God did not answer him**, he went in disguise to a woman in Endor, asking her to do the forbidden and **call up Samuel's spirit, who confirmed that God had abandoned Saul**. The next day many Israelites were killed in battle, including Jonathan. Saul was badly wounded, and fell on his own sword (31:2–6). **The Philistines mutilated his body** and displayed it at Beth Shan.

***SAUL AND THE WITCH OF ENDOR (1777), BY ANGLO-AMERICAN ARTIST BENJAMIN WEST***

BEFORE

David was saddened when he heard that Saul and Jonathan had died in a lost battle against the Philistines on Mount Gilboa.

**DAVID KILLING THE MESSENGER, ILLUSTRATED IN THE BRANTWOOD BIBLE (c.1260)**

### DAVID'S GRIEF

An Amalekite brought the news of the two deaths to David. The man **claimed he had killed Saul** (contradicted in 1 Samuel 31), and brought his crown as proof. David said he was wrong to kill a person anointed by God, and ordered him to be killed. David then composed a lament, regretting "How the mighty have fallen" (2 Samuel 1:19).

# David Becomes King

*With Saul dead, the way was open for David to become king. He ruled over Judah first; it was another seven years before he added the northern tribes to unite Israel under his leadership.*

**D**AVID ASKED GOD if he should go to Judah. God agreed, and told him to travel to Hebron, where David then settled with his two wives and the men who had gathered around him during his exile. The tribal leaders also travelled to Hebron, where they anointed David king over Judah, in a public recognition of the calling God had given him so many years earlier (see pp.150–51). Hebron, which had been strongly associated with Abraham, became David's capital for the next seven and a half years, during which time the city was expanded and fortified (see pp.78–79).

> " …the men of Judah came to Hebron and there **they anointed David king…** "
>
> 2 SAMUEL 2:4

The path to the throne of a unified kingdom was not straightforward, however. After Saul's death, his commander Abner had taken Saul's son Ish-Bosheth to Mahanaim and crowned him as Saul's successor.

The following years saw many skirmishes between the two sides. In one instance, Abner, accompanied by Ish-Bosheth's men, met Joab, who led David's men, at the Pool of Gibeon. Abner said to Joab, "Let's have some of the young men get up and fight hand to hand in front of us" (2 Samuel 2:14). But what had begun as friendly rivalry led to fierce fighting and ended in victory for David's men. A truce was eventually called at Gibeon, but the power struggle between the followers of David and Saul continued for many years. David became progressively stronger while Ish-Bosheth grew weaker.

### Abner's defection and death

Meanwhile, "Abner had been strengthening his own position" (3:6); he even challenged Ish-Bosheth's authority by sleeping with a royal concubine. When Ish-Bosheth questioned this, Abner was furious and threatened to "transfer the kingdom from the house of Saul and establish David's throne over Israel and Judah" (3:10). Abner then sent messengers to David, saying that he would bring Israel "over to you" (3:12) if they could reach an agreement. David demanded the return of his wife Michal, who had been left behind when David fled Saul (see pp.156–57), and this was done. Abner negotiated with the elders of

### JOAB KILLING ABNER

A 13th-century stained glass window in Strasbourg illustrates the moment of Joab's revenge on Abner for his brother's death. Joab had pretended to want a private interview, luring Abner to his death.

### CANAAN UNDER DAVID

According to biblical texts, David's kingdom extended over all the lands originally given to the 12 tribes of Israel (see pp.74–75).

Israel and Benjamin, calling on them to make David their king. Upon their agreement, he went to David at Hebron and offered to "assemble all Israel for my lord the king" (3:21). David was pleased, and sent Abner on his way in peace.

When Joab returned from a raid and heard that Abner had visited David, he was angry – Abner had killed his brother at Gibeon. Joab had Abner found and killed, but when David found out he cursed Joab and his house for ever.

Abner's death was a disaster for Israel. Two of Ish-Bosheth's men assassinated Ish-Bosheth and took his head to David in an attempt to stabilize the situation, but David was outraged and had the men killed. However, the path was now clear for David to become king of a united nation. So it was that the elders of the north came to Hebron, affirming their allegiance, and recognizing God's promise to make David ruler of Israel. They made a covenant with David before God and anointed him king.

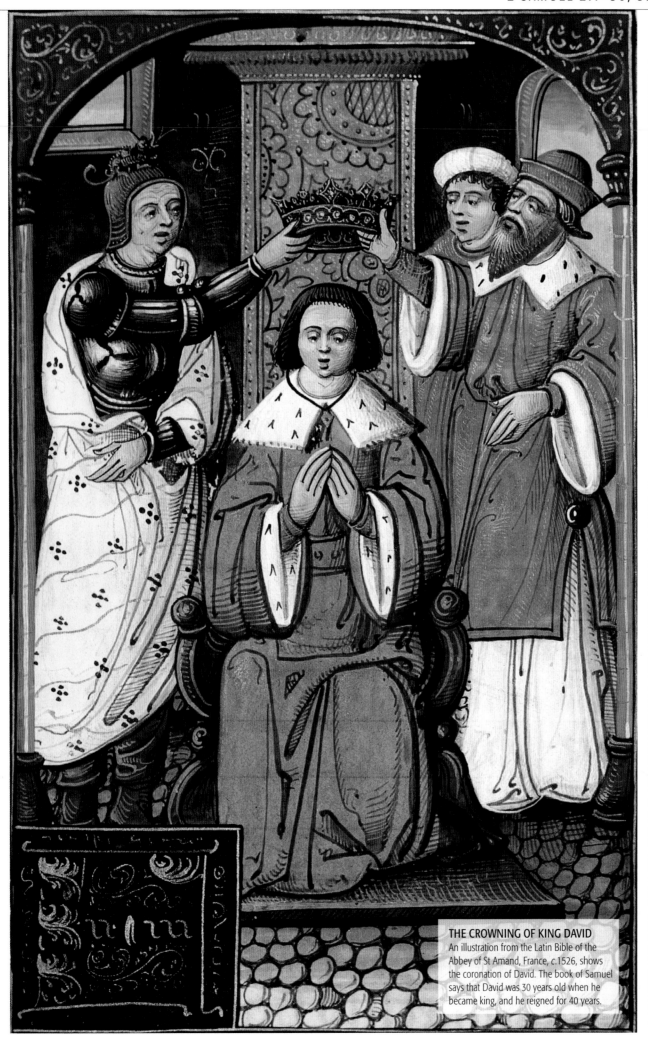

**THE CROWNING OF KING DAVID**
An illustration from the Latin Bible of the Abbey of St Amand, France, c.1526, shows the coronation of David. The book of Samuel says that David was 30 years old when he became king, and he reigned for 40 years.

## JOAB

David's nephew Joab, son of his sister Zeruiah, was a loyal commander and a skilful fighter in the long wars against Saul's followers under Ish-Bosheth and Abner. He led a daring attack on Jerusalem, after which he became commander-in-chief (1 Chronicles 11:6–8). Joab was hot-headed, as revealed by his killing of Abner, but utterly loyal; he arranged Uriah's death in battle as David requested (2 Samuel 11), because David had made Uriah's wife, Bathsheba, pregnant (see p.166–67).

Joab was instrumental in David's reconciliation with his son Absalom, but later killed Absalom to protect David. At the end of David's life, Joab supported Adonijah as David's successor, which cost him his life (1 Kings 1:7). David asked Solomon not to allow Joab's "grey head [to] go down to the grave in peace" (1 Kings 2:6).

## AFTER

Hebron had been a useful capital, but it was too far south for the new kingdom, so David needed a new one.

### THE NEW CAPITAL
**Jerusalem (Jebus) 162–63 »** was a Canaanite enclave that Israel had been unable to capture. Situated on the main east–west road through the Judean hills, and right on the border of Judah and Benjamin, it was the ideal position for a new capital. David **conquered it by sending men through a secret water shaft** that ran into the city from the Spring of Gihon, to attack the inhabitants (2 Samuel 5:6–9).

In **naming Jerusalem "the City of David"**, David adopted the practice of naming a capital after the monarch as well as claiming it as his own. The city sat on an artificial platform supported by terraces over 15m (50ft) high, with walls 3m (10ft) thick. David strengthened the fortifications and then had a palace built on top.

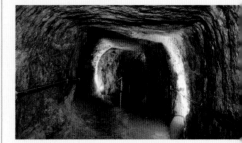

**THE WARREN SHAFT, CONNECTING THE CITY OF DAVID WITH THE SPRING OF GIHON**

## ISRAEL'S HOLY CITY  Origins 4th millennium BC

# Jerusalem

## "Great is the LORD… in the city of our God, his holy mountain."

PSALM 48:1

**THE GOLDEN GATE, TEMPLE MOUNT**
Also known as the Gate of Mercy, this gate is renowned in Jewish tradition as the gate through which the Messiah will enter Jerusalem.

**T**HERE HAS been a settlement at Jerusalem since the late fourth millennium BC, but it developed into a fortified city only in the Middle Bronze Age (c.2100–1550 BC). When the Israelites invaded Canaan around 1406 BC – according to the Bible and the ancient Egyptian Amarna tablets, – they failed to take Jerusalem; it remained in the hands of a Canaanite tribe known as the Jebusites (Judges 21). The city then covered an area of around 5 hectares (12 acres); it was bounded to the east by the Kidron Valley and to the south and west by the Tyropaean Valley, so it was secure on three sides. As the prophets noted, enemies had to approach from the north (Jeremiah 1:13–15).

### David rules Jerusalem

King David was the first to capture the city for the Israelites, and he made it his new capital. David strengthened its fortifications, built a palace and rebuilt the Jebusite citadel of Zion – whose name later became synonymous with the city. The Bible says that David brought the Ark of the Covenant into the

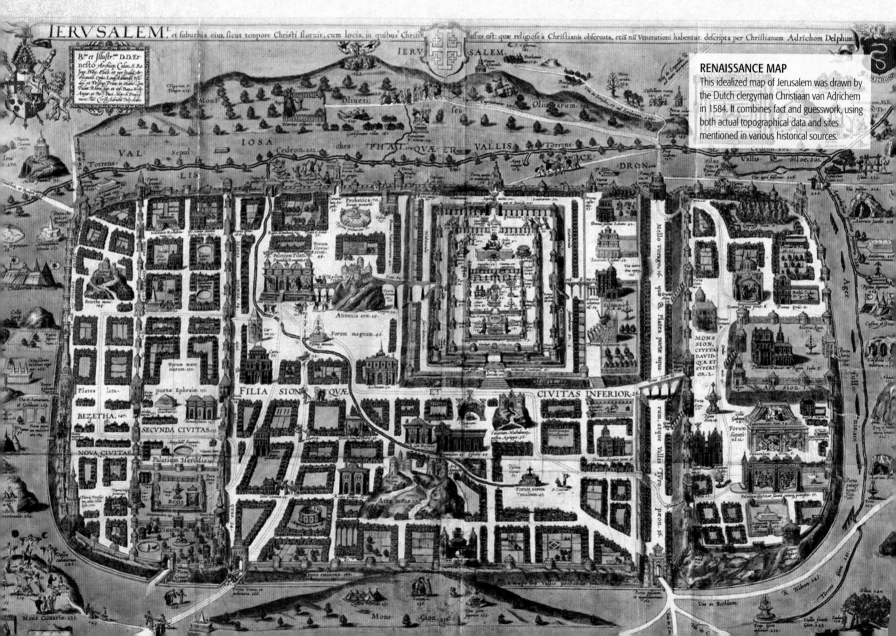

IERVSALEM, et suburbia eius, sicut tempore Christi floruit, cum locis, in quibus Christi passus est: quae religiose à Christianis obseruata, etiā nū Venerationi habentur. descripta per Christianum Adrichom Delphum.

**RENAISSANCE MAP**
This idealized map of Jerusalem was drawn by the Dutch clergyman Christiaan van Adrichem in 1584. It combines fact and guesswork, using both actual topographical data and sites mentioned in various historical sources.

city (see pp.164–65), making Jerusalem the religious and political centre of Israel. Biblically, it was now seen both as home to David and his descendants, and as God's chosen dwelling (Psalm 132:13). Yet Jerusalem would also be seen as a symbol of judgment (2 Kings 23:27), showing it was not the city itself that was special to God, but the life that the people within it were meant to live.

## Expansion after David

King Solomon is said to have expanded Jerusalem to around three times its size under the Jebusites, though archaeological evidence is scarce. Over the coming years successive kings expanded the city, adding new walls, towers, and gates, the last of which were often named after the activities associated with them, such as the Sheep and Fish Gates.

After the fall of Samaria, c.722–721 BC, a flood of refugees rapidly increased the city's population and Jerusalem grew hugely. King Hezekiah (r.716–686 BC) extended the city to the west and built a tunnel from the Gihon Spring to the Pool of Solomon, ensuring a permanent water supply. He also fortified the city in anticipation of an assault by the Assyrians, who did beseige the city in 701 BC, but eventually agreed to a treaty – the Bible says they were forced to withdraw when God sent a terrible plague among them.

> **" I saw the Holy City,** the new Jerusalem **coming down out of heaven** from God…"**
>
> **REVELATION** 21:2

## Between two powers

A period of calm ended with King Josiah's death in 609 BC, after which Judah's kings found themselves threatened by both Egypt and Babylon. In 605 BC the Babylonians defeated Egypt and besieged Jerusalem; a puppet government was installed but it rebelled, and in 597 BC the Babylonians attacked

**FALL OF JERUSALEM**
This illustration from a medieval French translation of *Antiquites Judaiques*, c.1470, depicts the Temple in Jerusalem being attacked by Nebuchadnezzar's forces in 587 BC (see pp.236–37).

again, taking 10,000 Israelites into exile. Finally, in 587 BC, the Babylonians under Nebuchadnezzar entered and set fire to Jerusalem, destroying the Temple, taking its treasures, and exiling its remaining people to Babylon (see pp.238–39).

According to the Bible, the prophets had warned against the people's arrogant belief that they were "safe to do… detestable things" (Jeremiah 7:10). God had vowed to destroy Jerusalem and its Temple if the people did not alter their wicked ways (Jeremiah 7:1–11).

The Temple was rebuilt when the Persian king Cyrus the Great allowed the Jews to return home in 538 BC. However, the city walls remained in ruins until the middle of the next century, when they were restored by Nehemiah (a governor installed by the Persian king Artaxerxes), who wrote the biblical book of Nehemiah. By then, Jerusalem had shrunk back to its size at the time of Solomon.

## Shifting rule

Cycles of destruction and renewal followed. In 332 BC Jerusalem surrendered peacefully to Alexander the Great, but then endured painful wars of succession. The Egyptian Ptolemaic dynasty seized it c.312 BC, ruling it for around 100 years; then the Greek Seleucids conquered the city. Freed in the Maccabean revolt that followed, Jerusalem once again flourished under the Judean Hasmonean dynasty. Around 500 years after the building of the Second Temple, Judea and Jerusalem came under the rule of the Romans, and Herod the Great.

### THE THREE ABRAHAMIC FAITHS

Jerusalem is sacred to the world's three great monotheistic faiths (those that hold that there is a single god). In Judaism, the Western (or "Wailing") Wall is recognized as the only remaining part of the Second Temple and is a holy place for prayer, while the Mount of Olives is seen as the place where the dead will rise first. For Christians, Jerusalem is where Jesus was crucified, buried, and then rose again. Muslims believe that Jerusalem is where Abram

nearly sacrificed Ishmael (not Isaac, as the Bible records), and where Muhammad ascended to heaven.

**DOME OF THE ROCK MOSQUE, TEMPLE MOUNT**

---

### CHRONOLOGY IN BRIEF

- **4th millennium BC,** first settlements.

- **c.2085 BC,** ruled by the priest-king Melchizedek, to whom Abraham gave a tithe: "a tenth of everything" (Genesis 14:18–20).

- **c.1406 BC,** the Israelites, led by Joshua, arrive in Canaan, but cannot dislodge the Jebusites from Jerusalem (Joshua 15:63).

- **c.1002 BC,** conquered by David and becomes his capital. The Ark of the Covenant is said to later be brought here (2 Samuel 6).

- **c.970 BC,** Solomon succeeds David; he expands the city and builds the Temple (1 Kings 5–9).

- **c.930 BC,** remains the capital of Judah after the kingdom is divided (1 Kings 12).

**13TH-CENTURY STAINED-GLASS DETAIL OF KING HEZEKIAH, FROM CHARTRES CATHEDRAL, FRANCE**

- **c.701 BC,** besieged by the Assyrians; Hezekiah prays and army withdraws (2 Kings 18,19).

- **Symbolic in the words of the prophets** as the focus of God's kingdom and rule (Isaiah 2).

- **Hezekiah constructs** a water tunnel from the Gihon Spring (2 Kings 20:20).

- **c.605 BC,** first besieged by Babylonians.

- **c.597 BC,** King Johoiachin surrenders to Babylonian king, Nebuchadnezzar.

- **c.587 BC,** Babylonians destroy city and Temple (2 Kings 25).

- **c.539 BC,** King Cyrus of Persia captures Babylon and a year later allows the Israelite exiles home.

- **c.536–516 BC,** the returning Jewish exiles rebuild the Temple (Ezra 3,4).

- **c.445 BC,** Nehemiah rebuilds the city walls and gates (Nehemiah 2,3).

- **c.332 BC,** Greece, under Alexander the Great, conquers Palestine, including Jerusalem.

- **c.198 BC,** Ptolemy V loses Jerusalem and Judea to the Seleucids.

- **c.168 BC,** walls destroyed and Temple defiled by Antiochus IV Epiphanes.

- **164 BC,** Maccabean rebellion.

- **63 BC,** Roman leader Pompey the Great captures Jerusalem.

**1ST-CENTURY MARBLE BUST OF POMPEY THE GREAT**

# The Ark is Brought to Jerusalem

*The Ark of the Covenant, containing the Ten Commandments, had remained in Kiriath Jearim throughout Saul's reign. David wanted to bring it to his new capital, Jerusalem, to demonstrate that he intended God to be at the heart of his kingdom. The first attempt failed, but the second was successful.*

**D**AVID TOOK 30,000 men to Kiriath Jearim, where the Ark had rested since the Philistines returned it to the Israelites (see pp.144–45). The men carried the Ark on a new cart, just as the Philistines had done, and started out for Jerusalem in a procession of singing and dancing. Abinadab's sons, Uzzah and Ahio, were guiding the cart, and when the oxen stumbled, Uzzah reached out to steady the Ark, but God saw this as irreverent and struck him down – "he died there beside the ark of God" (2 Samuel 6:7). This made David angry but also afraid, and he doubted his plan to take the Ark to Jerusalem. So instead he directed it to the home of Obed-Edom the Gittite, where it stayed for three months, and God blessed Obed-Edom and his family.

### Celebrating success

When David heard of the blessing, he realized what they had done wrong – Levites should have carried the Ark on poles as God had commanded (1 Chronicles 15:2). So, accompanied by Levites, musicians, soldiers, and elders, they went to fetch the Ark. After they had taken six steps, David sacrificed a bull and a calf in thanks. Wearing only a linen ephod (see p.110), he danced before God as the procession advanced, causing his wife Michal, Saul's daughter, to despise him.

### The blessing of David's line

The Israelites put the Ark in the tent that David had prepared, and David made offerings to God. When he returned home, Michal rebuked him for dancing "half-naked in full view" (2 Samuel 6:20). David said he had been dancing for God, not her or anyone else, and reminded her that God had chosen him, not one of Saul's family, as ruler. The Bible notes that Michal remained barren, signalling that Saul's line was to play no further part in Israel's story. The blessing lay in King David's line, now strengthened by the presence of the heavenly king – represented by the Ark of the Covenant – in the royal city.

> ## "David was afraid of the LORD that day and said, 'How can the ark of the LORD ever come to me?'"
>
> 2 SAMUEL 6:9

**DAVID BRINGS THE ARK TO JERUSALEM**
The Flemish embroidered wall-hanging *Tapestry of David and Bathsheba* (c.1510–15) includes a section titled "Transportation of the Ark of the Covenant". This shows the consecrated Levites carrying the Ark, and David dancing barefoot.

**DAVID AND BATHSHEBA**
Gazing out of the window of his palace, David first saw Bathsheba when she was bathing. He was immediately struck by her beauty, as imagined in *David and Bathsheba* by Lucas Cranach the Younger (1515–86).

## BEFORE

**When David wanted to build a house for God, God said that he would build a house for David.**

### GOD'S COVENANT
David had **brought the Ark of the Covenant to Jerusalem << 164–65**, but it remained in a tent. David felt it was inappropriate for him to have a palace while God only had a tent, so he planned to build a temple. Although Nathan (see panel, right) had initially encouraged him to go ahead, **God told Nathan to inform David that he had never needed nor asked for a temple.** Instead, he said, "the LORD himself will establish a house for you" (2 Samuel 7:11) – a house of descendants that would never end and a kingdom that would last for ever. **God would establish Israel and its king, and would never remove his love, as he had with Saul << 149**, although the king would be disciplined when necessary. David praised God and asked for his blessing.

# David's Failings

*David was a good king, but he was not perfect. His many mistakes are recorded in the latter part of the second book of Samuel. Unlike Saul, who covered up his sins or blamed others, David openly confessed to his.*

**I**N THE SPRING, David sent his commander Joab out on a campaign against the Ammonites, while he stayed in Jerusalem. One evening, he was walking on the roof of the palace when he saw a beautiful woman bathing. Despite discovering she was the wife of a soldier, Uriah the Hittite, he sent for her, slept with her, and she became pregnant.

David tried to hide the adultery. He asked Joab to send Uriah back from the frontline and when he arrived, David encouraged him to go home to see his wife. However, Uriah was unwilling to go home "to eat and drink and make love to my wife" (2 Samuel 11:11) when the soldiers he had left slept in tents, so instead of returning home, he slept at the entrance to the palace with the servants. The following night David made Uriah drunk, but still the soldier would not go home to his wife. So David sent Uriah back to the front with a note for Joab, which said, "Put Uriah out in front where the fighting is fiercest. Then withdraw from him so that he will be struck down and die" (11:15). Joab followed his orders, and sent the news of Uriah's death to David. After a short period of mourning, Bathsheba married David and they had a son, "but the thing David had done displeased the LORD" (11:27).

### The prophet's parable
God sent the prophet Nathan to tell David a parable of a rich man who had plenty of livestock but snatched a poor neighbour's pet lamb for a feast instead of using one of his own animals. David was

PEOPLE

## NATHAN

Nathan was a prophet to David and Solomon, who also wrote records of events (1 Chronicles 29:29). He proved a true friend to David on three key occasions. First, when he told David that his plan to build a temple was misguided (see Before panel, left). Second, when he confronted David after his adultery with Bathsheba, causing David to repent. Third, when Adonijah tried to usurp the throne towards the end of David's life. Nathan told Bathsheba of the plot and advised a course of action, and so ensured Solomon's succession to the throne.

**KING DAVID AND NATHAN BY CLAUDE VIGNON (1593–1670)**

outraged and said, "The man who did this must die! He must pay for that lamb four times over" (12:6). Then Nathan said, "You are the man!" (12:7) and exposed all that David had done to Uriah. David confessed and God forgave him, but said that Bathsheba's child would die as a consequence. The baby fell ill, and despite David's prayer and fasting, died after a week. David acknowledged the punishment, and comforted his wife, who later gave birth to another son: Solomon.

### A weak father

David was not a strong father; he appeared to be afraid to discipline

### THE DEATH OF ABSALOM

As Absalom's men travelled to fight David, Absalom's hair caught in a tree. Joab seized the moment to plunge three javelins into Absalom's heart, as depicted in this 16th-century painting by an unknown artist.

his children. His son Amnon raped his half-sister Tamar and would not marry her, so she was forced to live with her brother Absalom. David was enraged but did nothing, so Absalom grew increasingly angry. Two years later Absalom took his revenge: he killed Amnon and fled into exile. David mourned Amnon, and longed to go to Absalom, but they were not reconciled for another three years, and only then through the intervention of Joab.

Absalom started to curry favour with the people. For four years he stood outside the city gate every morning, telling people that the king would not hear their woes, whereas if he were king, they would receive justice. If anyone tried to bow before him, he reached out and kissed him, and soon "stole the hearts of the people of Israel" (15:6). The conspiracy erupted when he travelled to Hebron and had himself crowned king. David fled Jerusalem, fearing Absalom's men, and it was left to Joab to kill Absalom, quash the revolt, and ultimately stir David into returning to Jerusalem.

### A punishing plague

Later in David's reign, and against Joab's advice, David ordered a census of fighting men of Israel and Judah, which took more than nine months. Joab thought it foolish and eventually David saw the folly of what he had done. He asked God to forgive him, and "take away the guilt" (24:10). God gave him a choice of judgments: "Shall there come on you three years of famine in your land? Or three

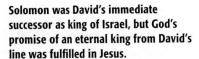

### DAVID AS A SHEPHERD

Nathan's parable of a rich man stealing his neighbour's lamb offended David, who had been a shepherd as a youth, as depicted in this 4th-century sculpture.

months of fleeing from your enemies while they pursue you? Or three days of plague in your land?" (24:13). David chose the plague, as it put him into God's merciful hands rather than man's, but even so, 70,000 people died. David cried to God that he had sinned, so he should be punished, but not his people. The plague

stopped at Araunah's threshing floor, where David built an altar – the site of the future Temple.

David's final weakness was a lack of clear direction over who should succeed him, leading to a dispute between his sons Adonijah and Solomon. But ultimately David appointed Solomon, and shortly afterwards his 40-year reign ended.

> " I am in deep distress. **Let us fall into the hands of the** LORD, for his mercy is great; but do not let me fall into human hands. "
>
> 2 SAMUEL 24:14

**AFTER** »

Solomon was David's immediate successor as king of Israel, but God's promise of an eternal king from David's line was fulfilled in Jesus.

### SOLOMON BUILDS THE TEMPLE

After David's death, his son **Solomon built the Temple in Jerusalem 172–73** », as God had foretold: "I will raise up your offspring to succeed you... He is the one who will build a house for my Name" (7:12,13). It took seven years and more than 180,000 men to build it.

### DAVID'S DESCENDANTS

Judah's king was always a descendant of David, just as God promised. Although Davidic rulers ceased with the **exile to Babylon 238–39** », the prophets had said that **the Messiah 353** », or chosen one, would be descended from David (Isaiah 11). In the New Testament, the gospels reveal that this would be true of **Jesus 286** », "the son of David" (Matthew 1:1) . For Christians, **Jesus is the fulfilment of God's promise of an eternal ruler**.

## « BEFORE

The struggle between two of David's sons over who would succeed to the throne reflected the existence of regional tensions within the kingdom.

**EARLY 20TH-CENTURY PHOTOGRAPH OF EN ROGEL**

### VYING FOR POWER

Adonijah drew much of the support for his claim for his father's throne from **among the tribes of Judah**, which had seen their influence reduced since the establishment of the royal city-state of **Jerusalem «« 162–63**. As David ailed, Adonijah gathered his supporters at the Stone of Zoheleth near En Rogel, in the vicinity of Siloam, to **make his bid for the kingship**.

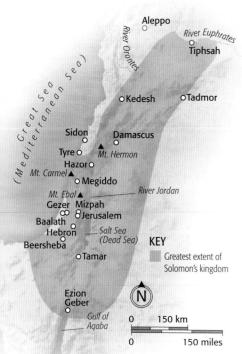

### KEY

Greatest extent of Solomon's kingdom

| 0 | | 150 km |
| 0 | | 150 miles |

### SOLOMON'S REALM

This map shows the probable extent of Solomon's kingdom around 940 BC, based on 1 Kings 4:21–24. Solomon reorganized the state into 12 districts that deliberately cut across tribal boundaries and power.

# Solomon Becomes King

*David's eldest surviving son, Adonijah, attempted to prevent Solomon coming to the throne, but David moved quickly to fulfil his earlier promise that Solomon would succeed him as king.*

**K**ING DAVID grew old and "could not keep warm even when they put covers over him" (1 Kings 1:1). It was clear that his powers were waning and he would not live much longer, so his son and heir-apparent, Adonijah, made a bid for the throne. As the eldest surviving son, Adonijah felt he had a more legitimate claim than David's favoured son Solomon, who many deemed unworthy because of the circumstances in which David had taken Bathsheba, Solomon's mother, as a wife (see pp.166–67).

David had alienated some powerful people during his reign, especially those who were involved in the death of his son Absalom (see p.167), and they rallied to Adonijah's cause. Drawing support from a group of his father's estranged advisors, including the former general, Joab, Adonijah was hailed as king by his attendants, who gathered near En Rogel – not far from Jerusalem – to celebrate his anticipated accession.

### Bathsheba acts

Adonijah's coup was to prove short-lived and the celebrations premature. David's loyal servant Nathan the prophet informed Bathsheba, Solomon's mother, of the plot, and reminded her that David had promised the throne to her son. Bathsheba moved quickly, coming before King David and lying prostrate at his feet. She acquainted David with Adonijah's plot and reminded him of his commitment that Solomon should be king after him. While she was doing this, Nathan arrived and also challenged David, in case he was considering reneging on his promise. Nathan pointed out that neither Solomon nor David's loyal supporters had been invited to Adonijah's "coronation".

David then declared: "As surely as the LORD lives, who has delivered me out of every trouble, I will surely carry out this very day what I swore to you by the LORD, the God of Israel: Solomon your son shall be king after me, and he will sit on my throne in my place" (1:29,30).

### David takes action

Although he was extremely frail, David acted immediately to secure Solomon's place on the throne. David commanded his key officials – Zadok the priest, Nathan, and Benaiah the soldier – to rally a crowd, proclaim Solomon king, and bring him to sit on David's throne. This made David's choice of successor unquestionably clear to the nation.

Each rosette held a turquoise

Zadok anointed Solomon with oil and, as his reign began, the new king was acclaimed by the people.

Adonijah's supporters became puzzled when their own festivities were interrupted by the greater noise coming from Solomon's coronation. When news reached them that Solomon had taken his seat on the royal throne, Adonijah's guests fled in alarm. Adonijah was fearful and sought assurances that he would not be put to the sword.

**ROYAL CORONATION**
A stained glass window depicts Queen Victoria's coronation. Since AD 973 the Bible passage from 1 Kings 1:38–40 has been read at British coronations as the sovereign is anointed.

"Tree of life" decorated with rosettes and pendants

## SYMBOLS

### ANOINTING WITH OIL

**At Solomon's coronation, Zadok used oil to anoint the new king.**

Anointing oil was described in Exodus 30:22–33 and consisted of olive oil scented with spices – myrrh, cinnamon, calamus, and cassia. It was used by Moses to anoint Aaron as high priest (Leviticus 8:12) and by Samuel to anoint Saul and David as kings (1 Samuel 10:1; 16:13). The primary symbolism was of God's Spirit equipping the person for office. Those chosen to be a servant of God, who were to be channels

of his peace, were sometimes called "Anointed One". The term is especially used of Jesus the Messiah (Luke 4:18; Acts 4:26,27; 10:38).

Jesus' disciples anointed sick people with oil to heal them (Mark 6:13). The Early Church continued to anoint the sick (James 5:14), and the rite of marking someone with oil is still practised in many churches today.

**IVORY HORN FOR HOLDING OIL, 15TH CENTURY BC**

> " Zadok the priest **took the horn of oil** from the sacred tent and **anointed** Solomon. Then they **sounded the trumpet** and all the people shouted, 'Long live King Solomon!' "

**1 KINGS** 1:39

### SYMBOL OF AUTHORITY

Crowns symbolize legitimate authority but also reflect the transience of earthly power, passing from one monarch to the next. Solomon's father, David, conquered Rabah and "took the crown from their king's head, and it was placed on his own" (2 Samuel 12:30). The gold crown pictured here was buried with a nomadic princess in Afghanistan in the 1st century AD.

**AFTER** »

**The final wishes of King David concerned loyalty to God and the perpetuation of his dynasty.**

### SECURING THE FUTURE

David had reigned for 40 years and died "**at a good old age, having enjoyed long life, wealth, and honour**" (1 Chronicles 29:28). The dying king's final act was to issue words of advice to Solomon – **to be faithful to God and his covenant**. Without such fidelity, there could be no prosperity and no guarantee that David's dynasty would continue. The events of **Solomon's reign 170–78** » would prove David's words to be true: "The LORD highly exalted Solomon in the sight of all Israel and bestowed on him **royal splendour such as no king over Israel ever had before**" (1 Chronicles 29:25).

In response, Solomon stated: "If he shows himself to be worthy, not a hair of his head will fall to the ground; but if evil is found in him, he will die" (1:52). Adonijah came and bowed before Solomon, who sent him home.

### Solomon's reign secured

In his parting speech, David briefed Solomon on matters of state, advised him on the handling of certain people, but above all, he encouraged him to remain faithful to God, walking in God's ways and obeying God's laws and commandments.

Meanwhile, Adonijah persisted in his folly by sending Solomon's mother Bathsheba to speak to her son on his behalf, to ask that David's beautiful attendant, Abishag, be given to Adonijah as his wife. Had his request been granted, it would have put Adonijah in a position of great influence due to Abishag's access to the royal court. Solomon saw through Adonijah's appeal, exclaiming to his mother, "Why do you request Abishag the Shunammite for Adonijah? You might as well request the kingdom for him" (2:22). He swiftly had Adonijah executed.

Solomon took firm action to secure power. Other rebels were banished, killed, or sentenced to house arrest. The kingdom was firmly in Solomon's hands.

# The Wisdom of Solomon

*At the start of his reign, God offered to grant Solomon whatever he wanted. Solomon asked for wisdom to help him govern well. God duly granted this request, which was immediately put to the test.*

**W**HEN DAVID DIED and Solomon succeeded him as king, his first act was to call a great assembly of Israel's leaders at Gibeon. This place was chosen because the tent in which Moses had regularly consulted God and the old bronze altar that had stood in the forecourt of the Tabernacle were located there.

## BEFORE

**Solomon offered sacrifices at the shrine at Gibeon because the Temple had not yet been built in Jerusalem.**

### THE HOME OF THE TABERNACLE
After entering Canaan, **the Tabernacle ‹‹ 112–13** was first located at Gilgal, then Shiloh. Some parts of it, such as the bronze altar, were later moved to Gibeon, together with the **Tent of Meeting ‹‹ 110–11** in which Moses had consulted God.

It is unclear how much of the Tabernacle was at Gibeon. By David's time it may have been mostly worn out, or he may have erected the Tabernacle in Jerusalem.

**THE CITY OF GIBEON**

### A COMPASSIONATE VERDICT
At the centre of Pier Franceso Foschi's 15th-century *Judgment of Solomon* are a live baby and a baby whose death caused his mother to claim the living child as her own. Solomon's solution was clever and just.

During the gathering, Solomon offered a thousand burnt offerings on that same altar.

### God appears in Solomon's dream
In those days, God often communicated with the people he had chosen for special tasks through their dreams. Accordingly, at Gibeon God appeared to Solomon during the night in a dream and instructed him: "Ask for whatever you want me to give you" (1 Kings 3:5).

Solomon's answer was suitably statesmanlike. Thanking God for his kindness to David and humbly describing himself as inexperienced in how to govern such a large and great nation, Solomon only had one request: that God would provide him with the wisdom he needed for the responsibilities he had undertaken.

God was pleased with this answer. After all, Solomon could have asked for personal gain or glory, for wealth or victory in war. Instead he demonstrated the wisdom he claimed to lack by asking for "discernment in administering justice" (3:11). In return, God granted Solomon not only the wise and discerning heart he desired, but also wealth and honour that would have "no equal among kings" (3:13) in his lifetime.

### A demonstration of wisdom
The need for wisdom was tested immediately. Two prostitutes who lived in the same house were brought to the king, each having given birth and both claiming to be the mother of the same baby boy. They asked the king to determine

whose son he really was. No real evidence existed; it was simply one woman's word against the other.

Solomon demonstrated his shrewdness by suggesting that the child should be cut in half. He knew that the real mother would want the child's life to be saved, even if it meant that he was given to the other woman. Sure enough, the real mother revealed herself by giving up her rights to the baby and pleading instead that he be spared. Solomon judged in her favour and sent her home with the boy.

When the news of this case spread, the verdict of the public was that the king was indeed wise: God had surely answered his prayer and granted him wisdom.

Solomon had passed his first test. However, from the very beginning of Solomon's reign there was a hint that not everything was perfect. Solomon entered into an alliance with the pharaoh of Egypt and sealed it by marrying his daughter. By having foreign wives who worshipped other gods, he lit a fuse that was to ignite trouble later in his reign (see p.175).

**THE PROVERBS**
Proverbs, pictured here on a Hebrew scroll, is part of the books that make up Jewish wisdom literature. The authorship of this collection of proverbial sayings is traditionally assigned to Solomon.

**ANALYSIS**

### EVENTS AT GIBEON

The Gibeonites had been made to serve as woodcutters and water-carriers after they used a ruse to avoid Gibeon being destroyed (Joshua 9:3–27). Once David had secured his kingship by defeating Saul's supporters at the pool of Gibeon (2 Samuel 2:12–16), the Gibeonites were permitted to execute seven of Saul's descendants to avenge their treatment.

**THE POOL OF GIBEON**

## AFTER

**Solomon reorganized the government of the kingdom of Israel, but at a cost.**

### THE PRICE OF REFORM
Solomon proved to be an expert administrator. Having appointed a group of personal advisors to various government responsibilities, he **reorganized the country into 12 tax districts**, each administered by a governor (1 Kings 4:1–19). The changes were motivated in part by the need for huge amounts of food at Solomon's court.

Each of the 12 new districts was responsible for providing a month's supplies in turn (1 Kings 4:7). However, the new boundaries did not relate to **Joshua's settlement of the land ‹‹ 124–24** and rode roughshod over the ancient tribal structure of Israel.

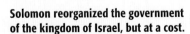

**BEFORE** «

David wanted to build a permanent home for God, but God had forbidden him to do so because of the blood shed in wars the king had waged. Therefore he prepared for the Temple to be built by his son.

**PLANNING A HOUSE OF GOD**

David made all the necessary arrangements for the construction of the Temple. He **moved the Ark of the Covenant to Jerusalem « 164–65**, purchased Araunah's threshing-floor (1 Chronicles 22), where the Temple was eventually built, began to put the finances aside, assembled a compulsory labour force, collected the building materials, and **gave his son instructions about the project**.

# Solomon's Temple

*One of Solomon's greatest achievements was the building of a magnificent Temple in Jerusalem, which housed the Ark of the Covenant and a massive bronze altar for sacrifice.*

G OD HAD PROMISED King David that his son Solomon could build a temple, so the new king made this task a priority at the start of his reign. It was an enormous project that took seven years to complete, although the building of Solomon's palace took 13 years. Solomon embarked on the undertaking with characteristic organization, forming a partnership with his father's old friend, King Hiram of Tyre.

### Supplies and workers

Hiram willingly agreed to supply the cedars, pines, and skilled carpenters and carvers needed to build the Temple, in return for food, olive oil, and a grant of territory. Solomon also conscripted 30,000 men to work on the Temple from his non-Israelite peoples, the descendants of the Hittites, Amorites, and others (2 Chronicles 8:7,8). The craftsmen prepared the timber and stone away from the construction site – "no hammer, chisel, or any other iron tool was heard at the temple site" (1 Kings

6:7). By building this holy place, Solomon would centralize Hebrew worship in Israel.

## The building

The central shrine of the Temple consisted of a massive oblong building, surrounded by side rooms on a number of levels, which in turn were surrounded by colonnaded cloisters. In front of the Temple was a courtyard. Two tall, decorated, and imposing pillars stood at the entrance, creating an appearance of grandeur.

Inside the Temple, there was a smaller inner sanctuary called the "Most Holy Place", in which the Ark of the Covenant, containing the tablets of the law of Moses, was kept. The Ark had lodged at Bethel,

Gilgal, and Shiloh, before David brought it to Jerusalem. A high point of the dedication ceremony of the Temple was the placement of the Ark in the Most Holy Place.

Everything in the Temple was decorated ornately, using the best available materials, such as gold and bronze. The altars, ritual baths, basins, and other furniture greatly surpassed the splendour of the items in the old Tabernacle.

The magnificence of the Temple was a reflection of the wealth Solomon accumulated as king. Reports of the lavish adornment support the claim that he was "greater in riches... than all the other kings of the earth" (1 Kings 10:23). His wealth came from taxes, tribute, commerce, and the many

### TRANSPORTING TIMBER
The 8th-century BC Khorsabad relief from the palace of the Assyrian ruler Sargon II shows Phoenician vessels carrying exports of cedar. This durable timber was highly prized in the ancient world and an essential material for the construction of the Temple.

gifts he received. Solomon's possessions included buildings, land, forests, horses, chariots, ships, and beautiful household objects, such as his gold and ivory throne.

## The dedication ceremony

When the building was completed, Solomon presided over a solemn dedication ceremony. This included a lengthy prayer, summarizing the need to observe God's covenant with care. It stated the perils for not doing so, and repeated God's promise to secure David's dynasty on the throne of Israel.

As the ceremony came to a climax, smoke filled the Temple – a sign of God's glory residing in this temple. Then the sacrifices began.

After 14 days the celebrations ended. The next day God appeared to Solomon and told him: "I have heard the prayer and plea made before me; I have consecrated this temple, which you have built, by putting my Name there for ever. My eyes and my heart will always be there" (1 Kings 9:3).

### HISTORY AND CULTURE

## THE "TRADERS IN PURPLE"

Famed in the ancient world for its control of a dye made from sea snails (used to colour royal clothing purple), Phoenicia was a major maritime trading nation situated on the coastal strip of northern Canaan, in modern-day Lebanon and Syria. Composed of various city-states, such as Tyre, Sidon, and the capital, Byblos, Phoenicia was at its most prosperous during Solomon's time, using galleys to transport timber, glass, and slaves in addition to the dye. Many of Phoenicia's art motifs, such as the sphinx, were derived from foreign cultures, and Solomon used its craftsmen and finishings for his Temple.

**8TH-CENTURY BC PHOENICIAN ART**

**AFTER** »

> " ...The **heavens**, even the highest heaven, **cannot contain you**. How **much less this temple I have built!** "
>
> **1 KINGS** 8:27

### SOLOMON'S TEMPLE
This coloured print from a copper engraving made in 1630 by Matthus Merian was inspired by the description of the Temple in 1 Kings 6. The Israelites had little experience of temple building, and the design of the structure owed much to Phoenician examples.

The Ark of the Covenant was Israel's most sacred object and it symbolized the nation's covenant with God.

#### ARK BROUGHT TO THE TEMPLE
A huge crowd gathered to **witness the Ark's procession to the newly built Temple**, where it was placed with great ceremony and animal sacrifices in the Most Holy Place. After this, Solomon dedicated it with a prayer of praise. What happened to the Ark of the Covenant afterwards is unknown, but it was probably lost or destroyed when the **Babylonians demolished the Temple 236–37 »** in 586 BC.

#### CHANGING FORTUNES
The Temple was rebuilt c.538 BC, desecrated by Epiphanes in 167 BC, **restored to glory by Herod the Great 382–83 »** in 20 BC, then finally destroyed by the Romans in AD 70.

**TRANSPORTING THE ARK**

**BEFORE**

In addition to the construction of the Temple and palace, Solomon developed trade to make Israel wealthier and more powerful.

**SOLOMON'S COMMERCIAL ACTIVITY**

Capitalizing on Egypt's weakness, Solomon **built a merchant navy** that developed the north–south trade route in the Red Sea. The Phoenician king, **Hiram of Tyre ‹‹ 172,** provided Solomon with sailors. The ships **exported smelted copper from southern Israel** and returned every three years with gold, ivory, silver, and apes and baboons.

**BAS-RELIEF OF PHOENICIAN TRADING VESSEL**

**ANALYSIS**

**WHY DID THE QUEEN VISIT?**

Ostensibly curious about accounts of Solomon's wisdom, the Queen of Sheba's visit was likely motivated by economic interests – she brought large quantities of gold, spices, and precious stones to present to the king, and already controlled existing trade routes between southern Arabia and Israel. As suggested by her gifts, much of Sheba's tax revenue came from incense trading (1 Kings 10:2,10 mention "spices", which would have included frankincense and myrrh), an activity threatened by the expansion of Israel's commercial interests.

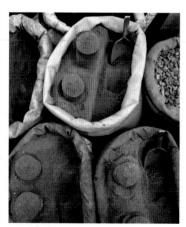

**TRADE IN SPICES WAS A LUCRATIVE BUSINESS**

# The Queen of Sheba

*The famous wealth and wisdom of Solomon provoked the Queen of Sheba's curiosity. She visited him and found his reputation justified. The visit also served their respective commercial interests.*

**S**OLOMON'S reputation as the fount of godly wisdom soon spread throughout the region. The Queen of Sheba, most likely a territory in southwest Arabia, decided to make a journey of some 1,900km (1,200 miles) to Jerusalem to see Solomon in person. According to 1 Kings 10:1, she wanted to test his wisdom by posing difficult problems for him to solve, but the Queen's lavish gifts were also intended to impress.

### The Queen arrives

The Queen's immense delegation arrived with a lengthy caravan of camels, all weighed down by spectacular gifts from her kingdom of spices, gold, and precious stones, which she presented to Solomon. The questions that the Queen of Sheba posed did not prove difficult for Solomon – nothing was too complex for him to explain to her, so she was quickly impressed by his intellect. The Queen was also astounded by what she saw of Solomon's royal court. His opulent palace, the lavish provisions on his table, the number of his servants, the uniforms they wore, and the number of sacrifices they offered overwhelmed her.

### Praise for Solomon

The Queen of Sheba's verdict was that the reality of Solomon's wisdom and his wealth far exceeded the rumours she had

> " The **report I heard** in my own country **about your achievements and your wisdom is true.**"
>
> **1 KINGS** 10:6

### DESERT LANDSCAPE
This rocky formation forms part of a mountain range near Marib in Yemen, which is one of several possible locations for the biblical kingdom of Sheba, along with Eritrea and Ethiopia.

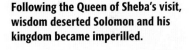

heard in her own country. She said that she would not have believed it possible if she had not seen it with her own eyes. Solomon and his people, she concluded, must be very happy. However, the Queen attributed his prosperity not to Solomon's own skills, but to God's love for his people and his delight in Solomon. Her complimentary words reminded Solomon that the king's task was "to maintain justice and righteousness" (1 Kings 10:9). The Queen then presented Solomon with her magnificent gifts: "120 talents [about 4 tons] of gold, large quantities of spices, and precious stones" (1 Kings 10:10). Never again, it was written, were so many spices brought in as those the Queen of Sheba gave to King Solomon. In return, Solomon gave her "all she desired and asked for, besides what he had given her out of his royal bounty" (1 Kings 10:13), for his generosity outdid hers. Then the Queen of Sheba returned to her own country.

### Trade and simmering tension
The Queen's gift of gold was generous, but it was less than a fifth of what Solomon received each year in revenues from the governors of his territories in Israel, and from merchants, traders, and the kings of Arabia. With this precious hoard of gold, Solomon made hundreds of decorative shields for his palace, goblets, household articles, and a throne like of which had never "been made for any other kingdom" (1 Kings 10:20).

### Solomon's wealth
Rulers came from near and far to visit the king: "All the kings of the earth sought audience with Solomon to hear the wisdom God had put in his heart" (2 Chronicles 9:23). His visitors presented him with precious metals, robes, weapons, spices, and horses and mules, and Solomon's wealth grew year upon year. His reign saw such prosperity that "silver [became] as common in Jerusalem as stones, and cedar as plentiful as sycamore-fig trees" (2 Chronicles 9:27).

### SOLOMON THE TRADER
This map shows the principal trade routes in and out of Solomon's kingdom. As well as trade with his neighbours, the Bible credits Solomon with establishing trade relations with Chittim (the "west"), and Ophir (possibly the African coast of the Red Sea).

### DESERT TRAIN
Trains, or caravans, of camels – shown here in the Sahara, Morocco – have long been used as transport across deserts. The Queen of Sheba arrived with a "great caravan – with camels carrying spices" (1 Kings 10:2).

**AFTER** »

Following the Queen of Sheba's visit, wisdom deserted Solomon and his kingdom became imperilled.

#### THE SEEDS OF REBELLION
God had warned the Israelites not to marry foreign women "because they will surely turn your hearts after their gods" (1 Kings 11:2). Solomon's devotion to his wives **duly led him astray** (1 Kings 11) and compromised his devotion to God.

This provoked God's anger. When Solomon refused to repent, God fomented trouble using men such as Hadad and **Jeroboam 194 »**. Although the kingdom held together during Solomon's reign, this folly contributed to the **break-up of his kingdom 192–93 »** immediately after his death.

#### SOLOMON AND JEROBOAM

HISTORY AND CULTURE

# Trade and Commerce

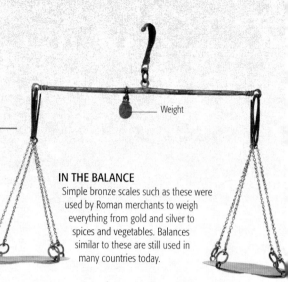

"The LORD **detests dishonest scales** but **accurate weights** find **favour** with him." PROVERBS 11:1

**IN THE BALANCE**
Simple bronze scales such as these were used by Roman merchants to weigh everything from gold and silver to spices and vegetables. Balances similar to these are still used in many countries today.

O nce a network of trading towns began to develop in the Mesopotamian region (see pp.214–15) in the 4th millennium BC, markets became highly significant, starting at the local level. The markets were generally located by town gates and became the hub of village life. Here farmers sold and bartered their produce, such as grain and olive oil, and craftsmen such as potters and smiths also sold their wares.

Gradually, foreign merchants began to appear with more exotic goods: spices from the Indus region in the east, or glass jugs from Phoenicia to the west. By New Testament times, markets were dotted across the city of Jerusalem, and temple authorities appointed market inspectors to ensure that weighing scales were accurate and business deals were fair – just as Jewish Law required.

**OLD MARKETPLACE**
Street traders offer their wares at the market at Damascus Gate in the Old City of Jerusalem.

## LUXURY GOODS

Merchants from the Phoenician port of Tyre (see p.168) and the inland city of Babylon (see p.238) dominated international trade in Old Testament times. However, the major trade routes, which ran down the Mediterranean coast and east of the River Jordan, bypassed the capitals of what would become the kingdoms of Israel and Judah, so international trade did not figure highly in ancient Jewish life.

This situation began to change in the reign of King Solomon, for several reasons: Israel's expanded territory now included key trade routes; crafts were developing that required imported raw materials; and kings and their entourages desired luxury goods. The Bible describes how Solomon

**PEACOCK FEATHER**
The growth of wealthy upper classes fuelled a desire for more and more exotic goods, such as colourful peacock feathers.

established a trading fleet manned by Phoenicians, which brought back exotic goods such as gold, silver, precious stones, ivory, peacocks, and apes (1 Kings 10:22). By land, Solomon's traders imported tin, lead, silver, timber, linen, spices, and gold. Israel slowly began to export its own products, including wheat, honey, oil, wine, and balma.

By the New Testament period, Rome had become the commercial centre of the Mediterranean, and

**SAFFRON STAMENS**
Derived from the saffron crocus, this costly spice was used in cooking, in medicine, and as a fabric dye.

**PHOENICIAN GLASS**
Highly prized for their beauty, Phoenician glass vessels were exported far and wide by Tyrian merchants.

most leading merchants were Roman. Galilee's trade developed and it became more prosperous – partly due to the fishing industry that had sprung up around the Sea of Galilee, and partly because of the main north–south trade route that cut through the region.

## TRADE AND TAXES

In Israelite society, the tithe – a 10 per cent income tax – was an amount paid to support the priests and the Temple. With the rise of the monarchy, however, taxes

**TAX** Tax collectors were especially despised by the Israelites – they were viewed with suspicion and were also seen as collaborators with Rome.

were imposed by Israel's kings, just as Samuel had warned (1 Samuel 8:11–17), to pay for their lavish lifestyles (1 Kings 4:22–28). This proved to be a significant factor in the ultimate division of the kingdom into Israel and Judah (see pp.194–95).

In New Testament times, Israelites had to pay taxes to Rome or, for those in the client kingdom of Judea, to Herod. Besides a land tax (a percentage of the harvest) and a periodic housing tax, tolls and customs duties were also charged on goods. These were

collected through tax farming: the selling to the highest bidder of the right to collect taxes and duties in a particular district. The tax farmer, supported by Roman soldiers, then charged highly inflated rates to make a profit.

Brass dupondius, worth 2 asses

Gold aureus, worth 25 silver denarii

Bronze as

Brass sestertius, worth 4 asses

Silver denarius, worth 16 asses

**COMMON CURRENCY**
Although most cultures had their own money, Roman coinage was the official currency of the Empire, which made trade between its provinces much easier.

## CARAVANS

International traders travelled overland in caravans (convoys of camels and donkeys) that passed through Israel from all directions (see p.175). Joseph was sold by his brothers to a caravan of passing Midianite traders on their way to Egypt (Genesis 37:28), and when the Queen of Sheba visited King Solomon from Arabia,

she was accompanied by a huge caravan. Caravans were usually quite large (300 donkeys were not uncommon) and they often had guards for protection against bandits and thieves.

Camels were favoured by merchants when crossing deserts because of the animal's ability to cope with desert life. Its nostrils close to thin slits to keep out sand, while long eyelashes protect its eyes, and its leathery tongue and mouth allow it to eat whatever scrub and vegetation manage to grow in such harsh conditions. In addition, the camel was a valuable source of milk and meat.

**BEAST OF BURDEN**
A descendant of the wild ass, the donkey was domesticated in the Middle East before 3,000 BC. This Roman bronze shows a braying donkey with panniers.

---

## MODES OF TRANSPORT

### PACK ANIMALS
Families that could afford them had an ass or donkey as a pack animal. Caravans used both donkeys and camels; the latter could carry 200kg (440lb) and go for days without water.

### RIDING
The donkey and ass were the most common beasts for riding. Horses began to be used for riding from the 9th century BC. Roman messengers rode horses to carry despatches; milestones every 1,000 paces told them where they were on their journey, and inns were built at intervals of a day's riding.

### WHEELED VEHICLES
In early times, wheeled transport was mostly limited to simple carts for heavy goods and crops, pulled by oxen or donkeys. Later, the Egyptians, Assyrians, and Israelites made use of horse-drawn chariots (see p.219).

### SAILING
Early Egyptian boats were made from reeds, later ones from wood. Phoenician boats had cedar masts, oak oars, cypress decks, and linen sails. By Roman times, large grain ships, up to 55m (180ft) long, also transported up to 300 passengers.

KING OF ISRAEL Born c.1011 BC Died c.931 BC

# Solomon

> ## "**And Solomon** ruled over all the kingdoms from the River Euphrates to the land of the **Philistines,** as far as the **border of Egypt.**"
> 1 KINGS 4:21

**K**ING DAVID had several sons, but Solomon was to become his chosen heir and successor. David had an adulterous affair with a woman named Bathsheba, and she became pregnant (see pp.166–67). His sin was compounded by the fact that his troops, including Bathsheba's husband, Uriah, were at war. David tried to engineer things so that Uriah would think he was the father of the child, but when this failed, David arranged for Uriah to be killed in battle.

### Solomon's birth

Soon afterwards, the prophet Nathan confronted King David with his sin and told him that the boy he was expecting with Bathsheba would not live. Although David grieved and prayed for his son, who the Bible does not name, the infant did not survive beyond seven days.

David then had another son by Bathsheba, called Solomon. This child was loved by God and given a second name, Jedidiah, as instructed by God through Nathan the prophet (2 Samuel 12:25). Although Solomon was not his oldest son, David designated him as the heir to the throne.

**SOLOMON THE WISE**
This regal, wise-looking Solomon was imagined by Justus van Ghent in c.1474. "Solomon's wisdom was greater than the wisdom of all the people of the East, and greater than all the wisdom of Egypt" (1 Kings 4:30).

---

**ANALYSIS**

### A LITERARY LEGACY

Solomon was a patron of Israel's poetry, songs, philosophy, and pragmatic wisdom. Several Old Testament books are associated with him, including Psalms 72 and 127, Ecclesiastes (see 1:1), the Song of Songs, and Proverbs, which he edited into a single work, including two collections of his own sayings (Proverbs 10:1–22 and Proverbs 25).

David's first son, Absalom, had been killed when he rebelled against his father (see p.167). That left Adonijah as the oldest surviving son, who contested Solomon's accession (see pp.168–69). The attempted coup failed and David instructed his loyal advisors to anoint Solomon as king and rally the populace to the cause.

Solomon's reign started well. He recognized his own youthful inexperience and asked God for the wisdom "to distinguish between right and wrong" (1 Kings 3:9). In the early years, it seemed that this request had been granted.

## Solomon's achievements

Solomon succeeded in making Israel a united, prosperous, and influential kingdom, and the achievements of his reign were immense. He built a magnificent Temple and established a strong economy, opening up Israel to international trade, thanks to his partnership with King Hiram of Tyre. Solomon's personal wealth grew and his lifestyle became increasingly ostentatious. He also reorganized the administration of Israel and strengthened the nation's military defences, built a large army, and fortified strategically located cities on the country's borders.

Solomon is associated with more than 3,000 wise sayings (see panel, far left) and acquired an international reputation for wisdom. This made his opinion sought after by other leaders, such as the Queen of Sheba.

## Costs of the reign

However, Solomon's achievements were not without cost. His building projects meant that he imposed heavy taxes on his people and conscripted thousands into his labour force. While he primarily enlisted Canaan's former tribal inhabitants, the Israelites feared that Solomon was returning them

**THE DREAM OF SOLOMON**
A 1405 edition of Jerome's Latin translation of the Bible – known as the Vulgate – depicts God, in the form of an angel, appearing to Solomon in a dream early in his reign.

> " **God gave Solomon wisdom** and very great insight…"
>
> 1 KINGS 4:29

to the slavery they had previously experienced in Egypt. Even greater damage was caused by Solomon's marriages to numerous foreign wives, who introduced their native gods to Israel. After many years of commitment to God, Solomon's wives "turned his heart after other gods" (1 Kings 11:4). He was no longer as fully devoted to God as he once had been.

In spite of God warning Solomon to mend his ways, he remained stubborn. So the latter part of his reign was blighted by rebellions within. Solomon died after reigning for 40 years.

## Solomon's legacy

The most notable of a number of rebels was Jeroboam who, after Solomon's death, led ten of the 12 tribes of Israel to break away from the other two. The united kingdom thus came to an end and the country was now split into two kingdoms: Israel in the north, with its capital in Samaria, and Judah in the south, with its capital in Jerusalem. The unity, prosperity, and faithfulness to God that had been enjoyed during the reigns of kings David and Solomon were never to be recaptured.

**SOLOMON'S PILLARS**
The so-called "pillars" are naturally eroded formations of red sandstone, located in the Timna Valley, southern Israel, where there are copper mines some 6,000 years old. The remains of a temple erected by copper miners from ancient Egypt during the reign of Rameses III can still be seen.

# WISDOM AND PRAISE

"For the LORD gives wisdom; from his mouth come knowledge and understanding."

**S**ANDWICHED BETWEEN THE BOOKS that tell of the history of Israel and the patriarchs, and those that describe the writings of the prophets is a collection of five books – Job, Psalms, Proverbs, Ecclesiastes, and Song of Songs – that are known as the wisdom literature. The books focus in different ways on everyday life and ordinary human experience. Their varied styles range from dialogue and philosophic argument, to poetry, songs for use in corporate worship, and pithy sayings. However, they have in common two main, interweaving themes – wisdom and praise.

Wisdom is presented in the five books as the application of the belief in God to daily life. The books teach that well-being in life begins with reverence for God and the development of a God-centred worldview. Jewish wisdom teaching is particularly associated with King Solomon, but it also draws on sources outside the Jewish tradition; the tradition of spiritual teaching through wise sayings was widespread in the ancient Near East. Proverbs 22:17–24 is similar to ancient Egypt's *The Wisdom of Amenemope*, for instance.

In many cases, the experience of life evokes praise – the second central theme. In the light of God's creation and his unfailing love and faithfulness, the appropriate response is to sing and pray with gratitude and worship, using words such as those of the Psalms.

### THE INDIVIDUAL BOOKS
The book of Job addresses suffering. The central character, Job, has led a righteous life but even so, suffers immensely, which calls into question orthodox teaching that suffering is punishment for sin. Three "friends" try to explain his plight, until God reveals himself and shows how ignorant they are about divine plans and purposes.

The book of Psalms is a collection of poetry whose main theme is praise to God, but it also reflects the range of both Israel's national experience and individual experience. The Psalms formed an important part of Israel's worship, both at the Tabernacle and in the later Temples in Jerusalem.

The book of Proverbs is a compilation of wise sayings, especially those attributed to King Solomon, in concise maxims covering issues of everyday living. Above all, Proverbs encourages readers to trust in God.

Ecclesiastes muses on life's enigmas and the way in which meaning and satisfaction in life seem elusive. Even though it never clearly resolves all of the puzzles it poses, the book rejects easy answers and suggests that the solution lies in remembering one's creator.

Song of Songs is a series of intense poems, celebrating human love, in the form of an unrestrained conversation between lovers. It is often interpreted as an allegory of the relationship between God and his people.

Despite their varied approaches, the books deal with the questions of how to live wisely in the world when confronted by the good, the bad, and the routine.

# Worship in Israel

*In Israel's early history there were no set rituals or fixed places for worship, since there was no divide between sacred and secular in their world view. It was only later that specific places – first the Tabernacle, then the Temple – acquired special significance.*

**I**NFORMAL WORSHIP may well have continued had the Israelites, afraid after God's appearance on Mount Sinai, not begged him to speak in future through an intermediary (Exodus 20:18,19). God appointed priests to offer sacrifices on their behalf at his appointed sanctuary.

## Tabernacle and Temple worship

Israel's first specified place of worship was the Tabernacle (see pp.112–13), inside which stood the Ark of the Covenant that symbolized God's presence among them. Moses said it was to be erected at "the place the LORD your God will choose" (Deuteronomy 12:5), and could be mobile to suit the movements of the Israelites. Only there should the Israelites present their offerings, sacrifices, and gifts, rather than at any of the local sanctuaries of the existing Canaanite inhabitants of the Promised Land. It was obligatory for all Jewish men to visit the Tabernacle three times a year, at

PATRIARCHAL WORSHIP
Abraham – depicted in this 15th-century stained glass window from Great Malvern Priory, UK – worshipped God in a variety of places, since Tabernacle worship had not been established.

the festivals of Unleavened Bread, Pentecost, and Tabernacles (Deuteronomy 16:16).

When David brought the Ark to Jerusalem (see pp.164–65), he wanted to build a temple to house it, but God would not let him do so. It fell to his son

PASSOVER PRAYERS
Descendants of the Levites, God's appointed priests for the people of Israel, cover themselves with prayer shawls as they perform the priestly blessing during Passover festivities at the Western Wall, Jerusalem.

# "Who may ascend the hill of the LORD?... The one who has clean hands and a pure heart."

**PSALM** 24:3,4

### FESTIVAL OFFERING
God instructed Moses that the people of Israel should celebrate the festival of the Firstfruits, in which a priest was to wave "a sheaf of the first grain you harvest... on the day after the Sabbath" before the Lord (Leviticus 23:10,11).

Solomon to build the Temple (see pp.172–73), a magnificent building that became a focal point of worship in Israel. Its importance to the Israelites is reflected in its destruction by Babylon in 587 BC (see pp.236–37) and in its later reconstruction by the returning exiles (see pp.252–53). It was completely rebuilt on a far grander scale by King Herod in the 1st century BC, and by New Testament times (see pp.382–83) it lay at the very heart of Jewish religious life and worship, causing Jerusalem to be packed whenever the great festivals were celebrated.

In keeping with God's intolerance of idol worship, neither the Tabernacle nor the Temple had any idols or statues, for these were

### PILGRIMAGE TO JERUSALEM
By the time of Jesus, the Temple in Jerusalem was an important site of pilgrimage for Jews – particularly during the festivals of Passover, Pentecost, and Tabernacles – and its remains are the focus of pilgrimage today.

forbidden in the Jewish Law (for example, see Exodus 20:1–4).

### Synagogue worship
During the exile, Israel developed new patterns of worship. It was here that synagogues (Greek for "gathering") originated. They were formerly just open-air meetings (see Psalm 137:1–3), but gradually simple buildings developed. There were no sacrifices, for these could only be offered in the Temple, which now lay in ruins. Rather the Jews focused on reading the Law, sermons, and prayer. Synagogues continued after the return from exile and the rebuilding of the Temple, and by New Testament times every town had its own

### TABERNACLE WORSHIP
The Tabernacle – as depicted in this wall painting dating from c.AD 245 from a synagogue in Dura Europos, modern-day Syria – was central to worship in Israel before the Temple was built in Jerusalem.

synagogue. These became the focal point of local life, and increasingly so after the final destruction of the Jerusalem Temple by Rome in AD 70. Synagogues remain the focal point of Jewish community life today.

### Festivals and holy days
Honouring special days was a key part of Israelite worship. The weekly Sabbath (see p.319) was initially a day of rest, rather than a day of worship, but eventually became a day for visiting the synagogue too. It marked Israel out, for while other nations had annual festivals, only Israel had a weekly Sabbath.

Many of the annual festivals (see panel, left) had their origins in the Law. However, two developed much later – *Purim* (see p.257), during the exile, and *Hanukkah*, during the Maccabean revolt.

Fasting days – abstaining from food (and, exceptionally, from water) to seek God in prayer – were voluntary. The Law prescribed only one compulsory fast a year, on the Day of Atonement. Other fasts were introduced in later times.

### Expressions of worship
Worship was generally a joyful affair, such as when Miriam led the women of Israel in rejoicing "with tambourines and dancing" (Exodus 15:20), or when King David accompanied the Ark of

the Covenant, "leaping and dancing before the LORD" (2 Samuel 6:16). Solomon appointed musicians and choirs for the Temple's dedication (2 Chronicles 5:12–13).

For Israelites, the most common form of worship happened at home. Prayer (see p.318) was offered at meal times, but also in the morning, afternoon, and evening. This was also a means for parents to pass on Israel's sacred history to their children (Deuteronomy 6:4–25), a practice that is still followed today.

"Come, let us bow down in worship, let us kneel before the LORD our Maker."

**PSALM** 95:6

### READING THE TORAH
Festival and everyday worship still involves reading the Torah – such as the book of Esther during the *Purim* festival, seen here being read by a rabbi at the Synagogue of the Premishlan congregation, Israel.

# The Psalms

*The Psalms are a collection of 150 songs, of various lengths and styles, composed by multiple authors. They served as a major resource for Israel's worship in the Temple. While many of the Psalms focus on praising God, they cover the whole range of life's experiences and emotions.*

**T**HE TRADITION of composing songs to express thanks or petitions to God has its origin in the early days of Israel. Songs were written to celebrate victories in battle, such as the songs of Moses and Miriam in Exodus 15 (see pp.104–05) and the song of Deborah in Judges 5. The book of Numbers records a song of praise sung by the Hebrews to thank God for providing water for them at the well of Beer in Moab (Numbers 21:16–18).

### Who wrote the Psalms?

The word "psalm" comes from *psalmoi* – the term used in the Greek translation of the Hebrew Old Testament – meaning "a song to be sung". Before the Psalms were collected together, tradition has it that David (see pp.152–53) composed songs from his own experience as a fugitive and a king. In 1 Chronicles 16, he is said to have appointed people to praise God in words that are repeated in the Bible in Psalms 96, 105, and 106, including "Give thanks to the Lord, for he is good; his love endures forever" (106:1), a recurring phrase within the Psalms (such as 100, 107, and 118). The book of Psalms as we know it was composed over many years and edited into five sections, probably after Israel's return from exile in Babylon. Seventy-three psalms, including Psalms 51–65, carry the words "of David", although this denotes a broad association with King David rather than direct authorship. Similarly, Asaph, master of music

## BOOK OF PRAISE

Psalters, books containing the text of the Psalms along with musical notation and directions, are often beautifully decorated. The Mainz Psalter shown here (*c.*1457) was one of Europe's first printed books.

The Mainz Psalter was printed with inks on vellum, using Gutenberg's printing press

Illuminated initials appear throughout the Psalters

Accompanying music is interspersed with the text of the Psalms

at the dedication of Solomon's Temple, is credited with 12 Psalms, while Psalms 72 and 127 are attributed to King Solomon himself. The "Sons of Korah", a musical guild among the Levite Temple servants, are credited with 11 amongst Psalms 42–59. Many Psalms do not carry an attribution.

**MULTIPLE TRANSLATIONS**
Due to their importance for use in Christian worship, the Psalms – such as this Russian Orthodox version in Cyrillic script from c.AD 1020 – were amongst the first Scriptures to be translated.

## Psalms of praise

Praise and trust in God are the underlying themes of the Psalms. They underpin the two major types of Psalm: praise and petition. Psalms of praise celebrate God's creation, rule, salvation, righteousness, and his justice, which is exercized on behalf of the powerless. Examples include Psalm 23: "The LORD is my Shepherd, I lack nothing" (23:1) and Psalm 46: "God is our refuge and strength, an ever-present help

in trouble" (46:1). They also often retell Israel's story as an incentive to praise.

God's faithfulness in continuing to love Israel, as he promised in his covenant, is the basis for praise. Psalm 136 says give thanks… "to him who led his people through the wilderness; His love endures for ever" (136:16). These themes sometimes merge with a celebration of David's royal dynasty, as in Psalm 2: "You kings, be wise… Serve the LORD with fear and celebrate his rule with trembling" (2:10,11).

## Psalms of petition

Psalms of petition voice the need for help in times of distress, suffering, or failure, whether on a national or personal level, such as Psalm 121: "I lift up my eyes to the mountains – where does my help come from?" (121:1). Several involve confession of sin and seeking forgiveness, such as Psalm 51: "Against you, you only, have I sinned… Create in me a pure heart, O God" (51:4,10). Some cry out for God to act in the face of despair and injustice, while others reflect more meditatively on the wisdom of God's law and how humans can live wisely, or simply speak in reverence and awe, "You have searched me, LORD, and you know me… If I rise on the wings of the dawn, if I settle on the far side of the sea, even there your hand will guide me, your right hand will hold me fast" (139:1,9,10).

## How were the Psalms used?

Psalms were generally sung as part of worship, either by a choir or by the congregation. Psalms 24, 47, and 110, which are royal Psalms, were sung at processions and the king's coronation. Psalms 113–118 are associated with Passover. Psalms 120–134 were sung by pilgrims "going up" to the Feast of

Tabernacles in Jerusalem, so are called "Songs of Ascent". Many of the Psalms invite people to "Sing to the Lord" (96:1). Fifty-five are addressed to "the Director of Music" and others contain musical directions, such as a melody.

The Psalms mention 20 musical instruments – the last one names seven and finishes with a fitting conclusion: "Let everything that has breath praise the Lord" (150:6).

Some Psalms have headings that use literary or musical terms. *Miktam* (Psalm 16) is thought to be a silent prayer; a *maskil* (Psalm 32) is thought to be an artistic song; *al'gittith* (Psalm 81) is a musical instrument, while *selah* (Psalm 3) means "reflect on this".

### KEY PSALMS

| | |
|---|---|
| Anger: | 69, 94, 109 |
| Anxiety: | 3, 91, 94 |
| Bereavement: | 23, 30, 68 |
| Confession of sin: | 32, 51, 103 |
| Envy: | 37, 73, 131 |
| Joy: | 95, 100, 145 |
| Loneliness: | 38, 42, 121, 139 |
| Old Age: | 71, 91 |
| Sickness: | 22, 38 |
| Stress: | 46; 62 |
| Thanksgiving: | 66, 92, 103, 118 |
| Trust in God: | 40; 62; 146 |

> **"** I will **sing the LORD's praise,** for he has been **good to me. "**
>
> **PSALM** 13:6

### LITERARY TECHNIQUES

The Psalms use poetic techniques in their composition. Parallelism, where the second line repeats the first line, or reinforces it with a contrast, is the most common technique (see Psalm 1). Imagery is commonly used, where words are chosen to employ powerful metaphors that convey meaning, such as "The LORD is my rock, my fortress and my deliverer" (18:1). Puns are also common, although they are often lost in English translations. For example, the Hebrew verbs "turn back" and "put to shame" in Psalm 6:10 use the same letters in reverse: "sh-o-b" and "b-o-sh". Alphabetical acrostics (where each paragraph begins with the next letter of the Hebrew alphabet) include Psalms 9, 37, and 119. Some Psalms include refrains that invite the congregation to respond, as in Psalm 136.

**DAVID THE PSALMIST**
The tradition of composing Psalms for use in worship is attributed to King David, pictured here kneeling in praise outside the walls of Jerusalem in the *Book of Hours of Louis of Orléans*, c.1490.

**SINGING THE PSALMS**
Psalms have been used in Christian worship – such as the Vespers evening prayer service pictured here at Newark Abbey, USA – since the Early Church (see Ephesians 5:19).

## HISTORY AND CULTURE

# Writing and Language

"Take a **scroll** and **write** on it **all the words** I have spoken to you **concerning Israel**…" JEREMIAH 36:2

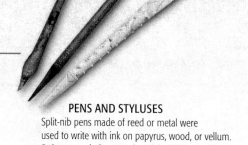

**PENS AND STYLUSES**
Split-nib pens made of reed or metal were used to write with ink on papyrus, wood, or vellum. Styluses, made from reed, metal, or ivory, had a pointed tip for writing on wax tablets. Some had a spatula end for smoothing the wax to erase mistakes.

**HEBREW SCRIPT**
A Yemenite scribe repairs an old Torah scroll. Only the hides of kosher animals are permitted in the manufacture of the parchment used for Torah scrolls, *Tefilin*, and *Mezuzahs*.

T he symbolic representation of language, writing first emerged in the 4th millennium BC. It is believed to have developed independently in five different areas of the world: Mesopotamia, Egypt, India, China, and Mesoamerica.

The Bible contains many references to writing, some from a very early period. For example, Moses, who was raised as the Pharaoh's scribe and was therefore well educated, is said to have written down the words of the covenant (see p.106) and other documents (Exodus 17:14, 24:4), and to have created a written record of the Israelites' journeys (Numbers 33:2). Joshua wrote a copy of the Ten Commandments on stones (Joshua 8:32) and part of the "Book of the Law of God" (Joshua 24:26). Samuel, too, is reported to have written a charter of kingship on a scroll (1 Samuel 10:25), and David wrote letters (2 Samuel 11:14) and kept records (2 Chronicles 35:4). The prophets kept records of their visions and prophecies (Isaiah 8:1; Jeremiah 30:2).

## CUNEIFORM

The first form of writing used pictures to communicate meaning. Around 3300 BC the Sumerians of Mesopotamia (see p. 244) developed writing in order to keep economic records, and they used pictures to symbolize the words that the scribes needed to represent. But the imperative for speed and

**TEMPLE RECORD**
This clay tablet was written in a temple in 3100–2900 BC. The script is proto-cuneiform – an early, pictorial stage of Mesopotamian writing.

precision meant that the pictorial symbols became less useful. By 2400 BC, the Sumerians had created cuneiform, a series of wedge-shaped lines formed by pressing a stylus into soft clay. Later forms of cuneiform used signs to represent not just words but syllables. Cuneiform was adopted by the Akkadians, who spread it across their empire.

## HIEROGLYPHICS

In Egypt (see pp. 84–85), a different system of writing developed from around 3200 BC: hieroglyphics ("sacred writing"). This involved pictographs that were initially direct representations of objects, but gradually came to express sounds, usually syllables. Hieroglyphs were in turn adapted into hieratic script, a cursive method of writing that used simpler symbols. By the 7th century BC, this had been transformed into demotic ("popular") script, an even more abbreviated form, which was used until the 4th century AD.

**EGYPTIAN HIEROGLYPHS**
When reading hieroglyphs the reader starts at the top on the side towards which the signs face, in this case left.

## HEBREW

The chief language of the Old Testament was Hebrew (apart from some small sections of Ezra, Daniel, and Jeremiah, relating to the exile, which were written in Aramaic). Hebrew is a Northwestern Semitic language; the word "Semitic" is thought to be derived from Shem, the name of Noah's eldest son. It probably developed from the ancient Canaanite language. The first record of the term "Hebrew" does not occur until the book of Jonah, dated to around the 4th century BC. So Abraham would not have spoken "Hebrew", but rather some form of Sumerian or Akkadian. Later Patriarchs probably spoke the Canaanite language.

## ARAMAIC

By New testament times, Jews were speaking Aramaic – a language that shares its roots with

Papyrus sheet

Aramaic script

**FREED SLAVES**
According to this document from Elephantine, Egypt, two slaves were granted their freedom on 3 July 449 BC.

Hebrew. Aramaic had become the language of trade in the ancient Near East in the 9th and 8th centuries BC. Jews adopted it during their exile in Babylon, and when they returned home few understood the Hebrew of their Scriptures (Nehemiah 8:8).

## GREEK

Although Jesus and his disciples spoke Aramaic, they probably also spoke some Greek, which was quite widespread. Greek had become the new international language of the Mediterranean world, as a result of Alexander the Great's conquests in the 4th century BC (see pp.264–65). It remained the chief language of the eastern Roman Empire until the Empire fell.

The New Testament was largely written in *Koine* (common) Greek, which was widely used from c.300 BC to AD 300.

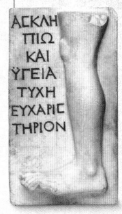

**GIVING THANKS**
This marble relief bears an inscription to Asclepius, the Greek god of medicine and healing, presumably in thanks for a mended leg or foot.

## ALPHABETS

In alphabetic scripts, each letter represents a single consonant or a vowel. The earliest alphabets, called Abjads, had sounds representing consonants but no vowels. They first appeared around the 18th century BC and developed over the next 400 years. Far fewer symbols are needed in alphabetic writing – usually around 26 – and this gradually led to cuneiform's decline in the 2nd century AD.

In Syria and Canaan alphabet-based Aramaic prevailed, along with Ugaritic and Phoenician. Greeks adopted the Phoenician alphabet and standardized their writing to read left to right, reversing usual Semitic practice (Hebrew is written right to left). The Romans then used this Greek alphabet, with some adaptations, to produce the Western European script used today.

## WRITING MATERIALS

Writers in biblical times used a wide range of writing materials to record events. Stone was used for monuments or for inscriptions that were intended to last, such as the Bible's famous stone tablets on which Moses wrote the Ten Commandments. Sometimes the stone would be coated with plaster, then inscribed with a stylus rather than being carved with a chisel.

**SCHOOLBOY'S WRITING SET**
These Roman writing utensils from the 1st century BC may have been used by a schoolchild. Classical Latin developed in the late Republic and early years of the Empire.

Wooden tablets were coated with soft wax that could be written on with a stylus. The writing could be erased so that the tablets could be re-used again and again. Wet clay tablets were engraved with a stylus or reed. When baked, the tablets became rock hard and the writing was preserved.

Stylus

Ink pot

Ostraca are fragments of pottery that have been recycled and inscribed with a metal stylus or written on in ink. They were often used for writing notes or short letters, and thousands have been found at archaeological digs.

Papyrus – the nearest thing to paper in the ancient world – was made by taking the pith of the papyrus reed, cutting it into strips, arranging them in two layers, one horizontal and one vertical, then pressing them into sheets. It was popular because of its smooth surface. Vellum or parchment is a thin material made from calfskin, sheepskin or goatskin. It was written on with a pen and ink. The Hebrew Scriptures were recorded in this way.

The book of Job is undated and no author is named, but clues in the text point to the time of the patriarchs being its likely setting, some 20 centuries BC.

**DATING EVIDENCE**

The dating of the book to the **patriarchal age « 46–47** is suggested by Job offering his own sacrifices, as the patriarchs did prior to Israel's developed sacrificial system. In addition, the pastoral lifestyle of Job and his family, and names such as "the land of Uz" and "the Chaldeans" fit that period. The idea of Satan entering God's heavenly court also belongs to the early patriarchal period.

**PEOPLE**

## SATAN

The name Satan means "adversary". His role is generally to oppose God and specifically to accuse people before God and tempt them to do wrong, as he does to both Job and David (1 Chronicles 21:1). Satan is one of a number of usually unseen evil powers that are mentioned in the Old Testament. These include the serpent in Eden and the dragon-like Leviathan mentioned by Job. Satan is part of an evil alliance that includes demons, evil spirits, idols, and false gods, and eventually he is presented as the head of this hierarchy. Isaiah 14:12–15 suggests that Satan may have been a fallen angel.

**SATAN, FRENCH MANUSCRIPT,** *c.*1450–70

**IN THE MIDST OF SUFFERING**
This illustration, from a mid-15th century Book of Hours, depicts Job in the depths of despair, being comforted by friends. They suggest that he must have sinned to have brought such woe upon himself.

# The Story of Job

*Job was a righteous man, who suddenly faced disaster and lost almost everything. He refused to blame God, and when God finally revealed himself, Job realized how little he had understood about him.*

J OB WAS a prosperous man who worshipped God, lived a blameless life, and enjoyed a large and happy family. One day Satan attended God's heavenly council, along with God's angelic advisors, and played his role as "the Accuser". He suggested that Job worshipped God only because it was in his interest to do so, asking, "Does Job fear God for nothing?" (Job 1:9). In response, God gave Satan permission to test Job, by removing the good things in life from him, providing only that he spared Job's life. So, one dramatic day, Job was faced with the tragic news that he had lost all of his animals, either to raiders or in a fire that "fell from the heavens" (1:16). This was swiftly followed by the news that his ten children had all been killed when the house they were in collapsed as a result of a mighty wind that had swept in from the desert. Job's response was to submit reverently to God, saying: "The LORD gave and the LORD has taken away; may the name of the

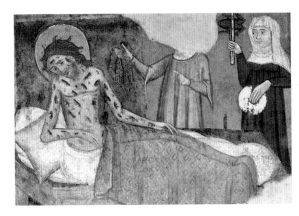

**AFFLICTED BY ILL HEALTH**
This 14th-century depiction of Job shows him sitting in misery on his bed, his body covered from head to toe in painful sores. He now had nothing – Satan had taken his children, his livestock, and his health.

LORD be praised" (1:21). Satan pressed Job's case with God who, being confident of Job's faithfulness, gave Satan permission to take away his health as well. So Job was inflicted with painful sores, "from the soles of his feet to the crown of his head" (2:7).

Job's wife wanted to blame their misfortunes on God, but Job refused to do so.

### Job's comforters

Three of Job's friends – Eliphaz, Bildad, and Zophar – came to comfort him. When Job had voiced his despair at what had happened, they each took it in turn to speak, although they largely said the same things but each adopting a slightly different tone. They claimed that innocent people did not suffer, therefore Job must have sinned – whatever his reputation. God was a powerful ruler who meted out retribution to the sinful, so Job's suffering must have been deserved. If only Job would admit it and repent, he could perhaps be freed from his suffering.

Job refused to accept their arguments and the conversation went around the circle three times, with each of his friends getting more frustrated that his arguments were not accepted. Throughout, Job begged God for relief and viewed himself as a victim of injustice. He was unwavering in protesting his innocence and believed, "Now that I have

### JOB THANKS GOD

This fresco by Bartolo di Fredi (1330–1410) shows Job thanking God, despite his great misfortune. He refuses to berate God for his suffering, but does begin to question why this fate has befallen him.

prepared my case I know I will be vindicated" (13:18).

Later, a young man called Elihu joined them. Having pompously corrected Job's friends, he too sought to correct Job, vigorously affirming God's justice. He warned them all that God was so mighty that they should be very careful what they said about him.

### God speaks

When the men finally fell silent, God himself spoke to Job: "Who is this that obscures my plans and words without knowledge?" (38:2). He asked Job a series of questions about creation: Where did it come from? How did it operate? How did the animals live? How did God's justice work? Job had no answer, and came to realize how little he had understood about God and his ways. Job confessed that he had spoken out of turn in doubting God. He now understood that he was accountable to God, not God to him.

God was angry with Job's friends for the foolish things they had said to Job, although he simply ignored Elihu. They were made to offer expensive sacrifices and were only redeemed when Job prayed for their forgiveness.

After all this, God blessed Job and "restored his fortunes and gave him twice as much as he had before" (42:10), amply restoring his animals and family to him. The later part of his life was more blessed than his earlier years had been. Job died at the age of 140, after being able to enjoy his great-grandchildren.

**ANALYSIS**

## SUFFERING

The book of Job is one of the stories in the Bible often studied in theodicy – the attempt to explain how a God who is good, all-knowing, and all-powerful can permit innocent people to suffer.

Many different answers to this central question have been offered by scholars. Some people focus on the free will that humanity enjoys, and argue that suffering is a deserved consequence of sin. However, the story described in the book of Job suggests otherwise.

Some people suggest that suffering is a result of the Fall, when the choice made by Eve and Adam affected the future for all humanity (see p.38). Others point out the positive value of suffering, which can sometimes achieve a greater good. Still others stress the limitations of our present human knowledge.

Job's story does not resolve this problem – suffering remains a mystery. Christians believe that God shared humanity's suffering through Christ's cross and that he bears the burden of suffering with us.

## "My ears had heard of you but now my eyes have seen you."

JOB 42:5

**AFTER**

**Two main approaches to the problem of evil developed in later Jewish thinking.**

### EVIL AS A CONFLICT OF POWERS

One strand saw evil as the result of people being caught up in the **cosmic struggle between God and Satan**, or the forces of good and wickedness. The clearest example of this is found in the apocalyptic writing of the **book of Daniel 250–51 ≫**.

### EVIL AS UNDER GOD'S CONTROL

The other approach saw evil as an **instrument of God's discipline**, or a refining process, and therefore fully under God's sovereign control. This was how some Psalmists understood it on a personal level (see Psalm 22, 38, or 51), and was how the prophets interpreted the exile 238–39 ≫.

**ARCHANGEL MICHAEL DEFEATS SATAN**

# Wisdom for Life

*Proverbs, Ecclesiastes, and Song of Songs lie at the heart of Israel's wisdom literature. Although different in style, they deal with how to live wisely – in ordinary life and in the search for meaning and love.*

**T**HE KINGS of Israel appointed professional sages for advice (Jeremiah 18:18). The tradition of wisdom literature gained particular stimulus from Solomon (see pp.178–79), who was famed for his wisdom.

## Proverbs

A compilation of several collections of wisdom sayings gathered from different sources, Proverbs deals with ordinary life. The first nine chapters contain the practical guidance of a father for his son about friendships and lifestyle. Wisdom is portrayed as a moral and spiritual quality that involves good decision-making and avoiding foolish behaviour, such as ill-discipline, laziness, sexual misconduct, violence, and destructive speech.

The main section of Proverbs – chapters 10 to 22 – contains the wise sayings of King Solomon. These pithy maxims cover every aspect of life, including speech, relationships, forward planning, dealing with people (from fools to neighbours), managing time, business integrity, family matters, reputations, death, wealth, and poverty. In all circumstances, they encourage people to live according to God's teachings.

The next section, chapters 22:17 to 23:35, is composed of "the sayings of the wise", who were probably professional royal advisors. Although distinctive, the structure and content betray the influence of wisdom literature from Egypt. A shorter collection of Solomon's wise sayings follows (Proverbs 25:1–29:27), before wise words from outside Israel, written by Agur and King Lemuel, are included. Proverbs concludes with a celebration of the value of a noble wife.

### The teachings of Proverbs

Proverbs presents a view of life centred around God. It assumes that there is a divinely ordained order in creation and that humans can choose to live either in the right way within it – and therefore find fulfilment – or to follow the wrong paths, and therefore experience life as uncomfortable and costly.

In chapters 1 to 9, wisdom is personified as a righteous woman. In addition to the value of her words, she claims a pre-eminent role in the cosmos as "the first of [God's] works" (Proverbs 8:22), before even creation itself. Not all

### THE WISDOM OF ELDERS

In Israel's wisdom literature, wisdom is equated with old age. The writer of Proverbs reminds his listeners that "Grey hair is a crown of splendour; it is attained in the way of righteousness" (16:31).

## KEY PROVERBS

**Contentment** 15:16,17; 19:23; 30:8,9

**Discipline** 3:11; 6:23; 15:5; 22:6

**Folly** 12:15; 10:23; 26:4,5

**Friendships** 17:17; 18:24; 27:6, 10

**Laziness** 6:6–11; 18:9; 21:25; 26:14

**Love** 3:3; 10:12; 15:17; 17:9

**The Poor** 11:24; 14:31; 19:17; 22:16; 31:9

**Riches** 3:9,10; 10:22; 22:2

**Speech** 12:17–19; 15:1,4; 18:21; 27:2

**Wisdom** 1:7; 3:7; 8:12–13; 9:10; 13:14

female figures are good, however – in Proverbs 5 Solomon warns his son against the seductive adulteress.

## Ecclesiastes

Unlike Proverbs, Ecclesiastes deals with the big questions of life. It perceives wisdom as personal intelligence and skill, a view that leads the writer into a dialogue about the apparent meaninglessness and absurdities of life. The "Teacher" who wrote it, traditionally thought to be Solomon, dismisses the ways that people find meaning – through work, leisure, wealth, or social advancement – as futile. Life is seen as fixed and unchangeable.

The writer incorporates wisdom sayings and concludes that, although life is an enigma, wisdom is better than folly. Ecclesiastes argues that, even if there are no answers, it is good for us to remember our creator, and to enjoy the life God has given us on Earth before we die.

> # "The beginning of wisdom is this: get wisdom. Though it cost all you have, get understanding."
>
> **PROVERBS** 4:7

### THE SONG OF SONGS

The Song of Solomon, shown here in a 15th-century Italian Bible, has been interpreted by some commentators as an allegorical representation of the relationship between God and Israel.

## Song of Songs

This poetic work is a positive celebration of life's richest experience – love. Two lovers address each another, their comments interspersed with those from friends. They celebrate the joy of love and sexuality without inhibition and speak passionately about a love that is "as strong as death... it burns like blazing fire" (Song of Songs 8:6). The lovers are conscious that they must actively maintain love, rather than take it for granted.

## THE FEAR OF THE LORD

To "fear the LORD" (Proverbs 2:5) does not mean being afraid of God, but showing a healthy respect or reverence for him by taking his instructions on life seriously and living in accordance with them. According to Proverbs, the lives of people who fear God will be marked by displaying the virtues of integrity, faithfulness, hard work, self-control, prudence, the rejection of temptation, and discipline – especially in their speech. The fear of God will lead to a contented and fulfilled life (Proverbs 19:23), as well as respect in the community.

**CLOCKWISE FROM TOP-LEFT: PRUDENCE, JUSTICE, TEMPERANCE, FORTITUDE**

# THE DIVIDED KINGDOM

"Jereboam did not change his evil ways... This was **the sin of the house of Jeroboam that led to its downfall** and to its destruction from the face of the earth."

1 KINGS 13:33,34

THE KINGDOM OVER WHICH David and Solomon reigned split apart when Rehoboam, Solomon's heir, came to the throne. The relationship between the two resulting kingdoms – Judah in the south and Israel to the north – was mostly tense and frequently gave rise to hostile action. The schism raised huge questions of a political and a spiritual nature. The story of the two kingdoms and their fluctuating fortunes is told in the books of Kings (1 Kings 12 to 2 Kings 25), and is revisited, with a different emphasis, in Chronicles (2 Chronicles 10–36).

After Solomon's death, people from the northern tribes petitioned his heir, Rehoboam, to relieve the harsh burdens of high taxes and slave labour that his father had imposed. Unmoved, Rehoboam threatened them with an even harsher regime – with the result that the ten northern tribes revolted, broke away from the kingdom based in Jerusalem, and invited Jeroboam to be their ruler in the northern kingdom of Israel.

### THE KINGDOM OF ISRAEL

Israel proved to be a fragile kingdom, led by a succession of kings who mostly "did evil in the eyes of the LORD" (1 Kings 16:25). They established alternative places to worship (because they had cut themselves off from the Temple, the one legitimate central place of worship in the united kingdom) and, more significantly, they often succumbed to the influence of Baal worship – idolatory that was condemned by the prophet Elijah.

For much of its history, Israel was ruled by the house of Ahab, whose capital was in Samaria. Although Israel sometimes allied with Judah against a common enemy, it was frequently in conflict with its former fellow citizens. Israel's location made it vulnerable to attack and so it regularly sought protection from stronger nations, frequently at some cost to its independence. After just over 200 years, the kingdom of Israel was brought to an end by Assyria, which is seen in the Bible as a just reward for its betrayal of the covenant with God.

### THE KINGDOM OF JUDAH

The two southern tribes that remained under the rule of Rehoboam considered the actions of the northern tribes to be a spiritual disaster. They saw the separatists as rebelling against God's promised plan to establish David's dynastic rule from his chosen place of Mount Zion (Jerusalem). Over time, however, the rulers and the people of Judah also showed varying degrees of faithfulness to God and varying levels of obedience to the covenant. In spite of a late spiritual revival under Josiah, God eventually invoked the disciplinary terms of the covenant and they were sent into a long period of exile in Babylon.

Judah was to survive as an independent kingdom for well over a century longer than Israel and – unlike Israel – following their exile the people of Judah were eventually restored to their land.

**ELIJAH CALLING DOWN FIRE**
In this 16th-century tapestry from Brussels, Belgium, the prophet Elijah takes on and defeats the priests of the false god Baal in a contest of offerings. In his victory, Elijah also ended the drought that had beset Israel.

**ROYAL SEAL**
This seal, thought to have belonged to one of Jeroboam's ministers, carries the name of the king along with a roaring lion – a symbol of the kingdom of Judah. Jeroboam became the first king of the northern kingdom of Israel after it split from the kingdom of Judah.

# Israel and Judah Split

*The northern tribes, represented by Jeroboam, asked Rehoboam to relieve the burdens of Solomon's reign. When Rehoboam refused, they broke away and formed the separate kingdom of Israel, bringing the united kingdom to an end.*

**S** OLOMON HAD presided over all Israel and his reign saw great advances in culture, prosperity, and territory. This progress had been costly, however, and the people suffered from heavy taxes and workloads. There was discontent before

## BEFORE

**The division of the kingdom was foretold by Ahijah the prophet.**

**A PROPHECY FOR JEROBOAM**
Jeroboam was one of Solomon's officials. He **rebelled against Solomon «  178–79** and fled to Egypt, but received a message from the prophet Ahijah. He predicted that Solomon's kingdom would be divided into two, with ten tribes on one side and two on the other, and that Jeroboam would lead the ten tribes. The division would be **God's punishment for his people's disloyalty**. Yet, because of his covenant with David, God would continue David's line in Jerusalem. Jeroboam was promised that, if he remained faithful to God, his **dynasty would endure**.

### ANALYSIS

### THE DIVIDED KINGDOM

The division of the kingdom of Israel into the northern and southern kingdoms had implications for the economic and political survival of the separated nations, but the Bible's interest lies in their spiritual history. In Kings, the stories of Israel and Judah are interwoven, whereas Chronicles tells everything from Judah's viewpoint.

Israel is presented as breaking God's covenant, and so becoming the home of impure worship and other evil practices. By contrast, Judah remained faithful to God, and continued with kings descended from David, God's chosen ruler. It saw Jerusalem, God's chosen city, as the sole centre of true worship.

---

Solomon died, but after his death Rehoboam, his heir, made decisions that would make life even harder for the people.

### Rehoboam takes advice

Soon after Rehoboam became king, Jeroboam, one of his father's former officials, returned from Egypt and on behalf of the people asked Rehoboam to help: "Your father put a heavy yoke on us, but now lighten the harsh labour and the heavy yoke he put on us, and we will serve you" (1 Kings 12:4).

Rehoboam promised to take advice, and asked Jeroboam to return after three days. His father's counsellors advised him to agree to the request. Rehoboam, however, had reservations, and consulted a younger, less-experienced group, whose advice he accepted. These people recommended the opposite – he should take a hard line and, far from lessening the load, should threaten to increase it.

### The kingdom breaks in two

When Jeroboam and the people heard this stubborn response and realized that the king would not listen to them, they returned home, dejected. The king sent out Adoniram, the civil servant in charge of forced labour, to collect taxes; the people reacted by stoning Adoniram to death and Rehoboam himself only just escaped with his life. Rebellion was in the air.

**CORONATION OF REHOBOAM**
This detail from an early 13th-century illuminated manuscript shows the coronation of Rehoboam as the new king of Israel, after he succeeded his father Solomon, following his death.

---

Jeroboam quickly became the focal point of the rebellion, and the people from ten of the tribes gathered to make him their king. Two of the tribes, Judah and Benjamin, however, remained loyal to Rehoboam, signalling the end of the united kingdom.

### The divided kingdom

The northern tribes initially set up their capital in Shechem, while the two southern tribes continued to have the city of Jerusalem as their royal seat. From then on, the northern kingdom was known as Israel, and the southern one as Judah.

Jeroboam realized that his people needed new centres of worship so that they would not have to visit the Temple in Jerusalem. He made two golden calves and built shrines for them at Dan and Bethel. Then he appointed priests and introduced new religious festivals. His actions confirmed Judah's view that the breakaway tribes were not in rebellion just against David's dynasty, but also against the covenant with God.

> **"** So **Israel has been in rebellion against** the house of **David** to this day. **"**
> 1 KINGS 12:19

---

*(Map of the region showing:)*
Great Sea (Mediterranean Sea)
PHOENICIA
ARAM
o Dan
Sea of Chinnereth (Sea of Galilee)
Megiddo
**KINGDOM OF ISRAEL**
Samaria o
Shechem o
Joppa o
Bethel o
AMMON
o Jericho
o Jerusalem
PHILISTIA
Lachish o
o Hebron
Salt Sea (Dead Sea)
**KINGDOM OF JUDAH**
o Beersheba
MOAB
EDOM
N
0    50 km
0    50 miles

**THE GREAT DIVIDE**
As related in 1 Kings 12, the nation of Israel split into the two kingdoms of Israel and Judah after Solomon's death. Israel was the largest in population and size, and had the most fertile land of the former kingdom.

## AFTER  **»**

**Jeroboam's new religion provoked condemnation from two prophets.**

**JUDAH'S FLAWED PROPHET**
As Jeroboam presided over the calf worship at Bethel, a prophet from Judah denounced him, saying the future king Josiah would **eradicate such idolatry 232–33 »**. Jeroboam pointed at the prophet and ordered his arrest; as he did so, his hand became paralyzed and he had to beg to be healed. The prophet suffered a violent end: on his way home he was **killed by a lion**.

**AHIJAH PROPHESIES AGAIN**
When Ahijah fell ill, Jeroboam sent his wife with a gift. Although blind, Ahijah identified his visitor and **sent a message for Jeroboam** saying that, because of his unfaithfulness to God, his **dynasty would collapse and his house would experience tragedy**.

**SACRIFICE TO THE GOLDEN CALF AT BETHEL**

**RAVAGED BY DROUGHT**
The drought that God sent on the land meant that even the brook in the Kerith Ravine – where Elijah was sheltering – dried up. Water shortages are still a risk in the Middle East, as shown in this parched landscape in Jordan.

« **BEFORE**

**The northern kingdom was ruled by a succession of kings who turned away from God.**

### RELIGION IN ISRAEL
After breaking away from Judah, Israel's kings **"did evil in the eyes of the Lord"** (1 Kings 16:25). They introduced their own forms of worship and erected shrines at Bethel and Dan, where people worshipped golden statues of calves. Israel's sixth king, Omri, "sinned more than all those before him" (see panel **208–09 »**) by further encouraging idolatry. His son, Ahab, was even worse, partly due to the influence of his wife Jezebel, from Sidon, who **forcefully propagated the worship of Baal**.

### POLITICAL CONFLICT
The period following Israel's split from Judah was characterized by **political instability**. Israel's size and location meant it could not escape conflicts between the powers surrounding it. The first threats came from Aram and **Egypt « 84–85** (1 Kings 14–16), but these powers were eclipsed by the **Assyrians 216–17 »**. There were victories, but the **future of Israel was precarious**.

# Elijah and the Drought

*The prophet Elijah told King Ahab that Israel would suffer a drought, and then fled in fear of his life. In the town of Zarephath, Elijah stayed in the house of a poor widow and was instrumental in two miracles.*

**D**URING KING AHAB'S reign, the people followed the king's example and abandoned the worship of Israel's God. Ahab had married Jezebel, daughter of the king of Sidon, and under her influence he built centres of worship for the gods Baal (see pp.198–99) and Asherah.

Then a prophet called Elijah, from Tishbe in Gilead, east of the River Jordan, came to see Ahab and announced, "As the Lord, the God of Israel lives... there will be neither dew nor rain in the next few years except at my word" (1 Kings 17:1). Soon after, a long drought struck the land.

### Elijah flees
Having made his prediction, Elijah was told by God to flee for safety, out of Ahab's jurisdiction.

First, God told Elijah to hide east of the Jordan, where water still flowed through the River Cherith.

**A PROPHET IN HIDING**
This 18th-century image of Elijah shows the prophet hiding from King Ahab in the desert. God ensured he would survive in this hostile landscape, instructing the ravens to bring him food.

God arranged for the ravens to supply Elijah with food, and they brought him bread and meat to eat. However, the drought was severe and in time even the water in the Cherith dried up. Elijah was then told by God: "Go at once to Zarephath in the region

## ACCESS TO WATER

**THE MEGIDDO WATER TUNNEL**

Israel lay in the arid eastern Mediterranean region, so securing access to water was vital. The towns of Jerusalem and Megiddo – a settlement 30km (19 miles) southeast of the Sea of Galilee – both lay near abundant springs, but these natural resources needed harnessing. A water channel was constructed near Megiddo in Solomon's reign, and during Ahab's time, a shaft and tunnel were added to bring water into the heart of the city. Jerusalem's early supply channel brought water from the Gihon Spring, but this was surpassed when Hezekiah built a tunnel, 533m (1,749ft) long, right into the western part of the city (see p.228).

**ELIJAH THE SAVIOUR**
In the second of Elijah's miracles in the home of the widow in Zarephath – depicted in this painting by Louis Hersent (1777–1860) – he cried out to God to restore the life of her son. God answered Elijah's call and resuscitated the boy.

of Sidon and stay there. I have instructed a widow there to supply you with food" (17:9). Although King Ahab searched for Elijah, he never found him.

### God will provide

Elijah met the widow gathering wood at the town's gate. When he first approached her and asked for bread and water, she explained that food was so scarce that she was collecting the wood for one last meal. She told him, "I don't have any bread – only a handful of flour in a jar and a little olive oil in a jug. I am gathering a few sticks to take home and make a meal for myself and my son, that we may eat it – and die" (17:12).

Elijah assured the widow that God would provide for her and for her son. The flour would not be used up and the oil would not run out until the drought came to an end. And so it proved to be – God kept his word.

### A second miracle

Some time later, the widow's son fell ill. His condition gradually worsened and he died. The widow immediately blamed Elijah for the boy's death, "Did you come to remind me of my sin and kill my son?" (17:18) she asked.

Elijah took the boy's corpse to a private room, prayed earnestly to God, and stretched himself out

over the boy three times. He cried, "LORD my God, let this boy's life return to him!" (17:21). God heard Elijah's prayers and restored the boy to life. Elijah carried the boy to his mother and showed him that he was alive. She declared that Elijah was a man of God, who spoke the true word of God.

> " The jar of **flour will not be used up** and the jug of oil will not run dry until ... the LORD sends rain."
>
> **1 KINGS** 17:14

## MIRACLES

The prophets Elijah and Elisha performed a number of miracles, or events that seem hard to explain by natural causes – such as Elijah's promise to the widow that, although her oil and water vessels were nearly empty, they would not run out during the drought. The Israelites had previously witnessed many miracles, both when they left Egypt and during their wilderness years. Moses had divided the Red Sea to allow the Israelites to cross (see pp.102–03); and when they were starving in the desert, God had provided manna for them to eat (see pp.104–05). Miracles such as these did not happen all the time, but they particularly occurred in times of crisis. They revealed God's supernatural power when human abilities were insufficient. Given the belief that God created the world from nothing, his occasional direct intervention in that world seemed reasonable to Israelite believers.

**OIL AND WATER VESSELS FROM CANAAN, 18TH CENTURY BC**

**Elijah returned to Ahab's court and gave Obadiah a message for the king.**

### GOD'S FAITHFUL SERVANT

Despite the severe famine in Israel, Jezebel continued to **eliminate God's prophets**. Obadiah, Ahab's chief of staff, however, remained true to God. He had even hidden a hundred true prophets in caves, and had provided them with food and water. God told Elijah: "Go and present yourself to Ahab, and I will send rain on the land" (1 Kings 18:1). When Elijah suddenly reappeared in Israel, he met a fearful Obadiah. He asked him to tell Ahab that Elijah was here, and that he had a message for him: the **drought was about to come to a spectacular conclusion 198–99 ≫**.

**CAVE OVERLOOKING THE DEAD SEA, ISRAEL**

### IDOLATRY AND PERSECUTION

Queen Jezebel had a signficant influence on Ahab's reign. She first convinced Ahab to turn away from the worship of Israel's God and instead **introduced the worship of Baal-Melqart ❬❬ 196**, the chief deity of Sidon, to Israel. She built up a huge following, including hundreds who served Baal and hundreds more devoted to the goddess Asherah. Jezebel also **persecuted God's true servants**, killing many and driving others underground, until only 7,000 people remained who were loyal to God. The **drought ❬❬ 196–97** was God's response to Israel turning away from him, an appropriate punishment, since Baal-Melqart was a fertility god.

# Elijah and Baal's Prophets

*After three years of drought, Elijah proposed a contest between himself, the prophet of Israel's God, and prophets of the gods Baal and Asherah. The most powerful God would ignite the fire on an unlit altar.*

**H**AVING BEEN in hiding for three years, Elijah reappeared in Israel to confront King Ahab about his betrayal of the God of Israel. Undeterred by being called the "troubler of Israel" (1 Kings 18:17), Elijah accused Ahab himself of being the true source of Israel's woes.

Showing himself to be in command, Elijah instructed Ahab to call the people of Israel together on Mount Carmel and to summon 450 representatives of Baal and 400 representatives of Asherah to meet him there. Elijah pointed out that he would be vastly outnumbered: "I am the only one of the LORD's prophets left, but Baal has four hundred and fifty prophets" (18:22). Nevertheless, he proposed that they should each sacrifice a bull to their deity – but they would not light these sacrifices in the normal way. They should pray to their respective deities to light the fires, unaided by human beings, and then

### THE CONTEST ON MOUNT CARMEL

Lucas Cranach the Younger's 1545 painting shows the dramatic moment when Elijah calls for God to ignite his offering, and the animal remains on the altar burst into flame.

## SYMBOLS

### DIVINE FIRE

In the Old Testament, God's power is often displayed in fire. He revealed himself to Moses at the burning bush (Exodus 3:2), and he descended to Mount Sinai in fire, covering the mountain with smoke (Exodus 19:18). God led Israel through the wilderness as fire in the clouds (Exodus 40:38), and Aaron's priesthood was confirmed when God sent fire to burn the offering on the altar (Leviticus 9:24). The angel of the Lord accepted Gideon's offering by consuming it with fire (Judges 6:21). A chariot and horses of fire took Elijah to heaven (2 Kings 2:11). God also used fire as capital punishment (Leviticus 10:2; 2 Kings 1:10). On Carmel, he was "the god who answers by fire" (1 Kings 18:24).

"The god who answers by fire – he is God" (18:24). Elijah believed that the true God of Israel would reveal himself and that the people would renew their allegiance to him.

Ahab made the arrangements and the contest began. As they assembled, the people remained stubbornly silent. The prophets of Baal went first. They asked Baal to light their sacrifice all morning. At noon, when nothing had happened, Elijah poked fun at them, suggesting that Baal was asleep. The prophets worked themselves into a frenzy, even injuring themselves as was their custom in their religious rites. However, still nothing happened.

### Elijah's altar

When it was obvious that nothing was going to happen, Elijah made his altar, building it from 12 stones to represent the tribes of Israel. He laid a bull on it and asked the people to drench the offering in water three times to make it harder for the offering to light. It was so wet that the surplus water ran off into a trench around the altar.

Then Elijah too prayed, just once, asking the God of his ancestors to light the fire and show himself to be "God in Israel". Without further rituals or prolonged praying, "The fire of the LORD fell and burned up the sacrifice" (18:38).

The people's response was immediate. Their silence gave way to acclamation as they shouted: "The LORD – he is God! The Lord – he is God!" (18:39).

### The aftermath

Once the result of the contest was clear, Elijah ordered the people to seize the prophets of Baal. Every one of them was taken to a place of execution in the Kishon Valley, where they paid for their treason with their lives.

The second consequence was more positive. Since the people had returned to following God, the drought was lifted. It took a little time for this news to be confirmed; in fact Elijah had to send his servant to a lookout seven times before the man spotted a small cloud. Soon, however, the clouds gathered and the rains came. As the storms broke, Elijah left Carmel and, with extraordinary energy, ran all the way to Jezreel, Ahab's capital, ahead of the king's chariot.

**IDOL WORSHIP**
This statue of the Canaanite deity Baal is believed to have been created in the 14th century BC. Queen Jezebel forcefully promoted the worship of Baal, and murdered prophets of Israel's God.

## HISTORY AND CULTURE

### BAAL WORSHIP

The name of Baal occurs frequently in the Old Testament. Baal was a Canaanite deity, who over time rose to be the chief god in the Canaanite pantheon. His name was often associated with the particular towns where he held sway. Baal was a storm god and thought to be in control of the fertility of the land, the animals, and people in the areas where he was worshipped. His followers practised rituals to encourage Baal to look favourably on their town; these rituals included prostitution and child sacrifice. Baal worship was often linked with the worship of Asherah, a goddess of the sea and consort of the high god El. The sensuous rituals of Baal worship were to prove a constant temptation for Israel.

**PROPHETS OF BAAL, 3RD-CENTURY AD FRESCO**

> "If the LORD is God, follow him; but if Baal is God, follow him."
>
> 1 KINGS 18:21

**AFTER** »

After the victory on Mount Carmel, Elijah faced opposition, but was soon recommissioned by God.

### GOD REFRESHES ELIJAH

When the news of Elijah's victory broke, Jezebel became angry and **threatened his life**. Elijah's courage deserted him and he fled. Wearily depressed, he told God that he had had enough, but God allowed Elijah to sleep. When he awoke, he found that **God had again provided for him**: he found bread and water next to him. Refreshed, Elijah went on a long journey to Mount Horeb – also known as Sinai – where God had previously revealed himself to Moses. There, Elijah **complained that he was the only one left serving God**. God ignored this complaint and re-commissioned him, not in a spectacular manner through wind, earthquake, or fire, but through "a gentle whisper". Elijah's task was now to **anoint a new generation of kings and prophets 202–03** » who would further God's plans for Israel.

**ELIJAH'S PLATEAU, NEAR MOUNT SINAI**

**PROPHET** 9th century BC

# Elijah

## "Elijah was a human being, even as we are."

JAMES 5:17

**E**LIJAH WAS ONE of the earliest prophets in Israel. He lived in the 9th century BC and prophesied in the northern kingdom of Israel during the reigns of King Ahab (*c*.874–853 BC) and his son King Ahaziah (*c*.853–852 BC). The Bible says that Elijah came from the town of Tishbe in Gilead, east of the Jordan, but otherwise we know nothing of his background.

### A brave and forceful prophet

Elijah was a courageous prophet who uncompromisingly challenged Israel's unfaithfulness to God, at great personal risk, and witnessed several miracles. He was also a strong, athletic man who travelled extensively in the fulfilment of his calling by God, and sometimes travelled lengthy distances at great speed on foot.

### Elijah and the drought

King Ahab's Phoenician wife, Jezebel (see p.205), vigorously promoted the worship of Baal, the god of her home territory, and of Asherah, and she severely persecuted those who remained loyal to the God of Israel. Elijah came before Ahab, unannounced, and informed him that God would punish Israel for submitting to Jezebel's

**ELIJAH THE PROPHET**
This statue of Elijah from St Peter's Basilica in Rome depicts the prophet in a striking pose, embodying his calling to declare that "Yahweh is my God", the meaning of his name in Hebrew.

**ANALYSIS**

## ELIJAH AND THE COMING MESSIAH

Elijah is mentioned later in the Bible, especially in connection with the coming of the Messiah. The prophet Malachi predicted that he would reappear "before that great and dreadful day of the Lord comes" (Malachi 4:5). In the New Testament, people asked John the Baptist if he was Elijah, returning to prepare the way for the day of judgment. His preaching, desert location, and diet suggested that he could be, but John himself denied it (John 1:21). Elijah later appeared alongside Jesus and Moses on the Mount of Transfiguration (see pp.354–55), where Jesus revealed his true identity to the apostles Peter, James, and John (Matthew 17:1–13; Mark 9:2–13; Luke 9:28–36).

**BYZANTINE ICON OF JOHN THE BAPTIST**

wickedness by sending a severe drought on the land, which would only be lifted at his command (1 Kings 17:1). During the drought, which lasted for three years, Elijah went into hiding outside Ahab's territory – first in the east, in the Cherith Ravine, and then in the west, at Zarephath in Phoenicia. Throughout this time Elijah experienced several miracles: he was fed by ravens at the brook at Cherith; then the widow who provided him with hospitality in Zarephath miraculously found that her meagre supplies of flour and oil never ran out during the famine. When the widow's son died from an illness, Elijah restored him to life.

## Mount Carmel

After three years, Elijah came out of hiding to bring the drought to an end. The rain came after he had mocked and defeated the prophets of Baal on Mount Carmel where, in contrast to their bone-dry altar, his water-soaked sacrifice was miraculously set alight by God (18:16–46).

Elijah's victory infuriated Jezebel, who threatened to have him assassinated. Elijah fled, exhausted and depressed (19:4), travelling a long way to Mount Horeb in Sinai. There, God sent an angel to him and restored him, again feeding him miraculously with bread and water, and sent him to perform further prophetic duties, including that of commissioning his successor, Elisha (19:19–21).

## Ahab and Ahaziah

Elijah had one final clash with King Ahab when the king greedily, and quite illegally,

### WITNESS OF THE PROPHETS
Giovanni Bellini portrayed Elijah and Moses in *The Transfiguration of Christ* (c.1487). This was the moment in the New Testament when Christ was revealed to James, Peter, and John in all his glory (see pp.354–55).

### ELIJAH'S ASCENSION
An illustration from a 16th-century Latin Bible from the Abbey of St Amand in France depicts Elisha holding on to Elijah's cloak as the great prophet is taken up to heaven in a chariot of fire.

took possession of Naboth's vineyard (21). Elijah accurately predicted that Ahab and Jezebel, together with their dynasty, would shortly face disaster.

Ahaziah, Ahab's son and successor, suffered a serious accident after falling from an upper storey and sent messengers to consult the prophets of Baal in Moab about his prospects. Elijah intercepted the messengers and challenged them as to why they were not consulting

an Israelite prophet. When Ahaziah sent a small military delegation to consult Elijah, the prophet caused fire to incinerate them. The same happened to a second delegation but, at the third attempt, Elijah sent the delegation back to the king with the message that he would never recover, but would die where he lay on his bed.

## The prophet's legacy

Elijah's departure from this world was fittingly spectacular. Walking one day with Elisha, his appointed successor, Elijah was caught up in a whirlwind to heaven, transported in a chariot of fire (2 Kings 2:1–18). Elijah's work was respected by other prophets of his day (2:15–18), but his reputation grew with time and he became the focus of the Jews' hopeful expectations. Elijah was subsequently considered to be one of the major prophets of the Old Testament, on a par with Moses, and was expected to return to herald the way for the Messiah.

> **" … these people will know** that you, LORD, are God, and that **you are turning their hearts back again."**
>
> 1 KINGS 18:37

« BEFORE

After Elijah had recovered from the conflict on Mount Carmel, God spoke to him and commanded him to undertake further tasks.

### KINGS AND A FUTURE PROPHET

God **appeared to Elijah on Mount Horeb** « 199 and asked him what he was doing there. Elijah replied that he was the **last of God's prophets** left, and his life, too, was in danger. Elijah was instructed to leave Horeb and travel to Damascus, where he was to **anoint Hazael as the future king of Aram, and Jehu as the king of Israel**. Hazael was to prove a thorn in Israel's side (2 Kings 10:32,33) and Jehu initially overthrew **Ahab**'s dynasty and destroyed **Baal worship**, but later betrayed God. Elijah was also told to **find Elisha** and appoint him as his successor.

**STORM GOD FROM THE COURT OF KING HAZAEL**

> "**Elijah** went up to him and **threw his cloak around him**. Elisha then left his oxen and ran after Elijah."
>
> 1 KINGS 19:19,20

### THE PROPHETS

This 11th-century relief from Bamberg Cathedral, Germany, shows the prophet Elijah (far right) talking with his follower Elisha. God appeared to Elijah on Mount Horeb and instructed him to find Elisha, son of Shaphat, and anoint him as a prophet, to continue the work that he had started.

# Elijah and Elisha

*Elijah resumed his work as a prophet and fulfilled God's command to anoint the next generation of kings. He also commissioned Elisha, who was to succeed him as God's prophet.*

**H**AVING LEFT Mount Horeb, Elijah followed God's instructions and made his way to the town of Abel Meholah, just west of the River Jordan. There he met a man called Elisha, whose name means, "my God is salvation".

The Bible does not tell us much about Elisha's background, only that he was from Abel Meholah and that his father's name was Shaphat; but he must have been wealthy because Elijah found Elisha ploughing his field with a large team of oxen.

What followed was somewhat unusual. Elijah did not anoint Elisha with oil – the usual act of commissioning – nor did he say that Elisha was to be his successor as God's prophet. Instead, Elijah went up to him and threw his cloak around Elisha's shoulders – a symbolic action that invested Elisha with the prophet's mantle that would eventually pass to him.

Elisha seems to have understood the significance of this event, as he responded by asking Elijah if he had time to go home and say farewell to his family. However, Elijah simply replied, "What have I done to you?" (1 Kings 19:20).

### Leaving home

In spite of this ambiguous reply, Elisha realized his life was about to change. He remained at home just long enough to slaughter his oxen, cook their meat on a fire that he had built from his ploughing equipment, and give the meat to the people in his household. By doing this Elisha cut his ties with his former life and removed any possibility of returning to support himself through farming. Then he set off to follow Elijah.

### Elisha's apprenticeship

Elisha became Elijah's follower; for the next few years, he served Elijah faithfully and learned from him. Literally and symbolically, Elijah's mantle would pass to Elisha, who served as a prophet in his own right for 50 years.

### The two prophets

The Bible goes on to show that Elijah and Elisha had much in common with one another. They were both courageous, and they frequently challenged royal power. Both worked miracles, and neither left a written record of their preaching, as later prophets did.

However, they appear to have been quite different characters. Elijah acted alone and seems the more aggressive in his challenging of authority. Elisha was more gentle in his relationships with kings and, although he often worked on his own, he also worked with a company of prophets. By the time they met, Elijah was weary and battle-scarred, while Elisha was young and eager. For all that, the similarities between them vastly outweigh any differences.

> "Let me **kiss my father** and **mother goodbye…** and **then I will come with you.**"
>
> 1 KINGS 19:20

**YOKE OF OXEN**
Elijah met Elisha while he was ploughing the field "with twelve yoke of oxen" (1 Kings 19:19). The 24 animals would have been yoked together in pairs, all pulling a single plough.

## ARAMEANS

At the time of Elijah and Elisha, in the 9th century BC, the Arameans – a semi-nomadic people – had settled northeast of Israel in a series of small kingdom states, of which Damascus was the most significant. Israel had mixed relations with Aram. David and Solomon fought against Aram, but Aram exploited the later division of their kingdom. The Aramean King, Ben-Hadad II, briefly allied with King Ahab, but Jeroboam II later defeated Damascus. Eventually Damascus became a province of the Assyrian Empire. The Arameans' greatest legacy was their language – Aramaic – which became the day-to-day language of Israel and was used by Jesus.

**SMALL STATUE OF AN ARAMEAN KING, 9TH-CENTURY BC**

## AFTER

Israel was repeatedly attacked by Ben-Hadad, the king of Aram, but, with the help of an unnamed prophet, gained the victory.

### BEN-HADAD

After Elisha left his family to become Elijah's attendant, Israel's **powerful neighbour**, the king of Aram, demanded tribute from Ahab, king of Israel. He replied, "Just as you say, my lord the king. I and all I have are yours" (1 Kings 20:4). However, when Ben-Hadad made a second demand, and threatened to sack Ahab's palace, **war ensued**. Assured of victory by an unknown prophet, Ahab fought Ben-Hadad and successfully defeated him. A year later, **Ben-Hadad sought revenge**, but he was again defeated by Ahab.

**9TH-CENTURY BC ARAMAIC INSCRIPTION DESCRIBING THE ATTACK ON ISRAEL**

**BEFORE** «

Having defeated Ben-Hadad, Ahab failed to kill him, and in doing so, condemned himself to death.

**A LIFE FOR A LIFE**

After Ahab of Israel's **second victory over Ben-Hadad «203**, the Aramaen king fled to the city of Aphek. From a hiding place in the city, he dispatched his officials to **appeal to Ahab to let him live**. Ahab agreed, and set free Ben-Hadad, a man who God had determined should die. An unnamed prophet confronted Ahab and exposed his failure: because Ahab had **disobeyed God** and had not executed Ben-Hadad, he **would soon lose his own life**.

**THE COVETED VINEYARD**

Naboth's vineyard in Jezreel, which he had inherited from his family, was close to the palace of Ahab and Jezebel, and was desired by the king as the perfect place to grow his vegetables.

# Naboth's Vineyard

*King Ahab coveted a vineyard, and Queen Jezebel devised a murderous plan to get her husband what he wanted. Their actions provoked God's condemnation, which was delivered by Elijah.*

**S**OMETIME AFTER his victories over Ben-Hadad of Aram, King Ahab visited his palace in Jezreel and spotted a vineyard nearby that would have served him as a wonderful vegetable garden. So he approached the owner, Naboth, and offered to purchase the vineyard from him or swap it for a better one elsewhere. Naboth refused, not because he was trying to be awkward, but because the practice of keeping property within the family and passing it on to children was a deeply held value at that time. He told Ahab, "The LORD forbid that I should give you the inheritance of my ancestors" (1 Kings 21:3).

### A sullen king

Whatever he tried, King Ahab could not get Naboth to agree to give up the vineyard. The king was not used to being rebuffed like this, and he went home to sulk and refused to eat. His wife, however, did not believe that a man like Naboth should stop Ahab getting what he wanted. She said to him, "Is this how you act as king over Israel? Get up and eat! Cheer up. I'll get you the vineyard of Naboth the Jezreelite" (21:7).

### Jezebel's plan

Jezebel forged letters from Ahab, instructing the city elders to invite Naboth to a civic dinner. Seated opposite him would be two scoundrels and, during the course

**PALACE RELIC**
This ornate fragment of ivory, believed to date from the 9th–8th century BC, was found in the remains of Ahab's palace, which is described in the Bible as being "adorned with ivory" (1 Kings 22:39).

of the dinner, they were to publicly accuse him of blasphemy against God and treason against the king. A charge of this nature could result in only one course of action – Naboth's execution. Jezebel's plan worked out exactly as she had intended, and, after being accused

of cursing God and the king, Naboth was stoned to death. With Naboth out of the way, especially in such circumstances, Ahab was able to seize the vineyard for himself.

### Elijah's message

In response to what had happened, God instructed Elijah to carry a message to the king. There was no love lost between Ahab and Elijah (see p.200–01), so when Elijah appeared Ahab sensed trouble, and greeted him with the words: "So you have found me, my enemy!" (21:20). Elijah replied that he had found Ahab because of his sins, and he then delivered his message from God. He denounced Ahab as a murderer and a thief and promised him that God would treat him in exactly the same way as Ahab had treated Naboth. Dogs, Elijah said, would lick up Ahab's blood from the soil and dogs would eat Jezebel's dead body in Jezreel. He added that "Dogs will eat those belonging to Ahab who die in the city, and the

**JEZREEL VALLEY**
The fertile agricultural land of the Jezreel Valley is bordered by Mount Tabor to the east and Mount Carmel to the south and west. The valley takes its name from the city of Jezreel, the location of Ahab's palace and Naboth's vineyard (1 Kings 21:1).

birds will feed on those who die in the country" (21:24), meaning that the royal house of Ahab would be brought to an end.

### Ahab repents

Ahab took Elijah's message seriously and humbled himself before God. He "tore his clothes, put on sackcloth and fasted. He lay in sackcloth and went around meekly" (21:27). As a result, God delayed the execution of Ahab's sentence, but promised to "bring it on his house in the days of his son" (21:29).

> ## "Let me have your vineyard to use for a vegetable garden, since it is close to my palace."
>
> **1 KINGS** 21:2

**AFTER** »

Queen Jezebel was assassinated when Jehu became king of Israel.

**JEHU BECOMES KING**
Ahab was killed in battle, during another conflict with Aram (1 Kings 22:29–40), but Queen Jezebel lived for a further ten years. God appointed Jehu to overthrow the house of Ahab, and he **killed King Joram**, the son of Ahab and Jezebel, and pursued Jezebel to Jezreel. The shameless Jezebel mocked Jehu's actions as treacherous. However, her servants, who supported Jehu, threw her out of the window. She died as she hit the ground, and **horses trampled on her corpse**. Jehu called to his servants, saying to them: "Take care of that cursed woman" (2 Kings 9:34). However, when the servants went to bury her, few bones remained, **fulfilling Elijah's prophecy** about her ignominious end.

**THE DEATH OF JEZEBEL**

**PEOPLE**

### JEZEBEL

The marriage of King Ahab of Israel to Jezebel, daughter of the priest-king of Tyre and Sidon, cemented a political alliance between the two countries. Jezebel was a fanatical worshipper of Baal-Melqart and the goddess Asherah (see pp.198–99) and was a dominating character who believed that the power of the monarchy was greater than Israel traditionally understood it to be.

The name of Jezebel developed negative connotations. In later Christian tradition, a Jezebel is a false prophet – a controlling and promiscuous woman.

**JEZEBEL AT THE WINDOW**

**ELIJAH LEAVES FOR HEAVEN**
At the end of Elijah's life, God took him to heaven in a chariot of fire drawn by horses of fire, as shown here in a painting from the Russian School, c.1600. Elijah's cloak fell to Elisha, who would take up his ministry.

BEFORE

Ahab's successor, his son Ahaziah, reigned only for a short time.

**JUDGMENT ON AHAZIAH**
Early in his reign, Ahaziah fell from an upper storey, hurting himself badly. He sent messengers to ask Baal's representatives in Ekron whether he would recover. **Elijah intercepted the messengers** and asked why Israelite prophets had not been consulted. He then called down fire from heaven to destroy two of the delegations sent by Ahaziah, before announcing to a third group that **the king would never recover** and that his death was **punishment for worshipping Baal**. As he had no sons, Ahaziah was succeeded by his brother, Joram.

ELIJAH BRINGS DOWN FIRE, 15TH-CENTURY ILLUMINATED MANUSCRIPT

> "Let me inherit a double portion of your spirit."
> 2 KINGS 2:9

HISTORY AND CULTURE

**THE DOUBLE PORTION**

When Elisha asked Elijah for a double portion of his spirit as a parting gift, he was in effect asking to become Elijah's heir. The term "double portion" came from Israel's inheritance laws (see Deuteronomy 21:15–17). According to these laws, when a father died his land would be shared out between all his sons, but the firstborn son would receive a larger share of two portions of land, confirming him as his father's primary heir and successor. The impact of this spiritual gift on Elisha was seen particularly in the miracles he went on to perform (see pp.210–11).

# Elijah and the Chariot of Fire

*Elijah's service as a prophet was brought to an end, not by his death, but when he was taken up into heaven in a spectacular manner. Elisha, his apprentice, assumed his mantle and became his natural successor.*

**E**LIJAH HAD SPENT his life on the move and, as he now came to the end of his time as a prophet, he went on one last journey. He had prophesied in the northern kingdom of Israel, but this final journey took him south to the cities of Bethel and Jericho, and eventually to the Jordan Valley. Elijah tried to discourage Elisha from accompanying him, but Elisha would not listen to him, and stayed at his master's side.

At each place they visited, they met other prophets, members of the local prophetic companies – groups of like-minded people who came together to preach and teach. These people knew that Elijah would soon be taken by God, and they warned Elisha about this. Elijah repeated his request for Elisha to leave him, but Elisha stayed with him to the end.

### Crossing the Jordan
When they came to the River Jordan, Elijah used his cloak to part the water, imitating Joshua's earlier crossing (see pp.120–21). Fifty prophets witnessed this miracle. Knowing that the end of his ministry was near, Elijah asked Elisha if he had any final request he could grant and Elisha requested a double portion of Elijah's spirit (see panel, left). Elijah replied that this request would be granted if Elisha witnessed his departure.

### Elijah is taken to heaven
As they walked, a chariot of fire appeared from nowhere and came between them. It caught up Elijah

**THE RIVER JORDAN**
Elijah, and Elisha after him, called upon God who parted the waters of the River Jordan to allow him to cross on dry land. This mirrored the parting of the river by Joshua, to allow the Israelites to cross.

and transported him to heaven, as if in a whirlwind. Elisha cried out "My father! My father!" (2 Kings 2:12) and tore his clothes in grief.

Having witnessed Elijah's departure, Elisha could now expect to become twice the prophet his master had been. Elijah had dropped his cloak and Elisha picked it up – literally inheriting Elijah's mantle. The cloak was put to immediate use when Elisha struck the River Jordan with it and crossed back over, repeating exactly what Elijah had done earlier. Those watching said: "The spirit of Elijah is resting on Elisha" (2:15), and he now began his ministry as a prophet in his own right.

These 50 prophets had observed everything that had happened from a distance. Even so, they were not convinced that Elijah had been taken to heaven and suggested that he may have been left by God on a distant mountain or valley. Reluctantly, Elisha agreed to let them send out a search party. As he anticipated, they returned after three days without having found Elijah.

AFTER

Elisha soon showed that he possessed a double portion of Elijah's spirit.

**A POWERFUL PROPHET**
Elisha quickly established himself as a credible successor to Elijah. He began to **perform miracles 210–11 »**, including restoring the purity of Jericho's water supply (2 Kings 2:19–22). He also cursed some young men in Bethel who mocked him, and they were mauled by bears (2 Kings 2:23–25). Elisha's later work was characterized by **prophecies of the future**.

ELISHA PUNISHES THOSE WHO MOCKED HIM

CAPITAL OF NORTHERN KINGDOM  Founded c.880 BC

# Samaria

## "He bought the hill of Samaria from Shemer… and built a city on the hill, calling it Samaria…"

1 KINGS 16:24

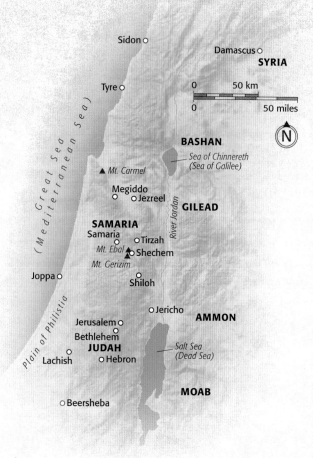

**F**OUNDED BY King Omri, Samaria was the capital of the northern kingdom of Israel. After the conquest by Assyria and then Babylon, it served as a provincial capital for both empires. The city was largely destroyed following the Maccabean Revolt (see pp.266–67), but was rebuilt by the occupying Romans

### SITE OF SAMARIA
The hill-top site of Samaria was an ideal location for a fortified city, since it was easily protected and had good access to regional trade routes. The city built by Omri and Ahab consisted almost entirely of royal residences.

(see pp.268–69), and prospered under Herod the Great. In New Testament times, the region of Samaria became a Roman toparchy – an administrative district – and was visited by Jesus.

### Strategic location
Situated on a hilltop 64km (40 miles) north of Jerusalem, Samaria lay near the main route leading north to the Esdraelon Plain. After reigning from Tirzah for some years, King Omri bought the hill as the site for his capital

### CITY OF SAMARIA
Part of Israel's hill country, Samaria lay to the south of the Mt Carmel range. It was capital of the surrounding country to which it gave its name. Samaria became synonymous with the Northern Kingdom.

city and named it after its former owner, Shemer (1 Kings 16:24), for two talents of silver. From his palace, which became known for its luxurious ivory decorations and furnishing, he would have been

able to see the Mediterranean Sea. His son and successor King Ahab completed the building of the city. From its inception, Israel was considered by the Judeans to be the home of illegitimate worship.

## KING OMRI

Omri is barely mentioned in the Bible but he was an important ruler – the first Hebrew king to rate a mention in Assyrian records. As an army commander, he overthrew Zimri in 885 BC to become king. He took time to secure control over Israel, initially reigning from Tirzah before building a new capital in Samaria. He built fortifications and began a palace, but chiefly used diplomacy to maintain peace. Omri was the founder of a new royal dynasty, all of whom did evil by worshipping Baal. He reigned for 11 years and was succeeded by his son, Ahab.

KING OMRI, 15TH-CENTURY ENGRAVING

---

Ahab turned it into a centre of idol worship by building a temple to Baal and other shrines, especially to the goddess Asherah. As a result, the prophets repeatedly denounced the city.

### Samaria in the Old Testament

Ahab defended Samaria against the attacks of Ben-Hadad of Aram, but was himself killed in the third round of hostilities between them. Under King Jehoram, the city was besieged by Aram and its population faced starvation until, as Elisha had prophesied, they experienced a miraculous delivery (2 Kings 7).

After Omri's dynasty came to an end, Israel suffered constant harassment and its fortunes fluctuated. When Jeroboam II was on the throne, the nation expanded and Samaria prospered, but in the 25 years following his reign, political instability and reckless rebellions meant that Israel was mostly at war. There were occasional brief respites, for example when Israel paid tribute to Assyrian king Tiglath-Pileser III.

In 721 BC, following a siege by the Assyrian king Shalmaneser V, Samaria finally fell to his brother

### ASSYRIAN TRIBUTE

The Black Obelisk is an Assyrian public monument that was erected in 825 BC, and shows King Jehu of Israel on his knees before Shalmaneser III.

and successor Sargon II. The new king deported more than 27,000 citizens from Samaria, then restored the city and settled it with non-Israelite subjects.

Under the Assyrians, Samaria became the capital of a province of the same name. After Assyrian rule gave way to the Babylonians and Persians (see pp.214–15), Samaria continued to be the capital of the province. After the exile, the Samaritans opposed the rebuilding of Jerusalem (see pp.260–61).

### Inter-testamental Samaria

Alexander the Great colonized Samaria with Greeks, and it became a centre of Greek culture. A temple was built on nearby Mount Gerizim and the city's defences were strengthened.

John Hyrcanus, the Hasmonean ruler of the Jews, led a revolt against the corruption of Judaism by Greek culture in c.108 BC. The city of Samaria, and the temple on Mount Gerizim, were destroyed.

Fifty years later the Romans rebuilt the city, repairing its fortifications and laying out a new pattern of straight streets. Samaria was greatly loved by King Herod the Great, who lavished resources

on it from 30 BC onwards. He renamed the city Sebaste – the Greek for "Augustus" – in honour of the Roman Emperor, who was thought to be divine. Where Omri's palace had stood, Herod built a temple to Augustus. Herod also brought new life to the city by building a stadium, theatres, and a forum, and also by resettling some 6,000 of his former soldiers there. Herod bequeathed the city to Archelaus, his son, who ruled ineffectively and briefly until the Romans took direct control. From then on, Samaria was ruled from the provincial capital, Caesarea.

### Samaria in the New Testament

The city of Samaria is not mentioned in the New Testament, although Jesus travelled through the region of Samaria (John 4:4) and encountered Samaritans. The Gospels illustrate the state of mistrust that existed between Jews and Samaritans.

Many Christians fled to Samaria to escape persecution in Jerusalem, and Philip, one of the deacons of the Early Church (see pp.422–23), went to the city to preach. Crowds gathered to see him, and he performed miracles. The apostles went to confirm Philip's work, and the Samaritan believers received the Holy Spirit (Acts 8:1–25).

The city of Samaria was ransacked during the first Jewish revolt of AD 66–70. Once again, it was restored and enlarged by the Romans between AD 180 and 230.

ALEXANDER THE GREAT

### PALACE RUINS

Archaeological artefacts including intricate ivory plaques have been found at the site of King Ahab's lavish palace, revealing the influence of Phoenician art and architecture.

- **c.880 BC,** Samaria is founded by Omri, king of Israel. Building work in the city, including the lavish and ambitious palace, is later completed by his son, Ahab.

- **c.874–853 BC,** Ahab rules Israel, enlarging his father's capital city at Samaria.

- **c.850 BC,** Samaria is repeatedly attacked by King Ben-Hadad of Aram. Ben-Hadad's siege leads to famine, and Ahab is killed in the fighting.

- **c.841–814 BC,** Jehu, who was anointed king to remove the line of Ahab, cleanses the kingdom of Israel of Baal worship.

- **c.814–798 BC,** Jehoahaz succeeds Jehu as king of Israel and leads the nation away from God. Allows an Asherah pole – a wooden symbol of the goddess Asherah – to stand in Samaria (2 Kings 13:6).

- **c.793–753 BC,** the city of Samaria expands under King Jeroboam II.

- **c.734–733 BC,** Tiglath-Pileser III of Assyria attacks Israel, but leaves Samaria intact.

- **c.725–722 BC,** Samaria is besieged by Assyrian King Shalmaneser V.

- **c.721 BC,** Samaria is conquered by Sargon II and repopulated with non-Israelites.

- **c.587 BC,** following the demise of Assyria, Nebuchadnezzar II of Babylon conquers Jerusalem. Samaria is a minor provincial capital.

- **c.559–530 BC,** Persian king Cyrus the Great defeats the Babylonians, taking control of the empire. Samaria is loyal to Persian rule and exercises the right to mint coins.

- **c.331 BC,** Alexander the Great destroys Samaria, then rebuilds it as a Greek city.

- **c.108 BC,** Samaria is destroyed by John Hyrcanus following the Maccabean revolt.

- **63 BC,** the Romans start to rebuild the city following Pompey's capture of Jerusalem in the same year.

- **From 30 BC,** the city is lavishly restored by King Herod the Great and renamed Sebaste.

- **AD 6,** under Herod the Great's son Archelaus, Samaria becomes a provincial capital of the Roman province of Judea.

- **c. AD 33,** the Church is founded in the region of Samaria – possibly in the city itself – following a visit by Philip the evangelist.

- **AD 66–70,** Samaria is destroyed during the Jewish revolt against Roman rule.

## BEFORE

**Joram succeeded Ahab as king and began to reform Israel's religion.**

### MOAB'S REBELLION
Joram started well by **removing the Baal shrine that his father Ahab had erected** ≪ **208–09**, but he did not continue the changes. Mesha, king of Moab, decided to
withhold the tribute he had been paying to Israel, and the Moabites commemorated this by producing the Mesha Stele, incised with details about their king.

**MESHA STELE, 9TH-CENTURY BC**

### ELISHA'S ROLE
**Israel moved to crush Moab**, enlisting the support of Judah and Edom. Victory was prophesied by Elisha and it **came about in a miraculous way**. Water flooded the Edom Desert, but the sun made it look like blood. The Moabites assumed that their enemies had turned against each other and when they advanced they were **cut down and defeated**.

# Elisha's Miracles

*Elisha followed in the footsteps of Elijah and was a prophet to Israel for more than 50 years, from the reigns of Ahab to Jehoash. As well as performing a series of miracles, Elisha led several schools of prophets.*

**E**LISHA ESTABLISHED his prophetic credentials, as the inheritor of the mantle of Elijah, in a series of miraculous acts. These included his cleansing of the polluted water supply in Jericho, and his cursing of youths who mocked him at Bethel – they were mauled shortly afterwards by bears (2 Kings 2:24).

Elisha's phrases, such as "this is what the LORD says" (3:17) and "hear the word of the LORD" (7:1), demonstrate the same passion for God's word as Elijah. However, whereas Elijah was more feared by those in authority, Elisha was more favourably disposed to Israel's rulers, who regularly sought and received his counsel.

### Personal miracles
In a miracle reminiscent of his master Elijah, Elisha provided a desperately poor widow with an unending flow of olive oil, so she could raise the money to stop her two sons being sold into slavery to pay for her debts (see panel, right).

He also made a prediction to a wealthy woman from Shunem, who, because she believed him to be "a holy man of God" (2 Kings 4:9), had regularly provided him with hospitality. He promised the

> "Don't be afraid... Those who are with us are more than those who are with them."
>
> **2 KINGS** 6:16

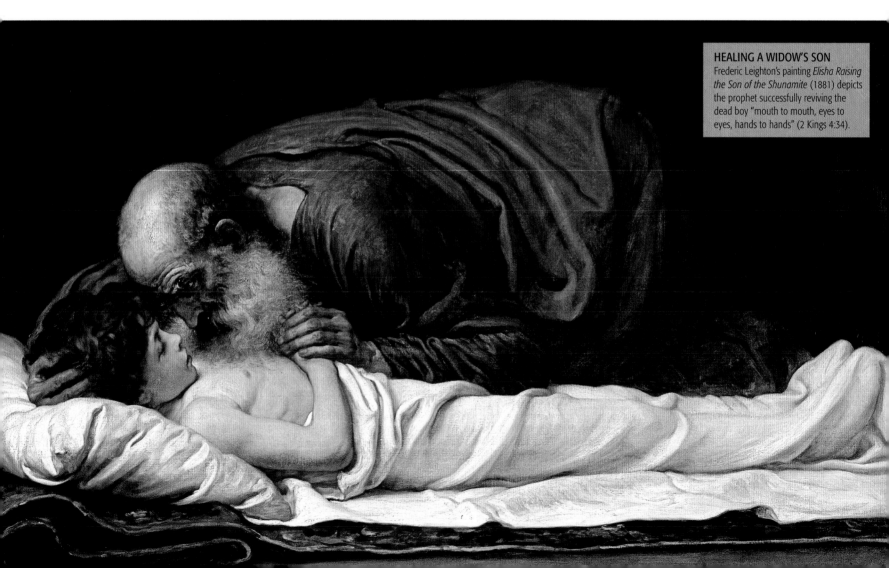

**HEALING A WIDOW'S SON**
Frederic Leighton's painting *Elisha Raising the Son of the Shunamite* (1881) depicts the prophet successfully reviving the dead boy "mouth to mouth, eyes to eyes, hands to hands" (2 Kings 4:34).

**IRON AXE HEAD**
In Elisha's day, an iron tool – such as this axe head, excavated in modern-day Israel – was expensive, so when he retrieved a borrowed axe head from a river, it was a valuable deed.

## HISTORY AND CULTURE
### DEBT SLAVERY

When Elisha thwarted a creditor who was coming to take a widow's two sons into slavery in lieu of money he was owed, he was preventing the loss of a poor woman's children into years of unpaid work.

Among the ancient Israelites, if other means of paying off debts failed, it was lawful for a creditor to take a family member as a slave until the debt was redeemed. The law on slavery is outlined in Leviticus 25, which stipulates that Hebrew slaves were to be treated differently from slaves from other nations: "They are to be treated as hired workers or temporary residents among you" (Leviticus 25:40). A relative could buy their freedom at any time, but if all else failed, they should be set free in the Year of Jubilee and their property should be restored. Such a year arose every "seven sabbath years – seven times seven years... a period of forty-nine years" (25:8).

woman, who was barren, that she would have a son. She became pregnant, but the child died when he was just a small boy.

When Elisha heard this terrible news, he commanded his servant, Gehazi, to go urgently to Shunem to restore the boy to life. Gehazi's intervention failed, but when Elisha arrived, prayed, and stretched over the boy's corpse, the boy was miraculously restored to life.

### In the company of prophets
Elisha lived with a group of other prophets. When they were eating a stew that mistakenly included poisonous ingredients, Elisha calmly removed the threat by adding flour to the pot. He also fed 100 people with 20 loaves of bread from the city of Baal Shalishah.

On another occasion, the group went to cut poles to build a larger meeting place. One man dropped a valuable iron axe head into the River Jordan, where it sank without trace. Elisha cut a stick and threw it into the river, and the metal axe-head floated up so that the man could pull it out.

### Aiding kings and generals
Political leaders often sought out Elisha for advice. When the kings of Israel, Judah, and Edom attacked the king of Moab, Elisha, inspired by music, assured them that they would be victorious, as indeed they were.

On another occasion, the king of Aram asked Joram, the king of Israel, to cure the leprosy that infected his general, Naaman. Joram was distressed, knowing that he could not do so, but Elisha volunteered to cure the general. He told Naaman to bathe seven times in the River Jordan. Naaman, angered at the perceived insult to his own country's rivers, did so reluctantly. He was healed, and said: "Now I know that there is no God in all the world except in Israel" (2 Kings 5:15).

Another miracle occurred when the king of Aram tried to capture Elisha, because his prophetic knowledge had been foiling his plans for ambush. As Aram's soldiers advanced on Elisha's hiding place, the prophet prayed to God to blind them. Elisha then led the blind Arameans right into the city of Samaria. However,

rather than demanding their execution, he asked the king of Israel to give them food and water, with the result that tensions eased between Aram and Israel.

Sometime later, the Aramean army again besieged Samaria, giving rise to a severe famine. Questioned by the king of Israel, Elisha told him that the siege would end within 24 hours. The following day God caused the beseiging Arameans to hear the sound of a great army, and they fled, mistakenly thinking they were being attacked by Hittite and Egyptian troops. Once more Elisha's prophecy had come true.

**CURING A LEPER**
The centre panel of a 15th-century Dutch triptych depicts the episode when Elisha cured Namaan, the commander of the Syrian army, of leprosy: "Go, wash yourself seven times in the Jordan, and your flesh will be restored and you will be cleansed" (2 Kings 5:10).

> "'Do not kill them... **Set food and water before them** so that they may eat and drink and **then go back to their master.'**"
> **2 KINGS** 6:22

**AFTER** »

**Elisha eventually died from illness but his influence continued to the end.**

**A FINAL PROPHECY**
When the **elderly Elisha fell ill**, King Jehoash came to pay his respects. Elisha asked the king to take his bow and shoot an arrow eastwards from a window; Elisha said that the arrow **represented victory over Aram**. Then he told the king to shoot more arrows. The king shot just three more arrows into the ground, then ceased; a furious Elisha told the king that he should have fired five or six arrows and his actions meant that Israel would defeat Aram only three times, not completely destroy it.

**A 19TH-CENTURY PAINTING BY WILLIAM DYCE DEPICTS JEHOASH SHOOTING ARROWS FOR ELISHA**

# Jonah and the Great Fish

*The prophet Jonah initially refused to obey God when sent to Nineveh to prophesy its destruction. But after being shipwrecked and rescued, he fulfilled his commission. Many people repented, but Jonah was displeased at God's mercy and sought to end his life.*

**J**ONAH, SON OF Amittai, was instructed by God to go to Nineveh and warn its citizens that their wickedness was known by God. Nineveh was the capital city of Assyria (see pp.216–17), an empire that was growing in power.

Instead of obeying, Jonah fled on a ship bound for Spain. God then sent a great wind "…and such a violent storm arose that the ship threatened to break up" (Jonah 1:4). The superstitious sailors cast lots to find out who on board was responsible for the storm. When they identified Jonah, he told them who he was running away from and that if they cast him overboard the sea would become calm.

Reluctantly, the sailors threw Jonah overboard, and a great fish swallowed him. He lived in its belly for three days, praying all the while for deliverance, before the fish spewed him up, alive, on the shore.

God then commissioned Jonah a second time; this time he obeyed, entering Nineveh and warning the people of God's imminent judgment. The people listened, fasting and putting on sackcloth in repentance. Seeing their reaction, God spared them. However, this angered Jonah, who believed that God should put justice before mercy.

Jonah sought shelter from the burning heat and welcomed the shade God supplied in the form of a plant. God then made it wither. When Jonah complained, saying he was so angry he would rather die, God rebuked him for being more concerned with the plant than for a city "in which there are more than a hundred and twenty thousand people" (Jonah 4:11), even if they were morally ignorant.

> ❝ **'Go to the great city of Nineveh** and preach against it, because its wickednes has come up before me.' **But Jonah ran away from the LORD** and headed for Tarshish.❞

JONAH 1:2,3

**THROWN INTO THE SEA**
A 13th-century illumination in the Book of Jonah shows the sailors pointing out Jonah as the one responsible for the storm; he is then pictured with the fish and seeking shade under the plant.

CONQUEST AND EXILE  Origins *c.*3300 BC  Decline 331 BC

# The Nations of Mesopotamia

> "The **God** of glory **appeared to our father Abraham** while he was still **in Mesopotamia,** before he lived in Haran."
>
> ACTS 7:2

**M**ESOPOTAMIA is Greek for "the land between the rivers", referring to the fertile area between the Tigris and Euphrates rivers, but it also came to describe the wider surrounding region. From Abraham's day, the movement of people and power in Mesopotamia had a major impact on the biblical story.

Ancient Mesopotamia was a diverse region, made up of many different tribes, peoples, and languages. It was a place of busy trade and active cultural growth, fostering such advances as the formation of city states and the development of written records.

## The Sumerians

The first complex society to develop in Mesopotamia was that of the Sumerians, who emerged as early as *c.*3300 BC in Sumer, in the southern half of contemporary Iraq. The Sumerians developed irrigation systems, invented counting and calendar systems as well as cuneiform writing, and composed epic literature. The language and customs of Genesis were greatly influenced by Sumerian civilization. The biblical story of the Tower of Babel names Sumer as "Shinar", the place where the tower was built (Genesis 11:1–9).

## The Assyrians

Originating in the north of Mesopotamia in the late 3rd millennium, the Assyrians (see pp.216–17) were a warlike people who came to dominate the region from the 10th century BC. They conquered territories, making them into vassal states; allegiance to Assyria and her deities was firmly enforced. Assyria appears in the biblical story at several points, most notably under Tiglath-Pileser III – named "Pul" in 2 Kings 15:19 – the Assyrian king who regained lost

**ASSYRIAN CITADEL**
Located at Mosul in modern-day Iraq, Nineveh was the third capital of the Assyrian Empire. At its heart was the palace of Sennacherib, which boasted limestone foundations and walls 20m (72ft) high.

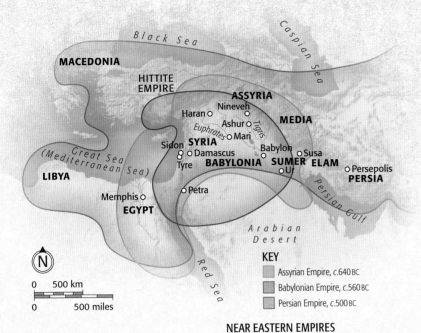

NEAR EASTERN EMPIRES
The empires of the great Near Eastern civilizations Assyria, Babylon, and Persia – centred on the fertile area between the Tigris and Euphrates rivers – are shown here at their maximum extents.

**KEY**
- Assyrian Empire, *c.*640 BC
- Babylonian Empire, *c.*560 BC
- Persian Empire, *c.*500 BC

## INSIGHTS FROM THE PAST

A number of Mesopotamian findings have shed light on the biblical story. A hoard of 4,000 clay tablets from Nuzi in modern-day Iraq contains details of the royal family and ordinary people in the 3rd millenium BC, describing customs similar to those of the Patriarchs. The Black Obelisk (see p.216) mentions King Jehu of Israel, and the Babylonian Chronicles are in line with the Bible's account of the period 625–595 BC. The Cyrus Cylinder includes details of the Persian king's conquest of Babylon and the return of the Jewish exiles.

**CYRUS CYLINDER, *c.*539–530 BC**

- **c.3300–3000 BC,** evidence of first Sumerian civilization.
- **c.1894–1595 BC,** Babylon's first Amorite ruling dynasty follows the break-up of Sumerian unity.
- **c.1792–1750 BC,** Hammurabi, the Amorite dynasty's sixth ruler, composes a law code consisting of 282 paragraphs.
- **c.1382–1374 BC,** in the first instance of Mesopotamian oppression of Israel recorded in the Bible, Cushan-Rishathaim of Aram rules over Israel for eight years before the Judge Othniel defeats the Aramean king (Judges 3:8–10).
- **c.885–860 BC,** Assyrian western expansion begins, leading to conflict with Israel.
- **c.859–824 BC,** Shalmaneser III extends Assyria's borders and receives tribute from Israel.
- **c.734–733 BC,** Assyrian king Tiglath-Pileser III attacks Israel, but leaves Samaria standing.
- **c.722 BC,** Samaria falls to Assyrian king Sargon II after a three-year siege (2 Kings 17:6). He deports the population and the nation of Israel ceases to exist.
- **701 BC,** Sennacherib of Assyria besieges Jerusalem, but withdraws when his army is slaughtered overnight by "the angel of the LORD" (2 Kings 19:35).

territory and pushed his empire into Israel and Judah in the 8th century BC. Jonah was sent by God to warn the people of the Assyrian capital, Nineveh, of their coming defeat by the Babylonians (Jonah 3). They fasted in repentance and the city was spared.

### The Chaldeans

Originally a semi-nomadic tribe, the Chaldeans settled in the lower reaches of the Euphrates by the 9th century BC. Chaldea features in the Old Testament in several discrete episodes: Abraham's family came from "Ur of the Chaldeans" (Genesis 11:28–31) and Job lost his camels to Chaldean raids (Job 1:16,17). Later biblical books – including Daniel, Isaiah, and Ezekiel – referred to the Babylonians as Chaldeans and viewed them as a threat to Judah. Ezekiel prophesied that King Hezekiah would be captured by Chaldeans (Ezekiel 12:13), and that "the Babylonians and all the Chaldeans" would punish Egypt (23:23).

### The Babylonians

Babylon – a city north of Sumer in central Mesopotamia – was a major force in the region in two distinct periods (see pp.244–45). The Old Babylonian period reached its zenith with the rule of the Amorite king Hammurabi in the 18th century BC. The Chaldeans took control of Babylon in 721 BC, and the later

Neo-Babylonian period emerged when this new dynasty, in a coalition with the Medes, attacked Assyria in 627 BC and destroyed the capital, Nineveh, in 612 BC.

Babylon (see pp.244–45) appears at several points in the Bible. Babylonian people had been resettled in Samaria (see pp.208–09) by the Assyrians in the 8th century BC. King Marduk-Baladan of Babylon tried to make an alliance with Judah in the late 7th century BC (2 Kings 20:12), and the prophet Isaiah foretold Judah's exile in Babylon (Isaiah 39:5–7).

The Babylonian King Nebuchadnezzar defeated the Egyptians at Carchemish in 605 BC, sacked Jerusalem in 597 BC, and carried its people into exile (see pp.236–39).

### The Persians

Migrating from central Asia in the 2nd millennium, the Persians settled in the eastern region of the Persian Gulf by the 9th century BC. King Cyrus II overthrew the Medes in 550 BC and conquered Babylon in 539 BC to form

the vast Achaemenid Empire, and created a new royal base at Pasargadae ("city of the Persians"). He liberated the Jews from exile in Babylon, permitting them to return to Jerusalem to begin rebuilding the Temple (2 Chronicles 36:22,23; Ezra 1:1–3; Isaiah 45:13). From 522 BC Darius I built palaces at Persepolis and Susa, and enabled the completion of the rebuilding of the Temple at Jerusalem and the city walls (Nehemiah 1–13). In the Book of Esther, Xerxes I (486–465 BC) chose Esther to replace Queen Vashti, and saved many exiled Jews from persecution. Persian rule came to an end in 331 BC after defeat by Alexander the Great.

**ASSYRIAN WINGED BULL, *c.*717–706 BC**

- **c.612 BC,** Assyrian capital Nineveh falls to Babylon after slow decline of empire.
- **c.609–608 BC,** Assyrian Empire ends and is replaced by the Babylonians.
- **c.605 BC and 597 BC,** first two deportations of Judeans to Babylon under Nebuchadnezzar II.
- **c.587 BC,** Jerusalem and its Temple destroyed by the Babylonians, and the third deportation of Judeans to exile.
- **c.539 BC,** Babylon falls to Persian King Cyrus II (the Great) of Anshan. Babylonian Empire ends. Cyrus decrees Judean exiles may return to Jerusalem a year later.
- **c.522 BC,** Darius I becomes king of Persia.
- **c.331 BC,** Persian forces are defeated by Alexander the Great. Some Jews choose to remain in Babylon (see pp.256–57), later compiling a Hebrew text, the Babylonian Talmud.

Head dress detailed with gold leaf

Necklace decorated with amber beads

**SUMERIAN SPLENDOUR**
Found at Ur in the tomb of Queen Pu-abi, the variety of precious metals and semiprecious stones in this head dress, necklaces, and earrings demonstrate the wealth and trading networks of the Sumerian city-state.

## BEFORE

**The Assyrians were the descendants of a group of scattered nomadic tribes, who settled in northern Mesopotamia around 2300 BC.**

### THE ORIGINS OF ASSYRIA

Assyria was first populated by Sumerian nomads, whose earliest settlements date from the 4th millennium. **They eventually built a number of independent city-states ‹‹ 214–15**, such as Ashur (or "Assur"), Nineveh, and Nimrud (the "Calah" named in Genesis 10:11,12 as "the great city", and founded by the grandsons of Noah). All these settlements were located in the **rich agricultural areas along the upper Tigris River**, with its abundant water supply. Nineveh was said to be so large "it took three days to go through it" (Jonah 3:3).

King Asshur-uballit I (1364–1329 BC) secured Assyrian independence from Mittani by defeating its ruler Shuttarna II. Asshur-uballit consolidated the city-states into one Assyrian nation that began its emergence as a powerful regional empire – one that would later temporarily rule **Babylon 244–45 ››**.

#### HAIL THE KING
The Black Obelisk, erected in 825 BC at Nimrud, bears scenes of tribute to Assyria's King Shalmaneser III. Here, a bowing Jehu, King of Israel, brings his offerings, said by an inscription to include chalices of gold.

HISTORY AND CULTURE

### ASSYRIAN MARTIAL TACTICS

Early adopters of the new military technologies of their age, the Assyrians had iron weapons when many enemies were still using bronze, and they were the first to use cavalry units. Their battle tactics were to shower the enemy with arrows, then use chariot and cavalry charges to divide them, and follow up with infantry.

Experts in siege warfare, using ladders, battering rams, and towers, the Assyrians had a fearsome reputation for the brutal suppression of defeated opponents.

**A 7TH-CENTURY BC STONE RELIEF FROM NINEVEH DEPICTS ASSYRIANS SEIZING A CITY**

# Threat From the East

*During the 9th century BC, a new superpower arose in Mesopotamia. The warlike Assyrians conquered a huge empire and remained the dominant power in the region for more than 200 years.*

**SSYRIA LAY TO** the northeast of Israel, between the Syrian Desert and the Persian Hills in modern-day Iraq. Its dramatic expansion threatened Israel, and eventually led to its downfall.

### Rise of the empire
An Assyrian city – Ashur – is first mentioned in the Bible in Genesis, in relation to the Garden of Eden. The third river said to flow from Eden is the "Tigris; it runs along the east side of Ashur" (Genesis 2:14). Assyria formed into a nation state in the 23rd century BC, when

it was part of a vast empire ruled over by Sargon of Akkad; when the empire fell c.2150 BC, the nation split into two kingdoms: Assyria in the north and Babylon in the south. From the 14th to the 11th century,

#### EXPANSION AND WORSHIP
The remains of a ziggurat – a stepped-pyramid temple – lie at the Assyrian city of Ashur on the west bank of the Tigris at an important crossing point for caravan routes. The temple was built c.1800 BC, under Shamshi-Adad I.

Assyria's rule by the great kings Asshur-uballit I (1364–1329 BC), Tukulti-Ninurta I (1242–1207 BC), and Tiglath-Pileser I (1114–1076 BC), made it the dominating power in

> **" We submitted to Egypt and Assyria** to get enough **bread**. Our ancestors **sinned and are no more**, and we bear their **punishment."**
>
> **LAMENTATIONS** 5:6,7

with Pul's support. There is both biblical and historical evidence that Pul went on to capture Damascus (2 Kings 16:9), and that under Hoshea's reign Israel was besieged and defeated, and its people taken into exile in Assyria (17:5,6).

### An unrivalled power

In 663 BC Assyria defeated Egypt at Thebes, and at this point it was acknowledged as a power without rival. Vassal states were forced to pay tribute, so the empire generated huge wealth, enabling the Assyrian kings to build grand palaces in Nimrud, Khorsabad, and other cities – Jonah attested to the "very large" city of Nineveh (Jonah 3:3).

the region. Its power then waned, but in 910 BC it again rose to conquer many nations, including Persia, Aramea, Judah, and Israel. The Assyrians had the most disciplined and well-equipped army of the time, and acquired a reputation for ruthlessly subjugating its enemies and executing their leaders.

Assyria's expansionist policies were continued by Tiglath-Pileser III (744–727 BC). Known in the Bible both as Tiglath-Pileser and Pul, he is said to have invaded Israel during the reign of Menahem (2 Kings 15:19), forcing the king to raise 1,000 talents of silver from his people to stay in power

#### TERRACOTTA MODEL OF AN ASSYRIAN WARRIOR

This Assyrian figurine – identifiable as a soldier by his shield and tall helmet – sits awkwardly on the horse's rump, which suggests that this model was made prior to the reign of Tiglath-Pileser III (744–727 BC), when a dedicated cavalry emerged.

Some Israelite kings were defiant: for example, King Ahab was in an alliance of 11 local kingdoms that fought against Shalmaneser III at the battle of Qarqar in 853 BC. Others tried to appease the Assyrians: King Jehu is depicted paying homage to Shalmaneser on an obelisk in the ancient Assyrian capital of Nimrud (see left); later kings also paid them tribute.

Occasionally, the Assyrian campaigns helped Israel. In 804 BC, an attack by Assyria on Israel's enemy, Aram, allowed King Joash to recapture some towns that had previously been lost to Aram. On the whole, however, Assyria was an ever-present threat.

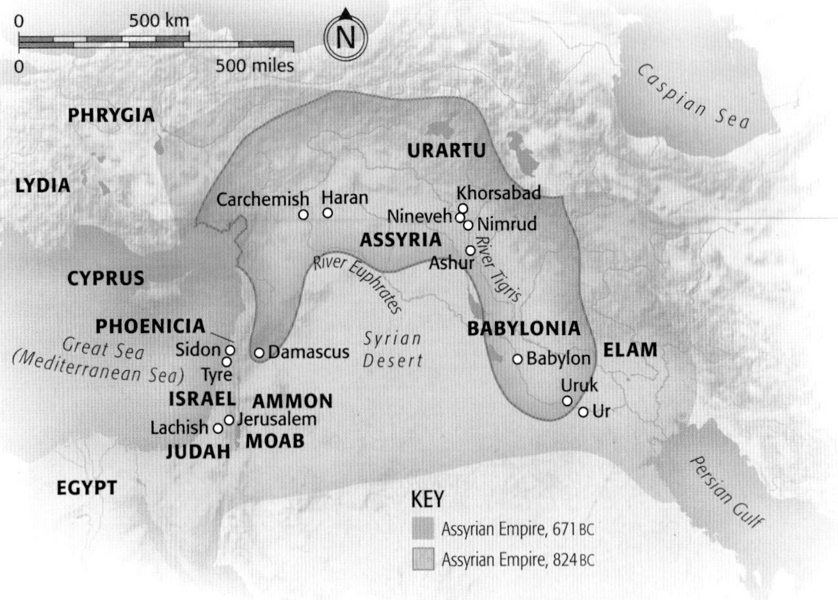

**DOMINANT EMPIRE**

This map shows the extent of the Assyrian Empire at the time of Shalmaneser III – fought by Israel's King Ahab and paid tribute by King Jehu – and Sargon II, who completed the defeat of Israel in c.720 BC.

Map labels: PHRYGIA, LYDIA, CYPRUS, URARTU, Carchemish, Haran, Nineveh, Khorsabad, Nimrud, ASSYRIA, Ashur, River Euphrates, River Tigris, PHOENICIA, Great Sea (Mediterranean Sea), Sidon, Tyre, Damascus, Syrian Desert, BABYLONIA, Babylon, ELAM, Uruk, Ur, ISRAEL, AMMON, Lachish, Jerusalem, JUDAH, MOAB, EGYPT, Caspian Sea, Persian Gulf

KEY
Assyrian Empire, 671 BC
Assyrian Empire, 824 BC

0   500 km
0   500 miles
N

> **"...Israel, prepare to meet your God."**
>
> **AMOS** 4:12

**AFTER**

**The Assyrian Empire collapsed when the resurgent Babylonians became the new power on the international stage.**

#### DEFEAT BY BABYLON

Assyria remained the dominant state in the region until the late 7th century BC, but **such an extensive empire was unsustainable**. Subject peoples began to form alliances to rebel against Assyria's power, and in the comparative weakness that followed the death of Ashurbanipal in 627 BC – and the outbreak of an internal power struggle to succeed him – they acted, including the vassal kingdom of Judah. **King Nabopolassar of Babylon played a key role in the empire's eventual downfall 244–45** ❯❯. In 625 BC, he led a force that expelled the Assyrians from Babylon. With his allies the Medes, he then captured the cities of Ashur (614 BC), Nineveh (612 BC), and finally Haran (610 BC), bringing Assyrian rule to an end.

# HISTORY AND CULTURE

# Warfare

> "In famine he will **deliver you** from death, and in **battle** from the stroke of **the sword.**"

JOB 5:20

**ROMAN PROJECTILES**
Iron ballista (catapult) bolts and lead slingshot pellets were just some of the missiles used by the Romans against their foes.

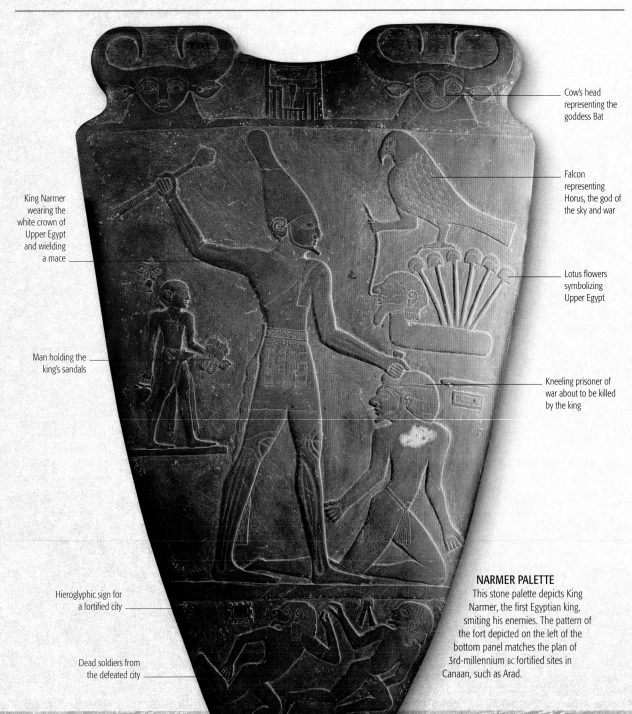

Cow's head representing the goddess Bat

Falcon representing Horus, the god of the sky and war

King Narmer wearing the white crown of Upper Egypt and wielding a mace

Lotus flowers symbolizing Upper Egypt

Man holding the king's sandals

Kneeling prisoner of war about to be killed by the king

Hieroglyphic sign for a fortified city

Dead soldiers from the defeated city

**NARMER PALETTE**
This stone palette depicts King Narmer, the first Egyptian king, smiting his enemies. The pattern of the fort depicted on the left of the bottom panel matches the plan of 3rd-millennium BC fortified sites in Canaan, such as Arad.

Canaan was a region often subject to war. Competition for agricultural land, water, and raw materials brought settled communities into conflict with one another, and prompted raids by nomadic pastoralists. Neighbouring major states expanded and fought on Canaan's soil. Even in the 3rd millennium BC there were strongly fortified cities, such as Arad, where excavations have revealed substantial defensive walls and towers. Egypt gained control of Canaan after 1550 BC. Its armies were kept busy fighting in the north to defend its conquests, first against the Mitanni and later the Hittites. From the 12th century BC the Philistines – the term for several groups of people who came from the Aegean region – settled in southern Canaan. They remained a potent political power until at least the 7th century BC.

The 1st millennium BC was a troubled time, with local conflicts and the menace of successive expanding superpowers. Israel and Judah were often in conflict with each other and with neighbouring tribes, city-states, and kingdoms. A succession of empires – Assyrian, Babylonian, Persian, Greek, Seleucid, and Roman – invaded the region. Under Seleucid and Roman rule, abuses of power and religious persecution sparked bloody revolts.

## WEAPONS AND ARMIES

Israel's first standing army was raised by King Saul (1 Samuel 13:2); his successors, David and Solomon, then created a fully professional army, which included foreign mercenaries. If necessary, the army could be supplemented by troops levied from the various tribes, as in earlier times. There were several reasons why a man could be excused from military service – for example, if he was betrothed or displayed cowardice that might affect others' courage (Deuteronomy 20:5–8).

Common weapons included arrows and simple bows, slings and stones (1 Samuel 17:40), and bronze daggers and spears. Members of the elite classes had bronze axes, helmets, and scale armour. The composite bow, made of three layers – of sinew, wood, and horn – greatly increased the range and penetration of arrows, but was not much used in Canaan until the time of David. In the 1st millennium BC bronze was largely superceded by iron, and the use of swords became more common.

Sickle sword

**CANAANITE WARRIOR**
This bronze figurine of a warrior holds a spear and a sickle sword, a weapon that has been found at several archaeological sites in Egypt and Canaan.

## HORSES AND CHARIOTS

The introduction of light horse-drawn chariots with spoked wheels revolutionized warfare. Developed in the 17th century BC, chariots were not much used in Canaan before 1000 BC. By this time they had become mobile firing platforms for one or two bowmen or spearmen. Bridles made it possible to control a horse while fighting, so cheaper and more manouverable cavalry began to replace chariots for fighting. The Israelites, however, still mainly used horsemen for rapid delivery of messages.

**EGYPTIAN CHARIOTEER**
This painting on Tutankhamun's casket shows him skilfully wielding a bow and arrow while driving his chariot at full speed.

## FORTIFICATIONS

Frequently threatened by local or international enemies, cities in Canaan were among the best defended in the ancient world. Stout walls and towers – often surrounded by a ditch and constructed on a mound with a glacis (smooth plastered slope) – prevented besiegers gaining access to city walls with their scaling ladders, siege towers, and battering rams.

Attackers often built ramps to bring siege engines close to the walls. Remains of the Assyrian siege ramp at Lachish in 701 BC have been excavated, along with arrows, slingshots, and a defensive inner mound that was built to counter attempts to undermine the city's walls.

**DEFENSIVE GATE**
The remains of this fortified gate with casemate walls at Tell Hazor, Israel, include two large, chambered towers with bulwarks on either side, flanking the road into the city.

The Romans introduced far more powerful and devastating siege weapons, including the ballista, which shot massive iron bolts or heavy stones, and the onager, which hurled rocks.

Sieges could be long: Samaria, for example, held out against the Assyrians for three years (2 Kings 17:56). A reliable supply of water was essential to the inhabitants of a besieged city. Innovative engineering in times of peace made this possible. Tunnels constructed under Jerusalem, for example, gave access to the Gihon spring (2 Kings 20:20).

## CONSEQUENCES OF WAR

In armed raids on towns and villages, men were slaughtered and livestock seized (Genesis 34:25–28). Defeated cities were often sacked and looted (2 Kings 14:13–14). Conquerors seized objects of national or religious significance, for symbolic and psychological effect. For example, King Nebuchadnezzar of Babylon looted the holy vessels from the Temple in 597 BC (Daniel 5:2–3), and the Second Temple's treasures were paraded in the Roman Triumph after the Jewish Revolt of AD 66–74 (see pp. 466–67).

A defeated state might simply be forced to pay tribute as a vassal (2 Kings 15:19–20). It was only after revolts against their authority that the Assyrian and Babylonians tortured and executed the leaders and deported many thousands of families to other parts of the empire (2 Kings 17:6; 24:10–16). Conditions for deportees varied: they were often enslaved under later Assyrian kings, but many of those deported to Babylon earned positions of trust and chose to stay there when the Persian King Cyrus offered to repatriate the Jewish exiles.

**PRISONERS OF WAR**
Jewish captives are led off to a life of slavery by a victorious Assyrian soldier.

# The Defeat of Israel

*With Assyria the dominant power in the region, Israel's position was increasingly precarious. Israel was conquered by Assyria in 720 BC and its people were dispersed, as God had warned would happen if they disobeyed him (Leviticus 26; Deuteronomy 4; 28).*

THE BIBLE explains the demise of Israel in religious rather than political terms, but its size meant that it had always been vulnerable to the attentions of its neighbour, Assyria, to the north. By the time that Menahem was king of Israel (c.752 BC) it was paying taxes to Assyria, where Tiglath-Pileser III had become king in 744 BC.

Pekah, who became king of Israel c.734 BC, formed an alliance against Assyria with Rezen, king of Aram. When the southern kingdom of Judah refused to join, war broke out. Tiglath-Pileser took advantage to seize territory, execute Rezen, and deport people to Assyria. Israel was initially spared, probably because Hoshea, the new king who had assassinated Pekah, gave tribute and land to Assyria.

When Hoshea attempted to form an alliance with Egypt in 724 BC, Shalmaneser V (Tiglath-Pileser's successor) attacked and seized Hoshea. Israel's capital, Samaria, was besieged until it was captured in around 722 BC by either Shalmaneser or his successor, Sargon II. After this, the kingdom of Israel ceased to exist and became a vassal state of Assyria. Thousands were deported from Samaria (see pp.208–09), and an Assyrian governor was appointed to rule over the lands.

Israel's downfall is described in 2 Kings 17:7–23. According to Kings, the Israelites had sinned against the God, "who had brought them up out of Egypt from under the power of Pharaoh king of Egypt" (17:7). They had refused to hear God's repeated warnings through the prophets, and had "worshipped other gods and followed the practices of the nations the LORD had driven out before them" (17:8). So God became angry with them and sent them into exile.

The ten tribes who formed Israel disappeared from the Bible story and from historical accounts after their exile. Some would have been resettled in Assyria or the cities of the Medes (modern Iran), while others would have dispersed further across the ancient world. Some remained in their home lands; they intermarried with the Assyrian settlers and became associated with the Samaritans – people who opposed Judah's resettlement after the exile and whom the Jews would despise in New Testament times (see p.308).

> "All this took place because the **Israelites had sinned against the LORD their God…**"
>
> 2 KINGS 17:7

**FALL OF A NATION**
Israel was conquered by the Assyrian kings Tiglath-Pileser III and Sargon II. This limestone relief, from Nimrud in northern Iraq, shows Assyrian soldiers attacking an enemy town c.737–727 BC.

## « BEFORE

Israel believed that God was not a "dumb idol" (1 Corinthians 12:2) but spoke through the prophets.

PROPHETS DEPICTED ON THE PORTAL OF STRASBOURG CATHEDRAL, FRANCE

### AN OLD TRADITION
In Israel there was a long-standing belief that God used prophets to bring his word to the people. Even **Abraham « 60–61**, Israel's founding father, was seen as a prophet (Genesis 20:7).

### THE PROPHET'S ROLE
Prophets **foretold the future** and called people to live in line with **God's covenant and law « 200–01**. Prophets also spoke to God on behalf of the people.

### PROPHETIC STYLE
The personality of each prophet influenced their language and style. Besides declaration, the prophets used **parables** (2 Samuel 12:1–14), **songs** (Isaiah 5), symbolic actions (Jeremiah 32), and **drama** (Ezekiel 4,5).

### THE TWELVE MINOR PROPHETS
John Singer Sargent (1856–1925) portrayed all the Old Testament prophets in his *Frieze of Prophets* (left to right): Zephaniah, Joel, Obadiah, Hosea, Amos, Nahum, Ezekiel, Daniel, Elijah, Moses, Joshua, Jeremiah, Jonah, Isaiah, Habakkuk, Micah, Haggai, Malachi, and Zechariah.

# The Twelve Minor Prophets

*Twelve prophets from the 9th to the 5th centuries BC were grouped in the Hebrew Bible on to one scroll, named "The Book of the Twelve". These important historical writings are minor only in terms of length.*

**E**ACH MINOR PROPHET wrote for a particular historical era, reflecting key aspects of life at that time (see panel, right, which lists the 12 in the order that they appear in the Bible). The most significant are Hosea, Joel, and Amos.

### Hosea and Israel's unfaithfulness
God told Hosea to marry a woman called Gomer, who would be unfaithful – a picture of the pain God himself felt about his people: "for like an adulterous wife, this land is guilty of unfaithfulness to the LORD" (Hosea 1:2). Hosea had three children, named as Jezreel

("God scatters"), Lo-Ruhamah ("not loved"), and Lo-Ammi ("not my people"), to express God's feelings towards Israel at the time.

Hosea's writings alternate between tales of his marriage and God's

## " I will raise up for them a prophet… from among their fellow Israelites"
DEUTERONOMY 18:18

### MOUNTING A WATCH
Prophets in the Old Testament were depicted as watchmen – as Isaiah 21:8 says, "I stand on the watchtower ",like this example in Samaria – warning the people about impending danger from foreign powers, and of words from God.

words concerning Israel's infidelity. The book records that Gomer was unfaithful to Hosea, so he rebuked her; it then gives God's words rebuking Israel for its unfaithfulness to him. Hosea divorced his wife, but God told him to marry her again, even though she deserved nothing; God says that likewise Israel is undeserving, but he will love her nonetheless. Hosea told his wife she must be faithful in the future; likewise God asks Israel to change its ways and repent: "You are destroyed, Israel, because you are against me" (Hosea 13:9). However, Israel need only "return… to the Lord your God" (Hosea 14:1), and God will again "love them freely"

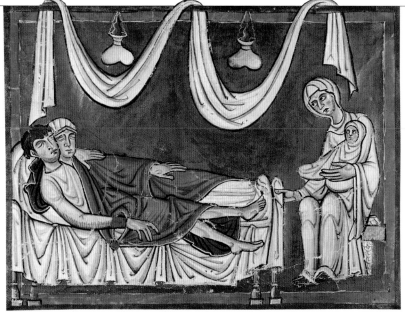

**HOSEA AND GOMER**
This illustration from the medieval Bible of St. André aux-Bois, shows Hosea the prophet in bed with his adulterous wife, Gomer, while someone else looks after their child. God ordered the marriage, saying it would be like Israel's faithless relationship with him.

> " Surely the Sovereign LORD does nothing without revealing his plan to his servants the prophets. "
> AMOS 3:7

**AFTER**

Prophecy disappeared between the Old and New Testaments, but it returned with John the Baptist, Jesus, and the Early Church.

**THE NEW PROPHETS**
John the Baptist's prophecies **prepared the way for the Lord,** and as the long-awaited Messiah, Jesus exercised the **gift of prophecy 308–09 »** and gave it to his followers. Acts and the New Testament letters show that prophecy was part of early church life. Paul, addressing members of the **church in Corinth 444–45 »**, wrote "you can all prophesy..." (1 Corinthians 14:31).

**JOHN THE BAPTIST (1438), BY DONATELLO**

(Hosea 14:4). He will deliver them from war and famine.

### Joel and the Spirit of the Lord
When a huge plague of locusts had devoured the crops across the land, Joel said this was a warning from God and a reminder of the coming "Day of the LORD" (Joel 2:28) when God would pass judgment on all nations. If the people repented and returned to God, he would restore to them all that had been destroyed. Moreover, a day would come when he would pour out his Spirit on all his people. The New Testament records this as being fulfilled on the day of Pentecost (Acts 2:14–21).

### Amos's call to righteousness
Although Amos came from Judah, God sent him north to Israel, to the town of Bethel, where King Jeroboam I had set up a shrine to false gods. Amos began prophesying by condemning Israel's neighbours. Then he turned on Israel, saying that they would also face God's judgment; even though they were God's people, they had acted wrongly when they knew better. Amos exposed unrighteousness, challenging corruption in the law courts and in the economy, and condemning those whose wealth came at the expense of the poor. He said that God does not tolerate false worship; "I despise your religious festivals; your assemblies are a stench to me" (Amos 5:21). No amount of religion could cover up such unrighteousness. Instead, what God was demanding of them was an immediate demonstration of justice: "let justice roll on like a river, righteousness like a never-failing stream!" (Amos 5:24).

# FALL, EXILE, AND RETURN

"When seventy years are completed for Babylon, **I will come to you and fulfil my good promise to bring you back to this place.** For I know the plans I have for you… plans to **prosper you and not to harm you**, plans to **give you hope and a future.** Then you will call on me and come and pray to me, and **I will listen to you.**"

JEREMIAH 29:10–12

 FTER SOLOMON'S DEATH in c.931 BC, the kingdom of Israel split into the southern kingdom of Judah, with Jerusalem as its capital, and the northern kingdom of Israel, whose capital was Samaria. Judah survived as an independent state until c.597 BC, when it finally succumbed to the Babylonians led by Nebuchadnezzar. The conquerors destroyed the city of Jerusalem and its Temple in c.587 BC and took almost its entire population to Babylon. The exiles were to remain there, in captivity, until King Cyrus II of Persia gave permission for them to return to Judah in c.539 BC.

After the division of the kingdom, Judah continued to be ruled by kings from the house of David. Some were good kings, such as Abijah, Asa, Azariah (or Uzziah), and the reforming Josiah, who, late in the day, led the nation in a spiritual revival. Others, such as Joash and Hezekiah were less benevolent, and some – such as Ahaz and Manesseh – ruled with evil intention. Increasingly, the nation proved unfaithful to God, which was to lead to its collapse.

### THE DOWNFALL OF JUDAH

During the power struggles in the region during the late 7th century BC, Judah looked to Egypt for support, but in c.605 BC the joint armies of Egypt and Assyria were defeated by the Babylonians at Carchemish, leaving Judah vulnerable. The first of three waves of exiles occurred at this point, when Judah's elite youths – including Daniel (see pp.242–43) – were taken to Babylon. The Babylonians attacked again in c.597 BC, and Judean King Jehoiachin surrendered. Ten years later King Zedekiah led a rebellion, but Babylon responded by destroying Jerusalem and taking almost all its people into exile in

c.587 BC. Most of the exiled Judeans settled into distinct communities in Babylon, observing their own customs. However, these were adapted to fit restrictions of the new environment: in the absence of the Temple, for example, worship became reshaped around the study of the Torah. The Kingdom of Judah, meanwhile, was left largely depopulated, and was ruled from Samaria.

### THE RETURN

In 539 BC Babylon fell to the Persians and their king, Cyrus II, decreed that the Judean exiles could go home. The Book of Ezra lists the names of the families, priests, and temple servants (Ezra 2) who returned to rebuild Jerusalem and the tiny province of Judea. With scarce resources, their difficult work was made harder by constant harassment from the Samaritans. It was only with the later intervention of Ezra and Nehemiah, who led parties to rebuild the temple and city walls in c.458 BC and c.445 BC, that the nation became established again. However, the future of Judea, like its past, was to be anything but settled.

**JERUSALEM IN RUINS**
The English artist William Brassey Hole's painting, *The Destruction of Jerusalem* (1910), illustrates the Holy City burning to the ground. It was attacked by Nebuzaradan, Nebuchadnezzar's commander, in c.587 BC.

**REBUILDING THE TEMPLE**
According to the Book of Ezra, the Persian King Cyrus appointed Sheshbazzar to rebuild the Temple on its old site (Ezra 5:16), as shown in this 13th-century Bible illustration.

**BEFORE** «

David and Solomon had ruled over all 12 tribes of Israel, but in 930 BC, Rehoboam's inept rule resulted in the division of the kingdom.

**14TH-CENTURY MANUSCRIPT ILLUMINATION OF REHOBOAM WITH THE ELDERS**

## THE SOUTHERN KINGDOM

The ten northern tribes split from the two southern ones to **form the breakaway kingdom of Israel «** 194–95. The two tribes that remained under the rule of David's family were Judah and Benjamin.

As the **dominant tribe, Judah** gave its name to the whole nation. **Jerusalem** remained its capital and **Solomon's Temple its sole place of worship «** 172–73.

# Good Kings, Bad Kings

*When the united kingdom broke up, kings from the house of David continued to reign over Judah from Jerusalem. However, increasingly they were unfaithful kings and eventually God's patience ran out.*

**A**LTHOUGH NOT ALL of Judah's kings were faithful followers of God, the Bible views them as the true heirs of David, in contrast to the kings of Israel. Judah's kings were believed to be the custodians of the nation's covenant with God and of the one divinely authorized Temple in Jerusalem.

The books of Kings intermingle the stories of the kings of Israel and Judah. Scholars have generally interpreted this account as presenting a view that rulers who are faithful to the covenant bring peace and prosperity (Judah remained comparatively stable), but those who neglect it bring trouble and disaster (Israel was continually in turmoil). The books of Chronicles that follow try, scholars believe, to present the kings of Judah in as good a light as possible, so as to emphasize the legitimacy of the line of David.

### The first kings of Judah

Rehoboam (*c*.930–914 bc), the first king, started out loyal to God but later erected shrines to false gods.

Abijah (*c*.914–911 bc), his son, continued these unrighteous ways, and was in continual conflict with Jeroboam, king of Israel (1 Kings 15:1–8). His son, Asa (*c*.911–870 bc), was a good monarch who removed false worship and led Judah to prosperity. He was also at war with Israel, but agreed a treaty with King Ben-Hadad of

> "**Nevertheless, for the sake of his servant David**, the Lord was **not willing to destroy Judah**."
>
> 2 KINGS 8:19

## JEHOIADA THE PRIEST

**12TH-CENTURY SPANISH MANUSCRIPT DEPICTS JEHOIADA ANOINTING JOASH AS KING**

After a brief reign, Ahaziah was killed by Jehu for following the idolatrous "ways of the house of Ahab" (2 Kings 8:27). Power was seized by Ahaziah's mother, Athaliah, who purged all opposition. However, she missed Joash, an heir who had been hidden. Six years later, a priest, Jehoiada, got military support to overthrow Athaliah, and he crowned Joash in the Temple. Jehoiada's action restored Judah as God's covenant people and Joash later repaired the Temple, which had fallen into ruin.

## RAMOTH GILEAD

Photographed a century ago, this city lies in the tribal territory of the Gad but was held by the Arameans. An alliance of Jehoshaphat of Judea and Ahab of Israel fought to retake it and Ahab was mortally wounded.

Aram, to the north of Israel, switching Aram's allegiance from Israel to Judah. This forced Baasha, king of Israel, to withdraw his forces (1 Kings 15:9–23).

### Devoted to God

Jehoshaphat (c.870–847 BC), Asa's son, reigned for 25 years and had "great wealth and honour. His heart was devoted to the ways of the Lord..." (2 Chronicles 17:5,6). He turned the people back to God by teaching the Book of the Law, and used tributes to strengthen his army, cities, and stores. He appointed judges and courts. Peace was achieved with Israel and Edom, with whom he joined forces against the Arameans to return Ramoth-Gilead to Israel. Judah was miraculously saved from a "vast army" invading from Moab and Ammon, but a later alliance with Ahaziah, king of Israel,

resulted in God destroying some newly-built trading ships (2 Chronicles 17–21).

Jehoshaphat married his son, Jehoram (c.847–842 bc), to Athaliah, daughter of King Ahab of Israel. Jehoram promoted pagan worship, and suffered defeat when Edom, a kingdom to the south under Judah's rule, rebelled.

Jehoram's son, Ahaziah (c.842–841 BC), was killed by Jehu when he took the throne of Israel from Joram, with whom he had joined forces. His mother, Queen Athaliah (c.841–835 BC), killed his heirs and ruled for seven years herself.

However, Ahaziah's sister Jehosheba had hidden his infant son and heir Joash (c.835–796 BC) in the Temple. Joash was crowned king when he was only seven (see panel opposite) and reigned for 40 years. He repaired the Temple, but abandoned God when his trusted advisers died, and was eventually assassinated. His son Amaziah (c.796–767 BC) took to the throne but suffered defeat by Israel, and was also assassinated.

### Turning to and from the Lord

Azariah (c.767–736 BC), also called Uzziah, was co-regent with his father Amaziah until the latter's death c.767 BC. Despite being a

great king who ruled for 52 years, God later made him leprous for burning incense in the Temple, an act that was reserved for the Levite priesthood alone. Jotham (c.752–732 BC), his son, was also a good king but Ahaz (c.732–716 BC), his successor, was one of Judah's worst – using pagan practices such as child sacrifice, and turning to the king of Assyria for help when Judah was besieged by Israel and Aram (2 Kings 16:7–9).

Hezekiah (c.716–686 BC) introduced religious reform and experienced a miraculous deliverance from the Assyrian army. Overcoming illness, he succumbed to pride and unwisely displayed his wealth to envoys from Babylon (see pp.228–29), which would have repercussions.

Manasseh (c.686–643 BC) was among the worst rulers (see p.229), but was humbled and repented (2 Chronicles 33:10–16). Amon (c.643–641 BC) worshipped idols and was assassinated.

### Judah's end

Josiah (c.641–609 BC) led a spiritual revival when the covenant of the Law was rediscovered (see p.232). However, Judah was set on a course of spiritual decline. During the short reigns of Jehoahaz (c.609 BC), his brother Jehoiakim (c.609–598 BC), Jehoiachin (598–597 BC), and Zedekiah (c.597–586 BC), Judah increasingly succumbed to idolatry as it was caught in conflicts between Assyria, Egypt, and Babylon, ending with the fall of Jerusalem and exile in Babylon (see p.244).

> " In his time of trouble, **King Ahaz** became even more unfaithful to the Lord."
>
> 2 CHRONICLES 28:22

### GALLERY OF KINGS

On the 13th-century West Front of Notre Dame Cathedral in Paris, France, 28 sculptures depict the kings of Israel and Judah. They date from the 19th century, having been carved to replace the originals, damaged by anti-monarchists during the revolution.

**AFTER** »

**God's people hoped for a day when the Lord would intervene to bring them deliverance from oppression.**

#### THE TRUE DAY OF THE LORD

The 8th-century prophets warned that "the day of the Lord" **would not be what people expected**: "Why do you long for the day of the Lord? **That day will be darkness,** not light. It will be as though a man fled from a lion only to meet a bear, as though he entered his house and rested his hand on the wall only to have a snake bite him" (Amos 5:18,19).

Rather than deliverance, the day would bring God's punishment, **through Babylon 236–39, 244–45 »**, for his people's disobedience. **Amos** was not a professional prophet, such as Elisha, but a **critic of social injustice**, which he believed was a breach of the covenant with God that would invoke his divine wrath. Amos's **message of divine judgment became a staple of prophetic writing**, as did his promises of restoration – when the **ploughman will overtake the reaper** and Israel would be planted "never again to be uprooted from the land I have given them" (9:15).

## BEFORE

Hezekiah's predecessor, Ahaz, presided over a disastrous time in Judah.

### A WEAK KING

Ahaz adopted the **false religious practices** of Israel and even sacrificed his own son, which was forbidden by God. After defeat by Israel and Aram, Ahaz **appealed to Assyria ≪ 214–15** for support. The Assyrians secured peace for him, but **depleted Judah's treasury** and took valuable articles from the **Temple ≪ 172–73** as payment.

AHAZ'S SEAL, c.732 BC

# King Hezekiah

*King Hezekiah "did what was right in the eyes of the Lord" (2 Kings 18:3), cleansing the Temple, reintroducing the Passover, strengthening Judah's infrastructure, and enjoying victory over his enemies.*

**H**EZEKIAH probably ruled from 729 BC as co-regent with his predecessor, Ahaz, who suffered from leprosy, and then reigned in his own right from c.715 to c.686 BC. He was a reforming king, and overturned his father's religious policies, which had encouraged idolatry and allowed the Temple to fall into neglect. He removed the high places where idols were worshipped, and destroyed Moses's bronze snake (see p.114), which had been a means of healing in the wilderness but had since become associated with idolatry. Next, Hezekiah repaired the Temple and removed the idolatrous symbols from it. He then reformed the priesthood, and reintroduced the offering of sacrifices that the Law required. When there were enough qualified priests to officiate, he invited the

**PRIDE BEFORE A FALL**
In this painting by Vincente López y Portaña (1772–1850), Hezekiah shows the treasures of his kingdom to a Babylonian visitor. His pride displeased God, who promised Hezekiah that it would all be taken away from him.

# "Hezekiah trusted in the LORD, the God of Israel. There was **no one like him** among **all the kings of Judah.**"

2 KINGS 18:5

people to celebrate the Passover, which they had not done for several years. People came to the celebration from all over Judah and from the northern kingdom of Israel. People gave generously towards these reforms.

### Other successes

Hezekiah was "successful in whatever he undertook" (2 Kings 18:7), and became very wealthy. He built new villages, strengthened Judah's defences, and built a tunnel to provide Jerusalem with water (see panel, below). He was also successful in battle, and gained victory over the Philistines.

### Threat from Assyria

During Hezekiah's reign, the dominant power in the region was Assyria. In 722 BC, the Assyrians had

conquered the northern kingdom of Israel. After this, Hezekiah joined an anti-Assyrian alliance with Egypt, but this provoked Assyria to attack Judah. Having lost several cities, Hezekiah bought peace, but at a heavy price. To pay the Assyrians as tribute, he gave "all the silver that was found in the temple of the LORD and in the treasuries of the royal palace" (2 Kings 18:15) and even stripped off the gold that had covered the Temple doors and doorposts.

### Jerusalem under siege

The peace did not last, however. The Assyrian king, Sennacherib, sent his troops to besiege

### SENNACHERIB PRISM

This 7th-century BC hexagonal clay document, buried in Sennacherib's palace foundations at Nineveh, was inscribed for posterity and for the gods with his achievements, and records his attacks on 46 cities of Judah and the siege of Jerusalem.

### LACHISH

A royal city in Judah, Lachish was destroyed by King Sennacherib of Assyria, as part of his assault on the fortified cities of the kingdom. Hezekiah was unable to prevent this attack, but hoped to broker peace by offering to pay a substantial tribute to Assyria.

Hezekiah "like a caged bird within Jerusalem his royal capital", as Sennacherib described it in his own account, recorded on the Sennacherib prism (see left). The Assyrian troops tried to intimidate Jerusalem's population into submission. However, the prophet Isaiah, who was Hezekiah's confidant, assured Hezekiah that Jerusalem would not fall, and when Hezekiah prayed for deliverance God answered in a remarkable way. The book of 2 Kings records that "the angel of the LORD went out and put to death a hundred and eighty-five thousand in the Assyrian camp" (2 Kings 19:35). Sennacherib's army withdrew and returned home. Jerusalem was free, but weakened.

### Hezekiah's final days

When Hezekiah fell ill and was dying, he prayed to God. Isaiah assured him that God had heard him and granted an extension to his life, and Hezekiah recovered. King Marduk-Baladan of Babylon sent a gift and good wishes to Hezekiah, and his envoys were shown Judah's great wealth of treasures during their visit. As a result, Isaiah prophesied that the time would come when all Hezekiah's possessions and some descendants would be carried off to Babylon.

## HISTORY AND CULTURE

### HEZEKIAH'S TUNNEL

Hezekiah knew the importance of a secure water supply for Jerusalem, especially if the city was ever besieged. So a tunnel, 530m (1,750ft) long, was dug from solid rock to bring water from the Gihon Spring to the Pool of Siloam in the west of the city. It was cut from both ends simultaneously and, remarkably, the diggers met in the middle. The city wall was extended to protect this new water supply and other supplies were cut off, so they could not be used by an enemy.

**HEZEKIAH'S TUNNEL**

## "This is what the LORD says: **Do not be afraid of what you have heard** – those words with which the **underlings of the king of Assyria have blasphemed me.**"

ISAIAH 37:6

### AFTER

**King Manasseh succeeded Hezekiah, and undid all the good work that his father had done.**

#### RELIGIOUS BETRAYAL

Manasseh **reinstated the idolatrous high places** and led people back to the worship of Baal and Asherah. Violence erupted in Jerusalem and many people were killed. Then God **punished Manasseh** with defeat and deportation to **Babylon 244–45 ⟩⟩** as a humiliated prisoner. However, Chronicles tells us that God responded to his prayers of repentance and **gave him a second chance**. So when he was restored to the throne, Manasseh **rebuilt Judah's defences and restored its pure worship**. Many of his subjects, however, continued with their pagan practices.

# OLD TESTAMENT EVANGELIST 8th century BC

# Isaiah

## "Here am I. Send me!"

ISAIAH 6:8

**O**NE OF THE most important and influential of the prophets, Isaiah prophesied in an unstable period during the reigns of four Judean kings, when Assyria was in the ascendency. Isaiah is mentioned in the books of Kings and Chronicles, as well as giving his name to the book of Isaiah, which records his sermons and his signs.

Isaiah lived in Judah during the 8th century BC. The Bible tells us little about his family background, only that he was the son of Amoz, about whom we know nothing, and that he was married to an unnamed woman who was a prophetess. Isaiah's name meant "God saves". His own two sons were also given names that served

as prophetic signs about their time: Shear-Jashub, who was taken to meet King Ahaz, meant "a remnant will return", while Maher-Shalal-Hash-Baz's name meant "swift to the plunder, quick is the spoil", referring to the overthrow of Damascus and Samaria.

According to a later Jewish rabbinic tradition, Isaiah came from royal lineage – he certainly had easy access to Judah's rulers and exercised considerable political influence.

### The call

In the year of King Uzziah's death, Isaiah visited the Temple in Jerusalem, where he had an awesome vision of God's throne and received his call to be a prophet. The mention of Uzziah (also known as Azariah) dates this event to around 736 BC. The vision led Isaiah to confess his sin and, once cleansed, to receive God's commission to preach – although God warned him that his message would not be warmly accepted (Isaiah 6).

### Challenging times

Isaiah was a contemporary of the prophet Micah and would therefore have been active as a prophet during the reign of Jotham as king of Judah. However, it was

**COMMISSIONED BY GOD**
A fresco from the 12th-century Catalan School depicts the commissioning of Isaiah. Six-winged biblical creatures called Seraphim appear to Isaiah above God's throne. One of the creatures touches Isaiah's lips with a burning coal, so freeing him from guilt and atoning for his sins.

**PROPHET ISAIAH**
This illuminated detail from the 12th-century Latin manuscript *Commentary of Saint Jerome upon Isaiah* shows the prophet as author, holding a scroll in his hands.

during Ahaz's reign that Isaiah really came to prominence. Ahaz did not follow the ways of God, and instead promoted idolatry and pagan practices (2 Chronicles 28:3). He refused to ally with Aram and Israel against Assyria

and equally refused to follow Isaiah's advice (Isaiah 7:12) and trust God for deliverance from Assyrian aggression (7:17). Instead, Ahaz sought Assyria's protection, which merely encouraged Assyria's king Tiglath-Pileser III to capture the neighbouring states and subject Judah itself to vassal status.

King Hezekiah, who succeeded Ahaz, chose a different path to his father. He introduced spiritual reform and invited the few people left in Israel to celebrate the Passover in Jerusalem. He rebelled against Assyria, then quickly sought to recover his position with them. When Sennacherib, King of Assyria, demanded that Jerusalem should surrender, Isaiah encouraged Hezekiah to resist and trust in God (37:6). Sennacherib's army withdrew without taking Jerusalem.

## Isaiah's message

Isaiah was a courageous prophet who denounced the sins of Judah and called for justice to be practised by God's people. He prophesied about both his own time and times to follow. His preaching was poetic and full of vivid imagery and he complemented his words with symbolic signs. His favourite term for God was "the Holy One of Israel", which encapsulated his emphasis on God's power, judgment, and salvation. Isaiah presented God as the sovereign of all the nations, so his prophecies condemned other nations as well as Judah, while also bringing promises of salvation (Isaiah 12:2).

Isaiah saw Assyria and Babylon as instruments used by God for disciplining the unfaithful people of Judah, climaxing in exile to Babylon. A "remnant" of the people would be restored to Jerusalem and experience God's renewed and enhanced salvation (10:21). This return would be accomplished

> " The Earth will be filled with the knowledge of the LORD…"
>
> ISAIAH 11:9

through Cyrus of Persia, whom Isaiah calls an "anointed one": "the LORD says… I will raise up Cyrus in my righteousness: I will make all his ways straight. He will rebuild my city and set my exiles free" (Isaiah 45:11,13).

Another of Isaiah's major themes is that of the "suffering servant", the person whose very suffering for God becomes the means to redemption (see Isaiah 52:13–15).

## The book of Isaiah

Many scholars believe that the book of Isaiah is a compilation of the prophecies of several individuals, rather than one "Isaiah". Chapters 1–39 relate to the 8th-century Assyrian period and the reigns of Ahaz and Hezekiah. From chapter 40 onwards the book relates to the background of the 6th-century exile in Babylon and later in the restored

**COMING OF THE MESSIAH**
Isaiah prophesized the Messiah's virgin birth. Later known as the "Old Testament Evangelist", Isaiah features in many depictions of the Annunciation, such as this painting by the Italian Neri di Bicci (1419–91), which shows the prophets David and Isaiah holding barrens or scrolls with Old Testament inscriptions.

### ISAIAH SCROLL
The Isaiah Scroll is the oldest complete version of the book of Isaiah, dating back to around 120 BC. It is one of the better preserved sections of the Dead Sea Scrolls discovered in caves near Qumran.

city of Jerusalem. Most of the book consists of Isaiah's prophetic messages, but chapters 24–27 are stylistically different and are known as "Isaiah's Apocalypse", while chapters 36–39 are a historical account of Hezekiah's reign, repeating the events covered in 2 Kings 18–20.

Isaiah's death is not recorded in the Bible, but later Jewish rabbis suggested that he died as a martyr during the reign of Manasseh.

## LISTS
### ISAIAH'S KEY PROPHECIES

1. The virgin will conceive and bear a son (Isaiah 7:14)
2. The government that brings peace will rest on a child's shoulders (9:6)
3. The wolf and lamb will live in harmony (11:6)
4. The desert and the wilderness will blossom (35:1)
5. Valleys will be raised, mountains will be levelled, and God's glory will be revealed (40:4–5)
6. The servant's wounds will bring healing (53:5)
7. The light has shone and God's glory has risen (60:1)
8. Good news to the poor (61:1–3)
9. The creation of a new heaven and earth (65:17)

## ◀◀ BEFORE

Solomon's magnificent Temple in Jerusalem had fallen into disrepair because of the polytheistic practices of much of the population under the rulers prior to Josiah.

### JOSIAH'S PREDECESSORS

Although he had repented, Manasseh had already aroused God's wrath as one of the most evil rulers of Judah (2 Kings 21:10–15).

Manasseh rebuilt the "high places" (where idol worship took place) that Hezekiah had destroyed ◀◀ 228–29, allowed pagan altars to Baal to be re-erected, made an Asherah pole just as Ahab had done ◀◀ 208–209 , built altars at the Temple to worship the stars and "sacrificed his own son in the fire, practised divination, sought omens, and consulted mediums and spiritists" (2 Kings 21:6). His son and successor Amon continued to defile the Temple during his short, two-year reign, so that it needed to be restored under Josiah.

Like Josiah later, both Joash ◀◀ 226–27 and Hezekiah had restored the Temple at the beginning of their respective reigns. However, Hezekiah had resorted to raiding Temple treasure to buy his kingdom protection from Assyria ◀◀ 216–17.

### FAMILY OF KINGS
A stained glass biblical window in the Corona Chapel of Canterbury Cathedral, UK, contains this depiction of King Josiah from a Tree of Jesse, c.1200. Josiah is one of the kings mentioned in the genealogy of Jesus in Matthew's gospel.

## ANALYSIS
### THE BOOK OF THE LAW

Josiah's revival stemmed significantly from the discovery of the "Book of the Law", which is an important landmark in the history of the religion of Israel because it reminded people of their covenant with God. Josiah was able to purge Judah's religion and thereby "fulfil the requirements of the law written in the book" (2 Kings 23:24).

The term "Book of the Law" could refer to the Pentateuch (see pp.16–17), the first five books of the Bible. However, many scholars believe that it was the book of Deuteronomy (see Analysis panel, p.115), which records the covenant treaty and stresses themes also emphasized in Kings: a central place of worship, no high places, the Passover, the need to obey God, and the need to avoid his curse.

# King Josiah

*Josiah was an exemplary king of Judah who is thought to have reigned in the late 7th century BC. With the rediscovery of the lost "Book of the Law", he renewed the nation's covenant with God and instigated a spiritual revival.*

**J**OSIAH BECAME KING at the age of eight. Both his father, Amon, and his grandfather, Manasseh, had turned from God, worshipping idols such as Baal and Molek, and thus had done "evil in the eyes of the LORD, following the detestable practices of the nations the LORD had driven out before the Israelites" (2 Kings 21:2). However, as Josiah grew up, he became steadfast in his search for God, and at the age of 20 he started a campaign to eradicate idol worship from his kingdom.

### Josiah's religious reforms
One day, Josiah sent his secretary, Shaphan, to the Temple in Jerusalem with instructions that the high priest, Hilkiah, should transfer the collection money to a large workforce engaged to repair the Temple building.

When Shaphan went to Hilkiah to deliver the message, the high priest told him that the building project had led to the discovery of a scroll – the "Book of the Law", the covenant document from the time of Moses.

### The "Book of the Law"
Shaphan took the book to the king and read from it in his presence. Josiah immediately expressed

## RELIGIOUS REFORMS
The archaeological site of Tel Beer Sheba contains the remnants of a cult centre that featured a large horned altar. This is one of the "high places" (2 Kings 18:3) that may have been destroyed by King Josiah or Hezekiah (Josiah's great-grandfather).

## PEOPLE

## WOMEN PROPHETS

Huldah, like Isaiah and Jeremiah, was a prophet who was protected by the king for speaking the word of God and foretelling the future. Other women named as prophets include Miriam (the sister of Moses); Deborah (the only woman judge); Isaiah's unnamed wife; Anna (see pp.290–91); Philip's four daughters (Acts 21:8,9); and women of the Corinthian church, in the New Testament.

**THE SONG OF MIRIAM, BY LUCA GIORDANO (1634–1705)**

# "'I have found the Book of the Law in the temple of the LORD.'"

2 KINGS 22:8

and none of the kings of Israel had ever celebrated such a Passover as did Josiah…" (2 Chronicles 35:18).

### Josiah's end
In Josiah's time, the Assyrian empire was disintegrating and Babylon's influence was rising. When the Egyptians marched to the Euphrates in support of Assyria, Josiah intervened and sought to stop them at Megiddo. Pharaoh Necho sent him a message telling him not to get involved since this fight was not his concern: "God has told me to hurry; so stop opposing God, who is with me, or he will destroy you" (2 Chronicles 35:21). Josiah stubbornly refused to listen and was determined to pursue the Egyptians. He went disguised into battle but, as Pharaoh had warned, he was wounded by an archer and died shortly after being taken from the battlefield.

sorrow that Judah had departed so far from God's law and realized that the nation deserved to face God's anger. "Great is the LORD's anger that burns against us because those who have gone before us have not obeyed the words of this book" (22:13).

Realizing that the nation was likely to be punished for its divergence from God's law, Josiah sent Shaphan and Hilkiah to visit the local prophet Huldah for help. She confirmed that God was angry, sending the message, "I am going to bring disaster on this place and its people" (22:16); however, because Josiah had shown such remorse, humility, and spiritual integrity, God's judgment would be postponed for a while.

Josiah went to the Temple and read out the "Book of the Law" to an assembled crowd. He publicly renewed the covenant with God on behalf of the nation, "to follow the LORD and keep his commands, statutes and decrees with all his heart and all his soul" (23:3), and then made the people renew their commitment to it as well.

To purge the nation, Josiah ordered the removal and destruction of all pagan shrines and objects of idol worship within the Temple and across Judah –

including the "high places" (23:5) where incense was burned to Baal, the sun, moon, and stars – and at Samaria in Israel. He also denounced and got rid of the "mediums and spiritists" (23:24).

### The Passover was celebrated
Josiah then revived the neglected feast of the Passover – the annual commemoration of the exodus from Egypt (see pp.102–03). He and his officials provided many of the people's sacrificial offerings from their own resources. The priests, Levites, gatekeepers, and musicians all played their part in a magnificent celebration. The writer of the book of Chronicles observed, "The Passover had not been observed like this in Israel since the days of the prophet Samuel;

> " Josiah… turned to the LORD… with all his heart and with all his soul and with all his strength…"
>
> 2 KINGS 23:25

## TEL MEGIDDO
This aerial photograph shows Megiddo, where King Josiah was fatally wounded by an arrow fired by one of Pharaoh Necho's archers. Josiah's officers took his body in a chariot back to Jerusalem for burial.

**AFTER**

**Josiah's humility had caused God to suspend the punishment that Judah's evil practices had merited.**

### JUDGMENT DESCENDS
Upon Josiah's death, **the people reverted to their idolatrous practices**. The four kings who followed Josiah all "did evil in the eyes of the Lord" (2 Kings 23:32,37; 24:9,19). Jehoahaz was carried off to Egypt. Under Jehoiakim, Judah became a vassal of Babylonia. Jehoiachin surrendered to Nebuchadnezzar and was taken captive to Babylon. Zedekiah rebelled against Babylon and caused the destruction of Jerusalem. God's judgment was realized.

**DETAIL OF A LION FROM BABYLON'S ISHTAR GATE, c.6TH CENTURY BC**

# The Prophet Jeremiah

*God often revealed his word to Jeremiah in the form of images that outlined the wrathful divine judgment to be visited upon Judah and ten other surrounding nations and kingdoms.*

J EREMIAH'S FATHER was a priest at Anathoth in Benjamin. As a young man in Josiah's reign, Jeremiah was called upon by God to serve as a special prophet to the nations: "I appoint you over nations and kingdoms to uproot and tear down,

**BEFORE**

Assyrian power was replaced by a rising Babylonian Empire.

**BABYLON ARISES**
The weakening **Assyrian empire ‹‹ 216–17 started to disintegrate when King Ashurbanipal died** in c.627 BC. Babylon claimed independence but joined forces with the Medes to attack Assyria in c.616 BC, and **by 610 BC all resistance was overcome**. Babylon controlled territory to the south and west of the River Tigris; the Medes took the east and north. **A marriage between their royal families set up the new empire**.

**THE RIVER TIGRIS NEAR ASHUR, A FORMER CAPITAL OF ASSYRIA**

to destroy and overthrow, to build and to plant" (Jeremiah 1:10). He continued to prophesy during the reigns of Josiah's four successors, a period from c.626 BC to c.587 BC.

### God's message of judgment
The early visions of Jeremiah were of an almond branch, representing God watching over the nation, and a boiling pot tilting from the north, representing the forces of Assyria and Babylonia bringing disaster. He warned the people that they had sinned by defiling the Temple, offering sacrifices to the Canaanite gods Baal and Molek, and following immoral lifestyles.

In another vision, the nation was depicted as a "thriving olive tree with fruit" (11:16) that would be broken by a storm, because the people of "Israel and Judah have done evil" (11:17). Drought, famine, and disease would follow.

### The nation is not consoled
Speaking through Jeremiah, God said: "Like clay in the hand of the potter, so are you in my hand, Israel" (18:6). Jeremiah was then instructed to go to Topheth (where children were sacrificed to Baal) and smash a clay jar in front of the gathered crowd to symbolize God smashing the nation (19:1–13).

Jeremiah's message was that God loves his people but demands their obedience. His warnings only angered the people. The priest

**EXCAVATED CISTERN**
This well leads into a cistern built in c.2500 BC in Arad, a city in the Negev. Jeremiah would have been thrown in such a cistern – an underground water tank – by Judah's officials when he tried to warn the king of impending disaster.

**BARUCH THE SCRIBE**
An early 14th-century fresco by Giotto, on the ceiling of Padua's Scrovegni chapel, depicts Baruch, a Jewish aristocrat and a friend of the prophet Jeremiah. Baruch wrote down Jeremiah's dictated prophecies.

of the Temple in Jerusalem had Jeremiah beaten and put in stocks; as a result, Jeremiah prophesied that Judah would fall to Babylon and its people would be exiled. Jeremiah advised Jehoiakim and Zedekiah (kings of Judah) to maintain good relations with their Babylonian governors, but both subsequently rebelled.

Jeremiah's refusal to preach messages of reassurance provoked hostility. He insisted that King Zedekiah would be duly punished. He saw two baskets, one with good figs and one with bad figs. The good fruit represented the people who would be exiled to Babylon; the bad fruit would be destroyed. The nation would be subjugated for 70 years and then Babylon would be punished. Jeremiah was called a traitor.

In Jehoiakim's time, Jeremiah faced the death penalty (26) and the scroll recording God's words to him that he dictated to Baruch (see fresco, above) was burned.

Later on, he was kept in a dungeon, a muddy cistern, and the palace courtyard.

Following King Jehoiachin's exile to Babylon (see p.238), Jeremiah sent a letter of encouragement to the exiles there: he advised them to "build houses and settle down" (29:5) and "increase in number" (29:6), for God would return them to Judah after 70 years (29:10). He bought a field to express this hope.

### Taken to Egypt
After Jerusalem fell to Babylon, Jeremiah was freed from the courtyard of the guards (39:11–14) and protected by the new governor, Gedaliah. When Gedaliah was assassinated, Jeremiah was later taken with Baruch to Egypt, where it is thought the prophet died.

## "Before I formed you in the womb I knew you… I appointed you as a prophet to the nations.'"
JEREMIAH 1:5

**DIFFICULT MINISTRY**
This painting of the *Prophet Jeremiah* (*c.*1442–45), is attributed to Barthélemy d'Eyck. Jeremiah's prophetic life was a difficult one: his role was to reveal the sins of the people and warn of impending disaster. He wrote many laments as a result, including one for Josiah.

**SYMBOLS**

## THE CUP OF GOD'S WRATH

God commands the nations to drink a "cup filled with the wine of my wrath" (Jeremiah 25:15), an act that brings disaster on them. This image is a symbol for judgment often found in the wisdom and poetic books (Job 21:20; Psalm 60:3), as well as in the prophecies of Isaiah (51:17–23) and Ezekiel (23:28–34). Jeremiah uses it more than once, and it occurs in Lamentations (4:21,22) when the people of Edom are warned about the coming judgment for their part in the downfall of Jerusalem.

When Jesus prayed in Gethsemane before his crucifixion, he asked for "this cup" (Matthew 26:42; Mark 14:36) to be taken away, in the hope of avoiding the punishment to follow. In Revelation, seven angels "pour out the seven bowls of God's wrath on the earth" (Revelation 16:1).

**A 9TH-CENTURY IMAGE DEPICTS AN ANGEL POURING OUT GOD'S WRATH FROM A CUP**

**AFTER**

**Upon taking control of Babylon, King Cyrus of Persia released the exiles.**

### JEREMIAH'S PROPHECY
The prophet Jeremiah had predicted that Judah would "become a desolate wasteland" (Jeremiah 25:11) serving the king of Babylon for 70 years. The **actual exile lasted from c.587 BC until c.539 BC, almost 50 years 238–39 ❯❯**.

Jeremiah was probably speaking in round terms, indicating the exile would be the equivalent of a lifetime. His wording may suggest he meant the time from **King Nebuchadnezzar's first subjection of Judah in c.605 BC** to the end of the exile. Jeremiah also prophesied that Babylon would then be repaid with enslavement (25:14).

# The Fall of Jerusalem

*Years after the city of Samaria, the capital of Israel, fell to the Assyrians, the Babylonians destroyed the city of Jerusalem, capital of Judah. Following Josiah, a series of short-lived and inept rulers surrendered power to Egypt and Babylon successively. An ill-judged rebellion by Zedekiah in c.587 BC finally ensured the city's downfall and the Jewish people's long period of exile.*

**J**UDAH'S FINAL king was Mattaniah, who was renamed Zedekiah by the Babylonian king, Nebuchadnezzar. In c.589 BC, "in the ninth year of Zedekiah's reign" (2 Kings 25:1), rebellious acts brought back the Babylonian army to Judah.

Nebuchadnezzar "marched against Jerusalem with his whole army" (25:1). They set up camp outside the city and built siege works all around it. Jerusalem was under siege for over two years, so famine set in and there was no longer any food to eat. Finally, the city wall was broken through by the Babylonians in c.587 BC, prompting Zedekiah and his army to flee from the city at night "through the gate between the two walls near the king's garden" (25:4). They were pursued by the Babylonian army and overtaken on the plains of Jericho. Zedekiah was captured and taken to Riblah, in the land of Hamath, where he was forced to witness the slaughter of his sons and nobles. "Then they put out his eyes, bound him with bronze shackles and took him to Babylon" (25:7).

Nebuzaradan, the Babylonian commander, ordered his soldiers to break up the bronze pillars, movable stands, and the Bronze Sea – a large ritual washing vessel – at the Temple. They took these pieces of broken bronze, together with the bronze service items, and the gold and silver from the Temple and the city, away with them to Babylon. The army broke down the city walls and set fire to all the buildings. The priests and remaining officials were taken to Riblah and executed. Those who were left, the remnant, were deported to Babylon, while the poorest people were left to work the fields. And so "Judah went into captivity" (25:21).

> **"They set fire to God's temple and broke down the wall of Jerusalem…
> and destroyed everything of value there."**
>
> 2 CHRONICLES 36:19

**JERUSALEM UNDER ATTACK**
Nebuchadnezzar, the warrior King of Babylon, is depicted besieging Jerusalem in the St. Jerome version of the Great Bible (c.1405). The Babylonians plundered the city, taking even the Temple treasures, and deported the people to Babylon.

# Exile to Babylon

*On three separate occasions people from Judah were taken into exile in Babylon, where they remained captive until the Persian king, Cyrus, defeated the Babylonians and allowed their return in c.539 BC.*

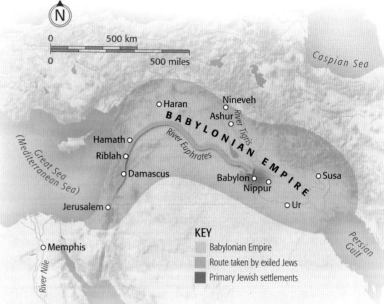

**THE FIRST EXILE** took place between *c.*605 and *c.*601 BC when King Jehoiakim of Judah was subject to Nebuchadnezzar, king of Babylon, after a previous period paying a heavy tribute to Pharaoh Necho of Egypt (2 Kings 23:35). Judah

rebelled, and the Babylonian king retaliated, taking Jehoiakim to Babylon, with members of the royal family, the nobility, and the Temple treasures (Daniel 1:1–2).

The second exile took place in *c.*597 BC when King Jehoiachin had been ruling for only three months. Once again Jerusalem was placed under siege and the king, his mother, his nobles, attendants, and officials all surrendered to King Nebuchadnezzar in person (2 Kings 24:12). All the army, artisans, craftsmen, and prominent people were taken to Babylon – "a total of ten thousand" (2 Kings 24:14) – with Jehoiachin and his entourage.

The third exile took place in *c.*587 BC – following the Fall of Jerusalem (see pp.236–37) – when

Zedekiah was ruling following Jehoiachin's exile. This time the Babylonians besieged Jerusalem for nearly two years before breaking in and destroying the city. Only the poorest people were left in Judah, under a new governor, Gedaliah, grandson of Shaphan (see p.218). Seemingly, the nation of Israel had come to an end.

## The city of Babylon

Babylon was a magnificent city of wide streets, canals, and sumptuous gardens, surrounded by a huge

### THE MARCH TO BABYLON
The route taken by the exiles into Babylon is not recorded in the biblical account (2 Kings 25), but would have probably followed the River Euphrates. The journey of over 1,600km (1,000 miles) would have taken several months to complete.

wall and entered by splendid gates (see pp.244–45). The exiles lived in their own communities in and around Babylon. Generally, they were permitted to live according to their own customs and so were able to maintain a separate identity. Some of the elite were educated for senior administrative posts and forced to assimilate.

## BEFORE

**The Babylonian empire was established.**

### THE ASSYRIAN DEFEAT
The demise of the Assyrian empire was assured from *c.*612 BC by **the capture of its capital, Nineveh**, by King Nabopolassar of Babylon. **Pharaoh Necho of Egypt reluctantly defeated King Josiah of Judah ❮❮ 232–33** on his way to support the Assyrians, but he was then defeated at the Battle of Carchemish in *c.*605 BC by Nebuchadnezzar of Babylon. The **new Babylonian empire used deportation** to weaken subjugated nations: their important leaders, skilled workers, and soldiers **were assimilated 243 ❯❯**. The city of Babylon was rebuilt and fortified as an emblem of its imperial might.

### CAPTURE OF LACHISH
The Assyrians destroyed Lachish, a city of Judah, in *c.*701 BC. This relief, from Sennacherib's Palace in Nineveh, shows booty being carted away. The city was resettled after the exiles' return from Babylon following Cyrus's decree in *c.*539 BC (see pp.252–53).

## LAMENTATIONS

The Book of Lamentations is read at evening services in dimmed synagogues on Tisha B'Av, meaning "the ninth day of Av" (usually August). This is a day of mourning that takes place at the end of a three-week Jewish festival of commemoration marking the destruction of the Temples of Jerusalem. Fasting takes place and solemnity is observed, with restrictions on all activities that would provide entertainment or comfort. People refrain from laughter and idle conversation, remembering the tragedies.

**12TH-CENTURY BOOK OF LAMENTATIONS SHOWING THE FALL OF JERUSALEM**

Jeremiah encouraged the exiles to work and pray for Babylon's prosperity, in order to secure the return to Judah.

The exiles had no temples and were forbidden to offer sacrifices, so new forms of worship developed that contributed to the emergence of the synagogue. The sacred space of the Temple was replaced by the observance of sacred time on the Sabbath. Study of the Torah became prominent and open-air prayer groups formed, such as the one at the River Kebar (see pp.240–41). Circumcision and food laws were once more emphasized.

### The Lamentations

Jerusalem's fall led to the writing of the Lamentations, five poems that expressed the reactions of the exiles to the tragedy. Their authors are not known, but they are thought to have been written around 586 BC. The first four poems are written as funeral songs in an acrostic form, with each verse starting with a different letter of the alphabet. The first poem is an expression of despair: "My groans are many and my heart is faint" (Lamentations 1:22). The second captures the anger towards God, "Look, Lord, and consider: Whom have you ever treated like this?" (2:20). The third is a meditation on the difficulties of serving God and of experiencing God's oppression; it offers a glimmer of hope but remains unforgiving. The fourth warns Judah's enemies that "to you also the cup will be passed; you will be drunk and stripped naked" (4:21; see Symbols panel, p.235). The final lament is a prayer: "Woe to us, for we have sinned!" (5:16). It asks God to renew his people: "Restore us to yourself, Lord, that we may return" (5:21).

### A GREAT CITY

The exiles were held in the magnificent city of Babylon, the monumental buildings of which were reimagined in this painting by the Dutch artist Adriaen van Nieulandt I (1584–1658).

## THE ARK OF THE COVENANT

The Ark of the Covenant was Israel's most precious religious object. It was a gold-plated wooden box containing the covenant tablets and was installed in the Most Holy Place at the heart of Solomon's Temple (see p.173). There is much speculation about what happened to it during the exile: it may have been hidden (tradition says Jeremiah hid it in a cave), mislaid, or broken up or stolen during the desecration of the Temple. Some claim that the Chapel of the Tablet in Aksum, Ethiopia, houses the Ark.

**ARK ON A STONE RELIEF FROM THE SYNAGOGUE AT CAPERNAUM, GALILEE**

# "Seek the peace and prosperity of the city to which I have carried you into exile. Pray to the LORD for it…"

JEREMIAH 29:7

AFTER

**Judgment falls on Babylon and the exiled people of Judah return home.**

#### THE RISE OF JEHOIACHIN

The new king of Babylon, Nebuchadnezzar's son Awel-Marduk, **released Jehoiachin** of Judah and "gave him a seat of honour higher than those of the other kings who were with him in Babylon" (2 Kings 25:28).

#### BABYLON'S FALL

Jeremiah predicted that God would take **vengeance on Babylon** by sending "an alliance of great nations from the land of the north" (Jeremiah 50:9). He foretold great suffering and terror: "**At the sound of Babylon's capture the earth will tremble**; its cry will resound among the nations" (50:46).

#### RETURN OF THE EXILES

Cyrus, king of Persia, captured Babylon in c.539 BC. **He allowed the exiles to return to Judah 252–53 >>** and rebuild their temple, on condition they remained loyal to the Persian empire. The city of Babylon was later destroyed by Xerxes in c.482 BC.

**BEFORE**

**Ezekiel was part of the first wave of deportations to Babylonia.**

**JUDAH IS VANQUISHED**
King Jehoiakim of Judah rebelled against Nebuchadnezzar's Babylonian empire **despite warnings from the prophet Jeremiah << 234–35.**

Jehoiachin succeeded his father as king of Judah in *c.*597 BC, but **he was forced to capitulate and was taken to Babylon with leading citizens including Ezekiel, a young man of 25 years old.** Clay tablets dating from 594–569 BC have been excavated from the royal residence of Nebuchadnezzar. Inscribed on them are the rulers in the region who are **living as captives in the palace,** including Jehoiachin and his sons, and receiving rations of grain and oil from King Nebuchadnezzar.

**CLAY TABLET LISTING
JEHOIACHIN'S RATIONS**

**CHARIOT OF GOD**
"Theophany" means the appearance of God to man, and Ezekiel was commissioned as a prophet by such an inaugural manifestation of God. Raphael's painting *Ezekiel's vision of God* (1518) interprets Ezekiel's description of God's chariot-like throne (Ezekiel 1).

# The Prophet Ezekiel

*Ezekiel was the major prophet and pastor of the period of exile from Judah. He comforted the exiles and inspired them with a vision of a renewed future and a rebuilt Temple.*

**E**ZEKIEL TRAINED TO be a priest like his father, but he was taken into exile before being able to serve in the Temple at Jerusalem. He was called to be a prophet in *c.*592 BC through a series of visions at the age of 30: "Son of man, stand up on your feet and I will speak to you" (Ezekiel 2:1). He spent part of his life amongst the Jewish community beside the River Kebar in Babylonia, where he was much respected by the elders.

Ezekiel had visionary experiences of rich, symbolic meaning, and adopted unusual methods to convey God's messages. He acted as a spiritual "watchman for the people of Israel" (3:17), delivering divine warnings to the people of Judah and other nations. He also prophesied the fall of Jerusalem, and guided the people towards a new future. The ability to make individual choices and accept responsibility for personal actions – whether to be faithful to God or to receive God's judgment – was a key theme of his teachings.

### The glory of God
Ezekiel's central message was the glory of the Lord. He had a vision of God's majestic throne of lapis lazuli "above the vault that was over the heads of the cherubim" (10:1), and then he looked on as "the glory of the Lord departed from over the threshold" of the desecrated Temple (10:18). The people had been sent into exile; but a purified remnant would return one day to the land God had given to them. His glory would return to Jerusalem and fill the rebuilt Temple.

Ezekiel encouraged the exiles to reconcile themselves to their situation by understanding its

cause. The exile was a time to trust in the sovereign God, not to doubt him or be angry with him. Calling for spiritual renewal, Ezekiel stressed the need for both individual and moral responsibility.

### Visions of the future
Ezekiel's message of hope was expressed in a number of vivid images. God himself would become Israel's shepherd, replacing the false shepherds who had destroyed the flock. Israel's mountains, currently barren and deserted, would become fruitful and prosperous again. God would breathe new life into the nation; the dried up bones of its people would join together again, flesh would be reformed, and "a vast army" (37:10) would come to life.

Joining two broken sticks together, Ezekiel predicted a reunited and purified nation under God's rule. God would defeat the forces of Gog (a figurative name for the enemies of God's people; see Ezekiel 38) in a climactic battle that would display his greatness over the nations.

### Visions of the Temple
The most detailed vision of the future concerned the rebuilding of the Temple in Jerusalem, a vision close to the heart of Ezekiel the priest. He not only envisaged a magnificent temple from which life would flow to all parts of the Earth,

**THE LORD IS MY SHEPHERD**
A shepherd tends her flock in the Judean desert, near the Wadi Qelt, a valley running from Jericho to Jerusalem. The Lord tells Ezekiel about rescuing his people from the darkness of captivity: "As a shepherd looks after his scattered flock when he is with them, so I will look after my sheep" (Ezekiel 34:12) – a recurring biblical metaphor.

but prophesied that the glory of the LORD would return to it "through the gate facing east" (43:4).

### Ezekiel's performances
Ezekiel sometimes adopted theatrical or non-verbal methods to convey his prophesies. He enacted the siege of Jerusalem using a brick and a pan, and the impending exile was represented by his bound body lying on the ground beside the assemblage for the number of days that expressed the years of sin totted up by the peoples of Israel and Judah. After wasting away like this for over a year, his head was shaved in disgrace and the cut hair burned and blown away, representing the coming murder, plague, and famine, until only a few strands remained – the surviving exiles.

# "Son of man, stand up on your feet and I will speak to you."
EZEKIEL 2:1

**VALLEY OF DRY BONES**
Tobias Fendt's *The Vision of Ezekiel* (1565) depicts Ezekiel's vision of dry bones brought to life. The prophet says that he was set down by God in a valley full of bones that when breathed on came to life as a vast army (Ezekiel 37:1–14).

## AFTER

**Ezekiel's visionary Temple was never built but his legacy was a lasting one.**

### GOD'S RETURN TO JERUSALEM
The book of Ezekiel concludes with a detailed description of **a perfect Temple,** that would represent God's redemption of the shamed nation and God's perfection. The account climaxes with "the glory of the Lord" (Ezekiel 43:5) arriving to fill the temple, and declaring: "This is where I will live among the Israelites for ever" (43:7).

### A VISION NEVER FULFILLED
Cyrus the Great, king of Persia, overthrew the Babylonians in 539 BC and **proclaimed that God had appointed him to build a temple at Jerusalem 252–53 »**. So Cyrus released the exiles from Judah to return with the "5,400 articles of gold and silver" (Ezra 1:11) taken from the Temple.
   **The rebuilding project suffered many setbacks,** not least owing to opposition from those who had not been exiled and from other ethnic groups in northern Israel, before its completion under King Darius I around 515 BC. It was less glorious than Ezekiel's vision, **prompting King Herod to redevelop it 382–83 »** in 19 BC.

### BEFORE

**Daniel had left Jerusalem as part of the first exile of Jews to Babylon.**

#### EXILED TO BABYLON
Following Egypt's defeat at Carchemish in 605 BC and Babylon's rise to power, **some Jews were taken to Babylon ≪ 238** (2 Kings 24:15, Daniel 1:1–3). Among these, Daniel and several of his friends were selected for **special treatment and education** and became trusted government officials. However, they resisted all attempts to eradicate their Jewish identities. Their **faithfulness to God and diligent service** led them to occupy important positions in Nebuchadnezzar's court.

**BABYLONIAN PRIEST**
This 7th-century seal shows a priest praying to symbols of Nebuchadnezzar's Babylonian gods. Marduk – the highest god – is symbolized by a spade; the writing tablet symbolizes Nabu, the god of wisdom; while Sin – the moon god – is the crescent moon.

#### PEOPLE
### NEBUCHADNEZZAR

Nebuchadnezzar, son of Nabopolassar, was king of Babylon 605–562 BC. His military successes secured the Babylonian empire. He fought campaigns against Tyre and Egypt, and first captured Jerusalem in 597 BC, when he took Jehoiachin prisoner. Ten years later, when his puppet king Zedekiah rebelled, Nebuchadnezzar destroyed the city (see pp.236–37). In the city of Babylon he built a magnificent palace and fortified the city's walls (Daniel 4:30). He built the Ishtar gate (see p.244) and rebuilt temples to Marduk and Nabu, Babylonian deities. The book of Daniel refers to a period of insanity towards the end of his life (see p.247), but Babylonian records do not mention this.

# Daniel and Nebuchadnezzar

*King Nebuchadnezzar had a disturbing dream and, as he believed that dreams conveyed important messages, he demanded that his advisors explain it. When they failed, he threatened to execute all the advisors, but Daniel intervened.*

**A** YEAR INTO his reign, Nebuchadnezzar had nightmares. So he called all his magicians, astrologers, and sorcerers, saying, "I have had a dream that troubles me and I want to know what it means" (Daniel 2:3). He then demanded, "If you do not tell me what my dream was and interpret it, I will have you cut into pieces and your houses turned into piles of rubble" (2:5). The wise men insisted that his request was impossible – no-one could reveal his dream except the gods. Their answer made the king furious, and he ordered the execution of all the wise men in Babylon.

### Daniel under threat
Daniel, a Jewish exile in Babylon, was one of Nebuchadnezzar's wise men and so was among the condemned. When commander Antioch came to execute him, Daniel asked his reason, and then went to the king to ask for some time to interpret the dream.

Returning home, he and his friends Hananiah, Mishael, and Azariah, prayed that God would reveal both the dream and its interpretation. The mystery of the dream and its interpretation was made known to Daniel in a vision.

He praised God for revealing this to him, and returned to the king.

### The dream
Daniel told the king that no man could reveal or interpret his dream, but there was a God in heaven who could. He told Nebuchadnezzar that God, "the revealer of mysteries" (2:29) had shown the king what would happen in the future, and God had now revealed the dream to Daniel, so he could interpret it for the king. In the dream, Daniel said, the king had seen an enormous statute made out of different metals: a head of gold, arms and chest of silver, stomach and thighs of bronze, legs of iron, and feet of iron and clay. A rock smashed the statue into little pieces that were blown away, while the rock itself grew into a huge, immovable mountain.

Daniel explained that the king and his empire represented the head of gold. He exercised real and widespread authority, but his empire would not last and would give way to another, inferior kingdom, which in turn would be replaced by a still-lesser kingdom,

**NEBUCHADNEZZAR'S PALACE**
In 1982, then-president of Iraq Saddam Hussein built a new palace on the ruins of Nebuchadnezzar's northern palace, then in Babylon. Original bricks still form the foundations, dating back 2,600 years.

and then a fourth. Ultimately, all these earthly kingdoms would come to an end and be replaced by God's kingdom, that "will crush all those kingdoms… but it will itself endure forever" (2:44). In thanks, the king bowed down to Daniel's "God of gods" (2:47) in worship and promoted Daniel and his friends to high office in Babylon.

### AFTER

**Daniel remained in service in Babylon for many years.**

#### A TRUSTED ADVISOR
Daniel stayed in Babylon and became a trusted advisor, but his loyalty was severely **tested during Darius' reign 248–49 ≫**.

#### A NOTED PROPHET
Daniel **received visions 250 ≫** of beasts, the "son of man", and supernatural forces, all of which spoke of the future. He also interpreted **the writing on the wall 251 ≫** for King Belshazzar.

> **"** During the night **the mystery was revealed to Daniel** in a vision. **"**
>
> DANIEL 2:19

## HISTORY AND CULTURE
# The Babylonians

> "The time will surely come when **everything in your palace...** will be carried off to **Babylon...**" 2 KINGS 20:17

**CITY OF POWER**
This partial reconstruction demonstrates the former glory of Babylon. At its height, it was reportedly the largest city in existence, covering 850ha (2,100 acres).

The empire we now refer to as Babylonia took its name from Babylon, one of the world's most famous ancient cities, situated in modern-day Iraq. Initially the capital of the southern Mesopotamian region, it was also the capital of the Neo-Babylonian Empire of the 7th–6th centuries BC. It was during this period that Babylon grew to be the largest city in the known world. The entire city was surrounded by a wide moat that encircled double walls: an outer one that was 16km (10 miles) long and 3.7m (12ft) thick, and an inner one that was 9km (5.5 miles) long and 6.5m (21ft) thick – wide enough for a four-horse chariot to turn around on. Towers stood at intervals of 17m (55ft) and there were eight fortified double gates.

Babylon may have been the home of the famous Hanging Gardens, which so impressed the Greek historian Herodotus that he praised them as one of the seven wonders of the ancient world.

Both Babylon and Babylonia's roots lay in the Sumerian civilization (see p.214–215), which dates back to before 3,000 BC.

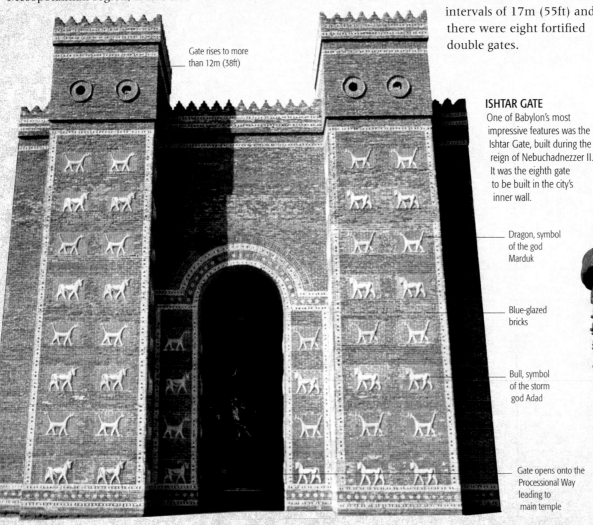

Gate rises to more than 12m (38ft)

**ISHTAR GATE**
One of Babylon's most impressive features was the Ishtar Gate, built during the reign of Nebuchadnezzer II. It was the eighth gate to be built in the city's inner wall.

Dragon, symbol of the god Marduk

Blue-glazed bricks

Bull, symbol of the storm god Adad

Gate opens onto the Processional Way leading to main temple

## SUMER AND AKKAD
During the 3rd millennium BC great cities and kings emerged, such as those that appear in the *Sumerian King List*, an ancient document that records the lengths of reigns of the rulers of Sumer. City-states flourished in Ur, Uruk, Shuruppak, and Kish, and these cultures came into frequent conflict with one another. Around 2350 BC Sargon I, king of Akkad in northern Mesopotamia, defeated Lugalzagesi of Umma, thereby uniting several city-states. He went on to create the world's first empire, which stretched from the

**EMPIRE BUILDER**
This life-size bronze cast is thought to be either of Sargon I, founder of the Akkadian Empire, or of his grandson, Naram-Sin, who extended the empire.

Persian Gulf to the Mediterranean. His grandson, Naram-Sim, extended the empire, but by 2154 BC it had collapsed.

In 2112 BC the city of Ur became the new centre of power under Ur-Nammu. The Third Dynasty of Ur (Ur III) reunited much of the region and saw a Sumerian cultural revival, including the building of the first ziggurat in Ur (see pp.44–45). In 2004 BC, after a series of famines, Ur fell to the Elamites, invading from the east.

## ASSYRIA AND BABYLONIA

The fall of the Ur III empire led to the rise of two empires – Assyria in the north of Mesopotamia and Babylonia in the south. In 1792 BC Hammurabi became king of Babylon. From 1760 BC, he embarked on a series of conquests, eventually making Babylonia the region's dominant state. He established Marduk

Bronze horned dragon head

### DRAGON GOD
The "snake dragon" was regarded as an emblem of Marduk, the chief god of Babylon and Babylonia.

as the national god and implemented a uniform legal code. His 42-year reign came to an end with his death in 1750 BC. The empire continued under his successors for another 200 years, when it began to decline, and in 1585 BC Babylon fell to the Hittites. The invaders left quickly and around 1570 BC the Kassites from the north took advantage of the power vacuum and established a new empire in Babylonia. Over the next few centuries, Babylonia's fortunes rose and fell and it was often dominated by Assyria.

## NEO-BABYLONIA

As a result of the power struggle that followed the death of Assyria's King Ashurbanipal in 627 BC, Nabopolassar became ruler of a newly independent Babylon in 626 BC, founding the Neo-

Clay impression of seal (left)

### HEBREW SEAL
This Hebrew seal dates from the Neo-Babylonian period. Seals such as this were probably used by merchants to "sign" messages or identify goods.

Babylonian dynasty. With the assistance of the Medes he invaded Assyria and captured Nineveh, the capital, in 612 BC. In 605 BC, the defeat of the Assyrian-Egyptian army at Carchemish by his son, Nebuchadnezzar II, signalled Assyria's fall. The Kingdom of Judah was part of Assyria and so was under the power of Babylonia.

## DECLINE AND FALL

Although he revitalized the empire of Babylonia, Nebuchadnezzar II was succeeded by a series of weak rulers. The empire's last king, Nabonidus, stopped worshipping Marduk and retreated to the desert to worship Sin, the god of the Moon, in 549 BC. His people blamed him for a series of plagues and famines, and although he returned to Babylon 10 years later, he was unable to prevent it falling to King Cyrus of Persia. The once-great kingdom of Babylonia now became part of the Persian Empire.

### PERSIAN CONQUEROR
Soldiers such as this Persian palace guard brought Babylonia under Persian rule.

## GODS AND DEMONS

Each city in Babylonia had a temple dedicated to its patron god, where its citizens gathered at festivals – although people more usually worshipped at local or domestic shrines. The cities' massive ziggurats may have been used for religious purposes as well as astronomy. Worship involved offering sacrifices or gifts to win the gods' favour or avert their wrath.

There were literally hundreds of Babylonian deities – a list discovered at the ancient city of Nineveh names more than 2,500. In addition, hundreds of demons were believed to be waiting to attack people at any moment, and were blamed for illnesses and other misfortunes. One of the most well-known was Pazuzu, king of the wind demons, and his image was thought to offer protection against other demons.

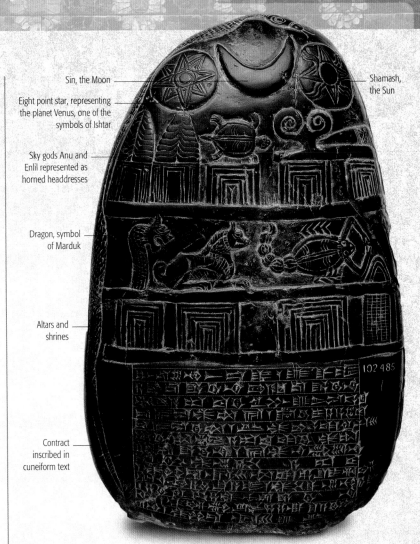

Sin, the Moon

Eight point star, representing the planet Venus, one of the symbols of Ishtar

Sky gods Anu and Enlil represented as horned headdresses

Dragon, symbol of Marduk

Altars and shrines

Contract inscribed in cuneiform text

Shamash, the Sun

### POWERFUL SYMBOLS
This boundary stone from southern Babylonia records a land grant to a man called Gul-eresh. The symbols of the gods give the land protection.

### CHIEF BABYLONIAN DEITIES

**Anu** King of heaven and father of the gods. His main shrine was at Uruk.

**Enlil** God of air, wind, and storms, who held the Tablets of Destiny, giving him power over mankind.

**Ea** God of the deep waters and wisdom. Revealed to humans how to know the minds of the gods.

**Ishtar** Goddess of war, fertility, and sexual love. Counterpart of the West Semitic goddess Astarte.

**Marduk** Creator of everything, and the city of Babylon's popular patron god.

**Sin** God of the Moon and seasons, whose image was a crescent Moon. Revered in Ur.

**Shamash** The Sun god; also the god of power, justice, and war.

**Nabu** The god of fate; also the scribe of the gods.

АГГЛЪ ХРАНИТЕЛЬ

АНАНЇ                    МИСАИЛЪ

« BEFORE

**Three friends from Judea were taken to Babylon after the siege of Jerusalem.**

BABLONIAN TABLET FROM 9TH CENTURY BC, DEPICTING THE SUN GOD, SHAMASH

### THREE EXILES

Nebuchadnezzar decreed that exiles from the Israelite nobility **be trained in the language and culture of Babylon** – including worship of Babylonian gods – and after three years, enter his service. Three friends – Hananiah, Mishael, and Azariah – were among this group. They received training and were given new names: **Hananiah became Shadrach, Mishael was called Meshach, and Azariah was named Abednego**. Their friend Daniel was renamed Belteshazzar.

---

### HISTORY AND CULTURE

## ANCIENT FURNACES

COPPER-SMELTING FURNACE, ISRAEL, 14TH CENTURY BC

Ancient furnaces were lined with bricks or stones, and generally used for smelting metals or making bricks. Often shaped like a bottle or dome, they had openings at the top and also at ground level, for introducing fuel and air. Nebuchadnezzar would have needed a view of the ground-level opening to see the men walking inside. Bellows could be used at that level to increase the temperature, which was normally around 900–1100°C (1652–1832°F). Charcoal made from acacia wood was the most likely fuel.

---

### THROWN INTO THE FURNACE

This 17th-century Russian icon depicts Shadrach, Meshach, and Abednego being thrown into the furnace. Nebuchadnezzar was astonished to see four men walking in the fire. Some Christians believe that the fourth figure was an appearance of Jesus.

---

# Shadrach, Meshach, and Abednego

*King Nebuchadnezzar erected a huge gold statue and commanded everyone to pay homage to it, on pain of death. When three Israelites refused, they were thrown into a furnace, but miraculously survived.*

**N**EBUCHADNEZZAR had a large gold statue built on the plain of Dura. The statue stood 27m (90ft) high and almost 3m (10ft) wide. He invited all the officials of Babylon to come to its dedication, where the image was unveiled with great ceremony. A herald proclaimed to the assembled peoples "of every language" that made up the gathering of prefects, governors, advisors, treasurers, judges and magistrates that they were to worship the image. He proclaimed that as soon as they heard the sound of the horn, flute, zither, lyre, harp, pipe, or any kind of music, they "must fall down and worship the image of gold that King Nebuchadnezzar has set up. Whoever does not fall down and worship will immediately be thrown into a blazing furnace" (Daniel 3:5). The people took heed, and everyone fell down and worshipped the image of gold as soon as they heard music.

### Into the furnace

Some astrologers came to Nebuchadnezzar and told him that three of the Israelites who had been given governing roles in Babylon were ignoring his edict.

Incensed, the king sent for the three men – Shadrach, Meshach, and Abednego – and reminded them of the punishment for not obeying. The men, however, stood firm – they refused to bow down to the gold image, and explained to the king that his threats had no hold over them, because if they were thrown into the furnace, their God would save them, and added, "But even if he does not… we will not serve your gods or worship the image of gold" (3:18).

Nebuchadnezzar was so angry that he demanded that the furnace be heated "seven times hotter than usual" (3:19), and commanded soldiers to tie up the men and throw them in. The soldiers who led the three friends were killed by the fire as they approached it, and Shadrach, Meshach, and Abednego fell into the furnace. The king leapt up in surprise, asking "weren't there three men that we tied up and threw into the fire?" (3:24). He told everyone to look into the fire – there were four men walking around within the fire, "and the fourth looks like a son of the gods" (3:25). He shouted to Shadrach, Meshach, and Abednego, "servants of the Most High God" (3:26) to come out of the fire. The men stepped out, and were seen to be untouched by the fire. The king praised their god, and decreed that anyone who spoke against him should be killed, "for no other god can save in this way" (3:29).

AFTER »

**According to the Bible, Nebuchadnezzar suffered from temporary insanity towards the end of his life.**

### NEBUCHADNEZZAR'S DREAM

The Babylonian king **had a dream about a large tree** that "was visible to the ends of the earth" (Daniel 4:11). But then it was felled, although the roots were left in the ground. Daniel told the king that the tree represented a human, driven to live among animals. He explained that **the king was the tree, who had been a great ruler, but also an oppressive and sinful one**. Until he repented – as he would, after "seven times" (4:25) had passed – he would be exiled from society, lose his mind, and live like an animal.

### THE DREAM FULFILLED

A year later, Daniel's prediction was fulfilled: **Nebuchadnezzar became mentally ill and lived like a beast** (4:33). At the end of the allotted time he looked to heaven and praised God, and was restored to sanity and his throne.

NEBUCHADNEZZAR'S MADNESS (1795), BY WILLIAM BLAKE

> "If we are thrown into the blazing furnace, **the God we serve is able to deliver us from it…**"
>
> DANIEL 3:17

# Daniel in the Lions' Den

*Daniel's qualities made his fellow officials jealous, so they conspired against him with the unwitting co-operation of the new king, Darius the Mede. Having fallen foul of a religious law, Daniel was sentenced to be thrown into a den of lions. However, the plot failed because God shut the mouths of the lions and delivered Daniel from their den.*

**K**ING DARIUS recognized Daniel's exceptional leadership skills and appointed him as one of three administrators over his 120 provincial governors, or satraps. Jealous of Daniel's appointment, the satraps sought to remove him from office. They soon discovered that his integrity meant he would never be dismissed justly, so they plotted against him.

The satraps persuaded the king to pass a law that for one month people should pray only to him; if anyone refused they were to be thrown to the lions. They thought this would cause Daniel a dilemma, because he would not compromise his allegiance to his own God.

As anticipated, Daniel continued his practice of praying to God three times each day. The conspirators went to the king and checked the terms of his law. Once the king confirmed it, they told Darius that Daniel had paid "no attention… to the decree" (Daniel 6:13). Darius had no option but to pass sentence on Daniel according to his law.

The king was distressed by the situation and tried to find a way around it, but the satraps reminded him that a king's edict could not be changed. Daniel's enemies seized him and threw him into the lions' den. Darius himself said to Daniel, "May your God, whom you serve continually, rescue you!" (6:16). The den was secured and sealed with the king's ring. There was no chance of escape.

The king hurried to the lions' den early in the morning. To his relief he found Daniel unharmed. "They have not hurt me, because I was found innocent in his [God's] sight. Nor have I ever done any wrong before you", said Daniel (6:22). "The living God", as Darius referred to him (6:20), had rescued Daniel, as Darius had hoped. Just as Shadrach, Meshach, and Abednego displayed no sign of burning when they came out of the blazing furnace (see pp. 246–247), no scratch was found on Daniel when he came out of the lions' den.

Those who had accused Daniel were thrown, with their families, to the lions, and overpowered swiftly. Darius then issued another decree, insisting that his people should revere Daniel's God for "He rescues and he saves; he performs signs and wonders" (6:27).

## "My God sent his angel, and he **shut the mouths of the lions.**"

DANIEL 6:22

**GOD PROTECTS DANIEL**
This detail from Briton Rivière's painting *Daniel's Answer to the King* (1890) depicts the royal advisor after falling victim to jealous rivals in King Darius's court. Despite the lions pacing behind him, Daniel stares peacefully into the light.

# Daniel

> **"God gave knowledge and understanding** of all kinds of literature and learning. And **Daniel could understand visions and dreams** of all kinds."

DANIEL 1:17

**D**ANIEL'S FAMILY belonged to Jewish nobility. He was deported to Babylon in *c*.605 BC by King Nebuchadnezzar, along with others from Jerusalem's elite, including his friends Hananiah, Mishael, and Azariah (Daniel 1:6). On arrival, officials selected them for special treatment on the basis of their nobility, intelligence, and physical stature. They were re-educated to become assimilated into Babylonian culture. This involved learning Babylonian language and literature – the means by which Babylon's values and worldview were communicated – and adopting Babylonian names. Daniel was renamed Belteshazzar. King Nebuchadnezzar's goal was to ensure that his officials included people who could liaise with the Judean exiles, even if they made no wider contribution to government.

## Observance of dietary laws

Daniel and his friends accepted most of these changes, but drew the line at consuming the food and drink served at the king's table. To repudiate their own dietary laws would have meant defiling themselves (1:8). When an official questioned this, Daniel proposed a test. For ten days they should be allowed to eat their own diet and then be examined to see whether they were physically and mentally healthier than those who ate the prescribed diet. They passed the test easily. "At the end of the ten days they looked healthier and better nourished than any of the young men who ate the royal food" (1:15).

## Daniel's qualities and battles

When the four young men were presented to King Nebuchadnezzar and he questioned them about wisdom, "he found them

**THE PROPHET DANIEL**
This 19th-century watercolour and gold painting of the prophet Daniel is a reproduction of a 13th-century mosaic from the altar-vault of the Basilica di San Marco, Venice, Italy.

### DANIEL'S LONG-RANGE PROPHECIES

Daniel's visions predicted that a succession of empires would follow Babylon, but none would survive. The visions fit the Maccabean period when the Seleucid heirs of Alexander's Greek empire corrupted Jewish faith and traditions. Antiochus Epiphanes desecrated the Jerusalem Temple as prophesied in Daniel: "...he will set up an abomination that causes desolation" (9:27) and "His armed forces will rise up to desecrate the temple fortress and will abolish the daily sacrifice" (11:31). The Maccabees fought zealously for Jewish purity and heroically endured extreme suffering for their cause (see pp.266–67).

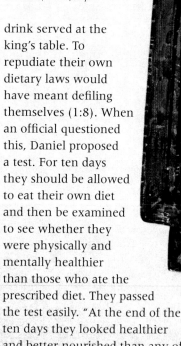

**DANIEL'S APOCALYPTIC VISION OF THE ANCIENT OF DAYS, BY WILLIAM BLAKE, 1794**

ten times better than all the magicians and enchanters in his whole kingdom" (1:20).

Nebuchadnezzar's usual counsellors failed to recall and interpret the king's dreams, Daniel was able to do so on more than one occasion. He alone was able to interpret the writing that appeared on the wall during one of Belshazzar's feasts (5:1–31). He was able to deliver messages about judgment without provoking the king's anger.

As a result of his ability to interpret dreams, Daniel became a senior royal advisor whose integrity and wisdom were trusted by several Babylonian kings. Daniel served these monarchs from the time of Nebuchadnezzar, until around 537 BC – the first year of rule of Cyrus the Persian, the conqueror of Babylon.

### Faithful and true

Throughout this period, Daniel showed courageous faithfulness to God. Although he lived in a society in which the people worshipped a diversity of Babylonian gods, the stories about Daniel demonstrate that he never deviated from practising his own faith or trusting in the sovereignty of his God.

Daniel remained homesick for Jerusalem, and chose a home in Babylon whose "windows opened towards Jerusalem" (6:10), although he remained in Babylon after the other exiles had left.

The true devotion of Daniel to God almost cost him his life, at least once. When he failed to observe the king's command that forbade prayer to any other deities than himself (see p.248), Daniel's jealous underlings betrayed him and he was sentenced to be mauled to death by lions. God had delivered Daniel, who

exclaimed, "My God sent his angel, and he shut the mouths of the lions" (6:22).

### The book of Daniel

The Old Testament book that bears Daniel's name is in two distinct parts. The first six chapters recount stories of Daniel and his friends, detailing their trials and their triumphs. Several record Daniel's ability to interpret dreams and prophesy about the future.

The second six chapters describe more mysterious visions and take the form of apocalyptic literature, a type of prophetic writing that is rich in symbol and imagery. These chapters contrast temporary earthly kingdoms with God's enduring kingdom. They encourage God's people to pray and seek wisdom in turbulent times.

**KING BELSHAZZAR**
Rembrandt's painting *Belshazzar's Feast* (c.1636), depicts the dramatic moment in the book of Daniel when a ghostly hand writes on the wall, predicting King Belshazzar's demise. None of the wise men and enchanters could read it, but Daniel did.

**THE TOMB OF DANIEL**
The Tomb of Daniel in Susa, Iran, is the most plausible of the possible locations for Daniel's tomb. There are five other sites: Mala Amir in Iran; Samarkand in Uzbekistan; and Kirkuk, Babylon, and Muqdadiyah in Iraq.

Some scholars argue that rather than being a historically accurate contemporary account of Daniel's life in exile, the book was compiled in the 2nd century BC when this type of writing became more common. The book certainly includes events that would occur in the 5th to 2nd centuries BC and would serve as an encouragement to those suffering persecution in the later Maccabean period (see pp.266–67).

**DANIEL'S VISION OF THE APOCALYPSE, 12TH-CENTURY MANUSCRIPT**

> **Daniel had a dream,** and visions passed through his mind as he was lying in bed.
>
> DANIEL 7:1

« **BEFORE**

Babylonian policy towards the exiles appeared to have been relaxed. They could live in their own settlements and, to some degree, keep their identity.

**JEWS WEEPING IN BABYLON, 13TH-CENTURY ITALIAN *PSALTERIUM BEATAE EISABETH*.**

### HOMESICK FOR JERUSALEM

However good their conditions, the exiles remained homesick for Jerusalem. Psalm 137:1 records them weeping when they remembered the city – referred to by the poetic name Zion, that symbolized the royal dwelling place of God – as the Babylonians taunted them. The **prophet Daniel** « **250–51** even prayed with his "windows opened towards Jerusalem" (Daniel 6:10).

# The End of the Exile

*Cyrus of Persia decreed that the exiles were free to return to restore the Temple. The task was arduous, especially in the face of local opposition, but those who did return gradually set about rebuilding.*

**C**YRUS THE GREAT captured Babylon in 539 BC, replacing Babylonian rule with the Medo–Persian, or Achaemenid, Empire. That same year, Cyrus decreed that exiled peoples taken captive by Babylon were free to return to their homelands. He gave permission to the Jews to rebuild their Temple in Jerusalem, and he encouraged his people to donate "silver and gold… goods and livestock, and… freewill offerings" (Ezra 1:4) towards the project. He also returned to the Jews some 5,400 gold and silver articles that had been taken from Solomon's Temple by the earlier Babylonian King, Nebuchadnezzar.

The Jews viewed Cyrus as God's "anointed" (Isaiah 45:1), who was fulfilling the words spoken to Jeremiah (Ezra 1:1). Cyrus's

> "Any of his people among you **may go up to Jerusalem**… and build **the temple** of the LORD, the God of Israel…"
>
> EZRA 1:3

PEOPLE

## KING CYRUS

Born into nobility, then abandoned and raised as a shepherd-boy, Cyrus reclaimed his throne and – as Cyrus II (reigned c.559–530 BC) – founded the Persian Empire that continued until the time of Alexander the Great in c.330 BC.

As king of the province of Anshan (Elam), Cyrus first brought the Persians under his rule, and by 550 BC united them with the Medes. In

546 BC he took control of Lydia (Asia Minor). He captured Babylon in 539 BC and was welcomed as a liberator, and governed benevolently. He granted the Jews and other exiled people their freedom. Isaiah speaks of Cyrus as God's "shepherd" (Isaiah 44:28). He was succeeded by his son, Cambyses II.

**THE INFANT CYRUS BY SEBASTIANO RICCI (1659–1734)**

proclamation, according to the Book of Ezra, was made in response to his heart having been moved by God (1:1,2).

### The returnees rebuild

For various reasons, some Jews chose to remain in Babylon, but Zerubbabel, the grandson of King Jehoiachin and now the governor of Judah, led a group of more than 42,000 returnees (2:64), including Joshua the priest. The returnees faced a difficult task, recultivating

neglected land and restoring ruined buildings. They began by rebuilding the altar on the site of the old Temple, so that burnt offerings could be resumed. A few months later, when the foundations of the Second Temple were laid, there was joyous celebration with trumpets, mingled with weeping by those who had seen the former Temple – "the sound was heard far away" (3:13).

### Stop and start

The inhabitants of Samaria offered to help with the project, only to be told, "You have no part with us in building a temple to our God" (4:3) – so they obstructed progress for more than 15 years by bribing officials to cause delays.

Later, opponents of the rebuilding programme sent a letter to Persia's King Artaxerxes, from the "judges, officials and administrators over the people" (4:9), reminding him that Jerusalem was "a place with a long history of sedition" (4:15). So, in the second year of the reign of Darius the rebuilding stopped.

### PALACE RUINS, PASARGADAE

Construction of Cyrus the Great's capital city of Pasargadae – remains of the palace's audience hall are seen here – began in about 546 BC. After Cyrus's death in 530 BC it was never finished, and his son, Cambyses II, reduced the city's significance.

**BABYLONIAN INSCRIPTION**
This 6th-century BC clay brick from Ur bears an inscription that reads: "Cyrus King of the World, King of Anshan... the great gods delivered all the lands into my hands and I made this land dwell in peace."

### TOMB OF KING CYRUS
This limestone tomb in modern-day Iran, located in Pasargadae, the capital of ancient Persia, is believed to be the final resting place of King Cyrus the Great of Persia.

However, almost a decade later, the prophets Haggai and Zechariah assured the people of Jerusalem that God wanted construction to continue, so the rebuilding recommenced. The provincial governor, Tattenai, investigated this breach of authority, and the Jewish elders requested that he send a report to the king, now Darius, and await a response. This report included their assertion that King Cyrus of Persia had ordered the rebuilding of the Temple.

Having searched the palace archives, Darius confirmed that the Jews had been given permission by Cyrus, and ruled that the work should go ahead without further interference. Within four years the new Temple was completed and dedicated with a sacrificial offering.

The new Temple was much plainer than Solomon's, with no gold or silver ornamentation, and on a much smaller scale, measuring less than 27m (90ft) wide and 27m (90ft) high (6:3,4). However, it served until Herod began to expand the Temple complex in c.20 BC (see pp.382–83).

> " Do not interfere with the work on this **temple of God**."
>
> **EZRA** 6:7

SYMBOLS

### EXILE

Exile is both an experience and a symbolic theme in the Bible. Individuals such as Cain, Jacob, Joseph, and Moses all went into exile; however, it is Israel's enslavement in Egypt and later exile in Babylon that form the two great exiles of the Old Testament period. Exile gave rise to emotions of lament and of seeking God in repentance, inspiring visions of a glorious homecoming. Jesus was exiled in Egypt as an infant, and the early Christians longed for a better, heavenly country (Hebrews 11:13–16; 1 Peter 1:1,4).

**AFTER**

**Israelites who were scattered under the Assyrians, and those Judeans who did not return after the exile, formed the Jewish Diaspora ("dispersal").**

### A PEOPLE DISPERSED
A sizeable colony of Jews remained in Babylon for centuries. Others formed communities in Egypt and elsewhere.

There were later dispersions and, by Paul's day, many Jews lived outside Palestine in cities throughout the Roman Empire. They paid the Temple tax and visited Jerusalem, **but had their own Old Testament translation, in Greek,** 270–71 » and developed distinctive religious practices. The experience of the Babylonian exile encouraged Jews to believe that it was possible to find God anywhere.

HISTORY AND CULTURE

# What People Wore

*"*Your cheeks are **beautiful** with **earrings**, your neck with **strings of jewels.**" SONG OF SONGS 1:10

**ORTHODOX HAIRSTYLE**
*Peyot*, or sidelocks, are worn by males in the Orthodox Jewish community, based on an interpretation of the Bible's injunction against shaving the "corners" of one's head.

**SPINNING WOOL**
A woman in Jericho winds sheep's wool onto a spindle, just as her ancestors would have done in Old Testament times.

The first "clothes" mentioned in the Bible are fig leaves, sewn together by Adam and Eve to cover their nakedness (Genesis 3:7), which were replaced by God with garments made of animal skins (Genesis 3:21). Clothes were made from sheep's wool, goat hair, or flax (for linen), which were spun and woven before being dyed. Black, blue, red, yellow, and green were all popular colours, while purple, which was a very expensive dye to produce, was used only by the wealthy. Clothing denoted not only the wearer's economic status but their religious status, too.

## MENS' CLOTHING

Men had a loincloth or waist cloth, over which they wore a calf-length wool or linen tunic – a length of material folded in half and sewn or tied at the sides, with holes for the head and arms. This was fastened at the waist with a leather or cloth girdle. Outdoors, a knee-length woollen cloak was worn, though this was generally removed when working. The rich wore more expensive linen undergarments and tunics and more elaborate cloaks than the poor. To protect the head and neck against the sun, a square of cloth was folded diagonally and secured on the head by a plaited wool band, with the folds draped over the neck. Sometimes the cloth was worn as a turban.

Sandals were the most usual form of footwear, although the poor went barefoot. The simplest sandal had a sole of leather, dried grass, or wood, and was secured by a leather thong passing between the big and second toes and tied around the ankle. Later on, the rich began to wear leather slippers. All footwear had to be removed before entering a house or holy place.

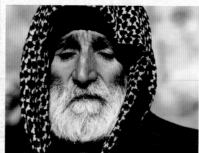

**COVERING THE HEAD**
Protecting the head from the fierce heat of the desert sun is as essential today as it was in biblical times and is often achieved with a simple piece of cloth.

## WOMEN'S CLOTHING

Women's clothing was similar to men's, although it was sufficiently different for Jewish Law to state that "a woman must not wear men's clothing, nor a man wear women's clothing" (Deuteronomy 22:5). They, too, wore a tunic, but it was ankle- instead of calf-length, and in wealthier households the tunics were often dyed and tied with ornate belts. By New Testament times, most women kept their heads covered in public.

**COLOURFUL TUNICS**
This scene from an ancient Egyptian tomb painting depicts Israelite women wearing vividly patterned woollen tunics.

## COSMETICS

From earliest times, ancient Near Eastern men and women wore dark eyeshadow, made by grinding minerals in oil or gum. Originally this had a practical purpose – to

**HENNA**
To stain skin, nails, or hair a reddish brown, powdered henna must be mixed into a paste then applied and left for a few minutes to several hours.

protect the eyes against the sun's glare – but it quickly became a fashion in Egypt, Canaan, and Mesopotamia. Lipstick was used, as was red paint, made from henna, on toenails and fingernails. Cheeks were rouged with red oxide, although in Mesopotamia they used yellow ochre.

Perfume, extracted from flowers, seeds, herbs, and fruit, was added to oil and rubbed on the skin, both to soothe it and to hide body odours. Imported perfumes, made from costly resins, such as frankincense, were kept in small alabaster jars.

## JEWELLERY

Jewellery was highly esteemed by both men and women in biblical times. It was used to display wealth, especially before coins came into common usage during the Persian period, given as gifts at social occasions, such as weddings, and claimed as booty in battle. Necklaces, bracelets, anklets, and rings (for fingers, ears, and noses) were all worn by the Israelites, particularly on special occasions. Gold, silver, and other precious metals were used as adornments and set with semi-precious stones such as jasper, agate, and carnelian. Ivory was used to make combs and brooches.

**GOLD EARRINGS**
These earrings, found at Tel El-Ajjul in present-day Palestine, and dated to the mid-2nd millennium BC, may have been worn by a man or a woman.

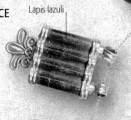

**ASSYRIAN NECKLACE**
Beautiful gems were an indication of wealth, but they were also believed to ward off sickness and protect the wearer from evil spirits.

Lapis lazuli

Fine gold work

Carnelian bead

While the wearing of jewellery is never condemned in the Bible, it can be interpreted as a sign of vanity, which is criticized. But the fact that the high-priests wore jewellery, and their garments were richly decorated, shows that the wearing of jewellery was not in itself deemed to be wrong and may have been an important marker of status.

## HAIR AND BEARDS

In Old Testament times, Jewish men often had long hair and beards, though some cutting seems to have been normal practice, apart from the Nazarites. Priests were forbidden to let their hair grow overly long, but neither were they permitted to shave it. Some men plaited or trimmed their hair, though Jewish Law forbade hair at the sides of the head from being cut (Leviticus 19:27), a practice that is still observed by Orthodox Jews. By New Testament times, some Jewish men wore their hair short and were clean-shaven in the Hellenic style. Women plaited, braided, or curled their hair, and wealthy women used ivory combs to keep it in place.

### HAIRSTYLES IN OTHER CULTURES

#### EGYPT

Most men wore their hair very short or shaved it off and were clean-shaven, although in early periods beards were fashionable. The pharaohs continued to wear beards (sometimes false) as they were deemed sacred. Although women initially had short hair, in the New Kingdom (1550 BC–1069 BC), long hair became fashionable and was plaited and decorated.

#### ASSYRIA AND BABYLON

Men cut their hair to shoulder length and grew their beards long, often oiling and tinting them. Although women usually had long hair, they sometimes wore it shorter than the men. Their hair was often shaped and dyed, and was curled by using heated iron curling bars. The styling of the hair denoted the wearer's social status.

#### GREECE AND ROME

After the 5th century BC, men abandoned long hair in favour of shorter styles. Women wore their hair long, often with corkscrew curls, but from c.650 BC they began tying it in a bun close to the neck. Hair was often dyed, or highlighted with saffron, and decorated with jewellery, flowers, and even gold powder. Some Roman women wore wigs.

# BEFORE

King Cyrus of Persia took control of the Babylonian Empire and established a policy of tolerance and repatriation.

## BABYLON CAPTURED
According to contemporary chronicles, Cyrus' troops entered Babylon in 539 BC via a dry riverbed while Belshazzar, oblivious to the threat, feasted.

## THE EXILES GO HOME
Cyrus permitted all exiled peoples to return home ≪ 252–53, but some Jews chose to stay, including Esther's family. Her story is set in Susa, the winter capital of Persia, around 80 years after Cyrus' decree, which is recorded on the Cyrus Cylinder ≪ 215.

# Esther Saves the Jews

*An edict was passed by Xerxes I of Persia ordering the annihilation of the Jews. With skilful diplomacy, his Jewish queen, Esther – supported by her cousin, Mordecai – saved them, leading to the celebratory festival of Purim.*

Hebrew script adorned with floral motifs

Ornately carved wooden handle

## KEEPING TRADITION
Reading the book of Esther – pictured here on an Italian 18th-century illuminated scroll – is an important component of the festival of Purim, which should "never fail to be celebrated by the Jews" (Esther 9:28).

**K**ING XERXES I, also known as Ahasuerus, ruled the Persian Empire from 486 to 465 BC. After banishing his queen, Vashti, from his presence because she refused to appear before him during a feast, Xerxes called to Susa the most beautiful young women from his realm. The king chose a new queen from among them – Hadassah, a Jewish woman who had been raised by her cousin, Mordecai. He advised her to conceal her ethnicity, and she took the name Esther.

### Jews under threat
Some time later, the king promoted a man named Haman, and said that everyone should bow down before him. Mordecai, however, refused to do this, and Haman was so angered that he conspired to rid the Persian kingdom not only of Mordecai, but also of his people, the Jews. By casting lots (*purim* in Hebrew), a date was set for the planned annihilation. Haman told the king that the Jews were a people who "do not obey the king's laws" (Esther 3:8), and asked that a "decree be issued to

## PURIM PROCESSION
The carnival-like festival is celebrated annually on the 14th or 15th of the Hebrew month of Adar. The book of Esther is read, feasts are held, and charity given to the poor.

destroy them (3:9). Xerxes handed Haman his signet ring, saying, "do with the people as you please" (3:11). Haman commanded the king's secretaries to write and send out orders to every governor of every province in the Empire, to kill all the Jews in their provinces on the 13th day of the 12th month.

### Esther intervenes
When the news of the edict reached the city of Susa, there was great distress. Mordecai told Esther what had happened and pleaded with her to intervene. Realizing she was risking her own life, she agreed, and formulated a plan. She invited King Xerxes and Haman to a banquet. She secured Xerxes' promise to grant her a wish, which she promised to make known to him at a second banquet.

Meanwhile, Haman plotted to kill Mordecai and built a gallows for the purpose. However, his plan was thwarted by the king. Xerxes was unable to sleep one night, and requested someone read the records of his reign to him. He found out that Mordecai had once prevented his assassination, but had received no recognition for this. To make amends, he ordered Haman to lead a parade honouring Mordecai for his loyalty to the king.

At the second banquet, Esther made known her wish: that the Jews be saved. She told the king

about Haman's plan and Haman was dragged away and executed on the gallows intended for Mordecai. In addition, King Xerxes gave the Jews the right to assemble, to protect themselves, and to exact vengeance on their enemies.

> " And who knows but that you have come to your **royal position for such a time as this?** "
>
> ESTHER 4:14

# AFTER

Following the reprieve for the Jews, Purim became an important festival, and Mordecai was promoted.

## A FESTIVAL OF CELEBRATION
Mordecai wrote "words of goodwill and assurance" (Esther 9:30) to all the Jews in all 127 provinces of the Empire, encouraging them to celebrate the festival of Purim.

## MORDECAI PROMOTED
Because he "spoke up for the welfare of all the Jews" (10:3), Mordecai was promoted to second-in-command by King Xerxes.

## PEOPLE

## MORDECAI

From the tribe of Benjamin, Mordecai was among those exiled from Jerusalem by King Nebuchadnezzar. He chose to remain in Susa after the Jews had been permitted to return to Jerusalem, raising his orphaned cousin, Esther. He was evidently a respected man who spent time in public affairs – he gathered at the "king's gate" (Esther 2:19) to be close to matters of state. Mordecai showed care and compassion for Esther. Though he pressed her to stand up for her people, he recognized the need for caution, such as concealing her Jewish identity.

ESTHER AND MORDECAI, 1685, AERT DE GELDER

## BEFORE

The first people to return from exile had made a valiant start on rebuilding their way of life, but their own officials were to lead the way in unfaithfulness.

### CONFESSION OF SIN

**The returning people of Israel ‹‹ 252–53** built homes, replanted fields, and rebuilt a modest Temple, in spite of much opposition. However, as time passed, they fell into old ways and became unfaithful to God.

By the time Ezra arrived, many had "not kept themselves separate from the neighbouring peoples with their detestable practices, like those of the Canaanites, Hittites... They have taken some of their daughters as wives" (Ezra 9:1,2). These marriages appalled Ezra, because, **as with Solomon's marriages ‹‹ 178–79**, the practice encouraged God's people to worship foreign deities.

## THE SCRIBES

**THE TORAH SCROLL BEING HANDWRITTEN BY A SCRIBE**

Scribes were valued early in Israel's history because of their writing skills. They formed guilds and exercised political influence.

During the period of exile, the priesthood was not able to offer sacrifices, so copying, teaching, and interpreting the Law became more prominent practices. Ezra epitomized the ideal scribe after the return to Judah.

By the time of Jesus, scribes had become a distinct class that preserved, interpreted, and taught the Law; acted as lawyers and theologians; and were the guardians of tradition. After the Romans destroyed Jerusalem in AD 70, many respected scribes migrated to Jamnia (or Yavne), near Ashdod, where Rabbi Ben Zakkai had recently founded a school of the Law.

### EZRA THE SCRIBE

This 3rd-century AD painting from the Dura-Europos synagogue in Syria shows Ezra reading the Law. He is traditionally identified as a writer, but also as the person who organized the books of the Old Testament.

# Ezra

*The teacher Ezra helped the returning exiles to re-establish their spiritual priorities, and was especially concerned about intermarriage. Committed to the Law, he was a key influence on post-exile Judaism.*

**E**ZRA WAS A "priest, teacher of the Law of the God of heaven" (Ezra 7:12), who was sent from Babylon to Jerusalem by King Artaxerxes I of Persia, in around 458 BC, on a mission to assess how well the Law of God was being upheld.

A large company made up of the heads of families, their kinsmen, and temple servants went with Ezra, generously equipped by the king with money and supplies. Artaxerxes wrote, "Whatever the God of heaven has prescribed, let it be done with diligence for the temple of the God of heaven. Why should his wrath fall on the realm of the king and of his sons?" (7:23). Ezra was authorized – "in accordance with the wisdom of your God" (7:25) – to appoint magistrates and judges to enforce "the law of your God and the law of the king" (7:26).

### Ezra's spiritual priorities

Ezra was a descendant of Aaron – a Levite, and Israel's first high priest – and was "well versed in the Law of Moses" (7:6), so he became known as Ezra the Scribe. His life was devoted to studying and teaching the Jewish Law. Ezra is credited with establishing an assembly of religious scholars where the Law could be studied authoritatively, and ensuring that adherence to the tenets of the Law lay at the heart of everyday life.

Ezra refused protection for his journey to Jerusalem, since this would have shown a lack of trust in God, and relied on prayer and fasting instead.

On his return Ezra found that the people, including the priests, had "mingled the holy race with the peoples around them" (9:2). This intermarriage was deemed unfaithful, because it contravened God's commands that had been outlined in Deuteronomy: "for they will turn your children away from following me to serve other gods, and the LORD's anger will burn against you" (Deuteronomy 7:4). Ezra was appalled, and deeply ashamed, "weeping and throwing himself down before the house of God" (Ezra 10:1).

Ezra's public grief soon inspired some to repent: "there is still hope for Israel. Now let us make a covenant before our God to send away all these women and their children…" (10:2,3). An enquiry was instigated and all the returnees were required to attend on pain of losing their property and suffering expulsion from the country. Those in mixed marriages pledged to "put away their wives" (10:19) and presented a sacrificial ram as a guilt offering. The whole process was settled within a couple of months, with the names of the guilty family heads recorded.

Later, when the people had finished rebuilding the wall of Jerusalem (see pp.260–61), Ezra gathered together an assembly of people to hear the Law read aloud, and told the people to spread its words around the land.

> ## " For Ezra had devoted himself to the study and observance of the Law of the LORD, and to teaching its decrees and laws in Israel."
>
> EZRA 7:10

**KING ARTAXERXES**
Naksh-e Rustam, near Persepolis, is thought to be the burial site of Darius I, Xerxes I, Artaxerxes I – pictured here in a relief outside his tomb – and Darius II. Building took place from the 17th century BC onwards.

**AFTER** »

Ezra and Nehemiah's desire for the purity of the Jewish people heightened existing tensions with the Samaritans.

**ONE BOOK, ONE SANCTUARY**
Shechem's resettlement and the building of the temple at **Mount Gerizim 308–09 »** nearby as an alternative to Mount Zion in Jerusalem exacerbated the friction between the peoples whose tales fill the first five books of the Old Testament. The tensions between the Jews and Samaritans are evident in the New Testament, where it is considered surprising for Jesus to visit Samaria and talk to a woman there (John 4).

**SAMARITAN PRIESTS AT PRAYER BEFORE THE SACRIFICE OF THE PASSOVER LAMB AT GERIZIM**

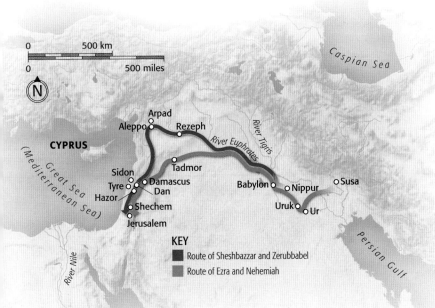

**RETURN OF THE EXILES**
The exiled Jews returned to Jerusalem in three groups. The first was led by Sheshbazzar and Zerubbabel, the second by Ezra the scribe, and the third by Nehemiah. Ezra and Nehemiah used the same (green) route.

**KEY**
■ Route of Sheshbazzar and Zerubbabel
■ Route of Ezra and Nehemiah

**BEFORE**

Although exiles had returned to Judah, now a province of Persia, the country had not regained its earlier stability.

EZRA IN FRONT OF THE SECOND TEMPLE, FROM A 13TH-CENTURY FRENCH BIBLE

### A CITY IN DISREPAIR

Early returning groups of exiles had rebuilt their houses and re-established some agriculture. **A modest Temple had been built ‹‹ 252–53** and, under Ezra, a legal system had been put in place. However, many problems remained, especially the indebtedness of the poor, and little progress had been made with much of Jerusalem's infrastructure. The city's walls remained broken, exemplifying its continuing weakness and vulnerability.

**PEOPLE**

### MALACHI

Malachi was a prophet who was active around the time of Nehemiah, when the people's observance of the Law was lax. His sermons reveal an agenda similar to Nehemiah's, about tithes and offerings, mixed marriages, divorce, social justice, and religious purity. His central theme is the need for people to repent for breaking the covenant. He develops a message of "the day of the Lord", which he speaks of both as a day of judgment on the unrighteous, and a day of hope and deliverance for those who revere God's name.

AN INITIAL "O" WITH THE PROPHET MALACHI FROM A GERMAN BIBLE, 1205

# Rebuilding Jerusalem

*Nehemiah was a governor of Judah who led the project to rebuild the walls of Jerusalem in 445 BC, in the face of great opposition. He shared many of Ezra's concerns for renewal, but focused on restoring civic life.*

**L**ITTLE IS KNOWN of Nehemiah's background except his father's name, Hakaliah, and that his family was from Jerusalem. He rose to become cupbearer to King Artaxerxes of Persia at the royal palace in Susa, which was a privileged position that brought him into close contact with the ruler.

### Nehemiah restores the city walls

On hearing from one of his brothers, who had returned to Susa from Judah, that Jerusalem remained a ruined and unprotected city, Nehemiah grieved. He prayed urgently to God, confessing "the sins we Israelites, including myself and my father's family, have committed against you" (Nehemiah 1:6), and asked for a favourable response from the king that day.

Seeing that Nehemiah was troubled, the king asked what was the matter. Fortunately, the king reacted helpfully, and sent him to Jerusalem with soldiers and cavalry for protection.

When he arrived in Jerusalem, Nehemiah inspected the city walls and set about organizing the rebuilding, with

**WINGED LION RHYTON**
This Persian *rhyton* (goblet) dating from the 5th century BC is the sort of cup Nehemiah would have used to serve wine to the ruler of Persia. It is made out of gold and decorated in the form of a regal winged-lion.

all the citizens working section by section. The people who lived in the areas around Jerusalem were "greatly incensed" (4:1) when they saw that Jerusalem's fortifications were being restored, because it served their interests to keep the city in a weakened state. Sanballat the Horonite, and Tobiah the Ammonite, at first ridiculed Nehemiah's work, but then became increasingly aggressive. Nehemiah courageously faced down their loud opposition, by ensuring that the task continued under the protection of an armed guard, formed out of half his workforce. Remarkably,

THE NEW TEMPLE
This vertical seam about 32m (105ft) to the north of the southeastern corner of the Temple Mount in Jerusalem shows the neat brickwork of the later Herodian Temple enclosure joining the earlier wall that was built in Nehemiah's time.

the whole wall with gates was repaired in 52 days.

The completed wall was rededicated in a joyful celebration, with processions around the walls, and the people also devoted themselves to obeying the Law, which was read out over seven days by Ezra (8:1–18).

### Nehemiah's other achievements

Nehemiah served as governor of Judah from 445 to 433 BC during which time he established an administration that supported the principles of the Law, such as the gathering of a tithe (10:37–39).

He built a fortress and official residences, and took steps to alleviate the condition of the poor by restoring lands that had been appropriated by officials, and by stopping the charging of interest

**HISTORY AND CULTURE**

### KEEPING RECORDS

The books of Ezra and Nehemiah contain many lists. One of the functions of scribes and administrators was to keep records to be placed in the royal archives (Ezra 5:17), in case of future need. For example, confirmation was needed that Cyrus had authorized the rebuilding of the Temple (see pp.252–53). Ezra records the precious objects returned to Jerusalem, those who returned with him and their sacrifices, and those guilty of intermarriage. Nehemiah lists the builders of the wall and other participants in Jerusalem's renewal, as well as the original returnees from exile.

> " And because **the gracious hand of my God was on me**, the king granted my requests. "
>
> NEHEMIAH 2:8

on loans. His integrity was beyond question, as he lived simply while providing generously for others.

After being recalled to Babylon, Nehemiah returned to Jerusalem for a second term of office – he reinforced compliance with the Law, which had become lax during his absence. Besides ejecting Tobiah the Ammonite from a room at the Temple, he insisted that the Levites should be provided for, that tithes should be given, and the Sabbath observed. Like Ezra and Malachi, he also criticized mixed marriages and passed a law forbidding them.

Nehemiah recognized that his achievements were only possible because God was blessing his endeavours.

## " We will not neglect the house of our God.' "

NEHEMIAH 10:39

### RAISED STONE BY STONE
A mason dresses stone and builds a wall in a way that has changed little for centuries. Sanballat, a Samaritan critic of Nehemiah's rebuilding project, mocked, "Can they bring the stones back to life from those heaps of rubble – burned as they are?" (Nehemiah 4:2). Against the odds, Nehemiah triumphed.

**The Book of Malachi, which closes the Old Testament, makes a final prophecy before a 400-year silence.**

*ST. JOHN THE BAPTIST PREACHING TO THE MULTITUDE*, BY ALLORI (1577–1621)

### THE COMING AGAIN
Addressing issues of unfaithful returning exiles, Malachi prophesied that Elijah would return, heralding "the great and dreadful day of the LORD" (Malachi 4:5). Jesus explained that this prophecy referred to **John the Baptist 298–99 ››** (Matthew 11:14; 17:12,13). Elijah appeared on the Mount of Transfiguration (see Mark 9:4).

# BETWEEN THE OLD
# AND NEW TESTAMENTS

"'**Surely the day is coming;** it will burn like a furnace. All the arrogant and every evildoer will be stubble…' says the LORD Almighty. '**Not a root or a branch will be left to them.** But for you who revere my name, the sun of righteousness will rise with **healing in its rays…Then you will trample on the wicked;** they will be ashes under the soles of your feet on the day when I act.'"

MALACHI 4:1–3

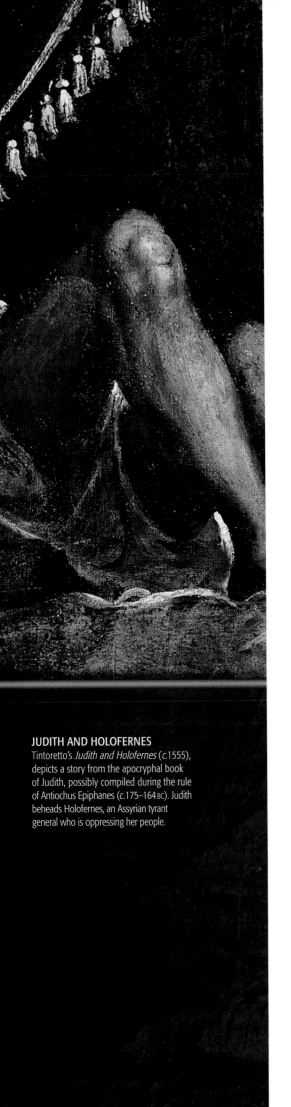

**JUDITH AND HOLOFERNES**
Tintoretto's *Judith and Holofernes* (c.1555), depicts a story from the apocryphal book of Judith, possibly compiled during the rule of Antiochus Epiphanes (c.175–164 BC). Judith beheads Holofernes, an Assyrian tyrant general who is oppressing her people.

 HE BIBLE IS LARGELY SILENT ON THE centuries between the prophet Malachi, active in the mid 5th century BC, and the birth of Jesus Christ. During that time the Greek empire exercised a lasting influence on Jewish culture. After the death of Alexander the Great, Samaria and Judea were ruled for a century by the Egyptian Ptolemies and then the Hellenistic Seleucid dynasty based in the city of Antioch (Antakya in modern-day Turkey), before Rome established its rule in 63 BC. The book of Daniel was probably compiled during this turbulent time, when the Jews struggled to preserve their identity.

Apart from Daniel's prophecies, notably his vision of "a son of man" with an "everlasting dominion" (Daniel 7:13,14), the Bible says nothing about the centuries directly before the birth of Jesus Christ. Yet these years provide the background to the cultural and religious context of the New Testament. At that time, the Jews had a Bible in Hebrew, as well as one in Greek, known as the Septuagint (see p.19), that was used by Diaspora Jews. The Septuagint contained 15 additional books, such as Judith and 1 and 2 Maccabees, which were later rejected by Judaism because they lacked a Hebrew original. However, those apocryphal books were incorporated by some Christian traditions into their versions of the Old Testament.

### ALEXANDER AND AFTER
The city-states of classical Greece were united under Philip of Macedon whose fabled son, Alexander the Great, extended the empire to the Himalayas. His sudden death in 323 BC left no clear successor and his empire fragmented. By then, Greek culture had powerfully impacted the cultures of the conquered territories. One of

Alexander's generals, Ptolemy, took over Egypt. Another Hellenistic dynasty, the Seleucids of Syria, ruled in the East and by 198 BC it controlled Samaria and Judea.

The Jews were permitted to practise their religion to begin with, but 30 years later Antiochus IV Epiphanes sought to impose Hellenistic culture and worship on them, which provoked resistance led by the priestly Hasmonean family. One of its number, Judas Maccabeus, organized a successful military campaign, although many Jews died. The eventual outcome of the revolt was that the Jews gained their independence under the leadership of John Hyrcanus around 134 BC. This was subsequently viewed as a golden era.

### THE COMING OF ROME
Jewish independence was not to last. When the reigning queen, Salome Alexander, died in 67 BC, civil war broke out between her two sons. General Pompey, who had been campaigning in the region on behalf of Rome, was invited by the warring parties to intervene and so the independent Jewish state became a part of the Roman Empire in 63 BC.

**HANUKKAH MENORAH**
A *Hannukiya*, or Hanukkah Menorah, lamp in Jerusalem, Israel. The candles are lit during the eight-day festival to observe the rededication of the Temple during the Maccabean revolt.

## HISTORY AND CULTURE

# The Impact of Greece

"I watched the ram as it **charged towards the west** and **the north** and **the south**… It did as it pleased and **became great**."

DANIEL 8:4

**ALEXANDER THE GREAT**
The son of Philip II of Macedon, Alexander was a brilliant general. By his death he had become the single most important ruler of his era.

The once powerful Persian Empire (see p.245) gave way to the Greeks in the time of Alexander the Great (356–323 BC). Although he was renowned for his military advances, the greatest legacy of Greece was social rather than political, as the Greek language and Hellenistic ideas and lifestyles shaped the cultures of the nations it ruled for many years after its decline.

Classical Greece, whose golden age began in the early 5th century BC, consisted of a number of independent city-states, such as Athens and Sparta, who governed themselves democractically. They occasionally allied with each other for defensive purposes, and this strategy allowed them to fight off the Persians in 480 BC.

Over a century later, the kingdoms of Macedonia, to the north of Greece, were united by Philip II. He went on to gain control of most of Greece.

When Philip II was assassinated in 336 BC, Alexander, his 20-year-old son, succeeded him. He expanded his father's empire, taking Egypt then Syria, and then defeated the Persians in their heartland in 331 BC, before pressing eastwards to India. Alexander never suffered a military defeat. He died of a fever in Babylon at the age of 32, having established an empire on three continents.

Without a designated successor, a 20-year power struggle ensued between four of Alexander's generals for control of his empire. Ptolemy ruled in Egypt and took over Judea in 301 BC. Seleucus gained the largest share of the empire, based on Syria. Judea was caught between the Seleucid and Ptolemaic dynasties and in 198 BC the Seleucids took control.

**LION HUNT**
This carving on Alexander's sarcophagus depicts Greeks and Persians (shown wearing leggings) hunting a lion together, reflecting his wish for the people under his rule to be culturally unified.

**ALEXANDER'S EMPIRE**
Alexander's conquests took him to the far corners of the Persian Empire. By 323 BC, his empire extended as far east as India.

# HELLENIZATION

Alexander, who had been tutored by the Greek philisopher Aristotle, adopted the policy of Hellenization, that is, the transformation of local cultures by Greek civilization ("Hellene" means Greek). To this end, he built around 70 new cities – such as Alexandria in Egypt and Antioch in Syria – which were Greek in their architecture, customs, and way of life. They boasted gymnasiums, theatres, and sports arenas. Greek became the language of officialdom, and numerous itinerant philosophers spread various Greek ideas.

Hellenistic influence became even more prominent after Alexander's death, and continued under the Romans, who admired Greece's

**PTOLEMY II PORTRAYED AS MEDUSA**
The Ptolemaic dynasty ruled as pharoahs in Egypt for 275 years. Their administration combined the best of Greek and Egyptian traditions.

achievements. The Greek language continued to be widely written and spoken by the Roman upper classes, who were often tutored by Greek slaves. Many Roman deities were equated with Greek gods and goddesses (see p.53).

Four pairs of Ionic columns flank main entrance to library

**GREEK CULTURE**
The Library of Celsus at Ephesus, in modern-day Turkey, was built in honour of one of the first men of purely Greek origin to become a Roman consul.

## THE GREEK LANGUAGE

After Alexander, Greek became the language of education, commerce, law, and politics throughout the region, and was a significant instrument of Hellenization. The dominant form of Greek from c.300 BC to AD 300 was a common dialect known as Koine Greek. The Greek translation of the Hebrew Bible – now known as the Septuagint – was used by most early Christians as the text of their Bible, and the New Testament was largely written in the everyday Greek of the people. Most New Testament writers were Jews, and their decision to use the Greek language demonstrates the

widespread ability to read and understand Greek across the Roman Empire. Paul, for example, claimed to be the "Hebrew of Hebrews", but he wrote well in Greek, which became a key vehicle for the spread of the Christian gospel around the world.

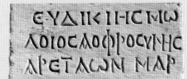

**GREEK INSCRIPTION, EPHESUS**

# THE IMPACT ON THE JEWS

Hellenization raised major questions for Judaism. Differing answers were given as to how far Jews could accommodate Greek ideas without compromising their faith. Some communities reacted by placing a stricter emphasis on the boundary markers of the Jewish faith, such as circumcision

Jumping weights

Javelin

Discus

**OLYMPIC PENTATHLETES**
The five events in the ancient Greek pentathlon included javelin and discus throwing, running, wrestling, and jumping.

and the Sabbath, by intensifying the study of the Torah, and by speaking only Aramaic. Others were more accommodating, especially among the Diaspora – the Jewish communities living outside Judea.

Jewish colonies in Egypt provide examples of Hellenization. In the city of Alexandria, Greek replaced Aramaic as the language of the Jews, and the Hebrew Bible was translated into Greek (see panel, left). Alexandria was also home to a Hellenistic Jewish philosopher called Philo (c.20 BC–AD 50), who sought to interpret Scripture from a Greek philosophical perspective. His writings were widely influential in the early Christian Church.

Hellenism is evident in the New Testament in the tensions between Greek-speaking and Aramaic-speaking Jews mentioned in Acts 6, in Paul's teaching in Athens (Acts 17), and in many of his letters,

which were addressed to the churches in the Roman province of Asia (modern-day Turkey) and in Greece itself.

The ancient Greeks believed that training the body was an important element in the development of a virtuous life. Athletic contests were therefore at the heart of their

community ethos. The Olympic games, first held in the 8th century BC, were religious contests in honour of Zeus, god of Mount Olympus. The Jews did not approve of such contests because the atheletes performed naked and the contests were held in honour of Greek gods, and the games are not directly mentioned in the Bible. Yet Paul, a Roman citizen in a Hellenized world, often uses athletic imagery to explain the Christian life, for example: "Everyone who competes in the games goes into strict training. They do it to get a crown that will not last; but we do it for a crown that will last forever" (1 Corinthians 9:25). This is probably an allusion to the Isthmian Games, held in Corinth as part of the Greek cycle of games.

## HISTORY AND CULTURE
# The Maccabean Revolt

> "His armed forces will **rise up** to desecrate the temple fortress and will **abolish the daily sacrifice**. Then they will set up the abomination that **causes desolation**."
>
> DANIEL 11:31

**FOUNDER OF A DYNASTY**
In 311 BC Seleucus I Nicator founded the Seleucid dynasty, which was to rule for almost 150 years. The Seleucids took control of Judea from the Egyptian-based Ptolemies in 198 BC.

The Seleucid dynasty, which derives its name from its Greek founder, imposed Hellenistic institutions and culture on the Jews in Judea until the actions of Antiochus IV Epiphanes provoked a revolt. The Hasmonean family of Jewish priests led the Maccabean rebellion from 167 BC, which witnessed many heroic acts of resistance and produced several martyrs. The revolt ultimately won the Jews their independence in 142 BC.

The Maccabees took their name from the nickname given to their leader Judas, who was called "Maccabeus" or the "Hammer".

## THE SELEUCIDS

When the Syrian-based Seleucid dynasty first took control of Judea in 198 BC, they permitted the Jews to maintain their laws and religious customs. That changed when Antiochus IV, known as Epiphanes, came to power in 175 BC. He sold Jerusalem's high priesthood to the highest bidder – as was the custom of the time, for it was also a political post – to a man called Menelaus, who was totally unqualified for office and a keen Hellenist. When Menelaus was ejected from office, Antiochus pulled down Jerusalem's walls and slaughtered many of its inhabitants in retribution.

In 167 BC Antiochus outlawed core Jewish customs, such as circumcision and Sabbath-keeping, on pain of death, and introduced "pagan" (in this case Greek) sacrifices into the Temple. His actions proved the catalyst for the Maccabean Revolt.

**BRONZE ARROWHEADS**
Several arrowheads dating from the period of the Maccabean Revolt have been found in the citadel in Jerusalem.

Diadem denotes kingship

**ANTIOCHUS IV EPIPHANES**
Epiphanes means "manifestation" in Greek and Antiochus IV promoted himself as a manifestation of a deity. His face adorns this rare gold tetradrachm – Greek coins were the currency of his empire.

## THE MACCABEES

An elderly priest called Mattathias, who fervently wished to uphold Jewish Law, sparked the revolt in 167 BC when he refused to offer a sacrifice to the Greek god Zeus and then killed a Jewish apostate (someone who had abandoned his religion) and a Seleucid officer as they did so. He then summoned his five sons to take to the hills and challenged others to join him, crying: "Let everyone who is zealous for the law and supports the covenant come out with me!" (1 Maccabees 2:27, *New Revised Standard Version*).

The rebels engaged in guerrilla warfare against the Seleucid army. When Mattathias died in 166 BC, leadership of the resistance force

### BURIAL GROUND
Several Maccabean tombs have been found near the modern city of Modi'in, which lies in the foothills of the Judean Mountains, to the west of Jerusalem.

### MACCABEAN FORTRESS
This former Maccabean stronghold at Beth Zur now lies in ruins. Judas Maccabeus defeated the Seleucid army led by General Lysias here in 164 BC and went on to take Jerusalem soon after.

passed to his son Judas Maccabeus. Antiochus was distracted by wars in the east of his empire and in 164 BC, when Judas recaptured Jerusalem, his regent was forced to withdraw the offensive laws. Judas reconsecrated the Temple (see panel, below) and re-established Judaism. Unfortunately, Jews elsewhere were still viciously persecuted and Judas' work was far from over. He died in a battle against the Seleucids in 160 BC.

The youngest brother, Jonathan, next took over the leadership of the Maccabees and continued the

fight against the Seleucid Empire, which had been weakened by internal factions following the death of Antiochus in 164 BC. Jonathan had himself nominated as high priest in 152 BC, then as general and governor of Judea in 150 BC, and was the first ruler of the Hasmonean Dynasty.

When Jonathan was murdered in 142 BC, Simon, Mattathias' only surviving son, led the Maccabean party and negotiated complete freedom from Seleucid taxation and virtual independence for the Jews. As a reward, the Jews installed Simon as their hereditary ruler and high priest. However, he was not from the traditional line of Zadok – the dominant priestly family descended from David's priest in Jerusalem – and this created a deep unease among pious Jews.

Simon Maccabee was assassinated in 134 BC and his son, John Hyrcanus, succeeded him as high priest and ruler of Judea. The Maccabees had succeeded in achieving political and religious freedom – but not for long.

## THE HASMONEAN DYNASTY

John Hyrcanus extended Judea's territory and occupied Samaria and Idumea, imposing Judaism on them. He was a good and generally respected ruler, but his successors were less distinguished.

It was during the Hasmonean period that several Jewish religious factions emerged, among them the Sadducees and Pharisees (see pp.366–67). Hyrcanus wanted his wife to succeed him as the head of the government, but when he died in 104 BC, his son Aristobulus seized power. He would rule for only one year, however, and on his death in 103 BC his brother Alexander Jannaeus succeeded him. The Pharisees opposed Jannaeus and in response he openly sided with the Sadducees.

His widow, Salome Alexandra, succeeded Jannaeus in 76 BC, but it was their elder son, Hyrcanus II, who held the office of high priest during her 11-year reign and he supported the Pharisees. When Salome died in 67 BC, her younger son Aristobulus II, a Sadducee, fought Hyrcanus for the throne. The resulting civil war left the way open for Rome to seize the chance to take control (see p.269).

### HASMONEAN COINS
These coins date from the time of Alexander Jannaeus, who ruled Judea from 103 to 76 BC. He was notorious for his ruthless cruelty.

### HANUKKAH

When Antiochus overran Jerusalem in 167 BC he defiled the Temple by setting up a Greek altar within it. Three years later, Judas Maccabeus ousted the Seleucids and recaptured the Temple. He then cleansed it and rededicated it to God. The event was later interpreted by non-Hellenistic Jews as being symbolic of the wider cleansing of the Jews from the pollution of Hellenism. Hanukkah is the Festival of Dedication and commemorates the miracle that the lamp in the Temple kept burning for eight days when there was only enough oil for one. Also known as the Festival of Lights, it begins on the 25th of the winter month Kislev, and is celebrated by the lighting of candles in Jewish homes. The New Testament says nothing about it except that Jesus attended the festival in Jerusalem (John 10:22) and was interrogated about his Messiahship.

**HANUKKAH MENORAH**

## HISTORY AND CULTURE

# Rome and its Empire

"Finally, there will be a fourth kingdom, **strong as iron**… and as iron breaks things to pieces, so it will **crush and break** all the others."

DANIEL 2:40

**GODDESS OF VICTORY**
To Romans, the spirit of military victory was a winged goddess, shown here holding a crown of laurel leaves, a symbol of victory.

From its foundation in the 8th century BC, the city of Rome fought to increase its influence over other cities and gain new territory in Italy through political alliances and military might. By 240 BC, the Romans controlled most of the Italian Peninsula. Victory in the First Punic War (264–241 BC) against the North African power of Carthage had brought Sicily under Roman rule; victory in the Second Punic War meant that by 202 BC Rome also controlled Sardinia and parts of Spain. By 120 BC, Greece and parts of Asia Minor had become Roman provinces.

Much of Rome's expansion was due to the ambitions of its generals. Pompey, for example, exercised huge authority in the east, imposing Rome's direct control over much of Asia Minor by 65 BC. In 64 BC he deposed Antiochus III, the last Seleucid king, making Syria a Roman province. This, together with the North African territories gained in 96 BC, meant Rome's power throughout the Mediterranean region was unrivalled.

**KEY**
- Roman territory 240 BC
- Roman territory 200 BC
- Roman territory 120 BC
- Roman territory 60 BC

GERMANIA

GALLIA

Aquileia

Massilia

Olisipo

HISPANIA

CORSICA

Rome

ITALY

ILLYRIA

Black Sea

Thessalonica

SARDINIA

Carthago Nova

MACEDONIA

Athens

Corinth

ASIA

Ephesus

ASIA MINOR

Antioch

SYRIA

Carthage

SICILY

CRETE

CYPRUS

JUDEA

Jerusalem

Sahara

Mediterranean Sea
(Great Sea)

Leptis Magna

Cyrene

EGYPT

**ROMAN EXPANSION 240–60 BC**
In less than 200 years, Rome expanded its territory to include Hispania and Gallia; parts of Germania, Illyria, North Africa; and much of Asia Minor. Judea became a Roman client kingdom in 37 BC.

## ROME AND JUDEA

Following his victory in Syria, in 63 BC Pompey became involved in the civil war in Judea. The Hasmonean brothers Hyrcanus II (who supported the Pharisees; see pp.366–67) and Aristobulus II (a Sadducee) were fighting over the right to rule in Jerusalem. Pompey intervened on Hyrcanus' behalf and laid siege to the city, resulting in much destruction and loss of Jewish life. After three months Jerusalem fell. On entering the city Pompey went into the Temple and viewed its treasures – something

that only the high priests were permitted to do under Jewish law. However, the Romans did not loot it, and the next day he ordered that it be ritually cleansed.

Although Jerusalem was permitted some independence under Hyrcanus' leadership, it was placed under Roman governorship and forced to pay tribute.

One of 1,200 columns in the colonnade

**GREAT COLONNADE**
The Syrian fortress city of Apamea was annexed to Rome in 64 BC. The great colonnade stood from the 2nd to the 11th century AD, when earthquakes struck.

## FROM REPUBLIC TO EMPIRE

Rome was a republic for almost 500 years, until 27 BC. Conflicting political interests in Rome led to three civil wars in the 1st century BC, which threatened to undermine the Republic's position on the world stage. The final civil war was fought between the supporters of Julius Caesar and Pompey, in 49–45 BC. Caesar's victories over his rival and his reformation of the army led to him being declared dictator in 48 BC, and in 44 BC he was given the office for life, but was murdered shortly after.

In 43 BC Caesar's great-nephew and adopted son Octavian took power with Mark Antony and Marcus Lepidus; this alliance lasted until 33 BC. When Mark Antony lost public support due to his relationship with Cleopatra, the Egyptian queen, Octavian seized his opportunity. He defeated them

**AUGUSTUS' EMPIRE, AD 14**
By the time of Augustus' death in AD 14 the Roman Empire had gained territories in all directions, but further expansion was yet to come.

in battle and made Egypt a Roman province. By 30 BC Octavian was sole ruler of the Roman world.

Knowing that Romans hated the idea of kings, Octavian proclaimed the restoration of the old Republic in 27 BC, with himself as its first, or leading, citizen. When the Senate responded by giving him several powers and the title *Augustus*, he became in effect the first emperor of Rome.

## THE HERODS

Alexander Janneus, member of the Hasmonean dynasty and king of Judea from 103 to 76 BC, had originally appointed Herod Antipater governor of the region Idumea during the brief time of territorial expansion that the Hasmoneans enjoyed. When the rivalry between Hyrcanus II and Aristobulus II erupted (see left), Antipater took Hyrcanus' side. Some years later, in 47 BC, Julius Caesar granted Antipater Roman citizenship, exempted him from taxation, and made him governor of Judea. He in turn appointed his sons Phasael and Herod the Great as governors of Jerusalem and Galilee respectively.

When the Parthians conquered Jerusalem in 40 BC Herod escaped to Rome. Three years later, the Romans retook the city and Herod was confirmed as king of Judea, making Judea a Roman client kingdom and bringing the Hasmonean dynasty to a close. Herod the Great reigned as a

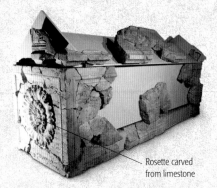

Rosette carved from limestone

**HEROD'S SARCOPHAGUS**
In 2008, the shattered remains of a red-tinted limestone sarcophagus were found at Herod's mausoleum in Herodium.

tyrant in Jerusalem for 33 years until his death. His cruelty, his lack of pure Jewish blood, and his favouritism towards Greek culture, reflected in his many building projects, meant the Jews were never at ease with him.

After his death, Herod's territory was divided between his three sons: Archelaus became ruler of Idumea, Judea, and Samaria; Herod Antipas became ruler of Galilee and Perea; and Philip ruled Trachonitis and other outlying territories.

## ROMAN POWER

Rome used various means besides military might to ensure stability and peace throughout its empire. It used diplomacy to enable subject states to negotiate their own rights

and privileges, and built loyalty by granting Roman citizenship to some people in its territories. Rome also imposed a common system of justice for its citizens.

The Romans built a vast network of robust roads connecting the Empire's towns and provinces. Pompey also improved travel conditions in the Mediterranean by clearing the sea of pirates. These measures promoted growing prosperity through trade and also facilitated the spread of the gospel by the early Christians.

**ROAD TO SUCCESS**
The Romans' sophisticated network of paved roads eventually covered 96,500km (60,000 miles), connecting Rome with all the important towns in its vast empire.

HISTORY AND CULTURE

# After the Hebrew Bible

**DEAD SEA SCROLLS**
Discovered in caves at Qumran, the Dead Sea Scrolls are biblical manuscripts and works of Jewish literature written in the century before and around the time of Jesus (see pp.22–23).

"For in everything, **O Lord**, you have exalted and **glorified your people**, and you have not neglected to **help them** at **all times** and in **all places**." WISDOM 19:22

T he rising influence of Greek culture, the revolt of the Maccabean Jews against the Seleucid dynasty, followed by the dominance of the Roman Empire all had a profound effect on the Jews. Much creative writing took place during the intertestamental period, as Jewish scholars pondered the ways of God in the world and encouraged their people to remain faithful to him.

Some of these writings include the Apocrypha (from the Greek, meaning "secret" or "hidden") – a collection of books found in some Christian Bibles but not in the Jewish canon.

## THE SEPTUAGINT

Early Christians and Jews alike used a Greek translation of Old Testament Hebrew texts called the Septuagint. The name comes from the Latin septuaginta, which means "70". Legend has it that the Egyptian ruler Ptolemy II Philadelphus requested a Greek translation of the Jewish Laws for his library at Alexandria in the 3rd century BC. As a result, 72 scribes, six from each tribe of Israel, went to Egypt; each worked in separate rooms, and after 72 days, each of the translations was identical to the rest. The Septuagint is also known by the abbreviation LXX – the roman numeral for 70 – as one version of the story has 70 rather than 72 scholars.

Further books from the Hebrew Old Testament were translated, by different people at different times and places, over the next three centuries, together with a number of other Hebrew deutero-canonical books (works that are secondary or of a later date) found in the Apocrypha. Although there is no fixed or agreed canon of the LXX, when the New Testament quotes the Old Testament, it is often a quotation from the LXX.

**ANCIENT SEPTUAGINT**
This fragment of an early copy of the Septuagint, written in Greek, also contains the name Yahweh in ancient Hebrew.

YHWY
(Yahweh)

## THE ESSENES

The Essenes were a Jewish sect that endeavoured to obey the command to "Be holy". They are not mentioned in the New Testament, but are known from the writings of Pliny the Elder, Philo, and Josephus. They flourished from around 100 BC to AD 100.

The Essenes lived in a commune under the direction of a leader. They underwent a three-year initiation period, remained celibate, and shared their property. They stressed Sabbath observance and ritual purity, and sought holiness through separation from ordinary society. Rising before sunrise to pray, they had a daily routine of work, ceremonial baths, and common meals. The Essenes were farmers and craftsmen as well as being devoted to studying the Scriptures. They rejected slavery, refused to make weapons, and did not offer sacrifices.

The Jewish sect at Qumran, home of the Dead Sea Scrolls, may possibly have been an Essene community (see pp. 22–23).

## THE APOCRYPHA

The Apocrypha normally refers to the 15 books of Jewish literature found in the LXX, which were written between 200 BC and AD 200 and reflect the concerns of this turbulent period. They are not in the Hebrew Bible, but twelve appear in Roman Catholic Bibles, as a result of their inclusion by Jerome in his Latin translation of the Bible, known as the Vulgate (the official version in the Roman Catholic Church, see pp. 23–24). Most of these are also in Bibles of the Orthodox Church.

Protestants have traditionally rejected these 15 books from their canon of Scripture, and therefore view them as Apocrypha. The 15 Protestant Apocrypha are: 1 and 2 Esdras, Tobit, Judith, additions to the book of Esther, book of Wisdom, Sirach, 1 Baruch, letter of Jeremiah, additions to the book

### GREEK ORTHODOX BIBLE
The Orthodox Old Testament includes nine of the books that are viewed as Apocrypha by the Protestant church, while the additions to Daniel are included in the book itself.

of Daniel (including the prayer of Azariah, Susanna and the Elders, and the story of Bel and the Dragon), prayer of Manasseh, and 1 and 2 Maccabees. The Roman Catholic Bible does not include 1 and 2 Esdras or the prayer of Manasseh. However, the other works are included; sometimes just as fragments, and often attached to books with which they are thought to be connected. Orthodox Bibles do not include 2 Esdras, additions to Esther, or the prayer of Manasseh.

The books in the Apocrypha can be grouped into four categories: Fictional, Wisdom, Historical, and

Apocalyptic. There are other Apocryphal works, both Jewish and Christian, which are included in some canons but not others. The book of Jubilees and several books of Enoch, for example, appear in the Ethiopian canon but not in the Western Christian tradition. In the New Testament, 2 Peter and Jude show knowledge of several of these apocryphal works.

## FICTIONAL

Tobit, Judith, Susanna, and Bel are now seen as fictional narratives that recount how God vindicates the righteous and punishes idolaters. The story of Susanna was

**DANIEL THE HERO**
When Susanna was falsely accused of adultery by two elders who had tried to rape her, Daniel intervened and Susanna's honour was vindicated.

added to the book of Daniel in most Greek and Latin texts. The stories of Bel and the Dragon are an addition to Daniel in the Septuagint, as is the prayer of Azariah. The prayer of Manasseh derives from 2 Chronicles.

## WISDOM

Wisdom literature (see p. 171) became increasingly popular in the intertestamental period. The books of Wisdom and Sirach (also known as Ecclesiasticus) are written in this style. Baruch, the name of Jeremiah's secretary, contains a considerable amount of prose but also has a poem concerning wisdom in the middle. Some versions include the letter of Jeremiah in Baruch, while others publish it separately.

**ECCLESIASTICUS**
Written by Jesus ben Sirach, a scribe of Jerusalem, about two-thirds of the Hebrew manuscript of the book of Sirach survives.

## HISTORICAL

The three historical books in the Apocrypha are 1 Esdras and 1 and 2 Maccabees, which recount various chapters in Israel's post-Exile story. The revolt against the Seleucids is told in 1 and 2 Maccabees (see pp. 266–67). The additions to Esther are 107 verses that Jerome found in the Greek version of the book of Esther, which derived from an earlier Hebrew text.

**DARIUS THE GREAT**
King of Persia from 522 to 486 BC, Darius appears in 1 Esdras when three of his bodyguards have a debate about the three greatest forces in the world.

## APOCALYPTIC

The final category of Apocrypha is apocalyptic, which became more prominent with the decline of classic prophetic literature and the rise of a sense of crisis among the Jews. Such writings record the dramatic revelations from God – of salvation or damnation – experienced by the authors in a vision. In the Bible, the two major apocalyptic works are Daniel (see

p. 250) and Revelation. The sole apocalyptic representative in the Apocrypha is 2 Esdras. This lengthy work is named after its central figure – Esdras is the Greek form of the Hebrew name Ezra. It consists chiefly of seven visions that assure the Israelites that their suffering is far from meaningless and that a Messiah will come.

MATTHEW · MARK · LUKE · JOHN · ACTS · ROMANS · I CORIN

GALATIANS · EPHESIANS · PHILIPPIANS · COLOSSIANS · I TH

1 TIMOTHY · 2 TIMOTHY · TITUS · PHILEMON · HEBREWS · JA

JOHN · 3 JOHN · JUDE · REVELATION

# 3

# THE NEW
# TESTAMENT

# New Testament Lands

*By the birth of Jesus, the world of the Bible had transformed almost beyond recognition. The landscape remained broadly the same, but the actors in the drama had completely changed.*

**E**GYPT REMAINED A significant economic and political power throughout the New Testament period. However, the dominant power in the biblical heartland was now Rome, which controlled Asia Minor, Syria, the lands of Galilee, Samaria, Judea, and Egypt. The Roman conquest had brought peace and prosperity – and

sometimes oppression – through the incorporation of the entire region into a single economic and political union; this allowed trade to flow freely, but at the cost of political independence.

The Romans also brought new technology, such as water-wheels and aqueducts to bring water into the hearts of the cities; they introduced larger, more sophisticated

ships to move cargo between countries; and they built a network of roads connecting the Empire's key towns. The advent of coinage had encouraged a shift towards a money economy, and coins from the many countries of the region enable scholars to trace the trade routes which converged on the biblical homeland. Coins also allow historians to follow the diaspora of

a people now called the Jews (a term first applied *c.*500 BC) as they spread across the Roman Empire.

The main events of Jesus' life as related in the gospels took place in Galilee and Judea in the eastern Mediterranean. After his death and resurrection, the apostles spread his teachings throughout the entire Mediterranean region, establishing many early Christian churches.

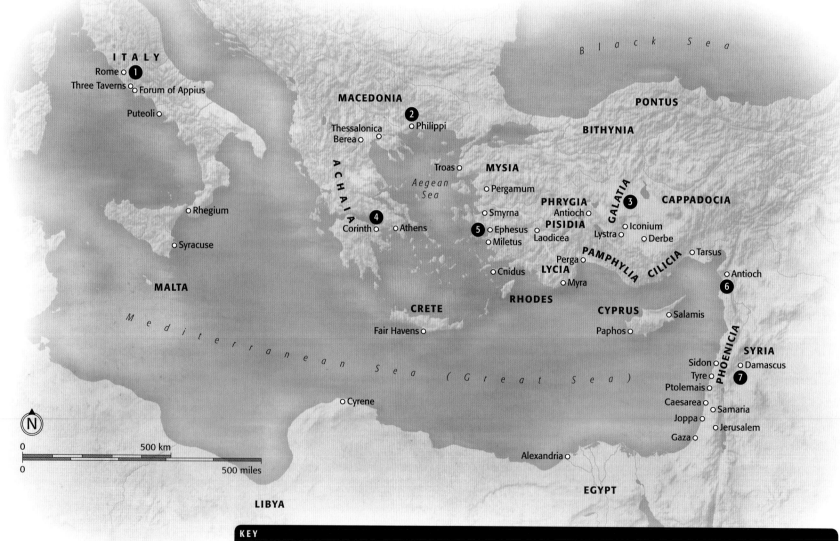

## THE MEDITERRANEAN

The gospels' story takes place entirely in the eastern Mediterranean, but Paul and other apostles spread Jesus' message far and wide. At the time, the Mediterranean was governed by the Roman Empire, which came to endorse Christianity in the 4th century AD under Emperor Constantine.

**KEY**

**1** Paul was imprisoned and tried in Rome during the time of Nero's persecution (see pp.458–59).

**2** The first Christian church in Europe was established at Philippi (see pp.442–43).

**3** Paul visited the Roman province of Galatia on his second and third missions (see pp.436–37).

**4** The church at Corinth was founded by Paul on his second missionary journey. Two of his letters are addressed to the community there (see pp.444–45).

**5** Ephesus is thought to be where the Gospel of John was written. Paul visited the city twice (see pp.446–47).

**6** Syrian Antioch is where many of the Christians persecuted in Jerusalem fled to. The word "Christian" was first used here (see p.436).

**7** It was on the road to Damascus that Saul of Tarsus (also called Paul) saw a vision of the risen Christ and became a Christian (see pp.428–29).

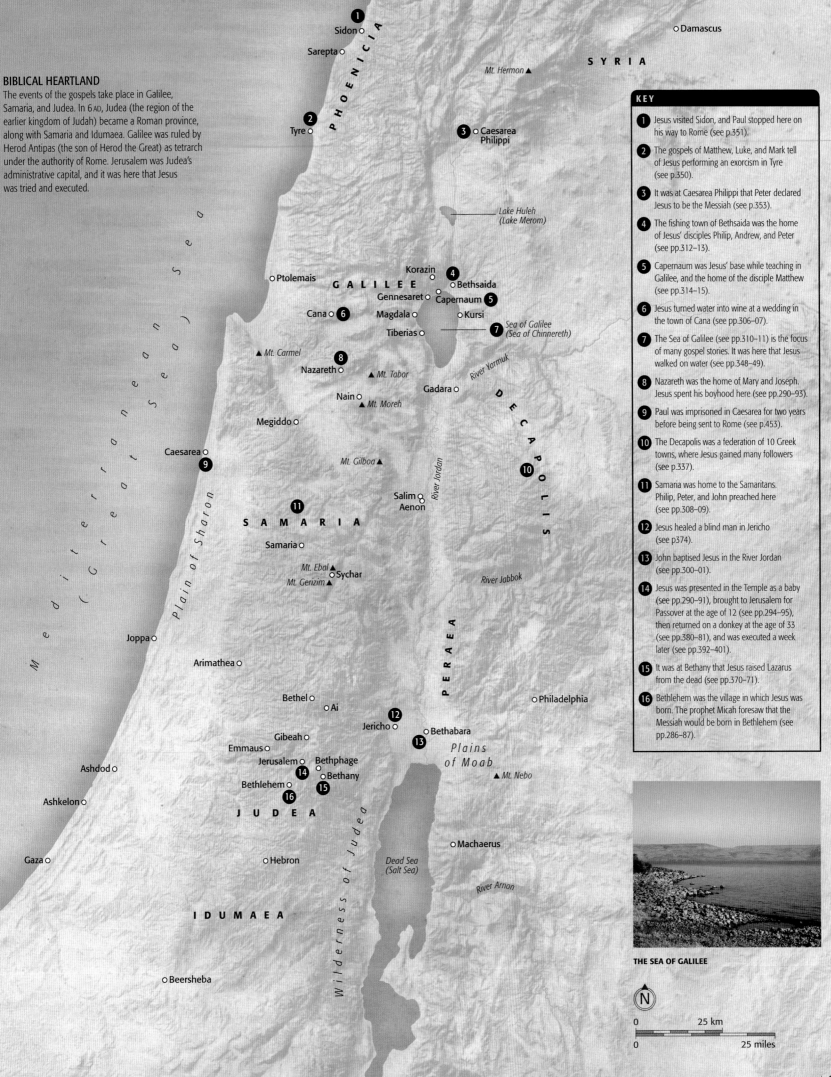

# BIBLICAL HEARTLAND

The events of the gospels take place in Galilee, Samaria, and Judea. In 6 AD, Judea (the region of the earlier kingdom of Judah) became a Roman province, along with Samaria and Idumaea. Galilee was ruled by Herod Antipas (the son of Herod the Great) as tetrarch under the authority of Rome. Jerusalem was Judea's administrative capital, and it was here that Jesus was tried and executed.

## KEY

1. Jesus visited Sidon, and Paul stopped here on his way to Rome (see p.351).

2. The gospels of Matthew, Luke, and Mark tell of Jesus performing an exorcism in Tyre (see p.350).

3. It was at Caesarea Philippi that Peter declared Jesus to be the Messiah (see p.353).

4. The fishing town of Bethsaida was the home of Jesus' disciples Philip, Andrew, and Peter (see pp.312–13).

5. Capernaum was Jesus' base while teaching in Galilee, and the home of the disciple Matthew (see pp.314–15).

6. Jesus turned water into wine at a wedding in the town of Cana (see pp.306–07).

7. The Sea of Galilee (see pp.310–11) is the focus of many gospel stories. It was here that Jesus walked on water (see pp.348–49).

8. Nazareth was the home of Mary and Joseph. Jesus spent his boyhood here (see pp.290–93).

9. Paul was imprisoned in Caesarea for two years before being sent to Rome (see p.453).

10. The Decapolis was a federation of 10 Greek towns, where Jesus gained many followers (see p.337).

11. Samaria was home to the Samaritans. Philip, Peter, and John preached here (see pp.308–09).

12. Jesus healed a blind man in Jericho (see p.374).

13. John baptised Jesus in the River Jordan (see pp.300–01).

14. Jesus was presented in the Temple as a baby (see pp.290–91), brought to Jerusalem for Passover at the age of 12 (see pp.294–95), then returned on a donkey at the age of 33 (see pp.380–81), and was executed a week later (see pp.392–401).

15. It was at Bethany that Jesus raised Lazarus from the dead (see pp.370–71).

16. Bethlehem was the village in which Jesus was born. The prophet Micah foresaw that the Messiah would be born in Bethlehem (see pp.286–87).

THE SEA OF GALILEE

0   25 km
0   25 miles

# COMING OF THE MESSIAH

"The Spirit of the Sovereign LORD is on me, because **the LORD has anointed me to proclaim good news to the poor.** He has sent me to **bind up the broken-hearted,** to proclaim **freedom for the captives** and **release from darkness** for the prisoners, to proclaim the year of the LORD's **favour...**"

ISAIAH 61:1,2

**VIRGIN AND CHILD**
In Lippo di Dalmasio's *The Madonna of Humility* (c.1390), the seated Virgin has a "crown" of 12 stars, like the book of Revelation's description of the Woman of the Apocalypse, whose son is the saviour who ushers in a millennium of peace.

 OR CENTURIES BEFORE THE APPEARANCE of Jesus, Israel had been a people of suffering and longing. The drama of their deliverance from bondage seemed unfinished. God had chosen them, rescued them from Egypt, and given them the Law and the land. He had driven them out for their chronic disobedience, but then (true to his promises), he had brought them back. Now, restored from exile in Babylon to the land God had granted to their ancestors, the people of Judah faced puzzling obstacles. Was life under a series of foreign oppressors – Persia, Greece, and now Rome – really what God had promised?

These external frustrations were not Israel's only concern. Jews who genuinely sought to live by God's Law looked to their own leaders and saw compromise and ungodliness.

Beneath these disappointments burned a deep-seated hope. The same God who had given Israel the Law and the land would, they believed, complete his plan by giving them a great deliverer: the Messiah.

### THE ANOINTED ONE

The Scriptures had promised Israel a human individual who would be the channel for salvation. He would be a priest like Aaron, a prophet like Elijah, and a king like David. He would be the Anointed One. The Hebrew word was "Messiah"; the Greek word was *Khristós* ("Christ".)

The prophets had said that this God-empowered champion would come, yet it had been five centuries since the return from Bablyon, and four since Malachi, the last recognized prophet.

Many people in Israel sustained their Messianic hope by recalling passages such as Isaiah 61, with its vivid picture of a Spirit-empowered liberator who would bring good news to the poor, healing to the broken-hearted, and release for captives and those in darkness – one who would "...bestow on them a crown of beauty instead of ashes, the oil of joy instead of mourning, and a garment of praise instead of a spirit of despair" (Isaiah 61:3).

When this long-awaited Messiah eventually came, he would restore Israel to what God intended it to be.

### WHAT KIND OF MESSIAH?

Those who looked for a Messiah had different notions. Some expected a political leader, others a military deliverer, or a priestly redeemer.

If a person became well known, "Messiah talk" would follow. If someone stood up to the Romans, or showed himself adept at preaching, or teaching, or healing, people would ask: "Is this the one?"

Uncertainty and yearning ruled the day, and both can be heard in the words of someone who did later meet Jesus: "Come, see a man who told me everything I've ever done. Could this be the Messiah?" (John 4:29).

**THE PROPHET**
This 13th-century window shows the prophet Isaiah, who predicted the coming of the Messiah: "...the Lord himself will give you a sign: the virgin will conceive and give birth to a son, and will call him Immanuel" (Isaiah 7:14).

# A Son for Zechariah

**HEROD THE GREAT, KING OF JUDEA**
Herod ruled from 37 BC to 4 BC. He **claimed Jewish ancestry and kingship over Israel**, both of which were disputed by many Jews of the day. Significantly, Luke gives more attention to Zechariah's credentials as a priest than he does to Herod's as king.

**SURPRISING SONS**
Barren Elizabeth giving birth to John recalls Hannah giving birth to **Samuel ≪ 142–43** (1 Samuel 1:20), and the **birth of Isaac ≪ 58–59** to aged Abraham and Sarah (Genesis 21:2). Samuel prepared the way for David; John prepared the way for Jesus.

STAINED GLASS DEPICTING THE BIRTH OF ISAAC

> **Do not be afraid** Zechariah; your prayer has been heard. **Your wife** Elizabeth will bear you a son…

LUKE 1:13

PEOPLE

**EMPEROR AUGUSTUS (63 BC TO AD 14)**

Although Caesar Augustus appears in just one verse in Luke (2:1), his rule had a profound impact on life in Israel. He was responsible for changing Rome from a republic into an empire, and in 27 BC was declared its first emperor. However, Luke's gospel deliberately focuses on unknowns such as Zechariah, Elizabeth, and Mary rather than the most politically powerful man of the day.

BUST OF AUGUSTUS, 1ST CENTURY AD

**Z**ECHARIAH and his wife, Elizabeth, were faithful people. Both had an honoured Jewish ancestry going back to Aaron, the brother of Moses and first high priest of Israel. Both were people of spiritual and moral integrity, and Zechariah served as a priest at the Temple. But they lived in difficult days: Israel was ruled by Rome and its puppet king, Herod.

### A childless couple

In the midst of all this, Zechariah and Elizabeth also had their own personal struggle: they were very old, and had no children. In any time and place, childlessness may bring disappointment and grief. In 1st-century Palestine, it also brought, as Elizabeth herself said, "disgrace" (Luke 1:25) – a painful sense of failure and shame.

### God intervenes

As a priest, Zechariah's job was to represent the people before God. The Temple in Jerusalem was God's dwelling-place on Earth, a model of his true dwelling in heaven (Hebrews 9:24). Priests entered the Temple and burned incense – which represented prayer ascending to heaven – in an act that was richly symbolic of Israel's relationship with God.

When Zechariah was priest-on-duty in the Temple, having been chosen by lot from among all the priests to burn incense, the angel Gabriel appeared to him. He came with a message from God: "Do not be afraid!" (Luke 1:13).

Elizabeth and Zechariah, Gabriel said, would have a son who would bring them joy, and they were to name him John. He would be a new Elijah (the most powerful of all the Old Testament prophets), and would prepare the way for the coming Messiah. John would "bring back many of the people of Israel to the Lord their God" (1:16). He would carry a power and authority to match his important place in God's plan. All the prophets had possessed the power of God's Spirit, but Gabriel declared that John would be "filled with the Holy Spirit even before he is born" (1:15).

### Zechariah's doubts

Zechariah was so surprised that he was not sure if he could believe the angel's words. "A child?" he wondered, "At our age? How can I know this will happen?" Gabriel rebuked Zechariah for his unbelief, and told him that he would be unable to speak until the baby was born. Yet, despite Zechariah's doubts, Gabriel declared that the promise would come true. Elizabeth would indeed have a son.

### A joy-filled ending

The story ended not with a rebuke, but with rejoicing. Elizabeth did conceive, and she knew that it was by God's power. She spent time in seclusion, worshipping God with psalms, such as Luke 1:25: "The Lord has done this for me... In these days he has shown his favour and taken away my disgrace among the people". An old woman, and now pregnant, she rejoiced that God was sending Israel a prophet and giving her a son.

**God's appearance to Zechariah had important implications, both for Israel and for the future life of his unborn son, John.**

**SILENCE BROKEN**
Israel had seen no prophets since Malachi – four centuries before the events of Luke 1. But now they would receive angelic appearances, miraculous births (**John 282–83 ≫ and Jesus 286–87 ≫**), that inspired prayers and worship. For Luke, **God was "silent" no more**.

**FAILED PRIEST, FAITHFUL PRIEST**
Luke set his story between two priests. The first was Zechariah, John the Baptist's father, who was **struck mute for his unbelief** when Gabriel spoke to him about the birth of his son John. The second priest was **the risen Christ**, raising his hands in priestly blessing as he **ascended into heaven 412–13 ≫** (Luke 24:50,51).

**NO STRONG DRINK**
According to Jewish religious customs, abstinence from alcohol applied to special times of dedication (see Leviticus 10:9; Numbers 6:1–3). Gabriel told Zechariah that John was to take no strong drink – a sign of his **radical obedience to God**.

JUDEAN WINE DECANTER

# The Annunciation

*Throughout Scripture, God sent angels to announce important events in his plan. His angel announced the exodus to Moses (Exodus 3) and, in an event known as the Annunciation, he sent Gabriel to Mary to announce the birth of the Messiah.*

**M**ARY, A YOUNG woman who lived in the village of Nazareth in Galilee, was engaged to be married to a man named Joseph. The angel Gabriel appeared to her, greeting her with an assurance of God's favour and presence with her. Gabriel told Mary that she would give birth to a son who she was to name Jesus, who would be great and whose kingdom would never end.

The promise of a child, however, seemed impossible. Mary asked Gabriel how this could happen, since she was a virgin. Gabriel's answer revealed the way: God's life-giving Holy Spirit would enable the impossible. The birth of this child would be a miracle, without the involvement of a human father. By the power of his Spirit, God would enable Mary to have a son – and he would be the "Son of the Most High" (Luke 1:32).

Gabriel's words recalled the creation story at the beginning of the Bible, when God's Spirit hovered above the waters (Genesis 1:2). In the same way, God's Spirit would bring about the birth of Jesus through Mary (Luke 1:35). This similarity of wording was not an accident – the birth of this child would do more than provide a king "reign over Jacob's descendants" (Luke 1:33), it would bring about a new beginning for all creation.

Mary hurried to the house of her relative Elizabeth, herself now six months pregnant with her own child. At the sound of Mary's voice, the child in Elizabeth's womb leaped for joy – she was filled with the Holy Spirit and spoke blessings over Mary and her unborn child.

Mary burst forth into praise, glorifying the Lord with rich, psalm-like poetry (1:46–55). In the original Greek, the word used for her song of praise means "magnify" (see p.285) – the act of showing how great someone is. In faith, Mary spoke of future events as already achieved – in the same way the Old Testament prophets showed their confidence in God's promises. She exalted God for what he would accomplish through her yet-to-be-born son – bringing down the mighty, but lifting up the humble. The word "humble" also meant poor or downcast. So Mary knew what God would do: in Jesus, God would bring down the forces that oppress and destroy – the King Herods of the world – and lift up all who are cast down.

> "Greetings, **you who are highly favoured!** The Lord is with you."
>
> LUKE 1:28

## A NEW BEGINNING

In Fra Angelico's altarpiece *The Annunciation*, c.1530, Mary bows in obedience before Gabriel. The scene also depicts Adam and Eve in a garden, hinting at the redemption of Eden – God's creation – through Mary's choice.

**BEFORE**

Luke's account set John's birth into the context of fulfilled prophecy and committed family relationships.

**"PREPARE THE WAY FOR THE LORD"**
As the precursor of the Messiah Jesus, John the Baptist, who would later preach in the desert, is the **fulfilment of the prophecy of Isaiah ‹‹ 230–31**: "A voice of one calling: 'In the wilderness prepare the way for the LORD...'" (Isaiah 40:3).

**LOVING RELATIVES**
The opening chapters of Luke's Gospel focus on two women: Elizabeth and **Mary 284–85 ››**. Elizabeth is described as Mary's "relative." Luke uses a Greek word that could mean a cousin, an aunt, or another female relation. The tender interaction between them during Mary's visit to Elizabeth's home is typical of Luke, highlighting the emotional, human-interest side of the events, and showing his interest in the **role of women** in the gospel story.

# The Birth of John the Baptist

*The prophet Isaiah had promised that, before the Messiah came, God would send a herald to "prepare the way for the LORD" (Isaiah 40:3). Although Israel needed to heed the herald's voice, it would be a voice in the wilderness.*

THE STORY OF JOHN the Baptist began before he was even born. His mother, Elizabeth, had long been childless. Then God intervened and gave her a son.

When Elizabeth was six months pregnant, she received a visit from Jesus' mother, Mary, who was now also pregnant. As Mary greeted her, John leaped for joy in Elizabeth's womb and she exclaimed loudly to Mary "Blessed are you among women, and blessed is the child you will bear!" (Luke 1:42). John's wondrous conception, his pre-natal welcome of the Messiah, and Elizabeth's greeting were all God's method of signalling to Israel that this child would be a vital part of their story as a people.

### Mary's canticle
Mary responded to Elizabeth with a great prayer in song (see p.285) in which she magnified a God who "has brought down rulers from their thrones but has lifted up the humble" and "has filled the hungry with good things but has sent the rich away empty" (1:52,53). As Zechariah was also to

**ELIZABETH AND MARY**

**CHURCH OF ST JOHN THE BAPTIST**
Although no one can be certain where John's birthplace really was, the Church of John the Baptist is built on the site where it is believed John was born to Elizabeth and Zechariah, in the small village of Ein Kerem, in Jerusalem, Israel.

experience and then to sing, this is a God who reorders his world and makes his light shine on his people.

### Joy and bewilderment
The day came for John to be born and everyone who knew Elizabeth and her husband, Zechariah, was (like John in the womb) overjoyed. However, on that happy day, everyone was to receive a shock.

Zechariah was mute – the penalty the angel of God had imposed on him for not believing God's promises about the birth of John. For the duration of Elizabeth's pregnancy, he had been unable to speak (see pp.278–79). Now, John was born. The family gathered to find out what Zechariah and Elizabeth would name their new son – everyone assuming they would name him Zechariah, after his father. To their surprise,

Elizabeth told them a different name: John. This was the name that the angel had given them, months before.

The family protested that John was not a family name. Someone gave the still mute Zechariah a slate to find out if he agreed with his wife about the name of the child. To the consternation of their relatives, Zechariah scratched on to the slate the name of his newborn son: John.

### Zechariah prophesies
Then, suddenly, Zechariah was once again able to speak. However, he did not just speak, he uttered the word of the Lord. He glorified God for bringing salvation from "our enemies and from the hand of all who hate us" (1:71), and prophesied what John would do: prepare the way for the Messiah, so that Israel might experience the mercy of God.

This baby, who had welcomed Jesus while he himself was still in the womb, would become the herald who would call the people of Israel to welcome Jesus. Zechariah's son John would "give his people the knowledge of salvation through the forgiveness of their sins" (1:77).

### God sets the stage
The setting for John's role was an unlikely place – "the wilderness" (1:80). Yet it was just as the prophet Isaiah had foretold, when he had declared that the desert was where the Messiah's herald would preach. According to Luke, that is precisely where the adult John went to live.

**HISTORY AND CULTURE**

## THE SONG OF ZECHARIAH

When John the Baptist was born, his father Zechariah burst into a rich psalm of praise, which begins "Praise be to the Lord, the God of Israel" (Luke 1:68), and is known in Christian liturgy as the *Benedictus* (Latin for "blessed"). Among other things, the *Benedictus* is used in the Roman Catholic Lauds, and in both the Lutheran and the Anglican service of Matins, or morning prayer.

**ZECHARIAH THE PRIEST**

### A PROPHET IS BORN
This 15th-century illumination, *Birth of Saint John the Baptist*, from a copy of the Bible, depicts the moment when Elizabeth's newborn baby is presented in swaddling to his mute father, Zechariah, who writes on a slate that his name is to be "John".

> " And you, my child, will be called a **prophet of the Most High**; for you will **go on before the Lord** to **prepare the way for him**…"
>
> LUKE 1:76

## AFTER ≫

**Many have wondered where John's desert was. It is possible that he lived among the Essene sect near Qumran.**

### THE VOICE IN THE DESERT
Luke says that after John left home "he lived in the wilderness **until he appeared publicly to Israel" (Luke 1:80) 298–99 ≫**. Some scholars believe that John may have been near Qumran in the Dead Sea region, and influenced by a group called the Essenes. The Essenes were zealous for spiritual purity, and emphasized a coming divine judgment. Although the gospel accounts never specifically identify John with the Essenes, the message he later preached was not unlike theirs.

**ARCHAEOLOGICAL REMAINS OF QUMRAN**

**THE VIRGIN MARY** Born *c.* 20 BC Died *c.* AD 45

# Mary, Mother of Jesus

> "From now on **all generations will call me blessed**, for the **Mighty One has done great things** for me – **holy is his name**."
>
> LUKE 1:48,49

**W**HEN WE READ her whole story, Mary is about far more than the typical Christmas-card images of a mother and baby. In the Scriptures, she is a second Eve, who obeys God whereas Eve did not. She is the human figure by whom God himself becomes human – so that humanity can be brought back to God. She is a model of confidence in God – even of personal sacrifice.

### A new Eve

The beginning of humanity's story involved the mother of the human race, Eve, making a tragic choice. Her decision to eat from the tree of knowledge (Genesis 3:6,7) meant setting her own will above God's – with consequences for all humanity. Mary did the reverse: She set God's will above her own, saying "I am the Lord's servant" (Luke 1:38). God chose and Mary obeyed. The Bible never tells us why God chose Mary – it just says he did. He sent his angel to tell her, and his Spirit to enable her.

Eve, by her disobedience, denied humanity eternal life. Mary became the mother of the new humanity, in Jesus – and through her obedience she held out the prospect of eternal life to all.

**CITY OF NAZARETH**
In the present-day cityscape of Nazareth – where Mary raised Jesus – the tower in the foreground is part of the Church of the Annunciation, which was built in 1969 on the site of a Byzantine church.

The gospel writers portray Mary as a disciple – someone who believed, yet was still learning to grow in that belief. Mary's challenges in adapting to her son's ways began early.

### Keeping up with her son

A Passover visit to Jerusalem with the 12-year-old Jesus turned into an awkward confrontation. Jesus went to talk with the elders in the Temple, and was missing for three days. When his distraught parents finally found the young Jesus, Mary admonished him for his insensitivity and lack of respect. He asked her if she did not realize that he had to be "in my Father's house" (Luke 2:49) – but neither Mary nor Joseph understood.

Later, when Jesus began his public ministry, Mary joined him at a wedding-feast (see pp.306–07). The wine ran short, and Mary thought that Jesus should intervene. Jesus said that his time had not yet come. She was learning to trust her son: "Do whatever he tells you," she said to the servants (John 2:5). Jesus proceeded to turn water into wine.

### A life yielded to God

In stories such as these, the gospels set Mary before us as a disciple learning to trust.

**THE VIRGIN IN PRAYER**
Giovanni Battista Salvi da Sassoferrato's *The Virgin Praying* (c.1640–50) uses traditional colours: white for purity; red for sacrifice; and blue, the heavenly colour to honour Mary, since it came from the costliest dye.

> **"'I am the LORD's servant,'** Mary answered. 'May your word to me be fulfilled.' Then the angel left her.**"**
> LUKE 1:38

**MADONNA AND CHILD WITH SAINTS**
This altarpiece by Sienese artist Bartolommeo Bulgarini (c.1310–78) shows the Virgin and the Child enthroned between angels and martyred saints, including John the Baptist.

Saying yes to God can not have been easy for young Mary. Up to this moment, things no doubt seemed to be going her way. She was betrothed to a godly young man and related to respected people, such as Elizabeth, the wife of Zechariah the priest. However, being pregnant before she was married would have changed everything, because of the fear that she would face public disgrace.

The difficulties did not stop there. When Joseph and Mary took the infant Jesus to Jerusalem to dedicate him to God, the devout Simeon warned Mary that her child was destined "to be a sign that will be spoken against… And a sword will pierce your own soul too" (Luke 2:34,35). Mary held an honoured place in God's plan, but it came at a price.

### How God became one of us

One of the greatest miracles in the Bible is what Christians call the Incarnation: God himself became a human being in Christ. How did this happen?

In several stories in the Old Testament, God had appeared on Earth as a man. He came in human form and he even ate with Abraham (Genesis 18:1–33). He also wrestled with Jacob (Genesis 32:24–30). However, these were temporary appearances as a man and not genuine incarnations.

Mary's obedience opened the way for something new. God the Son was conceived in a human mother, but without the involvement of a human father. He grew in her womb, was born, and lived a human life. He did not float down from heaven as a full-grown adult, but was "fully human in every way" (Hebrews 2:17).

---

**HISTORY AND CULTURE**

### THE SONG OF MARY

**MARY (IN BLUE) AND THE *MAGNIFICAT* IN LATIN**

When Mary greets the pregnant Elizabeth, carrying the son who will become John the Baptist, she utters a song (Luke 1:46–55) that is a glorification of God. It is known as the *Magnificat*, from the Latin for "magnify", because in older English translations it starts: "My soul magnifies the Lord". This canticle is one of the most ancient of Christian hymns, and has been sung for centuries to highlight God's majesty.

**BIOGRAPHY IN BRIEF**

- **c.20 BC,** Mary is born and, according to the beliefs of some Christians, is taken to the Temple by parents Joachim and Anne at the age of three.

- **Is pledged in marriage** to Joseph, a descendant of King David.

**JEWISH WEDDING RING**

- **While betrothed,** Mary is visited in Nazareth by the angel Gabriel, who announces that she will miraculously give birth to the Messiah.

- **Joseph finds out** about Mary's pregnancy and wants to break the engagement, but an angel tells him not to.

- **c.5–4 BC,** Mary marries Joseph.

- **c.4 BC,** Mary accompanies Joseph to Bethlehem during the Roman census and gives birth to Jesus there.

- **c.4–2 BC,** Mary goes with Joseph to the Temple in Jerusalem to dedicate Jesus to God.

- **c.2 BC,** the family flees from Bethlehem to Egypt to escape King Herod's death-squads. They later return from Egypt and settle in Nazareth.

- **c.AD 8,** Mary scolds the 12-year-old Jesus for getting separated from the family during the Passover festival in Jerusalem.

- **c.AD 30,** is a witness to Jesus' first public sign, at a wedding in Cana. Subsequently, she is sometimes in the crowds following Jesus.

- **c.AD 33,** sees Jesus' crucifixion and resurrection. The dutiful mother holding her dead son is later immortalized in Western art as the *pietà*.

- **Is a member** of the Early Church.

- **Upon her death,** although it is not recorded in the scriptures, many Christians believe she was assumed into heaven and commemorate her assumption on 15 August each year.

**MICHELANGELO'S *PIETÀ*, 1498–99**

# The Birth of Jesus

*The traditional account of the Nativity story is derived from only two of the gospels, but both agree that Joseph was descended from King David and that Mary conceived by the power of the Holy Spirit. Importantly, it is stressed that Jesus is a saviour for all humanity.*

**M**ATTHEW BEGINS his account of Jesus' birth with a genealogy. The lengthy list of names starts with Abraham, the father of Israel, and runs through King David all the way down to Jesus. It shows that Jesus was a true son of Israel and a descendant of Israel's greatest king.

Matthew also tells the story of the Magi from the east. They arrived, guided by a God-ordained star, and looking for a God-sent king. When they found the child in Bethlehem, they honoured him with gifts of gold, frankincense, and myrrh. The Magi were Gentiles. So before Matthew has written two chapters, he has shown his readers that this child was born to be both the king of Israel and lord of all the nations.

By contrast, Luke's story begins with an angel visiting Mary. She would conceive a child by the power of the Holy Spirit, the angel said. Then, during this miraculous pregnancy, the Roman emperor decided to order a census, which required everyone in the empire to return to their place of birth. For Mary's betrothed, Joseph, that meant travelling to Bethlehem. Behind this decision was God's plan, for the Old Testament had promised that a ruler of ancient lineage would arise in Bethlehem (Micah 5:2). Mary's pregnancy and Jesus' birthplace both came by the hand of God.

The census brought crowds to Bethlehem, and when Joseph and his pregnant wife arrived, there was no proper room for them. Mary had to lay her newborn baby inside a manger – a feeding trough for animals. Not a very dignified crib for a king, but fitting for this one, who would grow up to identify with the marginalized and the poor.

There were shepherds in the fields. An angel appeared to them, and his proclamation – recorded in Luke 2:11 – would become one of the best-known of Scriptures. He announced "good news that will cause great joy for all the people" (2:10) – a saviour-child had been born. The angel gave them a sign so they might recognize the baby – he would be "wrapped in cloths and lying in a manger" (2:12). As they went to the village, more angels appeared, crying out, "Glory to God in the highest heaven, and on earth peace to those on whom his favour rests" (2:14).

> **"Today in the town of David a Saviour has been born to you; he is the Messiah, the Lord."**
>
> LUKE 2:11

**WITNESSING THE NATIVITY OF JESUS**
Lorenzo di Credi's *Adoration of the Shepherds* (c.1510) depicts the moment in Luke 2 when, having been informed of the birth of the Messiah by an angel, the shepherds arrive to pay tribute to Jesus.

**BEFORE**

Matthew's telling of the story of the Magi contains echoes of several passages from the Hebrew Scriptures.

**THE GLORY OF ISRAEL'S KINGS**
The Magi story recalls the days of **Solomon** **《 178–79**, one of Israel's greatest kings: "All the kings of the earth... brought a gift – articles of silver and gold, and robes... and spices" (2 Chronicles 9:23,24).

**HALLEY'S COMET**

**WHAT WAS THE STAR'S MEANING?**
The star may have been a comet – such as Halley's Comet, which was regularly recorded in the ancient world and passed over the region in 12 BC – or a nova, or a convergence of planets. Matthew would have seen the star's Scriptural significance – recalling, perhaps, Numbers 24:17: **"A star will come out of Jacob; a sceptre will rise out of Israel."** The origin of the star – "in the east" in many translations – may also recall **Ezekiel's vision 《 240–41** of a coming **revelation of God's glory**: "I saw the glory of the God of Israel coming from the east. His voice was like the roar of rushing waters, and the land was radiant with his glory" (Ezekiel 43:2).

**SYMBOLS**

**GIFTS FOR A KING**

The Magi's gifts of gold, frankincense – a resin used as incense – and myrrh, an embalming oil, were symbolic of kingship, priesthood, and death.

The gifts were signs of the Magi's wealth and of Jesus' worth. Matthew reports that the Magi "worshipped" Jesus (Matthew 2:11), by bowing down before him and presenting him with gifts fit for a king. In a narrative device recognized by literary criticism of his Gospel, Matthew ends his story of Jesus on the same note – with Jesus worshipped by the 11 disciples after his resurrection (28:17). For Matthew, from beginning to end, Jesus was worthy of praise.

# The Visit of the Magi

*Scholars have debated whether "wise men" is the best translation of the word "Magi." But however we translate the word, the Magi who followed the star from the east were certainly wise in whom they came to worship.*

**T**HE FIRST PEOPLE who came seeking Christ, according to Matthew's Gospel, were not Jews – they were Gentiles. "Magi from the east came to Jerusalem and asked, 'Where is the one who has been born king of the Jews? We saw his star when it rose and have come to worship him'" (Matthew 2:1,2).

### In search of a king
Matthew does not explain how much the Magi knew about the Jews, or about Judaism. He does not tell us how they identified a particular star as "his star" – the star of Israel's newborn king. He does not tell us now many Magi there were, or what their names were. Nor does he explain exactly where "the east" was – although it may have been Babylon, where the Jews had once lived in exile (see pp.238–39). What he does tell us is how the Magi made their journey: they saw the king's star and they followed it. After a long journey they finally arrived in Jerusalem, and asked King Herod and the people where the king of the Jews had been born.

### A question for Herod
The Magi's question about a newborn king stirred up trouble. The land of Judea already had a king – Herod the Great, the former governor of Galilee who had been installed as a client king by the Romans in 37 BC. Matthew reports that Herod was disturbed by the Magi's news of a king of the Jews.

In the midst of this tension, the troubled Herod – himself a convert to Judaism – remembered the Jewish belief in a Messiah who would come to restore God's people, Israel. He summoned the chief priests and the scribes, and asked them where the coming Messiah would be born. They consulted the Scriptures and sent

> **" After Jesus was born in Bethlehem in Judea... Magi from the east came to Jerusalem "**
>
> MATTHEW 2:1

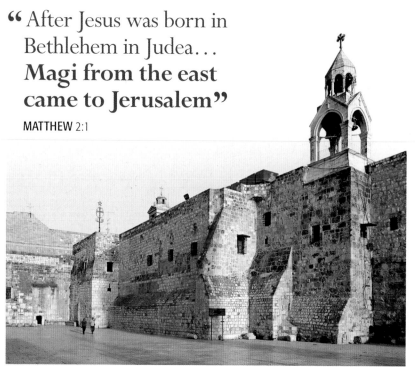

**PEOPLE**

**THE MAGI**

The word "Magi" had several meanings – from magicians to scientists – but Matthew seems to mean people who were wise in understanding the stars and their relationship to events on Earth. The Magi were from "the east" – possibly Babylon, where astronomy was practised as early as the 2nd millenium BC, or Arabia.

Matthew does not call the Magi kings, and the tradition of there being three visitors derives from the number of gifts presented to the infant Christ. The words "his star" (Matthew 2:2) suggest that the Magi saw Jesus' birth as the primary event, and the star as a sign rather than a cause. This would place their views not far from Hebrew wisdom literature, such as the book of Job (see pp.188–89), where God marshals the stars according to his purpose.

Herod the answer: Bethlehem. The prophet Micah had promised that from Bethlehem would come a ruler who would shepherd the people of Israel: "But you, Bethlehem... though you are small among the clans of Judah, out of you will come for me one who will be a ruler over Israel" (Micah 5:2). The idea of a ruler's arrival did little to quiet Herod's fears.

### A deceptive request
Herod summoned the Magi secretly, and asked when the star had appeared – a ploy to find out how old the child would be now – instructing them to report back to him when they had found the young king. That way, Herod said, he could go and worship him as well. Subsequent events would

**SACRED SITE**
The Church of the Nativity in Bethlehem was first built in AD 333. It is located over a cave that was believed by 2nd-century Christian historians to be the site of the birth of Christ.

prove that Herod's intentions were very different, and would have devastating consequences.

### The Magi find the king

The travellers left Jerusalem, bound for Bethlehem, and "the star they had seen when it rose went ahead of them until it stopped over the place where the child was" (Matthew 2:9). For the Magi, Jerusalem had been a place of tension and deception, but now the star moved clearly and truly before them. Herod had been a man full of fear, but when the Magi once again saw the star, they

were overjoyed. Their behaviour when they arrived at the place where Jesus lay also contrasted with that of the jealous Herod. He had already begun to scheme against this new king, but the Magi bowed down and worshipped Jesus, then presented him with gifts of gold, frankincense, and myrrh.

### A sudden departure

The Magi's arrival had been divinely led, and so was their departure – God warned them in a dream not to go back to Herod. They left Judea and returned to their own country by a different route.

**AFTER** »

Symbolic references in Matthew's Gospel point forward to significant aspects of the later life of Jesus.

**FRANKINCENSE AND MYRRH**
Aromatic incense had been used in **Hebrew worship** « **110–13** since the time of Moses, and is still used today in Jewish and Christian worship. Myrrh was one of the spices used to **embalm Jesus' body 402–03** » after his crucifixion.

**ONE LIFE FOR MANY**
The Bible records that after the Magi's visit, Herod ordered that all young boys in Bethlehem be killed. God warned Joseph to **flee to Egypt 292–93** », so Jesus was spared. But Matthew may also be hinting of **a time when Jesus would not be spared**.

**INCENSE BURNER FROM THE 15TH CENTURY**

**PRESENTED FOR DEDICATION**
Giotto di Bondone painted Jesus' presentation at the Temple by Mary and Joseph as part of his magnificent fresco cycle *Life of the Virgin* (1304–06) at the Scrovegni chapel in Padua, Italy.

**BEFORE**

Jews in 1st-century Palestine lived according to the laws God had given to Moses at Sinai.

### A TIME OF PURIFICATION

The Law ≪ 108–09 required ceremonial purification after loss of blood in menstruation and childbirth. Mary waited until her purification was over before travelling to Jerusalem (Luke 2:22).

### A SIGN OF IDENTITY

Jesus was circumcized when he was eight days old. Circumcision ≪ 50–51 went all the way back to Abraham, and was a God-given sign of Israel's distinct identity as the **covenanted people of God** (Genesis 17:11). Jesus' circumcision further confirmed him as a **true son of Israel**.

CIRCUMCISION TOOLS

**HISTORY AND CULTURE**

## SONG OF SIMEON

God had promised Simeon that he would die only when he had seen the Messiah. When he saw Jesus, Simeon – led by the Holy Spirit – knew that this child was the one. He took Jesus into his arms and uttered a hymn of praise now known as the *Nunc dimittis* ("now you dismiss") after its first words in Latin. Put to music, it has been used for evening worship, such as Compline, since the 4th century.

MONKS AT WORSHIP, 14TH-CENTURY FRESCO

# Jesus Presented in the Temple

*Joseph and Mary came to the Temple to make a humble sacrifice of two young pigeons. They also brought something far more important – their son – with the same intention as all Temple offerings: the praise and worship of God.*

JOSEPH AND MARY were ordinary, religiously observant Jews of their day – and they were poor. They lived by the Law of Moses, which included requirements such as circumcision, the dedication of firstborn sons, and the making of sacrifices and offerings at the Temple in Jerusalem.

### Faithful to their roots

When their newborn son was eight days old, Joseph and Mary had him circumcized and gave him the name Jesus. They then waited the required 33 days for cleansing from childbirth and made the trip to Jerusalem, to dedicate the young Jesus to God. They came to offer a pair of doves or pigeons – the Law's required sacrifice for the poor (Leviticus 12:8). The timing, the journey, the child-dedication, and the proper offering were all signs of Joseph's and Mary's roots in Israel's history, and of their obedience to God.

### Ancient hopes coming true

At the Temple in Jerusalem were two other godly people. The first was Simeon, an aged man of whom little is known other than the Bible's description as a devout man who "was waiting for the consolation of Israel, and the Holy Spirit was on him" (Luke 2:25). The Greek word that Luke used for "consolation" also meant "comfort" – a reference to the hoped-for Messiah, who would comfort the people of Israel. The same Holy Spirit who had earlier enabled Mary to conceive had also assured Simeon that he would not die until he himself had seen that Messiah.

Luke tells us that on the day Joseph, Mary, and their baby son arrived at the Temple, the Spirit led Simeon to go there as well. He met Mary and Joseph and seemed to know that the longed-for moment had come: this child was the comfort of Israel. He took little Jesus in his arms and asked God to dismiss him in peace from his long years of waiting – "For my eyes have seen your salvation" (2:30). That salvation lay with this tiny child. Simeon told Joseph and Mary that Jesus would bring God's light to both Israel and "Gentiles" – from the Latin *gentilis*, meaning all non-Jewish nations. However, he also warned that suffering lay ahead, and that a sword would pierce Mary's heart – a reference to the rejection Jesus would endure.

### Another voice

Someone else arrived at the Temple that day: aged, godly Anna. She was a prophetess and a faithful worshipper who was 84 years old, and had long-since been widowed after just seven years of marriage. Like Simeon, she saw more in Jesus than just another baby: "Coming up to them at that very moment, she gave thanks to God and spoke about the child to all who were looking forward to the redemption of Jerusalem" (2:38). The hope of Jerusalem, said Anna, was this one-month old boy from Nazareth in Galilee.

**AFTER**

Joseph and Mary returned home to the northern town of Nazareth.

### EVERYDAY PEOPLE

Following their visit to Jerusalem, Mary and Joseph **returned to Nazareth**, in the northern region of Galilee 310–11 ≫, a place many in their day saw as unsophisticated and rustic. **Joseph continued his work as a carpenter**, a trade in which Jesus may have been apprenticed as a boy (see Mark 6:3). Luke seems to stress that Joseph and Mary – and in many ways their son as well – were **everyday, ordinary people**.

CARPENTER AT WORK

> **" Joseph** and **Mary** took him to **Jerusalem** to **present him to the Lord. "**
> LUKE 2:22

**BEFORE**

The Old Testament prophet Hosea prophesied about God and Israel.

### OLD TESTAMENT ECHOES

Matthew linked the return of Jesus from Egypt with the words of the Old Testament prophet **Hosea ‹‹ 222–23**. Hosea described God's relationship with Israel in the 8th century BC, and his words in Hosea 11:1 also echo the flight of Israel from Egypt when **God parted the Red Sea ‹‹ 102–03**.

**CLOSING THE RED SEA ON THE EGYPTIANS**

# Escape to Egypt

*Israel's story involved escaping slavery in Egypt, so it may seem surprising that Jesus' early story took place there. Although partly to escape from Herod, it was God's way of setting Jesus in place to mirror the story of Israel.*

**M**ATTHEW'S STORY of Jesus' birth began with a miraculous star and the worship of the Magi – signs of the honour due to this God-appointed king. But after the Magi had left Bethlehem to return to their own country in the east, events took an ominous turn. An angel appeared to Joseph in a dream with an urgent warning of imminent danger: Joseph had to flee to Egypt with his family and stay there until he was told it was safe, because King Herod wanted to kill Jesus.

Herod had deceitfully instructed the Magi to report back to him when they had found the newborn king of Israel, so that he too could come and worship the child. But God had warned the Magi not to return to Herod, and they had left the land of Judea to go back to their own country.

Herod soon realized that he had been tricked. His anger at the Magi was mixed with his jealousy at the thought of another king. Herod had already shown that he was ruthless in preserving his own power, and had even executed members of his own family whom he perceived as political threats.

> **" Take the child** and his **mother** and escape **to Egypt."**
>
> MATTHEW 2:13

**FAMILY IN FLIGHT**
A family travels with their laden donkey across sand dunes in the Cappadocia, Turkey. Little is said of Joseph and Mary's journey in the gospels but their route to Egypt would have taken them through similarly arid terrain.

Herod's paranoia that he might lose power drove him to set a despicable plan into action: he sent his soldiers to kill all the boys aged two years and younger in the vicinity of Bethlehem. In describing this gruesome event, Matthew quoted an emotional text from Jeremiah 31:15 – "Rachel weeping for her children and refusing to be comforted, because they are no more" (Matthew 2:18). He also shaped his story to show the contrasts in the people involved. The Magi worshipped Jesus, while Herod wanted to kill him.

King Herod sent out death-squads, so the young Jesus had to flee by night, entirely dependent on his parents to keep him safe.

### Another exodus

Time passed, and King Herod died. He had ruled in Judea from 37 to 4 BC, having been designated King by the Roman senate in 40 BC. After his death, Joseph received guidance in another dream, in which he was told by an angel of God: "Get up, take the child and his mother and go to the land of Israel, for those who were trying to take the child's life are dead" (Matthew 2:20).

Matthew once again quoted from the Old Testament prophets: "Out of Egypt I called my son" (Hosea 11:1). In Hosea's original prophecy, this verse applied to the nation of Israel – God's covenant "son" – being brought out of Egypt by God. Matthew applied it instead to the young Jesus, pointing to him as the beginning of a renewed people of God, once again being brought out of Egypt.

### A new home

Joseph returned to Judea, probably intending to settle there. However, he discovered that King Herod's son, Archelaus, was now ruling Judea in his father's place. Joseph was uneasy about living

**PEOPLE**

## JOSEPH

Jesus' human father, Joseph, was descended from King David (see Matthew 1:6,16; Luke 2:4). This was an important link, since the Scriptures had promised that the Messiah would descend from David (Isaiah 16:5). Joseph was a carpenter by trade (Matthew 13:55). The gospel narratives of Jesus' birth portray him as a godly man (Matthew 1:19), who experienced divine dreams and angelic visitations, and who took steps to protect Jesus from King Herod (Matthew 2:14). Joseph is mentioned only in the stories of Jesus' birth and childhood – he is absent from the events in Jesus' life after he is presented at the Temple (Luke 2:41–52) – which may suggest that he died during Jesus' teenage or young adult years.

under the gaze of this particular member of Herod's family. Having been warned in a dream, Joseph instead took his family north to Galilee and began a new life in the village of Nazareth.

### Jesus, the new Israel

Matthew saw this move to the north as yet another fulfilment of the Old Testament Scriptures, telling the reader, "So was fulfilled what was said through the prophets, that he would be called a Nazarene" (2:23). Matthew told

this story with the intention of reminding his readers of Old Testament parallels. Joseph and his family's flight from Israel to Egypt recalls Jacob and his family's flight from famine to live in Egypt (see pp.86–87). What Israel did, Jesus had also done. His parents' actions to save Jesus from Herod recalled Moses' mother protecting her son from Pharaoh (see pp.94–95). What happened to Moses had also happened to Jesus. Just as Moses grew up to save Israel from slavery in Egypt, so Jesus would go on to

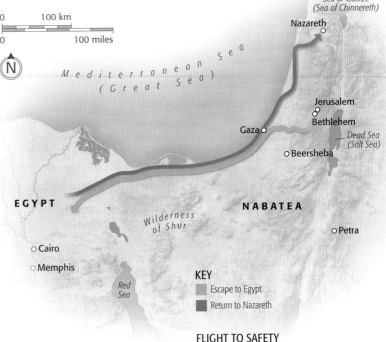

### FLIGHT TO SAFETY
Egypt was beyond the influence of Herod, but like Israel, also part of the Roman Empire, making travel between the two relatively safe. The principal route from Israel to Egypt was along the coast.

"save his people from their sins" (Matthew 1:21). And Jesus and his family leaving Egypt for the Promised Land recalled Israel doing just that, centuries before (see pp.120–21). For Matthew, none of these parallels with the Old Testament were accidents. They were historical pointers set in place by God himself, and lay at the heart of the story.

### MASSACRE OF THE INNOCENTS
Herod the Great hoped his murderous plan to remove the threat posed by Jesus, by sending his soldiers to kill all boys under the age of two in Bethlehem, would ensure he remained in power.

> " And so was fulfilled what the Lord had said through the prophet: 'Out of Egypt I called my son.' "
>
> MATTHEW 2:15

### AFTER

**Herod's son Archelaus succeeded him in Judea, while Herod Antipas ruled Galilee, where Jesus was raised.**

#### A CRUEL RULER
One of the sons of Herod the Great, Archelaus ruled Judea (in southern Israel) from 4 BC to AD 6. Like his father before him, **he was tyrannical and cruel**. A Jewish delegation travelled all the way to Rome to protest against the policies of Archelaus,

insisting that unless he were removed there would be an armed revolt. In AD 6, **Rome deposed Archelaus** and replaced him with a prefect appointed by the emperor.

#### UNDER HEROD'S DYNASTY
Galilee, the area that Joseph chose as a home for his family after returning from Egypt, was **ruled by Archelaus's brother Herod Antipas**. Antipas would become an admirer of John the Baptist **344–45 >>**.

**CHRIST IN THE TEMPLE**
A French stained glass window from the 18th century shows the moment when Jesus, not yet old enough in Judaism to have religious maturity, demonstrated to his elders his exceptional understanding of the Scriptures.

# In My Father's House

*A family trip to the Temple in Jerusalem confirmed Jesus' unique identity. He remained behind, conversing with the teachers. The event disclosed a loyalty greater than that to his earthly parents, and wisdom beyond that of his 12 years.*

## BEFORE

Parents, rabbis, and visits to the Temple would have been Jesus' main teachers in his early years.

### SPIRITUAL LEARNING

Jesus would have been expected to learn the Scriptures. The Mishnah (a written record from the first century BC of Jewish traditions), stated that, "At five years old [one is fit] for the Scripture… at thirteen for [the fulfilling of] the commandments… at twenty for pursuing [a calling]."

A 13TH-CENTURY GERMAN MISHNAH

WHEN JESUS WAS 12 years old, Joseph and Mary took him to Jerusalem to celebrate Passover. The trip may have seemed routine, part of an annual festival, but on this visit something unique was to take place. When the festival ended, Joseph, Mary, and their extended family left the city to return home to Nazareth. Jesus' parents both assumed that their son was somewhere among the retinue of their relatives, but after a day had gone by they began to wonder where he was.

Now anxious, Joseph and Mary went back in search of their son. It took them three days: he was in the Temple, seated among the teachers of the Jewish Law, asking questions and giving replies, and "Everyone who heard him was amazed at his understanding and his answers" (Luke 2:47).

### An uncomfortable revelation

There followed an awkward moment that provided insight into Jesus' true identity. Mary admonished him: "Son, why have you treated us like this? Your father and I have been anxiously searching for you" (2:48). Jesus' reply would become one of his most famous sayings: "'Why were you searching for me?' he asked. 'Didn't you know I had to be in my Father's house?'" (2:49).

This reply confirmed what Joseph and Mary already knew – that their son was unique. This had been revealed years before in the events surrounding Jesus' birth, but now their son's identity as God's son was confronting them in a personal way. Jesus' commitment to God and to his "Father's house" would take priority over social conventions, even family loyalties. He was not going to be a typical child.

Luke ends the Temple scene by highlighting Joseph and Mary's limited comprehension of their son's true identity. After Jesus questioned why his parents did not realize he had to be in the house of God, Luke writes that Mary and Joseph "did not understand what he was saying to them" (2:50).

### HISTORY AND CULTURE
### THREE TIMES A YEAR

The three great Jewish pilgrim festivals are Passover, Harvest, and Booths (see pp.318–19). Passover recalled the way that God had protected Israel's sons on the night of the judgment on the firstborn. Harvest (also known as Shavuot) celebrated God's goodness in providing annual crops. Booths (or Tabernacles) recalled God's provision when the Israelites lived in tents (booths or tabernacles) in the wilderness.

SAMARITANS CELEBRATING SHAVUOT

Now reunited with Jesus, Joseph and Mary then returned home to Nazareth. Luke concludes his account of this episode with a statement showing that, despite his divine authority and destiny, Jesus was still humble and willing to live under his parents' authority: "Then he went down to Nazareth with them and was obedient to them" (2:51).

## " And **Jesus grew in wisdom** and stature, and **in favour with God and man**."

LUKE 2:52

### WITH HIS TEACHER

By Jesus' time the Pharisees and others had established schools attached to local synagogues, where children could receive instruction in Jewish Law. Jesus may once have sat as attentively as this boy being taught by a rabbi.

## AFTER

Luke's Temple story is unique because it is the only story about Jesus' childhood retained in the Bible.

### INFANCY GOSPELS

Among other writings that did not become part of the Bible, the *Infancy Gospel of Thomas* reported that **the boy Jesus made clay birds, breathed on them, and brought them to life**. Another story featured a tutor teaching Jesus the Greek alphabet, beginning with the first two letters, Alpha and Beta. "Say 'Beta,'" the tutor said, to which Jesus replied, "First tell me **the meaning of Alpha**", which recalls **Jesus' declaration** 462–63 »

that he was "the Alpha and the Omega" (Revelation 1:8), meaning "the first and the last". In other scenes, **Jesus used miraculous power to bring judgment on people**, striking them blind.

### JESUS THE CARPENTER

Jesus' father, Joseph, was a *tekton* – the Greek word for a carpenter or stonemason (Matthew 13:55). Jesus himself was **later referred to as a carpenter** (Mark 6:3).

CARPENTER'S DRILL FROM EGYPT

# THE KINGDOM OF GOD

"After John was put in prison, Jesus went into Galilee, proclaiming the good news of God. 'The time has come,' he said. **'The kingdom of God has come near.** Repent and believe the good news!'"

**MARK** 1:14,15

**TURNING WATER TO WINE**
Paolo Veronese's *The Wedding at Cana* (1563), depicts the miracle when Jesus turned water to wine (see pp.306–07). The biblical episode is given a Venetian setting to reflect the painting's location at the Benedictine monastery of San Giorgio Maggiore.

HE "KINGDOM OF GOD" IS A PHRASE THAT does not appear in the Old Testament, although the notion of God's authority over all of his creation runs throughout. The kingdom that Jesus spoke about, and which is mentioned many times in the gospels of Matthew, Mark, and Luke, is not a physical place, but is God's dynamic rule where his grace, mercy, and power are experienced. The New Testament writers looked forward to this kingdom coming in its fullness, and yet they reported that the kingdom was already present in Jesus' ministry, steadily at work, just as yeast turns dough into bread.

People have always struggled in the face of suffering and evil. The book of Psalms reads, "When will you comfort me?" and "How long must your servant wait? When will you punish my persecutors?" (Psalm 119:82,84). The Scriptures promised that God would come and overrule everything that was contrary to his own goodness. The prophet Zechariah wrote, "The LORD will be king over the whole earth. On that day there will be one LORD, and his name the only name" (Zechariah 14:9).

### THE COMING KINGDOM
Against this backdrop, Jesus began his public ministry. He went into Galilee, a prosperous and well-populated region subject to Rome but ruled by Herod Antipas, announcing that the kingdom of God was approaching, and that it was time to repent and believe.

The idea of a "time" arriving recalled the hope of the prophets: the "day" that Zechariah had prophesied had begun. This required a response to repent and believe. Mark drew a parallel between the public arrival of Jesus (he "went into Galilee") and the establishment of God's reign ("the kingdom of God has come near"): the kingdom was dawning because the king had come.

Jesus did not just announce God's kingdom, he also demonstrated it. He drove out demons; he healed illness; he forgave sins; he overcame storms, by calming winds and waves, and even death, by raising the dead. At the end of his mission, Jesus himself would die and rise – defeating sin and death to reconcile humanity to God.

### NOW AND FOREVER
The kingdom was not just about power. Jesus told brief stories, or parables, about God's reign that pictured it in ordinary, everyday ways. It was like a tiny seed that finds good soil and grows into a large tree. It was like a wayward son whose father welcomed him home with a lavish feast. It was like people being invited to a wedding celebration – and needing to get ready. It was like allowing the weeds to grow alongside the wheat.

The kingdom would be given to the righteous on the day of judgment – when "the Son of Man comes in his glory" (Matthew 25:31) to transform the world for ever. "Then the King will say to those on his right, 'Come, you who are blessed by my Father; take your inheritance, the kingdom prepared for you since the creation of the world'" (25:34).

**THE MASTER AND HIS DISCIPLES**
This late 10th-century ivory plaque, from Germany, was originally set in a book cover. The intricate carving depicts the 12 apostles with Christ, who enlightened them about the glory of the kingdom of God.

**Prophet** Born *c.*7 BC Died *c.*AD 28–29

# John the Baptist

> "As it is written in the book of the words of Isaiah the prophet: **A voice of one calling in the wilderness, 'Prepare the way for the Lord…'**"
>
> LUKE 3:4

**L**UKE TELLS HIS readers that when Tiberius Caesar was emperor in Rome, Herod Antipas was tetrarch (ruler of one-fourth) of Galilee, and Caiaphas was high priest in Jerusalem, "the word of God" came to John in the wilderness (Luke 3:2). John began travelling around the dry region to the east of the River Jordan, preaching repentance and forgiveness of sins. He called on the large crowds who came to hear him to demonstrate their change of heart through baptism – a ritual immersion in water (see p.405).

### The "word of God"

Luke's telling of this story stresses that it started with the "word of God" – a divine message, like those given to Old Testament prophets. For Luke, the names of the political and religious leaders of the day set the historical stage for something more important – the coming of God's word. John's father, Zechariah, had been a priest in the Temple, the spiritual centre of Jewish life, and Zechariah himself had once

**THE JUDEAN WILDERNESS**
John the Baptist used to preach in the uncultivated, semi-arid desert of Judea to the north of the Dead Sea, attracting a large following with his messages of repentance and changing for the better.

received a message from God in that same place (Luke 1:11–22). By contrast, John lived far away from the centre of things, in the desert. Unlike his father, John was not a priest; he did not serve God in Jerusalem, but in a wasteland.

The word of God was a call to repentance. That call came out of Isaiah 40, a well-known passage in Israel's Scriptures, in which a voice in the wilderness says "prepare the way for the Lord" (Isaiah 40:3), referring to the arrival of God's Messiah. When people changed their hearts, received God's forgiveness, and submitted to baptism, that was what they were doing – preparing for the arrival of the Saviour sent by God.

**JOHN THE BAPTIST**
This painting by Giovanni Mazone, *c.*1466 shows John as he is often represented in Christian art – holding a thin staff made from a reed and topped with a cross, recalling his riverside ministry.

John's message was tough: "[He] said to the crowds coming out to be baptized by him, 'You brood of vipers! Who warned you to flee from the coming wrath?'" (Luke 3:7). Knowing that some people would take assurance in their Jewish ancestry and think themselves in no need of a change of heart, John warned them that repentance mattered more than genealogy. He used images from everyday life to picture God's judgment: "The axe has been laid to the root of the trees, and every tree that does not produce good fruit will be cut down and thrown into the fire" (3:9).

## So who was he?

John's growing fame brought an inevitable question: "Could this be the Messiah?" John's response was to point people to the real Messiah. He said that someone was coming who would be mightier than him and that he was not even worthy to untie this man's sandal straps. John baptized with water, but the Messiah would baptize with the Holy Spirit. John deflected people's focus away from himself, and on to Christ; he did it in a way that showed Jesus' unique authority as the one who would empower people to live for God.

## The spirit and the separation

However, baptism was not the Messiah's only task. John said that he would also carry a winnowing

fork – a farm implement used to toss harvested wheat into the air. The chaff would blow away in the wind, but the grain would drop back to the ground. The point of the image was separation – the separation of those who wanted to live for God from those who did not. John's picture of the coming Messiah was both sobering – his winnowing fork was in his hand – and full of hope: he would empower, with the power of God's Spirit, those who repented.

## Not afraid to speak out

The number of followers that John attracted caused Herod to fear that there could be trouble. John posed a threat partly because the "word

**GIVING A SERMON**
Giovanni B. Gaulli's 17th-century *The Sermon of St. John the Baptist* shows John preaching his message. John baptized people by immersing them in the waters of the River Jordan – an act that signified repentance from sin.

of God" that he bore was not reserved for the masses – John believed that it should also apply to the ruling powers.

John denounced Herod's marriage to Herodias, the former wife of his still-living brother, as a violation of Jewish Law. Herodias wanted John killed, but Herod imprisoned him.

Later, at a banquet, Herodias's daughter Salome danced so pleasingly for Herod and his guests that he said to her, "Ask me for anything you want, and I'll give it to you" (Mark 6:22). She asked for the head of John the Baptist on a dish. Not wanting to renege on his promise, Herod had John beheaded and his head was presented to Salome on a plate (Mark 6:14–29).

## John's importance

In fulfilling the prophecy of Malachi 3:1 – "I will send my messenger, who will prepare the way before me" – John provided a vital link between the Old Testament and Jesus' ministry. His considerable significance is reflected in the fact that, other than Jesus, he is the only character whose birth, life, and death are all recorded in the New Testament.

**ANALYSIS**

## JOHN ON REPENTANCE

John's fiery preaching prompted people to ask what they should do, so he gave them practical examples of repentance. If a man had two tunics, he should give one of them away. If people had more food than they needed, they should share it. Tax collectors should collect only what was legally required. Soldiers were told not to extort money from people, not to accuse people falsely, and not to complain about their wages.
The striking thing about this godly, pastoral teaching was that it came not from the Temple priests in Jerusalem, but from a radical in the desert.

**SOLDIERS OF THE PRAETORIAN GUARD**

**BIOGRAPHY IN BRIEF**

- **c.7 BC,** the angel of the Lord appeared to Zechariah and said that he and his wife, Elizabeth, would have a son, who should be called John.
- **John leaps in his mother's womb** when she (Elizabeth) hears the voice of her cousin, Mary, Jesus' mother (Luke 1:44).
- **Born to Zechariah and Elizabeth**, aged and godly members of the priestly tribe of Levi.
- **Controversy at his birth** over what his name should be. His parents obey the instructions of the angel Gabriel and name him John (Luke 1:13, 57–66).
- **John's parents** – old at his birth – probably die during his childhood.
- **John goes to live** "in the wilderness" until his public ministry begins.
- **During this time,** John may be in contact with the Qumran community (the Essenes), a zealous and ascetic Jewish group based near the Dead Sea.
- **Begins his public ministry** in the wilderness of Judea, some 32km (20 miles) east of Jerusalem. He preaches repentance, baptism, and forgiveness of sins, and large crowds come to hear him.
- **John's preaching** recalls zealous "repentance" prophets, such as Elijah, by saying, "The axe has been laid to the root of the trees, and every tree that does not produce good fruit will be cut down" (Matthew 3:10; Luke 3:9).
- **Clashes with** religious leaders, calling the Pharisees and Sadducees a "brood of vipers".
- **AD 27/28,** John baptizes Jesus in the River Jordan.
- **Rebukes** Herod Antipas for having married his brother's wife, Herodias: "It is not lawful for you to have your brother's wife" (Mark 6:18).
- **AD 28–29,** John is imprisoned by Herod. The historian Josephus says that John was kept in Herod's fortress at Machaerus, on the eastern shore of the Dead Sea.
- **While in prison,** he experiences a time of uncertainty about Jesus, but Jesus sends back evidence of his divine mission.
- **C.AD 28–29,** Herodias and her daughter Salome seek revenge against John. They force Herod into ordering his execution. John is beheaded in prison.
- **c.AD 30,** Jesus identifies John as the "second Elijah" mentioned in Malachi 4:5 (Matthew 17:12,13).

**BERNARDINO LUINI'S PAINTING OF JOHN BEHEADED, c.1510**

# The Baptism of Jesus

*Some 30 years after his birth, it was time for Jesus to begin his public mission. He did so in a surprising but defining way, by submitting to a rite intended for sinners – baptism.*

**J**ESUS ARRIVED at the River Jordan in order to be baptized – immersed in water – by John. John was surprised, saying it should be Jesus baptizing him, not the other way around. Jesus replied that it was necessary "to fulfil all righteousness" (3:15). John's reluctance was understandable. He had already spoken to the crowd of the "one" yet to come (3:11), who would baptize people with God's Spirit. Now here was Jesus, so why would he need to be baptized?

The story provides the answer. John preached "in the wilderness" and he baptized people in the River Jordan. For Israel, the wilderness and the Jordan were symbolic places. Their ancestors had travelled for 40 years in the desert, and then entered the Promised Land by crossing the Jordan. So the place of John's ministry represented an opportunity for Israel to renew its relationship with God – symbolically returning to the desert and then re-entering the Promised Land. Jesus – the one who would "save his people from their sins" (1:21) – joined them. Jesus saved the people not by standing aloof, but by becoming one of them – he joined the crowds in the desert and in the river, and submitted to baptism.

What happened next showed that Jesus' baptism was not only about Israel, but that it affected the whole world. As Jesus was coming up out of the water, "he saw the Spirit of God descending like a dove and alighting on him" (3:16). This description connects the scene to a biblical moment older than Israel and global in scope: the world re-emerging from the waters of the flood. As the world came out of the water, Noah's dove settled on it, representing God's new beginning for humanity (Genesis 8:8–12). Now Christ re-emerged from the waters, and the dove settled on him – the one in whom all humankind could begin again.

The Spirit empowered Jesus for the mission ahead. With God's Spirit came a voice from heaven, affirming that Jesus was the Son of God, loved by the Father (3:17). By setting this divine, heaven-sent declaration in front of his readers, Matthew exalted Jesus as the one trusted by God, and worthy of his readers' trust as well.

> "And a voice from heaven said, 'This is my Son, whom I love; with him I am well pleased.'"
>
> MATTHEW 3:17

**BAPTIZED BY THE BAPTIST**
*The Baptism of Christ* by Fra Angelico (c.1395–1455) shows John baptizing Jesus by the River Jordan, just as he would the sinners who came to him.

**BEFORE**

The symbolism of the wilderness features in several stories in the Bible, notably those of the Israelites, Elijah, and John the Baptist.

**JOHN WAS A SIGN**

The prophet **Elijah had lived for a time in the wilderness** ❮❮ 196–97, where he was miraculously fed by God, who sent ravens to supply him with bread and meat. The prophet Malachi had promised that a new Elijah would appear just before God's day of wrath and healing (Malachi 4:1–5). Thus, **John the Baptist appeared in the desert** ❮❮ 298–99 before Jesus began his mission – and he even dressed like Elijah (see Mark 1:6), with "a garment of hair and… a leather belt round his waist" (2 Kings 1:8). Jesus' temptation continues the symbolism.

**SYMBOLS**

**GOD AND THE DESERT**

In both the Old and New Testaments, the wilderness is portrayed as a place of hardship and salvation. There was no food, but God sent manna (Exodus 16). There was no water, but God brought water from a rock (Exodus 17). There were wild beasts, but God sent angels (Mark 1:13).

Many Christians have seen spiritual value in the desert as a setting in which to connect to the divine truth. In the 3rd century AD, Egypt's Anthony the Great, one of the leaders of the Desert Fathers and a hermit, sought the wilderness as a refuge from the corrupting influence of the world. Most of the Church's early monastic communities began in the desert, where solitude aided their devotion to God. Jesus' 40 days in the wilderness later became the model for the disciplines of Lent.

**THE DESERT TEMPTATIONS OF ST ANTHONY**

# Temptation in the Wilderness

*Following his baptism, Jesus was filled with the Holy Spirit. He left the River Jordan and travelled into the wilderness where he faced a great test – the devil tried three times to tempt Jesus into abandoning his mission.*

ISRAEL'S EXPERIENCE in the wilderness had been that of wandering – chiefly due to its people's disobedience (Numbers 32:13). Jesus' time in the wilderness was to have nothing to do with wandering – it was part of his God-appointed mission. His period in the desert lasted 40 days, recalling Israel's 40 years in the wilderness. Israel had passed through the Red Sea and faced testing in the wilderness. Jesus went through the Jordan at his baptism, and then – like Israel – faced a test in the desert. His story paralleled that of the Israelites, because in him Israel was being embodied and reborn. Luke tells us that Jesus was "led by the Spirit into the wilderness" (Luke 4:1).

Matthew's account of the event states that Jesus fasted, abstaining from food for 40 days. At the end of those 40 days he was very hungry (Matthew 4:2).

*Turning stone into bread*
Satan's first ploy was to use Jesus' hunger: "If you are the Son of God, tell this stone to become bread" (Luke 4:3). The devil's aim was to

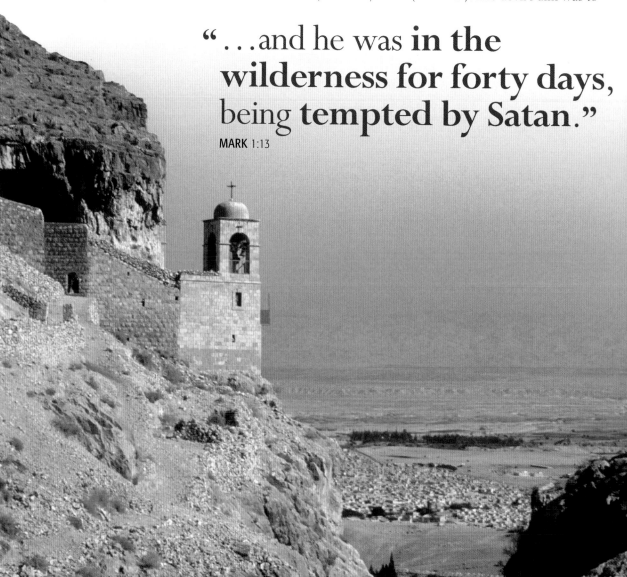

" …and he was **in the wilderness for forty days,** being **tempted by Satan.** "
MARK 1:13

## SATAN

The names "Satan" and "devil" primarily meant an adversary or accuser. Satan opposes God, his people, and his purposes. In the wilderness story, he tempts Jesus to exercise his authority in ways that dishonour God and undermine Jesus' own mission. In Acts, the story of Ananias shows how Satan can corrupt people's characters – Satan fills Ananias' heart, prompting

this disciple to lie to appear generous (Acts 5:3).

However, Satan's power is limited. In Revelation he is "an enormous red dragon" (12:3) that tried to devour Christ at birth (a picture of Herod, perhaps), but he was defeated by God. The dragon vowed to pursue God's people (12:17) but it found refuge in the wilderness.

**SATAN, 15TH-CENTURY TRIPTYCH**

**CHRIST BEING TEMPTED**
In *The Temptation of Christ on the Mountain*, c.1308–11, from the Maestá altarpiece by Duccio di Buoninsegna, a towering Jesus rejects the devil who is offering him the kingdoms of the world. The kingdoms are a metaphor for power, but in this painting of the second temptation, they strongly resemble the city of Siena in Italy, where the work was commissioned.

persuade Jesus to use his divine authority as a short cut in order to satisfy his own needs. Jesus replied quoting Deuteronomy 8:3: "It is written: 'Man shall not live on bread alone'" (Luke 4:4). He turned away from exploiting his power as an easy way out and chose the way of steady, human faithfulness, even if that meant going without food.

This moment had clear biblical echoes: Israel had faced hunger in the wilderness, complained against God ("we detest this miserable food"), and rebelled (Numbers 21:5). Adam had faced a longing for food in his desire for the fruit of the tree of knowledge, and he chose against God (see pp.36–37).

Those two previous temptations by food had led to rebellion, but this one did not, because this Son of Man was faithful.

### The kingdoms of the world
The next temptation involved much more than a loaf of bread. Satan took Jesus to a high place and showed him the world's kingdoms. "I will give you all their authority and splendour… If you worship me, it will all be yours" (Luke 4:6,7). This was another encouragement to take a short cut. Jesus could gain what God ultimately did want to give him as Messiah – dominion over the nations – but without dying on the cross. All he had to do was worship Satan. His response was simple and blunt, and again from Deuteronomy (6:13): "It is written: 'Worship the Lord your God and serve him only'" (Luke 4:8).

### Instant fame?
Finally, the devil took Jesus to Jerusalem and stood him on the pinnacle of the Temple. "'If you are the Son of God,' he said, 'throw yourself down from here'" (Luke

**THE MOUNT OF TEMPTATION**
The Orthodox monastery of Quruntal (or "Temptation") clings to the Mount of Temptation, overlooking the Jordan valley to the northwest of the town of Jericho. The exact location of the biblical temptation is not known, but it is traditionally identified with this limestone peak – one of the holy sites identified by Helena in the 4th century – on the road from Jerusalem to Jericho.

4:9). This time, it was the devil who used Scripture. He cited Psalm 91, which says that God will not let his faithful people strike their feet against a stone. By this, the devil was telling Jesus that he should do this daring act, because God promises him that he will not get hurt – and think of the adulation he would get.

Jesus saw through this trick, which promised him worship without the sacrifice that had to come first. It meant acting dangerously and presuming on God to intervene – what Deuteronomy 6:16 called "putting God to the test". Jesus refused to test God in this way and so rebutted the third temptation.

The story ended with both victory and realism: "When the devil had finished all this tempting, he left him until an opportune time" (Luke 4:13). The devil slunk away, defeated, if only temporarily; he would be back.

**AFTER** »

For a while, Jesus joined the followers of John the Baptist, although John had now acknowledged Jesus as "God's Chosen One" (John 1:29–42).

### POINTING TO JESUS
John the Baptist **pointed people to Jesus**. When Jesus stepped onto the public stage, a transition of loyalty began. One example was **Andrew; initially a disciple of John, he began following Jesus 312–13 »**, a man whom John called "the Lamb of God". Increasing numbers of people flocked to Jesus, and John stated: "A person can receive only what is given them from heaven. … He [Jesus] must become greater; I must become less" (John 3:27–30).

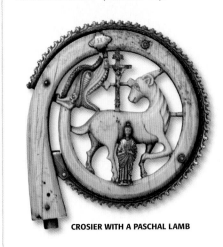

**CROSIER WITH A PASCHAL LAMB**

## HISTORY AND CULTURE

# Food and Drink

> "Go, **eat your food** with gladness, and **drink your wine** with a **joyful heart...**" ECCLESIASTES 9:7

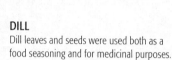

**DILL**
Dill leaves and seeds were used both as a food seasoning and for medicinal purposes. This herb is one of the traditional ingredients used to pickle cucumbers.

**B**reakfast and lunch were light meals in biblical times, such as the bread dipped in wine vinegar that Boaz shared with Ruth when she gleaned the harvest in his field

**WEDDING FEAST**
Bedouin prepare a wedding feast inside their home, a cave in Petra, Jordan. The meal includes flatbread made on an open fire.

(Ruth 2:14). The main meal was in the evening at the end of the working day, and the family sat down to eat together. After washing their hands, the diners used bread to pick up food from a common bowl. After the meal, and possibly before, a prayer of blessing was said (Deuteronomy 8:10) and everyone washed their hands again.

In patriarchal times, meals were eaten sitting on the ground, but in later periods rich people often sat on chairs at a table or reclined. By New Testament times, members of the middle and upper classes would have reclined on couches or mats around a low table, resting on their left elbow and using their right hand to eat.

The generous sharing of food and drink with others was a fundamental part of biblical culture. Eating was not just about satisfying hunger, but was an expression of friendship and acceptance, and this is why Jesus ate with people whom the Pharisees, concerned with ritual purity, would have felt obliged to avoid (Matthew 9:10–13).

### THE SYMBOLISM OF FOOD

During Passover (see pp.100–15), Jewish families gather together to eat a meal called *Seder* and to recount the story of the Exodus. The food served on the Seder plate symbolizes the story of the Israelites in ancient Egypt. Green vegetables (symbolizing spring) are dipped in salt water to represent the tears of the Jewish slaves; bitter herbs represent the bitter experience of slavery; *charoset* (a fruit and nut paste) represents the mortar Jewish slaves used to build cities; a lamb bone symbolizes the sacrifice of the first Passover, and an egg, a symbol of mourning, is a reminder of the destruction of the Temple.

*Pesach* is Hebrew for "Passover"

**SEDER PLATE**

## HOSPITALITY

Hospitality was (and remains) central to Middle Eastern culture. Strangers were welcomed and given food and drink, and perhaps the meat of a "choice, tender calf", as Abraham offered to his three visitors (Genesis 18:6–8). Travellers would wait in public places, such as by a well or at the city gates, until someone invited them home for the night (Genesis 19:1–3; Acts 16:13–15).

When Jesus sent out his disciples on their mission he instructed them to "Take nothing for the journey except a staff – no bread, no bag, no money in your belts" (Mark 6:8), because he was confident that someone would provide for them.

## BREAD

Bread was the staple of the ancient Near Eastern diet. Wheat made the best flour, though the poor used barley instead. The grain was ground into flour and mixed with salt, water, and olive oil to form dough. To make leavened bread, some previously fermented dough was added to the mix, which was then left to rise before being baked in an oven or on stones over hot coals.

The importance of bread is reflected in its presence in many religious festivals, such as Passover, when only flat, unleavened bread is eaten (Exodus 12:17–20), and in certain offerings (Leviticus 2:4–10). Twelve fresh loaves of bread, one for each tribe of Israel, were placed weekly on the table in the Tabernacle and Temple in recognition of God's provision of the grain.

Grindstone repeatedly rolled over grain

### GRINDING GRAIN
This model from the ancient Egyptian Middle Kingdom depicts figures grinding wheat and barley to make bread and beer.

## FRUIT AND VEGETABLES

Fruit and vegetables also formed a key part of the Israelite diet. Common fruits included grapes, figs, dates, pomegranates, melons, olives, and, by New Testament times, citrus fruits. Common

### FRESH FIGS
Figs are an excellent source of nutrition. They were eaten fresh when in season, but were also dried and stored. The large leaves served as wrappers.

vegetables and pulses included leeks, onions, cucumbers, lentils, and beans. Herbs included mint, dill, and cumin (Matthew 23:23).

## MEAT, FISH, AND POULTRY

Only the flesh of "clean" animals was permitted to be eaten (Deuteronomy 14:3–20), which included "any animal that has a divided hoof and that chews the

### PERMITTED FISH
Only fish with both fins and scales, such as sardines, were eaten. All other fish, shellfish, and other sea creatures were forbidden as food.

cud" (see p.319). Meat consumed in biblical times included mutton and goat, and birds such as chickens, pigeons, and quail. The poor could rarely afford meat; the wealthy also ate lamb, beef, and venison. Meat was normally boiled (1 Samuel 2:13), but the Passover lamb was roasted whole (Exodus 12:8).

By New Testament times, many people were keeping hens for their eggs. Fish now formed an important part of the diet, especially in Galilee (see pp.310–11). Small fish were dried in the sun, salted, and eaten with bread. Fresh fish was cooked over open fires (John 21:9–10). Salt, from the Red Sea, was used to season and preserve food.

### DOMESTICATED HEN
Birds' eggs, both domestic and wild, were a valuable source of food in Bible lands. Ostrich eggs were especially prized – the shells were sometimes used for ornaments and jewellery.

## DRINK

Wine was a popular drink, especially among the elite. Grapes were pressed in a wine-press, the juice strained, and the liquid allowed to ferment. It was then stored in jars or wineskins. Honey and spices were sometimes mixed with the wine for variety. Drinking wine was not forbidden in Jewish Law – in fact Jesus' first miracle was turning water into wine (John 2:1–11) – but drunkenness was condemned in both Old and New Testaments (Isaiah 28:1–8).

Barley, used in bread-making, could also be used to brew beer. Another staple drink was milk, taken from sheep, cows, goats, or camels. Milk could also be turned into yoghurt or cheese.

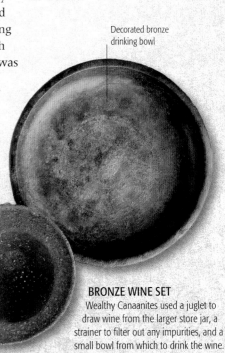

Decorated bronze drinking bowl

Strainer

Wine juglet

### BRONZE WINE SET
Wealthy Canaanites used a juglet to draw wine from the larger store jar, a strainer to filter out any impurities, and a small bowl from which to drink the wine.

## BEFORE

**Three days before Cana, Philip introduced Nathanael to Jesus.**

### FIG TREE AND STAIRWAY

When Nathanael met Jesus for the first time, Jesus said that he already knew him; he had "seen" him standing under a fig tree before Philip called him. Nathanael was amazed. Jesus told Nathanael that he would see greater things than that. He would witness "heaven open, and the angels of God ascending and descending on the Son of Man" (John 1:51). The image recalled **Jacob's "stairway" dream** ❮❮ **70–71**. The access to God that Jacob had foreseen would be fulfilled in Jesus himself.

**NATHANAEL UNDER A FIG TREE**

# The Wedding Feast at Cana

*Jesus' ministry was rooted in the Law, but it was also transformative. At a wedding celebration, he changed water for Jewish purification rites into wine, and revealed his divine nature to his disciples.*

THE SCENE OF Jesus' first miracle was an ordinary and joyful social event in Galilee – the wedding celebration of an unnamed couple. Jesus' mother was there and Jesus had been invited with his disciples.

### No more wine

The happy event suddenly became awkward when the wine ran out. Then, just as now, running short of wine at a wedding feast showed poor planning and was shameful for the families involved. Jesus' mother became aware of the problem and spoke to her son, telling him that the wine had run out. "'Woman, why do you involve me?' Jesus asked. 'My hour has not yet come'" (John 2:4).

The response of Jesus seems harsh to modern ears but referring to his mother as "woman" was not necessarily rude. However, Jesus' words were a sort of correction. And Mary's response shows that although she was his mother she was learning to be a disciple, or follower of Jesus. She turned to the servants and instructed them to do whatever Jesus told them.

### Symbolism of the jars

Standing nearby were six stone water jars, large enough to hold more than 80 litres (20–30 gallons) each. John mentions that they were jars for ritual washing – familiar, everyday receptacles for water, as well as symbols of the old covenant that God had made with

> ❝ **Fill the jars with water**…
> Now draw some out **and take it
> to the master** of the banquet. ❞
>
> JOHN 2:7-8

## CANA

Cana, near Nazareth, was also the setting for Jesus' second miracle: healing a royal official's son who lay sick some 30 km (20 miles) away in Capernaum. Nestled amid the rolling hills of Galilee, Cana was also the hometown of the disciple Nathanael.

## RITUAL CLEANLINESS

The rules of the old covenant included cleanliness in the sight of God. This was achieved through ritual immersion in a *mikveh,* a sunken pool holding holy waters that had powers of purification. Ceremonial washing enabled Israel to remain ritually pure and undefiled; it was also a symbolic pointer to obedience to the commandments and undiluted devotion to God. By Jesus' day, ritual cleanliness was a normal part of life for observant Jews, evident at Cana in the stone water jars of the kind "used by the Jews for ceremonial washing" (John 2:6).

*A MIKVEH RITUAL BATH AT MASADA*

Israel. The jars were made of stone, not pottery, because stone was easier to keep ceremonially pure for ritual purposes. Jesus told the servants to fill the jars with water.

### Something good and better

Jesus then told the servants to draw out some of the contents from the jars and take it to the master of the banquet (the head waiter). They did so, "and the master of the banquet tasted the water that had been turned into wine" (2:9). John points out that the banquet master did not know where this new wine had come from, "though the servants who had drawn the water knew" (2:9). When the banquet master tasted the wine he was surprised, and told the bridegroom that normally people used the best wine first and served the cheaper wine later, "after the guests have had too much to drink; but you have saved the best till now" (2:10). According to John, this was "the first of the signs through which [Jesus] revealed his glory; and his disciples believed in him" (2:11).

### Change and celebration

In Isaiah 62:5 and Hosea 2:14-23, the prophets had pictured the old covenant – the relationship between God and the Israelites – as a marriage, where God was the bridegroom and Israel the bride. "As a bridegroom rejoices over his bride, so will your God rejoice over you", said Isaiah (62:5). Therefore it was no accident that Jesus' first sign took place at a wedding.

At Cana, the water used for Judaic rituals was replaced by the choicest of wines. This was a sign that the existing religious customs and rituals had lost their meaning, and had been replaced by the true path to God – Jesus himself. Jesus later explained this explicitly to Thomas: "I am the way and the truth and the life. No one comes to the Father except through me" (John 14:6).

### STORING WINE

In Graeco-Roman times, wine was stored in large, ceramic jars called amphora. This terracotta amphora is from Beirut, Lebanon, and dates from the 4th century AD. The vase-like vessels typically had long, slender necks and two handles for carrying.

## THE SIGNS OF JESUS' DIVINITY

**1** **Turning water into wine** Jesus transformed ceremonial water into wine (John 2:1-11).

**2** **Healing the official's son** Jesus' power was not limited by distance (John 4:46-54).

**3** **Healing at the pool** In curing a 38-year disability, Jesus changed the unchangeable (John 5:1-15).

**4** **Feeding the 5,000** Jesus provided for his followers (John 6:1-13) as God had for Israel.

**5** **Walking on the sea** Jesus walked on the Sea of Galilee as Lord of nature (John 6:16-21).

**6** **Healing the man born blind** Jesus healed for the glory of God (John 9:1-6).

**7** **Raising Lazarus** The invincible enemy – death – met its match in Jesus (John 11:1-45).

### TURNING WATER INTO WINE

Julius Schnorr von Carolsfeld's *The Marriage at Cana* (1819) shows Jesus performing the first of seven miraculous signs that prove he is the Son of God. The Gospel of John describes all seven of these signs.

> ❝ **Everyone brings out the choice wine
> first** and then the cheaper wine after the
> guests have had too much to drink; **but
> you have saved the best till now.** ❞
>
> JOHN 2:10

**AFTER** 〉〉

After the wedding at Cana, John's Gospel describes Jesus driving traders from the Temple, and instructing Nicodemus, a member of the Jewish ruling council, on the Holy Spirit.

### CLEANSING THE TEMPLE

Jesus travelled to Jerusalem, where he found people trading animals and exchanging money within the Temple, and **drove them out in a fury 384-85 〉〉**.

### THE WINDS OF REBIRTH

The Pharisee **Nicodemus** came to talk to Jesus, who talked to him of the **life-giving power of the Spirit** – a holy wind that brings rebirth. Jesus told him, "The wind blows wherever it pleases. You hear its sound, but you cannot tell where it comes from or where it is going. **So it is with everyone born of the Spirit**" (John 3:8).

## BEFORE

The story of the woman at the well takes place in Sychar, a Samarian town on Jesus' route from Judea to Galilee.

### REASON FOR THE JOURNEY
Jesus and John the Baptist had been carrying **on parallel ministries ‹‹ 298** for some time. Then Herod Antipas imprisoned John and, according to Matthew 4:12, this event was the catalyst that persuaded Jesus to travel from Judea and head north towards his childhood home in Galilee.

### WOMEN AT WELLS
The Jewish Scriptures feature several stories of women who met their future husbands at wells: **Rebekah met the servant ‹‹ 62–63** seeking a wife for Isaac (Genesis 24:12–18), and **Zipporah met Moses** (Exodus 2:15–21). That may have been in John's mind as he told this story of a woman meeting Israel's true "bridegroom" at a well (John 3:29).

### HISTORY AND CULTURE
## JEWS AND SAMARITANS

**SAMARITAN PRIEST WITH PENTATEUCH**

Both Jews and Samaritans regarded the written Pentateuch as their Scripture, but whereas Jews looked to Jerusalem as their place for sacrifical worship, the Samaritans had Mount Gerizim, near Sychar.

In Jesus' day, Jews viewed Samaritans as ceremonially unclean, quasi-Gentiles. To share a cup with a Samaritan would make a Jew unclean. To avoid contamination some Jews detoured eastwards around Samaria. Jesus did not and his interaction with the Samaritan woman involved him crossing the geographical and cultural boundaries that existed between the two communities.

# Jesus and the Samaritan Woman

*At the site of Jacob's well, near the tomb of the patriarch Joseph, Jesus had a conversation with a woman who – not unlike the communities of Jews and Samaritans – had a history of troubled relationships.*

**W**HEN JESUS WAS on his way through Samaria, returning to the greater safety of his home territory of Galilee, he sat down by a well for a much-needed rest.

### A woman at the well
A Samaritan woman came to draw water from the source, and Jesus asked her to give him a drink. The woman was surprised for several reasons: Jews did not normally associate with Samaritans, whom they regarded as an inferior people (see box, left); conversations between unmarried men and women were socially improper; and she had come unaccompanied to the well in the midday heat – these were clues in the story that she was a shameful character. How could Jesus ask *her* for a drink, given that she was a Samaritan woman?

### Two kinds of water
Jesus did not let racial prejudice or social convention hold sway. He spoke about his own authority and about eternal life as a miraculous drink that he could provide: "If you knew the gift of God and who it is that asks you for a drink, you would have asked him and he would have given you living water" (John 4:10).

The woman did not understand. How would Jesus draw this water? – the well was a deep one and he did not even have a water jar.

### MOUNT GERIZIM
This view shows the western ridge of Mount Gerizim, believed by Samaritans to be the sacred mountain chosen by Yahweh for a holy temple. Today, many Samaritans live in the nearby village of Kiryat Luza.

Jesus replied that he was talking about a different kind of water – water that came from him and became an internal spring in the hearts of those who received it. Anyone who drank the water he could give them would never feel thirst again.

### Past and future
The woman then asked Jesus to give her this living water. Jesus in turn told her to return home and bring her husband back to the well, but the woman answered that she had no husband. So Jesus confronted her with the facts of her life: she had already had five husbands, he said, and was now living with her sixth. (The Greek word translated here as "husband" normally means "man" – she may never have been married at all.)

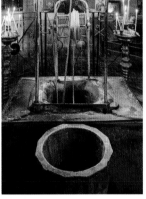

**JACOB'S WELL**
Modern-day Nablus (biblical Shechem, or Sychar) is the site of Jacob's Well. According to Jewish and Arab tradition, Jacob watered his herds here. The Samaritan woman in search of water met Jesus at this well.

Embarrassed by the revelation, the woman changed the subject, bringing up the historic dispute between the Samaritans and the Jews over the proper place to worship and sacrifice: the Jews said this was Mount Zion in Jerusalem; the Samaritans said it was Mount Gerizim.

### A new era dawns
Jesus did not let this source of rancour between the two comunities derail the conversation. The issue was not the location, Jesus said, but the heart: "… a time is coming when you will worship the Father neither on this mountain nor in Jerusalem… the true worshippers will worship the Father in the Spirit and in truth, for they are the kind of worshipers the Father seeks" (4:21–23). The woman then told Jesus that she knew the

Messiah was coming and that he would explain everything. Jesus replied: "I, the one speaking to you – I am he." (4:26).

### A hope that sparked life

Something in the woman changed; she put down her water jar, went back to the town, and told everyone, "Come, see a man who told me everything I've ever done. Could this be the Messiah?" (4:29). People came from the town and met Jesus for themselves, and at their urging he stayed several days in the town. The story ended with the remarkable testimony of the people: "… now we have heard for ourselves, and we know that this man really is the Saviour of the world" (4:42).

> " Jesus answered, 'Everyone who drinks this water will be thirsty again, but **whoever drinks the water I give them will never thirst**.'"
>
> JOHN 4:13,14

## JESUS' "I AM" SAYINGS

A key theme in John is the emphasis on Jesus' identity, shown especially in his seven descriptive "I Am" sayings. These recall God's words to Moses: "I AM WHO I AM" (Exodus 3:14).

**1** "I am the bread of life" (John 6:35, 48).

**2** "I am the light of the world" (8:12; 9:5).

**3** "I am the gate" (10:7,9).

**4** "I am the good shepherd" (10:11,14).

**5** "I am the resurrection and the life" (11:25).

**6** "I am the way, and the truth and the life" (14:6).

**7** "I am the true vine" (15:1,5).

**WATER FROM THE WELL**
A veiled woman carries water from a well on Socotra Island, Yemen. Tired from his journey, Jesus was resting at a well when the Samaritan woman came to draw water. By speaking to her, Jesus was challenging the prejudices of the day.

## AFTER

**Soon after the Samaria visit, a royal official came to Jesus and begged him to heal his son, who was dying.**

### AIDING THE ENEMY?

Jesus was **welcomed back to Galilee** by those Galileans who had heard of his acts elsewhere. He again went to Cana, and while he was there he was approached by a "royal official" who implored Jesus to cure his son, who lay close to death at Capernaum (John 4:46).

Jesus said, "**Unless you people see signs and wonders you will never believe**" (4:48), and then he declared that the boy was healed: "'Go,' Jesus replied, 'your son will live'" (John 4:50). Some distance away, at that moment, the son recovered. **The man and his entire household came to believe**.

The description "royal official" suggests that the father was employed by **Herod, ruler of Galilee 345 »**. Healing this man's son was, perhaps, a fitting postscript to visiting the "unclean" Samaritans.

**JESUS' HOME PROVINCE** Origins 15th century BC

# Galilee

> "**Jesus returned to Galilee in the power of the Spirit**, and news about him spread through the whole countryside."
>
> LUKE 4:14

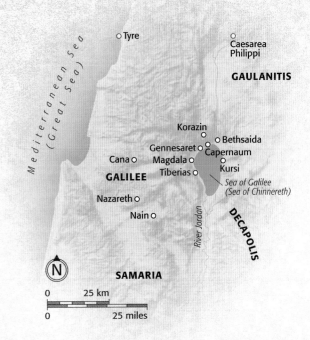

**G**ALILEE WAS the area promised to the tribes of Zebulun and Naphtali (Joshua 19:10–16,32–39). It shares its name with an inland lake, the "Sea" of Galilee, which was also known as the Sea of Chinnereth in the Hebrew Bible and, in Old Testament times, as the Lake of Gennesaret, for a town on its shore.

Although he was born in Bethlehem, Jesus grew up in Nazareth in Galilee. He would later spend most of his ministry teaching there, as Isaiah had prophesied: "[in] Galilee of the nations… The people walking in darkness have seen a great light" (Isaiah 9:1,2).

### Land of refuge and prayer
When the Israelites arrived in the land of Canaan after escaping from Egypt, they designated six cities as places of refuge, according to God's instructions. Here, anyone who killed unintentionally would not "be killed by the avenger of blood prior to standing trial" (Joshua 20:9). The city of Kedesh – meaning "holy" – in northern Galilee was one such city, and it was also an area for the Levites to live. Unlike the other tribes, the Levites had received no land-inheritance, because "the priestly service of the LORD is their inheritance" (Joshua 18:7). However, the other tribes gave them towns and pasture land (1 Chronicles 6:76).

### THE REGION OF GALILEE
Galilee was dominated by the inland lake that bears its name, both economically – supporting fishing and farming – and geographically. The key towns were clustered along the lake's western shore.

### Economic pawns
Galilee knew times of hardship. King Solomon gave 20 Galilean cities to Hiram, king of Tyre "because Hiram had supplied him with all the cedar and juniper and gold he wanted" (1 Kings 9:11) for his Temple and royal palace. Hiram was unimpressed with the gift and

---

**HISTORY AND CULTURE**

#### UPPER AND LOWER GALILEE

Upper – northern – and lower Galilee had very distinct characters. The northern region was a more mountainous area with a distinctly village culture, while the south was dominated by large towns, such as Capernaum and Tiberias, and had strong trading links with coastal towns. Both areas were relatively rich in resources. While parts of Galilee were forested, much of it was well suited to farming, and the Sea of Galilee boasted an abundant supply of fish, providing a livelihood and food source.

**FIELDS IN ZALMON VALLEY, LOWER GALILEE**

**THE SEA OF MIRACLES**
The Sea of Galilee was the setting for a number of miracles. Jesus calmed a storm on the lake, asserting his power over nature (see pp.334–35) and the feeding the 5,000 took place on its shores (see pp.346–47).

named it Kabul, meaning "displeasing" or "dirty". Some scholars believe that Hiram moved non-Israelites there from Tyre, which might explain the high percentage of Gentiles in the area.

## Political change

Jerusalem fell to Nebuchadnezzar in the sixth century BC (see pp.236–37), and the Israelites were sent to exile in Babylon. Following this, Galilee – along with the rest of Israel – changed hands many times. In 733 BC it was captured, along with the rest of the land of the tribe of Naphtali by King Tiglath-Pileser III (see pp.216–17), who "deported the people to Assyria" (2 Kings 15:29). Historians are unclear as to the scale of this deportation, since Galilee was later ruled by Persia, Greece, and then Syria and Egypt, during which time non-Israelite peoples repopulated the area.

From 110 BC Galilee had a brief period of Jewish leadership under the Hasmonean kings (see pp.266–67), but then came the Roman Empire. In 37 BC the Hasmonean kingdom yielded to one of Rome's puppet kings, Herod the Great, whose reign was succeeded by that of his son, Herod Antipas. Galilee was part of Israel, but Israel was part of the Roman Empire – between the time of the Old and New Testaments, Galilee was a place of strife.

## Jesus' mission from Galilee

This was the backdrop of the world into which Jesus was born. In Jesus' time a visitor to a Galilean market might have heard haggling in Greek, Hebrew, or Aramaic, and mixed with Jews, Syrians, Romans, and Parthians.

Jesus began his mission at home in Galilee (Matthew 4:12–25), then travelled south, ending his journey in Jerusalem, where the northern accent of Galileans was distinctive (Matthew 26:73; Acts 2:7). In Judea, Jesus faced the wealthy and powerful Sadducees (see p.366–67), a Jewish sect identified with the upper echelon of Judean society. However, in Galilee he confronted the more numerous Pharisees (see p.364), and their scrupulous concerns about Jewish Law (Mark 2:18–3:6).

The term "Galilean" was often used to refer to the early Christians in a contemptuous way, but Jesus accepted the epithet "Jesus of Galilee" (Matthew 26:69), and focused his teachings there, although his ministry moved to Jerusalem for its culmination. After he rose from the dead, he called his disciples to a mountain in Galilee, from which he commanded them to "make disciples of all nations"(Matthew 28:19).

**CALMING THE STORM**
This 19th-century window from Holy Trinity church in Fonthill Gifford, Wiltshire, UK shows Jesus calming a storm on the Sea of Galilee. Enveloped by hills and located below sea level, the lake was prone to squalls.

### CHRONOLOGY IN BRIEF

- **c.1400–1200 BC,** "Kedesh in Galilee" designated as one of God's "cities of refuge" and a Levite land-grant (Joshua 20:7; 1 Chronicles 6:76).
- **c.950 BC,** Solomon gives 20 towns in Galilee to Hiram, king of Tyre (1 Kings 9:11).
- **c.730 BC,** Assyria captures Galilee (2 Kings 15:29), then (seven years later) the entire Northern Kingdom (2 Kings 17:6). The area is now ruled from Megiddo (a new province instituted by Assyrian leader Tiglath-Pileser III).
- **c.700 BC,** Isaiah prophesies: "in the future [God] will honour Galilee of the nations" (Isaiah 9:1).
- **c.538–104 BC,** Post-exile Galilee under control of Persia, Greece, then alternately Syria and Egypt.
- **c.160 BC,** Jewish resistance leader Judas Maccabeus removes vulnerable Galileans south to Judea.
- **c.104 BC,** Jewish Hasmonean ruler, Aristobulus I, reconquers Galilee, bringing it temporarily back under Jewish control.
- **c.63 BC,** Roman general Pompey conquers Jerusalem.
- **c.40 BC,** Herod the Great becomes ruler of Galilee, later of Israel.
- **c.6 BC,** Jesus is born in Bethlehem and grows up in Nazareth, both in the province of Galilee.
- **c.AD 28,** Jesus begins his ministry: "Jesus went into Galilee, proclaiming the good news of God" (Mark 1:14).
- **c.AD 30,** Jesus dies and is raised from the dead. He returns to speak to the apostles, and summons them to a mountain in Galilee, where he tells them to baptise the people of all nations.

A 5TH-CENTURY MOSAIC OF LOAVES AND FISHES COMMEMORATES THE FEEDING OF THE 5,000 AT TABGHA CHURCH, BESIDE THE SEA OF GALILEE

- **c.AD 35,** Early Church prospers in Judea and Galilee (Acts 9:31).
- **c.AD 66,** Jewish War (revolt against Rome) begins.
- **c.AD 70,** Rome reacts to Jewish revolt, destroying the Temple and city of Jerusalem. From now on, Galilee becomes a centre of learning about the Jewish Law – along with Babylon – with the collection of the Masoretic texts integral to the preservation of the Hebrew Scriptures.
- **c.AD 75,** Historian Josephus writes *History of the Jewish War* (c.AD 37–101), describing his native Galilee as "encompassed with so many nations of foreigners" (Book 3: Chapter 3, section 2).

**BEFORE** «

Jesus had begun to set out his mission and the time had come to recruit followers to help him.

### CLEAR INTENTIONS

Jesus had announced that he had **come to preach good news to the poor and set free the oppressed** (Luke 4:16–19). He began to drive out demons and **heal the sick**. Jesus went on to find the people who could help him with the preaching.

### SIMON PETER AND ANDREW

Jesus had already met two of the men who were to become his disciples. Simon Peter and his brother Andrew went to listen to John the Baptist and Jesus was in the crowd (John 1:35–42). According to John's Gospel, it was at this meeting that **Jesus named Simon "Cephas",** Aramaic for "Peter", or rock.

# Jesus Calls his First Disciples

*Luke describes an event confirming the authority of Jesus that took place at Lake Gennesaret, or the Sea of Galilee. Jesus taught, brought about a miraculous catch of fish, and called four men to follow him.*

**J**ESUS STOOD AT the edge of the Sea of Galilee with the crowds pressing against him. Seeing two fishing boats at the edge of the water, he called to a fisherman, Simon Peter, got into his boat, and asked him to put out from the shore. Jesus then sat in the boat and taught God's word to the crowd: by sitting and teaching he revealed his authority (just as Moses had sat when he served as a judge for the people in Exodus 18:13). Jesus was also about to prove his authority with a sign of his Lordship over creation by performing a miracle on the Sea of Galilee.

### *The miraculous catch*

Jesus instructed Simon Peter to sail out into deeper water and to cast his nets. The fisherman replied,

### MIRACULOUS CATCH

*The Miraculous Draught of Fishes* (1516) by Raphael and his assistants, shows the two boats needed to deal with the great weight (or draught) of fish brought up from the Sea of Galilee.

## CALLING PETER AND ANDREW

*The Calling of SS Peter and Andrew* (1481), a fresco by Domenico Ghirlandaio, shows Jesus calling the two brothers to become his disciples – an event described in Mark's and Matthew's Gospels.

"Master, we've worked hard all night and haven't caught anything. But because you say so, I will let down the nets" (Luke 5:5) – showing not only faith but also obedience. The result was a huge catch, so big that when the fishermen tried to bring it in the nets tore and the boat began to sink. Simon Peter had to call his friends in another boat to help. For the witnesses of the event, this moment was a striking display of power, on a par with the mighty acts of God celebrated in the psalms: "The LORD does whatever pleases him… in the seas and all their depths" (Psalm 135:6).

### *Simon Peter is overcome*

Faced with the scale of Jesus' authority, Simon Peter was overwhelmed, as Luke's Gospel reveals: "When Simon Peter saw this, he fell at Jesus' knees and said, 'Go away from me, Lord; I am a sinful man!' For he and all his companions were astonished at the catch of fish they had taken, and so were James and John, the sons of Zebedee, Simon's partners" (Luke 5:8–10).

### *Isaiah recalled*

Simon Peter's words recalled Isaiah's cry in the Temple when he saw the majesty of God: "Woe to me… I am ruined! For I am a man

## "'Come, follow me', Jesus said, 'and I will send you out to fish for people.' At once they left their nets and followed him."

MARK 1:17,18

of unclean lips, and I live among a people of unclean lips, and my eyes have seen the King, the LORD Almighty" (Isaiah 6:5). Jesus reassured Simon Peter: "Don't be afraid; from now on you will fish for people."

### *Fishermen become followers*

The prophets of the Old Testament used images of "fishing for people" to illustrate inescapable judgment (Jeremiah 16:16; Ezekiel 29:4,5): the Babylonians were the fishermen, and the idolatrous Israelites were the fish. In this story, Jesus reverses the imagery: God will "catch" people and draw them to himself and into his family, and the "fishermen" will be the followers of Jesus.

### *Heeding the call*

Luke's story concludes: "So they pulled their boats up on shore, left everything and followed him" (Luke 5:11). By leaving their livelihoods, the four fishermen – Simon Peter, Andrew (the brother of Simon Peter), James, and John were giving themselves to the call of Jesus. Their new mission (to catch the souls of men, among both Jews and Gentiles) referred to Old Testament writings, such as the vision of Ezekiel in which he saw abundant fish in the Dead Sea (a place far too salty for fish), indicating the renewal of the world (Ezekiel 47:9,10).

**AFTER** »»

**Jesus moved to Capernaum and established an inner circle of disciples.**

### JESUS' HOME

After leaving Nazareth, Jesus lived in Capernaum on the north shore of the Sea of Galilee, **fulfilling the prophecy of Isaiah** (Matthew 4:15,16). The gospels mention the village no fewer than 16 times and Jesus **performed many miracles in or near Capernaum 314–15 »»**. The village was also home to his disciples Peter, Andrew, James, and John as well as Matthew.

A 12TH CENTURY MOSAIC SHOWING THE DISCIPLES JOHN, ANDREW, AND PETER

### ANALYSIS

## DISCIPLES AS LEARNERS

The Greek word for "disciple" appears 261 times in the New Testament and means "a learner". Traditionally, disciples were people who took the initiative to seek out a teacher or "rabbi" to train and mentor them. Learned rabbis welcomed would-be disciples who showed promise.

In contrast, Jesus sought out and chose his own disciples, who were ordinary, flawed people. Jesus described the heart of discipleship: "The student is not above the teacher, nor a servant above his master. It is enough for students to be like their teachers, and servants like their masters" (Matthew 10:24,25).

Although Jesus had scores of followers who are sometimes called "disciples", a number of whom donated money for the mission, the term is commonly used to refer specifically to "the Twelve", the inner circle of men. The 12 apostles (meaning those who were "sent out") all began as disciples (Matthew 10:1). So all apostles were disciples, but not all disciples became apostles (see pp.322–23).

**CAPERNAUM SYNAGOGUE**
The ruins of the synagogue at Capernaum date back to later than the time of Jesus. But excavations have also revealed an earlier structure at the site, with stone walls more than 1m (3ft) thick, which may have been where Jesus taught.

« **BEFORE**

**Jesus' presence in Capernaum began to attract large crowds.**

**NAHUM'S VILLAGE**
The name "Capernaum" seems to have derived from "Capher Nahum" – village of Nahum – and may have been **named after the Old Testament prophet Nahum** « **223**.

**OLD AUTHORITY**
Jesus's teachings were seen to be **in conflict with the teachers of the Law** – those who sat in synagogues in the Seat of Moses, an ancient symbol of authority.

**SEAT OF MOSES, WITH AN ARAMAIC INSCRIPTION, FROM THE SYNAGOGUE AT CHORAZIN, GALILEE**

# Miracles at Capernaum

*The coming of God announced by Isaiah was happening – the mission of Jesus had begun. He preached with great authority, emphasized by a number of miracles performed in his new home town of Capernaum.*

**J**ESUS ENTERED the synagogue at Capernaum and began to teach. Synagogues were meeting places where the Jews worshipped God, listened to the Scriptures, and received instruction from the teachers of the Jewish Law. Mark's Gospel does not record the lesson Jesus taught, but describes the response of the audience: "The people were amazed at his teaching, because he taught them as one who had authority, not as the teachers of the law" (Mark 1:22). Unlike the rabbis, who would always begin by referring to

the traditions of those who had taught before them, Jesus spoke directly and to the heart, without deference to anyone.

### Driving out demons and healing
In the synagogue there was a man possessed by an unclean spirit, a demon. The demon reacted sharply to Jesus, recognizing an invasion of its territory and the identity of the Messiah. "What do you want with us, Jesus of Nazareth? Have you come to destroy us? I know who you are – the Holy One of God!"(1:24). The people may have been slow to realize who Jesus

was, but the demons knew. Instead of rituals used by contemporary exorcists, Jesus' response was simple yet powerful. "'Be quiet!' said Jesus sternly. 'Come out of him!' The impure spirit shook the man violently and came out of him with a shriek" (1:25,26).

The great amazement of the crowd was a reaction to the miracle as well as to Jesus' ability to teach. The scribes in the synagogue could teach, but here was something radically new. News about Jesus' power and teaching spread quickly throughout the region of Galilee.

ANALYSIS

## DEMONS

The gospels and Acts mention demons many times. These entities are also referred to as "impure spirits" or "evil spirits" (Mark 1:23). They were represented as destructive and capable of inflicting terrible harm to people's bodies, minds, and emotions (Mark 5:1–5). Groups of demons seemed to be able to speak as a single spirit (Mark 1:21–26; 5:9).

**HAND OF MIRIAM JEWISH AMULET**

When driven out of a person, they could wander in "arid places", seeking a new body to inhabit (Matthew 12:43,44). Some thought Satan was their master (Mark 3:22–27). In Jesus' day Jews who performed exorcisms – the driving out of a demon – sometimes wore amulets, which were thought to confer protection. People distinguished demonic possession from "natural" illnesses.

> " The **people were all so amazed** that they asked each other, 'What is this? **A new teaching – and with authority**! He even gives orders to impure spirits and they obey him.' "
>
> **MARK** 1:27

Jesus left the synagogue and entered the house of his disciple Simon Peter. Simon's mother-in-law was bedridden with fever. Mark tells the story with brevity: Jesus took the sick woman by the hand and helped her up. "The fever left her and she began to wait on them" (1:31). Again, Jesus came in, and the fever went out. The events in the synagogue and this scene in Simon's house together showed Jesus' Lordship over both demons and sickness – both the spiritual and the physical realms. At sunset, "the whole town gathered at the door" (1:33). Jesus healed the sick and drove out demons. He forbade the demons to speak, since "they knew who he was". Scholars have debated why Jesus did this – possibly because if the crowds discovered at this early stage that he was the Messiah, his teaching ministry could become more difficult.(In John 7:8, Jesus indicates that there is both danger and a timescale within which he is working: "my time has not yet fully come".) Also, he did not want to be defined as a miracle worker.

### Jesus seeks solitude

Early the next day, while it was still dark, Jesus rose, left Simon Peter's house, and went to a quiet place to pray on his own. Simon Peter and his friends came looking for him. When they found him, they said "Everyone is looking for you!" (1:37). They wanted him to remain in Capernaum, but "Jesus replied, 'Let us go somewhere else – to the nearby villages – so that I can preach there also. That is why I have come'" (1:38). Jesus had left Simon Peter's house and would now take his message further afield. He had a mission from God and refused the request of the crowd to diverge from it, demonstrating his authority by refusing to let others dictate his actions. He went on and "...travelled throughout Galilee, preaching in their synagogues and driving out demons" (1:39).

#### HEALING AT A DISTANCE

John 4:46–54 records a miracle at Capernaum in which Jesus heals the (absent) son of a royal official. The official's pleading is recorded in *The Nobleman of Capernaum before Christ* by Veronese (1528–88).

**AFTER** ⟫

**After leaving Capernaum, Jesus tried to keep a low profile.**

#### CLEANSING OF A LEPER

In one of the villages around Capernaum, Jesus was stirred to **miraculously cleanse a man with leprosy**. Jesus was filled with compassion when the man "...came to him and begged him on his knees, 'If you are willing, you can make me clean'" (Mark 1:40). Jesus reached out and touched him and **the man was healed**. Jesus told him not to speak of this to anyone, but to go to the priest and fulfil the Jewish cleanliness customs. However, the man spread the news, and **Jesus' fame spread**.

## CHURCH OF THE BEATITUDES
The Mount of Beatitudes, near Capernaum, is where Jesus is said to have preached the Sermon on the Mount. The Franciscan church, overlooking the Sea of Galilee, was completed in 1938 and its octagonal floorplan represents the eight beatitudes.

## BEFORE

In his sermon Jesus draws on parallels with Moses to emphasise his authority for extending the spirit of the Law.

Moses was baptized in water, and **ascended a mountain to reveal God's truth <<< 106**.

**THE ROCK AS A SOLID FOUNDATION**
Moses called God himself a rock: "He is the Rock, his works are perfect, and all his ways are just" (Deuteronomy 32:4).

**THE SEAT OF JUDGMENT**
Moses "**took his seat** to serve as judge to the people" (Exodus 18:13) but then appointed others to help with this work.

**A TEACHER OF SPECIAL AUTHORITY**
Matthew reported that **God anointed Jesus with the Spirit <<< 301**.

## LISTS

### THE BEATITUDES

Jesus affirms the happiness of those who belong to his Kingdom, for their present suffering will not last. Happy are:

**1** The poor in spirit, who nevertheless turn to God.

**2** Those who mourn, who will be comforted.

**3** The meek, the lowly who do not thrust themselves forward at the expense of others.

**4** Those who hunger and thirst for righteousness, in themselves and in society.

**5** The merciful, who will be shown mercy.

**6** The pure in heart, whose whole hearts are opened to God.

**7** The peacemakers, who replace conflict with reconciliation.

**8** Those who are persecuted because of righteousness.

**JESUS TEACHING HIS FOLLOWERS**
This detail of Jesus addressing the crowd is from Cosimo Roselli's *Sermon on the Mount*, (c.1481–83), in the Vatican's Sistine Chapel. The young boy with the lamb is a reference to Jesus' sacrifice.

# Sermon on the Mount

*After Jesus had travelled throughout Galilee, teaching and healing, large crowds from across numerous regions gathered and followed him. So Jesus began to teach them a deeper understanding of the Scriptures.*

**W**HEN JESUS SAW the crowds from Syria, Galilee, the Decapolis, Jerusalem, Judea, and the region across the Jordan (Mathew 4:25), he went up a mountainside. He sat down and his disciples came to him.

Jesus began by teaching them eight "beatitudes" (see panel, left); these are statements that define, congratulate, and encourage God's faithful despite the challenges they face. Some echo the Old Testament promise of a healing redeemer who would bring "good news to the poor" and "comfort all who mourn" (Isaiah 61:1,2). Others state that those with little faith, the meek, and the persecuted who wait in faith for deliverance, all have reason to be happy despite their present circumstances, because they will be welcomed by God: "theirs is the kingdom of heaven" (Matthew 5:3).

### Jesus and Jewish Law

"Do not think that I have come to abolish the Law or the Prophets" (5:17). Jesus had come to fulfil the Hebrew Scriptures. His concern was to demonstrate that following the literal requirements of the Law was not sufficient; it was equally important to be faithful to God in one's heart and mind.

The Commandments said "You shall not murder" (5:21; Exodus 20:13), Jesus taught, but anger and contempt would also be judged; so reconciliation was important. "You shall not commit adultery" (5:27; Exodus 20:14), Jesus quoted, but for a man to look "lustfully" at a woman was adultery "in his heart" (5:28). A greater reward from God would be achieved for loving your enemies than loving those who you love already.

> **" But I tell you, love** your enemies and **pray** for those who **persecute you… "**
>
> **MATTHEW** 5:44

### Sermon for life

Jesus also taught about humility, non-retaliation ("turn… the other cheek", 5:39), giving to the needy (6:2,3), praying simply and privately (6:6–9), being forgiving and non-judgmental (6:14; 7:1), and trusting God to provide and not being driven by anxiety or seeking earthly wealth (6:19,25). "Ask and it will be given to you" (7:7). In all things, treat people as you would like to be treated (7:12).

Jesus warned of false prophets – "wolves in sheep's clothing" (7:15) – who would spread false teaching. Putting Jesus' words "into practice is like a wise man who built his house on the rock" (7:24, see Before panel); his life would have firm foundations. When storms came, the house would stand, unlike a house built on sand. The crowd was amazed that Jesus taught "as one who had authority", unlike their teachers of the law (7:29).

### ANALYSIS

#### THE LORD'S PRAYER

Jesus outlined a simple, private prayer. "This, then, is how you should pray" (Matthew 6:9). The opening line focuses on God and his honour: "Our Father in heaven, hallowed be your name" (6:9). Then came assertion of God's plan to establish his reign on Earth: "…your kingdom come, your will be done, on earth as it is in heaven" (6:10). Believers should ask for their needs: "Give us today our daily bread" (6:11). Forgiveness required a forgiving spirit: "And forgive us our debts, as we also have forgiven our debtors" (6:12). The prayer concluded with recognition of false paths and the need for deliverance: "And lead us not into temptation, but deliver us from the evil one" (also rendered as "from evil"; Matthew 6:13).

## AFTER

Jesus' Sermon on the Mount set a high standard for human conduct, but help with achieving this was offered by a compassionate Lord.

**GUIDANCE FROM JESUS**
The sermon outlined demands such that some listeners may have wondered, "Who can attain this?" However, later in Matthew another side to Christ's lordship is revealed: "Come to me, all you who are weary and burdened, and **I will give you rest**. Take my yoke upon you and learn from me, for I am gentle and humble in heart, and you will find rest for your souls. **For my yoke is easy and my burden is light**" (Matthew 11:28–30). Obedience to Jesus flowed out of knowing Jesus and finding strength, forgiveness, and rest in him.

## HISTORY AND CULTURE

# Jewish Rituals

> "For **six days work** is to be done, but the **seventh day** is a day of **sabbath rest**, holy to the LORD." EXODUS 31:15

**MEZUZAH**
This small case contains a piece of parchment inscribed with the words of the *Shema*. It is attached to the front door frame of Jewish homes, and sometimes on every door except the bathroom.

**SKULL-CAP AND TEFILLIN**
As well as a skull-cap, Jewish Orthodox men wear *tefillin*, bound to their head and left arm, at the morning synagogue service.

Leather strap made from the skin of a kosher animal

Passages from the Torah are sealed within each box

**J**ewish religious rituals changed considerably over the biblical period. Many started out as simple expressions of religious identity, but developed into more complex – and, for some Jews, essential – rituals of their religion involving things as diverse as childbirth, food, clothing, and prayer.

As it is in other religions, prayer is central to Judaism, and Jews are required to pray three times a day – in the morning, afternoon, and evening. On special occasions, a *tallit* (prayer shawl) may be worn by Jewish men (and in some traditions, by women) to cover their head when praying. It can be made of silk, linen, or wool – though never a mixture of materials – and must have a twined and knotted tassel (*tzitzit*) attached to each corner.

The *kippah* or skull-cap (also called a *yarmulke*) is probably the best-known item of Jewish apparel. It is used by Jewish men to cover their heads, as a sign of respect and to remind the wearer that God is constantly present. Some wear a *kippah* only when praying; the more orthodox always wear one.

The synagogue, the Jewish house of prayer, worship, and teaching, may have evolved during the Israelites' time in exile. It became central to religious and social life, especially after the destruction of the Temple in AD 70 (see p.467).

Embroidered and coloured stripes

Decorative fringe

**PRAYER SHAWL**
A *tallit* may be plain white or it may be embroidered and decorated, sometimes with black or blue stripes or with more elaborate patterns.

Tzitzit

## WASHING RITUALS

Unlike washing for reasons of hygiene, ritual washing makes a person clean from a specially defined "uncleanliness", and is a religious requirement the Jews shared with other cultures,

**WASHING CUP**
In ritual washing, water is poured onto each hand from a special cup three times.

including the Egyptians and Greeks (see p.339). Wide-ranging laws included the washing of hands and feet by priests (Exodus 30:17–21), washing after contact with a corpse (Leviticus 11:24–25; 17:15; Numbers 19:11–13), washing of clothes and body after recovery from skin diseases (Leviticus 14:1–9), and washing after bodily discharges (Leviticus 15).

Jewish Law requires that the hands be washed on a range of occasions, including at meals and before worship, using water from a special cup. However, on the occasions when full-body

**BEFORE PRAYER**
Orthodox Jewish men wash their hands before attending *Shabbat* prayers at the Western Wall in Jerusalem.

immersion is required, a *mikveh* is used, a specially constructed ritual bath connected to a natural water source such as a spring. For example, when a woman has finished menstruating each month, she must ritually clean herself in a mikveh.

## FOOD

The Bible's first food ritual stems from God's covenant with Noah after the flood when he was told he "must not eat meat that has its lifeblood still in it"(Genesis 9:3–4), so the blood must be drained from an animal after it has been slaughtered. Many centuries later, further food regulations were added as part of the Law given at Mount Sinai. Animals were divided into kosher or "clean" (permitted)

**AT THE TABLE**
Sharing a meal is an important part of Jewish life and traditionally each meal is begun with a blessing over the "breaking of the bread".

and "unclean" (forbidden) categories (Leviticus 11:1–47; Deuteronomy 14:3–21). Israelites were allowed to eat "any animal that has a divided hoof and that chews the cud", which included sheep, cattle, and deer, and excluded pigs. Fish were permitted if they had "fins and scales" and birds if they were not scavengers or birds of prey. While today such practices may be viewed as ensuring good hygiene, Jews also viewed these laws as an expression of holiness: a reminder that they should be different just as God was different (Leviticus 11:44–45).

Jewish dietary laws state that meat and dairy products cannot be eaten together, and a kosher household must have two sets of utensils and plates to keep them separate. While Jesus probably would have observed these dietary laws, he said that what came out of people's hearts rather than went into their stomachs was what made

## BABIES AND CHILDBIRTH

The ritual of circumcision, the removal of the foreskin, takes place when boys are eight days old. Though not exclusively a Jewish tradition, it remains an important ritual for many Jewish people and is considered to be a sign of being part of God's covenant (see p.51).

Naming, which would happen at a *Brit Milah* or circumcision ceremony, has always been extremely important, expressing either the parents' hopes for the child or the circumstances of his birth. The name may be in honour of a recently deceased relative.

When at least 30 days had passed since his birth, the firstborn son was presented in the Temple and then "redeemed" from priestly duties by the payment of five silver shekels. This practice, today called *Pidyon HaBen*, recalls the events of

the Exodus where the firstborn from each family was claimed by God for the role of priest.

Childbirth was thought to make the mother ritually unclean and so she had to undergo ritual purification. After 40 days for a boy or 80 days for a girl, she offered a sacrifice at the Temple to make herself ritually clean again.

**REDEMPTION OF THE FIRSTBORN SON**
A baby boy is draped in gold by his mother and family on presentation at the synagogue. He will be "bought back" for five pieces of silver.

### KEEPING KOSHER

There are many strictly kosher restaurants and fast food outlets where the Jewish dietary laws about ingredients and preparation are rigurously followed and closely monitored. At a kosher burger bar, cheeseburgers are not permitted as they mix meat and dairy.

them unclean (Mark 7:1–23). The early Christian Church eventually decided that such food laws were not binding for Christians (for example, Acts 10:11–15).

## THE SABBATH

The origins of the Sabbath are not certain – and before the Exile it seems to have been held once a month – but it is usually associated with the Creation story, where it is said that God rested after all his work, blessed the seventh day, and made it holy (Genesis 2:2–3). The word "rested" comes from the root of the Hebrew word for "Sabbath", *Shabbat*, and marks the divine pattern for living: six days of work, followed by one day of rest, a pattern still followed in Judaism and Christianity.

By New Testament times, Sabbath-keeping was strictly observed as a day of rest, renewal, and worship. Some Jewish leaders objected to Jesus healing people on a day of rest, but he replied: "The Sabbath was made for man, not man for the Sabbath" (Mark 2:27).

**BEFORE**

Jesus' ministry was all about restoration.

### THE PARALYSED MAN

Jesus was in **Capernaum 《 314–15** again and such large crowds gathered that when **a paralysed man was brought to him**, his friends had to lower him through the roof. Jesus declared the man's sins forgiven, and then commanded him to **get up and walk**. Spiritually and physically, the man was restored (Mark 2:1–12).

**HEALING THE PARALYSED MAN**

### FORGIVING THE TAX COLLECTOR

When Jesus joined a party at Levi the tax collector's house, the teachers of the Law took issue with Jesus **sharing a table with sinners**. He replied that **those with an illness need a doctor**; likewise, sinners (like Levi) need him to help them (2:13–17).

All of these scenes work together to portray the same message of **Jesus the restorer** – of life and health, of the relationship with God, **and of the Sabbath**.

**ANALYSIS**

### THE SABBATH

The Sabbath was not just a day of rest, but a sign that Israel belonged to God. Moses was instructed by God to tell the Israelites that: "You must observe my Sabbaths. This will be a sign between me and you for the generations to come, so you may know that I am the LORD, who makes you holy" (Exodus 31:13), meaning that God had set apart the people.

However, there were also man-made rules – strictly observed and enforced by the Pharisees – to prevent violation of the Sabbath. Tradition taught that a "Sabbath day's journey" (about 1km or ½ mile – the distance from the Mount of Olives to Jerusalem), was the maximum distance a pious Jew could walk on a Sabbath (see Acts 1:12). Yet the Law itself did not make such limitations.

# Challenges to the Sabbath

*The purpose of the Sabbath day was for people to be "restored" after six days of work (Exodus 20:8–11) and to be reminded of God's good creation. In this story, its true meaning became a flashpoint between Jesus and the Pharisees.*

**O**N A SABBATH day, Jesus and his disciples were walking through cornfields, and the disciples plucked some ears of corn. The Pharisees saw this and confronted Jesus, saying: "Look, why are they doing what is unlawful on the Sabbath?"(Mark 2:24). Such strict enforcement of the Sabbath was part of what Jesus called "human traditions" (7:8). The implication was that such traditions, created to ensure obedience to the Law and adherence to the Sabbath, could obscure its real intentions.

### Jesus answers his critics

Jesus replied from Scripture, asking his critics if they had forgotten the story of David (1 Samuel 21:1–6). Fleeing from Saul and desperate for food, David had taken some of the sacred bread "which is lawful only for priests to eat" (2:26). He had eaten the bread himself

> ## "The Sabbath was made for man, not man for the Sabbath. So the Son of Man is Lord even of the Sabbath."
> **MARK** 2:27,28

and given some to his companions on the Sabbath. The story Jesus referred to gives no sign of God's disapproval of David's act.

Jesus summed up his response to the Pharisees by stating that the Sabbath was made for man, and not vice-versa. People were not created to prop up the Sabbath – the purpose of the Sabbath was to lift burdens from them. It was a day for people to be physically, emotionally, and spiritually restored – a day of rest and recreation.

The second part of Jesus' response was a claim: "So the Son of Man is Lord even of the Sabbath" (2:28). He was stating that the Sabbath – the sacred day the Pharisees were dedicated to protecting – belonged to him as the Son of Man. In the next story, Jesus demonstrated this authority and emphasized the true purpose of the Sabbath.

### Sabbath power

On another Sabbath day, Jesus went into a synagogue. In the crowd was a man with a shrivelled hand. Jesus' opponents were watching him closely, eager to pounce on any violation of God's appointed day of rest. Healing this man would be such an offence.

Jesus told the man to stand up in front of everyone in the synagogue. Then he turned to the crowd and asked whether it was lawful to do good or to do evil – or to save someone's life or take a life – on the day of the Sabbath. The crowd remained silent. Jesus looked at the people and, "deeply distressed at their stubborn hearts,

**WORKING ON THE SABBATH**
Jesus' disciples were caught by the Pharisees plucking food from the fields on the Sabbath day. Jesus defended their actions, because they were doing so to satisfy their need, rather than because of greed.

## JESUS CURES AN INJURED MAN

This Byzantine mosaic shows Jesus healing the man's paralysed hand on the Sabbath. His action provoked anger from the Pharisees, who believed the Law did not allow healing on the Sabbath unless saving life.

### SYMBOLS

## HEALING THE SICK

Healing the sick was regarded by the gospel writers as a symbol of the advance of God's Kingdom in the world (Luke 10:9). Disease was variously interpreted, being seen as the work of Satan (Job 2:1–8), and also as a redemptive discipline from God (Isaiah 38:15,16). Blindness and deafness were sometimes seen as representing lack of spiritual understanding (Mark 8:18). Disease could make someone ceremonially unclean (Mark 1:40). Jesus healed by touch (Mark 1:41), by verbal command (Mark 2:11), by applying saliva (Mark 7:33), and by applying mud (John 9:6). Often he was moved with compassion for the needs of a sick person (Matthew 14:14, 20:34).

**THE HEALING OF THE LEPER**

### AFTER

**Jesus' mission placed him under increasing pressure.**

#### CRUSHED BY THE CROWD

The crowds that Jesus was attracting began to **impact on his activities**: "Because of the crowd he told his disciples to have a small boat ready for him, to **keep the people from crowding him**." (Mark 3:9). The word "crowding" here literally meant "crushing."

#### ENEMIES EARLY ON

The reaction to Jesus' synagogue healing was a **foretaste of things to come**. After Jesus had healed the paralysed man, "the **Pharisees 366–67 »** went out and began to **plot with the Herodians** how they might kill Jesus" (Mark 3:6). The Herodians were members of a political party who viewed Jesus' popularity as a threat.

said to the man, 'Stretch out your hand.' He stretched it out, and his hand was completely restored" (3:5). The use of the words "completely restored" is significant here – the man's hand was put back the way it was meant to be.

Therefore, in these two Sabbath stories, Jesus re-established the true meaning of the Sabbath: restoration. It was a response that angered the Pharisees (see 3:6).

> " Which is **lawful on the Sabbath**: to **do good** or to **do evil**, to **save life** or to **kill?**"

MARK 3:4

JESUS' CHOSEN MESSENGERS *c.* AD 27–30

# The Twelve Apostles

## "He appointed twelve that they might be with him and that he might send them out to preach…"

MARK 3:14–16

**PRAYERS ON THE MOUNTAIN**
Mount Arbel, overlooking the Sea of Galilee, may be the site at which Jesus prayed before choosing his apostles – an event reported in the gospels of Mark and Luke.

**T**HE GOSPELS OF Mark and Luke both tell the story of the appointing of the 12: "One of those days Jesus went out to a mountainside to pray, and spent the night praying to God. When morning came, he called his disciples to him and chose twelve of them, whom he also designated apostles" (Luke 6:12). In this way, Jesus asserted

**JESUS WITH THE APOSTLES**
This 15th-century German painting shows Jesus with his 11 apostles and Paul – holding a sword – who takes the place of Judas. Each apostle carries a symbol that has become associated with their life.

his authority: he decided how many, he chose them, he called them, he appointed them; and they showed obedience by coming to Jesus.

### What is an apostle?
Mark's gospel also says that Jesus "appointed" the 12. The idea of appointing was very different to the "calling" of the fishermen at Galilee (see pp.312–13). All of his followers were "disciples" (learners), but only the 12 were given this special authority. Mark emphasized three important aspects of apostleship: a close relationship

with Christ ("that they might be with him"); an authority to proclaim the gospel ("to preach"); and a special mandate from Jesus for spiritual warfare ("to have authority to drive out demons").

### Who were the apostles?
The 12 apostles are named in Mark's gospel: Simon (later known as Peter, or *Cephas* in Aramaic), James and John (brothers, also called *Boanerges*, or "sons of thunder"), Andrew (brother of Simon), Philip, Matthew (also called Levi), Bartholomew (also

called Nathanael), Thomas (also called *Didymus*, or "twin"), James son of Alphaeus, Thaddaeus (also called Judas son of James), Simon the Zealot, and Judas Iscariot. Almost nothing is known about the lives of Bartholomew, James son of Alphaeus, and Thaddaeus.

Simon was a fisherman from Capernaum to whom Jesus gave the name Peter, meaning "rock".

Jesus took Simon Peter – or Peter for short – with him to witness the Transfiguration (Mark 9:2). Simon Peter denied knowing Jesus after his arrest, but later he was restored to the chosen group, and is notable in the book of Acts as an important leader in the Early Church.

James and John, like Simon Peter, were fishermen, and were noted for their outspokenness. For example, when a Samaritan village denied Jesus and his disciples entry – since they were Jews travelling on the way to Jerusalem – James and John wanted to "call down fire" on the town (Luke 9:54–56).

Along with Simon Peter, James and John formed Jesus' inner circle; Jesus included the three of them in special moments of revelation and relationship with himself (Matthew 17:1; Mark 14:33). Traditionally, John has been identified as "the disciple whom Jesus loved" (John 13:23) and as the author of the fourth gospel, the book of Revelation, and the three epistles that bear his name.

Andrew was a fisherman and the brother of Simon Peter, whom he introduced to Jesus after following John the Baptist (John 1:35–41).

Philip came from Bethsaida (John 1:44) and is known for asking Jesus to show the Father to the disciples (John 14:8), and for his exclamation that not even eight month's wages would buy enough bread to feed the 5,000 (John 6:5–7).

Matthew was a tax collector (Matthew 9:9) at Capernaum, who would have collected taxes from the Jews for Herod Antipas. Christian tradition holds that he wrote the gospel that bears his name.

Thomas is best known as the doubter, since he believed in Jesus' resurrection only after seeing the scars of the risen Christ (John 20:24–29). Tradition claims that Thomas taught the gospel beyond the Roman Empire, as far as India.

Simon the Zealot receives little coverage in the gospels: he may have been a member of The Zealots – a radically anti-Roman group.

Judas Iscariot is described in Mark 3:19 as the man "who betrayed him [Jesus]". John sees Judas' role as in some inscrutable sense preeordained by God (John 17:12). After his betrayal of Jesus, Judas was seized with remorse and hanged himself (Matthew 27:5).

---

## SYMBOLS

### THE NUMBER 12

In Scripture the number 12 suggests fullness. The patriarch Jacob had 12 sons, who in turn became the fathers of the 12 tribes of Israel (Genesis 35:22, 49:28). When Jesus appointed 12 Israelites to be apostles, he was echoing this Old Testament story – and pointing to a renewed nation of Israel (Luke 22:30). Later, in the Book of Revelation, the perfection of the new Jerusalem is seen in its 12 gates and 12 foundations.

**THE FATHERS OF THE 12 TRIBES OF ISRAEL, FROM A 14TH-CENTURY BIBLE**

---

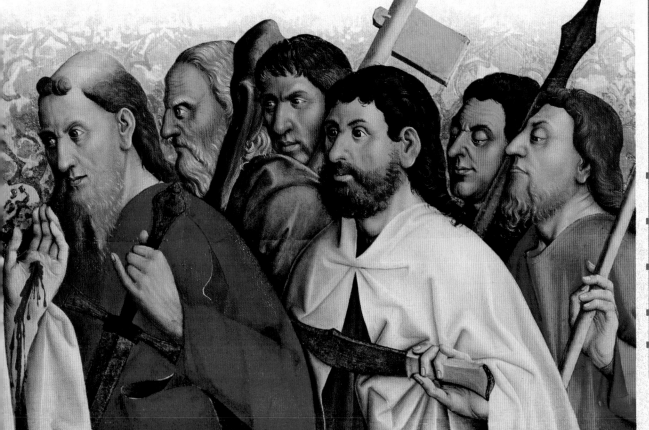

## « BEFORE

**Jesus healed the loyal servant of a Roman centurion at Capernaum. He was moved to heal the man because of the centurion's great faith.**

### RETURN TO CAPERNAUM
After preaching to the crowds in the countryside, Jesus made his way back to his home **in Capernaum « 313**.

### THE CENTURION'S SERVANT
A servant who was highly valued by his master became gravely ill. The master, a Roman centurion who knew of Jesus' reputation, sent messengers to **ask Jesus to come to his house**. When Jesus was not far from the house the centurion sent word, "Don't trouble yourself, for I do not deserve to have you come under my roof. That is why I did not even consider myself worthy to come to you. But **say the word, and my servant will be healed**. For I myself am a man under authority, with soldiers under me" (Luke 7:6–8). The Roman centurion's reasoning was that just as he could give orders to his soldiers, **so Jesus could command healing** to come to a sick man. He was right. Jesus granted the request and the servant recovered.

## LISTS

### DEAD BROUGHT TO LIFE

1 Elijah raises the son of the widow at Zarephath (1 Kings 17:21,22).

2 The son of the Shunammite woman is raised by Elisha (2 Kings 4:34,35).

3 The daughter of Jairus, a synagogue leader, is raised by Jesus (Luke 8:54,55).

4 Lazarus of Bethany is raised from his tomb after four days by Jesus (John 11:43,44).

5 Peter raises Tabitha ("Dorcas" in Greek), a charitable woman in Joppa (Acts 9:40).

6 Paul raises Eutychus after he falls from a third storey window while asleep (Acts 20:9–12).

**FUNERAL PROCESSION**
This 1st-century Roman relief shows a funeral procession. The grieving widow would have headed the procession, followed by men carrying the casket or "bier", which was forbidden to touch the ground. The casket would have been buried, the Jews believing cremation to be a heathen practice.

# The Widow's Son

*Travelling from town to town, Jesus met a widow, heartbroken by the death of her son. Filled with compassion, Jesus restored him to life and showed his superiority over the power of death.*

**J**ESUS WENT TO Nain, a small town on the slope of the Hill of Moreh in Galilee, accompanied by his disciples and a large crowd of followers. On arrival, he met another crowd leaving the town – this was a funeral procession led by a grieving widow, taking the body of her son for burial. It was customary for women to lead such processions, which often included professional mourners as well neighbours who believed that taking a body to its resting place constituted "good work". Burial grounds were usually located a short distance outside the town.

Luke condensed the opening of the story to a brief moment: "As [Jesus] approached the town gate, a dead person was being carried out." The dead man was "the only son of his mother, and she was a widow". Jesus responded emotionally to the plight of the bereaved mother, as Luke's gospel says: "When the Lord saw her, his heart went out to her and he said, 'Don't cry'" (Luke 7:13).

### Jesus the Lord
For biblical scholars, it is significant that Luke's gospel refers to Jesus as "the Lord" because the gospels do not often use this title for Jesus: "the Lord" usually means God. So the person whom the grieving woman met was not just another sympathetic neighbour, but the Lord – the embodiment of divine authority. Jesus' appeal to the woman not to cry was more than an expression of his compassion, but a preamble to victory – because "the Lord" was about to prove himself superior to the power of death – the first occurrence of a miracle in the New

> **"The dead man sat up** and began to talk, and **Jesus gave him back to his mother."**
>
> LUKE 7:15

**VILLAGE OF NAIN**
Around 40km (25 miles) southwest of Capernaum, Nain is mentioned only once in the Bible. Located on the hillside Givat Hamoreh ("the Hill of Moreh"), the village faces west towards the Jezreel Valley.

Testament where a dead person is brought back to life. The story also provides a contrast to the healing of the centurion's servant (see Before panel, left). The centurion was a Gentile, a powerful member of the ruling class, while the widow was of low status, suggesting that Jesus reached out to all people in his ministry.

### Raised from the dead
Jesus approached the coffin (which would most likely have been an open wicker container holding the shrouded body) and touched it. Then Jesus said to the man: "Young man, I say to you, get up!" (7:14). The immediate result was proof that Jesus was indeed "the Lord": the young man sat up and began to talk. In a final act of compassion, Jesus presented the son back to his mother.

### A sign of commitment
The crowd's response to the miracle provides another dimension to this biblical story. Luke reports that the witnesses to the event were filled with awe: "'A great prophet has appeared among us,' they said. 'God has come to help his people'" (7:16). For them, the miracle also showed God's commitment to Israel.

**RAISED FROM THE DEAD**
This scene from a 15th-century triptych shows Jesus raising the young man outside the town walls. The crowd is in awe because only the great prophets, such as Elijah and Elisha, had ever raised the dead.

ANALYSIS

## WIDOWS

**A STAINED GLASS PANEL BY WALTER CRANE (1845–1915) DEPICTING A WEEPING WIDOW**

Widowhood in the 1st century placed a woman low on the social scale. God commanded Israel to care for widows: "Do not take advantage of the widow or the fatherless" (Exodus 22:22). However, Israel did not always heed these laws, and widows were often exploited or neglected. Mercy to widows is a recurring theme in the Bible: for example, Elisha drew on God's power to save a widow from losing her children to a creditor (2 Kings 4) and Jeremiah warned that care of widows was a condition for the people of Israel remaining in the Promised Land (Jeremiah 7:6,7).

## AFTER

The scene that followed the resurrection at Nain suggests that John the Baptist – now in prison – was having doubts about Jesus.

### ARE YOU TRULY THE ONE?
**John sent messengers to Jesus** with a question: "Are you the one who is to come, or should we expect someone else?" (Luke 7:19). Luke's gospel suggests a possible reason why John may have asked the question: John as a Nazarite did not drink wine, but Jesus did (Luke 7:33,34) and **this may have offended John**. Jesus answered by highlighting his actions (the blind see, the lame walk): John needed only to remember the promise of Isaiah 61 and to recognize the deliverance that Jesus was bringing.

**JOHN THE BAPTIST BY FRANCESCO DA SANGALLO (1496–1576)**

## BEFORE

**The prophets foretold that God's people would be exiled but the Spirit would be restored to them.**

### RESCUING A FALLEN PEOPLE

God's people had failed to follow God's will ≪ **230–31:** "You have seen many things, but you pay no attention; your ears are open, but you do not listen" (Isaiah 42:20). Therefore they became a people "plundered and looted... **with no one to rescue them**" (42:22).

### THE LIGHT OF THE SPIRIT

Nothing remains hidden: "The human spirit is the lamp of the LORD that sheds light on one's inmost being" (Proverbs 20:27). **Isaiah prophesied that the glory of God would rise upon his people,** for their "light has come" (Isaiah 60:1). This redeemer would restore God's people by the power of the Spirit and then, across the world, "Nations will come to your light, and kings to the brightness of your dawn" (60:3). As the **prophet Ezekiel foretold ≪ 240–41,** "...I will put my Spirit in you** and move you to... keep my laws" (Ezekiel 36:27).

**A 2ND-CENTURY ROMAN LAMP WITH VICTORY STANDING ON A GLOBE**

## PEOPLE

### THE FAMILY OF JESUS

Jesus' lineage to King David, and ultimately Abraham, is attested by Matthew and Luke. Joseph was a direct descendant of David (Matthew 1:6–16,20), and some take Luke's description of Joseph as "son of Heli" (Luke 3:23) to be "son-in-law of Heli", which would make Mary a direct descendant from David.

Jesus' immediate family is far less clear. The Greek word used to describe his "brothers" – *adelphoi* – meant both brothers and close kinsfolk. James, Joseph, Simon, and Judas were all described as Jesus' "adelphoi" (Matthew 13:55). James became a leader in the church (Acts 15:13; see pp.440–41). Judas may have been the author of the epistle of Jude. Unnamed sisters are also mentioned: "Aren't all his sisters with us?" (Matthew 13:56).

# You are my Brothers and Sisters

*As Jesus' fame spread, some said that his actions and behaviour were the result of madness or possession. However, he reminded people about the Spirit of God and said that those who followed him would be his true family.*

**J**ESUS WAS BECOMING well known, and people quickly gathered around him. At one point, he entered a house and the crush of people was so intense that he could not eat. His family heard about this, and came quickly, saying, "He is out of his mind" (Mark 3:21).

Because Jesus had been curing people taken over "...by an impure spirit" (Mark 1:23), the teachers of the Law from Jerusalem thought they knew what was wrong with him: "He is possessed by Beelzebul! By the prince of demons he is driving out demons" (Mark 3:22).

### A house divided cannot stand

Jesus responded to the teachers gathered in the house, saying that it was ridiculous for Satan to drive out himself. For Satan to oppose himself was to weaken himself, and thus bring his own downfall.

Jesus continued that the house of a strong man could only be plundered if the man was first tied up. The implication was that Jesus was able to overpower the strong man (the devil).

Jesus questioned the teachers on their assumption that only a demon could drive out a demon, saying "by whom do your people drive them out?" (Matthew 12:27). Then he warned them that they should be careful about their suppositions: "if it is by the Spirit of God that I drive out demons, then the kingdom of God has come upon

**CHRIST AND THE DEMON**
This detail is from the doors of Pisa Cathedral, Italy. Cast by students of sculptor Giambologna, the doors replaced the originals that were destroyed by fire in 1595. Jesus is shown driving out a demon.

you" (Matthew 12:28). To call this power "an impure spirit" (Mark 3:30), to attribute the Spirit's work to the devil and so reject it, was the same as speaking "against the Holy Spirit" (Matthew 12:32). Jesus explained that this was blasphemy: "Truly I tell you, people can be forgiven all their sins and every slander they utter, but whoever blasphemes against the Holy Spirit will never be forgiven; they are guilty of an eternal sin" (Mark 3:28,29). God had put his Spirit on Jesus after his baptism (see pp.300–01).

### My true family listens

Jesus' family sent someone into the house. "Your mother and brothers are… outside, wanting to see you," he said. Jesus gestured about him, saying "My mother and brothers are those who hear God's word and put it into practice"(Luke 8:20,21).

By presuming to describe Jesus as out of his mind, his family set themselves outside Jesus' circle,

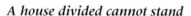

> " If a **kingdom** is **divided against itself,** that kingdom **cannot stand.** "
>
> **MARK** 3:24

emphasized by their physical separation from him outside the house. Those inside the house showed trust by sitting in a circle about Jesus, ready to be taught. These people were his family.

## AFTER

**Jesus predicted that he would be the cause of families being divided against each other (Luke 12:51–53).**

### THE NEW FAMILY

In the New Testament, **Christians became part of the "family of Jesus"** – but they had to become his disciples first. Jesus' response to his waiting family may seem abrupt, but was an example of how he saw the world differently – family included.

Jesus stated that his Father was the one that the people claimed as their God (see John 8:54), and he echoed the warning of **John the Baptist ≪ 298–99** to the Jewish crowds not to rely on their lineage from Abraham to save them: God could "raise up children for Abraham" from the stones on the ground, John had said (Luke 3:8). Belonging to the family would require obedience and faith **360–61 ≫ "Whoever belongs to God hears what God says.** The reason you do not hear is that you do not belong to God" (John 8:47).

## BEFORE

Jesus' criticism of the Pharisees was a response to their refusal to be baptized by John.

### REJECTING GOD'S PURPOSE

The scene in Simon's house was part of a bigger picture. **On one side were the many people, including tax collectors 374–75 》,** who had obediently humbled themselves and "acknowledged that God's way was right, because they had been baptized by John" (Luke 7:29). On the other side were "**the Pharisees 366–67 》** and the experts in the law [who] rejected God's purpose for themselves, because they had not been baptized by John" (7:30). Jesus' words addressed their disapproving comments about John ("He has a demon") and Jesus ("a friend of... sinners"). Jesus compared the people to children in a market saying to each other "We played the pipe for you, and you did not dance..." (7:32). **God would embrace those who accepted his purpose** in John and Jesus, for "wisdom is proved right by all her children" (7:35).

**A 4TH-CENTURY SILVER AND BRONZE *AULOS* OR WIND INSTRUMENT**

ANALYSIS

## MONEYLENDING

The Bible took a guarded view of lending money. It was forbidden to charge interest on a loan to a fellow Israelite. Even the taking of pledges (such as a man's cloak) was closely regulated – the pledge had to be returned the same day, "by sunset" (Exodus 22:25–27).

However, the charging of interest to a non-Israelite was permitted (Deuteronomy 23:20). During the rebuilding of Judah after the Exile, Nehemiah spoke out against Jews who kept their brothers in debt through the charging of interest on loans (Nehemiah 5:6–13).

When giving his disciples the Lord's Prayer, Jesus used debt cancellation as an image of forgiveness: "And forgive us our debts, as we also have forgiven our debtors" (Matthew 6:12). The same idea stood behind the two debtors parable in Luke 7.

### IN THE HOUSE OF SIMON

A 14th-century painted panel from a folding altar, made in Nuremberg, depicts Jesus dining with Simon the Pharisee at the moment when a woman dries Jesus' feet with her hair, before anointing them with perfume.

# A Woman Anoints Jesus' Feet

*Occurring early in Jesus' ministry, while he is still in Galilee, this story about a woman washing Jesus' feet with her tears and perfume signifies that Jesus' message is open to everyone – sinners included.*

A PHARISEE NAMED Simon invited Jesus to his house for a meal. As Simon and his guest were reclining at the table, a woman in the town who "lived a sinful life" (Luke 7:37) learned that Jesus was there and came and stood behind him with an alabaster jar of perfume. She began weeping and her tears fell on his feet. "Then she wiped them [his feet] with her hair, kissed them and poured perfume on them" (7:38).

Something – Luke's Gospel does not say what – had prompted the woman to come to Jesus. Perhaps she had heard him preach. She may have heard him teaching "love your enemies … and lend to them without expecting to get anything back" (6:35). Or she may have heard about God being "kind to the ungrateful and wicked" (Luke 6:35), and had realized this meant that God could and would forgive even her.

### The debtors' parable

Jesus' host took offence at the woman's presence, and when he saw what she had done he said to himself, "If this man were a prophet, he would know who is touching him and what kind of woman she is – that she is a sinner" (7:39). Jesus sensed the

**DECANTING PERFUME INTO A VIAL**
According to classical tradition, the gods were famously sweet scented. Roman women, as in this 1st-century fresco, carried perfume in vials.

Pharisee's criticism and posed a question to his host. A certain moneylender had two debtors, Jesus said. One owed a large sum, the other a much smaller one. When neither could pay him back, the creditor cancelled both their debts. Which of the debtors would love their creditor more?

The Pharisee replied, "I suppose the one who had the bigger debt forgiven" (7:43). The answer was the correct one, and Jesus said so.

However, Jesus pressed on, describing the stark contrast between the tepid welcome Simon had given him – no water to wash

his feet, no kiss as a greeting, no oil for his head – and the demonstration of love shown by the woman. She had wet his feet with her tears, dried them with her hair, kissed them, and anointed them with perfume.

The parable of the two debtors illustrated what was taking place at the table. A sinner, the debtor with the large debt, had come with an act of extravagant love. A comparatively upright man, the debtor with a smaller debt, had come with a love that was restrained and lukewarm. The sinner showed that she understood what it was to be forgiven, but the upright man did not.

### A parting benediction

"Your sins are forgiven" (7:48), Jesus told the woman. Another translation renders his words "Your sins have been forgiven", pointing to something that had already taken place. Jesus was seeing her love as the love of one whose debt was cancelled; the woman already knew that she had been forgiven. She did not wash Jesus' feet to be forgiven, but because she knew she already was.

Some of the guests took offence at Jesus' declaration, saying "Who is this who even forgives sins?" (7:49). Jesus ignored them, and said to the woman: "Your faith has saved you; go in peace" (7:50). Her trust in God had served to close off the past ("Your faith has saved you"). Now, God's Son, with words of forgiveness, was authorizing her to start again, to go on her way, and to live her life on the right terms with God: "Go in peace."

> " Therefore, I tell you, **her many sins have been forgiven – as her great love has shown**. But whoever has been forgiven little loves little. "
>
> LUKE 7:47

## A SINFUL WOMAN

The image of the prostitute is used in the Bible as a symbol of the sinful nation, from Genesis 38:21 to Proverbs 7:10 to Hosea 4:14. Perhaps the most serious references compared idolatrous Israel to a prostitute, and the false gods to her clients (Ezekiel 6:9; 16:25). However, the same prophet also promised redemption: "I will cleanse you from all your impurities and from all your idols" (Ezekiel 36:25). Grace for those selling sexual services was also reflected in Jesus' rebuke of the chief priests: "Truly I tell you, the tax collectors and the prostitutes are entering the kingdom of God ahead of you" (Matthew 21:31).

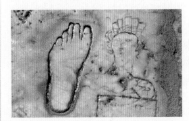

**A 1ST-CENTURY STREET ENGRAVING AT THE ENTRANCE TO A BROTHEL IN EPHESUS**

## AFTER

After the story of the anointing, Luke's Gospel makes it clear that women played a vital role in Jesus' ministry.

### LOYAL SUPPORTERS

Luke revealed that **many women responded to Jesus' message** by helping to finance his ministry. Among those travelling with Jesus and the apostles "from one town and village to another" (Luke 8:1), places such as Tiberias and Magdala, there were "also some women who had been cured of evil spirits and diseases… [who] were helping to support them out of their own means" (8:2,3). They included **Mary Magdalene 331 »**, Joanna wife of Chuza, and Susanna (8:3).

**AN EARLY 20TH-CENTURY PHOTOGRAPH OF TIBERIAS**

# The Sower and the Seed

*Jesus travelled, proclaiming the good news about the Kingdom of God, and large crowds gathered to listen. One day he likened his message to potent seed that could produce an amazing harvest, if it took root in its hearers.*

**E**ARLY ON, JESUS drew around him a collection of people of different backgrounds, all of whom had embraced his message. Mark records that in addition to the 12 apostles, there were several women. Some of the women had been cured of evil spirits and diseases (such as Mary Magdalene, see panel, right), while others were women who supported the group "out of their own means" (Luke 8:3), such as Susanna and Joanna, the wife of the manager of Herod Antipas's household.

### A farmer went out to sow

One day, as a large crowd gathered around him by a lake, Jesus said, "Listen!" (Mark 4:3). He then told a story about a farmer who went into his fields and scattered seed.

«

### BEFORE

Jesus' parables used everyday images to visualize spiritual realities.

**LANGUAGE OF THE GARDEN**
In biblical times most families – even non-farmers – would have had modest garden-plots. So images of hard-packed paths, birds stealing seed, rocky soil, fruitful soil, and so forth would have been familiar to those listening to Jesus. The story would also have reminded them of agriculture-based festivals such as **the Feast of Harvest (see Exodus 23:16)** « 182.

Some fell on the path, and the birds came and ate it. Some fell on shallow, stony earth where there was no moisture – the plants sprouted, but then withered. Some of the seed fell among thorns, and got choked by them. But some seed fell on good soil and yielded crops "thirty, some sixty, some a hundred times" more than was sown (Mark 4:20). Then Jesus called out, "Whoever has ears to hear, let them hear" (4:9).

### God's word

The disciples asked him what this parable meant. So Jesus went on to explain that the seed was God's word – the gospel, the good news of the Kingdom. The various landing places for the seed were groups of people with particular responses to the word. The people represented by the hard-packed path were those for whom the word remained on the surface; the birds (the adversary) came and stole the word. The rocky ground represented those people who initially embraced the gospel but had no root. When they were tested, they fell away. The thorny ground represented those people who were preoccupied with "life's worries,

> " The **knowledge** of the secrets **of the kingdom of God** has been given to you, but **to others I speak in parables…** "
>
> LUKE 8:10

riches and pleasures" (Luke 8:14) – they bore no lasting fruit. But in contrast to all these, there was a fourth group, "those with a noble and good heart, who hear the word, retain it, and by persevering produce a crop" (Luke 8:15).

### The names of the good

Some scholars believe that Jesus' description of this last group may have been intended to reflect the mixed group that accompanied him – the men and women described by Luke at the beginning of the scene (Luke 8:1–3).

The inclusion of this list of people may not be an incidental detail, but part of the message Luke aimed to communicate. He is emphasizing the importance of being a faithful recipient of the word, whatever one's background might be.

The parable of the sown seeds invited people to reflect on what could hinder the acceptance of a powerful, liberating

**THE SEED-SOWER**
A farmer sows pomegranate seed by hand in the Shephelah region of Israel, just as the sower in Jesus' parable would have done. Jesus said his parables were for those who "though seeing, they may not see; though hearing, they may not understand" (Luke 8:10)

message – not everyone's quality of character led to a fruitful response. The parable's main point was encouraging – what would have astonished its listeners was the amazing potency of the seed in good soil. A tenfold yield was considered a good harvest, but a hundredfold return was now possible.

### The power of parables

"Jesus spoke all these things to the crowd in parables; he did not say anything to them without using a parable" (Matthew 13:34). As a seed would need to grow and mature, so a believer would need to be able to listen and understand.

Animal horn or other spike scratched through the stony soil, rather than turning it over

A piece of strong wood, such as oak, cut from a young tree

### ANCIENT PLOUGH
On this simple scratch plough from the ancient Near East, the wooden frame mounts a spike of wood, animal horn, or even metal. By telling parables that his audience could relate to, Jesus engaged the peasant farmers in the villages of Galilee.

## SOWING THE SEED

A stained glass window (c.1880s) from St. Mary's church, South Walsham, UK, depicts the sower of the seed. The seed is shown being ploughed into the ground in the left panel, while the right depicts a hopeful future though a symbolic rainbow.

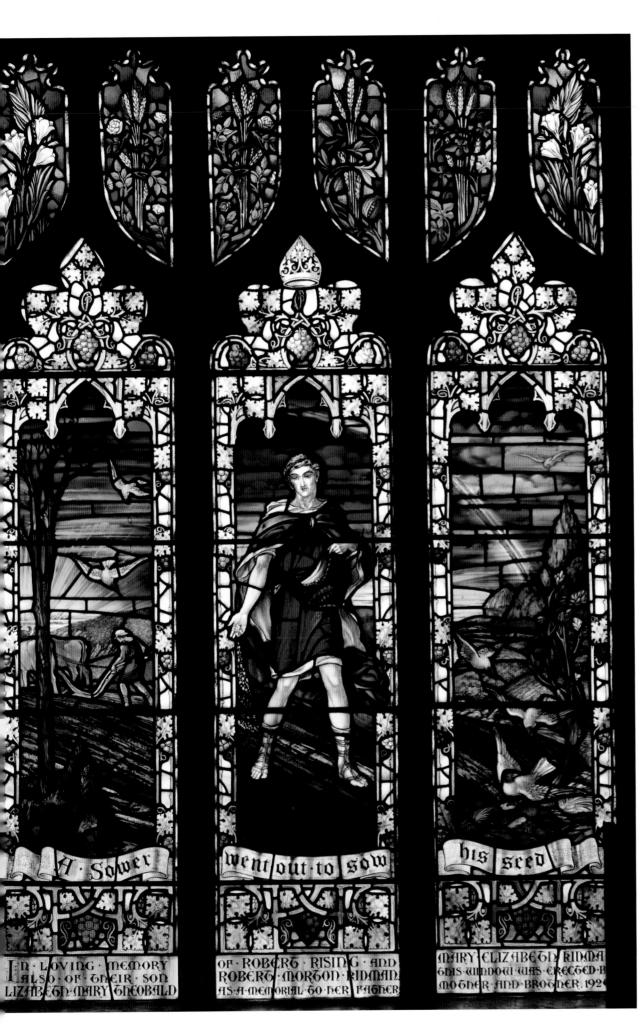

A Sower went out to sow his seed

IN · LOVING · MEMORY ALSO · OF · THEIR · SON LIZABETH·MARY·THEOBALD

OF · ROBERT · RISING · AND ROBERT · MORTON · RIDMAN AS · A · MEMORIAL · TO · HER · FATHER

MARY·ELIZABETH·RIDMAN THIS·WINDOW·WAS·ERECTED·BY MOTHER·AND·BROTHER·192⟨

### PEOPLE

## MARY MAGDALENE

*THE REPENTANT MAGDALENE*, **BY EL GRECO**, c.1577

Mary, or "Miriam" in her own Hebrew, came from a fishing village on Lake Galilee called Magdala. She was thus known as "the Magdalene" to indicate her origins. If she had been married, she would have been called after her husband. Jesus delivered her from "seven demons" (Luke 8:2) and she then accompanied him as part of the mixed group described by Luke. Mary was one of the women who watched Jesus' crucifixion "from a distance" (Mark 15:40), and she was present when he was buried (see Mark 15:47). As the first to see the risen Christ at the tomb, she was sent as his messenger to inform the disciples (see John 20:1–17).

## AFTER

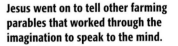

**Jesus went on to tell other farming parables that worked through the imagination to speak to the mind.**

### GERMS OF BELIEF

The parable of the growing seed (see Mark 4:26–29) describes **how the Kingdom of God grows once planted**. That of the mustard seed (see Mark 4:30–32; Matthew 13:31) explains that the Kingdom begins very small but becomes great when fully grown. In the parable of the weeds (see Matthew 13:24–43), followers should **leave the judgment of unfruitful companions to God**, who would separate out his harvest at "the end of the age" (13:40).

HISTORY AND CULTURE

# Farming and Fishing

"I will send you **rain in its season**, and the **ground shall yield its crops** and the **trees** their **fruit**." LEVITICUS 26:4

**FIELDS OF BARLEY**
Barley was ground to make flour for bread or fermented to make beer. Like millet and wheat, it was cultivated from wild varieties of grass.

**PLOUGHING**
Teams of oxen were commonly used to work the land in the ancient Near East, breaking the soil in preparation for sowing crops. This wooden Egyptian model dates from 2000 BC.

The farming year began with the "former" or early rains falling in early October and softening the ground. Fields were ploughed with a bronze or iron ploughshare, usually pulled by oxen. This was followed by sowing, when seed was scattered on to the ground by hand, often by people following the plough. Crop growth was aided by the main rains in January. During this time, peas, lentils, melons, and cucumbers were planted. The "latter", or later, rains in March and April helped grain crops to swell in preparation for harvest. Barley and flax were cut in April and May, wheat in June. After threshing, the mixture of grain and chaff was winnowed – tossed into the air so the straw was blown aside while the heavier grain fell to the ground.

**THRESHING**
Separating grain from its stalks was accomplished either by beating the stalks with sticks or by running over them using a threshing sledge (below). Such wooden sledges are still in use in parts of modern Egypt.

## THE FARMING YEAR

| | | |
|---|---|---|
| 1 | **Nissan** (March/April) | The latter rains |
| 2 | **Iyar** (April/May) | Barley harvest begins |
| 3 | **Sivan** (May/June) | Vine-tending; wheat harvest |
| 4 | **Tamuz** (June/July) | Grape harvest begins |
| 5 | **Ab** (July/August) | Full heat of summer |
| 6 | **Elul** (August/September) | Date and fig harvest |
| 7 | **Tishrei** (September/October) | Former rains; ploughing begins |
| 8 | **Marcheshvan** (October/November) | Ploughing; olive harvest |
| 9 | **Kislev** (November/December) | Wheat and barley sowing |
| 10 | **Tevet** (December/January) | The main rains |
| 11 | **Shebat** (January/February) | Almonds blossom |
| 12 | **Adar** (February/March) | Citrus harvest; flax harvest |

**90** The minimum percentage of people who survived by working the land. Even those who did not cultivate crops were dependent on the land to provide food and clothing.

## GRAINS AND PULSES

Cereals were crucial, as bread made from wheat or barley flour was a staple of the Israelite diet (see p.305). The earliest varieties of wheat were covered with a tough husk, which was difficult to remove by threshing, so they were replaced by durum wheat, which has naked grains. Lentils could be combined with grains and ground into flour to make cakes. They were also used in soups, pastes, and purées.

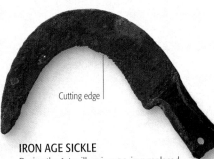

Cutting edge

### IRON AGE SICKLE
During the 1st millennium BC, iron replaced bronze in the manufacture of sickles, used to harvest grain, but the shape remained unchanged.

## FRUIT CROPS

Grape vines were grown in vineyards and, later, over trellises on rooftops. The grapes picked from them were consumed in a variety of ways: eaten fresh, dried as raisins, or turned into wine. Other cultivated fruits included melons, pomegranates, apples, and dates. Figs were eaten fresh or dried into cakes. Olives were eaten fresh or pickled, or were crushed to produce cooking oil, lotions, and lamp oil.

### POMEGRANATES
The fruit of the pomegranate was prized for its bitter-sweet juice. Its image was also used for decorative purposes: the pomegranate was carved on the pillars of Solomon's Temple.

## HERDS AND FLOCKS

Keeping animals as pets was a rare practice in Israel, although a common one for Romans and Greeks. For Israelites, animals existed either for work or for food.

Sheep were vitally important to the Israelites. They were kept for wool, which was spun and woven to make clothing; they were also killed for food or used as sacrifices. Goats were kept for their milk, which was drunk or turned into cheese, as well as their meat. Goat-hair was woven into coarse cloth, and their skins were used as water bottles. Goats were often offered as sacrifices. Cattle provided milk, meat, and leather. Introduced to Israel from India via caravans of traders, domestic fowl were also common (see p.305).

The main draught animals were oxen, used to pull ploughs, carts, and threshing

### LIVESTOCK AS WEALTH
The more sheep and goats a family owned, the richer they were. Both species, often tended in mixed flocks, are well suited to the rocky hills of Israel.

sledges. They were also offered as sacrifices by the wealthy. Donkeys and mules served as pack animals and occasionally for riding. Camels, which were owned primarily by traders, were able to carry huge loads and travel for days without water. Yet the camel also provided many other essentials: its dung was used as fuel, its milk was drunk, and its hair was used for making clothes. Only the rich owned horses, which were also used by kings and warriors in battle.

## FOOD FROM THE SEA

Unlike the Phoenicians and Egyptians, the Israelites were not great fishermen during the Old Testament period. But by New Testament times a thriving fishing industry had developed around the Sea of Galilee (actually a freshwater lake), and fish had become an important part of the Israelite diet. Fishing on the Sea of Galilee was dangerous, however: fierce storms rose suddenly when the wind rushed through the surrounding valleys. Fishermen frequently worked through the night, sorting and cleaning their catch the next morning, cleaning and drying the nets, then taking the fish to market.

FISH **The three most common fish in biblical times were probably the sardine – said to have been the "small fish" that fed the 5,000 – the barbel, and the musht.**

Four ways of fishing are mentioned in the Bible. Spearing was often done at night: a light or

### CAST-NET FISHING
Casting a weighted net into fertile fishing waters was an effective method of pulling in many fish at once. It is still used in many countries today.

"fire basket" was used to attract the fish to within spearing distance. Slightly more common was the line-and-hook method, where a bone or iron hook was attached to a line, baited, and thrown into the water. Cast-net fishing involved throwing a small, circular, weighted net into the water, which sank, trapping

### FISHING HOOK
This Roman-period fishing hook was found during excavations on the northeastern shore of the Sea of Galilee. Once fish had been caught, they had to be cooked immediately or else preserved. Salt curing was the most common method.

the fish. It was then dragged back to the shore or boat. The larger drag-net, up to 450m (1,500ft) long, had floats at the top and weights at the bottom and was dragged between two boats, or between a boat and the shore. As it was drawn into the boat or back to land, it trapped the fish.

**CALMING THE STORM**
Matthew described the dramatic moment when the storm broke: "Suddenly a furious storm came up on the lake, so that the waves swept over the boat. But Jesus was sleeping." (Matthew 8:24).

« BEFORE

Jesus had been travelling "from one town and village to another" (Luke 8:1), proclaiming the good news.

## CURING THE WOMEN
Luke records that shortly before Jesus calmed the storm, he **cured some of the women who were accompanying him** of various "evil spirits and diseases" (Luke 8:2). Jesus healed Joanna the wife of Chuza; Susanna; Mary Magdelene "from whom seven demons had come out" (8:2); as well as many other unnamed women.

## JESUS SETS OUT THE COSTS
Jesus met a disciple on the shore of the Sea of Galilee. The disciple wished to follow Jesus, but said to him "Lord, first let me go and bury my father" (Matthew 8:21). Jesus replied: "Follow me and let the dead bury their own dead" (8:22).

## SYMBOLS

### GOD AND THE WATERS

The Bible portrays God in effortless control of the Earth's waters: "'God said, Let the water under the sky be gathered to one place…' And it was so" (Genesis 1:9). In Exodus 14, God parted the Red Sea, and in Joshua 3, God stopped the River Jordan from flowing, so the Israelites could cross (3:13). In Revelation's "new earth", "there was no longer any sea" (Revelation 21:1). Jesus' calming of the storm confirmed him as Lord of the sea.

**DANIEL DREAMED THAT GOD'S ENEMIES AROSE AS FOUR BEASTS FROM THE SEA**

# Jesus Calms the Storm

*In the Old Testament, wind and waves often seem to represent chaotic forces beyond human control. When Jesus shows he has the power to save the disciples' storm-tossed ship, it leaves them fearful of him.*

**M**ARK'S STORY OF the calming of the storm began with Jesus suggesting a trip across the Sea of Galilee: "That day when evening came, he said to his disciples, 'Let us go over to the other side'" (Mark 4:35). For Mark, it was significant that Jesus had instigated this journey; it was not a whim of the disciples or a random happening. Jesus said, "Let us go".

Before long, however, there was trouble. A fierce storm arose; waves were breaking over the side of the boat and it was filling with water. Then Mark described one of the key images of the story: in the midst of the wind and the waves (forces outside the disciples' control) Jesus was sound asleep. Mark highlighted this moment with a detail none of the other gospels mentioned – Jesus was "sleeping on a cushion" (Mark 4:38). The pillow seems to emphasize the fact that Jesus was calmly at rest in the face of chaos and danger.

### Waking up the Lord
The disciples were frightened and unsure what to do. At a loss, they woke Jesus up and said to him, "Teacher, don't you care if we drown?" (Mark 4:38). Jewish believers hearing this story might have recalled the psalmist's cry, "Awake, Lord! Why do you sleep? Rouse yourself! Do not reject us for ever" (Psalm 44:23).

Jesus then performed one of his most dramatic displays of authority; he got up from his cushion, and delivered a short rebuke to the wind and waves, "Quiet! Be still!" (Mark 4:39). At this command, the storm died down until the sea was once more completely calm. Jesus then said to the disciples: "Why are you so afraid? Do you still have no faith?" (Mark 4:40).

Jesus' command to the sea to "be still!" recalls another group of storm-tossed sailors, described in Psalm 107: "He stilled the storm to a whisper; the waves of the sea were hushed. They were glad when it grew calm…" (Psalm 107:29,30). The disciples on Galilee during the storm were afraid of the sea, just as those whose tale was related in the psalm. But in this case there was also a second form of fear: an awe-filled fear in the face of Jesus' own authority, which

**STORM ON THE SEA OF GALILEE**
Winds whip up waves on the Sea of Galilee, recalling the conditions in which the disciples feared for their lives. Jesus' power to still the storm echoes God's power over the Red Sea (Exodus 14:26–28).

demonstrated power on a scale beyond their imagining. Mark's final description of the scene suggests this: "They were terrified and asked each other, 'Who is this? Even the wind and the waves obey him!'" (Mark 4:41).

### The question
"By ending the scene with a question – "Who is this?" – Mark is drawing attention to the major issue in the story: the identity of Jesus. Jesus wanted the disciples to grasp this, and Mark wanted his readers to do the same.

AFTER »

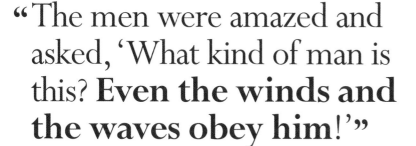

" **The men were amazed and asked, 'What kind of man is this? Even the winds and the waves obey him!'** "

MATTHEW 8:27

**Not long after the incident of the storm, Jesus again calms tempestuous waters.**

### TURBULENT SEAS
Following the miraculous **feeding of the 5,000 346–47 »**, Jesus sent his disciples by boat to Bethsaida, while he went up a mountain to pray. Jesus later saw the disciples struggling against the wind and **walked out on the water 348–49 »**, climbed into the boat, and stilled the storm. The disciples still needed to be persuaded of Jesus' power.

### THE SHIP OF SOULS
The early church **adopted the ship as a symbol of itself** – subject to storms of disbelief and persecution, but preserved by Christ's sovereign authority.

**BEFORE**

To have one's body possessed by an evil spirit had a parallel – in the nation controlled by an alien power.

### UNDER FOREIGN CONTROL

In Israel in Jesus' day **Rome's legions were part of daily life ‹‹ 268–69**. Possessed people can be seen as a spiritual example of "enemy occupation". Joshua had **defeated and driven out the Canaanites and their idols ‹‹ 128–29**; Jesus was taking a campaign of liberation to all the nations.

The wild boar symbol of the Roman Tenth Legion Fretensis

**CLAY BRICK STAMPED WITH THE EMBLEMS OF THE TENTH LEGION**

**ANALYSIS**

## DEMONS AND POSSESSION

**ST FRANCIS EXPELLING DEVILS AT AREZZO IN GIOTTO'S 13TH-CENTURY FRESCO AT ASSISSI**

### THE BIBLE AND "DEMONS"

The gospels contain a number of references to malevolent powers, called either "demons" (Matthew 8:31) or "impure spirits" (Matthew 12:43), which could cause severe emotional and physical disturbance (Mark 5:1–5, 9:20–27), and seem in some sense to have been controlled by Satan (Mark 3:22–27). These demons could speak (Mark 5:7) and they had emotions (Mark 5:7; James 2:19). They needed a host to inhabit (Matthew 12:43,44; Mark 5:12) and expelling them required "authority" (Mark 3:15), and sometimes "prayer" (Mark 9:29). Some churches today continue the ministry of exorcism (expelling evil spirits).

# Demons and the Herd of Pigs

*Jesus' victory over "Legion" – an army of demons that had possessed a man – demonstrated Jesus' authority over the spiritual realm. It followed his victory over the storm, a physical realm.*

THE "REGION OF THE Gerasenes" (Mark 5:1) was a Gentile territory where the people kept animals, such as pigs, which the Jews considered to be ritually unclean. This meant that the area was unsuitable for observant Jews to visit because it was regarded as spiritually tainted (see p.307). Scholars believe that for Jesus to sail across Lake Galilee and continue his ministry there showed commitment to a larger mission than ethnic Israel, and a lack of concern about becoming unclean.

### A ministry for all

Mark's account links Jesus' arrival in Gerasa (see panel, right) with his meeting of the "man with an impure spirit" (5:2). This has been interpreted to mean that the focus of Jesus' journey was to extend his ministry to all people, beyond cultural or spiritual limits.

### A man in torment

The demented man was an outcast. He lived in a graveyard, a place for the dead. He was so violent that people had chained him up, but he had broken the chains – "No one

**ANCIENT GADARA**
According to Christian tradition, the casting out of the evil spirit took place in the village of Umm Qais, or ancient Gadara. The site, now in Jordan, is marked by the ruins of a semi-circular Roman building, converted into a church in the Byzantine period.

was strong enough to subdue him" (5:4). His torment was such that, "Night and day among the tombs and in the hills he would cry out and cut himself with stones" (5:5).

### A sudden change

Jesus stepped from the boat onto the land. The demon-tormented man left the tombs and ran to Jesus, where he fell down before

**EXORCIZING THE DEMON**
This early 11th-century illumination depicts Jesus driving out the demons and the pigs rushing into the lake. The image is from the Codex Aureus of Speyer, also known as the Gospels of Henry III, the Holy Roman Emperor. The manuscript was later acquired by King Philip II of Spain, who donated it to San Lorenzo del Escorial monastery.

him. Scholars have argued that this symbolizes leaving the way of death – the tombs – and turning to Jesus, the source of life.

Jesus commanded the spirit to come out of the man, and the impure spirit recognized who Jesus was: "What do you want with me, Jesus, Son of the Most High God?" (5:7). It submitted to him, pleading, "In God's name don't torture me!" Jesus asked the spirit to reveal its name, another sign of his authority, and it answered that it was Legion, because "we are many" (5:9). Then it appealed to Jesus "again and again not to send them out of the area" (5:10).

Nearby, there was a herd of about 2,000 pigs. "'Send us among the pigs;' said Legion, 'allow us to go into them'" (5:12). So Jesus did, and the demons left the man and entered the pigs. At this, the herd ran down the hill, charged into the lake, and drowned.

### Echoes of the Exodus

Jesus had calmed the storm on the way to the region of the Gerasenes, and had drowned the demon army on arrival. Already, the disciples had asked themselves who Jesus was, and the two incidents together can be interpreted as an answer: they were seeing a re-enactment of the Exodus from Egypt – with Jesus as deliverer, just as God had delivered Israel (see pp.98–99).

Meanwhile, the pig-keepers ran away to report what had taken place. People came to see this miracle, and found the formerly demon-possessed man "sitting there, dressed and in his right mind" (5:15). Such a contrast made them afraid, and the people "began to plead with Jesus to leave their region" (5:17).

Before departing to re-cross Lake Galilee, Jesus sent the cured man on a mission: "Go home to your own people and tell them how much the Lord has done for you, and how he has had mercy on you" (5:19,20). So the man went back to the Decapolis and said how much Jesus had done for him, and the people were amazed.

**HISTORY AND CULTURE**

### THE DECAPOLIS

"Decapolis" means "Ten Cities" and it referred to ten cities along the eastern border of the Roman Empire that shared a common Greek or Roman ("Hellenistic") culture and whose inhabitants were mainly non-Jewish or Gentile. Each was a city-state able to govern its own affairs. Mark set the "Legion" incident in "the region of the Gerasenes" (Mark 5:1), which was the area around Gerasa – now named Jerash – one of the ten cities. This region was east of the River Jordan and located halfway between Lake Galilee and the Dead Sea. Matthew places the story on the eastern side of the Sea of Galilee in "the region of the Gadarenes" (Matthew 8:28), based around another of the cities, Gadara.

**WILD SOW**
This 2nd-century AD bronze model of a sow is Gallo-Roman in origin, from Cahors, France. A wild sow was one of the monsters guarding the entrance to the underworld in the Greek myth of Theseus.

> " Then Jesus asked him, 'What is your name?' '**My name is Legion**,' he replied, '**for we are many**.'"

MARK 5:9

**AFTER**  »

**More dramatic healings and exorcisms, using only words of power, were carried out by both Jesus and those appointed by him.**

### CASTING OUT DEMONS

Like Jesus, the twelve Apostles went out preaching and "drove out many demons..."

(Mark 6:13). **This aspect of their ministry would continue into the early church 418–19** », with the disciples healing those in Jerusalem and Samaria who were brought to them "tormented by impure spirits" (Acts 5:16) and where "with shrieks, impure spirits came out of many, and many who were paralysed or lame were healed" (8:7).

## BEFORE

Jesus sailed back from the Gentile region of Gergesa to the western shore of the Sea of Galilee.

### RETURNING HOME

By returning to his base in Jewish territory, Jesus showed his sustained commitment to the Jews – **the people of God's covenant**.

### THE PARALYZED MAN

The tale of Jairus' daughter is prefaced in Mark by Jesus **calming the storm** « 334–35 and **casting demons from a man** « 336–37. In Matthew, these two events are followed by Jesus healing a paralyzed man. At first, Jesus said that the man's sins were forgiven, but some **accused him of blasphemy**. He asked then which they thought more difficult: telling someone his sins were forgiven, or telling a paralyzed person to walk? He then told the paralyzed man to **pick up his mat and go home**, which he did, and the crowd was **"filled with awe"** (Matthew 9:8).

## LISTS

### CLOTHING IN SCRIPTURE

In Scripture, garments could represent the authority of their wearers, and many passages in the Bible make use of this symbolism.

"Now Israel loved Joseph more than any of his other sons, because he had been born to him in his old age; and he made an ornate robe for him" (Genesis 37:3).

Elisha took Elijah's cloak and struck it on the river: "...it divided to the right and to the left, and he crossed over" (2 Kings 2:14).

"I put on righteousness as my clothing; justice was my robe and my turban" (Job 29:14).

"God did extraordinary miracles through Paul, so that even handkerchiefs and aprons that had touched him were taken to those who were ill, and their illnesses were cured..."(Acts 19:11,12).

### THE HEALING CLOAK

*Healing the Woman with the Issue of Blood* by Paolo Caliari (also known as Veronese,1528–88) illustrates the moment when Jesus turns to see who has touched his cloak, to find a woman on her knees.

# Jairus' Daughter

*Jesus demonstrated his authority over illness and death by healing a woman and a child. The woman's chronic bleeding was draining her of life, while the young girl had already died, but Jesus revived her.*

**J**AIRUS, A LEADER of a synagogue, arrived on the shore where Jesus was teaching. He pleaded with Jesus to go with him to his dying daughter, saying that Jesus need only put his "hands on her so that she will be healed and live" (Mark 5:23). Jesus readily went with him, accompanied by a crowd that continually pressed against him.

SYNAGOGUE IN GALILEE
Jairus' synagogue was almost certainly simpler than this synagogue in Baram in Upper Galilee, which dates from the 1st century AD.

### Jesus heals a believer

Among the crowd was a woman "who had been subject to bleeding for twelve years"(5:25). She had consulted many doctors, at great cost, but her condition had only become worse. The woman had heard about Jesus and his power to heal, and believed that she could receive God's mercy through him. She came up through the crowd and touched Jesus' cloak, because she thought, "If I just touch his clothes, I will be healed" (5:28). Immediately, her bleeding stopped and she could tell that her long suffering was over. Jesus also noticed that something had happened; he sensed that "power had gone out from him... and asked, 'Who touched my clothes?'" (5:30). His disciples looked at the crowd pressing all around him, and wondered at the question, but Jesus continued to look around him, until the woman – realizing what was happening – came forward. She fell at his feet, "trembling with fear" (5:33) and told him the truth. Jesus said, "Daughter, your faith has healed you. Go in peace and be freed from your suffering" (5:34).

> " He went in and said to them, 'Why all this commotion and wailing? **The child is not dead but asleep.'"**
>
> MARK 5:39

### A child dies

Just after Jesus had spoken to the woman, servants arrived from the synagogue leader's house. They told Jairus that his daughter had died, and suggested that there was no reason to "bother the teacher any more" (5:35). However, Jesus overheard what they said and, turning to Jairus, told him, "Don't be afraid; just believe" (5:36).

Jesus set off for Jairus' house, accompanied only by his three disciples, Peter, James, and John, the brother of James. When they arrived at Jairus' house, the scene was chaotic – people were crying and wailing loudly. Immediately, Jesus took charge. He proceeded to drive out the wailing mourners, admonishing them for causing a

**RAISED FROM THE DEAD**
In 1809, Johann Friedrich Overbeck (1789–1869) founded a group of artists known as the Lukasbrüder, who believed art should serve a religious or moral purpose. His *Raising of Jairus' daughter* was painted around this time.

commotion. He declared that the child was not dead, but simply sleeping. The Gospel of Mark notes that at this point, "the people laughed at him" (5:40). Jesus disregarded them and proceeded to the girl's room, taking only her parents and his three disciples with him.

### "Talitha koum!"
Jesus took the child's hand and spoke to her in Aramaic, saying: "*Talitha koum!*". The Bible translates these words as, "Little girl, I say to you, get up!" (5:41). The New Testament was written primarily in Greek (see pp.18–19),

so it is unusual to find Jesus' words transcribed here in Aramaic. However, the majority of Jews spoke Aramaic at this time, so it is likely that Jesus himself spoke in this language.

Jairus and his wife were "completely astonished" (5:42) when their daughter stood up immediately at Jesus' command, and began to walk about the room. Jesus instructed her parents to give the child something to eat, and told everyone present not to talk about the episode, because he did not wish to reveal himself as the Messiah at this early stage in his public ministry.

**AFTER** »

After leaving Jairus' house, Jesus returned to Nazareth, his home town in Galilee, and started to send out the disciples.

**THE POWER OF FAITH**
In Nazareth, Jesus began to teach in the synagogue, where many who heard him already knew him. They questioned his wisdom and the miracles he was performing, asking, "Isn't this the carpenter? Isn't this

**MUSTARD SEEDS PROVE, SAID JESUS, THAT TINY CAN BECOME LARGE**

Mary's son and the brother of James?" (Mark 6:3). In response, Jesus said to them that the only places that a prophet is "without honour" (6:4) is in his own town, among his relatives, and in his home. Jesus was amazed at the **lack of faith in the people of Nazareth 340–41** ». He was unable to perform miracles there, but he was able to "lay his hands on a few people who were ill and heal them" (6:5).

339

**BEFORE**

Jesus returned to Galilee and spent much time teaching in synagogues where the Hebrew Bible was studied.

*THE PROPHET ELISHA CLEANSING NAAMAN, BY VASARI, 1560–1570*

**LEARNING FROM THE SCRIPTURES**
Synagogue attendants often translated Hebrew readings into the commonly spoken Aramaic. The usual practice was to teach by means of stories from the Scriptures. Jesus described **Elijah saving a widow from starvation ‹‹ 196–97** in 1 Kings 17:8–16, and to **Elisha healing the leper, Naaman ‹‹ 210–11** in 2 Kings 5:1–14.

**THE SCRIPTURE FULFILLED**
*Jesus Unrolls the Book in the Synagogue*, from a series of Bible illustrations called *The Life of Christ*, by James Tissot (1836–1902). In Luke's telling, Jesus declares himself the fulfilment of Isaiah's words.

# A Prophet Without Honour

*The people of Nazareth responded positively to Jesus at first. However, when Jesus anticipated their demand for signs and reminded them how God's prophets helped outsiders, they rose up to kill him.*

**J**ESUS CAME TO the town of Nazareth, where he had been brought up, accompanied by his disciples. It was the Sabbath, so Jesus entered the synagogue to teach, as was his custom. He stood up to read, and the attendant handed him the scroll of Isaiah. Jesus unrolled it and read out the passage in chapter 61 where Isaiah prophesied the coming of the Messiah: "The Spirit of the Sovereign LORD is on me, because the LORD has anointed me to proclaim good news to the poor" (Isaiah 61:1). He went on to read, "He has sent me to proclaim freedom for the prisoners and recovery of sight for the blind, set the oppressed free, to proclaim the year of the Lord's favour" (Luke 4:18,19).

Jesus then rolled up the scroll, handed it back to the attendant, and sat down.

### The Messiah
Afterwards, everyone looked at Jesus expectantly, their eyes "fastened on him" (4:20), and he said, "Today this scripture is fulfilled in your hearing" (4:21). Jesus was telling his listeners at

## WHERE HE PREACHED

The Synagogue Church in Nazareth was built by the Crusaders in the 12th century. According to tradition, this is the location in Nazareth of the synagogue where Jesus read from Isaiah on the Sabbath, which so angered the people.

the synagogue that the Messiah had come – he himself was the Anointed One.

### From applause to rejection

Initially the people spoke well of Jesus, and were amazed at the "gracious words that came from his lips" (4:22), but then they began to question his background. "'Where did this man get this wisdom...?' they asked. 'Isn't this the carpenter's son? Isn't his mother's name Mary...?'" (Matthew 13:54,55). Having identified him, they began to take offence at his reading. Jesus had known the people's acceptance

would not last and that they would soon begin to demand miraculous proof. He said, "Surely you will quote this proverb to me: 'Physician, heal yourself!' And you will tell me, 'Do here in your home town what we have heard that you did

in Capernaum'. Truly I tell you... no prophet is accepted in his home town" (Luke 4:23,24).

### Elijah and Elisha

Jesus went on to recall the story of Elijah and Elisha. Israel had many widows in Elijah's day, but God did not send Elijah to any of them and instead sent him to a widow in the Gentile town of Zarephath.

Israel had many lepers (or people with afflictions of the skin) in Elisha's day, but God did not send Elisha to any of them. Instead he sent him only to a Syrian army general named Naaman.

The gospels of both Matthew and Mark mention that Jesus had concluded that the people of Nazareth had a "lack of faith" (Matthew 13:58, Mark 6:6). Scholars believe that Jesus' point was that God sent Elijah and Elisha out of Israel because unbelieving Israel had not trusted them as

> ## "The Spirit of the Lord is on me, because he has anointed me to proclaim good news to the poor.'"
>
> LUKE 4:18

prophets – Jesus too was a prophet, and Nazareth was rejecting him. The people in the synagogue took offence at Jesus' argument, and they became violently angry. They forced Jesus out of Nazareth and up to the top of a nearby hill, intending to throw him off a cliff. However, according to Luke's gospel, Jesus "walked right through the crowd and went on his way" (4:30). The gospels do not explain how he did this, but they do make it clear that Nazareth had rejected him.

## ANALYSIS

### YEAR OF THE LORD'S FAVOUR

When Jesus spoke about proclaiming "the year of the Lord's favour" (Luke 4:19) he was quoting from Isaiah, "to proclaim the year of the LORD's favour and the day of vengeance of our God, to comfort all who mourn" (Isaiah 61:2). Isaiah in turn was echoing Leviticus, in which it is written, "Consecrate the fiftieth year and proclaim liberty throughout the land to all its inhabitants. It shall be a jubilee for you; each of you is to return to your family property and to your own clan" (25:10).

The jubilee – in Leviticus, God's instruction to Israel to celebrate, every 50 years, a year of emancipation and restoration – referred to the cancelling of debts; those whose debts had cost them their land were restored to their land (25:28). Isaiah – and Jesus – saw in this a picture of God cancelling sinners' debts and restoring freedom to their lives. Peter looked forward to a final jubilee when he preached that Jesus would remain in heaven "until the time comes for God to restore everything" (Acts 3:21).

### AFTER

**The first Christians continued to worship by attending synagogues, and they looked for and found Christ in the Hebrew Scriptures.**

#### IMITATING THE MASTER

After his **conversion during his journey to Damascus 428–29 >>**, Paul followed Jesus' example and, "At once he began to preach in the synagogues that Jesus is the Son of God" (Acts 9:20). Paul's preaching astonished

those who attended the synagogue, and he **"baffled the Jews living in Damascus by proving that Jesus is the Messiah"** (9:22).

#### APOSTLES AND THE SCRIPTURES

The apostles interpreted texts as prophecies, such as the verse from Isaiah: "he was oppressed and... yet he did not open his mouth; he was led like a lamb to the slaughter" (53:7), which was seen **to refer to Jesus' death 400–01 >>** (see Acts 8:32–35).

#### MOUNTAIN OF THE LEAP

This hillside south of Nazareth has been identified as a possible location of the cliff from which the angry mob meant to push Jesus to his death (Luke 4: 29). He simply walked through the crowd and away.

# Jesus Sends Out his Followers

*The gospels highlighted Jesus' authority. People were amazed that "he taught them as one who had authority, not as the teachers of the law" (Mark 1:22). His own disciples were in awe of his power, but Jesus did not reserve this authority for himself. He imparted it to his followers.*

**J**ESUS WAS NOW travelling through the villages, teaching, healing, and driving out demons as he went. The sending out of the 12 apostles (see pp.322–23) can be seen as an expansion of his mission. Jesus called the disciples to him and then sent them out in pairs, assigning to them "authority over impure spirits" (Mark 6:7).

Jesus gave them instructions: "Take nothing… except a staff – no bread, no bag, no money in your belts. Wear sandals but not an extra shirt" (Mark 6:8). The lack of comfort, or the means to purchase supplies, meant that the apostles had to rely on the guidance of God and the hospitality of people.

Jesus' instructions reinforced the idea of his representatives having authority. He advised that "if any place will not welcome you or listen to you, leave that place and shake the dust off your feet as a testimony against them" (Mark 6:11). Although these new apostles were ordinary people in one sense, they were extraordinary in another. They had been sent by Jesus, which meant their mission carried weight.

### The preaching of the 12

The apostles "went out and preached that people should repent" (Mark 6:12). By going, they showed obedience to Jesus and an alignment with his mission. Their preaching showed that the imperfect words of flawed, ordinary people would convey God's power. Their message of "good news" (Luke 9:6) was one people hoped to hear, but repentance also meant a change in direction, a change in thinking, and a change of heart.

In parallel with this message, the apostles brought a power to conquer spiritual darkness, and deliver freedom from sickness: "They drove out many demons and anointed with oil many people who were ill and healed them" (Mark 6:13).

> **"So they set out** and went from village to village, proclaiming the good news and healing people everywhere."
>
> LUKE 9:6

**THE SENDING OF THE 12**
This detail from a late 15th-century illuminated book of sung service responses is an initial letter E decorated with Jesus sending out the 12 apostles to "preach the kingdom of God and to heal the sick" (Luke 9:2).

**BEFORE**

Both Jesus, by observing festivals, and John, by confronting authority, showed links with the Old Testament.

**AN 18TH-CENTURY GERMAN *MIZRAH* ILLUSTRATING MAJOR JEWISH FESTIVALS**

### UP TO JERUSALEM
John's Gospel states that Jesus went to Jerusalem for a **festival ❮❮ 182**, an activity he did regularly. He **healed a man who had been crippled for 38 years** (John 5:1–15).

### PROPHETS AND AUTHORITY
**Elijah ❮❮ 200–01** had stood up to King Ahab and his idolatrous wife, Jezebel.

**ANALYSIS**

**SALOME'S DANCE**

*THE FEAST OF HEROD* (1461–62), BY BENOZZO GOZZOLI

### THE DANCING GIRL
The gospels do not give Herodias's daughter a name, but the historian Josephus called her "Salome". She was Herodias's child by her first husband, King Herod Philip I, who was a half-brother of Herod Antipas. At the time of her stepfather's feast, Mark referred to her as a girl, using the same word he had used for Jairus's 12-year-old daughter (Mark 5:42). Later paintings depicting a voluptuous woman owe more to artists' imaginations than they do to historical evidence. Salome married twice: first to her father's half-brother Herod Philip II, the tetrarch of Trachonitis; and then to Aristobulus, king of Chalcis, with whom she had three sons.

# Death of John the Baptist

*The gospels represented John the Baptist as "more than a prophet" (Luke 7:26) and a second Elijah (see Matthew 17:12). As Elijah had rebuked the powers of his day, so did John and he paid with his life.*

**J**ESUS HAD RECENTLY sent out the 12 apostles to preach and to drive out evil spirits (see pp.342–43). This generated some attention: "King Herod heard about this, for Jesus' name had become well known" (Mark 6:14).

### Herod and John the Baptist
The reason this news interested Herod Antipas was because of his difficult relationship with another well-known preacher, John the Baptist (see pp.298–99), the "voice of one calling in the wilderness"

(Matthew 3:3). Herod Antipas had courted Herodias, the wife of his brother Philip, and she subsequently left her husband to marry him – while Philip was still living. John had condemned this arrangement, saying to Herod, "It is not lawful for you to have your brother's wife" (6:18). In response, Herod had John arrested and imprisoned.

### Herodias seeks revenge
Herod's wife Herodias, meanwhile, wanted a greater punishment for John than incarceration. She wanted him dead. Herod stood

in her way, because he "feared John and protected him, knowing him to be a righteous and holy man" (6:20).

### The fateful party
Herodias's chance for revenge soon came. Herod gave himself a birthday party, and invited "his high officials and military commanders and the leading men of Galilee" (6:21). During the banquet, Herodias's daughter came in and danced for the guests. Her performance so pleased the party that Herod promised to give the girl anything she wanted: "Whatever you ask I will give you, up to half my kingdom" (6:23).

The daughter asked her mother what she should request. The answer from Herodias was quick and gruesome: "The head of John the Baptist" (6:24). The girl returned to the assembled dignitaries and told the king: "I want you to give me right now the head of John the Baptist on a dish" (6:25).

### A king under oath
Herod was trapped. Despite John's condemnation of his immoral behaviour, Herod had a personal regard for this man of God. He had imprisoned John, but he was afraid to take John's life. He was now captive to a public pledge, and caught between his conscience, his honour, and his familial loyalty. He ordered that an executioner

> **"When Herod heard John, he was greatly puzzled; yet he liked to listen to him."**
>
> MARK 6:20

**MARTYRDOM OF JOHN THE BAPTIST**
This late 14th-century altar panel, *Beheading of Saint John the Baptist*, by Flemish sculptor Jacques de Baerze, is from an altar of the Champmol Charterhouse, a monastery in Dijon, France.

**MACHAERUS FORTRESS**
This aerial view shows the fortified hilltop palace built by Herod the Great, to the east of the Dead Sea in modern-day Jordan. According to Jewish historian Josephus (AD 37–c.100), this is where John the Baptist was imprisoned and executed.

be sent to the prison. The man followed the king's instructions and returned with the prophet's head – on a platter. "He presented it to the girl, and she gave it to her mother" (6:28). Mark ended the account: "On hearing of this, John's disciples came and took his body and laid it in a tomb" (6:29).

When reports reached Herod's court about another holy man performing miracles and gaining fame – Jesus of Nazareth – he was intrigued and confused.

### Raised from the dead?

The gospels report conflicting opinions and widespread confusion about who Jesus was. Some people were saying, "John the Baptist has been raised from the dead, and that is why miraculous powers are at work in him [Jesus]" (6:14). Others said that Jesus was a prophet, "like one of the prophets of long ago" or, more specifically, that "He is Elijah" (6:15).

Hearing this, Herod feared that despite his execution, John the Baptist had returned. He said, "John, whom I beheaded, has been raised from the dead!" (6:16).

Jesus later told the disciples that "Elijah has already come" and they understood that he was talking about John the Baptist (Matthew 17:12,13), whose death foreshadowed Jesus' crucifixion.

**AFTER** »»

**Jesus sent out even more disciples, telling them to announce the arrival of the kingdom of God (Luke 10:9).**

### REJOICE IN GOD'S KINGDOM

Jesus appointed this larger group of 72 disciples and **he sent them out in the same manner as the 12 apostles ‹‹ 323** saying, "The harvest is plentiful but the workers are few" (Luke 10:2). **When they returned to him rejoicing that they had expelled demons,** Jesus reminded them that it is better to rejoice that their "names are written in heaven" (Luke 10:20).

---

**PEOPLE**

### ANTIPAS AND HIS WIFE

Herod Antipas (4 BC–AD 39) was a son of Herod the Great. On his father's death, Antipas was made tetrarch over Galilee and Perea. Antipas divorced his first wife to marry Herodias, who was (due to complex family relationships) his niece and his brother's wife. John the Baptist condemned the union. Jesus once referred to Herod as "that fox" (Luke 13:32) and was questioned by him hours before his crucifixion (see pp.396–97). Antipas died in Gaul in AD 39, where he was in exile with Herodias, after being accused of plotting against Emperor Caligula.

*HEROD AND HERODIAS AT THE FEAST OF HEROD (16TH-CENTURY, FLEMISH)*

## BEFORE

**God had provided nourishment and placed authority on his Son, as testified by John before his death.**

### GOD'S PROVISION

God showed compassion by offering meat and bread to the Israelites grumbling to Moses **in the wilderness ‹‹ 104–05** (Exodus 16:11) and by **feeding 100 people ‹‹ 210–11** with the 20 loaves of barley bread given to Elisha by the man from Baal-Shalishah (2 Kings 4:42–44).

**POOL OF BETHESDA, JERUSALEM**

### HONOURING THE SON

In **Jerusalem 362–63 ››**, the Jewish leaders questioned Jesus about **curing a lame man** at the pool of Bethesda **on a Sabbath ‹‹ 320–21**. His response was an assertion of his own divine authority: the Father had **"entrusted all judgment to the Son,** that all may honour the Son just as they honour the Father" (John 5:22,23). This had been supported by John the Baptist (John 5:33).

# Feeding the 5,000

*Many of Jesus' miracles are recounted in one or two of the four gospels. Only one appears in all four: the miracle of the five loaves and two fish. This may be an indication of its importance to the Early Church.*

**J**ESUS' DISCIPLES had just returned from a preaching mission, and the demands of their ministry were so intense that "they did not even have a chance to eat" (Mark 6:31). So Jesus said, "Come with me by yourselves to a quiet place and get some rest" (Mark 6:31).

### Uninvited guests

Jesus and the apostles went away by boat "to a solitary place" (Mark 6:32), which is identified by Luke as Bethsaida. They had been spotted, however, and many people had run ahead or followed them along the shore. By the time the boat reached the place, a large crowd had already gathered. Jesus was moved by the sight of these people, who seemed like lost sheep. Jesus healed those who were ill and addressed the spiritual hunger of the crowd by "teaching them many things" (Mark 6:34).

The day wore on, and the disciples came to him: "'This is a remote place,' they said, 'and it's already very late'" (Mark 6:35). (In Mark's account, this is the third reference to the isolation of the

**BREAD AND FISH**
Early Christian frescoes of the bread and fish symbol, such as this example from the Catacomb of Callixtus, Rome, were signs of God's abundance and his ability to satisfy people's material and spiritual hunger.

place, signifying its importance.) The disciples asked Jesus to send the people away to the nearby villages so that they could buy themselves something to eat. But Jesus surprised them by suggesting instead: "You give them something to eat" (Mark 6:37). The disciples protested that feeding such a large crowd would cost "more than half a year's wages!" They questioned whether he intended them to spend so much on bread to be handed out to the crowd. In response, Jesus told them to go and count how many loaves they had. The answer came back: "Five – and two fish" (Mark 6:38), which was certainly not enough to feed the large crowd of followers.

> **"When Jesus… saw a large crowd, he had compassion on them, because they were like sheep without a shepherd."**
>
> MARK 6:34

### Feeding the sheep

Jesus was about to perform another miracle: he would multiply the meagre resources on hand and feed thousands of people. But Mark's account supplies a detail that gives the meaning of the whole scene.

The disciples were asked to "have all the people sit down in groups on the green grass" (Mark 6:39). The Greek word used here means both "sit" and "recline", so it appears that the crowd were asked to recline (or lie down) in green pastures. This recalls the words of Psalm 23, in which the psalmist wrote: "The LORD is my shepherd, I lack nothing. He makes me lie down in green pastures, he leads me beside quiet waters, he refreshes my soul" (Psalm 23:1–3). It goes on to describe a shepherd who "prepare[s] a table" (Psalm 23:5). In the story of the feeding of the 5,000, Jesus was the shepherd who fed his hungry flock with the word and with actual food, in a location that seemed totally isolated.

### Breaking bread

The huge crowd was asked to sit down in groups of 50 or 100 people. Meanwhile, Jesus continued his preparation: "Taking the five loaves and the two fish and looking up to heaven, he gave thanks and broke them" (Luke

## ANALYSIS

### SHEPHERD AND SHEEP

The metaphor of the "good shepherd" runs throughout the Bible to illustrate God's care. "For he is our God, and we are the people of his pasture, the flock under his care", says Psalm 95:7. "He tends his flock like a shepherd", says Isaiah 40:11. In the New Testament parable of the lost sheep, the sinners are sheep and Jesus is the searching shepherd (Luke 15:1–7). John records Jesus as explaining: "I am the good shepherd. The good shepherd lays down his life for the sheep" (John 10:11).

**SHEEP BESIDE THE SEA OF GALILEE**

9:16). Early Christians might have recognized the allusion to a later meal here – the Lord's Supper – when Jesus took the bread, gave thanks and broke it (Mark 14:22). By using the same words in both episodes, Mark once more conveys the idea that the Lord of the church remains a source of comfort even in a "desolate place" (Jeremiah 3:12) of despair.

### The Lord's abundance

Jesus then gave the food to the disciples to hand out to the crowd. After they had all eaten and "were satisfied" (Mark 6:42),

Jesus asked the disciples to "Gather the pieces that are left over. Let nothing be wasted" (John 6:12). The disciples collected up the remaining food, and found that they still had 12 basketfuls of bread and fish. It is at this point that

Mark records: "The number of the men who had eaten was 5,000" (6:44). This story is about compassion and also "abundance": the numbers of loaves, people, and baskets indicate the magnitude of Jesus' ministry and the scale of his authority, as well as the scope of his care. John records that the people once more questioned the identity of Jesus (John 6:14).

**MIRACLES OF CHRIST**
This centre panel of a 15th-century Flemish tryptich depicts the feeding of the 5,000, which in conjunction with the miracle of the feeding of the 4,000, became known as "Feeding the multitude".

SYMBOLS

### BREAD OF LIFE

**BREAD SYMBOLIZES DAILY NEEDS**

Bread is often used to represent sustenance in the Bible, from the Old Testament story of God providing manna in the desert during the Israelite flight from Egypt (Exodus 16), to the two New Testament stories of miraculous feasts for thousands of people (Mark 6:30–44; 8:1–10).

Jesus used bread as an emblem of his own body in the Last Supper (Mark 14:22), where he asked the disciples to take bread, because "this is my body". Jesus is the essential nourishment; as he says: "I am the bread of life, whoever comes to me will never go hungry" (John 6:35).

## AFTER

**Jesus' miraculous feasts were statements about the nature of his spiritual kingdom.**

### WHAT KIND OF KINGSHIP?

After Jesus fed the 5,000, he realized that the people wanted to "make him king by force" (John 6:15). It has been suggested that this was because the feeding of the 5,000 was the **long-awaited miracle signalling the arrival of the Messiah,** who would re-establish the kingdom of the Jews. To avoid confronting this situation Jesus "withdrew again to a mountain by himself" (John 6:15). This withdrawal has been interpreted as a rejection of the people's mistaken view of kingship.

### WHY A SECOND FEAST?

A second miraculous feast – for 4,000 people – took place in the Decapolis area on the southeastern shore of the Sea of Galilee (Mark 8:1–10). This story **demonstrated Jesus' Lordship beyond Israel** and his compassion towards all; the crowd was mainly Gentile and yet he was concerned that they had been with him for three days without eating.

**BEFORE**

Jesus had been using a boat both for transport and for preaching at a small distance from the crowds.

**THE ROLE OF THE BOAT**
In the **calming of the storm** ❮❮ 334–35 the disciples' boat was their means of mission. Jesus taught from a boat (Luke 5:3) prior to the **miraculous catch of fish** ❮❮ 312–13.

**PRAYING ON THE MOUNTAINS**
Jesus **went up on a mountainside** by himself to pray before **appointing the 12 apostles** (Luke 6:12) ❮❮ 322–23.

**FISHING ON THE SEA OF GALILEE**

> ❝ When the disciples saw him **walking on the lake,** they were terrified. **'It's a ghost,'** they said, and cried out in fear. ❞
>
> MATTHEW 14:26

**ANALYSIS**

**FLAWED FAITH**

Peter's faith certainly wavered once he found himself standing on stormy waters. However, Peter had addressed Jesus ("Lord, if it is you..." Mark 14:28) while the rest of the disciples thought they were seeing a ghost. He also knew who to cry out to for help, so while he lost faith in his own abilities, his faith in Jesus remained firm. John the Baptist had recently been executed by King Herod Antipas (Mark 6:14–29), and when this event occurred there was much speculation as to who could be the Son of Man. This event prepared Peter for the faith that enabled him to see who Jesus really was (see pp.352–53; Matthew 16:16).

# Jesus Walks on Water

*This was not Jesus' first contest with the stormy sea. He had already won over the wind and waves with the command: "Quiet! Be still!" (Mark 4:39). This time he demonstrated his authority over the sea in a more vivid way – by walking on it.*

AFTER THE 5,000 had finished eating, Jesus made the disciples get into the boat and go on ahead of him across to the other side of the Sea of Galilee (Matthew 14:22), while he dismissed the crowd (Mark 6:45). They set off towards Capernaum (John 6:17), but this time – unlike the earlier boat journeys across the water – Jesus did not accompany them. Instead, "he went up on a mountainside by himself to pray" (Matthew 14:23).

### Walking on the water
The disciples' sea journey became increasingly arduous as the wind escalated from the opposite shore. While Jesus was praying on land alone, the disciples were rowing hard against the wind, "straining at the oars" (Mark 6:48) as they tried to make headway through the night. Just before sunrise, Jesus saw them struggling and went out to them, walking on the surface of the lake. All the disciples saw him and were terrified, thinking they were seeing a ghost. But Jesus responded quickly to their cries, calling across: "Take courage! It is I. Don't be afraid" (Matthew 14:27).

### Jesus defeats chaos
The disciples misunderstood what they were seeing for, as Mark wrote, "their hearts were hardened" (Mark 6:52). Jesus was demonstrating who he really was: Lord over the sea. The story places the disciples' failure to believe their eyes – and their lack of faith – alongside Jesus' triumph. The scale of Jesus's accomplishment here is easily lost on modern readers, who are likely to think of the sea as no more than a geographical feature. In the Old Testament, the sea is a symbol of chaos and crisis: "I have come into the deep waters;" wrote David, "the floods engulf me" (Psalm 69:2). In this story, during a storm that had raged all night, Jesus walked easily across the wind-tossed sea.

This was not a feat carried out before crowds, such as the 5,000 Jesus had recently fed; it was a demonstration of victory to the disciples alone, who are said in Mark to be "completely amazed, for they had not understood about the loaves". It recalls the Old Testament notion that God "alone treads on the waves of the sea" (Job 9:8), and his "footprints were

**HISTORY AND CULTURE**

**NIGHT WATCHES**

Jesus came to his disciples "shortly before dawn", which is a translation of the Greek expression "during the fourth watch" (Matthew 14:25). "Watches" were time assignments for night-duty sentinels. The Hebrew system had three watches: sunset to 10pm, 10pm to 2am, and 2am to sunrise. The Romans introduced a four-watch system: 6pm to 9pm, 9pm to midnight, midnight to 3am, and 3am to sunrise. According to Matthew, it was during the fourth watch, that Jesus walked on the sea. The prophets were called watchmen and the Lord "watched over" his subjects all night. Devices like water clocks were used to measure watches, with markings to indicate the time as water drained through a hole.

**EGYPTIAN WATER CLOCKS DATED FROM AROUND 1400 BC**

not seen" on the path "through the mighty waters" (Psalm 77:19). Chaos and crisis were – literally and spiritually – under Jesus' feet, and did not disturb him.

### A test of faith
As Jesus stepped on to the boat, the wind died down, and in Mark and John this is the end of the story – "immediately the boat reached the shore where they were heading" (John 6:21). In Matthew, however, the story continues, pinpointing the nature of belief and its true role in this narrative. In answer to Jesus's reassurance, Peter said, "Lord, if it's you… tell me to come to you

**THE SEA OF GALILEE**
The landlocked "sea" of Galilee is today designated a lake and is known as Kinneret. It is the largest freshwater lake in Israel, and supplies drinking water to Israel and Jordan.

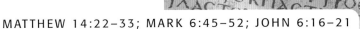

### A TEST OF FAITH
Peter alone of the disciples had sufficient faith to step on to the water, but faltered as he became aware of the wind. He was held safe by Jesus, as shown in Philipp Otto Runge's *Peter Walks on Water* (1806).

on the water" (Matthew 14:28). Jesus simply replied, "Come". Bravely, Peter stepped over the side of the boat, "walked on the water and came towards Jesus" (Matthew 14:29).

But then Peter noticed the wind, became afraid, and began to sink. He cried out, "Lord, save me!" (Matthew 14:30). Immediately Jesus reached out and caught Peter by the hand. "'You of little faith', he said, 'why did you doubt?'" (Matthew 14:30).

Jesus and the sodden Peter climbed into the boat. As they did so, the wind died down. Then the disciples realized what had taken place: "those who were in the boat worshipped him" (14:33) and declared that Jesus really was the Son of God. The boat had begun as a means of mission, a way of delivering Jesus' message about the kingdom of God, and had become a place of worship.

## "Truly you are the Son of God."

MATTHEW 14:33

---

**AFTER** ≫

Once Jesus and the disciples crossed the lake, Jesus healed the sick and then criticized the teachings of the Pharisees.

### HEALING IN GENNESARET
When the boat anchored in Gennesaret, Jesus was recognized by the locals and "they sent word to all the surrounding country" (Matthew 14:35). People **came from miles around to receive healing**. Ironically, unlike the disciples in the boat, the crowds had "recognized Jesus".

### AUTHORITY ON THE LINE
**The Pharisees 366–67 ≫** asked why Jesus' disciples did not respect the special traditions and rules of behaviour relating to Jewish worship and custom. Jesus **showed his authority over these traditions** and their teachers by quoting Isaiah: "their worship of me is based on merely human rules" (Isaiah 29:13). By not honouring God with their hearts, they had become "blind guides" (Matthew 15:14) and Jesus set out a new path.

**THE PLAINS OF GENNESARET BESIDE THE SEA OF GALILEE**

## BEFORE

**Jesus was challenged by the Pharisees over the behaviour of his disciples.**

### WHAT DEFILES?

The **Pharisees complained to Jesus** that his disciples were not following some traditions about ritual purity, since they **were eating food having not first washed their hands** ❮❮ 304–05. They asked him, "Why don't your disciples live according to the tradition of the elders instead of eating their food with defiled hands?" (Mark 7:5). Jesus responded that **nothing that entered a person from outside** could defile them. The evils that truly defile a person **come from that person's heart** (7:14–23); "it is what comes out of a person that defiles them" (7:15).

### IN HIDING

Jesus "withdrew to the region of Tyre and Sidon" (Matthew 15:21), suggesting that he knew the **Pharisees and Herodians were plotting to kill him** (Mark 3:6) after he called the Pharisees hypocrites and criticized their teaching (Matthew 15:7).

## ANALYSIS

### GIVING TO THE DOGS

Jesus' statement, "it is not right to take the children's bread and toss it to the dogs", was an example of "rabbinic exaggeration", or hyperbole. This was a common teaching device of the time. Elsewhere, he told disciples that if one of their eyes caused them to stumble, they should gouge it out and throw it away (Matthew 5:29). He also told them that if they did not hate their families, they could not be his disciple (Luke 14:26). This was to emphasize the cost of discipleship but did not imply literal action. Here, he used similarly stark language to highlight Israel's privileged identity. The length of Jesus' journeys to visit and heal Gentiles ("dogs") indicates the importance of his inclusive mission.

**c.2ND-CENTURY ROMAN MOSAIC OF A DOG**

# Jesus in Tyre and Sidon

*In successive miracles performed away from Galilee on visits to Gentile regions, Jesus healed a little girl in the grip of "an impure spirit" and a man who could neither hear nor speak.*

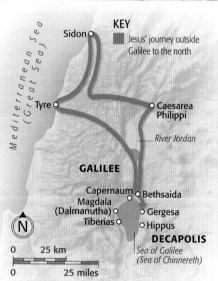

KEY

■ Jesus' journey outside Galilee to the north

**J**ESUS HAD been healing the sick in Genneraset on the western shore of the Sea of Galilee – a Jewish area. He then headed to the Gentile town of Tyre, on the Phoenician coast, where he healed a possessed girl. From there, he travelled about 80km (50 miles) southeast back through Galilee, across the Sea of Galilee, to the Decapolis – a group of ten Graeco-Roman cities that were Gentile territory. There he

healed a man who could neither hear nor speak. These two miracles involved different kinds of healing (one spiritual, the other physical) but had something in common: they were granted to Gentiles, people who were outside the covenant with Israel.

### Hard words?

The first healing took place in Tyre. A Greek woman, born in Syrian Phoenicia, had a daughter who

### BEYOND GALILEE

Jesus' route from Galilee towards the northern edge of the Promised Land, and then southeast to the Decapolis, is detailed in Mark 7:24–37 and shown on the above map.

was in the power of an evil (or "impure") spirit. The mother came to Jesus and fell at his feet, pleading for him to drive a demon out of her daughter. He answered: "First let the children eat all they want... for it is not right to take the children's bread and toss it to the

### ROMAN REMAINS
The Phoenician city of Tyre (meaning "rock") had almost been destroyed by the Assyrians in the 6th century BC. In 64 BC it came under the rule of the Romans, who built this triumphal arch and colonnaded street.

# "'He has done everything well', they said. 'He even makes the deaf hear and the mute speak.'"

**MARK** 7:37

Ultimately God's blessings would flow out through Israel to all the world (Genesis 12:2,3), but Israel would be first. Alongside the priority of Israel, however, was the value God set on faith. The woman with the demon-possessed little girl was determined in her desire for Jesus' blessing. This mirrors one of the most striking "faith" stories in the Old Testament: Ruth, a destitute Gentile widow (see pp.136–37), overcame hard times and remained loyal to her family and God (see Ruth 1:16,17), for which God rewarded her.

### A second miracle
Travelling outside the area under the authority of Herod Antipas (see p.345), Jesus moved from Tyre to Sidon, a city further up the coast. He then headed southeast via Caesarea Philippi to the Decapolis, east of the River Jordan. This was also Gentile country. Here, people brought to Jesus "a man who was deaf and could hardly talk" (Mark 7:32), and asked him to help. Jesus took the man to one side, away from the crowd. He placed his fingers in the man's ears and then spat saliva onto the fingers of his other hand and touched the man's tongue. Jesus looked up to heaven, sighed deeply, and said to the man, "*Ephphatha!*" (Mark 7:34) – Aramaic for "Be opened!" At this, the "man's ears were opened, his tongue was loosed and he began to speak plainly" (7:35).

The scene concluded with Jesus admonishing the formerly deaf and mute man, and those who had witnessed the miracle, not to tell anyone about what had happened. Scholars have debated why Jesus did this: some believe he did not wish to become famous as a "miracle man".

dogs" (Mark 7:27). Despite this puzzling response (see panel, left), the woman persisted: "'Lord,' she replied, 'even the dogs under the table eat the children's crumbs'" (7:28). Jesus was impressed by her answer, and told the woman that he had healed her daughter: "For such a reply, you may go; the demon has left your daughter" (7:29). The mother returned to her home and found the girl well, "and the demon gone" (7:30).

This awkward conversation revealed the intersection of two biblical themes: the priority of Israel in God's plan, and the place of stubborn faith in that plan. Israel was unique: the heir to the blessings of God, and God's appointed channel of blessing on all the nations of the Earth (the people of Tyre included).

### JESUS IN TYRE
During his visit to Tyre on the Phoenician coast, Jesus was asked by a local woman to heal her daughter, as shown here in an illustration from the illuminated manuscript *Codex de Predis* (1476).

## AFTER

**Jesus' opponents demanded that he should perform a "sign". He answered that he would – in God's time.**

### A DEMAND WITHOUT FAITH
"The Pharisees and Sadducees came to Jesus and tested him by asking him to show them a sign from heaven" (Matthew 16:1). They **wanted Jesus to prove himself** in a way that they could understand. He answered: "A wicked and adulterous generation looks for a sign, but none will be given it except the sign of Jonah" (16:4). His answer made no sense to them, although they knew the story of Jonah. **Jesus would indeed provide a sign**: the supreme sign of being swallowed up by the grave just as **Jonah had been swallowed by the fish** « **212–13**, and then **coming forth again in resurrection 404–05** ». Jesus was unwilling to be manipulated, performing miracles on demand to sceptical audiences. His submission was to God alone.

**JONAH AND THE GREAT FISH, 11TH-CENTURY STONE RELIEF FROM CAPUA CATHEDRAL, ITALY**

## BEFORE

**Before they realized that Jesus was the Messiah, the disciples often failed to understand his words.**

### UNABLE TO SEE CLEARLY

Jesus warned the disciples to be on their guard against the "yeast of the Pharisees" (Mark 8:15), **who were spiritually blind to Jesus' message**. The disciples thought Jesus meant that they needed more bread, but he rebuked them for not understanding that he was warning them against false teachings. Jesus asked, **"Do you have eyes but fail to see, and ears but fail to hear?"** (8:18).

At Bethsaida, a blind man was brought to Jesus, who touched him and asked, "Do you see anything?" (8:23). The man replied, "I see people, they look like trees walking around" (8:24). Jesus touched him again, and **"His eyes were opened, his sight was restored..."** (8:25).

**JESUS CURES THE BLIND, 19TH-CENTURY STAINED GLASS**

### CAESAREA PHILIPPI

The discussion about who Jesus was took place in the "villages around Caesarea Philippi" (Mark 8:27). Located at the foot of Mount Hermon near the Banias stream, a source of the River Jordan, this Galilean city was an ancient centre of Baal worship, identified by historians with "Baal Gad" (see Joshua 11:17). Josephus reported that there was also a cult here dedicated to the Greek god Pan between the 3rd and 1st centuries BC. Under Rome, Herod Philip rebuilt the area and dedicated it to Caesar ("Caesarea") and to himself ("Philippi"). A place once dedicated to false gods and human demagogues became the place were Jesus first confessed that he was the Messiah.

**THE CAVE OF BAAL GAD AT CAESAREA PHILIPPI OVERLOOKS THE BANIAS STREAM**

**KEYS TO HEAVEN**
Meister der Katharinen-Legende depicted Jesus literally handing Peter the keys to his kingdom in *Handing of Keys to St. Peter* (*c*.1470), which also features other scenes from the New Testament.

# Who Do You Say I Am?

*Jesus was halfway through his public ministry. He had taught, preached, healed the sick, cast out demons, and walked on the sea. But the moment came when he needed to address a more important issue – who he was.*

**J**ESUS AND THE disciples were travelling among villages in the vicinity of Caesarea Philippi, when Jesus one day turned to them and asked "Who do people say I am?" (Mark 8:27). The disciples mentioned some of the theories in circulation: "Some say John the Baptist; others say Elijah; and still others, one of the prophets" (Mark 8:28). The number of popular ideas about Jesus showed the extent of his fame.

Jesus pressed the issue. Rather than hearing popular views of people he did not know, he wanted to know what the disciples thought, and whether they themselves had formed an opinion. "'But what about you?' he asked. 'Who do you say I am?'" (Mark 8:29). Jesus used the plural of "you", showing that he was speaking to all the disciples.

Peter answered first, and his is the only answer recorded, so he seems to be speaking for the

group. "You are the Messiah, the Son of the living God" (Matthew 16:16) he said. By calling Jesus the Messiah, Peter was referring to him as the Anointed One, who the prophets had promised would come and restore Israel to God (see panel, right).

### How Peter knew

The Gospel of Matthew supplies additional information about this scene that is not recorded in Mark. According to Matthew, Jesus replied to Peter, "Blessed are you, Simon son of Jonah, for this was not revealed to you by flesh and blood, but by my Father in heaven" (Matthew 16:17). Jesus meant that an understanding of this kind – that Jesus was "the Son of Man" – could only be possible by God's revelation. Peter had not

guessed who Jesus was; he had been shown. This was a gift, and there was a reason that Peter had been privileged with this revelation; he was to be the "rock [on which] I will build my church" (Matthew 16:18). Peter was to live up to the name given to him by Jesus, who had renamed him Cephas, meaning "rock" (John 1:42). When the New Testament was written, the Aramaic word *Cephas* was translated as the Greek *Petros* or "Peter".

Jesus told Peter that he was going to give him "the keys of the kingdom of heaven; whatever you bind on Earth will be bound in heaven" (Matthew 16:19). Peter was learning from Jesus and through revelation, which would allow him to open the kingdom to those who believed, and close it to others. Then Jesus spoke to all the gathered disciples, telling them not to reveal to anyone else that he was indeed the Messiah.

**EMPEROR TIBERIUS**
Tiberius became Roman emperor in AD 14, and is the Caesar after whom Caesarea Philippi was named. He ruled the Roman Empire during the ministry and death of Jesus, and died as an unpopular ruler in AD 37.

**PALACE OF AGRIPPA II**
Herod Agrippa II had a grand palace – shown here in ruins – at Caesarea Philippi. Jesus told Peter at Caesarea that his own kingdom would withstand everything: even "the gates of Hades will not overcome it" (Matthew 16:18).

> " …he ordered his disciples **not to tell anyone that he was the Messiah.**"
>
> MATTHEW 16:20

## ANALYSIS
### THE MEANING OF "MESSIAH"

Messiah was a word with a rich history. In Peter's day, there were centuries of promises and hope behind this title. The word meant "anointed", and anointing signified the power of God resting on someone – a prophet (Isaiah 61:1), a priest (Exodus 30:30) or a king (1 Samuel 16:1–13).

The prophets had written that God would yet send "the Anointed One" (Daniel 9:25–27), someone who would, by the power of the Spirit, bring old covenant promises to new covenant fulfilment. Although he "will be put to death" (Daniel 9:26), he will also "confirm a covenant with many" (Daniel 9:27).

Peter realized that the Anointed One had now come, and said so (Matthew 16:16). Professing Jesus as Messiah was a vital aspect of faith and discipleship, as seen with Peter, Martha – "I believe that you are the Messiah, the Son of God" (John 11:27), and with all believers (John 20:31).

> " 'But what about you?' he asked. **'Who do you say I am?'** Peter answered, **'You are the Messiah.'** "
>
> MARK 8:29

### AFTER

**Jesus painted a stark picture of what was to come for the Messiah.**

#### SUFFERING AND DENIAL
Jesus told the disciples that as the Son of Man he would have to suffer greatly, be rejected by the elders, priests, and teachers, **be killed and "after three days rise again"** (Mark 8:31) 404–05 >>.

When Peter said that he refused to allow this to happen, Jesus was blunt and rebuked **him**, saying "**Get behind me, Satan!** ... You do not have in mind the concerns of God, but merely human concerns" (8:33). Jesus explained, "Whoever wants to be my disciple must **deny themselves and take up their cross and follow me**" (8:34).

**BEFORE**

**13TH-CENTURY FRESCO SHOWING ELIJAH IN HIS CHARIOT, ANAGNI CATHEDRAL, ITALY**

**The prophet Elijah was a key figure in Israel's history.**

**THE NEW ELIJAH**
The book of Malachi ended with the promise of **a new Elijah ‹‹ 200–01**: "See, I will send the prophet Elijah to you before that great and dreadful day of the LORD comes" (4:5).

**JESUS' PROPHECY**
Peter had **declared Jesus to be the Messiah ‹‹ 352–53** (Mark 8:29). Jesus told him of the suffering, death, and resurrection to come, but Peter "rebuked him" (8:31,32).

---

**ANALYSIS**
## MOSES AND ELIJAH

**FRESCO BY RAPHAEL (1483–1520) SHOWING MOSES RECEIVING THE TEN COMMANDMENTS**

The appearance of Moses and Elijah underlined the important link between the people of the Covenant and the followers of Jesus. The Law of Moses was God's gift to his people – it gave them the rules for living correctly and specified the sacrifices necessary for the forgiveness of sins (see pp.106–11). The appearance of Moses and Elijah at the transfiguration pointed to Jesus as the embodiment of all Israel's righteousness, forgiveness, and hope. When Luke said they spoke about his departure, the word he used for "departure" was the Greek *exodos*, or exodus, which links Jesus' death, resurrection, and ascension with Israel's departure from Egypt.

---

# The Transfiguration

*Jesus took his inner circle of apostles on a journey up a mountain. There, the Old Testament figures of Elijah and Moses appeared alongside him. God spoke, telling the apostles that Jesus was his son, and to listen to him.*

T HE OLD TESTAMENT describes how Moses was called upon to climb Mount Sinai, where "the glory of the LORD settled… For six days the cloud covered the mountain, and on the seventh day the LORD called to Moses from within the cloud" (Exodus 24:16). In the New Testament, the scene of Jesus' transfiguration was to echo much of this earlier scene, and – like Moses – Peter, James, and John would see God's glory, but in a new way.

### Jesus is transformed
The story of the transfiguration is told in all the synoptic gospels – these are the gospels of Matthew, Mark and Luke, which tell many of the same stories about Jesus' life. Matthew and Mark both begin the story by saying: "After six days Jesus took Peter, James, and John with him and led them up a high mountain, where they were all alone" (Mark 9:2). All the synoptic gospels then describe the moment when Jesus was transfigured before the men. Matthew says that Jesus' "face shone like the sun" (Matthew 17:2). Mark reports that Jesus "was transfigured" (Mark 9:2), or visibly transformed – using the Greek verb that forms the root of the word metamorphosis. Mark also describes that Jesus' "clothes became dazzling white, whiter than anyone in the world could bleach them" (Mark 9:3).

### Old testament heroes appear
As the apostles watched in wonder, Elijah and Moses appeared beside Jesus, talking with him. According to Luke's gospel, they spoke about Jesus' departure, "which he was about to bring to fulfilment at Jerusalem" (Luke 9:31). Peter said to Jesus: "Rabbi, it is good for us to be here. Let us put up three shelters – one for you, one for Moses and one for Elijah" (Mark 9:5), but Mark notes that Peter "did not know what to say, they were so frightened" (Mark 9:6).

A cloud appeared and covered Jesus, Moses, and Elijah. A voice issued from the cloud, saying, "This is my Son, whom I love. Listen to him!" (Mark 9:7). When the

**MOUNT HERMON**
The snow-capped Mount Hermon on the border between Lebanon and Syria rises to 2,814m (9,232ft) above sea level. It is believed to be one of the possible locations for Jesus' transfiguration.

apostles heard God's voice they fell to the ground, terrified. They remained like this until Jesus walked over to them and touched them. "Get up,' he said, 'Don't be afraid" (Matthew 17:7). When the apostles looked up, there was no one there but Jesus. As they walked down the mountain together, Jesus tolds them to say nothing of what they had seen "until the Son of Man had risen from the dead" (Mark 9:9).

**AFTER**

**After his transfiguration, Jesus identified the new Elijah.**

**UNDER WRAPS?**
The apostles wondered what Jesus meant by "risen from the dead" (Mark 9:9,10). Not until after Jesus' **sacrifice on the cross 398–99 ››** and his subsequent **resurrection 404–05 ››** would his glory – revealed in the transfiguration – be fully explained. Jesus **revealed John the Baptist to be the new Elijah** (Matthew 17:12,13). The role of Elijah was that of supreme teacher – the one who would come again (as John had) to signal the arrival of the Messiah.

> " As he was praying, **the appearance of his face changed**, and his clothes became **as bright as a flash of lightning**."
>
> LUKE 9:29

**EXORCIZING THE DEMON**
Jesus said anything was possible for one who believed, and drove out the impure spirit from the afflicted boy as shown here in an illustration on vellum from the *Codex de Predis*, produced in Milan, *c.*1470s.

## BEFORE

**After the Transfiguration, Jesus explained the importance of Elijah to Peter, James, and John.**

### ELIJAH CAME FIRST
After Jesus appeared **alongside Moses and Elijah ❮❮ 354–55**, the apostles asked Jesus, "Why do the teachers of the law say that Elijah must come first?" (Mark 9:11), referring to the prophecy of Malachi, which says Elijah will be sent before judgment day to restore righteousness (Malachi 4:5,6). The apostles believed this should be enough, and did not understand why Jesus needed to suffer. Jesus agreed that "Elijah does come first, and restores all things" (Mark 9:12), but another set of events also had to occur before that day. Just as Elijah's fate had been "written", so had it been "written that the Son of Man must suffer much and be rejected" (9:12).

# Healing a Boy of an Evil Spirit

*Following the Transfiguration, a change in focus occurred in Jesus' ministry. Repeated miracles gave way to teaching about Jesus' death – and the cost of following him.*

**W**HEN JESUS, PETER, James, and John came down from the mountain, following the Transfiguration (see pp.354–55), they encountered a loud argument between Jesus' other disciples and the teachers of the Law, or scribes. Jesus asked his disciples what the dispute was about. A man in the crowd answered, "Teacher, I brought you my son, who is possessed by a spirit that has robbed him of speech. Whenever it seizes him, it throws him to the ground. He foams at the mouth, gnashes his teeth, and becomes rigid. I asked your disciples to drive out the spirit, but they could not" (Mark 9:17,18).

Jesus' reaction recalls another mountain descent. When Moses came down from Mount Sinai, he found the people of Israel mired in unbelief, and reacted in disgust by smashing the stone tablets on which God had given him the Ten Commandments (Exodus 32, see pp.108–09). Jesus' reaction to the crowd was just as intense: "You unbelieving generation… how long shall I stay with you? How long shall I put up with you? Bring the boy to me" (Mark 9:19).

### Belief and unbelief
So the people brought the boy to Jesus, and when "the spirit saw Jesus, it immediately threw the boy into a convulsion. He fell to the ground and rolled around, foaming at the mouth" (9:20).

There followed a conversation between Jesus and the boy's father, who implored him to do something if he could. Jesus said to him, "'If you can?'… Everything is possible for one who believes" (9:23).

The troubled man cried out, "I do believe; help me overcome my unbelief!" (9:24). Then Jesus directly addressed the evil spirit in the boy: "You deaf and mute spirit, I command you, come out of him and never enter him again" (9:25). With a violent shriek the spirit left the boy. At first the boy was so drained that people thought he was dead, but Jesus took him by the hand and he stood up. When the disciples were indoors, away from the crowd, they asked him, "Why couldn't we drive it out?" (9:28). Jesus answered, "Because you have so little faith. Truly I tell you, if you have faith as small as a mustard seed, you can say to this mountain, "Move from here to there,' and it will move. Nothing will be impossible for you." (Matthew 17:20,21).

**QUESTIONING JESUS' AUTHORITY**
In Mark 11, scribes questioned Jesus' authority to do the things he did, such as casting out demons. In doing so, the scribes denied their original purpose – their lineage traced back to the faithful Ezra, shown here in the Codex Amiatinus (8th century, UK).

### The second prediction
They continued on their journey, but Jesus had not yet finished teaching. For the second time, he talked of the destiny that awaited him, "The Son of Man is going to be delivered into the hands of men. They will kill him, and after three days he will rise" (Mark 9:31).

Just as when Jesus had earlier predicted the Son of Man's rejection, suffering, killing, and rising again (Mark 8:31), the disciples did not understand and were afraid to ask, so they argued among themselves. At Capernaum, Jesus asked what they had been arguing about. The disciples remained quiet, because it had been a dispute over who was "the greatest" – perhaps meaning the most important or valued disciple among them.

Jesus explained that anyone who wanted to be first must put themselves last, and be a servant to all. Then he found a child in the gathering, and taking the child in his arms, said to the disciples, "Whoever welcomes one of these little children in my name welcomes me; and whoever welcomes me does not welcome me, but the one who sent me" (9:37).

## ANALYSIS
### TAKE UP YOUR CROSS

In Mark's account of Jesus' mission there are two overriding themes: power and service. Mark's first eight chapters describe Jesus' many signs and miracles (displays of power). The story's turning point is when Jesus asked, "But what about you? Who do you say I am?" and Peter answered, "You are the Messiah" (8:29).

Jesus began to tell the disciples what lay ahead, to correct their notions of the Messiah and power. He told them he would suffer to save others – the ultimate act of service – and what would be required of them. Every follower of Christ would be called to follow his example of putting the needs of others above their own. "Whoever wants to be my disciple must deny themselves and take up their cross and follow me. For whoever wants to save their life will lose it, but whoever loses their life for me and for the gospel will save it" (Mark 8:34,35).

> "Anyone who **wants to be first must be the very last,** and the servant of all.'"
> MARK 9:35

**DEMON-TRAPPING BOWLS**
These 5th-century AD ceramic "incantation bowls", with protective magic inscriptions in Aramaic, were in widespread use in the Middle East into late antiquity. Similar bowls were used in ancient Jewish magic rituals to trap evil spirits.

Resembling a stylized owl, this figure may represent the demon to be trapped by the spells

### AFTER

**Jesus began his journey to Jerusalem amid questions and controversy.**

**DETERMINED TO MAKE THE JOURNEY**
Luke's gospel says, "As the time approached for him to be taken up to heaven, Jesus resolutely set out for Jerusalem" (Luke 9:51), even though Jesus knew about **the suffering and death that awaited him there 398–99 ».**

**FOR OR AGAINST JESUS?**
The disciple John told Jesus, "Teacher, we saw someone driving out demons in your name and we told him to stop…" (Mark 9:38). Jesus said, "Do not stop him… whoever is not against us is for us" (9:39,40).

**PAYING THE TEMPLE TAX**
At Capernaum, Jesus told Peter to catch a fish and look in its mouth – there "you will find a four-drachma coin. Take it and give it to them for my tax and yours" (Matthew 17:24–26).

# The Good Samaritan

*One of the great treasures unique to Luke's gospel is the parable of the Good Samaritan. In a story of kindness coming from a surprising source, Jesus expanded the meaning of "neighbour".*

**O**NE DAY WHEN Jesus was teaching, an expert in Jewish Law stood up to test him saying, "Teacher... what must I do to inherit eternal life?" (Luke 10:25). Jesus directed his questioner back to the Scriptures, "What is written in the Law?" he replied. "How do you read it?" (Luke 10:26). The expert wisely quoted from the Old Testament, paraphrasing Deuteronomy 6:5 and Leviticus 19:18: "Love the Lord your God with all your heart and with all your soul and with all your strength and with all your mind", and "Love your neighbour as yourself" (Luke 10:27). Jesus replied, "You have answered correctly... do this and you will live" (Luke 10:28). However, the conversation was not over – the man wanted to prove and justify his position as an expert in the Law, so he asked Jesus, "who is my neighbour?" (Luke 10:29). Jesus answered his question by telling a parable about two men who failed to help their neighbour, while a stranger went out of his way to be a good neighbour.

### BEFORE

« BEFORE

**Earlier scenes in Luke's gospel tell of the cost of discipleship.**

#### REJECTIONS AND EXCUSES

When a Samaritan village did not welcome Jesus "because he was heading for Jerusalem", **James and John « 322–23** wanted "to call fire down from heaven to destroy them" (Luke 9:53,54). Jesus rebuked them, and went to another village.

As they walked along the road, in a series of encounters with would-be disciples, **Jesus taught the cost of discipleship**; he said, "No one who puts a hand to the plough and looks back is fit for service in the kingdom of God" (9:62).

### ANALYSIS

#### LOVE THY NEIGHBOUR

Luke's gospel shaped the story of the Good Samaritan to emphasize mercy as an attribute of God, a gift of God, and a requirement of God for his people. The parable is about the important values of the kingdom: mercy and neighbourly love. Jesus embellished it with commentary on the religious scene of his day. In the parable, the two people who conspicuously failed in their duty were a Levite and a priest, both equipped with a knowledge of the Old Testament. These men ought to have known better – they should have helped their neighbour instead of bypassing him for fear of contracting ritual impurity. Their interpretation of the Law kept them from being good neighbours.

> ❝ Which of these three do you think **was a neighbour to the man who fell** into the hands of robbers? ❞
>
> LUKE 10:36

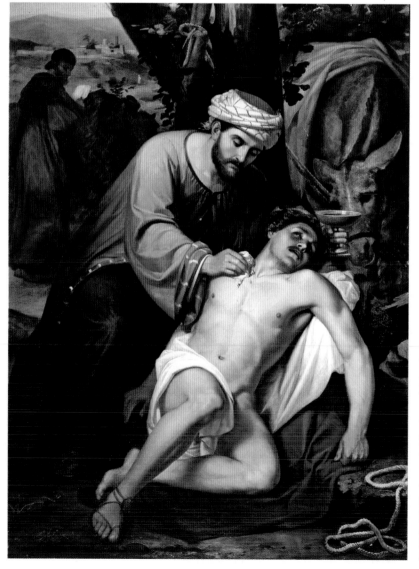

#### Attacked on the way to Jericho

Jesus began the story. A man travelling from Jerusalem to Jericho was attacked, viciously beaten, stripped of his clothes, and robbed. His assailants left him lying in the road, half-dead. A priest happened by along the same road. When he saw the wounded man, he passed by on the other side of the road. Next there came a Levite – a member of the tribe from which Israel's priesthood was descended. He too saw the injured man, and also crossed the road and passed by on the other side.

A third person, a Samaritan, then travelled along the road. The inhabitants of Samaria were viewed by the Jews as religiously and ethnically impure due to their mixed blood (see pp.308–09). A trip through the territory of Samaria was enough to make an observant Jew unclean.

When the Samaritan saw the helpless man, he took pity on him. He bandaged his wounds, pouring on oil and wine. Then he "put the man on his own donkey, brought him to an inn and took care of him" (10:34).

The next day, the Samaritan paid the equivalent of two days' wages for a labourer to cover the cost of the victim's stay at the inn, and

#### TENDING TO THE INJURED

Unlike the priest and the Levite who ignored the beaten man lying half-dead on the road between Jerusalem and Jericho, the Samaritan – pictured here in *The Good Samaritan* (1857) by Mexican artist Juan Manchola – stopped and tended to him.

said to the innkeeper, "Look after him... and when I return, I will reimburse you for any extra expense you may have" (10:35).

The surprising kindness of the despised but merciful Samaritan man was a model of what loving one's neighbour meant. Jesus continued, asking the expert in the Law which of the three passers-by was a neighbour to the man who fell into the hands of robbers.

Earlier, the expert had been evasive and had implied that he did not know who his neighbour was. Now, he replied, "The one who had mercy on him" (10:37). Jesus then told the man to go and follow this example.

Jesus' parable has been understood by commentators to demonstrate that keeping the spirit of the Law is something that outsiders can sometimes do better than those "experts" who might be expected to find it second nature. In this sense, it is a tale with an unexpected ending – akin to the parables of the prodigal son and shrewd manager (see pp.368–69) – that would have shocked listeners at the time.

> " The expert in the law replied, 'The one who had mercy on him.' Jesus told him, 'Go and do likewise.' "
>
> LUKE 10:37

**THE INN OF THE GOOD SAMARITAN**
Photographed c.1870, horses graze in and around the 19th-century Ottoman caravan camp which is known, in biblical tradition, as the Inn of the Good Samaritan, on the Jericho road near Jerusalem.

**AFTER** »»

The territory of Samaria proved fertile soil for the gospels.

**WITNESSES IN SAMARIA**
Jesus told the disciples "**you will be my witnesses in... Samaria**" (Acts 1:8). After his death and resurrection, the fledgling church there lacked the Holy Spirit, so disciples from Jerusalem – including John, who had wanted to punish a Samaritan village (Luke 9:54) – went to pray for the **Samaritans to receive the Holy Spirit 426–27** » (Acts 8:15).

**SEBASTIA NEAR NABLUS, IN FORMER SAMARIA**

**BEFORE**

**Jesus encountered several women who shed light on the meaning of faith.**

### THE FAITH OF WOMEN

In Mark's gospel there were four people – all women – whom Jesus commended for their faith. The woman with **chronic bleeding who touched Jesus' garment (Mark 5:25–34)** **《 338–39**; the Syro-Phoenician woman who begged Jesus to **heal her demonized daughter (7:25–30) 《 350–51**; the woman who put her **last two copper coins in the temple treasury (12:41–44) 384 》**; and the woman of Bethany who **anointed Jesus with expensive perfume (14:3–9) 386–87 》**.

Luke records the story of the sisters Mary and Martha (Luke 10:38–42). Mary **showed her faith by listening attentively at Jesus' feet**, while Martha, distracted by tasks, asked, "Lord, don't you care that my sister has left me to do the work by myself?" (10:40). He answered, "you are worried and upset about many things… **Mary has chosen what is better**…" (10:41,42).

# Jesus in Jerusalem

*Two stories in John's Gospel demonstrate Jesus' mercy and judgment. He spoke mercifully about the adulterous woman, and healed a man born blind. But in both stories, Jesus exposed the hypocrisy of his critics.*

J ESUS TOLD THE disciples to go to Judea for the Festival of the Tabernacles without him, saying that his "time had not yet fully come" (John 7:8). After they left, he followed on in secret.

One morning he went to the Temple to teach. People were gathered around when teachers of the Law and the Pharisees brought in a woman they claimed had been caught in adultery. The teachers made the woman stand before the group and they confronted Jesus. "'Teacher, this woman was caught

in the act of adultery. In the Law Moses commanded us to stone such women. Now what do you say?" (John 8:5,6). Their question was intended to be a trap, so that they would have a basis for accusing him.

### Writing on the ground

John's gospel reports that "Jesus bent down and started to write on the ground with his finger" (John 8:6). John does not say what he wrote or why he did so. Jesus may have been drawing an allusion to the time that Moses was given "the tablets of stone inscribed by the

finger of God" (Exodus 31:18, see pp.106–07). Or the gesture may have echoed Jeremiah's warning that those who forsake God would have their names "written in the dust" – an image of judgment and death (Jeremiah 17:13). By this interpretation, the people facing death would not be the woman caught in adultery, but her accusers.

### A challenge to the crowd

Jesus stood, turned, and issued a stark statement to the onlookers. He challenged anyone who was without sin to cast the first stone.

### THE FIRST STONE

When the Pharisees accused a woman of adultery – pictured in this painting by Nicolas Colombel in 1682 – Jesus said that anyone who had not sinned should cast the first stone. Everyone walked away without a stone thrown.

The woman's accusers drifted away. Jesus then asked, "Woman, where are they? Has no one condemned you?" (John 8:10). She replied "No one, sir"... Jesus responded, "Then neither do I condemn you... Go now and leave your life of sin" (John 8:11).

Jesus had exposed the duplicity of the woman's accusers. He was doing what – when his parents had dedicated him to God (see pp.290–91) – it had been prophesied he would do: to speak and act "so that the thoughts of many hearts will be revealed" (Luke 2:35).

### Kinds of blindness and sight

In chapter 9 of John's gospel, there is a strikingly similar story relating to sin. When Jesus met a man who had been blind from birth, his disciples asked, "Rabbi, who sinned, this man or his parents, that he was born blind?" (John 9:2). Jesus replied, "Neither this man nor his parents sinned, but this happened so that the works of God might be displayed in him" (9:3). With that, Jesus spat on the ground to make mud with his saliva, and then reached out his hand and put it on the man's eyes.

"'Go,' he told him, 'wash in the Pool of Siloam' [a Hebrew word meaning "Sent"]. So the man went and washed, and came home seeing" (John 9:7).

The healing happened on the Sabbath, which provoked the Pharisees: "This man is not from God," they said, "for he does not keep the Sabbath" (John 9:16). Others asked, "How can a sinner perform such signs?" When they asked the formerly blind man about Jesus, he said, "Whether he is a sinner or not, I don't know. One thing I do know. I was blind but now I see!" (John 9:25). The Pharisees threw the man out of the Temple.

When Jesus heard about this he went to find the healed man. Jesus asked if he believed in the "Son of Man" (John 9:35) and the man replied, "Lord, I believe" (John 9:38), and he worshipped Jesus. Then Jesus said, "For judgment I have come into this world, so that the blind will see and those who see will become blind" (John 9:39). Jesus told the Pharisees that by rejecting him, they stayed in the dark – "now that you claim you can see, your guilt remains" (John 9:41).

**POOL OF SILOAM**
This rock-cut cistern in Jerusalem – dating from the 5th century AD – is built over the site of the earlier Pool of Siloam, where Jesus told the blind man to wash after touching his eyes with saliva and mud.

> " When they kept on questioning him, he straightened up and said to them, 'Let any one of you who is without sin be the first to throw a stone at her.' "
>
> JOHN 8:7

### LISTS
### JESUS' VISITS TO JERUSALEM

John's gospel reports four visits by Jesus to Jerusalem, all for Jewish festivals:

**1** Passover – Jesus cleansed the Temple (John 2:15) and taught on the new birth (3:1–21).

**2** An unnamed festival – Jesus healed a crippled man (John 5:8) and claimed divine authority (5:17–47).

**3** Festival of Tabernacles – a feast celebrating God's provision in the wilderness. Jesus said, "...come to me and drink" (John 7:37).

**4** Feast of Dedication – "My sheep listen to my voice; I know them, and they follow me" (John 10:27).

### AFTER

Jesus' mission was a study in contrasts. He came to sow discord, but also to show a shepherd's care.

#### FIRE ON THE EARTH
**Jesus was controversial**. He said, "I have come to bring fire on the earth, and how I wish it were already kindled! But I have a baptism to undergo, and what constraint I am under until it is completed! **Do you think I came to bring peace on earth? No, I tell you, but division**" (Luke 12:49–51).

#### THE GOOD SHEPHERD
Jesus said, "The man runs away because he is a hired hand and cares nothing for the sheep. I am the good shepherd; I know my sheep and my sheep know me – just as the Father knows me and I know the Father – and I lay down my life for the sheep" (John 10:13–15). **Jesus was contrasting himself with the religious leaders 366–67 ≫**, and made it clear he cared for and knew his own followers.

**THE GOOD SHEPHERD, RELIEF FROM 3RD-CENTURY ROMAN SARCOPHAGUS**

361

**FOCAL POINT OF JESUS' MISSION** Rebuilding began 40 BC  Sacked AD 70

# Herod's Jerusalem

> "Jerusalem… **you who kill the prophets and stone those sent to you,** how often I have longed to gather your children together… **and you were not willing**."

LUKE 13:34

**J**ERUSALEM maintained its central role in the life of Israel after the exile (see pp.252–53). The returned exiles restored the city, and Jesus accomplished significant parts of his ministry there.

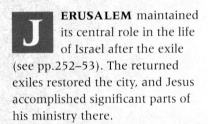

**ROOM OF LAST SUPPER**
In Jerusalem's Lower City, just outside the city walls, is one of the sites thought to be the "large upstairs room, furnished and ready" (Mark 14:15) that Jesus directed his disciples to for the Last Supper.

### Herod the builder
Famous for rebuilding Jerusalem's Temple (see pp.382–83), Herod the Great, Rome's client king of Judea, also provided an impressive house for himself. His Palace stood on an elevated site diagonally across Jerusalem from the Temple, in the southwest end of the city. It was a lavish building, demonstrating financial wealth and political power.

Herod's Palace stood in what the 1st-century AD Jewish historian Josephus called the "Upper City", a wealthy area that was the home of the political and religious elite. In Jesus' day, the Upper City took in the western half of Jerusalem. Its counterpart, the "Lower City", was some 500m (550yd) to the east, and just south of the Temple complex. It was "lower" geographically (situated downhill from the Upper City, and to its west) as well as economically, being the home of Jerusalem's poor. The "large room upstairs"

(Mark 14:15) where Jesus celebrated the Last Supper is thought to have been there.

### Jerusalem in the 1st century
Jerusalem sat at an elevation of around 750m (2,500ft) above sea level. Immediately to the city's east was the Kidron Valley, and to its west the Hinnom Valley. Most of the city's streets were too narrow for carts, and required the use of mules and camels. The city was a busy place, full of bazaars, markets,

and open-air shops. A customer could buy fresh fruit, meat, custom-woven fabric, sandals, clothes, and the services of letter-writers, fabric-dyers, carpenters, and metal-workers. One historian describes a rich trade in imported goods – some 118 different items – destined for Jerusalem's upper classes. Fine imported silks could literally fetch their weight in gold.

The Old and New Testaments highlighted the importance of Jerusalem as a destination for

---

**SYMBOLS**

### JERUSALEM THE HOLY

The New Testament contains many references to Jerusalem as a symbol of Israel's faith, history, and future. The temple-prophetess Anna described the child Jesus as coming "to all who were looking forward to the redemption of Jerusalem" (Luke 2:38) – a reference to the city as the home of God's people, the Jews. Jesus himself called Jerusalem "the city of the Great King" (Matthew 5:35) – recalling its historic greatness as "the city of David" (2 Samuel 5:7) and of God (see Psalm 48:2). In Revelation, the apostle John describes a vision of the future of the Earth by referring to Judaism's past – "the new Jerusalem, coming down out of heaven from God" (Revelation 21:2, see pp.464–65).

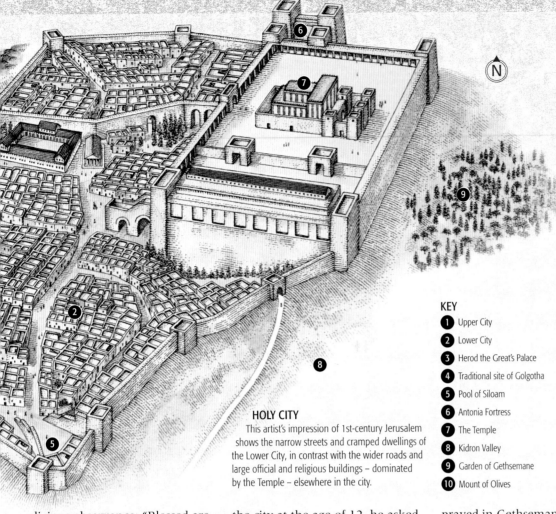

**HOLY CITY**
This artist's impression of 1st-century Jerusalem shows the narrow streets and cramped dwellings of the Lower City, in contrast with the wider roads and large official and religious buildings – dominated by the Temple – elsewhere in the city.

**KEY**

1. Upper City
2. Lower City
3. Herod the Great's Palace
4. Traditional site of Golgotha
5. Pool of Siloam
6. Antonia Fortress
7. The Temple
8. Kidron Valley
9. Garden of Gethsemane
10. Mount of Olives

## CHRONOLOGY IN BRIEF

- **63 BC,** Rome conquers Jerusalem.
- **40 BC,** Rome appoints Herod the Great as King of Judea, with Jerusalem as its capital.
- **c.20 BC,** Herod begins rebuilding the Temple.
- **4 BC,** birth of Jesus in Bethlehem, followed by dedication of Jesus at the Jerusalem Temple.
- **AD 8,** the 12-year-old Jesus visits Jerusalem with his family for Passover, and talks with elders at the Temple.
- **AD 26,** Pontius Pilate is appointed Roman Prefect of Judea.
- **AD 27–30,** Jesus visits Jerusalem for several unnamed "Feasts of the Jews" (see John 5:1, 6:4, 7:2, 7:11, 10:22).
- **AD 30,** Jesus deliberately chooses to go to Jerusalem for the climax of his mission (Luke 9:55, 13:33).
- **Jesus' makes his** triumphal entry into the city and cleanses the Temple (Mark 11:11–19).
- **Jesus teaches** about the destruction of the Temple and the end of the age (Mark 13).
- **The Last Supper** takes place somewhere in the Lower City (Mark 14:12–25).
- **Jesus prays in Gethsemane** (Mark 14:32–42).
- **Jesus is arrested,** interrogated, and sentenced to death (Mark 14:43–15:20).
- **Jesus is crucified** and buried, then rises again three days later (Mark 15:33–47;16:1–8).
- **The believers experience** the coming of the Spirit at Pentecost (Acts 2).
- **c.AD 30–35,** apostles proclaim the good news in and around Jerusalem (Acts 1–8).
- **AD 63,** Herod's Temple completed.
- **AD 70,** Herod's Temple and the city of Jerusalem sacked by Rome.

religious observance: "Blessed are those whose strength is in [the LORD], whose hearts are set on pilgrimage [to Zion]" (Psalm 84:5). The gospels make repeated references to "the feasts of the Jews" in Jerusalem. Acts 2 reports the presence of Passover pilgrims in Jerusalem from 15 different nations.

## Jesus in Jerusalem

Jerusalem was a focal point of Jesus' life and ministry, culminating in his death and resurrection. His parents took him there as a baby, to be dedicated to God (Luke 2:22, see pp.290–91). When he visited

### MODERN-DAY JERUSALEM
Temple Mount – pictured here from the Mount of Olives – is now home to the Al-Aqsa Mosque (centre-right) and the Dome of the Rock (centre). The old city walls are visible in the foreground.

the city at the age of 12, he asked precocious questions of the elders in the Temple (Luke 2:46, see pp.294–95). Midway through his public ministry, "Jesus resolutely set out for Jerusalem" (Luke 9:51), knowing full-well that suffering and death awaited him there: "I must press on today and tomorrow and the next day – for surely no prophet can die outside Jerusalem!" (Luke 13:33).

All four gospels describe Jesus' entry to the city, riding on a donkey, and being hailed by the crowds. The final days of Jesus' mission occurred in and around Jerusalem. It was there that he had his final Passover meal with his disciples (known as the Last Supper) and washed his disciples' feet (John 13:1–20, see pp.388–89),

prayed in Gethsemane (Mark 14:32–42, see pp.390–91), then faced arrest, interrogation, and crucifixion (Mark 14:43–15:47, see pp.392–99). And it was here that he rose again from the grave (Mark 16, see pp.404–05).

## Jerusalem and the Early Church

After rising again, Jesus sent out his disciples to preach "repentance and forgiveness of sins… to all nations, beginning at Jerusalem" (Luke 24:47, see pp.412–13). On the day of Pentecost, Jesus' followers were renewed in their faith by the coming of the Spirit (Acts 2, see p.417). The early days of the church in Jerusalem saw strong opposition, such as Stephen's martyrdom (see pp.424–25), but also the spread of the good news.

**ROAD TO CALVARY, SIMONE MARTINI (1284–1344)**

## BEFORE

When Jesus went to eat in the house of a Pharisee, he found a man suffering from abnormal swelling, due to dropsy. Jesus' response was controversial.

### HEALING ON THE SABBATH
The Pharisees considered healing to be work, and thus a **violation of the Sabbath ❮❮ 320–21** as a day of rest. Disturbed by the plight of the man, Jesus asked the Pharisees and experts in the law whether it was lawful to heal or not. They remained silent, so he healed the man and sent him on his way (Luke 14:1–4).

**JESUS CURES A MAN WHO HAS DROPSY**

**STONE CROCKERY**

# The Great Banquet

*Israel's covenant with God began with a feast at Sinai. Jesus described the kingdom of heaven as a banquet, where the Gentiles would "take their places at the feast with Abraham, Isaac, and Jacob" (Matthew 8:11).*

**T**HROUGHOUT this relationship, God's people are the guests and God is the host. It was against this cultural backdrop of God-ordained feasts that, one Sabbath, Jesus received an invitation to a meal at the house of an important Pharisee.

### One party, three parables
While Jesus was there, he observed the behaviour of the people at the party, and proceeded to tell three of his pithy, truth-packed stories, or parables. The first was for the people who were pushing their way into the best seats. The second was for the host of the meal. And the third was for a guest who spoke to him about "the feast in the kingdom of God" (Luke 14:15).

### Jostling for the best seats
As the people were being seated, Jesus noticed "how the guests picked the places of honour at the table" (14:7). He gave them some wise and godly advice, telling them that they should not grab the best seat at the table if they got an invitation to a wedding feast. The master of the feast may move you to the back row, he said, and you will feel humiliated. Rather, take the humble place. Who knows, you may get moved to a prominent place, and you will feel honoured.

As well as being good advice on avoiding embarrassment, this story teaches humility before God. In your relationship with God, the host of the banquet, take the humble seat. Jesus also warned that those who exalted themselves would be humbled, while those who humbled themselves would be exalted.

### Who is on the guest list?
Then it was the turn of the host of the party, described as "a prominent Pharisee" (14:1). The Pharisees and teachers of the law had muttered disapproval of Jesus eating with sinners (Luke 15:2). Jesus asked his host why he invited his relatives or his rich neighbours when he put on a meal. They would only return the favour and repay him for his hospitality. Why not invite "the poor, the crippled,

> ❝ Then you will be **honoured** in the presence of **all the other guests**. For all those who exalt themselves **will be humbled**, and those who humble themselves **will be exalted**. ❞
>
> LUKE 14:10,11

**A BANQUET WITH JESUS**
Paolo Veronese's *The Feast in the House of Levi* was originally painted in 1573 as a Last Supper, but after complaints that the feasting was irreverent the artist retitled the work after a story in Luke 5:29.

> " But when you **give a banquet, invite** the **poor**, the **crippled**, the **lame**, the **blind**, and you will be **blessed**. Although they cannot **repay you,** you will be repaid at the **resurrection of the righteous.** "
>
> LUKE 14:13,14

### PLACES AT TABLE
A 2nd-century BC sarcophagus shows an upper-class Roman woman in a *triclinium*, or formal dining room. She reclines on a cushioned couch known as a *lectus*. Couches were carefully arranged so that each person had equal access to the table.

the lame, the blind" (14:13)? These were the "unworthy" people – like the ones Jesus ate with. They could not repay the host, but God would.

### People making excuses
Finally, a man at the table said, "Blessed is the one who will eat at the feast in the kingdom of God" (14:15). Jesus replied with a third parable. A man planned a feast and sent out many invitations. Once the time for the banquet arrived, the man sent his servant to tell his guests, "Come, for everything is now ready" (14:17). However, the guests made excuses: they had bought a field, or bought new livestock, or just got married. They could not come. The host was angry, and sent his servants to "bring in the poor, the crippled, the blind and the lame" (14:21). The undesirable, marginalized people – the sort that Jesus rubbed shoulders with – were to be honoured at the feast. After the newcomers had arrived, the servant declared that there was still room. The host told him to go out and get more people to fill the house, vowing of those who were on his original guest list: "I tell you, not one of those who were invited will get a taste of my banquet" (14:24).

**AFTER**

**Jesus made it clear what it would mean to follow him, and foresaw how his listeners would respond.**

### COUNTING THE COST
Being a disciple was about **sacrifice**. Jesus told a crowd: "And whoever does not carry their cross and follow me cannot be my disciple" (Luke 14:27). In Jesus' day, to carry a cross did not mean to tolerate a problem, but to surrender to execution, **as Jesus would 398–99 ≫**.

*AGAPE* **FEAST, 3RD CENTURY MURAL, ROME**

### NEW GUESTS AT GOD'S TABLE
Jesus' admonition to invite the unfortunate was a hint at **the ultimate purpose of God**: the day when "many will come from the east and the west [that is, Gentiles], and will take their places at the feast with Abraham, Isaac, and Jacob in the kingdom of heaven" (Matthew 8:11). This idea of a **fellowship meal** was the purpose of the *agape* – "love" – feasts held by the early Christians.

### BANQUET IN ANTIOCH?
In the Early Church in Antioch, fearing the disapproval of conservative Jews, Peter **stopped eating with Gentiles 438–39 ≫**. Paul rebuked him (Galatians 2:11–14).

HISTORY AND CULTURE

# Sadducees and Pharisees

> "When he said this, a **dispute broke out** between the Pharisees and the Sadducees, and the **assembly was divided**."
>
> ACTS 23:7

**UPPER-CLASS DWELLING, JERUSALEM**
Sadducees were an aristocratic party made up of high priestly families and rich landowners. Their homes reflected their wealth and power.

A mong the many disparate factions of Judaism that existed during the time of Jesus, two religious groups stand out above the rest: the Sadducees and the Pharisees. It has been suggested that the word Sadducee derives from Zadok, the priest in the Temple during the time of David (1 Kings 2:35). Sadducees were theologically conservative and politically powerful. Pharisees were more democratic. Their name means "interpreters" and they were the forerunners of the rabbis.

**PHARISEES AND JESUS**
When the Pharisees called for Jesus to be arrested it was Nicodemus, himself a Pharisee, who tried to defend him. He later helped take Jesus down from the cross (below) and brought spices and oils to embalm the body.

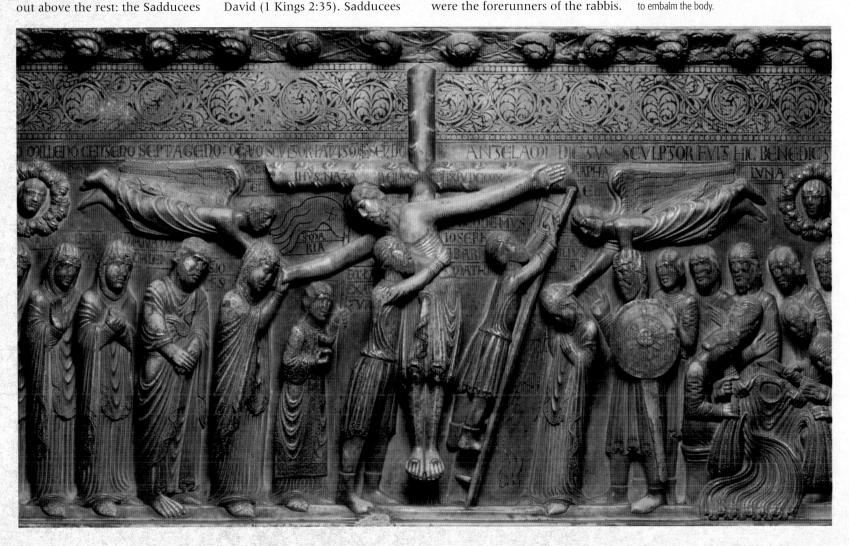

## THE SADDUCEES

No Sadducean writings have survived and the Sadducees do not appear in the portions of the gospels that take place in Galilee – perhaps because they were largely a Jerusalem-based elite. An upper-class movement that followed a strictly conservative theology based on adherence to the written Torah, the Sadducees were members of wealthy families and the aristocracy. The 1st-century Jewish historian Josephus (see p.467), suggests that the doctrines of the the Sadducees were "received but by a few, yet by those still of the greatest dignity".

In another passage, Josephus outlines the difference between the Pharisees and the Sadducees:

"...the Pharisees have delivered to the people a great many observances by succession from their fathers, which are not written in the law of Moses; and for that reason it is that the Sadducees reject them and say that we are to esteem those observances to be obligatory which are in the written word, but are not to observe what are derived from the tradition of our forefathers...".

Put simply, the Sadducees were the "Torah-only party": if it was not written in the "Law of Moses" – the first five books of the Hebrew Bible – then it was not doctrine. They did not accept the Oral Torah, developed by the Pharisees. For this reason, they rejected such concepts as angels and, in particular, the resurrection of the dead. "The doctrine of the Sadducees is this," wrote Josephus, "that souls die with the bodies."

Sadducees advocated loyalty to the state, to the Temple, and to Jewish Law, and were prominent until the destruction of the Temple in AD 70 (see pp.466–67).

**THE FIVE BOOKS OF MOSES**
In contrast to the Pharisees, who accepted an "Oral Torah", the Sadducees adhered strictly to the teachings of the written scripture alone.

## THE PHARISEES

In contrast with the Sadducees, the Pharisees made up the party of the masses. Its members formed a grassroots "holiness movement" popular in more rural areas and the poorer parts of the cities – precisely because they were attempting to redefine Judaism in a way that ordinary Jews could follow. Pharisees observed the teachings of the Torah, but added a wealth of oral guidelines and precedents in an attempt to help integrate observance of the Torah into everyday life.

Jesus sometimes disagreed with the Pharisees, comparing them, for example, to "whitewashed tombs" (Matthew 23:27), meaning people who looked pious but were not so. However, in many ways, Jesus' teachings were not dissimilar to those of the Pharisees. Both the Pharisees and Jesus wanted to make religion more accessible, but in different ways. Whereas the Pharisees believed they were helping people worship, Jesus charged them with burdening people with more needless regulations – as well as not living up to their own rules.

### THE TALMUD

The Talmud was compiled in the 5th century. As the Oral Law it is a multi-volume commentary on the Written Law (the five books of Moses).

Even so, Jesus and the Pharisees are frequently found together: they had significant common interests. There are many instances in which Pharisees come and listen to Jesus or ask him questions; they invite him to dine with them (Luke 7:36; 11:37; 14:1) and even

**STUDYING SCRIPTURE**
The study of the Torah was an important aspect of Judaism to both Sadducees and Pharisees, as it is to Jews today. They gather in a yeshiva, or educational centre, to study both the Written and Oral Torah.

warn him of a threat to his safety (Luke 13:31). And some of Jesus' followers, such as Nicodemus, were themselves Pharisees (John 3:1).

After the fall of the Temple in AD 70, the Sadducean movement effectively disappeared. In contrast, the rabbinic Judaism that developed in the decades that followed had its roots in the Pharisean movement.

## THE HERODIANS

The Herodians, as the name implies, were supporters of the ruling regime – in Jesus' time, those associated with Herod Antipas, son of Herod the Great. Followers ranged from friends and family to employees and officials appointed to provide local government. Their concern with Jesus was not religious but political.

Like the Pharisees, some of this faction became followers of Jesus, notably Joanna, the wife of Herod's steward, Chuza (Luke 8:3), and "Manaen (who had been brought up with Herod the tetrarch)", who became part of the church at Antioch (Acts 13:1).

**HEROD'S WINTER PALACE, JERICHO**

**BEFORE**

Jesus was travelling towards
Jerusalem, telling parables to
the crowds that gathered.

**TABLE SALT**
Shortly before Jesus told the three parables
of the lost and found, he said: "Salt is good,
but if it loses its saltiness, how can it be
made salty again?" (Luke 14:34). At the
time, **salt was hugely important ‹‹ 304–05**
– as a preservative, it prevented food from
decay. Jesus was showing **he was God's
"salt", who preserved life and defied
corruption**. He was the "saltiness" or faith
in his followers, who he referred to as the
"salt of the Earth" (Matthew 5:13).

**AMONG THE UNCLEAN**
In the parable, the younger son works with pigs
when he has no money left. Deuteronomy states that
pigs are "unclean" (14:8), yet the boy has less to eat
than they do; he is shown as sinking to the lowest
possible point before seeking help from his father.

# The Prodigal Son

*Jesus' religious opponents objected to him eating with sinners,
as meals were a sign of friendship. Jesus explained his actions
by telling three parables – the lost sheep, lost coin, and lost son.*

**J**ESUS SAT with the tax
collectors and sinners and
told them three linked
parables. He asked them to suppose
that one of them was a shepherd
who had 100 sheep, but had lost
one. Would that man not leave the
others to search for the lost sheep
until he found it? Jesus explained:
"I tell you that in the same way
there will be more rejoicing in
heaven over one sinner who
repents than over ninety-nine
righteous people who do not need
to repent" (Luke 15:7).

Then Jesus told a second story,
about a woman who had 10 silver
coins and lost one. She swept her
house, searching carefully until she
found it, then she called together
her friends to rejoice. Jesus added,
"In the same way, I tell you, there
is rejoicing in the presence of the
angels of God over one sinner who
repents" (Luke 15:10).

### The son who left
The third story, which forms the
climax of the biblical chapter, was
about a man and his two sons.

One day, the younger of the sons
came to his father and demanded
his share of his father's estate.
Soon afterwards, the son "set off
for a distant country and there
squandered his wealth in wild
living" (15:13). After he had spent
everything, the country was hit by
a severe famine, and things became
desperate. So he found work
feeding pigs. But as he fed them,
he started longing to eat their food
himself. The thought made him
come to his senses, and he
remembered that at home, his

## A SON RETURNED

In *Return of the Prodigal Son*, Palma Il Giovane (1548–1628) depicts the son on his knees; he will be raised up by his father literally and metaphorically.

father's servants had so much to eat, they had food to spare – "and here I am starving to death!" (15:17).

He resolved to go home and tell his father that he had sinned against him and against heaven, and that although he was no longer worthy to be his father's son, he would ask if he might become a servant. Acting on this impulse, he set off for home.

### The son's return

His father saw the returning boy from a distance and ran to him, filled with compassion, and threw his arms around his son. The son gave his rehearsed speech, but his father brushed it aside and commanded the household servants to bring the boy fine clothes and prepare the best of feasts, "For this son of mine was dead and is alive again; he was lost and is found" (15:24). The celebrations began.

However, not everyone was happy. The boy's older brother returned from the fields to find

> " But while he was still a long way off, **his father saw him and was filled with compassion** for him; he ran to his son..."
>
> LUKE 15:20

> " Bring the fattened calf and kill it. Let's have a feast and celebrate. For **this son** of mine **was dead and is alive again**; he was lost and is found. "
>
> LUKE 15:23,24

the party in progress. He asked one of the servants what was happening, and the servant told him that his brother had returned and the boys' father had "killed the fattened calf because he has him back safe and sound" (15:27).

The older son was furious and confronted his father. He pointed out that for years he had been "slaving" (15:29) for his father and had never disobeyed him, but had never been rewarded with so much as "a young goat so I could celebrate with my friends" (15:29). But on the other hand, when his brother returned, having "squandered your property with prostitutes… you kill the fattened calf for him!" (15:30).

His father heard his angry words, and tried to explain. He gently pointed out that the older son was not unrewarded: "you are always with me, and everything I have is yours" (15:31). He went on to explain that it was impossible not to celebrate the joyous return of the younger son, because it was as though "this brother of yours was dead and is alive again" (15:32).

As in the parables of the lost sheep and the lost coin, the boy was lost and then found. At the end of the two earlier parables, Jesus reminded the gathered crowd that there is always rejoicing in heaven over a repentant sinner. This is not stated again at the end of the tale of the prodigal son, because the tale itself demonstrates the possibility of repentance and the enduring love of a father who wants only his son's return.

## CULTURAL CONTEXT

The parable of the prodigal son was rich in detail and cultural background that would have shocked Jesus' audience.

### INHERITANCE

Asking for an inheritance before a parent had died would have been seen as a sign of disrespect – it seemed to signal that the boy wished his father were dead.

### UNCLEAN WORK

Pigs were seen as unclean animals that Jewish people were forbidden to eat. Working with them and coveting their food would have been seen as sinking to the lowest level.

### DIGNITY AND GRACE

The father ran to his son, yet at the time it was considered undignified for a man old enough to have grown sons to run in public. Jesus uses the figure of the father to reveal God's grace and forgiveness, and the importance of grace over dignity.

CAROB SEEDS WERE OFTEN USED AS PIG FOOD

## LOST AND FOUND

All three of Jesus' parables in Luke 15 had the theme of "lost and found" – the sheep that wandered off but was found by its master (15:1–7), the silver coin that was lost and then discovered after a woman's careful search (15:8–10), and the son who departed for a distant country but returned to his father (15:11–32). The parables would have had a strong resonance to the Jewish listeners, whose prophets had likened them to "lost sheep; their shepherds have led them astray" (Jeremiah 50:6) since the gradual decline of Israel. Jesus asserted that he was the good shepherd (see panel, p.346) who "was sent only to the lost sheep of Israel" (Matthew 15:24).

**SHEEP GRAZING IN THE SOUTHERN MOUNTAINS OF JUDEA, NEAR HEBRON**

## AFTER »

**Jesus continued to tell parables to the gathered crowd, made up of Pharisees and sinners.**

### THE SHREWD MANAGER

Jesus followed his prodigal son story with a parable **commending a man who used dishonest book-keeping** (Luke 16:1–9). Under threat of losing his job, a manager decided to improve his future prospects by cutting in half what was owed by debtors to his master. Jesus said that the master commended the manager, and went on to say that "the people of this world are more shrewd in dealing with their own kind than are the people of the light" (16:8). He then said, "I tell you, use worldly wealth to gain friends for yourselves, so that when it is gone, you will be **welcomed into eternal dwellings**" (16:9). This seems strange advice, but must perhaps be taken in context with what follows. He explained that "you cannot serve both God and money" (16:13). Turning to the Pharisees, who "loved money" (Luke 16:14), he pointed out that "**what people value highly is detestable in God's sight**" (16:15).

## BEFORE

**Throughout John's gospel Jesus is portrayed as the source of life.**

### WINTER IN JERUSALEM
In Jerusalem for the Festival of Dedication, or Hannukkah, Jesus was asked by Jews in the Temple courts to **confirm that he was the Messiah**. His answer anticipates the raising of Lazarus, "My sheep **<< 369** listen to my voice... I give them eternal life, and they shall never perish" (John 10:27–28).

### RETURN TO THE START
Jesus returned to the place where **John had baptized people << 300–01**. The people there realized that everything "John said about this man was true" (10:41).

### PEOPLE

#### MARY, MARTHA, AND LAZARUS

Jesus' friends Lazarus, Mary, and Martha appear several times in the gospels. They seem to have provided a home near Jerusalem for Jesus and his disciples. Luke's gospel describes Martha as preoccupied with domestic duties, while Mary was keener to listen to Jesus' teaching (see p.360). After Lazarus was raised from the dead, he and his sisters hosted a meal for Jesus. Mary later anointed Jesus with expensive perfume and wiped his feet with her hair (John 12:1–3, see pp.386–87).

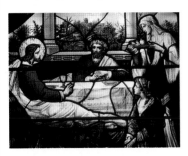

**JESUS, LAZARUS, MARY, AND MARTHA, 19TH-CENTURY STAINED GLASS WINDOW**

# Lazarus Raised from the Dead

*John's gospel tells the story of Jesus being called to the aid of his sick friend Lazarus, but delaying until Lazarus has died. This gives Jesus the opportunity to prove that he is the Messiah, with power over life and death.*

**J**ESUS' FRIEND Lazarus and his sisters Mary and Martha lived in the village of Bethany, in Judea. Lazarus fell seriously ill and the sisters sent word to Jesus telling him that his friend was sick. When the news reached Jesus, he said that Lazarus' illness would not end in death, rather: "it is for God's glory so that God's Son may be glorified through it" (John 11:4).

### Walking in the light
Jesus loved his friends, so two days later he called his disciples to follow him back to Judea. The disciples were worried, however, pointing out that not long before, the Jews there had tried to stone him. Jesus reassured them by saying that "anyone who walks in the day-time will not stumble, for they see by this world's light. It is when a person walks at night that they stumble, for they have no light" (11:9,10). He walked in the day-time of God's light, so had nothing to fear. He went on, "Our friend Lazarus has fallen asleep; but I am going there to wake him up" (11:11). The disciples were confused – thinking that he meant Lazarus was simply resting, they suggested that sleep might be good for the ill man. Then Jesus made himself clear: "Lazarus is dead, and for your sake I am glad I was not there, so that you may believe. But let us go to him" (11:14,15).

Bethany was less than 3km (2 miles) from Jerusalem, but by the time Jesus approached it, Lazarus had already been in his tomb for four days. Martha came to meet him, saying that if Jesus had arrived earlier, he could have saved her brother. Even now, demonstrating complete faith in Jesus, she asserted her belief that God would give him whatever he asked for. Jesus assured her that her brother would rise again. Martha agreed, mistaking his meaning; she told him that she knew Lazarus would indeed rise again in the resurrection at the last day. This had been promised in the Old Testament: "Multitudes who sleep in the dust of the earth will awake" (Daniel 12:2). But Jesus told her that this was not a hope for the future, "I am the resurrection and the life. The one who believes in me will live, even though they die; and whoever lives by believing in me will never die" (11:25,26). He asked if she believed this, and Martha replied that she believed he was the Messiah, "the Son of God, who is to come into the world" (11:27).

**TOMB OF LAZARUS**
The traditional site of the tomb of Lazarus can be visited today in Bethany, a Muslim and Christian village on the slopes of the Mount of Olives to the east of Jerusalem.

### Jesus moved to tears
Martha called to her sister Mary and told her that Jesus had come and was asking for her. Mary went to Jesus and fell weeping at his feet. She too said, "Lord, if you had been here, my brother would not have died" (11:32). When Jesus saw her weeping, and those around her also crying, he was deeply moved. He asked where they had laid Lazarus, and they

> **"Lord… if you had been here, my brother would not have died. But I know that even now God will give you whatever you ask."**
>
> JOHN 11:21,22

urged him to come and see. The Bible records his response in its shortest verse: "Jesus wept" (John 11:35). Some of the Jews, seeing this, remarked on how much Jesus must have loved Lazarus, but others were quizzical; Jesus had made a blind man see – could he not have prevented Lazarus from dying?

### Lazarus comes back to life

The tomb was a cave with a stone laid across its entrance. When the group arrived there, Jesus told them to take away the stone. Martha objected, fearful of the stench of decaying flesh, but Jesus insisted, saying, "Did I not tell you that if you believe, you will see the glory of God?" (11:40). When the stone was removed, Jesus looked up and thanked God for hearing his prayer – not for himself, but "for the benefit of the people standing here, that they may believe that you sent me" (11:42). Then he called out to Lazarus in a loud voice to come out of the tomb.

Miraculously, Lazarus emerged from the tomb. His hands and feet were still wrapped with strips of linen, and there was a cloth around his face. Jesus said to the astonished group, "Take off the grave clothes and let him go" (11:44). Many of the Jews who witnessed this began to believe.

## AFTER

**The action of bringing Lazarus back to life had significant repercussions.**

### AFTERSHOCKS

Some of the Jews who witnessed the raising of Lazarus were horrified and went to tell the Pharisees what had happened (John 11:46). They **called a meeting of the Sanhedrin** (the Jewish supreme court) to decide what to do. Some feared that Jesus' undeniable power and increasing fame would bring a hostile reaction from Rome (John 11:48), which would then take away "our temple and our nation" (11:48). Their high priest **Caiaphas 392–93 ≫** then rebuked the entire council, saying "You do not realize that it is better for you that one man die for the people than that the whole nation perish" (11:50). **One man dying for all 400–01 ≫** was the meaning of Jesus' mission. John's gospel goes on to say that Caiaphas, as high priest that year, prophesied that Jesus would die for the Jewish nation – and not only that nation, but all "the scattered children of God, to bring them together and make them one" (11:51,52).

**ITALIAN 1ST-CENTURY FIGURUINE OF A ROMAN STANDARD-BEARER, SYMBOLIZING ROMAN POWER**

**LAZARUS ARISEN**
In Fra Angelico's *The Resurrection of Lazarus* (c.1450), Jesus summons Lazarus from the tomb as the apostles, Mary, and Martha look on. The figures with halos are venerated as saints by most Christian denominations.

## BEFORE

**Jesus departed from Galilee and travelled south along the River Jordan towards Jerusalem.**

### ACROSS THE JORDAN
Jesus reached Perea (from the Greek for "land beyond"), the region on the eastern bank of the Jordan. He was **followed by large crowds and healed many people.**

### TESTED BY THE PHARISEES
Jesus was approached by a group of **Pharisees ‹‹ 336–37** who quizzed him on his interpretation of the Law regulating divorce (Matthew 19:1–12). Their intention was to lure Jesus into **contradicting the Law ‹‹ 106–09,** but he responded by questioning their interpretation of Scripture.

# Workers in the Vineyard

*Jesus' encounter with a rich young man provoked arguments among the disciples about riches and rewards. Jesus replied with a parable about God's surprising generosity, which transcended their notions of fairness.*

**J**ESUS MET A YOUNG man who asked him an important question: "What good thing must I do to inherit eternal life?" (Matthew 19:16). Jesus said "go, sell your possessions and give to the poor... then come, follow me" (19:21). The young went away deflated because he was rich and had many possessions. The encounter started a debate about riches and wealth among the disciples, during which Jesus told them that it would be easier for a camel to go through the eye of a needle than for a rich person to enter the kingdom of God.

### Sacrifice and reward
The disciples were baffled by Jesus' response. Peter said "We have left everything to follow you! What then will there be for us?" (19:27). Jesus answered that everyone who had made such sacrifices will gain their reward and inherit eternal life. But he added an enigmatic final point: "Many who are first will be last, and many who are last will be first" (19:30).

### The parable of the workers
Jesus told his disciples a parable to illustrate his point: "The kingdom of heaven is like a landowner who went out early in the morning to

## THE WORKERS RECEIVE THEIR PAY
In this Romanian manuscript from 1580, the workers are depicted toiling in the vineyard before receiving their pay from the vineyard manager, who takes instructions from the seated landowner.

## WINE AND VINEYARDS

Jesus used the image of wine or vineyards in many stories and sayings.

In the parable of the tenants in the vineyard (Matthew 21:33–41; Mark 12:1–9; Luke 20:9–16) the evil tenants kill slaves who come to collect the owner's produce. Eventually they kill his son too.

In the parable of the two sons (Matthew 21:28–32), two sons are asked to go and work in their father's vineyard, exploring the nature of true obedience and humility.

Jesus talks about not putting new wine into old wineskins (Matthew 9:17). The new wine would ferment, stretching the old leather beyond breaking point.

**GROWING VINES IN GALILEE**
Wine production has been an important industry in the Holy Land for thousands of years. In Jesus' day, vineyards were surrounded by walls to keep animals out, and overlooked by watch towers.

hire workers for his vineyard" (20:1). He agreed a wage with those whom he chose – one denarius for a day's work – and sent them into his vineyard.

The workers began their toil in the vineyard at six o'clock in the morning, the customary time for labourers to start their working day. Three hours later, the owner returned to the market place on the lookout for more workers. He saw those standing around without work and said to them "You also go and work in my vineyard, and I will pay you whatever is right" (20:4). So they also went to toil for the landowner. Still the landowner needed – or wanted – more workers, so he did the same thing at midday and again at three in the afternoon. Finally, at about five o'clock that afternoon he returned to the market place and saw the last few workers standing around. "Why have you been standing here all day long doing nothing?" (20:6) he asked them. They replied that no one had hired them, so he said to them: "You also go and work in my vineyard" (20:7).

### A fair day's pay

When evening came and it was time to stop work, the vineyard owner said to his manager, "Call the workers and pay them their wages, beginning with the last ones hired and going on to the first" (20:8). Those hired at about five o'clock in the afternoon received one denarius – a full day's pay. Those hired at six o'clock in the morning then came to be paid. They expected to receive more than the latecomers, but each also received one denarius.

These workers became indignant and began to complain to the vineyard owner. They argued that the last men had worked only one hour, yet had been paid the same as "us who have borne the burden of the work and the heat of the day" (20:12). The owner replied to one of them, "I am not being unfair to you, friend. Didn't you agree to work for a denarius?" (20:13). He told him to take his pay and go, asking "Don't I have the right to do what I want with my own money? Or are you envious because I am generous?" (20:15).

Jesus finished by reasserting his earlier point: "So the last will be first, and the first last" (20:16).

> ## "So the **last will be first,** and the **first will be last.**"
>
> MATTHEW 20:16

### THE VINEYARD OWNER

The denarius was a silver Roman coin and represented the usual day's wage for a labourer – subsistence pay. By comparison, a skilled scribe earned two denarii per day.

The vineyard owner was following the ancient Law, "Do not hold back the wages of a hired worker overnight" (Leviticus 19:13) – day-labourers earned just enough to see them through that day.

**DENARIUS COINS**

This parable addresses God's grace – or unmerited favour. The owner is usually interpreted as God, whose generous nature is to show surprising kindness to all people. It is up to God to bestow his generosity how he wishes. Jesus' point is that the kingdom of God does not run according to worldly principles – it is radical and transforming. There is no hierarchy – all people are welcomed unreservedly, and at any time.

Jesus continued his journey towards Jerusalem and taught his disciples further lessons about leadership and reward, and service and sacrifice.

### CAN YOU DRINK THE CUP?

The disciples James and John asked to sit at Jesus' left and right hand in positions of prestige and honour. "Can you drink the cup I am about to drink?" (Matthew 20:22) Jesus asked, to which they answered "We can". Jesus was referring to the **cup of suffering and martyrdom 390–91 ≫**. James was, indeed, to drink from the same cup – he was **martyred by Herod Agrippa 432–33 ≫**.

### HEALINGS IN JERICHO

Jesus and his disciples reached Jericho, where he met **two blind beggars who called out for mercy**. He touched their eyes and restored their sight (Matthew 20:29–34).

**BIBLICAL JERICHO WAS A RICH AND FLOURISHING TRADING TOWN**

**BEFORE**

Jesus spoke to his disciples about who could enter the kingdom of God.

### LITTLE CHILDREN

The disciples rebuked people for **bringing babies to Jesus to be blessed**, but Jesus said, "Let the little children come to me, and do not hinder them, for the kingdom of God belongs to such as these. Truly I tell you, **anyone who will not receive the kingdom of God like a little child will never enter it**" (Luke 18:16,17).

**CHRIST BLESSING THE CHILDREN, 16TH-CENTURY FRENCH SCHOOL**

### THE RICH

Jesus spoke to a rich young ruler, saying: "It is easier for a **camel to go through the eye of a needle** than for someone who is rich to enter the kingdom of God" (Luke 18:25). However, he reassured Peter that "No one who has left home...for the sake of the kingdom of God will **fail to receive many times as much in this age, and in the age to come eternal life**" (18:29,30).

# A Blind Man and a Tax Collector

*As Jesus travelled into Jericho, he met two men. One was physically blind, while the other was morally blinded by greed. But both men responded to Christ, and were saved.*

**J**ESUS WAS entering Jericho, with a crowd following him, when a blind beggar sitting by the roadside heard the commotion. He asked what was happening, and was told that "Jesus of Nazareth is passing by" (Luke 18:37). He seems to have known something about Jesus, because he called out to him using one of the names associated with the Messiah, appealing to him for grace: "Jesus, Son of David, have mercy on me!" (18:38). Some members of the crowd tried to silence him, perhaps feeling that he was an embarrassment, but he repeated his shouts for Jesus to grant him mercy. Jesus heard his cry and stopped, calling the man to come to him. He asked, "What do you want me to do for you?" (18:41). Luke's gospel does not give the blind beggar's name, but Mark's identifies him as Bartimaeus. He replied to Jesus, "Lord, I want to see" (18:41). Jesus answered back, "Receive your sight; your faith has healed you" (18:42). Bartimaeus's eyesight was immediately restored, and all those who had witnessed the miracle praised God with him.

> " Receive your sight; **your faith has healed you.** "
>
> **LUKE** 18:42

### The tax collector

Jesus and his entourage walked on and entered the city of Jericho. Knowing that Jesus was passing through, a wealthy tax collector named Zacchaeus struggled to see him, but he was too short to see over the crowds. He ran ahead and climbed a sycamore-fig tree to get a better view. When Jesus came past, he called up, "Zacchaeus, come down immediately. I must stay at your house today" (19:5). Zacchaeus climbed out of the tree straight away and welcomed Jesus.

### Zacchaeus repents

The crowd saw Jesus do this and were unhappy about it. They began muttering that Jesus had gone to the home of a sinner. Zacchaeus's response was swift and sincere. Speaking to Jesus – and in

front of the hostile onlookers – he offered to give half of everything that he owned to the poor, and to repay anyone he had cheated by four times the amount.

Jesus recognized that Zacchaeus's words were born out of genuine faith and genuine repentance. He spoke, significantly, not to the crowd but to the person that the

**HEALING THE BLIND**
*The Blind of Jericho (1650)* by Nicolas Poussin shows Jesus approaching two blind men. The painting may have taken inspiration from Matthew's account, which says that two blind men shouted to Jesus for mercy and were healed (Matthew 20:30).

**HISTORY AND CULTURE**

## TAX COLLECTORS

The Mishnah (a Jewish commentary on the Law) called tax collectors "unclean", while Jewish tax collectors were also despised and resented for collaborating with the Romans. Rome needed tax revenues and required a dependable means of tax collection, so they recruited Jews, because they thought that – as locals – they would know the financial health of those around them, and understand their customs. Zacchaeus was "a chief tax collector" (Luke 19:2), meaning that he oversaw a team of revenue gatherers for Rome. Tax collectors were widely suspected of lining their own pockets by charging more than Rome required – a charge that seemed accurate in the case of Zacchaeus.

**A TAX COLLECTOR AT WORK, SHOWN IN A 2ND-CENTURY MARBLE RELIEF**

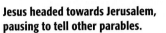

crowd had written off as a sinner, saying: "Today salvation has come to this house, because this man, too, is a son of Abraham" (19:9).

Jesus affirmed Zacchaeus as a "son of Abraham", an heir of the covenant. He then explained his actions in the context of his own mission, saying that the Son of Man came to seek and to save the lost. He had not told Zacchaeus to repay those he had cheated. For Jesus, Zacchaeus was not just a sinner, he was a Hebrew who had got lost. And it was the lost that God had sent Jesus to seek and to save (see pp.368–69).

### The two stories

There were parallels between the stories of Bartimaeus the blind man and Zacchaeus the tax

### THE CITY OF PALMS

Jericho is the world's oldest walled city, dating back at least 9,000 years. Described in Deuteronomy as the City of Palms (34:3), it was a welcome oasis in the desert in biblical times.

collector. Zacchaeus demonstrated his eagerness by climbing the tree, just as the blind beggar was insistent in shouting out to catch the attention of Jesus as he passed by. Neither was prepared to give up, and both had absolute faith. Jesus looked up in the tree and addressed Zacchaeus, just as he stopped and called for the blind man to come to him. Then Jesus publicly invited himself to Zacchaeus' house – in the face of the crowd's disapproval – just as he had disregarded those who tried to silence the blind man.

**TREE-TOP VIEW**
Zacchaeus peers down from a sycamore-fig tree to catch a glimpse of Jesus in Duccio di Buoninsegna's painted panel for Siena Cathedral, Italy (c.1308). The crowd is depicted remonstrating with him below.

AFTER »

**Jesus headed towards Jerusalem, pausing to tell other parables.**

**PILGRIM CROWDS**
Jesus was **surrounded by crowds in Jericho**. Many of those around him were clearly his disciples, but Passover was near, and thousands of people would have been **passing through Jericho en route to Jerusalem**. Some of those in the crowds would have been Passover pilgrims, with a variety of attitudes towards Jesus.

**THE KINGDOM OF GOD**
As he neared Jerusalem, Jesus paused to **tell more parables 376–77 »**, because "the people thought that the kingdom of God was going to appear at once" (19:11).

> "Today **salvation has come to this house**… For the **Son of Man came** to seek and **to save the lost.**"
>
> LUKE 19:9,10

**BEFORE**

**Jesus was in Jericho on his way to Jerusalem.**

**LOCAL RESISTANCE**
The historian Josephus, notes in *Antiquities* that c.4 BC a Jewish delegation travelled to Rome to ask Caesar not to make **Herod Archelaus king over them**. The parable of the ten coins echoes this opposition.

**HEALING THE BLIND**
As Jesus entered Jerusalem he **healed a blind man** begging by the road.

**ANALYSIS**
## JESUS AS JUDGE AND KING

This parable is a story that works at many different levels and has several messages. Most importantly, it highlights Jesus' future role as judge. Jesus had been a searching shepherd in an earlier passage (Luke 15:4), as he was in many biblical references, but in this parable he is both king and judge. The parable reminds followers that they are accountable to God, and that "we must all appear before the judgment seat of Christ" (2 Corinthians 5:10). It also reminds listeners that God will be the judge of all; both his servants and enemies.

The picture of the "man of noble birth" being appointed king was an allusion to Jesus' enthronement at God's right hand (Luke 9:31; 24:51; Acts 2:33). The parable affirms Jesus' forthcoming departure from Earth at the ascension (Luke 24:50–53) and return at the end of the age (21:27–28).

The story calls on Jesus' early followers, and later Christians, to put the resources God has given them to good use, rather than "playing safe" and hiding their beliefs.

# Parable of the Coins

*Jesus' parable of the ten valuable coins, or minas, drew together two important messages: everyone would be judged in the coming kingdom of God, and the disciples should spread God's message as widely as possible.*

**AS JESUS NEARED** Jerusalem, he told his followers a parable about God's ultimate judgment. Jesus sat down with the assembled people and began to tell them about a man of noble birth who went to a distant country to have himself appointed king. He planned to return at a later date, however, and before he left, he gathered ten of his servants and distributed money between them. Each received one mina (worth around three month's wages) and the nobleman ordered them to "put this money to work... until I come back" (Luke 19:13).

The nobleman then set out for the country where he was to be made king. Some of the people disliked him so intensely that they sent a delegation after him, to say that they didn't want him to be made king. Nonetheless, he was successful in being crowned, and returned home as a king.

### Honour and rebuke
On his return home, the new king called his servants together to see what they had done with the money he had given them, and in particular what they had gained.

**BURYING THE COINS**
A stained glass window at St Lawrence Church, Gloucestershire, UK, shows the third servant of the parable trying to minimize risk by burying his mina, instead of putting it to good use.

The first servant came to the new king and said, "Sir, your mina has earned ten more" (19:16). His master commended him, and appointed him to a place of honour, saying, "Well done, my good servant!... Because you have been trustworthy in a very small matter, take charge of ten cities" (19:17).

The second servant had not had the same measure of success, but even so his original mina had generated five more. Still his master rewarded him, saying, "You take charge of five cities" (19:18).

**SERVANT AT WORK**
This 3rd-century AD Roman mosaic depicts a slave serving a drink to his master. Roman slaves were able to buy their freedom, so the king in the parable of the coins may have been helping his harder working servants to freedom.

> **"He went on to tell them a parable, because he was near Jerusalem and the people thought that the kingdom of God was going to appear at once."**
> LUKE 19:11

Then another servant arrived and said, "Sir, here is your mina; I have kept it laid away in a piece of cloth. I was afraid of you, because you are a hard man. You take out what you did not put in and reap what you did not sow" (19:20,21). The master was not impressed, and said, "I will judge you by your own words, you wicked servant! You knew, did you, that I am a hard man, taking out what I did not put in, and reaping what I did not sow? Why then didn't you put my money on deposit, so that when I came back, I could have collected it with interest?" (19:22,23). The king turned to those standing nearby and told them to take the man's one mina and give it to the first man, who had amassed ten.

### King and judge
The people briefly protested, pointing out that the first servant already had ten minas. But the king explained to them that everyone who already had something would be given more, while those who had nothing would have what little they had taken away.

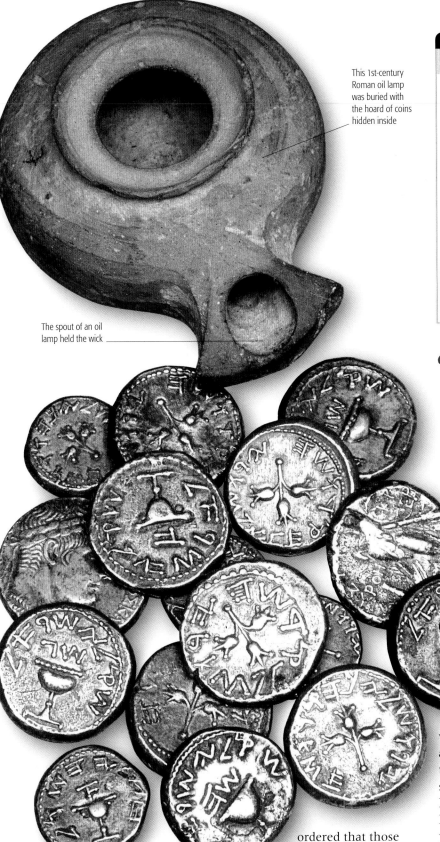

This 1st-century Roman oil lamp was buried with the hoard of coins hidden inside

The spout of an oil lamp held the wick

## MONEY AND WAGES

The gospel accounts mention several monetary units, particularly the drachma, mina, and talent. The drachma was the coin described in the parable of the lost coin (Luke 15:8). It was the daily wage for a day-labourer at the time, and roughly equivalent to a Roman denarius. The mina, referred to in this parable, was worth about 100 drachmae or 3 month's wages. A talent was worth around 60 minas or 6,000 drachmae. It was not a coin, but originally a value of weight, here representing a very large sum. Jesus refers to talents in his "parable of the talents", recorded in Matthew (25:14–30), which is a similar tale to the parable of the coins.

**A WATER-FILLED ROMAN AMPHORA WEIGHED THE SAME AS 80 TALENTS**

> " … I tell you that **to everyone who has, more will be given**, but as for the **one who has nothing, even what they have will be taken away**. "
>
> **LUKE** 19:26

The inscription on the shekels reads "Jerusalem the Holy"

### ANCIENT JUDEAN COINS
Shekels struck during the First Revolt of the Jews, c. AD 66, were decorated with a Temple chalice on one side and three pomegranates in transition from flower to fruit on the reverse.

### AFTER

After he left Jericho and neared Jerusalem, Jesus met both resistance and faith.

#### THANKFUL WORSHIP
Lazarus' sister Mary showed her love for Jesus by **pouring perfume on his feet** and wiping his feet with her hair – a gesture of worship after Jesus raised her brother from the dead **386–87 »**.

#### A FALSE CAUSE
Members of the Sanhedrin were **looking for a reason to put Jesus to death**. They were waiting for him to come to Jerusalem for the necessary ceremonial cleansing (ritual purification through immersion in water in a *mikveh*, or bath) before the Passover festival (John 11:55).

**THE ROAD TO JERUSALEM FROM JERICHO**

The parable closes with a sobering note that draws attention to the fact that the nobleman's power now extended beyond his servants to the rest of the people in the land – he was in a position to judge and sentence them. After awarding the third servant's mina to the first, he ordered that those who had rebelled against him, spreading news of their hatred towards him, be brought in front of him straight away and killed on the spot.

The most common understanding of this parable is that Jesus is the man of noble birth who would disappear for a while but return as king. He entrusted his disciples with his message (the minas) and wanted them to spread this as widely as possible. They should not play safe and hide his words, but take risks so that his message reached as many people as possible.

The final part of the story suggests that people who stand in opposition to Jesus' message will face a terrible judgment "on the day when God judges people's secrets through Jesus Christ" (Romans 2:16). On that day Christ's servants will be commended or reproved, and his enemies will be destroyed.

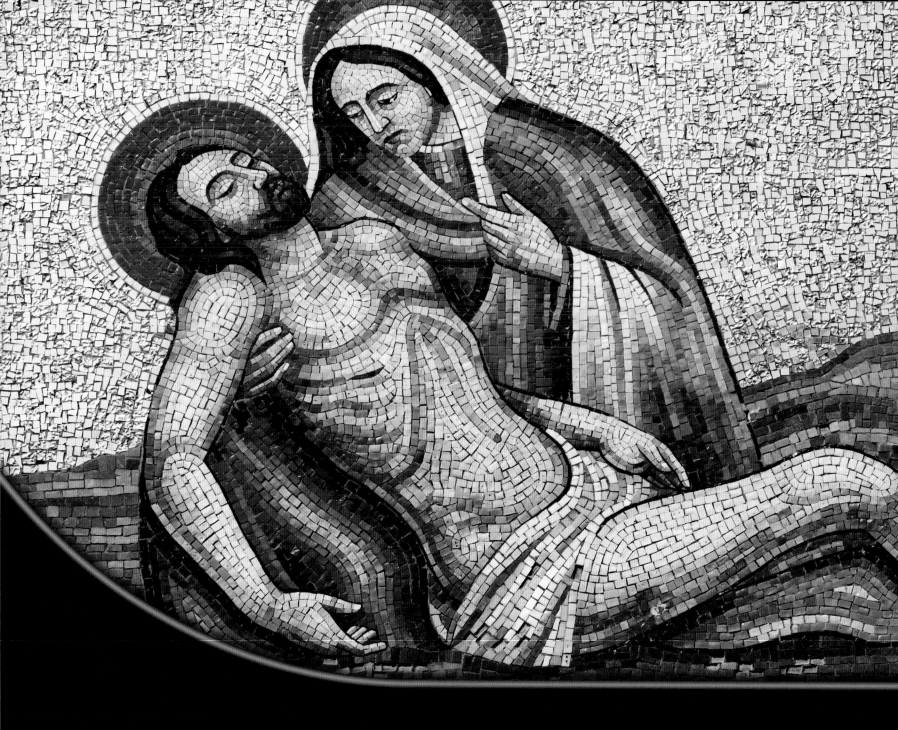

# THE CROSS AND THE TOMB

"What I received I passed on to you as of first importance: that **Christ died for our sins according to the Scriptures**, that he was **buried**, that he was **raised on the third day** according to the Scriptures."

1 CORINTHIANS 15:3,4

 HE EVENTS SURROUNDING JESUS' CRUCIFIXION AND resurrection form the climax of the story told by the four gospel writers. Each gospel spends more time describing how Jesus was betrayed, tried, executed, buried, and then discovered risen again three days later, than on any other event in his life. The first Christians recognized that what happened to Jesus during that single week had huge consequences – it fulfilled the ancient promises of God and opened up a new future for all the world.

Whereas much of Jesus' ministry had been based in the northern region of Galilee and the southern area of Judea, the key events of the last week before his death took place in the city of Jerusalem – the centre of Jewish national, religious, and political life. Jesus and his disciples arrived in Jerusalem amid the preparations for Passover – the festival that commemorates the Exodus from Egypt – when the city was full of devoted pilgrims eager to worship God for all his mighty acts in the past. However, that year the Passover pilgrims would experience God's activity among them at first hand.

### THE PASSION

Beginning with Jesus' triumphant entry into Jerusalem and ending with his death on a cross, the last week of Jesus' life is known as his "Passion", which comes from the Greek *pascho* meaning "to suffer". The Old Testament prophets had foretold that God's kingdom on Earth would arrive only after an intensely painful battle with evil. Jesus fulfilled all the prophecies: he was betrayed by a friend for 30 pieces of silver (Zechariah 11:12,13), spat upon and beaten (Isaiah 50:6), remained silent against false accusations and was led like "a lamb to the slaughter" (Isaiah 53:7), then executed (Zechariah 12:10). Jesus suffered all this on behalf of the world: as Isaiah said, "he took up our pain and bore our suffering… he was pierced for our transgressions, he was crushed for our iniquities… by his wounds we are healed" (Isaiah 53:4,5).

### NEW LIFE

Jesus' death was not the end of his life – after three days he rose again. Isaiah had prophesied about this too: "after he has suffered, he will see the light of life" (53:11). Jesus' resurrection fulfilled the promises of the Old Testament and showed God's desire to do away with sin, and breathe everlasting life into all things on Earth.

**CHRISTIAN SYMBOL**
For the first two centuries after Jesus' crucifixion, Christians used the image of a fish to symbolize their faith; by the end of the second century, the cross – like this example from 18th-century Zaire – had taken its place.

« BEFORE

Jesus' ministry was beginning to anger the Jewish authorities, but it was also fulfilling centuries-old prophecies.

**A THREAT TO AUTHORITY**
In the village of Bethany, near Jerusalem, Jesus had **raised his friend Lazarus from the dead** « **370–71**. Many people had come to see Lazarus and so Jesus' popularity grew. Because of this, the authorities had begun to plot how they might kill both Lazarus and Jesus (John 12:9–11).

**BETHANY**

# A King Astride a Donkey

*Just days before his arrest, trial, and execution, Jesus was welcomed into Jerusalem by a crowd of pilgrims. As he rode into the city on a borrowed donkey, the people hailed him as their long-awaited king.*

**J**ESUS AND HIS disciples were on their way to Jerusalem to celebrate the Passover. The roads were busy, because all male Jews who were able to travel were expected to make the pilgrimage to Jerusalem for this annual festival, which was one of the three main feasts of Judaism, together with Pentecost and the Feast of Tabernacles (see pp.182–83).

### Bethphage and Bethany

After the long climb from Jericho, Jesus and his followers stopped at the villages of Bethphage and Bethany, on the slopes of the Mount of Olives a short distance from Jerusalem. Jesus often stayed here because it was where his friends Mary, Martha, and Lazarus lived. Many other pilgrims would stay in such accessible villages whenever the major Jewish festivals were held because Jerusalem became too crowded.

Jesus told two of his disciples to go into the village ahead of them, where they would find a colt – a young male donkey – that had never been ridden. He instructed them, "Untie it and bring it here", adding that if they were stopped by any of the villagers and asked what they were doing, they should reply, "The Lord needs it and will send it back here shortly" (Mark 11:3).

The disciples went into the village and found a colt tied up at a doorway in the street, just as Jesus had said they would. They untied it and led the borrowed donkey out of the village to Jesus.

### A royal procession

When they returned, the disciples threw their cloaks over the donkey's back to form a simple saddle, and Jesus climbed onto it. The road ahead of them led down the western slope of the Mount of Olives, through the Kidron Valley to the gates of Jerusalem. It then climbed up to the Temple, the ultimate destination of all Jewish festival pilgrimages.

Sitting on the colt, Jesus began this short journey accompanied only by his disciples, but very soon a crowd of other pilgrims had gathered around him. These pilgrims recognized the significance of what Jesus was doing (see panel, right): he was entering Jerusalem as royalty by being astride an animal, but he had chosen to make this appearance in a modest fashion by riding a donkey rather than anything grander.

### Palm branches and blessings

Some of the people began to spread their cloaks out on the road in front of the colt. Others cut off palm branches from the trees in the neighbouring fields to lay on the road or wave in the air.

As the impromptu procession of pilgrims moved with Jesus towards Jerusalem, they shouted words of blessing from Psalm 118. These words were often used to bless pilgrims as they arrived in Jerusalem, but now they took on a deeper meaning as the crowd welcomed Jesus into the city as a sovereign: "Hosanna!" (an exclamation derived from the Hebrew *Hoshana*, meaning "Save!"), "Blessed is he who comes in the name of the Lord!", and "Blessed is the coming kingdom of our father David!" they shouted (11:9,10). Accompanied by these cries of joy and expectation, Jesus entered through the city gates and went up to the courts of the Temple.

## "'Blessed is he who comes in the name of the Lord!' 'Hosanna in the highest heaven!'"

MATTHEW 21:9

#### THE SAVIOUR COMES
*Entry into Jerusalem* by il Sassetta (1392–1450) depicts pilgrims waving palm fronds while others lay down their cloaks ahead of Jesus' colt. Many of the Jews may have recognized the acting out of a prophecy (Zechariah 9:9,10) that God's long-awaited king would arrive on a donkey's foal, rather than a warhorse, because he brought peace.

### HISTORY AND CULTURE
#### TRIUMPHAL PROCESSIONS

Throughout history, rulers have entered triumphantly into important cities. A military-minded king might have chosen to ride a warhorse, a symbol of power and prestige. Jesus chose to ride a donkey, an everyday working animal, and was welcomed by ordinary people. When enthroned as king of Israel, Solomon had ridden a humble mule (1 Kings 1:33–40).

The palm branches waved by the pilgrims were associated with Hanukkah, an annual festival that celebrates the successful revolt of Judas Maccabaeus (see pp.266–67) against the Syrian king, Antiochus IV, who had desecrated the Temple. In 164 BC the Temple was purified and rededicated; then the Jews processed triumphantly into Jerusalem, waving palm branches.

**PALM FROND**

### AFTER »

**After a joyful welcome into Jerusalem, Jesus arrived at the centre of Jewish national and religious life, the Temple.**

#### PALM SUNDAY
Christians today celebrate Jesus' arrival in Jerusalem on Palm Sunday, the Sunday before Easter Day. Some churches re-enact the joyful procession with palm branches or small crosses made from palm fronds.

#### GREEK-SPEAKING PILGRIMS
A group of Greek pilgrims in Jerusalem for the Passover sent a message to Jesus, asking to see him. Jesus replied that the time had come for him to be lifted up **(on the cross 398–99 »)**, and that he would draw all people to himself (John 12:20–36).

**GREEK NOTICE ON THE TEMPLE WALL BARRING GENTILES FROM ENTERING THE SANCTUARY**

JERUSALEM'S TEMPLE RESTORED  Work began *c.*20 BC  Destroyed AD 70

# Herod's Temple

## "Jesus entered the temple courts and drove out all who were buying and selling there."

MATTHEW 21:12

**MODEL OF HEROD'S TEMPLE**
This model shows Herod the Great's enlarged Temple, constructed from *c.*20 BC on Temple Mount in Jerusalem. The entrance pillars were called *Jakin* and *Boaz* after the names of the pillars in Solomon's Temple (2 Chronicles 3:17).

**T**HE TEMPLE – both Solomon's Temple (see pp.172–73) and the Second Temple (see pp.252–53), which was rebuilt and expanded by Herod the Great – was the focal point of Jewish national life. In Jesus' day, Herod's building work had made the Temple into a vast

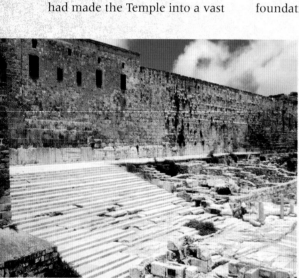

**GATES OF CHULDAH**
Jesus would have walked up the steps – a section of which has been restored – leading to the Huldah, or Chuldah, Gates, which was formerly a main entrance in the southern wall of Herod's Temple.

structure, occupying the most prominent location in Jerusalem, Temple Mount. It was known across the Roman world for its beauty.

Although the major reconstruction work had been completed between 20 BC and 10 BC, embellishments were added almost continuously until the mid-60s AD, providing valuable stimulus to the local construction industry. According to

Josephus, the renewed Temple, with its white stone and gold leaf, astonished people who visited it.

### Public space, sacred space

One of Herod's accomplishments was to enlarge the Temple complex, doubling the area of the original foundations. Engineers built up the area around the Temple – even filling in small valleys – to create room for a spacious plaza called the Court of the Gentiles. This was a public meeting place akin to a market bazaar – traders changed Roman coins into special Temple currency, while others sold unblemished animals required for sacrifices. This was the area from which Jesus drove out the traders (see pp.384–85). Teachers of the Law would use this space to instruct their students, as Jesus did during his ministry (see Matthew 21:23–27).

Each subsequent court in the Temple had restrictions. Only Jews could advance from the Court of the Gentiles into the Court of the Women. Next was the Court of the Israelites, which was only open to Jewish men. Here, they could hand sacrificial animals to the priests on duty, who would sacrifice them on the great altar (see 2 Chronicles 4).

Beyond was the sanctuary building itself, the most sacred space in the whole complex. Once inside the entry porch, it was divided into the Sanctuary and the Holy of Holies, separated by an embroidered curtain, which was torn in two when Jesus died (see p.401). Only priests could enter the Sanctuary, and only the high priest could enter the Holy of Holies, and even then, only once a year on the Day of Atonement (see pp.182–83).

### Levites and priests

The Temple was staffed by Levites and priests. Levites were members of the tribe of Levi, while the priests were Levites who were descended from Aaron (see 1 Chronicles 23,24). Priests had an array of duties, from the upkeep of the buildings and policing boundaries of the courts, to providing music

**HISTORY AND CULTURE**
**TEMPLE PRIESTS**

At the end of the 1st century AD, Josephus recorded that there were around 20,000 priests. Most were not wealthy and lived away from Jerusalem, except for when they were performing their duties. However, within Jerusalem there was a small group of powerful chief priests, drawn from a few families that included the Boethus and Kathros, who were notable members of the Jewish aristocracy.

**A STONE WEIGHT WITH THE NAME KATHROS**

for worship. They were available to help worshippers determine what kind of sacrifice they needed to provide, depending on the occasion of their offering (see 2 Chronicles 8:12–15). A central part of the priests' work was to make the sacrifices on the altar, and proclaim absolution and blessing to the worshipper; they would also perform purification rites for those who had recovered from disease or were considered to be ritually unclean. One of the highest honours for a priest was to burn incense in the Temple Sanctuary, as Zechariah, John the Baptist's father, had done (see pp.278–79).

By the 1st century AD, there were so many priests that they had to follow a rota for their duties. Priests were divided into groups and served in the Temple for two week-long

CHRONOLOGY IN BRIEF

- **c.1440s BC,** after the Exodus from Egypt, God instructs Moses to make the Tent of Meeting, a large tent complex that is to be the Israelites' place of worship.

- **c.1020s BC,** King David wants to build a permanent "house" for God, but God tells him that his son Solomon will build it. David buys the site from Araunah and declares, "The house of the LORD God is to be here, and also the altar of burnt offering for Israel" (1 Chronicles 22:1).

- **c.967 BC,** King Solomon starts building work on the Temple, having "conscripted 70,000 men as carriers and 80,000 as stonecutters in the hills and 3,600 as foremen over them" (2 Chronicles 2:2). He tells Hiram of Tyre, "The temple I am going to build will be great, because our God is greater than all other gods" (2 Chronicles 2:5).

**VAN LOO'S PAINTING (c.1640) OF ZERUBBABEL SHOWING CYRUS A PLAN OF JERUSALEM**

- **c.960 BC,** the Temple is completed and dedicated.

- **c.587 BC,** Solomon's Temple is looted and destroyed by the Babylonian army when it captures Jerusalem.

- **c.537 BC,** some Jews return from exile in Babylon and begin rebuilding the Temple, overseen by Zerubbabel.

- **516 BC,** Zerubbabel's Temple (also known as the Second Temple) is completed and dedicated.

- **167 BC,** the Syrian king, Antiochus Epiphanes, invades Jerusalem and desecrates the Temple.

- **164 BC,** Judas Maccabeus defeats the Syrians and reconsecrates the Temple.

- **20 BC,** King Herod the Great begins rebuilding the Second Temple, to be the most wonderful building the world has seen up to that point. Major work is completed by 10 BC, but continual additions are made.

- **c.AD 27–30,** Jesus visits the Temple a number of times during his ministry, and clears the Temple traders days before his death.

- **AD 66,** a Jewish revolt against the Romans puts a stop to embellishment work on the Temple.

- **AD 70,** the Temple is destroyed by the Romans when they crush the Jewish rebellion.

sessions every year. When they were not performing these duties, many priests went out into the villages and towns, where they taught the Law and gave guidance and advice in legal matters.

### The Temple in national life

Jews paid the Temple tax annually, a topic that Jesus spoke to Peter about (Matthew 17:24–27). It derived from God's command that every Israelite should give a half shekel for the

work of the Tent of Meeting (see Exodus 30:11–16), which had been used for sacrifice and worship before the Temple was built. The authorities who oversaw the work of the Temple were important people within Jewish life. Often, they were from wealthy families, and belonged to the party of the Sadducees (see pp.366–67) . The

**KEY**
1. Court of the Gentiles
2. Court of the Women
3. Court of the Israelites
4. Sanctuary, containing Holy of Holies
5. Nicanor Gate

final destruction of the Jerusalem Temple by the Romans in AD 70 was seen by many as a fatal blow to Jewish identity.

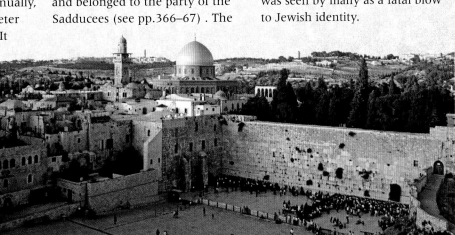

**THE WAILING WALL**
At the western side of the Temple Mount, this remnant of wall was once part of a retaining perimeter wall, built c.19 BC as part of the enlarged platform of Herod's Temple. For centuries, it has been a Jewish place of prayer.

**BEFORE**

In condemning the misuse of the Temple, Jesus was following prophetic tradition. Isaiah had spoken of the Temple as a "house of prayer" where all nations could meet with God, not just the Israelites (Isaiah 56:5–8).

### DEN OF ROBBERS

Centuries before Jesus, **Jeremiah ‹‹ 234–35** warned the Israelites not to make the Temple into a **"den of robbers"** (Jeremiah 7:11). God's people were committing all sorts of evil, but presumed they would be safe from judgment as long as they kept going to the Temple. Jeremiah reminded them that God **expected holy behaviour in the world**, not just in the Temple.

### THE BARREN FIG TREE

On his way to the Temple, Jesus saw a fig tree beside the road, **without any fruit**. He declared that this tree would never produce fruit again, and when he passed it the next day, the tree had withered away (Mark 11:12–14 and 20,21). The tree may have symbolized Israel's religious system, which **was not producing the good fruit that God expected**.

**FIG TREE**

### TRIBUTE COINS

When Jesus was asked whether taxes should be paid to Caesar (Mark 12:14,15), he asked for one of the "tribute-pennies" used to pay taxes. The coins bore the image of Tiberius Caesar and were controversial because images of humans were forbidden by Jewish Law. Even worse, as tokens of imperial religion they depicted Tiberius as high priest and son of the "divine Augustus" (the first Roman emperor). When Jesus replied that people should "give to Caesar what is Caesar's and to God what is God's", he was observing that the real issue was not about taxes, but whether to resist the blasphemous imperial religion and remain true to God.

# Driving out the Temple Traders

*After Jesus' royal entry into Jerusalem, he returned to the Temple, where his prophetic actions and teachings exposed the misuse of the Temple and pointed to its eventual destruction.*

**T**HE DAY FOLLOWING his triumphant entry, Jesus returned to the Temple with his disciples. As they arrived in the spacious outer court, they were greeted by the typical hustle and bustle of the Temple business. Money-changers were at their stalls, exchanging commonly used Roman coins for Temple currency. These special coins were needed in order to purchase the unblemished animals required for sacrifices, which were sold at other stalls in the Temple.

### Jesus acts

The sight of all this activity stirred Jesus to action. With unconcealed anger, he picked up some cords and, using them as a whip, drove out the traders and their animals (John 2:15).

As the sellers and buyers fled, Jesus overturned the stalls, pushing the money-changers' tables to the floor and scattering their coins everywhere. Jesus had effectively disrupted trade in the Temple. He then refused to let anyone carry any merchandise through the outer courts of the Temple.

### Jesus teaches and heals

Instead, Jesus began to teach the crowd that was gathering in the Temple. His words were a pointed criticism of the commercial activity he had just stopped. Jesus quoted first from Isaiah 56:7, then from Jeremiah 7:11, saying "Is it not written: 'My house will be called a house of prayer for all nations?' But you have made it 'a den of robbers'" (Mark 11:17). The Temple in Jerusalem was supposed to be the holy place where all people could meet with the God of Israel. Instead, it had become a bustling centre for profit at the expense of the poor.

As Jesus taught in the Temple, people who were blind or lame came to him. Some onlookers would have thought that such people did not belong there (citing Leviticus 21:18), but Jesus welcomed them and healed them.

### A real challenge

Children saw these wonderful things and began repeating the songs of joy and expectation from the procession into Jerusalem the day before: "Hosanna to the Son of David!" (Matthew 21:15). The Temple priests were indignant,

> **"My house** will be called **a house of prayer** for all nations.**"**
>
> **MARK** 11:17

since the reference to King David implied to the listeners that Jesus was the Messiah. They asked Jesus whether he had heard what the children were saying. Jesus replied, citing Psalm 8:2: "Yes, have you never read, 'From the lips of children and infants you, Lord, have called forth your praise'?" (Matthew 21:16).

The crowd of Passover pilgrims was in awe of Jesus' bold words and actions – he was confronting the religious authorities directly, on their own ground, in the Temple itself. By contrast, the chief priests and teachers of the law were furious, but they were afraid to arrest him in the Temple in case they started a riot.

**AFTER**

Teaching at the Temple that week, Jesus explicitly warned the crowd to watch out for the feigned piety of the teachers of the law (Mark 12:38–40).

### QUIET GENEROSITY

These teachers, Jesus said, liked to be greeted with respect and **take the places of honour at a banquet ‹‹ 364–65**. They would make a spectacle of their prayers, but at the same time swindle houses from widows.

Many rich people made a similar show of putting large sums of money into the Temple collection box, but when Jesus saw a widow quietly donate just two small coins (a mite) he praised her. Whereas the rich had only put in a little of their wealth, **she had given all she had** (Mark 12:41–44).

**A MOSAIC DEPICTING THE WIDOW'S MITE EPISODE**

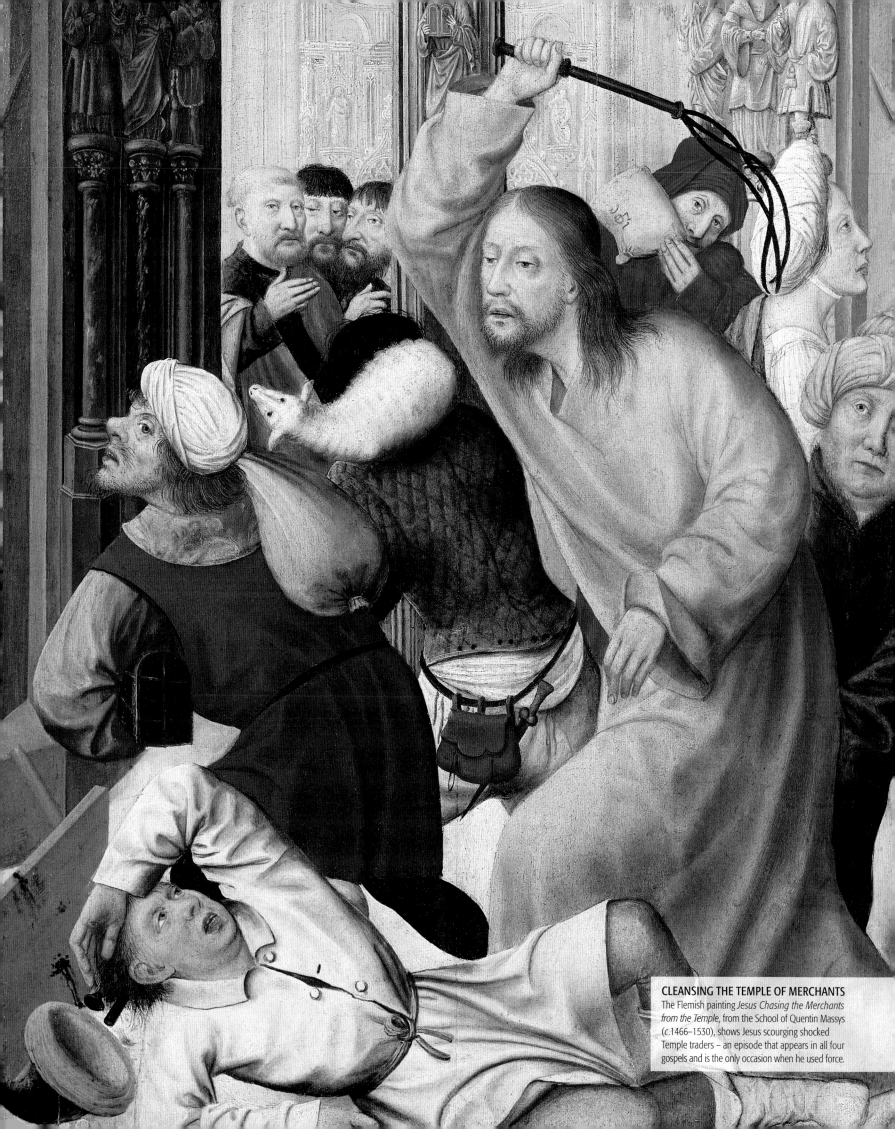

# The Anointing at Bethany

*While Jesus was sharing one of his last meals with followers and friends, a woman entered the room and anointed him with expensive perfume. This extravagant action pointed to Jesus' impending death.*

**J**ESUS AND HIS disciples were staying in Bethany, just outside Jerusalem. Two days before the Passover, they were invited to go for a meal at the house of a man called Simon, whose nickname was "the Leper", perhaps because he had once suffered from the skin disease. However, according to John's Gospel (12:1–8), the meal at Bethany was held not at the home of Simon the Leper, but at the home of Lazarus, and was attended by Mary and Martha.

### An unexpected interruption

As was customary at the time, Jesus and the other male guests were reclining around the meal table to eat. While they were still at the table, a woman came into the room, carrying an alabaster pot containing a very expensive perfumed oil. It would have been highly unusual for an uninvited woman to enter a room while men were eating. The woman moved directly to where Jesus was sitting. She broke the jar open and proceeded to pour all of the luxurious, aromatic perfume – described as nard (see panel, right) in Mark's account – on to Jesus' head.

The other dinner guests were horrified. Some of them, including some of Jesus' disciples, began to make angry comments. They knew that nard was so precious that even the small amount in the alabaster pot would have cost more than 300 denarii, which was at least a full year's wages. Instead of being poured over Jesus, they pointed out that the perfume could have been sold and the money used to help the poor. The dinner guests were soon rebuking the woman harshly.

### A beautiful action

Then Jesus spoke, causing the other guests to quieten down. "Leave her alone," he said, "She has done a beautiful thing to me" (Mark 14:6). Far from being wasteful, the woman's extravagant action had been entirely appropriate. By anointing him with perfume, she had prepared him for his burial, which would take

**POURED ON THE HEAD**
A frieze from St Mary the Virgin church in Oxfordshire, UK depicts a woman pouring perfume on Jesus' head. The woman is not named by Matthew or Mark, but John names her as Mary, sister of Lazarus (John 11:2).

## BEFORE

**Jesus and his disciples were staying in Bethany for Passover.**

**PLOTTING AUTHORITIES**
The Jewish authorities were now convinced that they had to **get rid of Jesus**, but his popularity with the crowds of **pilgrims at Jerusalem for the Passover 《 380–81** made this difficult. They decided they should wait until after the festival, **in case the people rioted** (Mark 14:1–2).

**OTHER ACCOUNTS OF ANOINTINGS**
Luke records that Jesus was anointed **much earlier in his ministry 《 328–29** (Luke 7:36–50). In John's Gospel, Mary anoints Jesus at the home of **Lazarus 《 370–71** (John 12:1–8).

**UNLEAVENED PASSOVER BREAD**

**PERFUME BOTTLES**
Roman-period vessels used to contain fine oils, perfumes, and cosmetics – the oil poured by the woman at the meal would have been held in a vessel that looked similar to these.

Alabaster vase with cobalt blue pigment, a popular colour in 1st century BC

Hellenistic-style glassware

## ANOINTING FOR BURIAL

Jewish burial tradition was to wash the body, anoint it with spices and perfume, then bind it up in cloth, ready for the tomb.

Spikenard was an exotic perfume with an earthy aroma. It is also known as muskroot or simply as nard, which is how John's Gospel describes it – "Mary took half a litre of pure nard, an expensive perfume" (John 12:3). The perfume is distilled from the spikenard plant, which grows around the foothills of the Himalayas. In the ancient world, spikenard was an expensive luxury.

The woman's action in anointing Jesus was full of significance, both as a portent of his death and a reminder of Jesus' status (see Anointing with oil panel, p.169).

place later the same week. After his crucifixion there would be no time to anoint his body with spices, as was the Jewish custom, before it would have to be put in a tomb.

As for the charge that the perfume should have been sold in aid of the poor, Jesus reminded the dinner guests that they would always have opportunities to help the poor, whereas he would soon be gone. "The poor you will always have with you, and you can help them any time you want. But you will not always have me" (Mark 14:7).

### Impending death
Despite Jesus' repeated predictions about his impending death, his disciples had still not understood that he would not be with them much longer. The woman, on the other hand, seemed to know that she needed to express her devotion and love to Jesus now, before it was too late.

Jesus said that wherever the news about him would be told, this woman's deed would be remembered as a lasting testament to her

**VIEW OF BETHANY**
The biblical village of Bethany is usually identified with the West Bank village now known as al-Eizariya, just over a mile from Jerusalem and home to the traditional site of Lazarus's tomb.

actions. The woman had taken her opportunity to act for Jesus while he was still alive. Jesus was declaring that although her name may not be known, her actions revealed that she had grasped who Jesus was and what he was about to do.

**SPIKENARD, A FLOWERING PLANT OF THE VALERIAN FAMILY**

Translucent coloured glass jug in the western Roman style

> " Truly I tell you, wherever the **gospel is preached throughout the world**, what she has done will also be told, **in memory of her.** "
>
> MARK 14:9

**AFTER** ≫

After the anointing, the arrangements were made for what would be Jesus' last day before his arrest.

**PASSOVER PREPARATIONS**
On the first day of the festival, Jesus asked his disciples to **make preparations for the Passover meal 388–89 ≫**. He told them to go into the city and there they would meet a man who would let them use a large upper room in his house (Mark 14:12–16).

**JUDAS' PRICE FOR BETRAYAL**
One of the disciples, Judas Iscariot, went to the chief priests. **In return for 30 silver coins** he agreed to watch for an opportunity to **hand Jesus over 391 ≫** (Matthew 26:14–16).

**JUDAS IS PAID BY THE CHIEF PRIESTS**

# The Last Supper

*During a meal with his disciples at the time of the Passover, Jesus explained the significance of his approaching death. Just as the Passover festival celebrated God's rescue of his people from Egypt, so this event, known as the Last Supper, was a thanksgiving for Jesus' forthcoming rescue of all people from sin.*

**J**ESUS AND his disciples gathered for their meal in an upper guest room in Jerusalem. The traditional Jewish Passover was an annual reminder of how God had delivered their ancestors from slavery in Egypt (see pp.102–03).

As the meal was beginning, Jesus got up, took off his robe, wrapped a towel around his waist, and began to wash his disciples' feet. It should have been the task of a household servant to wash the dusty feet of the guests, not that of Jesus, the honoured host. Jesus wanted to set a different example of leadership to his disciples: "Now that I, your Lord and Teacher, have washed your feet, you also should wash one another's feet" (John 13:14). Very soon, Jesus would prove the extent of his servant–leadership by dying for them.

As they reclined around the table, in the customary way, their celebration recalled the ritual of the Passover meal (see pp.100–01). However, when Jesus held up the unleavened bread, which had been the food for the escape from Egypt on the first Passover night, he gave it a startling new meaning. "Take and eat; this is my body," he said (Matthew 26:26). He broke the bread, just like his own body would be broken on the cross. Then he took a cup of wine: "This is my blood of the covenant, which is poured out for many for the forgiveness of sins" (Matthew 26:28). At the original Passover, a lamb's blood had been shed to prevent the death of the household's firstborn. Jesus said that his death would deliver many people, setting them free from the tyranny of sin.

Jesus told his disciples that one of them would soon betray him, which would mean certain death. However, his main concern was not for his own safety. Rather, he wanted his disciples to understand why he was going to his death – because of his love for them and for the whole world. Jesus told them that what he was about to do would bring them peace from God.

Jesus asked his disciples to share bread and wine together in future, in the same way as they just had. "… do this in remembrance of me," he said (Luke 22:19). Jesus' Last Supper is still celebrated today when Christians meet, in the Eucharist. This simple meal of shared bread and wine expresses how Jesus willingly gave up his life, so that the world might experience God's love, forgiveness, and peace.

> **"**As I have **loved you**, so you must **love one another**.**"**
>
> **JOHN** 13:34

**"ONE OF YOU WILL BETRAY ME"**
Pomponio Amalteo's 16th-century depiction of the Last Supper captures the reactions of the disciples to the revelation by Jesus (centre) that one of them will betray him. Seated opposite Jesus, Judas clutches a bag of money – his reward for this act of treachery.

« BEFORE

**Jesus had already talked to his disciples about what would happen after he was arrested.**

### WORDS OF WARNING

Jesus told the disciples to make sure they had purses, bags, and swords with them (Luke 22:35–38), even though they had never needed them before. With **Jesus arrested and then killed**, they would need to watch out for themselves. The words of the **prophet Zechariah « 222–23** would come true: the disciples would be **scattered like sheep** after Jesus their shepherd was arrested (Zechariah 13:7).

**ROMAN SWORD**

### OLIVE TREES AT GETHSEMANE

The most likely site of the Garden of Gethsemane in Jerusalem is today home to a small group of olive trees, several of which are claimed to be as many as 2,000 years old and still bearing fruit.

# Betrayal in the Garden of Gethsemane

*After the Last Supper, Jesus went to Gethsemane with his disciples. He prayed fervently about all that he was soon to face – his trial and crucifixion – before Judas arrived with armed guards to arrest him.*

JESUS AND the 11 disciples walked the short distance from the upper room in Jerusalem to an olive grove called Gethsemane, just outside the city. Leaving the rest of the group near the entrance, Jesus took Peter, James, and John, his inner circle of disciples, a little further into the grove. They noticed that Jesus was becoming distressed, as the impending events began to weigh heavily on his spirit. He told them, "My soul is overwhelmed with sorrow to the point of death" (Matthew 26:38). He asked them to stay awake and keep watch, while he went on alone to pray.

### Jesus prays

A little distance from the three disciples, Jesus fell down prostrate with his face to the ground. "My Father, if it is possible, may this cup be taken from me," he prayed (26:39). He was referring to his imminent death as a "cup" of suffering. In drinking "this cup" (26:39,42), he would not only experience the physical pain of crucifixion, but also the psychological distress of not being saved from suffering by God, his Father. Yet Jesus knew that by drinking "this cup", he would enable others to be rescued from sin and come into a relationship with God.

> " Then **Jesus went** with his disciples to a place called **Gethsemane,** and he said to them, '**Sit here** while I go over there and **pray.**' "
>
> MATTHEW 26:39

So he continued to pray to God, uttering the words "Yet not as I will, but as you will" (26:39).

### The disciples sleep

Jesus got up and went back to Peter, James, and John, only to find them fast asleep. "Couldn't you men keep watch with me for one hour?" he asked them (26:40). He knew that they were willing in spirit, but they were weak in their bodies, exhausted from sorrow and from the strain of what was about to happen. He told them once again to keep watch and to pray, while he walked a short distance away to return to his own prayers.

Again, Jesus fell on his face, both in anguish at the approaching events and in submission to God's will. Then he returned to the three disciples again, only to find them sleeping. He left them for a final time and went away to pray once more. Luke records that his distress was so great that his sweat fell to the ground like drops of blood. An angel from God appeared to Jesus and strengthened him for the hours that lay ahead (Luke 22:43,44).

### Judas arrives

When Jesus returned to the disciples for the third time, he roused them from their slumber. There were sounds of people approaching the olive grove: "Here comes my betrayer!" said Jesus. Then Judas arrived in Gethsemane with a crowd of armed soldiers, who had been sent by the Temple authorities. Judas had already arranged with the soldiers the signal he would use to identify Jesus in the darkness. He came up to Jesus and greeted him with a kiss. "Rabbi!" he said.

Astonishingly, Jesus neither rebuked Judas for his betrayal nor fled, but simply said, "Do what you came for, friend" (Matthew 26:50). Jesus knew that the time had come for him to face his opponents with the truth about God's kingdom, even if that would result in his own death on a cross. His prayer in Gethsemane had strengthened him to face the insults, accusations, and brutality to come.

**PEOPLE**

#### JUDAS ISCARIOT

Judas was the son of Simon Iscariot, "Iscariot" possibly referring to the family's home region of Kerioth. One of Jesus' 12 disciples, Judas Iscariot was a trusted member of the group and became its treasurer (John 13:29). However, he agreed to hand Jesus over to the Jewish authorities – the Bible does not tell us why. Judas had already been stealing from the disciples' moneybag (John 12:6), so perhaps the lure of 30 silver pieces had tempted him. Or perhaps he was disillusioned with Jesus and hoped to force him into revolutionary action against the Roman state. Whatever his motivation, the Gospel writers say that he was doing the work of Satan, the enemy of God. When Judas saw that Jesus had been condemned to death, he was filled with remorse and committed suicide (Matthew 27:3–10).

**THE KISS OF JUDAS**
This 6th-century mosaic from the basilica of Sant' Apollinare Nuovo in Ravenna, Italy, depicts the moment in Gethsemane when Judas embraced Jesus and revealed his identity to the arrest party.

> " Then he returned to the **disciples** and said to them, 'Are you still **sleeping and resting**? Look, **the hour has come**, and the **Son of Man** is delivered into the hands of **sinners**. Rise! Let us go! Here comes **my betrayer!**' "
>
> MATTHEW 26:45,46

**HISTORY AND CULTURE**

### THE GARDEN OF THE OIL PRESS

Although it is sometimes referred to today as a garden, Gethsemane was more accurately a small grove of olive trees (as part of it still is today), complete with a press for crushing the fruit to produce oil. The Hebrew name Gethsemane means "oil press". Gethsemane lay just outside the eastern wall of Jerusalem, across the Kidron Valley, on the slope of the Mount of Olives. The cultivation of olives (see pp.332–33) was widespread in Judea, yielding the region's biggest export – olive oil. This versatile and valuable product was used for cooking, medicine, to fuel lamps, for applying to hair, and as a base for lotions.

**ANCIENT OLIVE OIL PRESS**

**AFTER** »

**The disciples were distraught at the arrest of Jesus.**

#### MALCHUS'S EAR

When the group of soldiers and priests came to arrest Jesus, Peter realized what was happening. Trying to defend Jesus, he took his sword and sliced off the right ear of Malchus, **one of the servants of the high priest 394–95** ». **Jesus rebuked Peter** for trying to defend him, saying to him: "No more of this!" Jesus then healed Malchus (John 18:10; Luke 22:51). **The disciples ran away**, leaving Jesus with the soldiers. One young man who fled naked, his robe left in the hands of a soldier (Mark 14:51,52), is thought to be Mark himself, the writer of the second Gospel.

# Interrogation and Trial

*Jesus was questioned throughout the night by the Jewish authorities, who had hurriedly come together to debate his case. By early morning, they had settled on a verdict of guilty and a sentence of death.*

**T**HE SOLDIERS bound Jesus and led him from Gethsemane back to Jerusalem. First, they brought him to Annas, a former high priest and the father-in-law of the current high priest. He was still a highly regarded public figure, so his hasty assessment of Jesus' case would be valuable. Annas began questioning Jesus about his teaching, but Jesus refused to answer him. "I have spoken openly to the world... Why question me? Ask those who heard me"(John 18:20,21). At this, Jesus was accused of insolence and struck across the face. Jesus pointed out that he was speaking the truth: his teaching had never been secret, so it should be clear to all if he was guilty.

### The Sanhedrin debates

After this preliminary hearing, Jesus was led into the residence of the high priest, Caiaphas, where members of the Sanhedrin had gathered. They began to debate what charge they could bring against Jesus, seeking one that would require the death penalty according to Jewish Law. Although they had managed to arrest him secretly, they knew they needed a clear verdict of guilty in order not to inflame the crowds of pilgrims.

A number of people brought fabricated evidence against Jesus, but their accounts were contradictory. At last, two witnesses were found whose testimony was broadly the same. They mixed up some of Jesus' teachings and accused him of saying "I will destroy this temple made with human hands and in three days will build another, not made with hands" (Mark 14:57,58). This sounded like a threat against the Temple, as well as a claim to be acting with divine authority.

It was enough for the Sanhedrin. Caiaphas turned to Jesus, who had remained silent throughout. "Are you not going to answer?" (Matthew 26:62). As the whole Sanhedrin watched, Caiaphas questioned Jesus directly, and under oath: "Tell us if you are the Messiah, the Son of God" (Matthew 26:63). Did Jesus really claim to have divine authority?

At last, Jesus spoke. "You have said so," he replied; then he added, "... from now on you will see the Son of Man sitting at the right hand of the Mighty One and coming on the clouds of heaven" (Matthew 26:64). The Sanhedrin understood the incriminating implication: Jesus was claiming to be God's chosen one. They did not believe this could be true, so they called it blasphemy.

### The verdict is reached

Caiaphas, the high priest, tore his clothes in anger at Jesus' claim. The trial was over – the Sanhedrin had heard Jesus speak blasphemy in their presence. "What do you think?" asked Caiaphas. The religious authorities answered decisively: "He is worthy of death" (Matthew 26:66).

## BEFORE

**The high priest was drawn from an elite of Jewish families. As head of the Temple, this influential public figure sought to preserve Jewish institutions.**

#### WORKING WITH THE ROMANS
The high priest had always been important, because of his **role in the sacrificial rites** **《 110–11** at the Temple. However, under Roman rule he gained **increased political power**, because he worked closely with the Roman governor to maintain the status of the Temple and the peculiarities of Jewish law. The high priest lived in a residence in the upper city of Jerusalem, near the Temple.

> ❝ They **took Jesus to the high priest,** and all the chief priests, the elders and the teachers of **the law came together.** ❞
>
> MARK 14:53

## PEOPLE

### CAIAPHAS THE HIGH PRIEST

Joseph ben Caiaphas was appointed by the governor in AD 18 and remained in office until AD 36/37. A shrewd politician, he made sure the Jews and the Temple prospered, even under Roman rule – hence his response to the Sanhedrin: "...it is better for you that one man die for the people than that the whole nation perish" (John 11:50). In 1990, an ossuary bearing his name was unearthed in Jerusalem.

**ORNATE LIMESTONE OSSUARY OF CAIAPHAS**

**STEPS TO THE UPPER CITY**
Ancient steps in Jerusalem lead up Mount Zion, the former Temple Mount, to the church of St Peter in Gallicantu, which means "the cock's crow". According to tradition, the house of Caiaphas was located here.

## HISTORY AND CULTURE

### THE SANHEDRIN

The supreme council for all issues of Jewish life – religious, political, or legal, the Sanhedrin had 71 members, called elders, drawn mainly from among the chief priests and scribes, and it was presided over by the high priest. Many of its members belonged to the Sadducee party (see pp.366–67), which was more open to co-operating with the Roman authorities than the dominant group in Judaism – the Pharisees – was.

## AFTER

**Alarmed by the threat Jesus posed to social stability, the Sanhedrin planned to hand him to the Romans for trial.**

#### A CAPITAL CHARGE OF BLASPHEMY
Blasphemy was a grave offence under Jewish Law. However, for the full sentence – the death penalty – to be pronounced, Jesus would have to be **tried by the Roman authorities 396–97 》**.

Members of the Sanhedrin **spat in Jesus' face** as an insult. He was **blindfolded, and they struck him with their fists** and called out "Prophesy!" in mockery. Then the **guards took him and beat him** (Mark 14:65).

# Peter's Denial

*While Jesus was in the high priest's house, being interrogated by the Sanhedrin, his disciple Peter was outside in the courtyard, facing a series of questions about his own association with Jesus.*

**O**UTSIDE THE HIGH priest's residence, which was set in an elevated position on the Temple Mount, it was cold in the courtyard. The servants and officials of the household had lit a charcoal fire and were gathered around it, warming themselves. Peter also went over to warm himself, hoping to remain unnoticed in the shadows. Peter had not fled after Jesus' arrest, but had instead followed courageously at a distance, determined to see the outcome.

### Peter is recognized

Soon, though, one of the high priest's maids, who was sitting by the fire, thought she recognized him. "You aren't one of this man's disciples too, are you?" she asked. But Peter denied it: "I am not" (John 18:17). Despite the cold, he moved a bit further away from the fire, and stood in the gateway of the courtyard.

"This fellow was with Jesus of Nazareth," said another maid, pointing Peter out to the servants and officials around the fire. Peter could hear the accusation. He swore an oath and called back over, "I don't know the man!" (Matthew 26:71,72) The servants were not convinced. Peter spoke with a Galilean accent and, because Jesus had come down to Jerusalem from Galilee, it was hard to believe that Peter did not know who Jesus was.

As the night wore on, another of the high priest's servants came into the courtyard to warm himself by the fire. He had been with the armed band of soldiers who had arrested Jesus, and he was also a relative of the servant called Malchus whose ear Peter had cut off with his sword. This man was certain he had seen Peter at the arrest. "Didn't I see you with him in the garden?" he asked (John 18:26). "Surely you are one of them, for you are a Galilean," said others standing near (Mark 14:70).

### The cock crows

Peter could take it no longer. With curses he cried out, "I don't know this man you're talking about" (Mark 14:71).

At that moment, a cock crowed. Through an open window, Jesus came into view and Peter saw him – Jesus was looking straight at him. Immediately, Jesus' words from just a few hours earlier came flooding back to Peter. "Truly I tell you," Jesus had said, "this very night, before the cock crows, you will disown me three times" (Matthew 26:34).

Peter turned and ran out of the courtyard, weeping bitterly. He had indeed disowned Jesus, three times.

**WHERE THE COCK CROWED**
The Roman Catholic church of St Peter in Gallicantu, Jerusalem marks the traditional site of Peter's denial. Shrines have existed there since the Byzantine era and the current church was built in 1931 to replace a crusader chapel erected in 1102.

## BEFORE

Peter had declared that he was willing to follow Jesus wherever he went, even to prison and death.

### JESUS' PREDICTION
At the end of the **Passover meal ‹‹ 388–89**, Jesus told Peter that his faith was about to be **tested by Satan**. He explained what would happen: before the cock crowed, Peter would **deny that he knew Jesus**, not just once but three times (Luke 22:31–34).

### THE HIGH PRIEST'S COURTYARD
After **Jesus' arrest ‹‹ 390–91**, Peter and another disciple **followed at a distance**. The other disciple was known at the high priest's house, and was able to get Peter into the courtyard (John 18:15,16).

## AFTER

After Jesus' resurrection, Peter was forgiven and restored as a disciple.

### FOLLOW ME, PETER
Following the miraculous haul of fishes on the Sea of Galilee, when Peter was the only one to jump out of the boat, the risen Jesus **prepared a meal for his disciples 412 ››**. He took Peter aside and asked him three times, **"Do you love me?"** Each time Peter replied, "Yes, Lord, you know that I love you." Jesus told him, **"Feed my sheep."** Peter may have disowned Jesus, but Jesus was clear that he still wanted Peter to follow him (John 21:15–17).

Jesus then gave another prediction: in the future, Peter would not deny Jesus but would remain true to him, **even though it would mean his own death** (John 21:18,19).

### ANALYSIS
## WHY DID PETER DISOWN JESUS?

**CRUCIFIXION, A TERRIFYING PROSPECT FOR PETER**

Peter had reason to think that the Sanhedrin would hand Jesus over to the Romans for execution. Jesus had spoken several times about what would happen in Jerusalem: the Romans would crucify him as another Galilean rebel and a threat to the peace. Peter would have known about the fate of other revolutionary figures, who were always rounded up by the Romans, with their followers, and sentenced to the cruel penalty of death by crucifixion. Did Peter fear that the same thing would happen to him if he acknowledged his association with Jesus?

> ❝ Then **Peter remembered** the word Jesus had spoken to him: 'Before the cock crows twice you will disown me three times.' ❞
>
> **MARK** 14:72

**CHURCH OF ST PETER, BY THE SEA OF GALILEE**

**PETER DENIES JESUS**

*The Denial of St Peter* by Giovanni Canavesio forms part of a cycle of 15th-century frescos depicting the Passion of Christ. It decorates the shrine of the 1375 *Notre Dame des Fontaines* ("Our Lady of the Fountains"), La Brigue, France.

**BEFORE**

In order to have Jesus executed, the Sanhedrin needed to co-operate with the Roman authorities.

### HEROD AND THE DEATH PENALTY

As a Galilean, Jesus came under the jurisdiction of **Herod Antipas ‹‹ 345**, the ruler of Galilee and Perea, who had imprisoned and beheaded John the Baptist (Mark 6:14–28). At Passover, Herod was in Jerusalem. However, it is likely that the ability to authorize a death penalty was **restricted to the Roman governor**.

**RECONSTRUCTION OF HEROD'S PALACE, JERUSALEM, COMPLETED IN 23 BC**

# Jesus Before Pilate

*The Sanhedrin had found Jesus guilty of blasphemy, but they were unable to put him to death. They needed the Roman authorities to convict him, so they took Jesus to Pilate, the governor of the region.*

**A**S SOON as it was morning, the Sanhedrin escorted Jesus to Pontius Pilate, the Roman prefect or governor of Judea, who was at his residence in the Praetorium.

The Sanhedrin knew that Roman law would not accept their charge of blasphemy as a sufficient reason for imposing the death penalty on Jesus. Instead, they introduced him to Pilate as a political threat – Galilee having long been a centre of resistance to both Roman power and its client Jewish rulers. The council accused Jesus of subversive activity, saying that he had incited a rebellion against paying Roman taxes and had claimed to be a king (Luke 23:2).

According to John's Gospel, the appeal made by the Sanhedrin to Pilate took place to fulfil what Jesus had said about the kind of death he was going to have. In being crucified by the Romans, he would be "lifted up" (John 12:32) on the cross.

**CARVED IN STONE**
Roman games are carved into these paving stones, which once formed part of Fort Antonia in Jerusalem. Built by Herod the Great, this military barracks was the home of the garrison of Roman soldiers that took Jesus to be crucified.

### Questioned by Pilate

Pilate turned to Jesus, "Are you the king of the Jews?" he asked. Jesus replied simply, "You have said so" (Luke 23:3). Jesus' calm response did little to persuade Pilate that this man was a threat to Rome. Pilate announced that there was no basis for the charge of treason that had been brought.

The Sanhedrin would not give up. They insisted that Jesus had been disrupting the peace throughout the land, from Galilee in the north to Judea in the south. On hearing that Jesus was from Galilee, Pilate decided to send him to Herod Antipas, who was the ruler of Galilee and was in Jerusalem at that time.

### Jesus before Herod

Herod was delighted to see Jesus. He had heard much about Jesus' ministry and hoped that Jesus would perform some miracles for him. However, Jesus refused even to speak in Herod's presence. The Sanhedrin brought their accusations against him, but still Jesus did not say a word. Seeing that he was not going to get his wish, Herod started to mock and ridicule Jesus. The soldiers joined in. They dressed Jesus in an expensive royal robe, and sent him back to Pilate.

### Barabbas is freed

By now, a crowd had gathered at the Praetorium. The Sanhedrin again accused Jesus before Pilate, but Jesus remained silent. Pilate was amazed at Jesus' behaviour, and announced again that there was no reason to condemn him to death. Even Pilate's wife sent him a message that Jesus was innocent.

> **"** But Pilate answered, '**You take him** and **crucify him**. As for me, **I find no basis** for a charge against him.'**"**
>
> JOHN 19:6

### PONTIUS PILATE

Pilate's official title in Judea was Praefectus (Prefect). He was the fifth Roman to serve in the post, which was based in the provincial capital of Caesarea Maritima. Praefectus was a military term, which referred to his command of a company of around 500–1,000 auxiliary troops. His job was to keep the rebellious province of Judea in order. Pilate held office from AD 26 to AD 36/37, during which time, according to the historian Josephus and the commentator Philo, he regularly upset the Jews by disregarding their religious and social customs. He was removed from office after a complaint was made against him for needlessly killing a group of Samaritan pilgrims.

**RAVENNA MOSAIC OF PILATE IN JUDGMENT**

> **"** Wanting to **satisfy the crowd,** Pilate released **Barabbas to them.** He had **Jesus flogged,** and handed him over to **be crucified."**
>
> MARK 15:15

### THE DAY OF PREPARATION

According to John's Gospel, Jesus' trial occurred on the Day of Preparation, when Jewish families would prepare for the Passover feast by ridding their homes of leavened bread, in memory of their exodus from Egypt (see pp.102–03). It was a busy day in Jerusalem, with crowds of pilgrims staying in the city to celebrate their Passover meal. When the Jewish authorities took Jesus to Pilate, they refused to enter the Praetorium. Pilate was not a Jew, so entering his palace would make them unclean and mean they would not be able to celebrate Passover (John 18:28).

**PRAYING DURING PASSOVER**

## AFTER

**Herod Antipas and Pontius Pilate became friends (Luke 23:12). It served both their political interests to have Jesus put to death. In their custody, the captive Jesus was mocked.**

#### HAIL, KING OF THE JEWS!
Once Pilate gave the **order of execution**, Roman soldiers took Jesus into the Praetorium. The whole company of soldiers gathered around Jesus and began to mock him. He was dressed in a scarlet robe. They twisted together **a crown of thorn branches**, pushed it onto his head, and put a wooden staff in Jesus' hand. The soldiers knelt down in front of Jesus, mocking him, and calling out **"Hail, king of the Jews!"** Then they spat on him, and began beating him around the head with the staff (Matthew 27:27–31).

**CROWN OF THORNS**

The Sanhedrin was ready with a reply to persuade Pilate: "If you let this man go, you are no friend of Caesar" (John 19:12).

Every year, at the Passover festival, Pilate would pardon and release one prisoner, as an act of goodwill to the Jewish people. He now decided to let the crowd choose: did they want him to release Barabbas – a violent revolutionary who had committed murder – or Jesus? Much to his surprise and dismay, the crowd clamoured for Barabbas to be released – the religious authorities had been stirring them up against Jesus (Matthew 27:20).

### Jesus condemned to death
"What shall I do, then, with Jesus, who is called the Messiah?" asked Pilate. "Crucify him!" cried the mob. Pilate protested that Jesus was innocent. But the mob just shouted louder, "Crucify him!" Pilate suggested that Jesus should be punished and then released, but the crowd would not give in.

**PRESENTED TO THE CROWD**
Antonio Ciseri's *Ecce Homo*, 1871, portrays Pilate's presentation of Jesus to the crowd. The Roman governor's wife turns her back on the scene, having earlier urged her husband of Jesus' innocence.

Eventually, Pilate realized he would have to grant their request in order to avoid a riot. He took a bowl of water and washed his hands in front of the people, to show that he did not want to be held responsible for the crucifixion of Jesus. Even so, he gave the order for Jesus to be taken away, flogged, and executed by crucifixion.

## BEFORE

**After Jesus had been condemned to death, he was led out of the city.**

### BEARING THE CROSS

Victims of crucifixion were expected to take their cross to the place of execution. Jesus **began his last journey** with this heavy beam of wood bound to him. He stumbled from its weight, and from sheer exhaustion **after his trial and flogging ‹‹ 396–97**. The Roman soldiers grabbed a man who was entering the city – **Simon from Cyrene**, a city on the North African coast. They **forced him to carry Jesus' cross** to Golgotha (Luke 23:26).

**CHRIST STUMBLING WITH THE CROSS**

### HISTORY AND CULTURE

## VIA DOLOROSA

According to tradition, the route Jesus took to Golgotha is the one that became known as the Via Dolorosa, "The Way of Sorrow". Jesus was followed on his last journey by a crowd, which included many women wailing with sorrow. Jesus addressed them as "Daughters of Jerusalem", and, foretelling disaster for their city, he asked them not to weep for him, but rather for themselves and their children (Luke 23:28–31). They would experience the force of Roman punishment themselves, when Jerusalem was destroyed in AD 70.

**VIA DOLOROSA, JERUSALEM**

# The Crucifixion

*Jesus was taken to a place of execution on a hill just outside the city of Jerusalem where he was crucified along with two criminals. Throughout his ordeal, Jesus was mocked and humiliated by a crowd of onlookers.*

**P**ONTIUS PILATE'S soldiers led Jesus out of the city of Jerusalem to a place called Golgotha, from an Aramaic word that means "the skull" (Luke 23:33) and is translated into Latin as *calvaria*, which gives Calvary. A typical site for Roman executions, it was located on a hill beside a main road into the city. It was intentionally

public: those killed there were visible to all who journeyed in and out of Jerusalem. Their slow and painful deaths served as a reminder of what the Roman state would do

to any who challenged its authority. When they reached Golgotha, the soldiers offered Jesus a drink of wine mixed with myrrh (a type of gum; see also pp.288–89) and gall, or bile, which would have made the wine taste bitter. The mixture

**THE SON OF GOD ON THE CROSS**
This central panel of an ornately carved and gilded wooden triptych depicts the crucifixion. Carved in 1509–13, it adorns the Eglise des Cordeliers church in Fribourg, Switzerland.

# "Carrying his own cross, he went out to the **place of the Skull** (which in Aramaic is called Golgotha). **There they crucified him…**"

JOHN 19:17,18

**IN MEMORIAM**
The Church of the Holy Sepulchre on Calvary Hill was built on the site where tradition maintains that Jesus was crucified. The church also contains a shrine at the place where it is said he was buried.

was supposed to act as an anesthetic to make a prisoner more compliant for the ordeal of crucifixion that was to follow. Jesus tasted the sharp mixture, but refused to drink it (Matthew 27:34), and so remained fully conscious.

### Jesus is nailed to the cross

Then the soldiers placed him on the cross. A Roman cross typically had two beams of wood: an upright beam embedded into the ground, and a cross beam that locked into the top of the first, onto which the victim's arms were outstretched. Some victims were simply bound to the cross with ropes, but Jesus was nailed to his – the soldiers drove iron nails through his hands and ankles. This fulfilled the Old Testament prophecy "the one they have pierced" (Zechariah 12:10).

Pilate ordered a notice, or *titulus*, to be prepared and fastened to Jesus' cross, indicating why he was condemned to death. It was written in the languages of Aramaic, Latin, and Greek for all to read. In Latin this placard proclaimed *Iesus Nazarenus Rex Iudaeorum*: "Jesus of Nazareth, the King of the Jews" (John 19:19,20).

### The mocking crowd

A crowd of passersby soon gathered. Some of the Jewish authorities from Jerusalem had also come to watch the execution of their enemy, Jesus. When the people saw Jesus on the cross, they began to taunt him: "He saved others;" they sneered, "let him save himself if he is God's Messiah, the Chosen One" (Luke 23:35). "Come down from the cross, if you are the Son of God!" shouted others (Matthew 27:40). Even the Roman soldiers joined in. If Jesus really was the King of the Jews, they said, then surely he would be saved from this gruesome death. Where were his armed followers? But Jesus remained silent as the people mocked him. He knew what they had not yet realized:

that by accepting death on the cross, rather than escaping from it, Jesus was showing himself to be God's true King, who would even go through suffering and death to bring peace and salvation to his people.

### Jesus' promise

Two criminals had also been led out to Golgotha for crucifixion along with Jesus. They had earlier been condemned to death for robbery, and were probably involved in seditious activity against the Romans (both Matthew and Mark call them rebels). They were crucified on either side of Jesus.

Hearing the taunts of the crowd, one of the criminals joined in: "Aren't you the Messiah?" he jeered. "Save yourself and us!" The second criminal rebuked him: "We are punished justly, for we are getting what our deeds deserve. But this man has done nothing wrong." Then the robber spoke directly to Jesus: "remember me when you come into your kingdom" (Luke 23:39–42).

Despite all the insults hurled at Jesus by the crowds, the robber had recognized the truth – Jesus really was God's Messiah and his kingdom could not be defeated by death. Jesus answered the dying criminal with an amazing promise: "Truly I tell you, today you will be with me in paradise" (Luke 23:43). Because the robber had believed that Jesus was sent by God, he was promised a share in the rest and renewal of eternal life.

**ROMAN DICE**

## SYMBOLS

### THE CROSS

Death by crucifixion was the most dreaded method of execution in the Roman Empire. It was not only a painful torture, but also a public shaming and humiliation of the victim, who was crucified naked and offered up as a warning to others. Roman citizens were exempt – it was only used to execute slaves, foreigners, and provincial subjects. Victims were bound or nailed to a cross of wood, and left to die from starvation, exhaustion, and dehydration, which could take hours, even days. In *Epistle 101 to Lucilius*, Seneca described it as "long drawn-out agony". So dishonourable was this execution that it is absent from early Christian art. However, by the 2nd century this cross of shame had become the central symbol of the Christian faith – a constant reminder of Jesus being willing to die for the sins of the world.

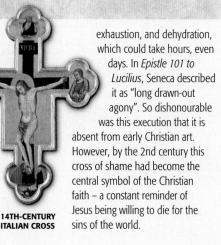

**14TH-CENTURY ITALIAN CROSS**

# Darkness at Noon

*At the end of Jesus' life, just as at its beginning, extraordinary events emphasized the significance of what was taking place: Jesus, God's Messiah and son, was dying for the world – a sacrifice for the sins of mankind. The world was changed for ever.*

**J**ESUS WAS CRUCIFIED on Golgotha at the third hour of the day, around 9am. By the sixth hour – midday, when the sun should have been at its highest point – an unexplained darkness shrouded the entire land. This eerie gloom only added to the horror of what was happening on the hill outside Jerusalem. Jesus, the man who had said about himself, "I am the light of the world" (John 9:5), was dying in the agony of crucifixion.

This dimness covered the land for about three hours. Towards the end of that period, at about 3pm, the ninth hour of the day, Jesus cried out in Aramaic with a loud, anguished voice: "*Eli, Eli, lema sabachthani*?" (Matthew 27:46). Translated as "My God, my God, why have you forsaken me?", these are the first words of Psalm 22.

Some of the people in the crowd that had gathered around Jesus' cross misunderstood his cry and thought he was calling for the great prophet Elijah, who had performed many miracles in the history of God's people, to come and rescue him.

But Jesus was not calling out for Elijah. He was expressing the horror of what he was experiencing. Throughout his life, he had known the closest of relationships with God, calling him "*Abba*", meaning father (Mark 14:36). Now, though, Jesus felt abandoned. He had been betrayed by Judas, deserted by his disciples, and denied by Peter. The authorities had falsely condemned him and the soldiers had tortured him. The world had abandoned Jesus because it had renounced God, and the weight of this sin was now on Jesus' shoulders (Isaiah 53:4,5). He felt deserted, or forsaken, by God.

Yet Jesus still did not relinquish his trust in God. Instead, just before Jesus died he cried out loudly, "Father, into your hands I commit my spirit" (Luke 23:46), and then he breathed his last.

Although many of those gathered around the cross did not realize the significance of Jesus' death, the physical world trembled at the enormity of what had occurred. At the moment of his death, an earthquake split open stone tombs around Jerusalem, and some of the dead were even shaken back into life (Matthew 27:52). In the Temple in Jerusalem, the curtain that separated off the Holy of Holies was torn in two. By enduring the God-forsakenness of the world, Jesus had opened up the possibility of a new relationship with God.

> "And when **Jesus had cried out** again in a loud voice, **he gave up his spirit.**"
>
> MATTHEW 27:50

**"FATHER, FORGIVE THEM…" (LUKE 23:34)**
Karel Dujardin's *Calvary* (1661) captures the dramatic light on Calvary during Jesus' final hours. Jesus' cross stands between those of two convicted thieves, one of whom asked Jesus "remember me when you come into your kingdom" (Luke 23:42).

## ⟪ BEFORE

Jesus died at about 3pm on Friday afternoon. He uttered a loud cry of torment that was accompanied by supernatural events and dramatic portents.

### CENTURION'S ASSERTION

When the centurion who was guarding the site of Jesus' crucifixion saw how he died, he said, **"Surely this man was the Son of God!"** (Mark 15:39).

### JESUS' SIDE IS PIERCED

To hasten their death, the soldiers **broke the legs of the two criminals** who had been crucified alongside Jesus. When the soldiers reached Jesus, they saw he was already dead so they did not break his legs. To make sure he really was dead, a soldier **pierced his side** with a spear, or *pilum*, which released a flow of blood and water (John 19:32–34).

***PILUM* HEAD**

---

### PEOPLE

### JOSEPH OF ARIMATHEA

A rich and respected man, Joseph came from the small Judean town of Arimathea, north of Jerusalem, and had a seat on the Sanhedrin – the Jewish ruling council (see pp.366–67). Called by Luke "a good and upright man", Joseph must have been of sufficient standing to have persuaded Pilate to commit the body to him. That Joseph ensured Jesus had a decent burial, something usually done by the deceased's close family, shows that not all Jewish religious authorities were opposed to Jesus.

**JOSEPH, WHO BURIED JESUS IN HIS TOMB**

# Placed in the Tomb

*Before the Jewish Sabbath day began at sunset, Jesus' body was taken down from the cross and placed in the newly hewn tomb of Joseph of Arimathea. This Sabbath was particularly significant because it fell during Passover week.*

J**ESUS HAD BEEN** crucified on a Friday, the day before the Jewish Sabbath. It was common for Romans to leave the bodies of crucified victims on their crosses until at least the next day, as a deterrent to other would-be criminals. However, under Jewish law, the Sabbath was a day of rest, on which no work could be done, even burial. More important still, it was the festival of Passover. The Jewish authorities were therefore eager that the bodies of Jesus and the two criminals should be taken down from their crosses before sunset, when this holy day began (John 19:31).

### Joseph of Arimathea's request

One of the members of the Jewish Sanhedrin was a wealthy man from nearby Arimathea, called Joseph. He had been a follower of Jesus, but had kept it secret from the rest of the Sanhedrin out of fear for what they would do to him. At Jesus' trial, Joseph had not given his consent to Jesus' execution, or joined in when Jesus was mocked. When Joseph discovered that Jesus' body would be taken down from the cross and put in a common criminal's grave, he decided to act. After such a horrific death, Joseph wanted Jesus to have a respectful burial.

Joseph went to Pontius Pilate to ask for Jesus' body to be released into his custody. Pilate was initially surprised that Jesus was already dead – death by crucifixion usually took many hours, sometimes days – and he summoned the centurion

#### THE DEPOSITION
*Descent from the Cross* (1612–14) by Peter Paul Rubens depicts the solemn moment when Christ's body was taken down from the cross. Rubens produced several varied compositions on the subject.

#### THE TOMB OF CHRIST
The Church of the Holy Sepulchre in Jerusalem is reputedly built on the site of Jesus' death and burial. Every year it is visited by Orthodox Christians who come to see the Miracle of the Holy Fire.

who had been in charge of the execution. The centurion then confirmed that Jesus was indeed already dead. So Pilate gave Joseph permission to take the body (Mark 15:43–45).

### Spices and a shroud

There was another secret follower of Jesus in the Sanhedrin, called Nicodemus, who went with Joseph to Golgotha to collect Jesus' body. Nicodemus brought with him some embalming spices – about 34kg (75lb) of myrrh and aloes mixed together (John 19:39). This was an extravagant amount of spices, fit more for a king (like the gift of the Magi) than a victim of crucifixion. However, for Nicodemus and Joseph, no cost was too great to

show their respect for Jesus. They wrapped Jesus' body in a linen shroud, along with the spices, in accordance with Jewish burial custom (John 19:40).

### The family tomb

Not far from Golgotha was Joseph of Arimathea's own tomb, which he had recently had hewn out of rock, set within a garden. Joseph and Nicodemus took Jesus' bound body to this tomb, and laid it inside. Since it was almost sunset, and Sabbath was about to begin, they rolled a large stone across the entrance and left.

> **"Joseph took the body,** wrapped it in a clean linen cloth, and **placed it in his own new tomb** that he had cut out of the rock. He rolled a big stone in front of the entrance to the tomb and went away.**"**
>
> MATTHEW 27:59,60

## HISTORY AND CULTURE
### BURIAL CUSTOMS

Jewish burials had two stages. First, the dead body would be washed, anointed with spices, and wrapped in a linen cloth. It would then be laid on a cool shelf inside a burial cave. After about a year, the remains would be gathered up, put in an ossuary, or bone box, and placed with the person's ancestors in a family tomb (see pp.406–07).

Jesus' body prior to burial is often depicted wrapped in a long shroud. For centuries, a piece of linen on display in Turin Cathedral has been venerated by some Christians as the shroud in which Jesus was buried. This mysterious cloth appears to bear the image of a man whose wounds are consistent with having been crucified, but radiocarbon dating has proved inconclusive.

**THE SHROUD OF TURIN**

## AFTER

**Jesus' burial was observed by a small group of faithful women.**

#### THE WOMEN AROUND JESUS
While Jesus' disciples had deserted him in the last hours of his life, the women who supported his ministry had **stayed close by "to care for his needs"** (Matthew 27:55). Among those who gathered at the cross were: Jesus' own mother Mary; Mary Magdalene; the mother of James and John, possibly called Salome; and the "other" Mary, probably the wife of Cleopas and mother of James and Joseph. Mary Magdalene and the "other" Mary followed Joseph of Arimathea and Nicodemus and saw where Jesus was buried. These women became **key witnesses of the events of Easter morning 404–05 ≫**.

**Jesus had already predicted that he would die and rise again.**

**THE THIRD DAY**
At the height of Jesus' popularity, he told his disciples that he would be rejected by the elders and chief priests and killed, but would be "raised to life" on the third day (Luke 9:22). At the time, **they did not understand what this meant ‹‹ 352–53**.

**SETTING A GUARD**
After Jesus' burial, the religious authorities were worried that the disciples might steal the body, and **claim that he had been raised from the dead**. Such a deception, they said, would "be worse than the first". Pontius Pilate duly authorized guards to **watch the tomb** (Matthew 27:62–66).

**ANALYSIS**

## CHARLEMAGNE GOSPELS

Some of the earliest manuscripts of Mark's Gospel end abruptly at Chapter 16 verse 8, with the statement that the women fled after the angel's message, telling no one what they had discovered because they were afraid. Many scholars have tried to explain why the Gospel finishes so suddenly.

Some scholars think the final column of text from the original manuscript must have been lost. Other manuscripts of Mark's Gospel attempt to supply what is missing: the women did tell their story and Jesus then appeared to his disciples. A version of this "longer ending" can be found in most Bibles. Perhaps Mark intended the abrupt ending, as a challenge to his readers. Having heard the news about Jesus' resurrection, would they keep it to themselves or go and tell others?

**SAINT MARK, FROM THE CHARLEMAGNE GOSPELS, c.800**

# The Empty Tomb

*After the horror of Jesus' crucifixion, and the finality of his burial, something truly astonishing happened: his tomb was discovered open and empty. Jesus rose from the dead on the third day, as he had foretold.*

THE WOMEN who had seen where Jesus was buried rested on the Sabbath, as the Jewish law required. They could do nothing; Jesus' body had been sealed in the tomb that belonged to Joseph of Arimathea. As soon as the Sabbath was over, just as the first day of the new week began to dawn, the women made their way back to the garden where the tomb was.

The group included Mary Magdalene, the "other" Mary, Salome (mother of James and John), and Joanna (Luke 8:3; 24:10), the wife of the manager of Herod Antipas's household – all of whom had followed Jesus throughout his ministry. They brought with them the spices they had prepared on Friday, planning to anoint Jesus' body properly, since his burial had been

so rushed in the minutes before the Sabbath began. As they made their way to the garden, they began to worry about how they would move the stone that had been rolled across the entrance of the tomb.

### An earthquake and an angel

Before the women reached the tomb, there was an earthquake that shook the ground – an angel had been sent by God to roll away the heavy stone from the tomb's entrance. The Roman soldiers who had been guarding the site on the Sabbath were so terrified when they saw the angel that they fell down paralyzed with fright (Matthew 28:2–4). When the women arrived, they were astonished to find that the tomb was open.

The women went into the cave, expecting to find Jesus' body lying on the stone shelf, bound in the linen shroud as it had been left on Friday evening – but it was not there. All that remained on the shelf were the linen cloths that had been wrapped around Jesus' body when he was buried.

Suddenly, while they were still reeling from shock, God's angel came and stood with them and said: "Do not be afraid, for I know that you are looking for Jesus, who was crucified" (Matthew 28:5). The angel invited them to come and see the shelf where Jesus' body had been lying. The women were then reminded of what Jesus had foretold long before he had made his final journey to Jerusalem: he would be betrayed and crucified, but he would rise to life again on the third day. It had all happened as Jesus had predicted (Luke 24:6,7).

Then the angel said to the women, "go quickly and tell his disciples: 'He has risen from the dead and is going ahead of you into Galilee. There you will see him.' Now I have told you" (Matthew 28:7). These women

### BURIAL CAVE

This Roman-era rock-cut burial chamber in Israel has a stone that can be rolled across its entrance. After his crucifixion, Jesus was buried (see pp.406–07) in a tomb that may have been similar to this.

became "apostles" in the literal Greek meaning of the word: they were "messengers sent out into the world" with the good news about Jesus' resurrection.

All the women except for Mary Magdalene hurried off – "afraid yet filled with joy" (Matthew 28:8) – to tell Jesus' disciples the news. Suddenly, on the way, the risen Jesus met them. "Greetings!" he said. They fell down before him and clasped his feet, worshipping him. Jesus told them to go and give the message to his disciples that he would see them soon in Galilee.

### Mary and the gardener

Mary Magdalene remained in the garden by the tomb, weeping. Could the message about Jesus' resurrection really be true? As Mary stood there she noticed a figure, standing beside her. "Woman, why are you crying? Who is it you are looking for?" he asked her (John 20:15). Mary assumed it was the gardener.

**THE WOMEN VISIT THE TOMB**
A detail from the Verdun Altarpiece (c.1320) in St Leopold's chapel at Klosterneuberg, Austria depicts the women at the sepulchre and the iconographic tradition known as *Noli me tangere*, when the risen Jesus appears to Mary Magdalene.

She thought that perhaps he had removed Jesus' body, not having realized that Joseph of Arimathea had authorized Jesus' burial in the tomb. So she said, "Sir, if you have carried him away, tell me where you have put him, and I will get him" (John 20:15). Then the figure spoke again: "Mary" he said. Mary

recognized the voice instantly – it was Jesus. He really was alive. She cried out in Aramaic, "*Rabboni*!", which means "Teacher". She was filled with joy and relief and amazement. Jesus told her not to cling to him – later translated in Latin as *Noli me tangere* – but to go and tell his disciples to go to Galilee, where they would see him again before he ascended to be with his Father, God. Mary ran to tell the disciples the wonderful news, "I have seen the Lord!" (John 20:17,18).

> " He is not here; **he has risen**, just as he said. **Come and see the place where he lay**."
>
> **MATTHEW** 28:6

---

**SYMBOLS**

## RESURRECTION AND BAPTISM

For the early Christians, Jesus' resurrection was central to their faith. It gave them hope for their own transformation and new life as followers of Jesus. Dying and rising again are symbolized in the Christian sacrament of baptism – including infant baptism and adult, full-immersion baptism – when the old sinful existence dies and a new life with God is born.

If the body of Jesus had remained in the tomb, Christian faith would be meaningless (1 Corinthians 15:14). The authorities tried to spread a story that Jesus' body had been stolen. Some suggested that in their grief the women went to the wrong tomb or that Jesus had not died on the cross, but revived in the tomb and escaped. However, the Romans had

made sure of Jesus' death by piercing his side. The disciples went on to die as martyrs because they were convinced Jesus had risen from the dead and was alive, never to die again.

**BAPTISM CEREMONY IN THE RIVER JORDAN**

**AFTER** »»

**Jesus' resurrection was such incredible news that it was difficult to believe.**

### PETER AND JOHN

When the women brought news of the empty tomb, **Peter and John** ran to the garden. They saw the stone shelf and the empty linen shroud, and **realized that Jesus was indeed risen** (John 20:3–9).

### DISCIPLES DISCREDITED

The Jewish authorities bribed the guards of the tomb to say that the disciples had **stolen Jesus' body** while they were asleep on duty (Matthew 28:11–15).

## HISTORY AND CULTURE

# Death, Burial, and Afterlife

> " After **my skin** has been **destroyed**, yet in my flesh **I will see God**; I myself will see him with my **own eyes…** " JOB 19:26–27

**STONE MARKERS**
Small pieces of rock and pebbles are placed on top of tombstones by visitors to the graves at this Jewish cemetery on the Mount of Olives, Jerusalem.

**B**eliefs about what happened after death changed during the biblical period, moving from little hope to huge confidence. Death in ancient times was generally more visible than it is today, and wherever possible, the relatives of a dying person would gather round to receive final blessings or instructions, as at Jacob's bedside (Genesis 49:29–33) and when David lay dying (1 Kings 2:1–11).

Life expectancy in biblical times was short, with half the population dying before the age of 18, often of an infectious disease. Surviving to 40 was seen as fortunate and living to old age was noteworthy. However, if someone reached 18 and was relatively wealthy, they had a good chance of achieving the psalmist's hope of a 70–80 year lifespan (Psalm 90:10).

Carved stone lid

Coffin usually about 80cm (31in) long

## NON-JEWISH BURIAL PRACTICES

### EGYPTIANS
Rich Egyptians were mummified, which involved removing the brain and large organs, packing the body in salt to dry it out, and filling the cavities with fragrant resin. The body was then covered with resin, wrapped in bandages, and placed in an elaborate wooden coffin. The poor, however, were simply buried in dry sand.

### ASSYRIANS
The Assyrians buried their dead, sometimes in clay coffins or in burial jars placed under the home. There is also evidence of cremation.

### GREEKS
The ancient Greeks initially buried the dead in their homes, but later used burial grounds outside the town or even on islands. Cremation became an alternative to burial from the 11th century BC.

### ROMANS
Romans disposed of bodies by either burial or cremation. The funerals of dignitaries were very grand affairs.

### CHRISTIANS
Christians followed Jewish practice and buried their dead.

**JEWISH OSSUARY**
During the Roman period, the practice of two burials was widespread. The first burial stage was complete once the embalmed body was laid in the tomb. After the body had decayed, the bones were collected into a short stone coffin, or ossuary.

## JEWISH BURIAL

Israelites were normally buried with their ancestors. The wealthy were buried in a family tomb, carved out of the rocks. Sarah, Abraham, Isaac, Rebekah, Leah, and Jacob were all buried in the family vault in the cave of Machpelah. Here, archaeologists have discovered up to 100 burials in a single tomb. The poor could not afford tombs and were buried in shallow graves outside the city.

**CAVE OF COFFINS**
Beit She'arim National Park in Galilee has a large number of ancient Jewish tombs. Jewish symbols decorate the limestone walls.

Burial occurred within a day because of the heat. The body was washed, anointed, wrapped in linen, and carried to the burial place on a bier, accompanied by mourners (2 Samuel 3:31). Cremation was not practised, apart from in extreme situations (1 Samuel 31:12–13), and was condemned in later rabbinic writings. The mourning period usually lasted seven days.

After the flesh had decomposed, which could take two years in Israel's dry climate, relatives gathered the bones into a stone ossuary (see left), which created space for more bodies. Joseph of Arimathea and Nicodemus placed the body of Jesus, wrapped in strips of linen with a mixture of myrrh and aloes, in "a new tomb, in which no one had ever been laid" (John 19:41).

## MOURNING THE DEAD

Mourning practices were similar across the ancient Near East, and many survive to this day. Wailing was a usual expression of grief, and professional mourners or "wailers" were hired by the wealthy to lament at the funeral and during the mourning period. They were often women: "Call for the wailing women to come; send for the most skilful of them" (Jeremiah 9:17). Mourners would express their grief in a variety of ways. Beating the head or the chest, tearing at clothes, wearing sackcloth made from rough camel or goat hair (sometimes only a loincloth), and putting ashes on the head or body would all demonstrate the desperation and grief felt by the mourner. Some of these mourning practices carried an extra significance: wearing painful or uncomfortable clothing would irritate the skin and mirror the mourner's inner pain and turmoil; and daubing with ashes symbolized feeling downcast and recalled that mankind was made of dust. Songs of lament were performed to mourn the dead, as David did for Saul and Jonathan. Putting stones on graves is a more recent Jewish mark of mourning.

**GRIEVING WOMAN**
This Jewish clay figure of a mourning woman clutching her head in grief dates from the 7th century BC.

**MOURNING THE TEMPLE**
Orthodox Jews wearing sacks over their clothes pray at the Honi Ha'Magel tomb in memory of the destruction of the Temple.

Large stones marked graves from earliest times, but pebbles are now placed on the grave both as a symbol of participating in the deceased's burial and to mark that someone has visited the grave.

Other forms of mourning in biblical times included women cutting off their hair, men not cutting their hair, tearing at one's beard, the removal of headdresses or shoes, observing times of silence, and fasting.

## AFTER DEATH

Most people believed that, at death, everyone (good and bad alike) went to the underworld. The Old Testament called this *Sheol* (in Greek, Hades), a place of shadowy half-life (see Job 10:20–22). Jews eventually came to see Sheol as the destiny of the wicked (though not as a place of punishment), but had little idea of what happened to the righteous. Although there are early glimpses of hope for an afterlife (Psalm 49:15;

**KIDRON VALLEY**
Absolom's Pillar is one of a number of tombs and monuments in Kidron Valley, Jerusalem.

Job 19:25–27), for most Jews that hope lay in the belief that they would live on through their children and grandchildren.

In later Old Testament times, the idea of life after death grew stronger (see Isaiah 26:19; Ezekiel 37:11–13; Daniel 12:2). The idea developed further in the Second Temple period (c.500 BC–AD 70), though there were widely divergent views, as reflected in the conflict between the Sadducees, who rejected resurrection, and the Pharisees, who accepted it (Matthew 22:23–32). Some Jews began to believe that Sheol had two zones: one for the righteous and one where the wicked awaited judgment.

**THE UNDERWORLD**
The ancient Greeks believed that deceased mortals went to the underworld, which was ruled by the god Hades and his consort Persephone (above centre).

Jesus proclaimed clear hope for an afterlife for the righteous (for example, Matthew 25:31–46; John 14:1–4). His death, resurrection, and ascension broke any fear of death for his followers and convinced them of the reality of a future life (1 Corinthians 15:50–57; Philippians 3:7–14; 1 Thessalonians 4:13–18).

« BEFORE

**Jesus had often taught his disciples while they travelled.**

### EMMAUS

Known in the Bible by the Latin form of its Hebrew name *Hammat* – "warm spring" – Emmaus was a **village near Jerusalem**. Several places today claim to be the site, but the exact location remains uncertain.

### TEACHING ON THE ROAD

The gospels present Jesus as a **wandering rabbi**, or teacher. Jesus had used his last journey to Jerusalem to teach his disciples many things about God's Kingdom, as Luke describes from 9:51 onwards.

**JESUS AS A WALKING RABBI, 11TH CENTURY**

> " They asked each other, 'Were not our hearts burning… while he talked with us… and opened the Scriptures to us?' "
>
> LUKE 24:32

### JOURNEY TO EMMAUS

A Romanesque sculptural relief adorning the cloister of the Benedictine monastery of Santo Domingo de Silos in Burgos, Spain, depicts Jesus walking the road to Emmaus with his unsuspecting followers. Jesus is shown with the pouch and stick of a pilgrim – in Latin, *peregrinus*, or "stranger".

# The Road to Emmaus

*On the afternoon after Jesus' resurrection, two of his followers were leaving Jerusalem, travelling home to Emmaus. The risen Jesus met them on the road, and walked with them to the village.*

**M**ANY OF THE pilgrims who had come to Jerusalem for Passover were now returning to the surrounding towns and villages. A man named Cleopas and his companion, who had both been followers of Jesus, were heading to the village of Emmaus, about 11km (7 miles) away. As they were walking along, they were talking about all that had happened in Jerusalem over the past few days.

## Walking and talking

A man joined the two companions as they travelled along the road and asked them what they were talking about. Cleopas turned to the stranger, saying with a heavy heart, "Are you the only one visiting Jerusalem who does not know the things that have happened there in these days?" (Luke 24:18).

Cleopas and his companion described the events as they had happened: Jesus' powerful teaching and miracles, his rejection by the Jewish authorities, his night-time trial and condemnation, and his crucifixion by the Romans. They had hoped he was God's promised Messiah, but their hopes had been dashed by Jesus' death. They told the man about Jesus' empty tomb, which the women had discovered earlier that morning. Cleopas and his companion found the turn of events strange and confusing.

## The stranger responds

"How foolish you are!" said the man who was walking with them, "and how slow to believe all that the prophets have spoken!" Then the man began at the beginning of the Jewish Scriptures and worked his way through to their end, explaining how all that had happened to Jesus in Jerusalem had been prophesied long ago. "Did not the Messiah have to suffer these things and then enter his glory?" the man said (24:26).

Soon the travellers came close to Emmaus. The man looked as if he was going to keep on travelling, but Cleopas and his companion urged him to stay the night. So the man agreed.

Later, as the three sat around the supper table, the man took up the loaf of bread. He gave thanks for it and broke it, passing it to them. As he did this, Cleopas and his companion recognized the familiar actions, the familiar voice, the familiar person – this was Jesus.

At the moment the pair realized this, Jesus was gone. The men were amazed, and commented on how they had felt as Jesus explained the Scriptures to them. Even though it was late, they hurried back to Jerusalem to tell the disciples how the risen Jesus had met them.

**LANDSCAPE OF EMMAUS**
Carem, or Ein Karem, lies just to the west of Jerusalem, overlooking the valley of Qalunya, and is one possible location for the unknown village of Emmaus.

> **" Then their eyes were opened and they recognized him... "**
>
> **LUKE** 24:31

**AFTER**

**BREAKING BREAD WITH DISCIPLES**
Caravaggio's *The Supper at Emmaus* (c.1596–1602) depicts Jesus in the gesture of blessing when breaking bread at the table, thereby revealing himself after his resurrection, much to the surprise of his seated companions.

**Cleopas and his unnamed companion were not the only ones to meet the risen Jesus.**

### NOT A GHOST
The two companions from Emmaus returned to Jerusalem that night. While they were still talking with the disciples, **Jesus was suddenly there 411 >>**, standing among them. "Peace be with you," he said (Luke 24:36). The disciples were afraid, thinking that he must be a ghostly apparition, but Jesus invited them to touch him so that they would believe he was **real flesh and bones**. The disciples were full of joy and amazement.

### TEACHING AGAIN
Jesus explained to the gathered disciples how the Jewish Scriptures pointed towards his death and resurrection. He reminded them that he had already told them to **expect his death and resurrection** in Jerusalem.

JOHN 20:24-29

# Jesus Appears to Thomas

*Jesus' resurrection is the starting point for Christian faith. Christianity does not just rely on an account of Jesus' empty tomb, but on the testimony of those who met with the risen Jesus.*

**T**HE FIRST WITNESSES of the risen Jesus were women – Mary Magdalene and the others who went to Jesus' tomb early on Easter morning (Matthew 28:8–10). After that, Jesus appeared to his other disciples while they were gathered together, and ate with them (Luke 24:43).

However, Thomas was not present and when the other disciples told him the wonderful news, he refused to believe them: "Unless I see the nail marks in his hands and put my finger where the nails were, and put my hand into his side, I will not believe" he said (John 20:25).

A week later, the disciples were together again, and Thomas was with them. The doors to the room were locked. Jesus came and stood among them: "Peace be with you!" he proclaimed (John 20:26). Then Jesus turned to Thomas and offered him his hands and his side. In an instant, Thomas knew it was Jesus, alive, standing before him. He fell down and worshipped, "My Lord and my God!" (John 20:28). Jesus responded that all who believed in him without seeing him – as Thomas had – would be blessed.

About 20 years after Jesus' resurrection, the apostle Paul wrote a list of some of those to whom the risen Jesus had appeared. The list included Peter and the other disciples, along with more than 500 people, some of whom were still alive (1 Corinthians 15:5–8). This was important information for the early Church: Jesus' resurrection was not a delusion in the disciples' imaginations – many people had encountered Jesus alive again, and their testimony could be checked.

Throughout history, Christians have believed that those first witnesses really did meet Jesus after his crucifixion. His body had been changed by the resurrection – for example, he could appear in the middle of a locked room – but it was still a real body of flesh and blood. Christians believe that this indicates the transformation that will happen to all who follow Jesus into God's kingdom.

> **"**Because you have seen me, you have believed; blessed are those who have not seen and yet have believed.**"**
>
> JOHN 20:29

**THE DOUBTING DISCIPLE THOMAS**
Thomas found it hard to accept the resurrection testimonies. Caravaggio's *The Incredulity of St. Thomas* (1602–03) depicts the moment when Jesus invites Thomas to touch his wounded hands and side.

411

**PLACE OF WORSHIP**
The Bible states that the Ascension took place at the Mount of Olives, outside Jerusalem. Today there are several churches on the Mount including the Chapel of the Ascension at the highest point (see opposite) and the domed Church of Mary Magdalene (upper left).

# The Ascension

*Jesus continued to meet with his followers after his resurrection. Before ascending into heaven while his disciples looked on, he commissioned them to proclaim the gospel to the world.*

### ANALYSIS

## ON EARTH AS IN HEAVEN

The ascension of Jesus is an important part of Christian teaching, with implications for where the risen Jesus is now, and what he is doing. Although Jesus "ascended", heaven is not a location up in the sky. For Christians, heaven is better understood as God's dimension of reality, where all is ordered according to his good will.

In his ascension, Jesus fulfilled the prophecy of Daniel 7:14, entering God's presence as the one who had defeated sin and death, and was given divine authority to inaugurate God's kingdom on Earth. Christians believe that it is from heaven – God's dimension of reality, where Jesus is – that the renewal of the world will come.

**T**HE RISEN JESUS spent 40 days with his disciples, teaching them many things about the kingdom of God. Now that Jesus' death and resurrection had taken place,

## BEFORE

Several miracles were performed by Jesus in the presence of his disciples after his resurrection, to convince them that he was the Messiah.

### JESUS IN GALILEE

Some of Jesus' post-resurrection appearances happened **in Galilee ‹‹ 310–11**, where he and his disciples had spent much of their time. On one occasion, after the disciples had been fishing all night without success, a man appeared on the shore and told them to drop their net on the other side of the boat. The net filled with 153 large fish but did not tear. The disciples **realized it was the risen Jesus**, and Peter jumped into the water to go to Jesus. When they reached the shore, Jesus had prepared a breakfast of bread and fish for them (John 21:1–14).

**THE MIRACULOUS CATCH OF FISH**

aspects of his teaching that had seemed confusing before became clearer to his disciples. Jesus showed them how the Jewish Scriptures foretold his sufferings and death, as well as his resurrection. At the end of the 40 days, they were utterly convinced that he really was alive again, and that he was God's promised Messiah.

### A great commission

Jesus now gave his disciples a new task. They were to be his witnesses, going out into the world to proclaim the incredible things that God had done through him. They were to explain how Jesus' death and resurrection had made it possible for people to make a new start with God, receiving forgiveness for their sins (Luke 24:47). They were to call on all people everywhere to become followers of Jesus and to believe what God had accomplished (Matthew 28:19,20; Mark 16:15).

To mark this entry into a new way of life, people were to be baptized in the name of Jesus, his Father, and the Holy Spirit (Matthew 28:19). The disciples would begin this great task in

**ASCENSION CHAPEL**
The octagonal Chapel of the Ascension on the Mount of Olives surrounds the rock upon which it is believed Jesus stood just before he ascended to heaven.

Jerusalem, but the mission would soon spread out into Judea, then into Samaria, and then "to the ends of the earth" (Acts 1:8).

Jesus' disciples needed to be his witnesses because he himself was going to leave them, to return to his Father in heaven. But they would not be alone in this commission. Jesus told them about the gift of the Holy Spirit, which they would soon receive to give them the power they needed to be his witnesses on Earth. (Luke 24:49; Acts 1:5,8).

### Jesus withdraws

One day, Jesus took his disciples to the Mount of Olives, near Bethany, just outside Jerusalem. The disciples knew something important was about to happen. They asked, "Lord, are you at this time going to restore the kingdom to Israel?" (Acts 1:6). Their question showed that they had not grasped the radical nature of Jesus' life and teaching. They clung to the hope that God's rule would be established as a political kingdom, centred on Israel.

**CHRIST IN HEAVEN WITH MUSICIAN ANGELS**

Jesus replied that they were not to know the time or date when God's kingdom would fully come; but it was not yet that time. Instead, their present task was to share what they had seen with the rest of the world.

Then Jesus raised his hands and blessed his disciples. As he was doing so, he was lifted up in front of them, until a cloud hid him from their sight. Jesus had ascended into heaven, and his disciples worshipped him.

## AFTER

Although Jesus' post-resurrection appearances had ended, he would continue to empower his followers.

### THE HOLY SPIRIT

As Jesus' disciples were staring into the cloud where he had gone, **two angels came to them**. They reassured the disciples that the incarnate Jesus **would return one day** in the same way he had gone (Acts 1:10,11).

Jesus had told the disciples to wait in Jerusalem (Acts 1:4). He would **send them the gift of the Holy Spirit 416–17 ››**, which would clothe them with "power from on high" (Luke 24:49), equipping them to **go out and be his apostles**, or "messengers".

> " After he said this, **he was taken up before their very eyes,** and a cloud hid him from their sight."
>
> ACTS 1:9

# THE BIRTH OF THE CHURCH

"But you will receive power when the Holy Spirit comes on you;
and **you will be my witnesses** in Jerusalem, and in all Judea and Samaria,
and to the **ends of the earth.**"

ACTS 1:8

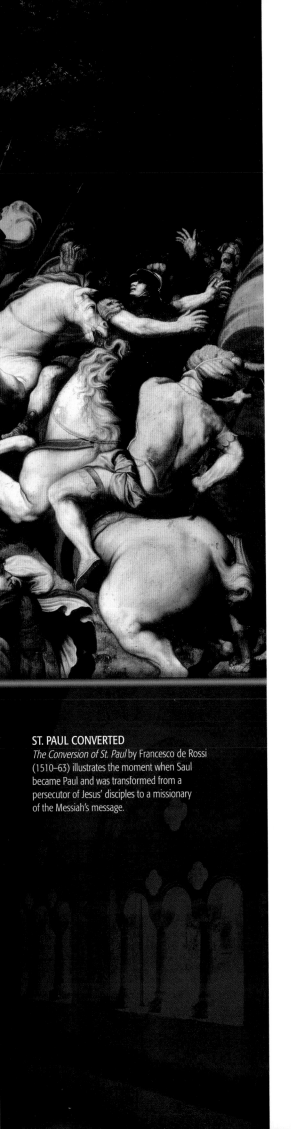

**ST. PAUL CONVERTED**
*The Conversion of St. Paul* by Francesco de Rossi (1510–63) illustrates the moment when Saul became Paul and was transformed from a persecutor of Jesus' disciples to a missionary of the Messiah's message.

ITHIN A FEW DECADES OF JESUS' DEATH AND resurrection, the good news about him had been spread throughout the ancient world, as far as Rome and beyond. Jesus had told his disciples to take the news out into the world – to become his "apostles", or messengers (the Greek word *apostolos* means "messenger" or "ambassador"). At Pentecost they were empowered for this great task by the gift of the Holy Spirit, which transformed them from fishermen into courageous campaigners. Wherever the message was heard, people formed communities of believers, heralding the emergence of the Church.

This movement was not intended as a new religion – initially, the apostles continued to worship at the Temple in Jerusalem. Rather, the fellowship of believers claimed to be the continuation and fulfilment of the story of Israel. Central to this was a conviction that Jesus was God's Messiah – the promised one the prophets of Israel had spoken of, who would bring the rule of Israel's God to the whole world.

The first apostles began preaching among Jewish communities, hoping that the chosen people would believe that Jesus was the Messiah. The apostles' preaching was accompanied by healings and acts of power that showed that the restoration of life promised by God was becoming a reality: "Crowds gathered also from the towns around Jerusalem, bringing those who were ill and those tormented by impure spirits, and all of them were healed" (Acts 5:16).

### A MISSION TO THE WORLD

However, the news about Jesus was not meant to remain within the Jewish world. Israel's Messiah wanted to bring all the nations of the world into the family of the one true God, so Jesus' message had to be spread to non-Jews – the Gentiles. Moreover, many Jews did not believe that this man Jesus, who had been crucified on a Roman cross, was their long-awaited Messiah. Soon, the followers of the Messiah (later known as Christians from the Greek translation, *Christos*) found themselves harassed by some Jewish authorities and thrown out of the synagogues.

In spite of this, the apostles continued their mission to preach, teach, and baptize groups of Gentiles, spreading the word throughout the ancient world. The new movement continued to grow, even reaching the centre of the Roman Empire itself, the mighty city of Rome. The news stirred up keen support, suspicion, and opposition along the way. However, many communities of believers were born and continued to grow with the spreading of the word of Jesus.

### TRIBULATIONS AND TRIUMPHS

The book of Acts in the New Testament is a thrilling account of the struggles, tensions, and successes of the developing Christian movement, such as the prosperous work of Barnabas at Antioch where "the disciples were called Christians first" (Acts 11:26). Alongside this book, the 21 letters, or epistles, of the apostles give us snapshots of life in the fledgling communities that formed the Early Church.

**ST. PETER CRUCIFIED**
This marble relief, *Crucifixion of Saint Peter*, was produced in 1438 by Florentine sculptor Luca Della Robbia as part of a commission for an altar.

# The Coming of the Spirit

*Jesus' disciples waited in Jerusalem, just as he had asked them to before the ascension. On the day of the festival of Pentecost, the Holy Spirit descended upon them and empowered them to go and tell the good news about Jesus to the pilgrims gathered there.*

**F**IFTY DAYS AFTER Passover was the Feast of Weeks or "Pentecost". Jewish people of many different nationalities gathered in Jerusalem to give thanks for the beginning of the harvest and remember how Moses had ascended the mountain of Sinai to receive God's law – the foundation of Jewish life.

Jesus' disciples were assembled in a house when suddenly it was filled with the sound of a mighty rushing wind that came from heaven, where Jesus had gone to be with his Father. In this wind, they saw what looked like tongues of fire that rested on each of them (Acts 2:1–3). God's Holy Spirit filled them, just as Jesus had promised. God's Spirit was going to carry the disciples across the world with the message about Jesus, just as the wind carries ships across the water. The Spirit would purify their lives, and flood them with the light of God's truth and the warmth of his love. As the disciples moved through the world, the Spirit would spread from person to person, spreading the good news about Jesus.

Straight away, the disciples began speaking in languages they didn't even know (Acts 2:4). A crowd of pilgrims gathered around to hear, amazed that they could understand the disciples' words. The presence of God's Spirit was reversing the confusion of language that had begun at Babel (Genesis 11:9).

Peter stood up and told the crowd that God had raised Jesus from the dead and was forming a renewed community around him. Whereas Moses had gone up a mountain to receive the Law, Jesus had gone into heaven itself, and had sent the gift of the Holy Spirit to renew his people's lives from the inside out (Acts 2:17–36). The apostles baptized 3,000 people that day, and the Church was born.

> "They saw what seemed to be tongues of fire… **All of them were filled with the Holy Spirit and began to speak in other tongues as the Spirit enabled them.**"
>
> ACTS 2:3,4

**THE MIRACLE**
Giotto's *Pentecost* (c.1305), a fresco in the Scrovegni Chapel in Padua, Italy, depicts the moment that the Holy Spirit descended on the gathered apostles, whose faces reveal their astonishment.

## BEFORE

The new community of people who believed in Jesus as the Messiah was growing day by day.

### A FELLOWSHIP OF BELIEVERS
Those who were **baptized on the day of Pentecost ≪ 416–17** began meeting with the apostles regularly for teaching and prayer. They also shared food together, especially to celebrate the **Last Supper ≪ 388–89** that Jesus had told them to repeat to remember the significance of his death. The believers shared all they had. Their lives were living proof that Jesus had inaugurated God's kingdom (Acts 2:42–47).

### REPLACING JUDAS ISCARIOT
After **the suicide of Judas ≪ 391**, the remaining 11 disciples wanted to make their number up to 12, a symbolic number for God's people because of the 12 tribes of Israel. Any replacement had to have shared their experience of Jesus, from the start of his ministry through to his **Ascension ≪ 412–13**. Two men, Joseph and Matthias, were nominated, and Matthias was the one chosen by God (Acts 1:12–26).

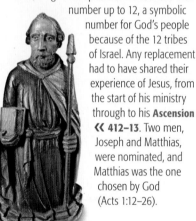

**SAINT MATTHIAS**

### A MIRACULOUS CURE
In *St. Peter and St. John Healing the Paralytic* (1783), Francisco Javier Ramos y Albertos depicted the moment of healing. Peter is merely a conduit; his hands bridge the gap between the crippled beggar on the ground and God in heaven above.

# A Lame Beggar Healed

*The Holy Spirit not only empowered the apostles to proclaim the good news of Jesus, it also enabled them to perform miracles of healing, just as Jesus had done. However, this brought them into confrontation with the religious authorities, just as it had for Jesus.*

ONE AFTERNOON, shortly after Pentecost, Peter and John went to pray at the Temple in Jerusalem. It was three o'clock, one of the times of daily prayer, and many other people were also making their way to the Temple. Among them a group of friends carried a man who

was more than 40 years old and who had been lame from birth. Every day they left him at the Temple gate to beg for money.

### An unexpected healing
The lame man had just been left at the gate when Peter and John arrived. Seeing the pair, the

man called out for money in his usual way. Instead of tossing him a coin, Peter and John stopped and spoke to him.

"Look at us!" Peter said, seizing the expectant man's attention. Peter explained that he did not have any silver or gold, but would give him what he did have – then

commanded him, "in the name of Jesus Christ of Nazareth, walk" (Acts 3:5,6). With these words, Peter took hold of the lame man's right hand. As he lifted him up, the man's feet and ankles instantly became strong. Amazed, the man jumped up and began to walk. Peter and John continued into the

> " Then **Peter said**, 'Silver or gold I do not have, but what I do have I give you. **In the name of Jesus Christ of Nazareth, walk.'**"

ACTS 3:6

Temple, and the man went along with them. He could not contain his joy – he was jumping in the air and praising God.

### Peter's sermon

The people gathering for prayer recognized the man as the person they normally saw begging at the gate, but here he was inside the Temple, leaping for joy. They were astonished, and rushed to Peter, John, and the man to find out what had happened.

Peter began to teach the crowd. "Fellow Israelites, why does this surprise you? Why do you stare at us as if by our own power or godliness we had made this man walk?" (3:12). Peter went on to tell them that the man had been healed through the power of Jesus, whom they had rejected and disowned before Pilate. They

had "killed the author of life", but God had raised him from the dead (3:15). Peter called the crowd to turn away from their old way of life, to trust in Christ, and to discover God's blessing in the new community. Many responded to Peter's message, and the number of believers grew to around 5,000.

### Before the Sanhedrin

The noise of people celebrating the lame man's healing quickly drew the attention of the Temple authorities, the Sanhedrin (see p.393). When they heard Peter and John teaching, they seized the two apostles and put them into prison.

The next morning, Peter and John were brought before the Sanhedrin, who demanded an explanation: "By what power or what name did you do this?" (4:7).

(see p.393)

**BEING INTERROGATED**
A miniature from a 14th-century vellum manuscript of the Bible, produced in Paris, shows Peter and John (far left) under questioning from the high priest and the Sanhedrin. The courage of the disciples greatly worried the religious authorities.

---

## HISTORY AND CULTURE
### BEGGARS AT THE TEMPLE GATE

In the ancient world, the sick or handicapped relied entirely on the charity of their family, friends, and others within their community. This charity – often known as almsgiving – was positively encouraged by the Jewish faith, which placed a strong emphasis on caring for one another. People who needed to beg for alms, or help, often gathered around the gates of the Temple, hoping that devout Jews on their way to make sacrifices and to pray would take pity on them and give them some money.

The gate at which the lame man sat day after day was called the "Beautiful Gate", but we cannot be certain today which gate

this was. Any of the outer gates leading to the Temple complex was an ideal spot for beggars to ply their trade and seek help from those seeking to give back to God.

**MODEL RECONSTRUCTION OF NICANOR GATE**

---

Once again, Peter declared that the man had been healed in the name of Jesus of Nazareth, God's Messiah. The Sanhedrin did not know what to say. They did not believe that Jesus was the Messiah, yet the man who had been lame was walking in the Temple. He was living proof that Jesus' name was powerful and could heal, and the news was spreading quickly. In an attempt to stop this, the authorities called Peter and John in again and "commanded them not to speak or teach at all in the name of Jesus" (4:18). But Peter and John said that they would rather obey God than the Sanhedrin. They had to speak about what they had seen and heard God doing through Jesus and the Holy Spirit.

> " By faith in the name of Jesus, this man whom you see and know **was made strong**."

ACTS 3:16

---

### AFTER

After being released from prison, Peter and John returned to their own people and told them all that the priests and elders had said.

#### A PRAYER FOR BOLDNESS
Powerful people were trying to threaten the commission that Jesus had given his followers, so **they prayed for boldness for themselves, and signs of God's power for others**. The Holy Spirit filled them just as it had at **Pentecost**.

#### ANANIAS AND SAPPHIRA
Ananias and his wife Sapphira wanted to be seen as generous, so they sold property and **gave some of the money to the community**. But they said that they had given away everything that they had received. When Peter rebuked them for deception, **they fell down dead** (Acts 5:1–11).

**THE DEATH OF SAPPHIRA**

**ST. PETER**
This statue of St. Peter stands outside St. Peter's Basilica in Rome; unveiled in 1847, it replaced a 15th-century statue. The keys are symbols of the power promised to Peter by Jesus in Caesarea (Matthew 16:19).

**DISCIPLE** Born C.AD 10  Died C.AD 65–67

# Peter

" ... you are **Peter**, and on this rock **I will build my church,** and the gates of Hades will not overcome it."

MATTHEW 16:18

**P**ETER WAS ONE of Jesus' most important and best-known disciples, and he is the one mentioned most frequently in the gospels. However, when he first met Jesus, his name was not Peter, but Simon. He grew up in the small town of Bethsaida, on the northern shores of the Sea of Galilee and as a young man, he married and settled further along the shore in Capernaum, with his wife and mother-in-law.

## Simon meets Jesus

Together with his brother Andrew, Simon worked as a fisherman. The pair had a boat and a small fishing business on the Sea of Galilee, and often joined with other fishermen, including James and John, the sons of Zebedee.

Simon and Andrew travelled to the Jordan region to hear John the Baptist preach. While they were in the crowds, John the Baptist saw Jesus walking by and called out, "Look, the Lamb of God!" (John 1:36). Andrew heard this and went to tell his brother. The two men went to Jesus, who took one look at Simon and announced, "You are Simon son of John. You will be called Cephas" (John 1:42).

*Cephas* is Aramaic for "rock", which is translated into Greek as *Petros*. He became known as Simon Peter, which was later shortened to Peter. Simon Peter and a few other disciples went with Jesus back to Galilee, where they attended a wedding in Cana (see pp.306–07), before arriving in Capernaum (John 2:12).

## The impulsive disciple

The brothers returned to their fishing for a short while. One day, Jesus found them casting their nets at the Sea of Galilee: "Come, follow me... and I will send you out to fish for

**CALLED BY JESUS**
This detail of a relief from one of the three doors of the 12th-century church of Saint-Pierre de Montmartre in Paris, France depicts the calling of Peter.

## HISTORY AND CULTURE

### PETER AND THE CHURCH

According to Christian tradition, Peter died in Rome during the persecution of Christians by Emperor Nero. It is likely Peter spent some time in the city before his death and possible that Mark wrote his gospel at this time, basing it on Peter's recollections. The letter Peter sent to the churches in Asia Minor from Rome reads: "She who is in Babylon, chosen together with you, sends you her greetings, and so does my son Mark" (1 Peter 5:13). "Babylon" is probably a reference to Rome. Peter's leading role as bishop ("overseer") in the church at Rome became the basis of a later tradition that traces the office of the Pope back to Peter himself. After his death, Peter's body was buried in the city, possibly under the future site of St. Peter's Basilica in the Vatican City.

**ST PETER'S BASILICA, VATICAN CITY, ROME**

people", he said (Matthew 4:19). Simon Peter and Andrew left their fishing and became part of Jesus' closest group of disciples, or followers, the 12 (Matthew 4:18–20).

Peter, James, and John quickly became Jesus' most intimate friends. They were with him when he raised Jairus's daughter (Mark 5:37), at his transfiguration (Mark 9:2), and in the garden of Gethsemane just before his betrayal (Mark 14:33).

Peter was often impulsive. Once, when he saw Jesus walking across the water on the stormy Sea of Galilee towards the disciples' boat, he immediately wanted to go to Jesus, even though that meant stepping out onto the water (Matthew 14:28,29). Once out of the boat, his nerve failed him, and Jesus had to save him from drowning. Later, just before Jesus'

**PETER'S HOUSE**
The ruins of a 1st-century house in Capernaum have been identified – by tradition – as having belonged to St. Peter. Inscriptions mentioning Simon Peter and Jesus have been found on the walls.

death, Peter announced that he would stay at Jesus' side, whatever happened – "Even if I have to die with you…" (Matthew 26:35). Yet, within a few hours, Peter had denied three times even knowing who Jesus was.

However, Peter's impulsiveness sometimes led to moments of great faith. He was the first disciple to declare that he believed Jesus was the Messiah promised by God (Matthew 16:16). Jesus reaffirmed that Simon was indeed Peter, "the rock" – the solid foundation of his faith in Jesus was the rock on which Jesus' church would be built.

### The bold apostle

After the resurrection, Jesus made a special point of meeting with Peter. Jesus asked Peter three times if he loved him, before reaffirming him as his messenger to the world, despite his past failures (John 21:15–19). On the day of Pentecost, when all the apostles were filled with the Holy Spirit, Peter was the first to stand up and preach to the crowd (Acts 2:14).

In Acts, Peter is the daring apostle, spreading Jesus' news to ordinary people, the Jewish authorities, and

even non-Jews, or Gentiles. Peter was clearly a leader in the Early Church, and was present at the important Council of Jerusalem in around AD 50 (Acts 15). According to tradition, he was associated with the church in Antioch in Syria, the Roman capital of the eastern Mediterranean region, from where he probably travelled extensively on missionary journeys.

Peter faced prison at least twice because of his faith in Jesus, but he still did not stop telling the world about what he had seen and heard. Church tradition maintains that he eventually reached the city of Rome, where his preaching led him to be condemned to death by crucifixion. It also records that he asked to be crucified upside down, because he felt unworthy of suffering the same death as Jesus.

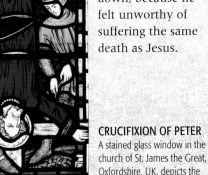

**CRUCIFIXION OF PETER**
A stained glass window in the church of St. James the Great, Oxfordshire, UK, depicts the martyrdom of Peter, crucified head downwards.

## BEFORE

**The activities of the Christians were attracting great interest in Jerusalem.**

### SIGNS AND WONDERS
News spread in the city that the apostles were **performing miracles ‹‹ 418–19**. People arrived from the surrounding villages and towns, bringing their sick or demon-possessed for healing. Some were healed by Peter's shadow falling across them as he passed (Acts 5:12–16).

### LIBERATED FROM PRISON
The Jewish authorities **arrested the apostles and locked them in jail**. But during the night, an angel from God freed them. When the guards came to take the apostles to the authorities, the jail was empty. The apostles were **back in the Temple courts, teaching people the news about the Messiah**. One member of the **Sanhedrin ‹‹ 393**, called Gamaliel, advised the council to wait and see what would happen to the new movement (Acts 5:17–40).

GAMALIEL AND HIS STUDENTS, DEPICTED IN A CASTILIAN *HAGGADAH*, 1300

# The Word Spreads

*The apostles first began to share the news about Jesus the Messiah in Jerusalem, and very soon the church began to grow. With the growth came additional pressures and work, so the apostles appointed deacons to help them.*

**A**S THE CHURCH in Jerusalem grew, the apostles found themselves responsible for supporting and feeding a large number of widows. Usually, the welfare of a widow was the task of close family members; however, within the Early Church there were many widows who lacked such a family network. Scholars have speculated about why this was the case. A widow may have been disowned by her family because she believed in Jesus as the Messiah; or she may have been attracted to his ministry precisely because of the concern that Jesus expressed for widows' poverty and unfortunate social position (see pp.384–85).

### A problem emerges
The widows who were being cared for by the church came from two distinct communities in Jerusalem. The first were the Hebraic, or Hebrew, Jews. Deeply immersed in the culture of Palestine, they spoke Aramaic and preserved local customs. The second were the Hellenistic Jews, many of whom had settled in Jerusalem after living in Jewish communities throughout the wider and

HELLENISTIC CULTURE
This Greek inscription was found in Jerusalem at the large *Nea* (Greek for "New") church. The inscription states that the building of the church was carried out "by our most pious Emperor Flavius Justinian" and completed in AD 543.

**❝** Brothers and sisters, **choose seven men** from among you who are **known to be full of the Spirit and wisdom. ❞**

ACTS 6:3

predominantly Greek-speaking world. These women were less willing to embrace Hebraic customs, and preferred to combine their Jewish identity with the customs of the Hellenistic world.

The two groups appear to have been distrustful of each other: the Hellenists felt like outsiders, while the Hebraic Jews thought that the Hellenists had watered down their Jewish identity.

Even though members of both Jewish groups were now part of the same Christian community, suspicions remained. Hellenistic Christians felt that their widows were not being supported as well as the Hebraic widows, and they started to complain that they "were being overlooked in the daily distribution of food" (Acts 6:1).

### The apostles' solution
Much of the apostles' time was taken up with practicalities, such as arranging food for the widows. Yet this was not the task that Jesus had given them. They were called to spread the message about Jesus, which required them to devote

time to prayer and preaching. "So the Twelve gathered all the disciples together and said, 'It would not be right for us to neglect the ministry of the word of God in order to wait on tables'" (6:2).

Instead, the apostles suggested that the community appoint seven helpers who would take over responsibility for the distribution of food and other practical tasks, so the apostles could give their "… attention to prayer and the ministry of the word" (6:4). These helpers, who were to become known as *diakonai*, or deacons (1 Timothy 3:8–12), needed to be full of God's Holy Spirit and wisdom like the apostles, but they would use their gifts in a different way (Acts 6:3).

### Seven deacons appointed
The believers agreed that this was a wise proposal, and chose seven men from among their number. The apostles prayed over the men and commissioned them as deacons – an innovation that enabled the Christian community to continue to grow.

**❝** So **the word of God spread.** The number of disciples in Jerusalem increased rapidly, and a large number of priests **became obedient to the faith. ❞**

ACTS 6:7

**SERVANTS OF GOD**
*St. Stephen and the Twelve Apostles*, c.1370, by Anovelo da Imbonate, belongs to a cycle of frescoes in the Oratory of St. Stephen – one of the first seven deacons – at Lentate sul Seveso in northern Italy.

## JEWISH DIASPORA

The first seven deacons appointed by the church were Stephen, Philip, Procorus, Nicanor, Timon, Parmenas, and Nicolas (Acts 6:5). Their Greek names suggest that they were drawn from the Hellenistic group.

Many of those Jews had once lived in the Jewish communities scattered around the ancient world in predominantly Greek or Roman cultures, known as the Diaspora. While they retained their faith, they also embraced some local customs. When Diaspora Jews came to Jerusalem, they were recognizably different, and even had their own synagogues – for example, the Synagogue of the Freedmen had members from Cyrene and Alexandria as well as the provinces of Cilicia and Asia (6:9).

### AFTER

**The church in Jerusalem soon faced intense persecution.**

#### THE CHURCH SCATTERED
After the authorities had **killed the deacon named Stephen 424–25 ≫**, pressure was put on the other believers in Jerusalem. While the apostles stayed in the city, many believers scattered throughout Judea and Samaria (Acts 8:1).

#### DEACONS
Throughout history, the Christian church has continued to **appoint deacons to help with practical aspects of its life**. Such helpers are considered to be as important to the work of Jesus' great commission as the apostles.

ROMAN CATHOLIC DEACONS ORDAINED AT ST. PETER'S BASILICA, THE VATICAN, ROME

# Stephen Martyred

*Opposition to the early Christian movement was growing and the authorities were eager to halt the spread of the news about Jesus. When Stephen was arrested in Jerusalem, officials took their opposition to the extreme, resulting in his death.*

**S**TEPHEN WAS ONE of those chosen to help with the rapidly growing Christian community in Jerusalem. The Holy Spirit empowered Stephen to perform "great wonders and signs among the people" (Acts 6:8) just as he had empowered the disciples.

Stephen's ministry attracted the attention of some members of a synagogue in Jerusalem who tried to argue against him, but his wisdom, and "the wisdom the Spirit gave him" (6:10), were too great for them. They persuaded some men to claim that Stephen had spoken against the central tenets of Judaism: the law of Moses, the Temple, and God himself (6:11–14). This was enough for Stephen to be brought before the Jewish ruling council, the Sanhedrin (see p.393).

"Are these charges true?" demanded the high priest. As Stephen began to speak, the Sanhedrin saw that his face looked like an angel, a messenger from God. Instead of defending himself against the charges, Stephen gave them a lesson in their own history. He pointed out that the people had always rejected God's messengers, including Moses. The religious authorities of Stephen's day were no different – they had rejected and killed God's promised Messiah and were now trying to stamp out his message (7:2–53).

The members of the Sanhedrin could not believe what they were hearing: Stephen had publicly accused them of disobeying God. As he spoke he looked up and saw a vision of heaven. "Look," he exclaimed, "I see heaven open and the Son of Man standing at the right hand of God" (7:56).

The Sanhedrin could no longer contain their anger. This was blasphemy. They seized Stephen, dragged him out of the city, and began to stone him. As they did this, Stephen's final words echoed those of Jesus on the cross. He prayed that Jesus would receive his spirit, and that God would not hold this sin against his executors. Then he died, becoming the first Christian martyr (see pp.450–51). Jesus had warned his disciples that they would face persecution or death, just as he had (John 15:20,21).

> **" 'Lord Jesus, receive my spirit.' Then he fell on his knees and cried out, 'Lord, do not hold this sin against them.'"**
>
> ACTS 7:59,60

**STONED TO DEATH**
An illustration from a French gospel (c.1200) depicts the imprisonment and then the stoning of Stephen, an event attended and approved of by a young man called Saul (the future apostle Paul).

## BEFORE

**In the face of persecution in Jerusalem, the disciples went out to areas nearby.**

### PHILIP THE EVANGELIST
Philip, one of the **seven deacons << 422–23**, became an evangelist, **preaching and healing in Samaria**. Many people believed and were baptized (Acts 8:5–8,12).

**14TH-CENTURY DEPICTION OF SIMON MAGUS**

### SIMON MAGUS
One of the new believers from Samaria was Simon Magus, a magician, who was amazed by Philip's miraculous powers. When Peter and John came from Jerusalem to **pray for the Holy Spirit to come upon the new believers**, Simon offered to pay them for this power. Peter rebuked Simon for trying to buy the Spirit's power – it was **freely given by God** (Acts 8:9–24).

---

**HISTORY AND CULTURE**

### ETHIOPIA AND THE CHURCH

The man Philip met on the road to Gaza was the chief finance minister to the Ethiopian royal court. Ancient Ethiopia was a wealthy kingdom, situated in what is now northern Sudan and modern Ethiopia, over 1,600km (1,000 miles) from Jerusalem, with diplomatic and trade links across the world. Affairs of state were managed by "Kandake", which is not a name but a title, denoting a queen or the regent's mother. The king had a more ceremonial and religious role. Some church traditions suggest that when the Ethiopian returned home, he began sharing the good news and a church was founded, which perhaps included Kandake. Christianity took hold in Ethiopia early in the 4th century, when it became the state religion.

### BAPTIZING THE EUNUCH
This 16th-century painting, *St. Philip the Apostle Baptizing the Eunuch*, depicts the first Ethiopian embracing Christianity. As the two men travelled, the eunuch said to Philip, "Look, here is water. What can stand in the way of my being baptized?" (Acts 8:36).

# Philip and the Ethiopian

*Jesus' message had now spread far beyond Jerusalem, just as he had said it would. When a God-fearing government official from Ethiopia decided to become a Christian, it was clear that the news was also spreading beyond Jews.*

**CHURCH OF BETE GIYORGIS**
The Ethiopian Orthodox church of St. George is the best preserved of 11 churches dating from the 13th century, each one hewn from the rock at the pilgrimage site of Lalibela, in northern Ethiopia.

**P**HILIP THE EVANGELIST, one of the seven Greek-speaking Jews elected by the Early Church and approved of by the apostles, had been preaching in Samaria. One day, an angel appeared to him and said: "Go south to the road – the desert road – that goes down from Jerusalem to Gaza" (Acts 8:26). Philip was given no further direction, but he set out for Gaza, about 96km (60 miles) away.

**HILLS OF JUDEA**
Philip met the Ethiopian eunuch while on his way along the road through the desert hills of southern Judea, travelling southwest from Jerusalem to Gaza (the Philistine city in Canaan).

### A puzzled Ethiopian
An important royal courtier from Ethiopia was travelling in a chariot on the same road. The official had been to Jerusalem on a pilgrimage to one of the Jewish festivals. The Ethiopian was attracted to the Jewish faith, but he was a eunuch – he had been castrated as a sign of his loyalty to Kandake, queen of Ethiopia (see panel, left). Under Jewish Law, eunuchs were not allowed to participate in Jewish worship (Deuteronomy 23:1). Even so, the Ethiopian was interested in the Jewish Scriptures and was reading the Book of the Isaiah when he met Philip.

The Holy Spirit told Philip: "Go to that chariot and stay near it" (Acts 8:29). As Philip got close, he heard the man reading from Isaiah. Philip asked if he understood what he was reading. The Ethiopian said that he was puzzled, and invited Philip to explain the text to him.

### Philip talks about Jesus
The Ethiopian was reading a passage that began, "He was led like a sheep to the slaughter" (Acts 8:32), and ended with "For his life was taken from the earth" (8:33) . The man asked Philip whether the prophet was talking about himself or someone else. Philip explained that the prophecy was about Jesus, who had suffered and died in order to bring God's forgiveness and new life to the world. He explained that Jesus was God's Messiah and may also have pointed the Ethiopian to Isaiah 56:4,5 in which God says: "To the eunuchs who keep my Sabbaths… I will give them an everlasting name that will endure forever."

### An impromptu baptism
The eunuch was overjoyed when he heard the news: he could belong to the family of Israel's God after all, because Jesus, God's Messiah, had opened the kingdom to him too.

As they continued their journey they came to some water. The Ethiopian ordered the chariot to stop, and asked Philip to baptize him. Philip and the eunuch went down into the water and Philip baptized him as a believer in Jesus. Then the Ethiopian went on his way, rejoicing.

> " The eunuch asked Philip, 'Tell me, please, **who is the prophet talking about,** himself or someone else?' Then **Philip… told him the good news about Jesus.** "
>
> ACTS 8:34,35

**AFTER**

After the Ethiopian courtier's baptism, God's Spirit "suddenly took Philip away" (Acts 8:39) from the scene and the eunuch did not see him again.

**PHILIP IN CAESAREA**
Having reappeared at Azotus (or Ashdod), Philip continued to **spread the message about Jesus** as he travelled north along the Mediterranean coast, until eventually he reached and settled in the Roman port of Caesarea on the coast of northern Israel.

Some time later the **apostle Paul 448–49 »** and his companions stayed with Philip on their **journey from Ephesus to Jerusalem 452 »**. Philip had four unmarried daughters who lived with him and who were regarded as **possessing the gift of prophecy** (Acts 21:8–9).

---

**ANALYSIS**

## PROSELYTES AND GOD-FEARERS

Most Jews had inherited their faith by being born to Jewish parents, and all males were circumcised on the eighth day. However, it was possible for people to convert to Judaism, provided they met certain conditions.

Known as "proselytes", full converts were required to be circumcised (if male), obey the whole of the Jewish Law, and could participate fully in worship at the Temple. As a eunuch, the Ethiopian could not have become a proselyte.

Those known as God-fearers included people who simply respected the Jewish faith as well as others who were on their way to becoming proselytes. Unlike proselytes, God-fearers were not allowed into the inner courts of the Temple.

**A GREEK INSCRIPTION RESERVING SEATING AT MILETUS THEATRE "FOR GOD-FEARING JEWS"**

**‹‹ BEFORE**

**Christian communities were growing outside Jerusalem.**

**THE CHURCH IN DAMASCUS**
Jews from Damascus had been in Jerusalem for Pentecost. Some may have become believers in Jesus after **hearing Peter's sermon ‹‹ 416–17**. When they returned, a small community of believers was formed. Other Christians may have joined them after **persecution broke out in Jerusalem**.

**SAUL THE PHARISEE**
Saul studied under the rabbi **Gamaliel ‹‹ 422**. He was also a Pharisee, and enthusiastically upheld the law of Moses as the proper way to obey God.

**PEOPLE**

**ANANIAS**

A respected member of the Jewish community in Damascus, Ananias was also a believer in Jesus as the Messiah. When God told him to visit Saul, Ananias was confused because he had heard that Saul was persecuting the Christians. But when God reassured him, Ananias obeyed, and went to the house of Judas in Straight Street, where Saul was staying, to heal Saul and deliver Jesus' message: "The God of our ancestors has chosen you… You will be his witness to all people of what you have seen and heard" (Acts 22:14,15). According to Christian tradition, Ananias was martyred for his beliefs.

ANANIAS BAPTIZING SAUL

# Saul on the Road to Damascus

*One of the most influential figures in the Early Church was the apostle Paul, originally known as Saul of Tarsus, who had persecuted Jesus' followers. Saul's life changed when the risen Jesus met him on the road to Damascus.*

**W**HEN STEPHEN WAS stoned to death (see pp.424–25), a young Pharisee named Saul had been standing by; he had even looked after the coats of those who were throwing the stones (Acts 7:58). What Saul saw convinced him that he should "…do all that was possible to oppose the name of Jesus of Nazareth" (26:9), and he became one of the strongest opponents of the Christian movement. With the authorization of the Jewish chief priests, he visited the homes of known believers, dragged them away to prison, and even supported their being put to death (26:10).

ROMAN CITY GATE, DAMASCUS
Paul is believed to have fled from Damascus after his conversion near this Roman-era gate, which still stands today by the Christian quarter of the old city.

### The road to Damascus
As the believers in Jesus dispersed to other regions, Saul followed (26:11). The Sanhedrin wrote letters of introduction to synagogues in other cities, and gave Saul permission to hunt down any Jewish followers of Jesus and return them to Jerusalem (22:5). One of the cities he went to was Damascus, northeast of Israel.

As Saul neared the city, a blinding light struck him and his travelling companions. They all fell to the ground, and Saul heard a voice asking why he persecuted him. Saul knew that the voice had come from heaven. "Who are you, Lord?" Saul asked. "I am Jesus, whom you are persecuting," came the reply. Jesus told Saul to go into Damascus and wait there for instructions. Saul and his companions rose to their feet. "The men travelling with Saul stood there speechless; they heard the sound but did not see anyone" (9:7). Saul opened his eyes, but he could see nothing at all; the brilliant light had blinded him (9:8).

### Ananias brings a commission
Saul was led to a house in the city, where after three days he was visited by a local believer called Ananias. He put his hands on Saul, saying "Brother Saul, receive your sight"; then what looked like scales fell from Saul's eyes and he could see. Ananias told Saul that Jesus was appointing him an apostle and Saul was then baptized as a believer.

**AFTER ››**

**Saul's life was completely transformed by meeting the risen Jesus.**

**THE PLOT AGAINST SAUL**
After recovering his sight, Saul applied his expertise in the Jewish law to **teach others about Jesus**. In Damascus's synagogues he offered persuasive scriptural interpretations to prove that Jesus was the Messiah whom God had promised long ago (Acts 9:20–22).

The Jewish authorities in Damascus were furious that Saul had become **the champion of the Christians**, and was gaining more followers. They plotted to kill him as he left the city, and so kept watch on the gates. Saul heard of the plan, and one night his followers **hid him in a basket and lowered him through a window** in the city wall. Saul escaped to Jerusalem (Acts 9:23–25).

SAUL ESCAPES FROM DAMASCUS IN A BASKET

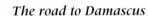

**❝** … suddenly a **light from heaven flashed** around him. He fell to the ground and heard a voice say to him, '**Saul, Saul, why do you persecute me?**' **❞**

ACTS 9:3,4

**THE CONVERSION OF SAINT PAUL**
Caravaggio's 1601 painting shows a blinding light striking Saul's face. Later, by which time his name had changed to Paul, the evangelist wrote that he had seen Jesus during his conversion (1 Corinthians 9:1).

## BEFORE

**Peter travelled around the countryside telling "the good news" about Jesus.**

### HEALING AENEAS

While Peter was visiting the Christian community in the town of Lydda, **he met a man called Aeneas who had been paralyzed and bedridden for eight years**. Peter said to him, "Jesus Christ heals you" (Acts 9:34) and the man stood up. Jesus healed many sick people in a similar way (Matthew 8:3, 8:13, 8:14, 9:22) **and gave this power to his apostles ≪ 342–43**.

### TABITHA RAISED TO LIFE

While Peter was in Lydda, **a woman named Tabitha became ill and died in Joppa**. She had been generous to many people, making items of clothing for the poor or widowed. The Christians sent for Peter, who knelt beside her and prayed, then called out, "Tabitha, get up" (Acts 9:40). Tabitha opened her eyes and stood up. There are several examples of Jesus bringing the dead back to life (such as Matthew 9:18–25).

**PETER RESURRECTING THE WIDOW TABITHA, HENRI TESTELIN (1652)**

## ANALYSIS

### CLEAN AND UNCLEAN

God's law told Jews to keep themselves "clean", and outlined which kinds of practices and foods were "clean" and "unclean". Pork, for instance, was said to be an unclean food, and Jews were forbidden to eat it. Leviticus 11 lists the animals, fish, and insects that are unclean and may not be eaten (see pp.304–305). This concern for purity later led to the formation of traditions that prohibited Jews from eating with non-Jewish people.

### GENTILES

Cornelius was the first Gentile convert. The term "Gentile" – from the Latin word *gentilis*, meaning "belonging to a clan" – is used in the Bible to refer to non-Jewish nations or peoples. Gentiles were considered "unclean" because they did not follow the laws of the Jewish faith. Relations between Jews and Gentiles were often good, but sometimes their different beliefs and customs caused mutual distrust and suspicion.

**PETER'S VISION**
The Italian baroque artist Domenico Fetti portrayed Peter's strange vision of foods descending from heaven in *Peter's Vision of the Unclean Beasts* (1619).

# Peter and Cornelius

*Jews understood themselves to be God's chosen people, who kept themselves "clean" by following special customs and laws. Peter had a strange vision and an encounter with a Roman that challenged his views about purity.*

**P**ETER WAS STAYING in the port town of Joppa, in the house of a leather-worker named Simon. One day, around noon, Peter was on the roof of Simon's house, praying. He began to get hungry, and while the food was being prepared, he had a strange vision. He saw heaven opened, and something like a large sheet being let down to Earth by its four corners. The cloth was full of creatures: "all kinds of four-footed animals, as well as reptiles and birds" (Acts 10:12). Then Peter heard a voice from heaven saying, "Get up, Peter. Kill and eat" (10:13). Peter was shocked, because according to Jewish law some creatures were clean and could be eaten, while

## HISTORY AND CULTURE

### CAESAREA

Cornelius was based in Caesarea (later known as Caesarea Maritima), which was the Roman administrative capital of the province of Judea. An ancient settlement on the site had been rebuilt as a major trading port by Herod the Great between 22 and 9 BC. Archaeologists have found evidence of a vibrant city, with palaces, an amphitheatre, and a hippodrome. When it was annexed by the Romans in 6 BC, Caesarea became the base for the Roman procurator (governor). It was ideal as a garrison city, and the Italian Regiment of the Roman army was stationed there.

**CAESAREA MARITIMA, ISRAEL**

others were unclean and could not be eaten (Leviticus 11). The sheet from heaven contained an assortment of both clean and unclean creatures.

"Surely not, Lord!" he exclaimed (10:14). He had never eaten any unclean thing before, and he was reluctant to do so now. But the voice said: "Do not call anything impure that God has made clean" (10:15). Twice more the voice called out "Get up, Peter. Kill and eat" and twice more Peter questioned the command. Both times he received the same reply as earlier: "Do not call anything impure that God has made clean." Then the sheet full of creatures was taken back into heaven.

### Cornelius's request

While Peter was wondering about the vision, three messengers came to the house looking for him. God's Spirit directed Peter to greet them. The three men – a Roman soldier and two servants – told Peter that they had been sent by their master Cornelius, a centurion from the Italian Regiment of the Roman army based in Caesarea (10:1), which was a coastal town 48 km (30 miles) away. Although he was a Roman, Cornelius greatly

### CONVERSION OF CORNELIUS
The sarcophagus of the "Miraculous Source", carved in the 4th century AD shows Cornelius at Peter's feet in reverence. It was extraordinary for a Roman centurion to bow down before a simple fisherman.

admired the Jewish faith, and had gained a good reputation among Jews in Caesarea for being devout and God-fearing, and for his generous gifts to those in need (10:2). The previous afternoon, Cornelius had been visited by an

angel, who had told him to send some men to Joppa to find Peter and bring him back. The men explained this to Peter, who agreed to go with them to Caesarea.

### Peter's message

As Peter and the men set out the next day, a few Jewish Christian believers from Joppa joined them. Meanwhile, at Cornelius' house, the centurion's family and friends gathered in expectation. When Peter entered, Cornelius fell at his feet in worship, but Peter asked him to get up, saying "I am only a man myself" (10:26).

Peter told Cornelius that although Jewish law forbade a Jew from visiting a Gentile house, "God has shown me that I should not call anyone impure or unclean" (10:28). He asked why Cornelius wanted to see him, and Cornelius recounted his visit from the angel. Peter then began to speak to the gathering. He

## " ... God does not show favouritism but accepts ... the one who fears him and does what is right."

**ACTS** 10:34,35

said that he now realized that God did not favour any race or people, but accepted everyone into his faith. Paul went on to tell them about Jesus' life and his death on the cross, and how he had been raised back to life by God. The risen Jesus, Peter said, had commanded the apostles to testify that he was the Messiah, and to preach that Jesus would forgive the sins of everyone who believed in him, Jews and non-Jews alike.

As Peter was saying these things, the Holy Spirit filled everyone who heard them; Cornelius and his guests began "speaking in tongues and praising God" (10:46). Seeing this, Peter said "Surely no one can stand in the way of their being baptized with water. They have received the Holy Spirit just as we have" (10:47), and he ordered that they should all be baptized.

### AFTER

**News of what had happened in Caesarea spread quickly.**

**PETER'S EXPLANATION**
A group of Jewish Christians in Jerusalem criticized Peter, because **they had heard he had entered the house of an unclean Roman and eaten with him**. Peter explained everything that had taken place, from his vision on the roof of Simon's house to the coming of the Holy Spirit on Cornelius and his household. When they heard this, all the believers began to praise God.

**CHRISTIANS IN ANTIOCH**
The message about Jesus **continued to spread north to Antioch 434–45 >>**, a multi-cultural city in Syria, where believers in Jesus first came to be called "Christians".

**THE ENTRANCE TO ANCIENT ANTIOCH**

**BEFORE**

**The church outside Jerusalem was growing stronger all the time.**

**SAUL AND BARNABAS**

Many people in the city of Antioch were becoming believers. **Barnabas was sent from Jerusalem** to help to teach the new Christians (Acts 11:22). Finding that he needed help, he travelled to Tarsus to persuade Saul to return with him and help teach the people. "The disciples were called Christians first at Antioch" (Acts 11:26).

**FAMINE PREDICTED**

A prophet in Antioch named Agabus prophesied that there would be **a severe famine throughout the Roman Empire** (Acts 11:28). The believers in Antioch decided to support the Christians in Judea, sending their gifts through Barnabas and Saul.

**HISTORY AND CULTURE**

**HOUSE CHURCHES**

The first Christians often met secretly because of the threat of persecution. Rather than meeting in official places, they gathered in one another's homes to pray, read scriptures, and eat together (Romans 16:1–5, 23). Over time, some house owners modified or extended rooms to accommodate these Christian gatherings. Later, when it was safer to meet, many of these house churches became sites for public church buildings.

**THE RUINS OF AN EARLY HOUSE CHURCH IN ROME, BENEATH THE CHURCH OF ST CECILIA**

# Peter Freed by the Angel

*It seemed that nothing could stop the Christian message from spreading far beyond the Jewish nation. In Jerusalem, some religious leaders were intent on stopping the movement, but even King Herod and his soldiers could not silence the apostles.*

**M**ANY JEWISH pilgrims were gathering in Jerusalem for the feast of Passover, causing the authorities to worry that the Christian message would spread to more people. Herod Agrippa decided to arrest some of the believers and put them in prison. Among them was James, the brother of John and son of Zebedee. He had been one of Jesus' closest disciples, and was a well-known figure in the Jerusalem church. Herod ordered the beheading of James as a public deterrent.

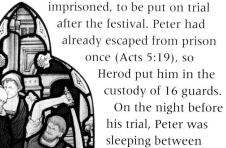

**HEROD BEHEADS ST JAMES**
A stained glass window in the medieval church of St James, Pembrokeshire, UK, depicts the beheading of St James the Great. The act was to make him the first martyr among the apostles.

### Peter put in prison

When Herod saw that many Jews approved of James' execution, he decided to hunt down another of Jesus' closest apostles. Peter was in Jerusalem for the Festival of the Unleavened Bread (which includes the celebration of Passover), so Herod had him arrested and imprisoned, to be put on trial after the festival. Peter had already escaped from prison once (Acts 5:19), so Herod put him in the custody of 16 guards.

On the night before his trial, Peter was sleeping between two soldiers, bound by two chains, and two guards stood at the entrance to his cell. Suddenly, the room was filled with light, as an angel from God appeared. Peter was still asleep, so the angel hit him on his side to wake him up. "Quick!" said the angel, "Get up!" (Acts 12:7). The chains that had been shackled to Peter's wrists fell away, and he sleepily rose to his feet. He thought he was having a dream.

The angel hurried him on: "Put on your clothes and sandals" (12:8). After Peter had wrapped his cloak around him, the angel told him to follow. The soldiers were still asleep in the cell, and those guarding the door did not stir as they went out. Bemused, Peter kept following the angel until they arrived at the iron entrance gate of the prison. Mysteriously, the gate swung open unaided, and the angel and Peter walked out into the city. At the end of the first street, the angel disappeared. Suddenly Peter came to his senses. It was not a dream; he was no longer in prison. "Now I know without a doubt that the Lord has sent his angel and rescued me from Herod's clutches" (12:11), he said.

### Surprise and joy

Peter hurried through the dark streets to the house of Mary, the mother of John Mark, where he knew some believers would be

> **"King Herod arrested some** who belonged to the church… He had **James,** the brother of John, **put to death with the sword."**
>
> ACTS 12:1,2

> "Suddenly **an angel of the Lord appeared…** 'Quick, get up!' he said, and **the chains fell off Peter's wrists**."
>
> ACTS 12:7

**PETER'S PRISON**
It is thought that Peter was probably imprisoned in the four-towered Fortress of Antonia (model shown above). This was a palace and also the Roman barracks, where 600 soldiers were garrisoned.

gathered. He knocked on the door, and waited for the servant, called Rhoda, to answer. When Rhoda heard Peter's voice, she was so overjoyed that she ran back into the house to tell the others, without even opening the door to let Peter in. "Peter is at the door!" she exclaimed (12:14). But the others did not believe her, and

thought she was hallucinating. As she continued to insist they wondered if it was Peter's angel and he had already been executed.

Peter kept knocking. Eventually, the believers opened the door, and

were astonished to see Peter himself outside. Peter explained how the angel had freed him from prison, and told them to let the other believers in Jerusalem know what had happened. Then he left the city. In the morning, Herod learned of Peter's escape – he was so angry that he cross-examined and then executed the guards.

**MIRACULOUS RESCUE**
Peter could barely believe his eyes as an angel appeared between the guards, telling him to get dressed and leave. Jacob de Backer illustrated Peter's surprise in *The Liberation of St Peter* (1560).

### PEOPLE

### MARY AND MARK

Mary, the mother of John Mark, seems to have been a prominent member of the church in Jerusalem, and her home was spacious enough to be used for gatherings. Her upper room may have been the one that was used by Jesus for the Last Supper. It is assumed she was a wealthy widow, who could use her property to help the Christian movement. Her son, John Mark, became a companion of Saul (later the apostle Paul; see Acts 12:25) and Peter (1 Peter 5:13). He is thought to be the same Mark who wrote the Gospel of Mark.

### AFTER ››

**God was keeping his apostles safe so they could continue their work.**

**HEROD AGRIPPA'S DEATH**
Following a speech by Herod in Caesarea, some of his subjects flattered him by **claiming he was a god**. Herod accepted their praise, but was immediately struck down by an illness, which led swiftly to his death (Acts 12: 23).

COIN OF HEROD AGRIPPA

**ANOTHER ESCAPE**
Paul and Silas were later **imprisoned in Philippi 442–43 ››** for taking away a female slave's ability to foretell the future. They too were miraculously freed, when **God sent an earthquake** that shook open the prison doors in the middle of the night (Acts 16:26). They baptized the jailer – relieved that **none of the prisoners had taken the opportunity to escape** – and his whole household.

## BEFORE

**Saul and Barnabas took gifts of money from Antioch to the poor in Jerusalem, before returning to the city.**

### A GIFT FROM ANTIOCH

Some prophets visited Antioch from Jerusalem. Among them was Agabus, who **prophesied that there would be a severe famine** throughout the Roman Empire. The believers in Antioch supported the Christians in Judea, many of whom were poor. They sent **Saul and Barnabas ‹‹ 432**, a Cypriot believer who had introduced Saul to the apostles, to **deliver a gift of money** for the believers in Jerusalem, to help them during the time of famine (Acts 11:27–30).

### JOHN MARK

While they were in Jerusalem, the two companions had met **John Mark, the son of Mary ‹‹ 433** and the cousin of Barnabas. John Mark travelled with Saul and Barnabas on their return to Antioch.

ANALYSIS

### MAGIC AND MAGICIANS

Many people in the ancient world believed that there were good and bad spirits, whose power could be harnessed to accomplish miracles. Elymas Bar-Jesus was a Jewish magician, who invoked this power to exorcise demons and to cast spells for protection and good fortune. This had earned him a prestigious position as an attendant to the Roman governor of Cyprus, Sergius Paulus. Elymas recognized that the Christian message threatened his practice of magic.

The early Christians did not need complicated formulas or incantations – the name of Jesus the Messiah was power enough since Jesus had defeated evil by his resurrection. Wherever the Christian message spread, it released people from the fear of evil and the need for mysterious magic.

**AMULET WORN BY ROMAN CHILD TO WARD OFF EVIL**

### SALAMIS

Acts relates that Saul and Barnabas visited the synagogue in the Roman city of Salamis – seen here are the columns of the city's ruined gymnasium – on the east coast of Cyprus as part of their mission to bring the word of God to the island's people.

# Mission to Cyprus

*Antioch in Syria was becoming a thriving centre for the Early Church, and its believers were prompted by the Holy Spirit to send two of their strongest leaders with the good news to Cyprus, a Roman province.*

THE PERSECUTION of Jewish believers in Jerusalem following Stephen's death (see pp.424–25) caused some believers to uproot to Antioch, the third largest city of the Roman world, situated around 485km (300 miles) north of Jerusalem. Many Greeks there had responded to the Christian message, and when the Jerusalem church heard about these new followers, Barnabas was sent to instruct them in their faith.

Barnabas was "a good man, full of the Holy Spirit and faith" (Acts 11:24) who was able to bring the word of God to many people. The church in Antioch continued to grow under the direction of five leaders who were also prophets and teachers – Barnabas, Simeon, Lucius, Manaen, and Saul.

### A special commission

One day, as these teachers were fasting and worshipping, God's Holy Spirit told them to send Saul and Barnabas away to undertake missionary work. So, after fasting and praying, the Christians placed their hands on the two men to commission them, and sent them on their way.

Saul and Barnabas took John Mark (see Before panel, left) as their helper, and travelled to the port of Seleucia, about 25km (15 miles) away. They boarded a boat that was sailing to the island of Cyprus, which was where Barnabas had originally come from (see Acts 4:36).

### A magician on Cyprus

The three companions arrived at Salamis, a commercial port on the east coast of Cyprus. They went directly to the Jewish synagogue in the city, as they would do in all the other places they visited, and preached that the Jewish Messiah had come, and he was Jesus. The Messiah was now calling all people everywhere, including Gentiles, to belong to God's family,

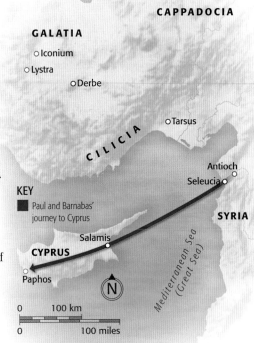

CAPPADOCIA
GALATIA
○ Iconium
○ Lystra
○ Derbe
○ Tarsus
CILICIA
Antioch
Seleucia ○
KEY
■ Paul and Barnabas' journey to Cyprus
SYRIA
Salamis ○
CYPRUS
○ Paphos
Mediterranean Sea (Great Sea)
N
0 ———— 100 km
0 ———— 100 miles

### THE FALSE MAGICIAN BLINDED

Raphael's 16th-century painting *The Blinding of Elymas* shows Saul miraculously blinding the false magician Elymas because he had tried to hinder Sergius Paulus from hearing God's message.

Paulus "wanted to hear the word of God" (13:7), but Elymas knew that the Christian message was a threat to his influence, so he opposed the missionaries' message.

However, Saul – who from this point in Acts is known by his Roman name of Paul (13:9) – spoke directly to Elymas, warning him that he was "full of all kinds of deceit and trickery" (13:10) and was not following the "right ways of the Lord" (13:10). He declared that Elymas was "an enemy of everything that is right" (13:10).

As a result, Paul said that God would temporarily hide the light of the Sun from Elymas. Immediately, the magician was unable to see, and fell about the room. When Sergius Paulus saw what had happened, he was amazed and believed the Christian message.

### FROM ANTIOCH TO CYPRUS

According to Acts 13, Paul and his companions sailed to Cypus from the port of Seleucia. They visited Jewish synagogues and ventured widely across the island before leaving for Galatia.

which knew no boundaries. Saul, Barnabas, and John Mark travelled across the island with the good news. At Paphos, the provincial capital on the southwest coast, they were summoned by Sergius Paulus, the Roman governor, or proconsul, of Cyprus (see panel, below). He listened to the three Christians and was impressed with their message. Nonetheless, a Jew named Bar-Jesus, also called Elymas, began to argue with the three missionaries. Elymas was a magician who used his skills to entertain the governor. Sergius

> " When the proconsul saw what had happened, he believed, for he was **amazed at the teaching about the Lord.**"
>
> ACTS 13:12

### PEOPLE

### SERGIUS PAULUS

References to a Roman governor (or proconsul) called Sergius Paulus have been found on several inscriptions. One was discovered near Paphos in Cyprus in 1877, and recorded that the events inscribed on the monument took place during the time of the proconsul Paulus. Within a decade, a memorial stone was found in Rome that recorded the appointment of Sergius Paulus in AD 47 as one of the officials in charge of maintaining the banks and channels of the River Tiber.

**1ST-CENTURY INSCRIPTION BEARING THE NAME SERGIUS PAULUS**

**AFTER** »

The journey to Cyprus was the beginning of a series of missionary travels for the apostle Paul.

**PAPHOS COASTLINE, CYPRUS**

### SAUL OR PAUL?

It was common for people who lived in the provinces of the Roman Empire to have **both a local name and a Roman name**. As Saul began travelling and teaching throughout the Roman world, he apparently stopped using his Jewish name "Saul", and became known simply as **Paul, the apostle**. After Paul left Cyprus, his name "Saul" is not used in Acts to describe his life as a Christian.

### ONWARD JOURNEY

Paul, Barnabas, and John Mark sailed northwest from Paphos to the **mainland of Asia Minor**. They landed at the port of Attalia, then walked about 14km (9 miles) inland to the **city of Perga**.

**BEFORE**

**Paul, Barnabas, and John Mark had arrived in Asia Minor from Cyprus.**

**MARK LEAVES**
At Perga in Pamphylia, **John Mark left the others** to return to his home in Jerusalem. Paul and Barnabas travelled on to Pisidian Antioch, but Paul felt that John Mark had deserted the mission at a crucial time (Acts 13:13; 15:38). As a result, he would later choose to take Silas, rather than John Mark, to **Derbe and Lystra 442 »**.

**SPREADING THE WORD**
On arriving in Pisidian Antioch, **Paul and Barnabas went to the synagogue** where they were encouraged to speak. Paul took the opportunity to remind the gathering of Israel's history and to tell them that Jesus was the Messiah (Acts 13:16–41).

**PERGA, TWICE VISITED BY PAUL**

# Paul and Barnabas in Galatia

*Paul and Barnabas preached the good news about Jesus in the major cities of southern Asia Minor. Wherever they went, both Jews and Gentiles responded to their message. However, some people opposed them and stirred up trouble.*

**M**EMBERS OF the Jewish synagogue in Pisidian Antioch were intrigued by the message that Paul and Barnabas had brought. They invited them to return the following Sabbath to teach them more about Jesus, the Messiah that God had promised long ago. When they returned one week later, news about them had spread so widely that almost the whole city gathered at the synagogue to hear them speak – both Jews and Gentiles. When some of the Jews saw how popular Paul and Barnabas were, they became jealous (Acts 13:45), and began to speak against Jesus, contradicting what Paul was saying. Paul turned to address them directly. He pointed out that he had begun by preaching to them, but since they were rejecting his message, he and Barnabas would now go to preach to the Gentiles. God had commanded him to bring salvation to everyone. Hearing this, the Gentiles in the crowd were overjoyed, and many of them became Christians.

**MISSION TO GALATIA**
The route followed by Paul and Barnabas from Paphos in Cyprus, into Galatia, and back to Syrian Antioch is detailed in Acts 13:13–14:28 and summarized in the map above.

*Map labels: ASIA MINOR, Pisidian Antioch, CAPPADOCIA, GALATIA, Iconium, Lystra, Derbe, Attalia, Perga, PAMPHYLIA, LYCIA, Myra, CILICIA, Tarsus, Antioch, Seleucia, SYRIA, CYPRUS, Salamis, Paphos, Mediterranean Sea (Great Sea), N, 0 100 km, 0 100 miles*

**KEY**
■ Journey of Paul and Barnabas to Galatia
■ Return journey to Antioch

### Facing opposition
The Jewish authorities were furious at the spread of the message about Jesus. They persuaded the leaders of the city to oppose the two apostles, and eventually they were expelled from the region as troublemakers. As they left, Paul and Barnabas shook the dust off their feet, just as Jesus had told his disciples to do when people rejected them (see p.343). It was a warning to the people in Pisidian Antioch not to reject the great salvation that God was now offering in Jesus.

**PISIDIAN ANTIOCH**
The ruins of Pisidian Antioch, a Roman colony in the ethnic area of Phrygia, within Galatia, can be visited today in Turkey. Pisidian Antioch was the first city to have a fully Gentile Christian community.

Paul and Barnabas travelled east to Iconium, and began speaking about Jesus there, starting as usual at the synagogue. Nearly everyone in the city had an opinion about Paul and Barnabas's message. Once again, a great number of people believed that Jesus was God's Messiah, citing the miracles that the two missionaries were performing as proof of their message. But others opposed Paul and Barnabas, and began to plot how they might get rid of them, even considering stoning them to death. Before they could do anything, however, the believers heard about the plan, and Paul and Barnabas left the city.

### Lystra and Derbe
Travelling a short distance south, Paul and Barnabas arrived in Lystra. Among the crowd who listened to their message was a

> **" Therefore, my friends, I want you to know that through Jesus the forgiveness of sins is proclaimed to you."**
>
> ACTS 13:38

## HEALING A CRIPPLE

*Paul Heals a Lame Man in Lystra* (1663), by Karel Dujardin, shows Paul reaching out to heal the cripple. The clouds behind him recall those that were said to form the gate to Olympus, home to the Greek gods, including Zeus and Hermes.

### HISTORY AND CULTURE

## THE GODS HAVE COME DOWN

Around 50 years before Paul and Barnabas visited Lystra, the Roman poet Ovid wrote his great narrative poem *Metamorphoses*. This included the legendary tale of a visit to Phrygia – which neighboured Lystra – by the Greek god Zeus and his son Hermes (also known as the Roman gods Jupiter and Mercury). An elderly peasant couple offered them hospitality, but 1,000 people had refused them, so the gods punished everyone but the old couple with a flood. Thinking that Barnabas and Paul were the two gods come again, the people of Lystra gave them an enthusiastic welcome.

**REPLICA OF A 1ST CENTURY SCULPTURE OF THE GREEK GOD, ZEUS**

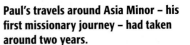

### AFTER

**Paul's travels around Asia Minor – his first missionary journey – had taken around two years.**

#### MEETING TIMOTHY

It was on this journey that Paul **met a young man called Timothy** from Lystra for the first time. He would later become one of Paul's closest companions 442–43 ❯❯.

#### RETURNING HOME

Paul and Barnabas **returned to their home** in Antioch, Syria, where they gathered people together and told them all that had happened during their journey. They said that through observing what God had done in Asia Minor, they had come to realize that God had "opened **a door of faith to the Gentiles**" (14:27).

lame man, who had never been able to walk. Paul turned to him and said, "Stand up on your feet!" (14:10). The man did so, and the surprised crowd thought that Barnabas and Paul must be the gods Zeus and Hermes, visiting the city in human form. The priest hurried from the temple of Zeus with all that he needed to make a sacrifice to the two apostles. But when Barnabas and Paul realized what was happening, they cried

out to stop the crowd, shouting: "Friends, why are you doing this? We too are only human, like you. We are bringing you good news, telling you to turn from these worthless things to the living God" (14:15). Even so, it proved hard to prevent the crowd from performing sacrifices to them.

However, some of the Jews from Pisidian Antioch and Iconium then arrived and began to stir up the crowd against the two missionaries.

Paul was stoned and dragged out of the city, where he was left for dead. The disciples gathered around him, and he recovered enough to stand up and return to the city.

The next day Paul and Barnabas left for Derbe, where many people responded to their message and became believers. Afterwards, they retraced their steps through Lystra, Iconium, and Pisidian Antioch, helping believers to appoint elders to oversee their work.

BEFORE

**The church in Antioch welcomed Barnabas and Paul back from their missionary journey.**

**REPORTING BACK**
Barnabas and Paul gathered the **Antioch church «434–35** together and told them what had happened in Cyprus and southern Asia Minor. The Antioch Christians were **overjoyed to hear of the new communities**, and especially of the many Gentiles who had put their trust in Jesus. God "had opened a door of faith to the Gentiles" (Acts 14:27).

**PETER IN ANTIOCH**
The **apostle Peter «420–21** spent some time in Antioch with the believers. He shared his meals, one of the most intimate

**ST PETER'S CHURCH, ANTIOCH, CREATED c.AD 30.**

social activities, with Gentile Christians, just as he had with **Cornelius and his family many years earlier «430–31.**
The church in Antioch made no distinction between Jewish and Gentile believers – **they were all equal in God's new family of faith.**

**"** …God made a choice among you that **the Gentiles should hear** from my lips the **message of the gospel** and believe.**"**

ACTS 15:7

# The Council of Jerusalem

*The influx of Gentile believers into the Early Church caused a stir among Jewish Christians. When a fierce dispute broke out in Antioch, the issue was taken to a council of apostles and elders in Jerusalem.*

A GROUP OF JEWISH Christians travelled from Judea to Antioch. When they arrived, they saw that the church in Antioch was made up of both Jewish and Gentile believers who worshipped together and shared meals.

### A fierce dispute
The Christians from Judea were aghast. The Judeans began to teach the believers in Antioch that if they wanted to receive the salvation that God was offering in Jesus, they first had to be circumcised and become Jews. Jesus was the Jewish Messiah,

after all. It seems that even the apostle Peter was influenced by their teaching; he stopped eating with Gentile believers, for fear of what the Judeans might say (see Galatians 2:11–13).
Paul understood the danger of what was happening, and began to dispute with the Judean Christians. He told Peter and the church in Antioch that Jesus had brought in new conditions for belonging to God's family – circumcision was no longer necessary for Gentiles, only a belief in Jesus as the Messiah (see Galatians 2:16). It was therefore

wrong to force Gentiles to convert to Judaism before including them in the Christian community. The debate was so heated that the believers decided to send

River Jordan, flowing into the Dead Sea

Walled city of Jericho, ringed with palm trees

Land of Ephraim and Benjamin

Holy city of Jerusalem, with its walls, gates, and main road visible

Land of Judah

**MADABA MAP OF BIBLE LANDS**
This east-oriented map was produced in the 6th century as a floor mosaic in the church of St. George at Madaba, Jordan. At that time, Madaba was home to Aramaic-speaking Christians, Gentiles who were direct beneficiaries of the decisions made at the Council.

a delegation to the leadership of the church in Jerusalem, to have the matter settled once and for all.

### The deliberation

In Jerusalem, Paul and Barnabas told the apostles and elders of the church about the great things that were happening among both Jews and Gentiles in Antioch, and in the new churches that had sprung up in Asia Minor as a result of their work. However, some of the Jerusalem Christians who were also Pharisees – experts in the Jewish law – stood up to make their case: "The Gentiles must be circumcised and required to keep the law of Moses" (Acts 15:5).

Opinion was divided, so the apostles and elders met together to decide what to do. The Law of Moses commanded circumcision for all of God's chosen people. Not long before, many Jews had died during the Maccabean revolt (see pp.266–67) to defend the practice.

Peter stood up. He reminded the council that Cornelius and his household had been accepted into God's family without the need for circumcision. "God, who knows the heart, showed that he accepted them by giving the Holy Spirit to them, just as he did to us" (Acts 15:8), he said, referring to Pentecost (see pp.416–17). The Jewish law was a heavy load to carry, even for Jews. The good news was that salvation had come to all simply through faith in Jesus. "We believe it is through the grace of our Lord Jesus that we are saved, just as they are" (15:11).

### A decision and a letter

After considering the Scriptures, James (see pp.440–41), the leader of the Jerusalem church, made his judgment. It was clear that God was welcoming Gentiles into his family, and it would be wrong to hinder them by forcing them to be circumcised. Instead, Gentile Christians would be told "to abstain from food polluted by idols, from sexual immorality, from the meat

**JUDAIZERS AND GENTILES**
This illustration from the *Annals of Hainaut* by Jacques de Guise (1334–99) depicts the council deliberating, with James seated in the centre. After the ruling, the council sent Judas and Silas to Antioch with a letter that outlined the decision the council had made.

of strangled animals and from blood" (Acts 15:20). With these simple guidelines in place, Jewish and Gentile Christians could eat and worship together, just as they had done before, as equal members of God's family.

> "It is my judgment… that we should **not make it difficult for the Gentiles** who are turning to God."
>
> ACTS 15:19

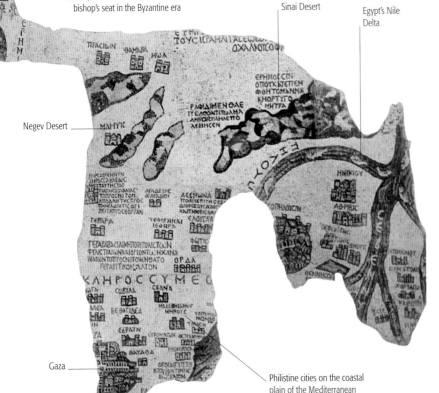

Zoar, where Lot lived, became a bishop's seat in the Byzantine era

Sinai Desert

Egypt's Nile Delta

Negev Desert

Gaza

Philistine cities on the coastal plain of the Mediterranean

**AFTER**

**Paul and Barnabas decided to visit the churches they had set up on their first missionary journey.**

**CYPRUS, SYRIA, AND CILICIA**
Barnabas wanted to take John Mark (who had returned with them from Jerusalem) on the mission but **Paul disagreed because Mark had deserted them in Pamphylia ❮❮ 436** during the previous trip. So Barnabas took Mark and sailed for Cyprus. Paul travelled northwards instead, taking as a new companion **one of the leaders from Jerusalem – Silas**. They visited Syria, then passed through the Taurus Mountains to Cilicia (see Acts 15:40,41).

**THE "CILICIAN GATES", A PASS THROUGH THE TAURUS MOUNTAINS OF MODERN-DAY TURKEY**

# James the Just

> **"James, a servant of God and of the Lord Jesus Christ,** to the twelve tribes scattered among the nations: **Greetings."**
>
> JAMES 1:1

**J** AMES THE JUST was not one of Jesus' original disciples, but became an influential leader of the Jerusalem church. He is described as "the Lord's brother" by the apostle Paul (Galatians 1:19), but his kinship to Jesus is debated by some Christians. The gospels record that Jesus had brothers and sisters: Mark 6:3 names James (or Jacob in Hebrew and Greek), Joseph, Simon, and Judas – thought to be the author of the New Testament Book of Jude – as his brothers. Some Christians hold that Mary remained a virgin after Jesus' birth; they translate "brothers" as "kinsfolk", seeing them as Jesus' cousins, or as children of Joseph from a previous marriage.

Jesus' family lived in Nazareth in Galilee, where Joseph worked as a carpenter. When Jesus left home to begin his ministry of preaching and healing in the surrounding region, James and his brothers did not believe in what he was doing. But when Jesus continued to work miracles, they began to get excited by the crowds he was drawing. They suggested he should go to Jerusalem, where he would attract much more attention (John 7:3–5). They did not understand Jesus' mission, and were not regarded as disciples during his ministry (see Matthew 12:46–50).

The name James was a common one among Jews in the 1st century AD. There were at least two other important figures by this name in the Early Church. The first, often called James the Great, or Greater, was the son of Zebedee and, along with

**JAMES THE JUST**
This Orthodox icon depicts James, leader of the Jerusalem church. He was accorded the epithet "the Just" on account of his wisdom and good deeds among the Early Church.

> **"'…You have faith; I have deeds.'** Show me your faith without deeds, **and I will show you my faith by my deeds."**
>
> JAMES 2:18

his brother John, a member of the inner group of Jesus' disciples (see pp.322–23). Herod ordered his execution around AD 44, when he was "put to death with the sword" (Acts 12:2). The second James was also one of Jesus' 12 disciples, but little is known about him, except that he was the son of Alphaeus; he is often called James the Less.

## James and the Early Church

The attitude of James changed following the crucifixion, death, and resurrection of Jesus. The risen Jesus appeared to him, an incident recorded by Paul in 1 Corinthians 15:7. In that meeting – also recounted in the Gospel of the Hebrews, a book not included in the Christian Bible but later cited by Jerome – James realized the full truth of who Jesus was: he was God's Messiah. Jesus' miracles and teaching had not been mere entertainment for the crowds, as he had once thought, but rather moments of God's salvation breaking into the world. James shared this insight with his brothers. After Jesus had ascended into heaven, James and the brothers assembled with Jesus' disciples in Jerusalem, while they waited for the gift of the Holy Spirit. On the day of Pentecost, he was filled with the Spirit. James became an active member of the growing Christian community in

Jerusalem. His relationship to Jesus already gave him a privileged position within the church, but his deep faith and wisdom meant he was soon recognized as a leader alongside the apostles. When Paul came to Jerusalem to begin his work as a missionary, James joined Peter and John in giving him approval (Galatians 2:9).

When the other apostles left Jerusalem to take the good news about Jesus to the rest of the world, James stayed behind. He became the leader of the Christians in Jerusalem and the surrounding area, later becoming the city's first bishop. At the Council of Jerusalem (see pp.438–39), James used his position of authority to support Paul's mission to the Gentiles (Acts 15). Although he himself worked primarily among Jewish Christians, he was glad that the message about Jesus was spreading effectively into the Gentile world.

### THE HOLY FAMILIES
The Master of Uttenheim's painting *The Holy Families* (c.1470) depicts – seated from left to right – Elizabeth with the infant John and James the Great; Anne, mother of Mary, with the Virgin Mary and Jesus; and Mary, wife of Cleopas with James the Just, Joseph, Simon, and Judas.

## James martyred

Remaining in Jerusalem, James both taught and encouraged the Christians. But when Porcius Festus, the Roman governor of Judea, died, enemies of James in the Sanhedrin took the opportunity to destroy him. While a replacement for Festus was being appointed, the high priest in Jerusalem – Annas the Younger, the brother-in-law of Caiaphas, who had handed Jesus to the Romans for crucifixion – seized James and put him on trial for breaking the Jewish Law by teaching that Jesus was the Messiah. Condemned by the court, James was stoned to death.

### THE LETTER OF JAMES

The New Testament letter of James, attributed to James the Just, may date from the late 40s AD. As leader of the mostly Jewish church in Jerusalem, James wrote to encourage and instruct Jewish Christians scattered across the Roman world. The letter draws upon the rich tradition of Old Testament wisdom, encouraging believers to live wise, mature, and careful lives, in the midst of a dangerous world, and to let their faith guide their actions and deeds. Whereas Paul often emphasized the roots of Christian faith, James stressed its fruits, or works.

**PARCHMENT IN GREEK FROM THE 12TH CENTURY, RECORDING THE LETTER OF JAMES**

- **Known as James,** brother of Jesus.

- **c. late-20s AD,** observes Jesus' ministry of preaching, teaching, and healing. He encourages Jesus to go to Jerusalem, for larger crowds.

- **Becomes a believer** after the risen Jesus appears to him (recorded by the apostle Paul in 1 Corinthians 15:7).

- **c.AD 30,** at Pentecost, receives the gift of the Holy Spirit in Jerusalem with other believers.

- **Recognized as** a leader of the church in Jerusalem.

- **Welcomes Paul (Saul)** to Jerusalem after he becomes a believer on the road to Damascus.

- **c. late-40s AD,** authors the biblical letter of James for Jewish Christians scattered throughout the Roman world.

- **Affirms Paul,** alongside Peter and John, in his mission to go as an apostle to the Gentiles.

- **Christians arrive** in the city of Antioch claiming to have come from James in Jerusalem (see Galatians 2:12). James becomes implicated in the controversy over circumcision that engulfs the Early Church.

- **c.AD 49–50,** described by Paul, writing in Galatians, on the way to Jerusalem for the Council as one of those in the church who are "esteemed as pillars" (Galatians 2:9) .

- **c.AD 50,** chairs the Council of Jerusalem, which resolves the Gentile controversy (circumcision not required to join the church). James decrees, "It is my judgment, therefore, that we should not make it difficult for the Gentiles who are turning to God. Instead we should write to them, telling them to abstain from food polluted by idols, from sexual immorality, from the meat of strangled animals and from blood" (Acts 15:19,20).

**A 12TH-CENTURY RELIQUARY PLAQUE DEPICTS PAUL DISCUSSING MISSION TO THE GENTILES WITH JAMES AND THE APOSTLES**

- **AD 57,** greets Paul on his last visit to Jerusalem, where Paul was arrested and sent to Rome.

- **c.AD 62,** arrested by Annas the Younger, the high priest, condemned, and stoned to death.

- **After his death,** James was regarded as a saint by the Early Church, and was known as "James the Just" or "James the Righteous" because of his exemplary lifestyle of faith, wisdom, and good works. It was said at the time that James had prayed so much that his knees were "as tough as camels' knees".

### RESTING PLACE
In 2002 this ossuary – a stone vessel for holding bones – from the 1st-century AD, found in a family burial cave in Jerusalem, became famous because it bears an Aramaic inscription "Jacob son of Joseph brother of Jesus". Many experts claim that the last three words were added later.

**BEFORE**

Together with Silas, who was one of the "leaders among the believers" (Acts 15:22), Paul revisited the churches in southern Asia Minor.

Paul arranged for Timothy, **a highly regarded believer in Lystra**, to join him and Silas on the next stage of their journey. God's Spirit was **directing the journey of the three missionaries**. When they tried to take the good news into certain places, such as Bithynia, "The Spirit of Jesus would not allow them" (Acts 16:7) and they travelled onwards instead.

**14TH-CENTURY IMAGE OF PAUL AND TIMOTHY**

# Paul in Macedonia

*The message about Jesus continued to spread into new territory. Paul and his companions crossed the Aegean Sea, bringing the good news to the mainland of Europe. Once again, they encountered a mixed response.*

P AUL, SILAS, AND Timothy had reached the western border of Asia Minor – the Aegean Sea at Troas. They were uncertain where they should travel next. One night, Paul had a vision. A man was beckoning him, and asking Paul to come to Macedonia. The missionaries knew Paul's vision was no coincidence. God's Spirit was directing them to the next place where they were to preach about Jesus.

### The work starts in Philippi
They crossed the Aegean Sea to the province of Macedonia, travelling first to Neapolis and then to the city of Philippi. This was a Roman colony, and the most important city in the district. Unusually, it had no Jewish synagogue.

Paul, Silas, and Timothy went outside the city gates and down to the river, where some women had gathered to pray. The men began to tell the women the good news about Jesus. One of the women, named Lydia, came from Thyatira, a city famous for its dye; she was a trader in expensive purple-dyed cloth. She was not Jewish, but when she heard Paul's message, she believed in Jesus the Messiah. She and her whole

household were baptized, and then – as "a believer in the Lord" (16:15) – she invited Paul and his companions to stay at her house.

### Paul and Silas arrested
In Philippi, there was a slave girl who was possessed by a spirit that enabled her to predict the future. She began to follow Paul and Silas – Timothy is not mentioned again – around day after day, shouting out, "These men are servants of the Most High God, who are telling you the way to be saved" (16:17). It was true; the missionaries were bringing a message from God. But the spirit-possessed girl was attracting the kind of attention that was not helpful to the believers.

Finally, Paul turned to the girl and commanded the spirit to come out of her. Immediately, the spirit left and the girl became quiet. The girl's owners were furious, because they had been making a considerable amount of money from her fortune-telling. They seized Paul

**A ROMAN COLONY**
The ruins of Philippi show that it was the urban centre of a Roman colony that stretched over 180,000 hectares (700 square miles). Historical records show that most of its inhabitants were Roman war veterans.

**KEY**
- Paul, Silas, and Timothy journey to Macedonia
- Paul, Silas, and Timothy in Macedonia
- Paul's journey to Athens and Corinth

*Aegean Sea*

Philippi · Amphipolis · Neapolis · Thessalonica · Berea · Apollonia · Troas · Delphi · Corinth · Athens · Sparta

N

0        100 km
0        100 miles

**PAUL'S TRAVELS**
The above map shows Paul's route through Macedonia and down the east coast of Greece as descibed in Acts 16:8–18:4.

and Silas and dragged them before the city magistrates, accusing them of causing an uproar and undermining their Roman way of life. The magistrates had Paul and Silas stripped and flogged, then thrown into prison.

### Miraculous events in prison
Around midnight, as Paul and Silas were praying and singing hymns, there was suddenly a mighty earthquake. It shook the prison so violently that all the cell doors swung open and the prisoners' chains fell loose. The jailer woke up, and seeing the doors open, he presumed the prisoners had escaped. As he drew his sword to kill himself, Paul called out, "Don't harm yourself! We are all here!" (16:28). The jailer rushed to Paul and Silas, and fell trembling before them. Then he led them from the prison and asked: "What must I do to be saved?" (16:29) They replied

**PAUL IS GIVEN DIRECTION**
Paul's vision of a man from Macedonia calling him to help forms part of a mural at St Paul's memorial – the Bema – in Veria, Greece. Veria was once known as Berea, where Paul went to preach shortly after Philippi (see After panel, right).

> " …**Paul had a vision of a man** of Macedonia standing and **begging him, 'Come over to Macedonia** and help us.'"
>
> ACTS 16:9

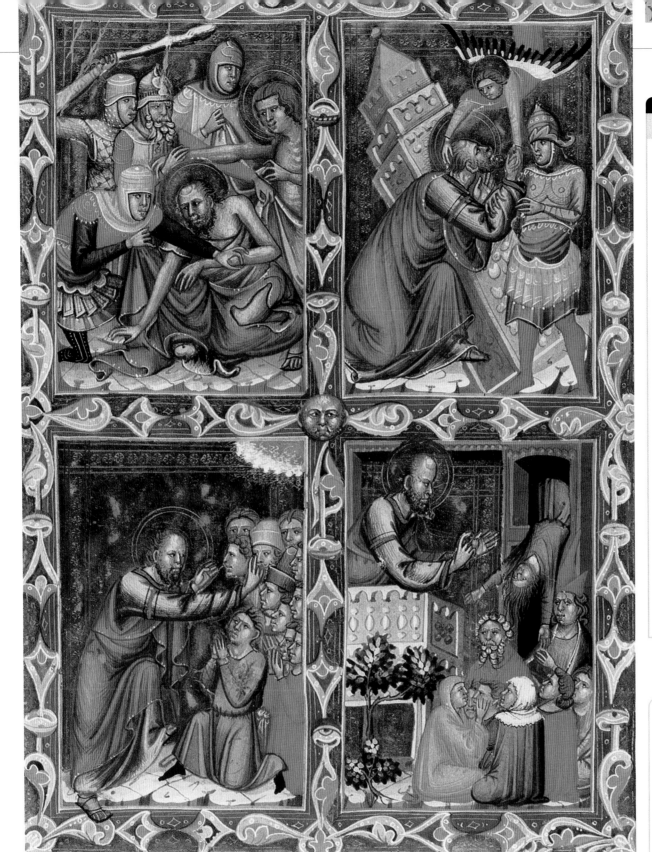

## PEOPLE

### TIMOTHY

Timothy, the son of a Greek father and Jewish mother, had been taught the Jewish Scriptures by his mother and grandmother. They all lived in Lystra, and had become Christian believers on Paul's first visit. By Paul's second visit, Timothy was a young man, highly regarded by the congregation. Paul recognized that Timothy's many gifts would be useful in his mission work, and arranged for Timothy to join him. Timothy became a valuable assistant, and later Paul appointed him to oversee the growing church in Ephesus. According to tradition, near the end of his life, Paul wrote two letters to Timothy, encouraging him in his ministry (see 1 and 2 Timothy).

**SAINT TIMOTHY**

**AFTER** »

**Paul, Silas, and Timothy continued to travel south through Macedonia.**

### THESSALONICA
In Thessalonica, some people were persuaded by the missionaries' message, but others were angry, and **started a riot.** They dragged some believers who had been helping the missionaries before the city officials, accusing them of saying "that there is another king, one called Jesus" (Acts 17:7). Hearing this, the crowd was thrown into turmoil and let the believers go.

### BEREA
Paul, Silas, and Timothy left the night that Jason was mobbed and travelled to Berea, where both **Jews and Gentiles warmly received the news about Jesus**. When troublemakers arrived from Thessalonica, the believers sent Paul away to Athens (Acts 17:10–15).

**LIFE OF ST PAUL**
Paul's days in Philippi were illustrated in *Scenes from the life of Saint Paul*, a 15th-century manuscript that shows his imprisonment, the earthquake and release from prison, conversion of the jailer, and preaching in Rome.

at once: "Believe in the Lord Jesus" (16:31). They explained the message about Jesus to the jailer and his household. The jailer took them and washed their wounds, then he and his whole household were baptized. Afterwards the new believers shared a joyful meal with Paul and Silas.

When morning came, the authorities sent word to the jailer that Paul and Silas were to be released. But Paul refused to leave until the magistrates had come in person. After all, said Paul, he and Silas were Roman citizens, which meant they should not have been beaten and imprisoned without a trial. On hearing that the two men were Romans, the magistrates were alarmed and tried to appease them; they escorted the two companions from the prison and asked them to leave the city.

After leaving the prison, Paul and Silas went to Lydia's house, where they met with the new believers and encouraged them. Later they left the city and travelled west towards the provincial capital of Macedonia, Thessalonica.

Paul left Silas and Timothy in Macedonia, and travelled south down the coast of Greece to Athens, which had many temples to different gods.

**PREACHING BEFORE THE AREOPAGUS**
The philosophers of Athens thought Paul was bringing two new gods – "Jesus" and "Resurrection". So they took Paul to the Areopagus, the city's highest council of authorities, named after an area of high ground where it met. When Paul explained his message, some said it was nonsense, but **others became believers**.

**A TAPESTRY DEPICTION, c.1557–1559, AFTER RAPHAEL, OF PAUL PREACHING IN ATHENS**

# Paul in Corinth

*Paul did not usually stay in any place for a long time but he remained in Corinth for more than a year. Here, a ruling by the governor meant that the Christian message could be proclaimed without persecution.*

**P**AUL TRAVELLED west from Athens to Corinth, the capital of the province of Achaia. When he arrived in the city, he quickly befriended a Jewish couple called Aquila and Priscilla. They too had recently arrived in Corinth, having travelled east after leaving Rome.

According to writers such as the Roman historian and biographer Suetonius, there had been "constant disturbances" among the Jewish population in Rome. It is not known why, but there may have been arguments about the message or status of Jesus. The Emperor Claudius did not want a riot within his imperial capital, so he expelled all the Jews to avoid the risk that it might happen. Aquila and Priscilla had set up a small business in Corinth, making tents and other leather goods. Paul was "a tentmaker" (Acts 18:3), so he joined them in their work, staying in their house.

### Fruitful work in Corinth
Paul began preaching the message about Jesus at the Jewish synagogue in Corinth. After a little while, Silas and Timothy arrived from Macedonia, where Paul had left them. With their help, Paul continued to explain to the Jews in Corinth that God's Messiah was Jesus. However, some rejected the message, and began to oppose Paul. He stopped preaching in the synagogue, having fulfilled his responsibility to tell the Corinthian Jews them about God's Messiah. He said to the Jews, "From now on I will go to the Gentiles" (Acts 18:6).

The small group of believers began to meet in the house of Titius Justus, who lived beside the synagogue. However, not all members of the synagogue had

## PAUL ON TRIAL

The Roman proconsul Gallio – pictured here in *The Trial of the Apostle Paul* by Nikolai K.Bodarevski (1850–1921) – refused to judge a dispute between Paul and the Jews because it was based on "words and names and your own law" (Acts 18:15).

Eventually, some of the Jews who had rejected Paul's message united and decided to try to stop the Christian movement.

### A legal triumph

A new Roman proconsul of Achaia, called Gallio, had recently arrived from Rome. The Jews took Paul to the proconsul's court. They accused Paul of teaching people to worship God in an illegal way. While the Jewish faith had authorized status within the Roman Empire, Paul's opponents hoped that the proconsul would declare Christian belief illegal, and outlaw its practice.

However, Gallio was not interested in their complaint. He did not even wait to hear Paul's defence, but simply dismissed the case. If they had been bringing a serious criminal charge against Paul, Gallio would have been obliged to investigate. However, as far as he was concerned, their dispute was about different interpretations of the Jewish faith – one that said Jesus was the Jewish Messiah, and one that said he was not. Gallio declared, "since it involves questions about … your own law – settle the matter yourselves" (18:15), making it clear he did not want to judge a religious discussion. Even when the Jewish group started to cause

a commotion in the court by beating their new synagogue leader – Sosthenes – Gallio took no notice.

This set an important precedent. At least for the next few years, Christians in Corinth, and all of Achaia, could live and worship under the same legal protection as Jews. Paul continued his work, without persecution, until it was time to return to the church in Antioch.

> " The Jews… made a **united attack on Paul**… 'This man… is persuading the people to worship God in ways **contrary to the law.**'"
>
> ACTS 18:12,13

rejected the message. Crispus, who had been the leader of the synagogue, and his entire family believed the good news and were baptized.

Paul, Silas, and Timothy began to think about where they would travel next to spread the Christian message. In other cities, some Jews had quickly risen up against them and made their work impossible. However, one night, Paul had a vision, in which Jesus told him not to be afraid to stay in Corinth, "For I am with you," said Jesus, "and no one is going to attack… you, because I have many people in this city" (18:10).

No one would harm Paul and his companions there, and the Corinthian church would grow with their good work. Encouraged by this vision, Paul stayed in the city for about 18 months.

### CORINTH, GREECE

The *bema* – a platform in the *agora*, or main square, upon which Roman officials stood when making their public appearances – is the site in Corinth where Paul stood accused before Gallio in AD 51–52.

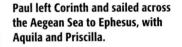

### AFTER

Paul left Corinth and sailed across the Aegean Sea to Ephesus, with Aquila and Priscilla.

#### PAUL'S REPORT

Although the **Jews in Ephesus 447 》** asked Paul to stay to teach them more about Jesus, he had to return to Syria. He **left Aquila and Priscilla in Ephesus**, and travelled back across the Mediterranean, staying in Jerusalem before **returning to Antioch**.

#### APOLLOS

A Jewish believer called Apollos arrived in Ephesus. He was an **excellent teacher, and began to share what he already knew about "the way of the Lord"** (Acts 18:25) at the synagogue. Christian teaching was often called "the way" because it was not purely theoretical, but a practical way of living. **Aquila and Priscilla invited Apollos to their home 446 》** to give him a fuller account of "the way of God" (Acts 18:26).

**‹‹ BEFORE**

There were already a few believers in Ephesus, including Paul's friends Aquila and Priscilla.

**AQUILA, PRISCILLA, AND APOLLOS**
Paul had gone to Antioch, leaving **Aquila and his wife Priscilla ‹‹ 444–45**, whom he had befriended in Corinth, in Ephesus. There the couple met a new arrival from Alexandria, a Jew named Apollos. "**He was a learned man, with a thorough knowledge of the Scriptures**" (Acts 18:24). They explained to him the way of God "more adequately" (18:26), then Apollos went to the province of Achaia, where he was an effective teacher. Paul returned from Antioch to Ephesus, travelling overland through Asia Minor, just **as he had promised** when he passed through on his way from Macedonia (Acts 18:19–21).

**SAINT PAUL AT EPHESUS**
In *St. Paul at Ephesus* by Maarten de Vos (1568), the moment is depicted when, after word had spread widely that "the name of the Lord Jesus" (Acts 19:17) was powerful, those who "practised sorcery" (19:19) burned their scrolls.

# Paul in Ephesus

*Ephesus was one of the great cities of the ancient world, and would become one of the centres for the early Christian movement. Before that, Paul had to deal with difficult disciples, powerful spiritual forces, and a violent riot.*

**T**HERE WAS ALREADY a small group of disciples in Ephesus who had heard the teaching of John the Baptist about the imminent arrival of the Kingdom of God, and had responded by being baptized.

When Paul arrived in the city, he went to speak with the group. He asked them, "Did you receive the Holy Spirit when you believed?" They replied, "No, we have not even heard that there is a Holy Spirit" (Acts 19:2).

It soon became clear that their baptism had been a baptism of repentance and that they did not know that Jesus had fulfilled the prophecies of John the Baptist. The disciples in Ephesus had not heard about the day of Pentecost (see pp.416–17), when God had filled Jesus' disciples with the promised Holy Spirit.

Paul explained to the group that John had "told the people to believe in the one coming after him, that is, in Jesus" (19:4), who was God's Messiah. On hearing this, the disciples believed in Jesus and were baptized in his name. "When Paul placed his hands on

**SCENE OF THE RIOT**
The angry crowd dragged Paul's travelling companions Gaius and Aristarchus to the amphitheatre at Ephesus, in complaint at the damage that Paul's teaching was doing to the trade associated with the goddess Artemis and also with her temple.

**GODDESS ARTEMIS**
A marble statue of Artemis of Ephesus, dating from the 2nd century AD. Distinct from the Greek Artemis, her symbols of fertility testify to her origins as a Near Eastern mother goddess.

> " ...they were furious and began shouting: 'Great is Artemis of the Ephesians!' Soon the whole city was in an uproar. "
>
> ACTS 19:28,29

## HISTORY AND CULTURE
### TEMPLE OF ARTEMIS

Ephesus, a harbour city on the western edge of Asia Minor, was one of the leading cities of the Graeco–Roman world. The populous city was dominated by the chief temple of the goddess Artemis (known as Diana by the Romans), which dated from the 6th century BC. Reputed to have been the first Greek temple built of marble, this enormous building was one of the seven wonders of the ancient world.

Ephesian religion was a distinctive form of the worship of Artemis, which included mystery, magic, and astrology. A local industry depended on the temple, creating images of the goddess and shrines for worshippers and tourists.

Ephesus later became an important centre for Christianity (one of the key churches of Asia), and Christian tradition suggests that Jesus' mother Mary settled near Ephesus, along with the apostle John.

them" (19:6), they were filled with the Holy Spirit, and began to speak in other languages, as had happened to the disciples at Pentecost.

## Paul's ministry

For the next three months, Paul spoke regularly at the synagogue, telling the Jews about Jesus. Some believed, but others were obstinate and began to oppose him, publicly slandering his message. Paul left the synagogue and started to teach in a lecture hall owned by a Gentile called Tyrannus.

For the next two years, Paul taught and debated every day in Tyrannus's venue. Jews and Gentiles came from all over Ephesus and the surrounding area to hear him, and many of them became believers.

It was not only Paul's words that were powerful – God enabled him to perform many "extraordinary miracles" (19:11). Even pieces of clothing or handkerchiefs that had been touched by Paul brought a cure to people who were ill and freedom to those who had been possessed by demons.

## A cautionary tale

These miraculous healings happened because of the power of the name of Jesus. Other itinerant healers soon wanted to use this power themselves. On one occasion, seven brothers, the sons of Sceva, a Jewish chief priest,

tried to exorcize an evil spirit by calling upon "the name of the Jesus, whom Paul preaches" (Acts 19:13). Instead of leaving the man, the evil spirit spoke back to them, "Jesus I know, and Paul I know about, but who are you?" (19:15). The possessed man suddenly jumped on the seven brothers, and gave them such a beating that they ran away.

News of this soon spread throughout Ephesus. Many people began to believe in Jesus as God's Messiah. Some, who used to practise magic, decided to burn publicly all their magic scrolls and written charms, as a sign of their new way of life. The value of what they burned was 50,000 days' wages.

## A riot in Ephesus

So many people were now beginning to follow Jesus that local craftsmen and traders, whose

livelihoods depended upon people worshipping at the temples in Ephesus, began to worry. Paul's message was a threat to business.

One craftsman named Demetrius, who made silver idols of the main Ephesian goddess, Artemis, called a meeting to complain about Paul. Soon, he had stirred up a crowd, which began to declare allegiance to Artemis, whose temple dominated the city.

The furious throng marched to the public theatre, which could hold 25,000 people, shouting aloud the name of the goddess Artemis again and again, for two hours. Paul wanted to speak to the crowd, but he was persuaded by the disciples and provincial officials that it was too dangerous.

Finally, "the city clerk quietened the crowd" (19:35). He rebuked them for their behaviour – if they had evidence that Paul had broken the law, then they should make a formal complaint to the courts and press charges. Their rowdiness would not accomplish anything. In fact, they were in danger of being prosecuted themselves for disturbing the peace. The crowd finally dispersed, and Paul decided it was time to leave Ephesus.

## AFTER »

**Paul left Ephesus to revisit the Christian congregations in Macedonia and Greece, collecting money for the poor Christians in Jerusalem.**

### MACEDONIA AND CORINTH
Paul **encouraged the churches in Philippi, Thessalonica, and Berea**. In Macedonia he wrote a letter (2 Corinthians) to the church in Corinth, where there had been some objections to his leadership. When Paul finally **returned to Corinth**, he stayed for three months, dealing personally with the church's difficulties. During his time in Corinth, **he wrote a letter (Romans) to Christians in Rome 454–55 »**.

### RETRACING HIS STEPS TO PHILIPPI
Paul intended to sail from Corinth to Syria, taking the money to Jerusalem. However, to thwart **a plot against him by some Jews** (Acts 20:3), he travelled overland to Philippi.

### ANALYSIS
## PAUL'S LETTER TO THE EPHESIANS

While he was imprisoned in Rome, Paul wrote a letter to be circulated around the congregations that he had established in the area surrounding Ephesus.

Paul knew that the local culture was powerfully influenced by magic and mystery. Paul reminded the Christians that the power God had displayed in Jesus Christ was far stronger than

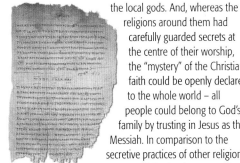

**A 3RD-CENTURY MANUSCRIPT OF PAUL'S LETTERS TO THE EPHESIANS**

the local gods. And, whereas the religions around them had carefully guarded secrets at the centre of their worship, the "mystery" of the Christian faith could be openly declared to the whole world – all people could belong to God's family by trusting in Jesus as the Messiah. In comparison to the secretive practices of other religions, following Jesus was like living in the light.

**THE MAIN ROAD THROUGH ANCIENT CORINTH**

**THE GREAT EVANGELIST** Born C.AD 5–10 Died C.AD 64–65

# Paul

> ## "I want to know Christ – yes, to know the **power of his resurrection** and participation in **his sufferings…**"
>
> PHILIPPIANS 3:10

**P**AUL, ALSO KNOWN by his Jewish name Saul, was born into a family of devout Jews who had settled in Tarsus, a coastal town in the region of Cilicia in southern Asia Minor. His ancestry could be traced right back to the tribe of Benjamin (Philippians 3:5), and the young Saul was named after the most famous member of that tribe, the first king of Israel (see pp.146–47). Saul's parents were Roman citizens, so Saul was thus both a Jew and a Roman citizen by birth. As a Jew, Saul was taught to speak

**SAINT PAUL**
A sculpture of St. Paul by René Michel Slodtz (1705–64), adorning the porch of Saint-Sulpice church in Paris. The bearded Paul is holding a book – "the epistles" – and a cruciform sword, used as his symbol from the 10th century onwards.

Hebrew and Aramaic, and to observe the laws and customs of Judaism. However, he also learned Greek, and was familiar with the Roman way of life.

## Saul the Pharisee

Saul was trained in the trade of tent-making. However, as a teenager, Saul was sent to Jerusalem to be educated "under Gamaliel" (Acts 22:3). The rabbi Gamaliel was the grandson of the renowned rabbi Hillel, who had pioneered a new way of interpreting the Jewish Scriptures in order to apply them to the life of contemporary Jews. Saul would have learned these techniques, and it soon became clear that he was an outstanding pupil.

Nevertheless, Saul did not share all the same views as his rabbi. Gamaliel had a generally liberal attitude to the application of the Jewish law. In contrast, Saul was more radical, and willing to

**TARSUS**
Paul's birthplace, the city of Tarsus, in modern-day Turkey, was the capital of the Roman province of Cilicia and one of the ancient world's great centres of learning. Pictured is the 1st-century AD Roman stone road to the north, thought to be the one-time route to Cappadocia.

approve violence to maintain the distinctiveness and purity of Judaism at all costs. Saul's zeal and immense intellectual capabilities soon identified his potential as a leader among the Pharisees.

## Saul is transformed

When the Christian movement began to grow in Jerusalem and beyond, Saul the Pharisee saw it as a serious threat. With the blessing of the Jewish authorities in Jerusalem, he began to persecute Jewish Christians (Acts 8:1; 9:1,2), threatening them with death if they did not give up their belief that Jesus was God's Messiah. But in a dramatic encounter with the risen Christ on the road to Damascus (see pp.428–29), Saul's life was turned upside down – he too now believed. Jesus gave the once-strict Pharisee a special commission to take the message beyond the Jews to the Gentile world.

## Paul, apostle to the Gentiles

Saul threw himself into the Christian mission as zealously as he had tried to crush it. The Jews of Damascus were at first baffled and then furious that, far from arresting disciples, he was now "proving that Jesus is the Messiah" (Acts 9:22). There "was a conspiracy among the Jews to kill him" (9:23), so for his own safety Saul returned to Tarsus, where he stayed for about six years. During this time, Saul worked through his understanding of the Jewish Scriptures, coming to the conclusion that they pointed towards Jesus as God's Messiah.

It was now time to take this message to the Gentile world. Saul began to be known by his Roman name Paul. He moved to the church in Antioch in Syria, which became the base from where he was sent out on his three major missionary journeys. Wherever he went, Paul spread the message about Jesus the Messiah to Jews

Paul's stature in the early Christian movement is reflected by the use of 13 of his letters among the 21 in the New Testament. Many of these were produced with his missionary partners, Silas or Timothy, and written by a scribe (see Romans 16:22). In his letter to the Galatians (c.AD 49–50), Paul writes: "See what large letters I use as I write to you with my own hand!" (Galatians 6:11). Some letters, such as 1 and 2 Corinthians, give important guidance for the church's life; others, such as Romans and

**LETTER TO THE COLOSSIANS IN A 15TH-CENTURY BIBLE**

Colossians, contain wonderful explorations of the significance of Jesus as God's Messiah. In Galatians, Paul strongly affirms that Christ came as God's promised Messiah to deliver all people, without requiring Gentiles to submit to practices required by the Old Testament that marked people out as Jews. What counted most was being part of God's "new creation" (Galatians 6:15) and "faith expressing itself through love" (Galatians 5:6). In his day, championing the inclusion of Gentiles on the basis of faith alone was seen as radical.

> " I, Paul, **write this greeting in my own hand**, which is the distinguishing mark in all my letters. **This is how I write.** "
> **2 THESSALONIANS** 3:17

and Gentiles, establishing small communities of Christian believers, sometimes provoking commotions and riots. Paul writes of the difficulties and dangers he faced as he went about the work of Jesus' commission: floggings, stonings, shipwrecks, starvation, and overwhelming tiredness (see 2 Corinthians 11:23–28). Whenever

possible, Paul revisited or wrote to the churches he had established, encouraging them in their faith.

## Paul the martyr

After being arrested in Jerusalem, Paul was imprisoned in Caesarea for two years before being transferred to Rome for trial. He was probably released, and may even have taken the gospel to Spain, which had long been his intention. However, within two years, he was back in prison in Rome, facing execution by beheading. Paul had enthusiastically committed himself to the task Jesus had given him: to take the good news to the Gentiles. As a result of Paul's ministry, God's family expanded dramatically.

### DEATH OF PAUL
Tradition says that Paul's execution – pictured here by Sienese artist Ventura Salimbeni (1568–1613) – took place near Rome at a place called Aquae Salviae on the same day as that of Peter.

- **c.AD 5–10,** Saul (Paul) is born in Tarsus in Asia Minor.
- **c.AD 27–33,** in Jerusalem, training as a rabbi under Gamaliel, before joining the Pharisees.
- **c.AD 32–33,** observes the stoning of the martyr Stephen, and begins to persecute the Christian movement.
- **c.AD 33–34,** encounters the risen Jesus on the road to Damascus. He is commissioned to go to the Gentiles with the good news.
- **c.AD 34–41,** returns to Tarsus, having escaped the authorities in Damascus and Jerusalem.
- **AD 41,** brought to Antioch by Barnabas, where he teaches the growing church.
- **AD 42,** travels with Barnabas to Jerusalem with a gift of money for the poor Christians.
- **c.AD 44–47,** undertakes first missionary journey to Cyprus and Asia Minor, with Barnabas and John Mark.
- **c.AD 49–50,** writes Galatians letter, or epistle, on the way to Jerusalem for the Council.
- **Speaks to the Council** of Jerusalem.
- **c.AD 50–52,** undertakes second missionary journey to Macedonia and Greece, with his missionary partners Silas and Timothy, with whom he writes some of the letters included in the New Testament.
- **Writes the letters** 1 and 2 Thessalonians to believers in Thessalonica, while in the city of Corinth.
- **c.AD 53–56,** undertakes third missionary journey to Ephesus, Macedonia, and Greece.
- **c.AD 54,** writes 1 Corinthians letter from Ephesus.
- **c.AD 56,** writes 2 Corinthians letter on the way through Macedonia to Corinth. Writes Romans letter from Corinth.
- **AD 57,** arrested in Jerusalem, having brought a collection of money for the church.
- **AD 57–59,** imprisoned in Caesarea, awaiting trial.
- **AD 59–60,** transferred to Rome.
- **AD 60–62,** under house arrest in Rome.
- **AD 60–61,** writes letters Ephesians, Colossians, and Philemon from prison in Rome.
- **c.AD 62,** writes 1 Timothy and Philippians letters after his first hearing in Rome.
- **c.AD 62–63,** possible further journeys, including to Spain and Crete.
- **c.AD 64,** writes Titus and 2 Timothy letters from prison in Rome.
- **c.AD 64–65,** martyred near Rome.

**PENS FROM ANCIENT ROME**

HISTORY AND CULTURE

# Persecution and Martyrdom

"He sent still another, and that one **they killed**. He **sent many others**; some of them they beat, others they killed." MARK 12:5

**ICHTHYS, CHRISTIAN SYMBOL**
The fish was a symbol of early Christians. The five letters of the ancient Greek word for fish spell out the acronym Jesus Christ, Son of God, the Saviour.

From the beginning of the Church there were occasional localized outbreaks of persecution against Christians. Stephen was stoned to death by a mob c.AD 34–35 (see pp.424–25) and James, son of Zebedee, was executed by Herod Agrippa in AD 34 (see pp.440–41). Some Christians were beaten or imprisoned. In the early days of Christianity the threat of persecution came mainly from Jews who often regarded Christians as blasphemers against Jewish Law. Christians were later banned from synagogues, where they had previously preached, and took to meeting in their own homes, often in secret. Having previously been largely tolerated, Christians began to suffer at the hands of the Roman Empire from the mid-1st century AD.

**DEATH IN THE ARENA**
Romans enjoyed the spectacle of criminals being executed by being torn apart by wild animals, such as leopards. Many Christian martyrs suffered this grisly fate.

## EMPEROR NERO

On 19 July AD 64 a fire broke out in Rome. Spreading quickly through the dense, crowded streets, it burned for five-and-a-half days, resulting in massive destruction. People blamed the unpopular Emperor Nero – it was rumoured that he started the fire in order to clear the way for a new palace to be built. Nero sought to deflect

**BRUTAL LEADER**
Prone to acts of extreme cruelty, the Roman emperor Nero is infamous for having Christians thrown to wild animals, crucified, or even set alight to serve as torches.

this blame, and he found the perfect target: Christians, who, being a religious minority, were vulnerable. They were arrested, rounded up, tortured, and killed.

The following report comes from the Roman historian, Tacitus:

"Mockery of every sort was added to their deaths. Covered with the skins of beasts, they were torn by dogs and perished, or were nailed to crosses, or were doomed to the flames and burned, to serve as a nightly illumination, when daylight had expired… Hence, even for criminals who deserved extreme and exemplary punishment, there arose a feeling of compassion; for it was not, as it seemed, for the public good, but to glut one man's cruelty that they were being destroyed."
(*Annals* 15–44, c.AD 116)

Among the many victims were Peter, who was martyred by crucifixion in Rome c.AD 65–67, and Paul, who was martyred near the city c.AD 64–65.

## IMPERIAL WRATH

The Roman persecution begun under Nero was more brutal than any that had occurred before. Nero's actions set the tone for much of the next few centuries. While actual persecution was sporadic and rare, the possibility of it remained a threat, right up until the early years of the 4th century AD.

The Christians' refusal to participate in pagan ceremonies or worship the Roman emperor, and the widespread suspicion that they were cannibals who ate the body and drank the blood of Christ, meant that they were marginalized and viewed with hostility. Letters were written to encourage the persecuted, such as the anonymous letter to the Hebrews.

The persecution of Christians that continued under Emperor Domitian forms the background to the book of Revelation: the souls of those "who had been slain because of the word of God and the testimony they had maintained" cry out for justice (6:9–10). John's vision depicts Rome as a beast, with blasphemy dripping from its mouth, making war against the saints (Revelation 13).

The persecution ended in AD 313 when Emperor Constantine made Christianity a legal religion of the Roman Empire (see p. 455).

**AMPHITHEATRE OF THE THREE GAULS**
In AD 171 there was an outbreak of persecution against Christians in Lyons in Gaul (France). The remains of the Roman amphitheatre contain a memorial to those Christians who lost their lives.

## FAITH UNDER PERSECUTION

The threat of persecution meant that the Church had to be much more careful about how it spread its message. It could no longer stand in the marketplace and proclaim "the good news". Instead, Christians had to be quiet and discreet when preaching the gospel. As one contemporary writer, Marcus Minucius Felix (c.AD 250), succinctly put it: "We do not talk about great things; we live them" (*Octavius* 38:5). He was a Christian Apologist – that is, he wrote in defence of Christianity – and was one of the first to write in Latin; the *Octavius* was aimed at educated non-Christians.

By contrast, when Christians were publicly executed, they had a platform from which to express the faith that was otherwise denied them. The Christian author Tertullian, who lived in the latter half of the 2nd century, wrote that onlookers were struck by the manner in which the Christians died: "See, they say, how they love one another… how they are ready even to die for one another." He went on to describe how the public death of Christians served only to spread the Church: "We multiply whenever we are mown down by you; the blood of Christians is seed" (*Apologeticus* 39, 50).

### WORSHIP IN THE EARLY CHURCH

Christianity was carried on behind closed doors. Christians met in homes; there were no church buildings as such until the late 3rd century. Their numbers were small but everyone was involved in worship. As Paul wrote to the Church at Colossae: "When you come together, each of you has a hymn, or a lesson, a revelation, a tongue, or an interpretation" (1 Corinthians 14:26). Christians collected money for the poor, and, most of all, they shared meals together. Sharing bread during the Eucharist was central to the rite. It was a symbol of peace and unity within the Church, and signified the presence of the risen Jesus with his followers.

**EUCHARIST**

## EXECUTIONS AND MARTYRS

Persecutions continued at a sporadic pace. In AD 170 in Lugdunum (now Lyon, France), Christians were banned from public areas such as the baths and marketplaces. They also became the victims of mob violence and robbery. Eventually all the Christians in the city were rounded up, interrogated by the governor, and executed in the amphitheatre (left). Such localized executions culminated in the great persecutions under the emperors Diocletian and Galerius at the end of the 3rd and beginning of the 4th centuries. During this period, all Christians in the Roman Empire were commanded to sacrifice to the gods of Rome or face immediate execution. More than 20,000 Christians are thought to have died during Diocletian's reign alone.

**SAINT DOROTHEA**
Dorothea, the virgin martyr and patron saint of gardeners, was reputedly executed at Caesarea in Cappadocia on 6 February AD 311, during the reign of Galerius.

# Paul Arrested in Jerusalem

*Paul's ministry among the Gentiles turned the Jews in Jerusalem against him. Formerly their champion against the Christians, he was now their enemy, and an angry mob gathered against him.*

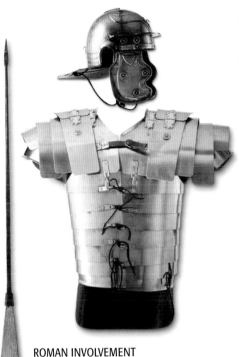

**ROMAN INVOLVEMENT**
The Roman soldiers based in Jerusalem probably wore segmented body armour, known as *lorica segmentata* and a helmet, and would have routinely carried a steel-shafted *pilum*, a kind of javelin.

## BEFORE

**Paul and some of the believers began to make their way from Philippi to Jerusalem for the feast of Pentecost.**

### DROPPING OFF
Leaving Phillippi by ship, Paul and his companions arrived at Troas on the coast of modern Turkey, where they stayed for seven days. One night in Troas, while Paul was speaking, a man called Eutychus fell asleep and tumbled out of a third storey window. **His fall killed him,** but Paul brought him back to life – and then **continued teaching until daylight** (Acts 20:7–12).

### MEETING AT MILETUS
Paul and his companions than set sail again down the Aegean coast. In his hurry to reach Jerusalem, Paul opted to by-pass **Ephesus ‹‹ 446–47**. However, **he did make landfall at Miletus, south of Ephesus and summoned the elders of the church at Ephesus to meet him there**. In an emotional speech he told them he would never see them again and that they must remain faithful and guard "the flock" (Acts 20:29).

### ON TO JUDEA
Paul put to sea again, travelling via Kos, Rhodes, and Cyprus before reaching Tyre and then Caesarea.

**P**AUL RETURNED to Judea, resting at the house of Philip in Caesarea. Here, a prophet called Agabus foretold that Paul would be imprisoned if he went on to Jerusalem. Nevertheless, Paul and his companions departed, and met James and the other elders in Jerusalem. Paul told them how he had spread the good news about Jesus among the Gentiles, and the elders were overjoyed. However, they could see trouble ahead. A rumour had reached Jerusalem, claiming that Paul was telling Jews in Gentile countries to give up their Jewish practices, including circumcision. Many Christians in Jerusalem still followed Jewish customs, and were angry that Paul seemed to be dismissing Judaism.

The Jerusalem elders had a plan. There was a Jewish custom in which a person could take a Nazirite vow (see p.135) to become especially holy for a specific period of time. The elders suggested that Paul should do this. This would prove that he was "living in obedience to the law" (Acts 21:24). Paul agreed, and he along with another four men had his head shaved, as a sign of the vow.

### A riot in the Temple
A few days later, when Paul was in the Temple, he was recognized by some Jews from Asia who were in Jerusalem for Pentecost. They seized him, shouting to the other worshippers, "This is the man who teaches everyone everywhere against our people and our law and this place" (21:28). Then they mistakenly charged him with bringing uncircumcised Greeks into

the Temple (because they assumed he had brought in Trophimus, an Ephesian Gentile, whom they had seen him with earlier).

The crowd erupted in fury; a mob grabbed Paul, surged out of the Temple, and beat him to the ground. He would have been killed were it not for the arrival of a squad of Roman soldiers, who restored order. Their commander arrested Paul and put him in chains. Then he turned to the crowd to try to find out what had caused the commotion, but could not hear what was said, because of the uproar. He told his soldiers to take Paul to the barracks, as the mob shouted, "Get rid of him!" (21:36).

### Paul speaks to the people
On the steps up to the barracks, Paul turned to the commander and asked to speak to the crowd. The

**PAUL AND THE GENTILES**
*The Prophet Agabus Predicting St. Paul's Suffering in Jerusalem* (1687) by Louis Chéron shows Agabus warning Paul that he will be bound and imprisoned.

commander was surprised, but agreed. Paul began to address the crowd in Aramaic, their own language. He told them how he had once persecuted Christians, but then had met the risen Jesus on the road to Damascus (see pp.428–29), which had transformed his life. The crowd listened quietly until Paul told them of the commission God had given him: "Go; I will send you far away to the Gentiles" (22:21). At this, the crowd began clamouring for Paul to be put to death.

### Under Roman control
The soldiers hurried Paul into the barracks to have him flogged and questioned. But as they stretched him out to flog him, Paul asked if it was legal for them to flog a Roman citizen. Disturbed by the fact Paul was a Roman, the commander took him to the Sanhedrin, the Jewish council, to find out why the Jews were accusing him. But as Paul made his case, the Sanhedrin divided in uproar, with some vociferously defending Paul and others calling out against him. The Roman commander feared for Paul's life and ordered that he be taken back to the barracks.

### PAUL UNDER ARREST
This detail from the 4th-century "Sarcophagus of Travellers", from the crypt of St Victor Basilica, Marseilles, France, shows Paul being arrested. The crypt is said to contain the remains of several saints.

## HISTORY AND CULTURE

### TENSION IN JERUSALEM

Paul's arrest in Jerusalem took place around AD 57, when tensions between Jewish inhabitants and the Roman government were running high. The Jewish religion had protected status under Roman rule, but the governors of Judea were not always sympathetic to Jewish concerns. A powerful nationalist movement wanted to defend the integrity of Judaism against Roman laws, customs, and taxes. Christianity was seen as a threat, because it included Gentiles as well as Jews. Jewish nationalists eventually rose up against Roman rule in the Great Revolt of AD 66–73 (see pp.466–67).

**DETAIL ON THE 1ST-CENTURY ARCH OF TITUS, ROME, SHOWING ROMANS LOOTING THE TEMPLE DURING THE GREAT REVOLT**

### AFTER

**Paul remained in prison in Caesarea for two years, during which he was called upon to speak to the authorities a number of times.**

After hearing from the Sanhedrin's high priest and from Paul himself, the **Roman governor Felix adjourned the trial** until more witnesses were brought. During this time, he and his wife often invited Paul to speak with them about the Christian faith.

After two years, **Porcius Festus replaced Felix** as governor, and the Jewish authorities in Jerusalem asked him to send Paul to Jerusalem, as they secretly planned to assassinate him on the way. Festus consulted with the Jewish King Agrippa, who said that although Paul was innocent, he had asked to stand trial before **Caesar rather than the Sanhedrin 458–59 »**.

That night, some Jews hatched a plot to kill Paul the following day, as he was taken back to the Sanhedrin. However, Paul's nephew heard of the plot, and told the Roman commander, who arranged for Paul to be taken that night to the Roman governor Felix in Caesarea Maritima, accompanied by an armed guard of 470 men.

> " I admit that **I worship the God of our ancestors as a follower of the Way**, which they call a sect. "
>
> ACTS 24:14

**IMPERIAL CAPITAL** Founded *c.*753 BC Sacked AD 410

# Rome

> "To all in Rome… **Grace and peace** to you from **God our Father** and from the **Lord Jesus Christ.**"
>
> ROMANS 1:7

**R**OME WAS one of the most magnificent cities of the ancient world. It was the centre of the Roman Republic and Empire (see pp.268–69), which reached its peak between 250 BC and AD 250, and stretched from northwestern Europe to the Near East, including the entire Mediterranean region. Rome's appearance in the Bible is limited to Paul's house arrest in the city before his trial (see pp.458–59). But as the centre of administration, culture, and religion, the city exercised a powerful influence on its provinces – including Judea and other Bible lands.

### Early history
According to legend, Rome was founded in 753 BC by Romulus and Remus, the twin sons of a human mother and the god Mars. After the twins had established the city on the banks of the River Tiber, they quarrelled over who should rule as king. Romulus killed Remus, and named the city Rome.
Over the next 250 years, Rome grew into a powerful city-state. In 509 BC the city became a Republic, ruled by annually elected officials. Rome fought to dominate the Italian peninsula, and engaged in wars with Greek states and Carthage, resulting in the gradual annexation of territory. By the 1st century BC Rome was the foremost power in the ancient world, with territories stretching north to Gaul (France), east to Greece and Asia Minor

**JEWISH CATACOMBS**
Dating from the 2nd century AD, the Jewish catacombs in Rome – such as the Villa of Torlonia (pictured) – predate their early Christian counterparts, but share some of the same iconography.

(Turkey), south to the African coast, and west to Hispania (Spain). But the Republic had grown so rapidly that its administration became difficult – order began to give way to chaos. Julius Caesar instituted a military dictatorship in 46 BC, and when he was assassinated two years later, the Republic came to an end. After a brief time of turmoil, his nephew Octavian restored order. It was during this period that Herod the Great was installed as king of Judea. In 27 BC Octavian declared himself Emperor, re-establishing political and social stability. Rome entered two hundred years of peace, known as *Pax Romana*.

### Rome's diverse ethnicity
As first the Republic and then the Empire expanded, people from across the known world settled in the great capital. Local inhabitants lived alongside provincial migrants, in a total population of around one million. Different cultures were allowed to retain their customs and identities – Rome embraced Greek philosophy and Persian art, Babylonian astronomy, and ultimately, the religions of Judaism and Christianity.

### Religion in Rome
After Augustus died in AD 14, he was proclaimed to be a god. Before long, his successors were also being worshipped as sons of gods. A new system of temples and priests and sacrifices was set up, alongside the more traditional gods of Rome. Willingness to participate in this new religion was seen as a sign of allegiance to the Empire. At this time, there were around 40,000 Jews in Rome; some had initially arrived as slaves from the Judean

(see pp.268–69)

---

**HISTORY AND CULTURE**

## THE CHURCH IN ROME

Christian faith was first brought to Rome by Jews who had heard the message about Jesus while attending the feast of Pentecost in Jerusalem (Acts 2:10). Both Peter and Paul spent time among the small network of house churches in Rome before their martyrdom. The church in Rome soon became an influential centre for the early Christian mission, not least because of its location in the well-connected imperial capital. After Christian worship was legalized in the 4th century AD, the church in Rome was given a special place in the Christian community.

**SAN CLEMENTE BASILICA, ROME, WAS BUILT ON THE RUINS OF AN ANCIENT HOUSE CHURCH**

### CHRONOLOGY IN BRIEF

**c.753 BC,** Rome founded, according to legend.

**c.509 BC,** creation of the Roman Republic, governed by senators and elected consuls.

**c.264–146 BC,** the Punic Wars give Rome control over Sicily, and parts of Spain, North Africa, and Greece.

**c.139 BC,** Jews who are not Italian citizens are expelled from Rome.

**c.135–50 BC,** Roman rule extends to Asia Minor, Crete, Cyprus, and Syria.

**46 BC,** Julius Caesar emerges as victor after Roman military generals fight with one another for supreme control of the Republic.

**44 BC,** the assassination of Julius Caesar.

**c.27 BC,** Octavian is made the first Emperor, and takes the name Augustus.

**8 BC,** Augustus orders a census of the Roman Empire. This is possibly the census in which Mary and Joseph go to Bethlehem, where Jesus is born.

**AD 6,** Rome annexes Judea as a Roman province.

**AD 14,** Augustus dies and is proclaimed a god.

**AD 19,** Emperor Tiberius orders the expulsions from Rome and the whole of Italy of all Jews who refuse to abandon their religion.

**AD 49,** Jews are expelled briefly from Rome by Emperor Claudius because they are creating disturbances in synagogues.

**c.AD 56,** Paul writes to the Roman Christians.

**c.AD 60,** the apostle Peter arrives in Rome, from where he is thought to have written the books of 1 and 2 Peter.

**AD 64–68,** Emperor Nero instigates persecution of Christians, after a great fire in the city. Apostles Peter and Paul are martyred.

**AD 70,** the Romans destroy Jerusalem, during the Great Revolt by Jews.

**AD 126,** Emperor Hadrian rebuilds Pantheon, a temple to all Roman gods. Later, in the 7th century, it was converted into a Christian church.

**AD 312,** Emperor Constantine embraces Christianity, and makes it a legal religion of the Empire with the Edict of Milan in AD 313.

**AD 380,** Rome adopts Christianity as its state religion under the Edict of Thessalonica.

**AD 410,** Rome is sacked by the Goths.

**AD 476,** Roman Empire ends when Rumulus Augustus abdicates to the Germanic warlord Odoacer.

**Eastern Roman Empire,** also called the Byzantine Empire, is spared the decline of the lands ruled from Rome, continuing until defeat to the Ottomans in 1453.

**EMPEROR CONSTANTINE**

military campaign of Pompey in 62 BC, while others had migrated to the growing metropolis. They were given special permission to meet in their own synagogues, and did not need to participate in the imperial religion. Although the Jewish community was well-established in Rome, it sometimes experienced racial discrimination and hatred.

### Christianity in Rome

In AD 49, some Jews were briefly expelled from Rome (Acts 18:1,2) and the Roman historian Suetonius offers evidence that the expulsion was due to unrest in synagogues, caused by Jewish Christians preaching that Jesus was the Messiah. Some Jews saw this as a threat to their Jewish identity. The Christian community would then have been fairly small – perhaps a few thousand believers at most. The church in Rome received a letter from the apostle Paul around AD 56, expressing his desire to visit the city (Romans 15:20) to encourage them in their faith, and to use it as a base for his missionary activity further west. He did not arrive until AD 60, and then he was under arrest.

In AD 64 there was a huge fire in Rome that destroyed around 70 per cent of the city. Looking for a scapegoat, Emperor Nero decided to blame the Christian community. From then on, Rome became a

**IMPERIAL ROME**
This scale model shows the area of Rome around the Colosseum during the reign of Emperor Constantine (AD 306–337). The Colosseum was the largest amphitheatre ever built in the Roman Empire.

**KEY**

| | |
|---|---|
| **1** Colosseum | **5** Circus Maximus |
| **2** Trajan Baths | **6** Roman Senate |
| **3** Roman Forum | **7** Capitoline Hill |
| **4** Palatine Hill, site of Imperial palaces | **8** River Tiber |

dangerous place for Christians (see pp.450–51). They met in hidden, secret places, such as catacombs (see top left). Numbers continued to grow, but they were unable to worship openly until Emperor Constantine, a Christian convert, made worship legal in AD 313. Church building soon took off in Rome and across its territories, often on the sites of earlier house churches. For the remaining years of the Roman Empire, the city of Rome was closely associated with the Church.

> " **Take courage!** As you have testified about me in Jerusalem, **so you must also testify in Rome.** "
>
> ACTS 23:11

# Paul at Sea

*A centurion named Julius escorted Paul to Rome, where he was to put his case before the emperor. Travelling with other prisoners, the gruelling journey across the Mediterranean Sea nearly ended in disaster.*

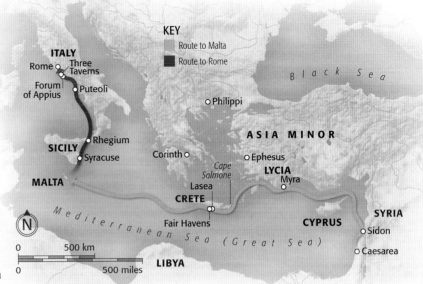

**KEY**
- Route to Malta
- Route to Rome

**ITALY** · Rome · Three Taverns · Forum of Appius · Puteoli · Rhegium · **SICILY** · Syracuse · **MALTA** · *Black Sea* · Philippi · **ASIA MINOR** · Corinth · Ephesus · **LYCIA** · Myra · Cape Salmone · Lasea · **CRETE** · Fair Havens · **CYPRUS** · **SYRIA** · Sidon · Caesarea · *Mediterranean Sea (Great Sea)* · **LIBYA**

«

## BEFORE

**Paul was being taken to the city of Rome. As a Roman citizen, he could ask for Caesar to adjudicate if he was charged with a serious crime.**

### A MESSAGE FROM JESUS
**After Paul's arrest in Jerusalem** « 452–53, Jesus appeared to him in a vision, telling him that he would not be killed in Jerusalem, but would eventually make it to Rome: "Take courage! As you have testified about me in Jerusalem, so you must also testify in Rome" (Acts 23:11).

**T**WO OF PAUL'S companions travelled with the small group of prisoners on the ship that had been secured by Julius, who served with the Imperial Regiment. These companions were Luke, who would later write down his account of the journey in the book of Acts, and another believer called Aristarchus. The ship sailed along the coast of Asia Minor to Myra in Lycia, a journey that took about two weeks.

At Myra, Julius found an Alexandrian ship, carrying grain from Egypt to Rome, and he transferred the prisoners on board for the voyage to Italy. After days of struggling along the coast to Cnidus, the ship was blown off course towards the island of Crete.

**PAUL'S JOURNEY**
The route of Paul's voyage is detailed in Acts 27, 28. He sailed via Myra because prevailing winds would have made a direct northwest crossing of the Mediterranean impossible.

With some difficulty, they stopped at the harbour called Fair Havens (or Kaloi Limenes) on the southern coast of the island, near the town of Lasea.

### A disastrous decision
It was now the beginning of October ("after the Day of Atonement", Acts 27:9), which was considered a dangerous time

**SHIPWRECKED AT MALTA**
*St. Paul arriving at Malta*, by Pieter Mulier the Younger (1637–1701), shows Paul's ship stuck on a sandbank. His arrival in Malta began a Christian influence there that has continued down through the centuries.

> "But now I urge you to **keep up your courage**, because not one of you will be lost; **only the ship will be destroyed.**"

ACTS 27:22

## SEA VOYAGES

A 2ND-CENTURY FRESCO DEPICTS A ROMAN MERCHANT SHIP BEING LOADED WITH GRAIN

Paul was shipwrecked at least four times during his many journeys, and Acts 27 is one of the most detailed accounts of an ancient sea voyage. Travelling by sea was notoriously dangerous.

From late September onwards, the weather in the eastern Mediterranean was considered too unpredictable for safe passage, so ships usually wintered in harbours. Even during the months of the year when the weather could normally be relied upon to be fair, ships tended to stay close to the coastline, sheltering from the worst of the winds, and hopping from port to port. Although small by modern standards, Alexandrian grain ships – such as the one Paul travelled in – were the largest commercial vessels of the day, crossing the Mediterranean with grain from Egypt for Rome.

of year to set out on sea voyages, because stormy weather was more likely to cause difficulties. Paul warned his fellow travellers that the ship should stay in Fair Havens over the winter months. If they set sail, he said, they would lose both the ship and its cargo, and put their own lives in danger too.

However, Julius did not listen to Paul, but preferred to take the advice of the ship's crew and owner. Because the harbour was not suitable for winter mooring, they decided to sail further west to the safer harbour at Phoenix (believed to be modern-day Loutro), and spend the winter there. With a gentle south wind blowing, the ship raised anchor and set off along the coast of Crete.

### A violent storm
Shortly after their departure from Fair Havens, the gentle southerly breeze turned into a violent hurricane-force wind, whipping down from the hills of Crete. It pushed the small ship out into the open sea, towards the reef of deadly sandbanks at Syrtis, off the

northern coast of Libya. Everyone on board knew they were all in terrible danger. The crew tried to bring the ship under control, and tied it with ropes to hold it together. They dropped the sea anchor to slow the ship and threw some of the cargo overboard. On the third day, in desperation, they tossed out the ropes and pulleys, hoping to lighten the ship and lessen the chances of it running aground. Luke records the travellers' despair, "When neither sun nor stars appeared for many days... we finally gave up all hope of being saved" (27:20).

### The ship runs aground
One night, an angel appeared to Paul, reassuring him that although the ship would run aground, he and the rest of the passengers and crew would not drown. He would eventually get to Rome and stand trial before Caesar. After the angel left, Paul encouraged the others on the ship to keep up their courage and have faith that they would survive. The storm raged for 14 days, until one night, the sailors

checked the depth of the sea and realized they were nearing land. Afraid of being dashed onto rocks, they dropped anchors, and some of them tried to lower the lifeboat. Paul told the soldiers that the ship would need its crew in the coming hours. By now, Paul's calmness had won him the respect of all on board, and the lifeboat was cut adrift. Paul then urged everyone to have a hearty meal, to give them strength for what lay ahead.

As the day dawned, they saw a sandy beach not far away and headed towards it, intending to run aground. But the ship's bow stuck fast in a sandbank short of their target and pounding waves began to tear the ship apart. Sailors, soldiers, passengers, and prisoners – 276 in all – threw themselves into the water. Some swam, while others clung to pieces of the ship's wreckage, but everyone made it safely to the shore – just as the angel had said.

### ST PAUL'S BAY
An aerial view of St Paul's Bay, Malta, where Paul and his fellow shipmates are said to have landed after their vessel had hit a sandbank. The Roman soldiers had planned to kill the prisoners to stop them from escaping, but Julius prevented this.

**The storm had blown them to Malta where they stayed for three months.**

#### MIRACLES ON MALTA
Paul cured many Maltese who were ill, including the father of the local governor, Publius. Paul himself was **bitten by a poisonous snake but did not die**, and the islanders thought that he must be a god. Jesus had told his disciples that he would give them "authority to trample on snakes and scorpions and to overcome all the power of the enemy; nothing will harm you" (Luke 10:19).

#### ON TO ROME
When Paul and the others **boarded another ship heading towards Rome 458–59** », the grateful islanders gave them all the supplies they needed for the journey.

12TH-CENTURY MURAL OF ST PAUL AND VIPER, CANTERBURY CATHEDRAL, UK

**PAUL BEFORE THE EMPEROR**
The Roman Emperor Nero sentenced Paul to death by beheading, according to the historian Eusebius. The Italian artist Luca di Tomme (1330–c.1389) depicted Nero ordering Paul's death in *St Paul Led to Martyrdom*.

**‹‹ BEFORE**

**The Roman governor Festus put Paul on a ship to Italy.**

**SAILING TO ITALY**
Paul and some other prisoners were put on a ship to Myra in Asia Minor, where they transferred to an Alexandrian grain ship sailing to Italy. They were **shipwrecked in Malta ‹‹ 456–57**, but after three months they again set sail for Italy, arriving at Puteoli (now Pozzuoli) near Naples.

**RUINS OF THE MARKET PLACE AT PUTEOLI**

# Paul Under Arrest in Rome

*Paul finally entered Rome, the city he had long wanted to visit, after a difficult journey. Although he arrived as a Roman prisoner, not a free man, he still used every opportunity to speak about Jesus, God's Messiah.*

**P**AUL AND the other prisoners were under the command of a centurion named Julius and, after their arrival in Italy, he took them north along the Appian Way. About 69km (43 miles) from Rome they came to a market town called the Forum of Appius. A group of Christian believers from Rome had gathered there to greet Paul on his way to the city, and Paul felt encouraged by the sight of them. Further on, another group of Christians met Paul at a stopping place known as the Three Taverns. All of these believers travelled alongside the armed guards, escorting Paul into the city of Rome where Julius handed over his prisoners to local guards. As a Roman citizen, who had not yet been convicted of wrongdoing, Paul was allowed to live under house arrest, with one soldier to guard him.

### Preaching under guard
Paul wanted to speak first to the elders and members of the Jewish community. Three days after his

**ROMAN LICTORS**
Roman governors and magistrates employed lictors to enforce their decisions and sentences. When Paul and Silas were arrested in Philippi, the lictors had ordered that they be beaten with rods (Acts 16:22).

arrival, he called for their leaders to come to his house, since he was unable to visit them.

Paul explained to them why he was in Rome as a prisoner. The Jews in Jerusalem had accused him of corrupting the Jewish way of life. But Paul was innocent of this charge – he simply believed that the promises about God's Messiah had been fulfilled in Jesus. Because the Jerusalem authorities would not drop their charges against Paul, he had appealed to Caesar, and was now in Rome for a hearing. He assured the Jewish elders that he did not intend to bring any charge against the Jews: "It is because of the hope of Israel that I am bound with this chain" (Acts 28:20).

### Paul defends his teaching
The Jews in Rome were surprised by Paul's account of his recent troubles because none of the malicious rumours about him had reached Rome. So they agreed to gather the Jewish community and return, so that Paul could tell them his views, "for we know that people everywhere are talking against this sect" (Acts 28:22).

Paul willingly spent a whole day teaching them about Jesus and the kingdom of God. He told them how Jesus fulfilled all the promises of the Jewish Scriptures, referring to the Law of Moses and the words of the prophets.

### Roman converts
In his final statement, Paul quoted the Holy Spirit's words to Isaiah, telling him to go to a people who heard but never understood, because their hearts had become hardened. Paul found himself in the same position – he was to help people "understand with their hearts" (Acts 28:27), turn to God, and be healed. God's message had been sent to everyone, Paul said, and through him, it was to be sent to the Gentiles – "and they will listen!" (Acts 28:28).

Some of those who heard this were convinced by Paul's words and began to believe – they would go on to join the small group of Christian disciples in Rome. However, others rejected Paul's message, and left his house.

### Paul's letters
Paul spent the next two years living under house arrest in Rome waiting for his case to be heard by the Emperor, but imprisonment did not hinder his mission. He was visited by

"**And so we came to Rome.** The brothers and sisters there had heard that we were coming."

ACTS 28:14-15

both Jews and Gentiles, and he welcomed them all and told them about Jesus and the kingdom of God. Paul also wrote letters of encouragement to the churches he had established in his previous missionary activity; these were written c.AD 60–61 and recorded in the books of Colossians, Philemon, Ephesians, and Philippians.

### Trial in Rome
Eventually, Paul's case was heard in Rome. At first, Paul felt that he had been deserted by his fellow believers, because no one came to the initial hearing to speak in his defence (2 Timothy 4:16). But support for Paul soon arrived. His friend Timothy came to Rome to be with him, and in his letter to the Philippians (2:25), Paul gave thanks for the supplies that were sent to him by the church in Philippi via a believer called Epaphroditus.

There is no further mention of Paul in the Bible, though scholars believe that Paul survived one trial, only to face another (see panel, below).

**HISTORY AND CULTURE**
## IMPRISONMENT IN ROME

**CHURCH ON THE SITE OF MAMERTINE PRISON, ROME, WHERE PAUL WAS IMPRISONED**

In the Roman world, a person charged with wrongdoing could be detained for months or years before being tried. There were several types of prisons: dedicated buildings (as in Philippi); secure rooms within a military barracks (as in Jerusalem) or official residence (as in Caesarea); or a private house under guard. Under house arrest in Rome, Paul would have had to pay for his accommodation and food. The Christian community provided for this.

**AFTER** ⟫

Later events in Paul's life are recorded in historical documents.

**CONTINUED MINISTRY**
Based on historical writings, such as those by Eusebius of Caesarea, some scholars believe that **Paul was freed by Emperor Nero** after his trial and continued to preach in Rome or in countries to the west. He was later **rearrested by Nero in Rome** and then imprisoned in the Mamertine prison, before **being beheaded**. Several sites claim to be his resting place.

**SAN PAOLO FUORI LE MURA, ROME, BUILT OVER ONE OF THE POSSIBLE SITES OF PAUL'S BURIAL**

**BEFORE**

As Christianity grew, Jewish Christians found that they were increasingly excluded from the synagogues.

## CHRISTIANS AND SYNAGOGUES

The early Christians who believed in Jesus as God's Messiah were often ostracized by their friends and family. For some, this was a significant setback, which shook their faith. **In his gospel, John recounts how Jesus foretold these difficulties**. The Jewish authorities had rejected Jesus, so it was no surprise that they were rejecting Jesus' followers too: "...anyone who acknowledged that Jesus was the Messiah would be put out of the synagogue" (John 9:22).

### HISTORY AND CULTURE
## CHALLENGE OF GNOSTICISM

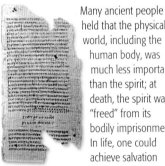

Many ancient people held that the physical world, including the human body, was much less important than the spirit; at death, the spirit was "freed" from its bodily imprisonment. In life, one could achieve salvation by learning great spiritual secrets.

**A FRAGMENT OF THE GOSPEL OF THOMAS**

These ideas developed into Gnosticism, from the Greek *gnosis,* or "knowledge". Many Gnostic writings were revealed for the first time in the 1940s when a cache of texts was unearthed at Nag Hammadi, Egypt, which included the Gospel of Thomas, containing many sayings of Jesus.

# John Fights False Teachers

*By the late 1st century* AD, *the churches in some areas of the ancient world were already well established. However, it was not long before the original message of the apostles was being challenged.*

THE CHRISTIAN congregations in Asia Minor associated with the apostle John were being threatened by confusion and division. Some teachers had arrived, claiming to bring a better version of the Christian message than that taught by John and the other early missionaries, but it distorted both the identity of Jesus and the implications of belief in him.

### Danger within
Recognized today by the term Gnosticism (see panel, left), this new message existed in a confusing variety of forms, and presented early Christianity with its greatest challenge from around AD 150 to 300. Gnosticism reinterpreted Christian faith as a set of spiritual principles that had little

> " ...do not **imitate** what is evil but what is good. Anyone who does what **is good is from God.**"
>
> **3 JOHN** 1:11

to do with Jesus' bodily life. The Gnostics rejected the significance of Jesus' death and resurrection because they had to do with his physical body, which they thought was unimportant. John made it clear that true Christian faith recognized divine life in Jesus' human body: "The life appeared; we have seen it and testify to it, and we proclaim to you the eternal life, which was with the Father and has appeared to us" (1 John 1:2).

However, some of the believers in John's community were persuaded by Gnostic arguments and tried to win over the others.

### Warning letters
John wrote his first two letters to warn the churches about the danger of accepting the new ideas, saying "I write this to you so that you will not sin" (1 John 2:1). Despite John's warnings, some followers persisted in their distorted beliefs, and eventually left the community. He encouraged those who stayed, and told them that they should live out their faith in Jesus by obeying God (1 John 5:1–3).

"I ask that we love one another. And this is love: that we walk in obedience to his commands" (2 John 5,6). In his third letter, John wrote to an elder named Gaius, warning him about a church member named Diotrephes, who was opposing the message of the apostle and leading others astray.

Other letters in the New Testament warned Christian communities about the perils they faced. A short one from Jude, brother of James the Just (see pp.440–41), asks believers to remain faithful to the genuine message about Jesus, despite the presence of "ungodly people" (Jude 4).

**AFTER**

Distorted teaching continued to be a problem for the growing church.

#### CONFUSING WRITINGS
Just like the genuine apostles, the false teachers instructed their followers through letters and **writings, such as the Gospel of Thomas ‹‹ 22–23**, many of which were circulated around the ancient world.

#### NEW TESTAMENT
In order to avoid confusion, **Christians began to identify gospels and letters** that taught the genuine message about Jesus. Over time, this became the New Testament.

**THE 4TH-CENTURY CODEX SINAITICUS IS THE EARLIEST WHOLE COPY OF THE NEW TESTAMENT**

**EPHESUS COLONNADE**
Ephesus, in modern-day Turkey, was one of the great spiritual centres of the ancient world. In Revelation, Ephesus is cited as one of the seven churches of Asia, and it may have been where the gospel of John was written. These are the remnants of the colonnade, which leads downhill to the Library of Celsus.

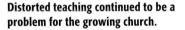

**BEFORE** «

The Roman Emperor Domitian persecuted members of the Christian church throughout the last decade of the 1st century AD.

**ISLAND EXILE**
The apostle John, who had been living in Ephesus, was **arrested and exiled to Patmos** (Revelation 1:9), a small island off the west coast of Asia Minor that the Romans used as a place of imprisonment.

**THE ISLAND OF PATMOS, GREECE**

# Sunday Morning on Patmos

*The Book of Revelation is one of the strangest books of the Bible, featuring weird creatures and violent events. Importantly, it reassured persecuted Christians that Jesus is Lord over all and will bring God's Kingdom to Earth.*

**D**URING HIS internment on Patmos, the apostle John continued to pray and worship God. Sunday was a significant day, because it was the day of the week on which Jesus had risen from the dead. One Sunday, when John was praying and praising God, he heard a loud trumpet-like voice behind him, summoning him to take note of all that was about to happen. "Write on a scroll what you see", it said, "and send it to the seven churches: to Ephesus, Smyrna, Pergamum, Thyatira, Sardis, Philadelphia and Laodicea" (Revelation 1:11), the seven important cities in Asia Minor.

John turned to find out who had spoken with such authority, and found himself facing an awesome figure, standing among seven golden lampstands. The figure looked like a human, but his hair was brilliant white, his eyes gleamed like a blazing fire, and his face shone like the midday sun.

**ST JOHN ON PATMOS**
The painting *St John on Patmos* by Spanish artist Juan Mates (1370–1431) shows John receiving the revelations in forced exile. He was sent to the Greek island of Patmos for refusing to stop preaching the gospel.

**ANALYSIS**

## THE SEVEN LETTERS

Jesus instructed John to write letters to seven churches: Ephesus, Smyrna, Pergamum, Thyatira, Sardis, Philadelphia, and Laodicea. He often used a notable aspect of the local area to illustrate his point. For instance, Laodicea was situated near hot springs, and water travelled to the city via a long aqueduct.

When it arrived, the water was lukewarm and sometimes made people ill. In the letter to Laodicea, Jesus said the church's lukewarm faith had the same effect on him (Revelation 3:16). The city was also famous for eye ointment; Jesus said the church needed to use his ointment to heal their spiritual blindness.

His long, flowing robe was tied with a golden sash, and his feet looked like bronze glowing in a fiery furnace. In his right hand he held seven stars. His voice was like the sound of rushing waters, and a double-edged sword came out of his mouth.

### Jesus speaks

John fell down in worship before the figure. A reassuring hand was placed on him and a voice said, "Do not be afraid… I am the First and the Last. I am the Living One; I was dead, and now look, I am alive for ever" (1:17–18). The figure said that he held "the keys of death and Hades" (1:18) – the place of the dead in Greek mythology. These descriptions pointed to the true identity of the figure: it was God's Messiah, Jesus, who had defeated death by his resurrection (see pp.404–05).

### Messages for the churches

Jesus told John that the seven lampstands were symbols of the seven churches, and the seven stars in his hand were the angels of those churches. Jesus instructed John to write down the individual messages that he wanted to give to each of the seven churches.

Each message began with a description of one aspect of John's

> ## "'I am the Alpha and the Omega', says the Lord God, 'who is, and who was, and who is to come…'"
> REVELATION 1:8

mystical vision of Jesus, such as this, to the church in Ephesus: "These are the words of him who holds the seven stars in his right hand" (2:1). Each description was followed by Jesus' commentary on the state of that particular church, both praising and encouraging the healthy aspects of its life, such as enduring hardships, and warning it where it had gone astray, such as by losing its first love.

### A throne and a lamb

Suddenly, John's vision changed. The dazzling image of Jesus was gone, and in its place, John found himself in a throne room, where 24 crowned elders sat on thrones. All were turned to the middle of the room, where there was a central throne, surrounded by four amazing creatures, each with six wings. They were declaring in worship: "Holy, holy, holy is the Lord God Almighty" (4:8). John understood at once – this was the throne room of God.

### The lamb of God

A radiant figure sat upon the central throne, and in his right hand there was a scroll. This contained all of God's plans for the world, but it was sealed tightly shut. A great cry went around heaven, "Who is worthy to break the seals and open the scroll?" (5:2). John began to weep, because it seemed there was no one capable of opening the scroll and accomplishing God's plans.

However, one of the elders told him not to weep because "the Lion of the tribe of Judah, the Root of David, has triumphed" (5:5). John looked up and saw not a lion, but a lamb, looking "as if it had been slain" (5:6), standing at the centre of the room. The lamb took the scroll from the figure on the central throne, and all the living beings fell down before it. The lamb was Jesus.

All those around the throne burst into song, "You are worthy to take the scroll and to open its seals, because you were slain, and with your blood you purchased for God persons from every tribe and language" (5:9).

**THE ANGEL OF REVELATION**
John describes a mighty angel who plants his right foot on the sea and his left foot on the land, then raises his hand to the heavens (10:1–3). William Blake depicted this in *Angel of Revelation*, c.1805.

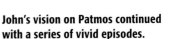

**AFTER**

**John's vision on Patmos continued with a series of vivid episodes.**

**OPENING THE SCROLL**
The scroll containing God's purposes had seven wax seals holding it tightly shut. In John's vision, Jesus – as the sacrificed lamb – broke the seals open one by one (Revelation 6–8:1). As each seal was broken, **a different calamity fell upon the Earth**: war, murder, famine, plague, and earthquakes. These were warnings that the wickedness and unbelief of the world would ultimately lead to its destruction. God's people, however, would be kept safe.

**HERALDING DISASTER**
When the seventh seal was opened, **seven angels brought seven trumpets** into John's vision (8:2). The trumpets heralded more disasters, such as a third of the Earth burning up, a third of the sea turning into blood, and a third of the sun turning dark. When the seventh trumpet sounded, the 24 elders fell from their thrones to worship God, and John saw into the centre of God's temple in heaven.

**MONASTERY OF ST JOHN, PATMOS**
On Patmos, John is said to have lived in a cave situated below the hilltop temple of the Roman goddess Diana. The Monastery of St John was built around and above his grotto in 1088.

**BEFORE**

John's strange vision continued with some terrifying episodes.

### THE WOMAN AND THE DRAGON

A woman clothed with the sun was pregnant with **a child that a seven-headed dragon wished to devour** (Revelation 12:1–4). As the child was born, he was snatched up to God, and war broke out in heaven. The dragon and his angels were flung to Earth, where they pursued the woman, who had been given eagle wings. She escaped with the help of the Earth.

**THE GREAT PROSTITUTE, 14TH CENTURY**

### BABYLON FALLS

As John's vision reached its climax, he saw God's judgment on evil being poured from seven bowls on to the Earth. The city of Babylon – described as "the great prostitute" (17:1) – tried to fight back against God, but was reduced to a smouldering ruin. Satan, God's enemy, was imprisoned and God's people had **1,000 years of peace.**

### NEW JERUSALEM

The huge expanse of the golden city is revealed to John in this wood engraving (after the drawing by Gustave Dore, 1832–83) titled *The Angel Shows John the City of Jerusalem.*

**ANALYSIS**

**CREATION**

The theme of creation runs throughout the Bible. God's creative power brought the heavens and the Earth into existence in the first place (Genesis 1:1–2), and the people of Israel praised God for being the wise creator of the whole universe (Psalm 24:1–2). However, the Bible also recognizes that God's creation has been distorted by humans, who think that their way of giving order to life is better than God's way (see pp.36–38, Genesis 3). The whole story of the Bible, from Genesis to Revelation, recounts how God has been at work to deliver his whole creation from its bondage to death, and undo the effects of human sin. The central episode is the death and resurrection of Jesus. The resurrection of his body foretells God's plan for creation: he will bring about a new creation that is recognizably the same, yet transformed.

# New Heaven, New Earth

*The Bible began in Genesis with the creation of the heavens and the Earth. It ends, in the book of Revelation, with a vision of God's coming new creation: a new heaven and Earth in which all God's people will live in peace and joy.*

**A**S HIS VISION was reaching its conclusion, John saw a final attempt by Satan to defeat God's people. But God triumphed over his enemy, banishing him to a fiery lake of burning sulphur. Then John saw all the people who had ever lived on Earth being brought before God's throne. Books were opened, and the dead were judged according to what they had done, as recorded in the books. Another book, called the Book of Life, was also opened. Those whose names were not in this book were sent to the lake of fire. God was ridding the world of the enemies who had opposed him and his people. With their defeat, the whole of creation underwent a glorious transformation.

### New worlds

John watched as heaven and Earth completely disappeared: "the first heaven and the first Earth had passed away, and there was no

# " Then I **saw a new heaven and a new Earth**, for the first heaven and the first Earth had passed away... "

REVELATION 21:1–2

longer any sea" (Revelation 21:1). For Jews, the sea was a place of chaos and danger (see pp.348–49); but God's new world was to contain only peace and order.

As John watched, a city appeared in the new heaven, where God was enthroned. It was Jerusalem – but not the old city that John had known in Judea; this was a transformed Jerusalem, coming down from heaven to Earth. John saw that it was radiant and pure, "prepared as a bride beautifully dressed for her husband" (21:2).

Then John heard a loud voice, coming from God's throne, saying, "Look! God's dwelling-place is now among the people" (21:3). The new Jerusalem had not just been sent from God – God himself was coming with it, to live in the centre of his new world. Then God spoke to John, telling him that his faithful people would live with him in this new world, and God would make sure that death, pain, disorder, and sin would never disrupt their life together. "There will be no more death or mourning or crying or pain, for the old order

of things has passed away" (21:4). God instructed John to write down his words because they were true. He is "the Alpha and the Omega, the Beginning and the End" (21:6).

### A city of gold

As the vision continued, an angel carried John up to a mountain overlooking the new city of Jerusalem. Every detail of the city that John could see "shone with the glory of God" (21:11). The angel gave John a golden measuring rod so that he could measure the size of the new Jerusalem. It was 12,000 stadia (around 2,000km or 1,400 miles) in length, width, and height; there was plenty of room within it for all of God's people. The city was constructed

from pure gold, and decorated with all kinds of precious stones. The gates were inscribed with the names of the 12 tribes of Israel, and the walls with the names of the 12 apostles.

Unlike the old city of Jerusalem, the new city was not dominated by a temple. There was no need for it; the Temple had been the meeting point between God, who lived in heaven, and his people, who lived on Earth. But in the New Jerusalem God would live among his people. Heaven had come down to Earth.

### The river of life

Through the middle of the city, John saw a river, flowing out from God's throne. As the life-giving water flowed through the city, it watered the Tree of Life. This tree was constantly bearing fruit, all through the year, bringing healing to the nations of the world. God's presence in the city was a source of light, so there was no longer such a thing as "night" and there was no need for "the light of a lamp or the light of the sun" (22:5). Nothing impure would ever enter the city, and only those whose names were written "in the Lamb's book of life" (21:27) would live there.

The angel turned to John and told him to remember all he had seen. It would not be long before it all happened: God's new heaven and Earth were coming soon.

ALPHA AND OMEGA
This painting on wood dates from 1419 and derives from Tuscany, Italy, depicting Christ holding the book of life. The Greek characters Alpha and Omega are written on the book.

**SYMBOLS**

## APOCALYPTIC LANGUAGE

Some key phrases from Revelation have entered our everyday language, but their original meaning was often specific and symbolic.

**ABYSS:** A place of darkness and separation from God, where God's enemies are destroyed.

**ALPHA AND OMEGA:** One of the many titles given to Jesus. Alpha and Omega are the first and last letters of the Greek alphabet, just as God is the "Beginning and the End" (22:13). Jesus has authority over everything, from beginning to end.

**ARMAGEDDON:** The place in John's vision where the decisive battle between God and his enemies was fought.

**FOUR HORSEMEN OF THE APOCALYPSE:** Riders on white, red, black, and pale horses, who take war, murder, famine, and death throughout the world.

**LAMB'S BOOK OF LIFE:** In John's vision, this book contains the names of all those who believe in Jesus (the "Lamb" in 5:6) as God's Messiah.

**AFTER** »

The end of John's vision brings the whole Bible to a close.

### THE WEDDING FEAST
The arrival of God's new creation was to be like a great wedding: **the marriage of heaven with Earth**, and of Christ with his people, the Church. There would be a sumptuous wedding feast. All those who had believed in Jesus as God's Messiah would be part of this joyful celebration. In John's vision, everyone was invited.

### JESUS IS COMING
The last sentences of the Bible look forward to the return of Jesus. The first Christians believed that **Jesus would return very soon**, bringing the wonderful new creation envisioned by John in Revelation. The expectation that Jesus might return at any moment to complete the transformation of the world into God's Kingdom has been central to Christian faith through the ages.

HISTORY AND CULTURE

# The Jewish Revolt

> "Truly I tell you, **not one stone** here will be left on another; every one will be **thrown down**." MATTHEW 24:2

**EMPEROR VESPASIAN**
Vespasian ruled as emperor for ten years, until his death in June AD 79. He was the first Roman emperor to be directly succeeded by his son.

When Paul was arrested in Jerusalem in AD 58, the Romans assumed he was a revolutionary: "Aren't you the Egyptian who started a revolt and led 4,000 terrorists out into the wilderness some time ago?" the tribune asked him (Acts 21:38). This may have been a case of mistaken identity, but it reflects the anxieties and tensions of the time. The growing corruption of the Roman procurators, combined with nationalistic fervour and expectations of an imminent Messiah, meant that tensions were high in Judea. In addition, the success of the Maccabean Revolt of the previous century (see pp. 266–67) and the ensuing period of Jewish independence were almost within living memory. The stage was set for a Jewish clash with Rome.

**AERIAL VIEW OF MASADA**
At the beginning of the revolt, rebels took the palace-fortress of Masada, atop a steep-sided mesa 240m (800ft) above the Judean Desert floor. It was to be the last point of resistance.

## UPRISING

The breaking point occurred in the late spring of AD 66, when the corrupt Roman governor, Gessius Florus, helped himself to money from the Temple treasury. The Jews were outraged, and a riot broke out in Jerusalem. Tensions escalated rapidly: the Temple's daily sacrifice for the emperor ceased and the Roman garrison in Jerusalem was slaughtered. The uprising then began to spread, with sporadic fighting between Jews and Gentiles breaking out in cities in Judea and Syria.

**JEWISH SILVER COIN**
During the revolt, the Jews minted their own coins, bearing Hebrew symbols and inscriptions.

## ROMAN RETALIATION

In October/November AD 66, the Romans responded by sending an army from Antioch, led by the governor, Cestius Gallus. Gallus initially laid siege to Jerusalem, but withdrew his forces as winter began to set in. The retreating Roman forces were massacred in an ambush near Beth-Horon, and the Roman standard was captured. Encouraged by this success, revolution swept through the region.

The euphoria, however, was short-lived.

The Romans waited until spring AD 67, when Emperor Nero dispatched a huge army of 60,000 men commanded by his general, Vespasian. They retook Galilee and Samaria with ease, and then Vespasian set about "pacifying" the outlying territories as far south as the Dead Sea. It may have been during this time that the community at Qumran (see pp.23 and 270–71) was destroyed.

Protective cheek flap

**ROMAN HELMET**
Archaeologists have found bronze helmets in Israel, worn by soldiers in the Roman army.

### JOSEPHUS

Much of the information about Judea at this time comes from the work of Flavius Josephus, a 1st-century Jewish politician, soldier, and historian. He was born in AD 37 and was given the Hebrew name Joseph ben Mattityahu. He came from an aristocratic family, and at the age of 27 led a delegation to the court of the Roman emperor Nero. Two years later, however, he was fighting against the empire as general of the Jewish rebel forces in Galilee. Despite being captured, Josephus gained the support of Vespasian after predicting that the Roman general would become emperor. He is is best known for his histories: the *Bellum Judaicum* (or The Jewish War), which was published *c.* AD 75–80, and the massive *Antiquitates Judaicae* (Jewish Antiquities), published *c.* AD 90. Josephus died *c.* AD 100.

## TITUS VICTORIOUS

Vespasian's victory was followed by yet another – and major – delay. At the end of AD 68, news reached Vespasian at the port city of Caesarea that the emperor Nero had been assassinated. Rome fell into turmoil and the Senate recalled Vespasian to keep the peace. He returned to Rome, and was proclaimed emperor in July AD 69. Vespasian never returned to Judea; instead, he left his son, Titus, to finish the task of quelling the rebellion.

Titus resumed the attack on the Jews in AD 70, initially by marching to Jerusalem and surrounding it. He first allowed thousands of pilgrims into the city to celebrate Passover, then refused to let them leave. Conditions in the besieged city grew increasingly desperate. The unity of its defenders was undermined by bitter infighting between different factions: the rebels expended as much energy on killing one another as they did on killing the Romans. What grain reserves they had were destroyed in a fire – either as a result of the infighting, or as a deliberate attempt to force people to fight. After this, those who did not starve to death were crucified when they tried to escape.

Eventually, after a five-month siege, the Romans breached the outer wall of Jerusalem and the armies flooded through. They regained the Antonia Fortress to the north of the Temple. With the final defenders holed up in the Temple Mount, it was only a matter of time before the end came. In early August, the Temple Mount was captured and its population massacred. The Temple itself was burned to the ground and its treasures looted. The leaders of the revolt and 700 other prisoners were taken to Rome to appear in a humiliating triumphal procession.

Inscription dedicates the arch to Titus

Frieze depicts the triumphal 1st-century procession

**ARCH OF TITUS**
The Romans honoured Titus and Vespasian with a triumphal procession, commemorated by this Triumphal Arch in Rome.

## MASADA

The suppression of the revolt continued for a further three years. Under the command of General Lucilius Bassus, the Romans subdued the fortresses of Herodium and Machaerus, and captured the desert fortress of Masada in spring AD 74, bringing more of Judea under Roman rule. According to Josephus, the final defenders, Jewish rebels known as Sicarii (meaning "assassins with daggers"), who had retreated to the fortress, chose to commit mass suicide rather than face defeat. However, archaeological evidence suggests that some of the Sicarii fought the Romans to the death.

**STONE PROJECTILES**
Many stone missiles have been found at Masada. They may have been catapulted at the Romans or used by the Romans themselves.

THE REVELATION FROM JESUS CHRIST, WHICH GOD GAVE

MADE IT KNOWN BY SENDING HIS ANGELS TO HIS SERVANT

WORD OF GOD AND THE TESTIMONY OF JESUS CHRIST. BL

PROPHECY, AND BLESSED ARE THOSE WHO HEAR IT AND T

JOHN, TO THE SEVEN CHURCHES IN THE PROVINCE OF ASI

# 4

# REFERENCE

TO SHOW HIS SERVANTS WHAT MUST

HN, WHO TESTIFIES TO EVERYTHING HE

D IS THE ONE WHO READS ALOUD THE WO

TO HEART WHAT IS WRITTEN IN IT, BECAU

RACE AND PEACE TO YOU FROM HI

# People in the Bible

## A

### AARON
Elder brother and spokesman of Moses. He was consecrated as a priest, became the first High Priest of Israel, and was responsible for making the golden calf. Aaron opposed Moses on some occasions, and died before the Israelites entered Canaan.
EXODUS 4–12; 28; 32; NUMBERS 12; 16–17; 20:22–29

### ABEDNEGO
One of Daniel's friends who was exiled to Babylon. He was thrown into a furnace on the orders of Nebuchadnezzar, but was protected by God and survived the flames.
DANIEL 1:3–7; 2:49; 3

### ABEL
Second son of Adam and Eve. His offer of an animal sacrifice was preferred to the cereal offering of his brother, Cain, who then murdered him.
GENESIS 4:1–8; HEBREWS 11:4

### ABIATHAR
Son of Ahimelech and a priest of Nob who joined David and became a priest alongside Zadok. He escaped Saul's massacre of priests. On David's death, Abiathar supported Adonijah against Solomon and Solomon stripped him of his office.
1 SAMUEL 22–23; 2 SAMUEL 8:17; 1 KINGS 1–2

### ABIGAIL
Wife of Nabal, who appealed to David to spare her husband's life. She later married David.
1 SAMUEL 25; 30:5; 2 SAMUEL 2:2; 3:3

### ABIJAH
■ Son of King Jeroboam I of Israel, he died according to a prophet's prediction as a sign of God's punishment of his family.
1 KINGS 14
■ Son and successor of King Rehoboam of Judah.
1 KINGS 15; 2 CHRONICLES 13; MATTHEW 1:7

### ABIMELECH
■ Philistine king of Gerar to whom Abraham pretended that Sarah was his sister in order to protect himself.
GENESIS 20
■ Philistine king of Gerar to whom Isaac pretended that Rebekah was his sister.
GENESIS 26:7–11
■ Son of Gideon who murdered all of his 70 brothers, with the exception of Jotham.
JUDGES 8:31; 9

### ABIRAM
Conspirator against Moses with his brother, Dathan, and Korah, a Levite, while in Sinai. They, their families, and their cattle were all swallowed up by the earth.
NUMBERS 16

### ABISHAI
Brother of Joab and one of David's 30 warriors. He urged David to kill Saul, but David refused.
1 SAMUEL 26

### ABNER
Commander of Saul's army, killed by Joab, who did not trust his professed loyalty to David.
1 SAMUEL 14:50; 2 SAMUEL 2–3

### ABRAHAM
Originally known as Abram. Terah's son and Lot's uncle; called by God to leave Haran. He is known for his faith and obedience to God. God promised that Abraham would found a great nation, would be blessed, and would bring blessing to the whole Earth. God's covenant with Abraham included protection, land, and many descendants. He had his son Ishmael by Hagar, his servant, and in old age, his son Isaac by his wife Sarah. God tested Abraham by commanding him to offer Isaac as a sacrifice. Abraham pleaded with God for the cities of Sodom and Gomorrah. He was buried near Mamre. In the New Testament Abraham is noted for his faith and righteousness, and is described as father of God's people, and God's servant and friend.
GENESIS 11–25; MATTHEW 1:1–2, 17; 3:9; LUKE 16:22–30; JOHN 8:39–40, 52–58; ACTS 7:2–8; ROMANS 4:1–25; GALATIANS 3:6–9; HEBREWS 11:8–12; JAMES 2:23

### ABSALOM
Third son of David. He murdered his half-brother Amnon, who had raped Absalom's sister Tamar, and then fled, fearing his father's anger. David's general, Joab, interceded for Absalom and he was forgiven. Later, Absalom led a rebellion against his father. Despite David's orders to spare him, he was killed by Joab.
2 SAMUEL 13–19

### ACHAN
One of the tribe of Judah who stole from the spoils set apart for God when the Israelites conquered Jericho. As a result of this act, the Israelites' attack on Ai failed and Achan was later stoned to death.
JOSHUA 7

### ADAM
The first man, created by God, and given responsibility in the Garden of Eden. He was given Eve as a helper and then wife. Adam and Eve disobeyed God, bringing sin into the world. Jesus Christ is referred to as the last Adam.
GENESIS 1–3; ROMANS 5:12–19; 1 CORINTHIANS 15:45

### ADONIJAH
Fourth son of David, who tried to take the throne meant for Solomon. He later asked for David's servant Abishag as his wife, but was refused and killed by Solomon.
1 KINGS 1–2

### ADONI-BEZEK
Canaanite king who cut off the toes and thumbs of 70 kings. When defeated by Simeon and Judah, the same punishment was exacted on him.
JUDGES 1:4–7

### AGRIPPA I see Herod Agrippa I

### AGRIPPA II see Herod Agrippa II

### AHAB
Son of Omri; king of Israel who set up an altar for Baal worship in Samaria and set himself against Elijah; he married Jezebel. He joined Judah in war against Syria, murdered Naboth and stole his vineyard, and was killed at Ramoth Gilead.
1 KINGS 16:29–22:40

### AHASUERUS see Xerxes

### AHAZ
King of Judah, son of Jotham, and father of Hezekiah. He introduced pagan worship and took away some temple treasures out of deference to King Tiglath-Pileser of Assyria. He built a copy of the pagan altar at Damascus for the temple in Jerusalem.
2 KINGS 15:38–16:20; ISAIAH 7

### AHAZIAH
■ Ahab's son, king of Israel. Became a worshipper of Baal like his father.
1 KINGS 22:51–53; 2 KINGS 1
■ Son of Jehoram, King of Judah; he was murdered by Jehu.
2 KINGS 8:24–30

### AHIJAH
Prophet who tore his robe into 12 pieces to show how Solomon's kingdom would be divided. He gave ten pieces to Jeroboam to show that he would rule over ten of the twelve tribes of Israel.
1 KINGS 11:29–39; 14:1–18

### AHIMELECH
Priest of Nob, killed for helping David when he was escaping from Saul.
1 SAMUEL 22:1–19

### AHITHOPHEL
David's trusted adviser, who betrayed him to support Absalom. He committed suicide.
2 SAMUEL 16:15–17:23

### AMALEK
Grandson of Esau and Amalekite ancestor.
GENESIS 36:12; EXODUS 17:8–13; DEUTERONOMY 25:17–19

### AMASA
Nephew of David and commander of Absalom's army, he was killed by Joab.
2 SAMUEL 17:24–25; 19; 20:4–13; 1 KINGS 2:5, 32; 1 CHRONICLES 2:17

### AMAZIAH
Son of Joash, king of Judah. Having defeated Edom, he challenged Israel but was routed. He was exiled to Lachish and murdered by his people.
2 KINGS 14:1–22; 2 CHRONICLES 25; AMOS 7:10–17

## AMNON
David's eldest son, who raped Tamar and was killed by Absalom.
2 SAMUEL 13

## AMON
Son of Manasseh; king of Judah.
2 KINGS 21:19–26; 2 CHRONICLES 33:21–25

## AMOS
Prophet from Tekoa who prophesied against Israel.
AMOS

## ANAK
Ancestor of a race of giants (the Anakim).
NUMBERS 13; DEUTERONOMY 9:1–2; JOSHUA 15:14

## ANANIAS
■ Man who sold a piece of property but who gave only a part of the amount to the apostles. He was challenged by Peter and fell down dead, as did his wife Sapphira.
ACTS 5:1–11
■ Christian at Damascus, sent to Saul by God to cure Saul's blindness after his vision on the road to Damascus.
ACTS 9:10–19
■ High priest in Jerusalem who ordered a guard to hit Paul after his arrest in Jerusalem.
ACTS 23:2–3; 24:1

## ANDREW
Apostle and fisherman, brother of Simon Peter. The first disciple to be called by Jesus. Told by John the Baptist that Jesus was the "Lamb of God", Andrew later told Simon he had found the Messiah.
MATTHEW 4:18–20; 10:2; MARK 1:16; 3:18; 13:3; LUKE 6:14; JOHN 1:35–42; 12:22; ACTS 1:13

## ANNA
Prophetess in the temple at the time that Jesus was presented. She recognized Jesus as the Messiah and told others about him.
LUKE 2:36–38

## ANNAS
Jewish high priest, father-in-law of Caiaphas before whom Jesus stood trial. Although deposed by the Romans in AD 15, he was still recognized as high priest by the Jews. He opposed the apostles in Jerusalem after Jesus' resurrection.
LUKE 3:2; JOHN 18:12–24; ACTS 4:5–7

## ANTIOCHUS IV EPIPHANES
King of Syria and Asia Minor in the time between the Hebrew Bible and the New Testament. He desecrated the temple and forbade the Jewish faith to be practised. This led to the Maccabean uprising, the purification of Jerusalem, and the rededication of the temple in AD 164. An enemy of God's people, he foreshadowed the Antichrist. He is identified with the little horn of Daniel's prophecy.
DANIEL 7:8–11; 8:9–14; 11:28; 1 MACCABEES 1:20–23; 2 MACCABEES 3–4

## ANTIPAS *see Herod 2*

## APOLLOS
Learned Jew from Alexandria, instructed in Christianity by Aquila and Priscilla. A powerful preacher and leader of the church at Corinth.
ACTS 18:24–28; 19:1; 1 CORINTHIANS 1:12; 16:12

## AQUILA AND PRISCILLA
Jewish Christian couple whose work was tent-making. They instructed Apollos and served the church in various places, including Ephesus and Rome.
ACTS 18:1–3, 18–26; ROMANS 16:3; 1 CORINTHIANS 16:19; 2 TIMOTHY 4:19

## ARAUNAH
Man whose threshing floor David bought, on which David built an altar that later became the site of the temple.
2 SAMUEL 24:16–25; 1 CHRONICLES 21:18–30

## ARCHELAUS *see Herod Archelaus*

## ARCHIPPUS
Christian leader in Asia Minor.
COLOSSIANS 4:17; PHILEMON 2

## ARISTARCHUS
Paul's companion and fellow worker who accompanied him on his last visit to Jerusalem and Rome, and stayed with him when he was imprisoned in Rome.
ACTS 19:29; 20:4; 27:2; COLOSSIANS 4:10

## ARTAXERXES
King of Persia who ordered the rebuilding of the walls of Jerusalem to stop. Later he supported Ezra. Many families returned to Jerusalem during his reign. His cupbearer was Nehemiah, whom Artaxerxes appointed as governor of Judah. There were several Persian kings with this name.
EZRA 4:17–23; 7; NEHEMIAH 2:1–10

## ASA
Third king of Judah, reigned for 41 years. He worshipped Yahweh, removed pagan shrines, and reformed worship.
1 KINGS 15:8–24; 2 CHRONICLES 14:1–16:14

## ASAHEL
David's nephew, and one of his 30 warriors. Killed by Abner.
2 SAMUEL 2:18; 23:24; 1 CHRONICLES 11:26

## ASAPH
Levite responsible for music in the temple. Composer of several psalms.
1 CHRONICLES 6:39; 15:17; 16:5, 7, 37; 25:1; PSALM 50; 73–83

## ASHER
One of Jacob's 12 sons. His mother was Zilpah, the servant of Leah. Ancestor of the tribe of Asher.
GENESIS 30:12–13; 35:26; 49:20; JOSHUA 19:24–31

## ASHURBANIPAL
Last of Assyria's great kings.
EZRA 4:10

## ATHALIAH
Daughter of Ahab and Jezebel, who married Jehoram of Judah and seized the throne after her son Ahaziah's death.
2 KINGS 11; 2 CHRONICLES 22:10–12

## AUGUSTUS CAESAR
Roman emperor who ruled from 27 BC to AD 14 and who ordered the census that brought Joseph and Mary to Bethlehem.
LUKE 2:1

## AZARIAH *see Uzziah*

# B

## BAASHA
King of Israel; he took the throne of Israel from Nadab, Jeroboam I's son.
1 KINGS 15:16–16:7

## BALAAM
Prophet called on by Balak to curse the Israelites during their time in the wilderness. An angel stopped Balaam and warned him only to say what God told him. Instead of cursing the Israelites, he blessed them three times. Balaam was killed when the Israelites attacked the Midianites.
NUMBERS 22–24; 31:8; JOSHUA 24:9; NEHEMIAH 13:1–3

## BALAK
Moabite king who hired Balaam to curse Israel.
NUMBERS 22–24

## BARABBAS
Robber released instead of Jesus. Pilate initially tried to set Jesus free, but the priests stirred up the crowd against Jesus, forcing Pilate to release Barabbas instead.
MATTHEW 27:15–26

## BARAK
Deborah's commander of the Israelites in the defeat of Sisera and the Canaanites.
JUDGES 4–5

## BAR-JESUS
Also known as Elymas, Jewish sorcerer and false prophet in Paphos, Cyprus, who was temporarily blinded as a punishment for opposing Paul's message.
ACTS 13:6–12

## BARNABAS
Originally a Levite from Cyprus, Barnabas was commissioned for missionary service with Paul by the church at Antioch. Known as "son of encouragement", Barnabas sold his land and gave the money raised to poor Christians. He later parted company with Paul, who refused to allow John Mark, Barnabas's cousin, to accompany them again.
ACTS 4:36; 9:27; 11:22–30; 12:25; 13–15; 1 CORINTHIANS 9:6; GALATIANS 2:1; COLOSSIANS 4:10

## BARTHOLOMEW
One of the 12 apostles, probably "Nathanael" in John's Gospel.
MATTHEW 10:3; ACTS 1:13

## BARTIMAEUS
Blind beggar from Jericho who was healed by Jesus as Jesus travelled to Jerusalem for the Passion.
MARK 10:46–52

## BARUCH
Jeremiah's secretary who wrote down Jeremiah's prophecies. A book in the Apocrypha is named after him.
JEREMIAH 32:12–16; 36; 43:1–7; 45; BARUCH

## BARZILLAI
Faithful friend of David during Absalom's rebellion.
2 SAMUEL 17:27; 19:31–39

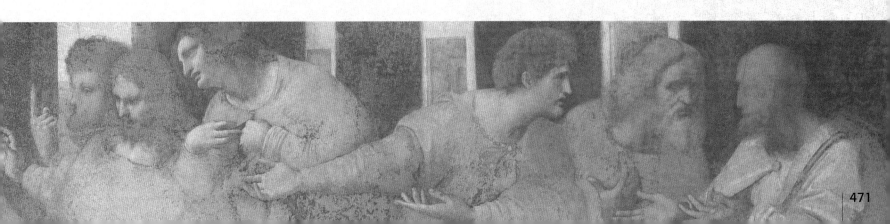

## BATHSHEBA

Wife of Uriah the Hittite. David committed adultery with her and later married her. She was the mother of Solomon.
2 SAMUEL 11; 1 KINGS 1–2

## BELSHAZZAR

Ruler (co-regent) and last king of Babylon. His death was predicted by the writing on the wall.
DANIEL 5; 7–8

## BELTESHAZZAR

Babylonian name given to Daniel.
DANIEL 1:7

## BENAIAH

One of David's officers responsible for proclaiming Solomon king. He became commander of Solomon's army.
2 SAMUEL 8:18; 1 KINGS 1–2; 1 CHRONICLES 11:22–25

## BEN-AMMI

Ancestor of the Ammonites. Son of Lot's younger daughter, incestuously fathered by Lot.
GENESIS 19:38

## BEN-HADAD

Name of three rulers of Syria c.900–800 BC. The name means "son of Hadad", who was the Syrian storm god.
1 KINGS 20:1–34; 2 KINGS 6:24–8:14; 13

## BENJAMIN

Youngest son of Jacob; Rachel died giving birth to him. After the disappearance of his brother Joseph, he became his father's favourite. Ancestor of the tribe of Benjamin.
GENESIS 35:16–18; 43–45; 49:27

## BERNICE

Sister of Herod Agrippa II, who was with him when he heard Paul's case at Caesarea.
ACTS 25:13

## BEZALEL

Craftsman called by God to construct the tabernacle and its furnishings during the wilderness period.
EXODUS 35:30–36:2; 37:1; 38:22; 2 CHRONICLES 1:5

## BILDAD

One of Job's three friends who tried to comfort him.
JOB 2:11; 8; 18; 25; 42:9

## BILHAH

Rachel's servant, given to her by Laban on Rachel's marriage to Jacob; mother of Dan and Naphtali.
GENESIS 29:29; 30:3–7

## BOAZ

Wealthy landowner from Bethlehem; he became Ruth's husband and ancestor of David.
RUTH 2–4

# C

## CAESAR see Augustus Caesar

## CAIAPHAS

High priest at the time of Jesus' arrest, before whom Jesus was interrogated. He prophesied Jesus' death without understanding its significance. He found Jesus guilty and sent him to Pilate for sentencing. He was also the high priest in Acts who persecuted the first Christians.
MATTHEW 26:3, 57; LUKE 3:2; JOHN 18:13–14, 24, 28; ACTS 4:5–7

## CAIN

Eldest son of Adam and Eve. He was a farmer, and his brother Abel was a shepherd. His cereal offering to God was not accepted. Cain murdered Abel and was forced to live the rest of his life as a nomad, although protected by God.
GENESIS 4

## CALEB

Sent by Moses to explore Canaan. Of the 12 spies, only he and Joshua believed wholeheartedly that God would bring them into the Promised Land. They were therefore the only two allowed to settle in Canaan. Later the area around Hebron was given to Caleb.
NUMBERS 13–14; 26:65; DEUTERONOMY 1:35–36; JOSHUA 14:6–15; 15:13–19

## CANDACE

Queen of Ethiopia (Nubia) whose treasury official (eunuch) met the evangelist Philip.
ACTS 8:27

## CHRIST see Jesus Christ

## CLAUDIUS

Roman emperor who reigned from AD 41–54.
ACTS 11:28; 17:7; 18:2

## CLEOPAS

One of two disciples who met the risen Jesus on the road to Emmaus after Jesus' resurrection.
LUKE 24:13–35

## CORNELIUS

God-fearing Roman centurion to whose household Peter was sent to preach the gospel. He was converted, becoming the first recorded Gentile Christian.
ACTS 10

## CRISPUS

Ruler of the synagogue in Corinth, who was converted through Paul's ministry.
ACTS 18:7–8

## CUSHAN-RISHATHAIM

Mesopotamian king said to have ruled over the Israelites in the time of the Judges. Probably not an actual person.
JUDGES 3:8–10

## CYRUS

Persian king who allowed the Jews to return from exile and rebuild the temple in Jerusalem. He returned items stolen from the temple by Nebuchadnezzar, and financed the building work.
2 CHRONICLES 36:22–23; EZRA 1–6; ISAIAH 44–45

# D

## DAMARIS

Woman from Athens, converted by Paul.
ACTS 17:34

## DAN

Son of Jacob by Bilhah, ancestor of the tribe bearing his name.
GENESIS 30:4–6; 35:25; 49:16–17

## DANIEL

Nobly born Hebrew taken into exile in the court of Babylon. He refused to eat unclean food and was given the ability to interpret Nebuchadnezzar's dreams. Daniel's friends were thrown into a furnace on the orders of Nebuchadnezzar but were protected by God and survived. Daniel held high offices and maintained a godly and prayerful life, refusing to obey the king's command, for which he was thrown into the lions' den. He received visions of hope reminding God's people of his presence and predicting an eternal kingdom.
DANIEL 1–12

## DARIUS

■ Darius the Mede. He became ruler of Babylon.
DANIEL 5:31; 9:1
■ Darius I, the Great, king of Persia 522–486 BC. He allowed the returned Jews to rebuild the Jerusalem temple.
EZRA 4–6; HAGGAI 1:1; ZECHARIAH 1:1

## DATHAN see Abiram

## DAVID

Shepherd and youngest son of Jesse; founded the royal line from which the Messiah was to be born. David had several wives including Michal, Abigail, and Bathsheba. Solomon was among his children. David reigned in Hebron for seven years and in Jerusalem for thirty-three years. Samuel anointed him in Bethlehem and he served Saul as a musician. David killed Goliath but provoked the jealousy of Saul, who tried to kill him. David's friendship with Saul's son Jonathan meant that he survived Saul's threats on his life. David united the northern and southern tribes as king over all Israel, and he captured Jerusalem from the Jebusites, installing the Ark of the Covenant in Jerusalem. God promised David that his dynasty would last for ever. David is described as "a man after my [God's] own heart". His weakness is seen, however, when he committed adultery with Bathsheba and then had her husband Uriah killed. David was rebuked by Nathan and the child David and Bathsheba conceived died. David's son, Absalom, conspired against David but Absalom's men were defeated, and Absalom himself was killed. David then made Solomon king. David is remembered for his Psalms, many of which concern his life. In the prophetic books, the expectation of a Messiah is linked to David's family line. In the Gospels, Jesus is referred to as the "Son of David", establishing Jesus as the Messiah.
1 SAMUEL 16–30; 2 SAMUEL 1–24; 1 KINGS 1–15; 1 CHRONICLES 11–29; PSALM 3–9; 11–41; 51–70; 108–110; 131–145; MATTHEW 1:1, 6, 17; 12:3; 22:42–45; JOHN 7:42; ACTS 13:22; ROMANS 1:3

## DEBORAH

Prophet in the time of the Judges, who appointed Barak to attack Sisera and the Canaanites.
JUDGES 4–5

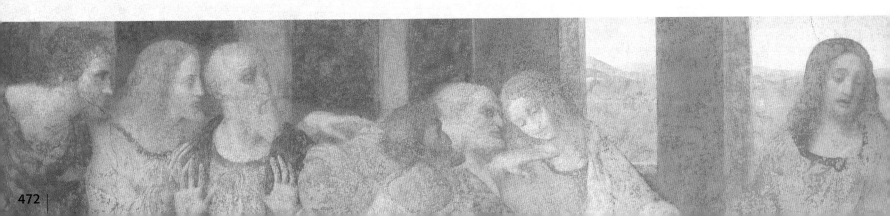

## DELILAH
Mistress of Samson, who betrayed him to the Philistines after finding that the source of his strength was his hair. She cut off his locks before he was blinded and enslaved.
JUDGES 16:1–22

## DEMAS
Paul's fellow Christian worker who was imprisoned with Paul in Rome but later deserted him.
COLOSSIANS 4:14; 2 TIMOTHY 4:10

## DEMETRIUS
Silversmith at Ephesus who made silver shrines of Artemis. He organized a riot against Paul.
ACTS 19:23–41

## DINAH
Jacob's daughter, whose rape by Shechem was avenged by her brothers, Simeon and Levi.
GENESIS 34

## DIONYSIUS
Member of the Areopagus (a powerful court in Athens) who became a Christian after meeting Paul.
ACTS 17:34

## DIOTREPHES
Church leader criticized by John for refusing to welcome Christian brothers.
3 JOHN 9–10

## DOEG
Edomite official of Saul, who informed him that Ahimelech had given David provisions in his flight from Saul. As a consequence, Ahimelech was killed by Doeg.
1 SAMUEL 22:9–23

## DORCAS *see Tabitha*

## DRUSILLA
Herod Agrippa I's youngest daughter, and wife of the governor Felix, who heard Paul's case.
ACTS 24:24

# E

## EBED-MELECH
Cushite official in Zedekiah's palace who saved Jeremiah's life and whose own life was saved by God as a result.
JEREMIAH 38:7–12; 39:16–18

## EGLON
Moabite king who defeated the Israelites and ruled them for 18 years before being killed by Ehud.
JUDGES 3:12–26

## EHUD
Israelite judge who killed Eglon of Moab. Once Eglon was dead, he defeated the Moabites and freed the Israelites.
JUDGES 3:12–30

## ELAH
The fourth king of Israel, who was succeeded by son Baasha, and who was killed by his chariot commander, Zimri.
1 KINGS 16:6–14

## ELASHIB
Steward of Hezekiah's household, who negotiated with Sennacherib's officers.
2 KINGS 18:18; ISAIAH 36:1–37:7

## ELEAZAR
Aaron's third son, who became high priest after Aaron died. He was leader of the Levites and had responsibility for the tabernacle.
NUMBERS 3:2, 32; 4:16; 27:2; JOSHUA 14:1

## ELI
Priest at Shiloh, who raised young Samuel. His sons were rebellious and as a result Eli's house was cursed. Both sons were killed in battle against the Philistines, and the Ark of the Covenant was stolen. When Eli heard the news, he collapsed and died.
1 SAMUEL 1–4

## ELIAB
Eldest son of Jesse, and brother of David.
1 SAMUEL 16:6; 17:13, 28

## ELIAKIM
The palace administrator under Hezekiah, who negotiated with Sennacherib's officials.
2 KINGS 18:18; ISAIAH 22:20–24; 36:3, 11, 22; 37:2

## ELIEZER
Abraham's servant and heir, who was sent to find a wife for Abraham's son Isaac. He found Rebekah.
GENESIS 15:2

## ELIHU
A fourth friend of Job, who suggested that Job look to God to explain his suffering.
JOB 32–37

## ELIJAH
A 9th-century-BC prophet in Israel who predicted a drought. He was miraculously fed by ravens at Kerith. Elijah challenged the prophets of Baal on Mount Carmel to prove the existence of their god. He denounced Ahab over Naboth's vineyard and prophesied God's judgment on Ahaziah. He is known for such miracles as raising a widow's son from the dead and dividing the River Jordan; he did not die but was taken up to heaven in a chariot of fire and whirlwind. In the New Testament, he appeared with Moses at Jesus' transfiguration and was identified with John the Baptist.
1 KINGS 17–21; 2 KINGS 1–2; MATTHEW 11:13–14; 17:2–3, 11–13; JAMES 5:17

## ELIMELECH
Husband of Naomi; his daughter-in-law was Ruth.
RUTH 1–2

## ELIPHAZ
One of Job's three friends who tried to comfort him.
JOB 4–5; 15; 22

## ELISHA
Elijah's successor as prophet of Israel. He carried out the task set by Elijah to anoint Hazael and Jehu as kings-to-be in Syria and Israel. He performed a number of miracles, including purifying bad water, providing oil for a widow, bringing a Shunammite woman's son back to life, and healing Naaman, a Syrian general, of his leprosy.
1 KINGS 19:16–21; 2 KINGS 2–9; 13:14–20

## ELIZABETH
Wife of Zechariah and mother of John the Baptist. The cousin of Jesus' mother, Elizabeth visited Mary when they were both expecting sons. She knew that Mary's child would be the long-awaited Messiah.
LUKE 1:5–57

## ELKANAH
Father of Samuel, and husband of Hannah.
1 SAMUEL 1

## ELYMAS *see Bar-Jesus*

## ENOCH
Descendant of Adam's son Seth and father of Methuselah. He was taken into God's presence without dying.
GENESIS 5:18–24; HEBREWS 11:5; JUDE 14–15

## EPAPHRAS
Paul's friend and fellow worker who founded the Christian church in Colossae.
COLOSSIANS 1:7–8; 4:12; PHILEMON 23

## EPAPHRODITUS
Christian sent to Paul by the Philippian church, and who brought a gift from the Philippians to Paul at his Roman prison. Paul's trusted fellow worker.
PHILIPPIANS 2:25–30; 4:18

## EPHRAIM
The younger of Joseph's two sons, who received a greater blessing from his grandfather Jacob than his brother, Manasseh. Ancestor of the tribe of Ephraim.
GENESIS 41:52; 48

## ERASTUS
■ Paul's assistant, sent to Macedonia with Timothy.
ACTS 19:22; 2 TIMOTHY 4:20
■ Christian city-treasurer from Corinth.
ROMANS 16:23

## ESARHADDON
King of Assyria who succeeded his father Sennacherib. Ruled 680–669 BC.
2 KINGS 19:37; EZRA 4:2

## ESAU
Son of Isaac and Rebekah, and older twin brother of Jacob. He sold his birthright in return for some stew and lost the blessing as the eldest son. He was later reconciled with Jacob, and became the ancestor of the Edomites.
GENESIS 25–33; 36; MALACHI 1:2–3; ROMANS 9:13; HEBREWS 12:16

## ESTHER
Jewish woman originally named Hadassah and who lived in Persia. Brought up by her cousin Mordecai, she became Xerxes's queen. She discovered a plot by Haman to exterminate the Jews, risked her life in approaching Xerxes and revealed Haman's plot. The Jews celebrated their victory, initiating the feast of Purim.
ESTHER

## EUNICE
Jewish mother of Timothy.
2 TIMOTHY 1:5

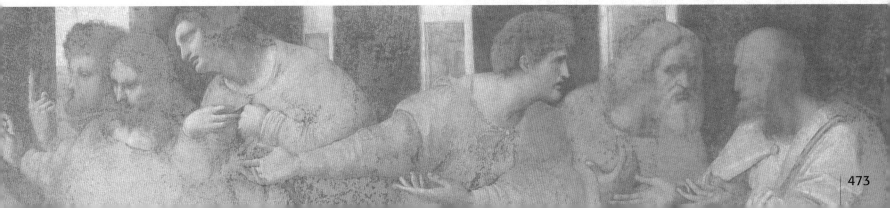

## EUTYCHUS

Young man who fell to his death from a window during Paul's sermon at Troas, and whom Paul restored to life.
ACTS 20:7–12

## EVE

The first woman in the biblical accounts, created by God from Adam's rib. Helper and then wife of Adam, she gave in to the serpent's temptation and then encouraged Adam to give way to temptation too. Her children included Cain, Abel, and Seth.
GENESIS 2–4; **2 CORINTHIANS** 11:3; **1 TIMOTHY** 2:13

## EZEKIEL

Priest and prophet who was deported to Babylon, he was called to be a prophet while in exile. His wife died suddenly but he was not allowed to mourn for her. Ezekiel is known for his bizarre dramas acting out his prophecies (for example, eating a scroll and lying on his side) and his visions, especially of the valley of dry bones and the new temple in Jerusalem.
EZEKIEL

## EZRA

Priest and teacher of the law; Ezra led a return of the exiles from Babylon to Jerusalem, with King Artaxerxes providing resources for temple worship. In Jerusalem, Ezra reformed the people's moral and religious life, establishing Jewish law as the basis of community life, reading the Law at the Feast of Tabernacles, and participating in the dedication of the city walls.
EZRA 7–10; **NEHEMIAH** 8; 12

# F

## FELIX

Roman procurator *c.*AD 52–60 who kept Paul in prison at Caesarea for two years.
ACTS 23:23–24:27

## FESTUS

Successor to Felix as procurator of Judea. He heard Paul's case at Caesarea and agreed that Paul was innocent.
ACTS 25–26

# G

## GABRIEL

Archangel sent to interpret Daniel's vision. He announced the birth of John the Baptist to Zechariah and the birth of Jesus to Mary.
DANIEL 8:15–16; 9:20–27; **LUKE** 1:11–20, 26–38

## GAD

■ Son of Jacob and Leah's servant Zilpah; ancestor of a tribe of Israel whose territory lay to the east of the River Jordan.
GENESIS 30:9–11; 49:19
■ Prophet who advised David to leave Moab for Judah.
1 SAMUEL 22:5; **2 SAMUEL** 24

## GALLIO

Governor of Achaia in AD 51–52 (and brother of the philosopher Seneca, the tutor of Nero) who declared that the charges the Jews were bringing against Paul were an internal matter for them to settle, giving them more freedom.
ACTS 18:12–17

## GAMALIEL

Influential Pharisee, rabbi, member of the Sanhedrin, and tutor of Saul of Tarsus. He advised cautious handling of the apostles when they were arrested, suggesting that if they were doing only human work, nothing would come of it, but if they were doing God's work, opposition would be futile.
ACTS 5:34–40; 22:3

## GEDALIAH

Governor of Judah appointed by Nebuchadnezzar. He was assassinated after only a few months.
2 KINGS 25:22–26

## GEHAZI

Servant of Elisha, who falsely obtained money from Naaman, whom Elisha had cured of leprosy. As a punishment, Gehazi himself caught leprosy.
2 KINGS 4–5; 8:1–6

## GERSHON

Levi's first son; founder of the Gershonite clans, one of the three Levitical families that served in the Temple of Jerusalem.
EXODUS 6:16–17; **NUMBERS** 3:17–18

## GIDEON

One of Israel's judges, who delivered the nation from the Midianites. He was called to action by an angel, and he asked for a sign from God using a fleece. His army was reduced to 300 men who attacked the enemy. In their fear, the Midianites turned on each other, and then fled the land. There was then peace for the rest of Gideon's life.
JUDGES 6–8

## GILEAD

Grandson of Manasseh, whose name was given to the land east of the River Jordan.
NUMBERS 27:1; 36:1; **JOSHUA** 17:1, 3; **1 CHRONICLES** 7:14–17

## GOG

A chief prince of Meshek and Tubal, in the land of Magog. Ezekiel describes God's defeat of the forces attacking Israel that Gog led; he is possibly to be identified as Gyges, the king of Lydia. The name is used symbolically in Revelation to represent one who opposes God.
EZEKIEL 38–39; **REVELATION** 20:7–8

## GOLIATH

Philistine giant who challenged Israel and was killed by a stone from David's sling. David then beheaded Goliath.
1 SAMUEL 17

## GOMER

Hosea's unfaithful wife, who was forgiven by Hosea to represent God's readiness to forgive unfaithful Israel.
HOSEA 1–3

# H

## HABAKKUK

Prophet to Judah during the period of the Babylonian rise to power.
HABAKKUK

## HADAD

Edomite who fled to Egypt and married the queen's sister. On hearing that both David and Joab were dead, he returned to Edom and opposed Solomon.
1 KINGS 11:14–25

## HADADEZER

King of Zobah, defeated by David.
2 SAMUEL 8–10; **1 CHRONICLES** 18–9

## HAGAR

Egyptian servant of Abraham's barren wife, Sarah, who gave Hagar to Abraham so that she might bear him a child. Hagar then gave birth to Ishmael. Sarah began to treat Hagar so badly that she fled, but an angel of the Lord brought her back.
GENESIS 16; 21:8–20; **GALATIANS** 4:21–31

## HAGGAI

Prophet who encouraged the returning exiles to rebuild the Temple.
EZRA 5:1; 6:14; **HAGGAI**

## HAM

Noah's youngest son, who was saved in the ark but later disgraced Noah. The father of Cush (Ethiopia), Egypt (Mizraim), Put (Libya), and Canaan, from whom the Canaanites descended.
GENESIS 5:32; 6:10; 9:18–19; 10:6–20

## HAMAN

Villain of the book of Esther, who plotted against the Jews because he had been slighted by the defiance of Mordecai. Haman was subsequently hanged when Esther exposed his plot to destroy the Jewish people.
ESTHER 3–9

## HANAMEL

Jeremiah's cousin, who sold him the field at Anathoth during the Babylonian invasion. Jeremiah bought the field to show that one day Judah would no longer be under the power of Babylon.
JEREMIAH 32:6–12

## HANANI

Brother of Nehemiah, who travelled to Susa to tell Nehemiah that Jerusalem was still in ruins despite the return of the exiles. He was made governor by Nehemiah once the walls of the city had been rebuilt.
NEHEMIAH 1:2; 7:2

## HANANIAH

False prophet denounced by Jeremiah because he spoke lies that the people wanted to hear.
JEREMIAH 28

## HANNAH

Mother of Samuel, who was childless for many years before she prayed and finally gave birth to a son, Samuel, whom she dedicated to God.
1 SAMUEL 1–2

## HARAN

Abraham's brother, who died in Ur before Terah and Abraham left the city. He had three children: Lot, Milcah, and Iscah.
GENESIS 11:26–31

## HAZAEL

King of Syria who murdered Ben-Hadad following a prediction by Elisha. Hazael waged war against Israel and Judah in the 9th century BC.
1 KINGS 19:15–17; 2 KINGS 8:7–9:15

## HEBER

Husband of Jael, who killed Sisera, the Canaanite general.
JUDGES 4:11–21; 5:24

## HEROD

■ Herod the Great, King of Judea when Jesus was born. He received the Magi and ordered the killing of all newborn baby boys in Bethlehem.
MATTHEW 2:1–22; LUKE 1:5
■ Son of Herod the Great, also called Antipas. Ruler of Galilee. He took his sister-in-law, Herodias, as his wife, which evoked outspoken criticism from John the Baptist, whom he arrested and had beheaded. Pilate sent Jesus to him.
MATTHEW 14:1–12; MARK 6:14–29; LUKE 3:19–20; 9:7–9; 23:6–15

## HEROD AGRIPPA I

Grandson of Herod the Great, and ruler of Galilee, Judea, and Samaria. He had James killed and put Peter in prison. He was struck down by an angel and his body was eaten by worms.
ACTS 12:1–23

## HEROD AGRIPPA II

Son of Herod Agrippa l before whom Paul gave his testimony at Caesarea.
ACTS 25:13–26:32

## HEROD ANTIPAS *see Herod*

## HEROD ARCHELAUS

Son of Herod the Great; he succeeded his father as ruler of Judea.
MATTHEW 2:22

## HERODIAS

Wife of Philip who left him to marry Herod Antipas. She prompted her daughter Salome to ask for the head of John the Baptist.
MATTHEW 14:1–12; MARK 6:17–29; LUKE 3:19

## HEZEKIAH

King of Judah and contemporary of Isaiah. Known for his godliness, he set out to rid his land of idol worship and reform religious worship. However, he was rebuked by Isaiah for relying too much on Babylonians. He rebelled against the Assyrians but the constant threat from the north made him realize the possibility of a siege. When the Assyrian king Sennacherib threatened the people of Jerusalem to trust him rather than Hezekiah and God, Hezekiah wept, prayed, and asked Isaiah's advice. Isaiah reassured Hezekiah that the Assyrians would not defeat them. He prayed and received God's help. He cut the Siloam tunnel to ensure Jerusalem's water supply.
2 KINGS 18–20; 2 CHRONICLES 28–32; ISAIAH 36–39; MATTHEW 1:9–10

## HILKIAH

High priest at the time of King Josiah. He discovered the Book of the Law in the temple and brought it to the king.
2 KINGS 22:4–23:24; 2 CHRONICLES 34:9–22

## HIRAM

King of Tyre who supplied materials for the building of David's palace, made a treaty with Solomon, and supplied cedar and skilled labour for the Temple. His sailors served in Solomon's navy.
2 SAMUEL 5:11–12; 1 KINGS 5; 9–10

## HOLOFERNES

Captain of Nebuchadnezzar's army who was killed by Judith.
JUDITH 2–7; 10–15

## HOPHNI

Corrupt son of Eli; a priest at Shiloh, he was killed when the Philistines captured the Ark of the Covenant.
1 SAMUEL 4:4–17

## HOSEA

Prophet to Israel; he emphasized God's faithfulness to his people. His relationship with his adulterous wife, Gomer, and his forgiveness of her reinforced his message.
HOSEA; ROMANS 9:25–26

## HOSHEA

Last king of the northern kingdom of Israel. Hoshea killed King Pekah and appointed himself as ruler. He was imprisoned by Shalmaneser, and a few years later Samaria – the capital of Israel – fell, and the people were exiled to Assyria.
2 KINGS 17:1–6

## HULDAH

Prophetess consulted by Hilkiah after he discovered the Book of the Law.
2 KINGS 22:14–20; 2 CHRONICLES 34:22

## HUR

Israelite leader after the Exodus; worked with Aaron; he held up Moses' hands (expressing trust in God) when Joshua was fighting against the Amalekites.
EXODUS 17:10–12; 24:14

## HUSHAI

David's friend who persuaded Absalom not to take Ahithophel's advice. Hushai's misleading advice led to Ahithophel hanging himself, and to Absalom marching across the Jordan to his death.
2 SAMUEL 15–17

## HYMENAEUS

False teacher who was disciplined by Paul for unsettling people's faith.
1 TIMOTHY 1:20; 2 TIMOTHY 2:17

# I

## ICHABOD

The grandson of Eli; the son of Phinehas; his name means "no glory".
1 SAMUEL 4:12–22

## ISAAC

Son of Abraham, and the heir of God's promises to Abraham. Abraham was prepared to offer Isaac as a sacrifice but God provided a ram instead. Isaac married Rebekah and fathered twins, Esau and Jacob. Issac was deceived by Rebekah and blessed Jacob, not Esau, as the firstborn.
GENESIS 17–28; EXODUS 3:6; HEBREWS 11:17–19

## ISAIAH

Prophet to Judah in the 8th century, Isaiah received a vision of God. He prophesied judgment on the nations but also good news: the possibility of salvation for all people and Israel's role as a light to the nations. He emphasized trust in God rather than in man, and reassured Hezekiah in his illness. He prophesied deliverance from Assyria, the coming of God's servant to save his people, and the return of the people from exile. Tradition has it that he was sawn in two under King Manasseh.
2 KINGS 19–20; ISAIAH; MATTHEW 13:14–15; MARK 1:2–3; ACTS 8:28–33; HEBREWS 11:37

## ISH-BOSHETH

Saul's son, made king by Abner. He ruled over much of Israel while David was king of the tribe of Judah. He was murdered by two of his generals.
2 SAMUEL 2–4

## ISHMAEL

Son of Abraham and Hagar (Sarah's servant). He was blessed by God, but God's covenant was through Isaac, Ishmael's half-brother. Ishmael's descendants became great.
GENESIS 16–17; 21:8–21; 37:25–28; GALATIANS 4:21–31

## ISRAEL

The name God gave Jacob after they wrestled at the Jabbok River. The name, meaning "the man who fights with God", was then given collectively to the 12 tribes descended from him ("the sons of Israel"). Later, it became the name for the land occupied by these 12 tribes, which grew into a kingdom under David and Solomon. After the Kingdom of Israel divided, "Israel" came to refer to the more northerly of the two new kingdoms.
GENESIS 32:22–28; 34:7; 35:9–10; 49:7, 28; DEUTERONOMY 17:4, 20; 18:6; 1 KINGS 11:31, 35; 2 KINGS 17

## ISSACHAR

Son of Jacob by Leah. Ancestor of the tribe of Issachar.
GENESIS 30:17–18; 35:23; 49:14–15

## ITTAI

Philistine from Gath who stood by David during Absalom's rebellion. As a reward for his loyalty, David made Ittai the commander of a third of his army.
2 SAMUEL 15:19–22; 18:5

# J

## JABEZ

A descendant of Judah, known for praying to request the Lord's blessing – a prayer which God answered.
1 CHRONICLES 4:9–10

## JABIN

King of Hazor whose army was defeated by Joshua.
JOSHUA 11:1–11

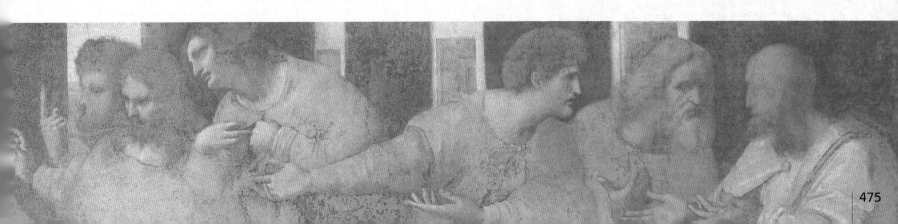

## JACOB

Son of Isaac; his older twin brother was Esau. Favoured by Rebekah, he deceitfully bought the birthright from Esau and tricked Isaac into blessing him as the firstborn. He had a dream of a stairway ("Jacob's ladder") at Bethel, where God assured him he would inherit the promises given to Abraham. He worked for Laban for seven years to marry Rachel but was tricked into marrying Leah. He then married Rachel in return for further work. He wrestled with God and his name was changed to Israel. He showed favouritism towards his son Joseph, and was led to believe Joseph had died but was eventually reconciled with him and settled in Egypt. He blessed his sons shortly before he died.

GENESIS 25–50; MATTHEW 1:2; LUKE 1:33; 3:34; JOHN 4:5–6, 12; ACTS 7:8–16; ROMANS 9:13; HEBREWS 11:9, 20–21

## JAEL

Wife of Heber, who killed Sisera, the Canaanite general, with a tent peg.

JUDGES 4–5

## JAIRUS

Ruler of the synagogue at Capernaum, whose 12-year-old daughter was restored to life by Jesus.

MARK 5:22–43

## JAMES

■ Son of Zebedee, brother of John, one of the 12 apostles; known as James the Great to distinguish him from James the Less. He and his brother John were called "men of thunder" by Jesus. Part of Jesus' inner circle of close disciples with Peter and John. Sentenced to death by Herod Agrippa I.

MATTHEW 4:21–22; 17:1–2; 26:36–38; ACTS 12:2

■ Son of Alphaeus, another of the apostles, called James the Less or James the Younger in Mark 15:40.

MATTHEW 10:3; MARK 15:40; ACTS 1:13

■ Brother or half-brother of Jesus, who became leader of the Jerusalem church.

MATTHEW 13:55; ACTS 12:17; 1 CORINTHIANS 15:7; JAMES

## JAPHETH

One of Noah's three sons. He survived the Flood to become ancestor of a number of nations.

GENESIS 5:32; 7:13; 9:18–19; 10:2

## JASON

Host of Paul and Silas when they visited Thessalonica.

ACTS 17:5–9

## JEDUTHUN

Levite appointed by David to be one of the leaders of the temple music.

1 CHRONICLES 16:41–42; 25:1; 2 CHRONICLES 5:12

## JEHOAHAZ

■ Son of Jehu, and king of Israel. He tolerated idol worship, and Israel was oppressed by Syria for part of his reign.

2 KINGS 13:1–9

■ Son of Josiah and king of Judah for three months. He was captured by Pharaoh Neco II and taken to Egypt. Called Shallum by Jeremiah.

2 KINGS 23:31–34; 2 CHRONICLES 36:1–4; JEREMIAH 22:11–17

## JEHOASH

Son of Jehoahaz. The 12th king of Israel. He was aided in territorial battles by Elisha.

2 KINGS 13:10–14:17

## JEHOIACHIN

Son of Jehoiakim, king of Judah for three months. Taken as a captive to Babylon by Nebuchadnezzar.

2 KINGS 24:8–17; 25:27–30; 2 CHRONICLES 36:9–10; JEREMIAH 52:31–34

## JEHOIADA

Name of a number of individuals, notably the priest responsible for the coup that dethroned Athaliah and placed Joash on the throne of Judah.

2 KINGS 11–12; 2 CHRONICLES 23–24

## JEHOIAKIM

Son of Josiah, king of Judah, originally called Eliakim, and put on the throne by Pharaoh Neco II. He burnt Jeremiah's scroll of prophecies and later rebelled against Babylonian control. He died on the way to captivity.

2 KINGS 23:34–24:7; 2 CHRONICLES 36:5–8; JEREMIAH 22:18–23; 26; 36; DANIEL 1:1–2

## JEHORAM

■ Son of Ahab of Israel, see Joram.

■ Son of Jehoshaphat and King of Judah. He died of disease after he reverted to idol worship.

2 KINGS 8:16–24; 2 CHRONICLES 21:4–20

## JEHOSHAPHAT

Son of Asa, king of Judah, allied by marriage to Ahab of Israel, but committed to God. He fought with Ahab against the Syrians at Ramoth Gilead. He discouraged the worship of idols, and ensured his people learned God's laws.

1 KINGS 22; 2 KINGS 3; 2 CHRONICLES 17–21

## JEHOSHEBA

Daughter of King Jehoram of Judah and wife of the priest Jehoiada, who saved the life of Joash by hiding him from Athaliah.

2 KINGS 11:1–3; 2 CHRONICLES 22:11–12

## JEHU

King of Israel, anointed by Elisha to destroy Ahab's line. He killed his predecessor Joram and Jezebel before restoring the worship of Yahweh and eradicating Baal worship.

2 KINGS 9–10

## JEPHTHAH

One of Israel's principal judges whose rash vow to God resulted in his daughter's sacrifice.

JUDGES 11:1–12:7

## JEREMIAH

Prophet to Judah; needed God's reassurance as a prophet because he was fearful and knew his own weaknesses. His prophecies warned of exile to Babylonia and challenged false prophets. He suffered persecution by being put in the stocks, threatened with death, imprisoned, and thrown into a cistern. He continued to prophesy when his scroll was burned, and promised future restoration and a new covenant. He was taken to Babylonia and Egypt.

2 CHRONICLES 35:25; JEREMIAH; LAMENTATIONS 1–5

## JEROBOAM

■ Jeroboam I, king of Israel. First king of the northern kingdom. He rebelled against Solomon and became an exile in Egypt before returning to lead the ten northern tribes against Rehoboam.

1 KINGS 12:25–14:20

■ Jeroboam II, king of Israel. He re-established Israel's political power and material prosperity, but the social evils and empty ritual of his reign were attacked by the prophet Amos, who predicted the fall of Samaria as a result.

2 KINGS 14:23–29; AMOS 2; 5–7

## JESSE

David's father, grandson of Ruth and Boaz.

1 SAMUEL 16–17

## JESUS CHRIST

The Gospels of Matthew and Luke trace Jesus' earthly genealogy; John's Gospel asserts the eternal nature of Jesus Christ, with God taking on human flesh and becoming a man. The Gospels tell of Jesus' birth in Bethlehem, his presentation in the temple as a baby, his upbringing in Nazareth, and his visit to the Temple at Jerusalem. Aged about 30, Jesus' baptism by John marked the beginning of his ministry. He taught, healed, and performed other miracles to show his authority and compassion. He mentored and delegated authority to his disciples. Peter acknowledged him as the Christ and his closest disciples Peter, James, and John saw him transfigured. The Gospels devote much space to his last week in Jerusalem, including his triumphal entry into the city; his cleansing of the temple; his sharing of the Last Supper with his disciples; his prayer in Gethsemane; his arrest and trials; his death by crucifixion; and his burial. After dying, Jesus was raised back to life and appeared to many of his followers. He promised them the gift of the Holy Spirit, and then ascended to heaven.

MATTHEW; MARK; LUKE; JOHN; ACTS 1:1–11; 1 CORINTHIANS 15:1–34

## JESUS SON OF SIRACH

Greek form of the name of the author of the book of Sirach; Latin name Ecclesiasticus.

SIRACH

## JETHRO

Midianite priest and father-in-law of Moses. Sometimes known as Reuel. He advised Moses to delegate his authority for the administration of justice by appointing other leaders.

EXODUS 3:1; 4:18–19; 18

## JEZEBEL

Wife of Ahab, king of Israel. She introduced the worship of Baal into the kingdom and was responsible for Naboth's death. Elijah predicted her violent death and, on the orders of Jehu, she was thrown from an upstairs window. In Revelation her name symbolizes idolatry.

1 KINGS 16:31; 18:4, 13, 19; 19:1–2; 21; 2 KINGS 9:30–37; REVELATION 2:20

## JOAB

Nephew of David and commander of his army. He helped reconcile David and his son, Absalom, but later killed Absalom against David's orders. Joab had earlier murdered his army rival Abner, and was put to death by Solomon for it.
2 SAMUEL 2:13–3:31; 10–11; 14; 18–20; 24:1–4; 1 KINGS 1:15–2:34

## JOANNA

Wife of one of Herod Antipas's officials. She was one of the women who provided for Jesus from their own resources, and who found the tomb of Jesus empty on the morning of the resurrection.
LUKE 8:1–3; 24:1–10

## JOASH

Rescued from Athaliah's massacre, he became king of Judah at the age of seven. Guided by Jehoiada during much of his reign, he repaired the temple and obeyed God's laws. After Jehoiada's death, he allowed the worship of Baal, and killed Jehoiada's son. He was finally murdered by his officials.
2 KINGS 11–12; 2 CHRONICLES 22:10–24:27

## JOB

God-fearing man whom God permitted to be tested by Satan. He suffered the loss of his family and wealth, and endured much physical affliction. Throughout, Job remained patient and faithful to God, honestly expressing his thoughts. He declared his innocence when challenged by his friends, who claimed his suffering must be due to his sin. God eventually vindicated and healed him, giving him even greater wealth than before.
JOB; JAMES 5:11

## JOEL

Prophet who describes the coming of a plague of locusts as depicting the coming of the Day of the Lord – the people are to turn back to God, who will have mercy, restore them, and give them his Spirit.
JOEL; ACTS 2:16–21

## JOHANAN

Name of several Old Testament men, notably the Jewish leader who warned Gedaliah of the plot to kill him. He ignored Jeremiah's advice and led the people to Egypt.
JEREMIAH 40–43

## JOHN MARK see Mark

## JOHN THE APOSTLE

Fisherman and son of Zebedee; he was especially close to Jesus. John was present at Christ's transfiguration, and was in the Garden of Gethsemane before Jesus' death. After the ascension, John became a leader in the churches at Jerusalem and Ephesus. He is thought to be the author of John's Gospel, the three letters that bear his name, and Revelation.
MATTHEW 4:21–22; MARK 3:17; 5:37–43; 10:35; 14:33; LUKE 9:28–54; JOHN 13:23; 19:26–27; ACTS 3–4; GALATIANS 2:9; 1 JOHN; 2 JOHN; 3 JOHN; REVELATION 1:9

## JOHN THE BAPTIST

Son of Zechariah and Elizabeth; cousin of Jesus, who was sent to prepare the people for the coming Messiah. He baptized Jesus; and criticized Herod Antipas for marrying Herodias, so was arrested and killed.
MATTHEW 3:1–15; 11:2–19; 14:1–12; MARK 6:17–29; LUKE 1:5–80; JOHN 1:6–36; 3:27–30

## JONAH

Prophet while Jeroboam II was king of Israel. God called him to preach to Nineveh but he ran away from God. A storm broke out and Jonah was thrown overboard from the ship he was in, to be swallowed by a great fish. He was vomited out onto dry land and obeyed God's second call to go to Nineveh, but was angry at Nineveh's repentance.
2 KINGS 14:25; JONAH; MATTHEW 12:39–41; 16:4; LUKE 11:29–32

## JONATHAN

■ Saul's eldest son, who became a close friend of David. He was a brave warrior who fought against the Philistines and saved David from being killed by Saul. Together with Saul, he was killed when the Israelites were defeated by the Philistines.
1 SAMUEL 13–14; 18–20; 23:16–18; 31:1–2; 2 SAMUEL 1
■ Son of Abiathar the high priest. He delivered vital information to David that helped David in his feud with Absalom.
2 SAMUEL 15:27–36
■ Brother of Judas Maccabeus.
1 MACCABEES 9:19–13:25; 2 MACCABEES 8:21–22

## JORAM

Son of Ahab of Israel, killed and succeeded by Jehu at the instigation of Elijah.
2 KINGS 3:1–8:15; 9:14–29

## JOSEPH

■ The first son of Rachel, and eleventh son of Jacob, who favoured him above his brothers, giving him a special robe. This, together with Joseph's dreams, which he interpreted as showing his superiority over his brothers, aroused their hostility and jealousy. He was sold into slavery by his brothers and became the slave of Potiphar. He resisted the temptations of Potiphar's wife but was falsely accused of seducing her. In prison, Joseph interpreted the dreams of his fellow inmates and the Pharaoh, who then made him second in command of Egypt. By means of his role in Egypt, Joseph preserved his family line. He tested his brothers when they came to buy grain, eventually revealing his identity to them and settling his family in Egypt.
GENESIS 30:22–24; 37–50; HEBREWS 11:22
■ Descendant of David; the husband of Mary mother of Jesus. An angel told him not to divorce his pregnant fiancée and that his child would be called Jesus. He fled with his family to Egypt after hearing of Herod's plans to murder new-born Hebrew boys. He later returned to work as a carpenter in Nazareth.
MATTHEW 1–2; 13:55; LUKE 1–2; JOHN 6:42
■ Also called Joses, brother or kinsman of Jesus.
MARK 6:3
■ Joseph of Arimathea, secret disciple of Jesus and member of the Jewish council. After Jesus' crucifixion, Joseph asked Pilate for Jesus' body, which he wrapped in a cloth and placed in a new tomb.
MATTHEW 27:57–60; LUKE 23:50–56; JOHN 19:38–42
■ Joseph Barsabbas. Candidate to fill the place of Judas Iscariot as one of the 12 apostles. Matthias was chosen instead.
ACTS 1:23

## JOSHUA

■ Son of Nun; Moses' successor as leader of Israel; led the Israelites into Canaan. He was one of the spies who believed the conquest was possible. He directed the military campaign and ensured adherence to the Law of Moses. Joshua divided the Promised Land among the 12 tribes of Israel. Before his death, he reminded the Israelites of God's commitment to them in a renewal of the covenant at Shechem.
EXODUS 17:9–14; NUMBERS 13–14; JOSHUA
■ After the exile, the high priest who, with Zerubbabel, was responsible for re-establishing the temple and its worship.
HAGGAI 1; ZECHARIAH 3:1–10; 6:11–15

## JOSIAH

Son of Amon and king of Judah; known for his righteousness and religious reforms. After the Book of the Law was discovered, he wept because of his people's rebellion. He reformed religion, renewed the covenant, and was killed by Pharaoh Neco at Megiddo.
2 KINGS 22:1–23:30, 34; 2 CHRONICLES 34:1–36:1

## JOTHAM

Son of Uzziah, king of Judah. Defeated the Ammonites.
2 KINGS 15:32–38; 2 CHRONICLES 27

## JUDAH

Jacob's fourth son by Leah, who became the ancestor of the royal tribe of Israel. Judah persuaded his brothers to sell Joseph to merchants on the way to Egypt rather than have him killed. Ancestor of David. The territory of Judah eventually became the Roman province of Judea.
GENESIS 29:35; 37:26–27; 38; 44:18–34; 49:8–12; 2 SAMUEL 2:4; MATTHEW 1:2–3; HEBREWS 7:14; REVELATION 5:5

## JUDAS

■ Relation of Jesus, man to whom the letter of Jude is attributed.
MATTHEW 13:55; MARK 6:3; JUDE 1
■ Son of James, one of the 12 apostles. Known as such in Luke's Gospel and Acts; called Thaddeus in Mark and Matthew.
MATTHEW 10:3; MARK 3:18; LUKE 6:16; JOHN 14:22; ACTS 1:13
■ Judas Iscariot, disciple who betrayed Jesus. He was the treasurer for the disciples and agreed to betray Jesus for 30 pieces of silver, identifying him with a kiss. He later committed suicide.
MATTHEW 10:4; 26:14–16; 27:3–5; JOHN 6:70–71; 12:1–8; 13:21–30; 18:2–5; ACTS 1:16–25
■ Judas Barsabbas. Sent to Antioch by the Christians, together with Silas, Paul, and Barnabas, conveying the decisions of the Council of Jerusalem.
ACTS 15:22
■ Judas Maccabeus. Son of Mattathias, leader of a Jewish rebellion in response to the actions of the Greek king of the Seleucid Empire, Antiochus Epiphanes, who had ransacked Jerusalem and desecrated the temple. Antiochus wanted to force the Jewish people to adopt a Greek way of life. Judas died on the battlefield in 161 BC.
1 MACCABEES 2–9; 2 MACCABEES 2:19; 5:27; 8; 10–15

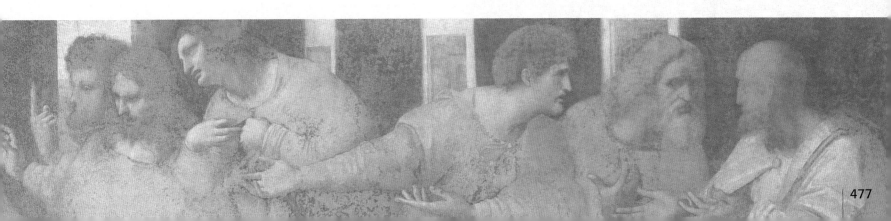

**JUDE** *see Judas*

## JUDITH
Beautiful, godly, and brave widow from Judah who cut off the head of Nebuchadnezzar's general, Holofernes. She decapitated him with his sword.
JUDITH

## JULIUS
Roman centurion charged with accompanying Paul to Caesarea from Rome.
ACTS 27:1, 3, 6, 42–44

## JUSTUS
■ Owner of the house Paul stayed in during his time in Corinth.
ACTS 18:7
■ Alternative name for Joseph Barsabbas.
*See also Joseph Barsabbas.*
ACTS 1:23

# K

## KEDORLAOMER
King of Elam who led a punitive raid against Sodom and Gomorrah. He was later pursued and killed by Abraham.
GENESIS 14

## KETURAH
Abraham's second wife, who he married after Sarah's death. Possibly the same person as Hagar, suggesting that Abraham may have sought her out after the death of Sarah.
GENESIS 25:1; 1 CHRONICLES 1:32–33

## KISH
Father of King Saul.
1 SAMUEL 9:1–5

## KOHATH
Son of Levi, head of the Kohathite clans, and an ancestor of Moses.
EXODUS 6:16; NUMBERS 3:17

## KORAH
Grandson of Kohath, a leader who conspired with Dathan and Abiram against Moses and Aaron. He died because of his rejection of God's chosen leaders. His descendants were singers and gatekeepers at the Temple of Jerusalem.
NUMBERS 16; 1 CHRONICLES 6:37; 9:19; PSALM 42; 44–49; 84–85; 87–88; JUDE 11

# L

## LABAN
Rebekah's brother and Jacob's uncle, who tricked him into marrying his elder daughter, Leah, instead of Rachel. Jacob was later able to cheat his uncle, with the result that his own flock of sheep and goats became larger and stronger than his uncle's. When Jacob secretly left for Canaan, Laban gave chase but God warned him in a dream not to harm Jacob and so they reconciled their differences and went their own ways.
GENESIS 24:29; 29–31

## LAMECH
■ Descendant of Cain and first man to commit polygamy.
GENESIS 4:18–24
■ Noah's father.
GENESIS 5:28–31

## LAZARUS
■ Brother of Martha and Mary, whom Jesus raised from the dead. His body had been in the tomb for four days when Jesus commanded the onlookers to roll away the stone in front of it. Lazarus walked free from the cave tomb.
JOHN 11:1–12:11
■ Beggar in Jesus' parable of the rich man and the beggar at his gate.
LUKE 16:19–31

## LEAH
Elder daughter of Laban, who became Jacob's first wife and mother of six of his sons and his daughter, Dinah.
GENESIS 29:16–35

## LEVI
■ Third son of Jacob and Leah, also called Matthew. He was cursed by his father when he killed the male inhabitants of Shechem with his brother Simeon in revenge for the rape of their sister Dinah. The tribe descended from him was responsible for the tabernacle.
*See also Matthew.*
GENESIS 29:34; 34; 49:5–7; NUMBERS 1:47–53; 26:57–62

## LOIS
Jewish grandmother of Timothy.
2 TIMOTHY 1:5

## LOT
Abraham's nephew, who chose to live in Sodom after parting from Abraham. Later, when Sodom was destroyed, Lot escaped, but his wife looked back at the city and was turned into a pillar of salt. Lot went to live in a cave with his daughters who, afraid of never finding husbands, seduced their father and bore him sons, Moab and Ammon (Ben-Ammi).
GENESIS 11:31–14:16; 19

## LUKE
Greek author of the third Gospel and Acts. A doctor and Paul's companion, he accompanied Paul on his missionary journeys.
LUKE; ACTS; COLOSSIANS 4:14; 2 TIMOTHY 4:11; PHILEMON 24

## LYDIA
Businesswoman from Thyatira who was converted by Paul's teaching at Philippi.
ACTS 16:14–15, 40

# M

## MAHER-SHALAL-HASH-BAZ
Son of the prophet Isaiah.
ISAIAH 8:3–4

## MALACHI
Prophet; author of the book of Malachi, his name means "my messenger".
MALACHI

## MALCHUS
Servant of the high priest whose ear Peter cut off as Jesus was arrested in the Garden of Gethsemane. According to Luke, Jesus then healed his ear.
LUKE 22:50–51; JOHN 18:10

## MANASSEH
■ Joseph's elder son; ancestor of one of the tribes of Israel, given land on both sides of the Jordan.
GENESIS 41:51; 48:13–20; JOSHUA 13:6–8, 29–31; 17:7–13
■ Son of Hezekiah, king of Judah. He encouraged pagan worship and persecuted prophets, but later he repented and reformed worship.
2 KINGS 21:1–18; 2 CHRONICLES 33:1–20

## MANOAH
Father of Samson, told by an angel that his barren wife would bear him a son.
JUDGES 13

## MARK
Cousin of Barnabas who joined him and Paul in Jerusalem and accompanied them on their missionary journeys. Barnabas separated from Paul to go his separate way with Mark after an argument with Paul. It is thought that Mark was the author of Mark's Gospel.
ACTS 12:12; 13:13; 15:37–39; COLOSSIANS 4:10; 2 TIMOTHY 4:11; PHILEMON 24

## MARTHA
Sister of Mary and Lazarus, in whose house Jesus stayed while in Bethany. Jesus restored Martha's brother Lazarus to life.
LUKE 10:38–42; JOHN 11:1–12:2

## MARY
■ Mother of Jesus and wife of Joseph. She was visited by the Archangel Gabriel, who told her that she would conceive a child by the Holy Spirit and give birth to a son who would be the Son of God and the Messiah. She witnessed Jesus' crucifixion and was entrusted to the care of John the apostle.
LUKE 1–2; JOHN 2:1–11; 19:25–27; ACTS 1:14
■ Sister of Martha and Lazarus; she anointed Jesus.
LUKE 10:38–42; JOHN 11:1–44; 12:1–8
■ Mary Magdalene, who was healed by Jesus and was first to see him after his resurrection.
MATTHEW 27:55–56; 28:1–10; LUKE 8:2; 24:1–10; JOHN 20:10–18
■ Mother of James and John; wife of Clopas and probably the sister of Mary mother of Jesus.
MATTHEW 27:56, 28:1; MARK 16:1; JOHN 19:25
■ Mother of Mark.
ACTS 12:12

## MATTATHIAS
Founder of the Maccabean (Hasmonean) dynasty.
1 MACCABEES 2

## MATTHEW
Son of Alphaeus; also called Levi. Matthew was a tax collector and became one of the 12 apostles. He was the author of the first Gospel.
MATTHEW 9:9–13; 10:3; LUKE 5:27–32

## MATTHIAS
Man chosen to take the place of Judas Iscariot as the twelfth apostle.
ACTS 1:21–26

## MELCHIZEDEK
Priest and king of Salem, who met and blessed Abraham. In the New Testament Jesus is described as a high priest and king like Melchizedek.
GENESIS 14:18–20; PSALM 110:4; HEBREWS 5:6–10; 7:11–17

## MENAHEM
One of the last kings of Israel, who approved idol worship. He paid the Assyrians money to remain in power.
2 KINGS 15:14–22

## MEPHIBOSHETH
Grandson of Saul and son of Jonathan, crippled from a fall but honoured by David for Jonathan's sake.
2 SAMUEL 4:4; 9; 16:1–4; 19:24–30

## MERARI
One of Levi's sons. He went on to form the Merarites.
EXODUS 6:16; NUMBERS 3:17, 33–37

## MESHACH
One of Daniel's friends who was exiled to Babylon. He was thrown into a furnace on the orders of Nebuchadnezzar but was protected by God and survived the flames.
DANIEL 1:3–7; 2:49; 3

## METHUSELAH
Grandfather of Noah; lived for 969 years.
GENESIS 5:21–27

## MICAH
Prophet in Isaiah's time who spoke out against injustice and idolatry, and declared a future of hope and restoration.
JEREMIAH 26:18–19; MICAH

## MICAIAH
Prophet summoned by Ahab for prophesying Ahab's defeat by the Assyrians, a prophesy which came true.
1 KINGS 22:1–37; 2 CHRONICLES 18:1–27

## MICHAEL
Archangel seen as the one who protects God's people; defeats Satan in Revelation.
DANIEL 10:13, 21; 12:1; JUDE 9; REVELATION 12:7–9

## MICHAL
Saul's daughter, the wife of David, who helped him escape Saul, but disapproved of him dancing before the Ark. She was condemned never to have a child.
1 SAMUEL 14:49; 18:20–29; 25:44; 2 SAMUEL 3:13–16; 6:16–23

## MIRIAM
Elder sister of Moses and Aaron. She saw Moses as a baby in the bulrushes, and sang in triumph at the crossing of the Red Sea when the Israelites left Egypt. She became jealous of Moses and was temporarily punished with a skin disease for her rebellion against him. Moses then asked God to forgive and heal her.
EXODUS 2:4–8; 15:20–21; NUMBERS 12; 20:1

## MOAB
Son of Lot's daughter fathered by Lot, and the ancestor of the Moabites.
GENESIS 19:36–37

## MORDECAI
Uncle to Queen Esther, who prompted her to act and save the Jewish people from massacre after he had heard of a plot to kill them. He led the Jewish people to celebrate their survival; the celebration became known as the feast of *Purim*.
ESTHER 2–10

## MOSES
Great leader and law-giver of the Jewish people, who fulfilled the roles of prophet, priest, and intercessor for the people. As a baby he was put into the River Nile in a basket, but was found and brought up by Pharaoh's daughter. As a young man Moses killed an Egyptian and fled to Midian where he married Zipporah. God called him at the burning bush and after some hesitation he accepted that call. He pleaded with Pharaoh to set the people free and God sent plagues as judgment on the Egyptians, after which Moses led the people out of Egypt. He was faithful to God and miraculously brought water out of a rock. God spoke the words of the Law to Moses on Mount Sinai, and Moses recorded them on stone tablets. However, Moses broke the tablets when he saw the Israelites worshipping the golden calf. He led God's people through the wilderness and oversaw the building of the tabernacle. He was criticized by Aaron, Miriam, and Korah. He sent spies to investigate Canaan but was not allowed to enter Canaan himself because of his disobedience to God.
EXODUS; NUMBERS; DEUTERONOMY; MATTHEW 17:3–4; 19:7–8; JOHN 1:17, 45; 3:14; 5:45–46; ACTS 7:20–44; 1 CORINTHIANS 10:2; 2 CORINTHIANS 3:7–15; HEBREWS 3:1–5; 11:23–28; 12:21; REVELATION 15:3

# N

## NAAMAN
Syrian army commander healed of leprosy by Elisha after his king sent him to Israel to find a cure.
2 KINGS 5

## NABAL
Husband of Abigail, and the landowner who refused David's request for hospitality. David planned to punish him, but Abigail appeased him. Nabal died soon after, and Abigail became David's wife.
1 SAMUEL 25

## NABOTH
Landowner who was killed so that Ahab could seize Nahboth's vineyard, which he coveted. Ahab's wife, Jezebel, persuaded religious leaders to convict Naboth of blasphemy. He was stoned to death, and Elijah warned Ahab that he and his family would be punished.
1 KINGS 21

## NADAB
■ Eldest son of Aaron, who became a priest but was later killed for dishonouring God.
EXODUS 6:23; LEVITICUS 10:1–3; NUMBERS 3:2–4; 26:60–61
■ Successor to his father, Jeroboam I, as king of Israel. He was assassinated by Baasha.
1 KINGS 15:25–31

## NAHOR
Abraham's brother, and son of Terah. He settled at Haran with his wife, Milcah. Nahor became the ancestor of several Aramaean tribes.
GENESIS 11:26; 22:20–24

## NAHUM
Prophet who prophesied against Nineveh.
NAHUM

## NAOMI
Mother-in-law of Ruth, from Bethlehem. She returned to Bethlehem with Ruth after the death of her two sons.
RUTH 1–4

## NAPHTALI
One of Jacob's 12 sons, ancestor of one of the tribes of Israel.
GENESIS 30:8; 49:21

## NATHAN
Prophet who declared God's promise to David of a dynasty that would last for ever, and who delivered God's judgment to David after he had committed adultery with Bathsheba. Nathan helped make Solomon king.
2 SAMUEL 7:1–17; 12:1–15; 1 KINGS 1; 1 CHRONICLES 17:1–15

## NATHANAEL
One of the 12 apostles named in John's Gospel; probably the Bartholomew mentioned by other Gospel writers.
JOHN 1:45–51; 21:2

## NEBUCHADNEZZAR
King of Babylon who captured Jerusalem, took Judah into exile, and destroyed Jerusalem. Daniel interpreted his dreams, and was made one of the king's courtiers. He was a great builder of temples, canals, and palaces. God humbled him with a temporary madness after which he honoured God.
2 KINGS 24–25; 2 CHRONICLES 36; JEREMIAH 21–52; EZEKIEL 26:7; 29:18–20; 30:10; DANIEL 1–5

## NEBUZARADAN
Nebuchadnezzar's head guard, who had the responsibility of sending the Judeans into exile in Babylon after Jerusalem had been captured. He burnt down the Temple, and the city was reduced to ruins. He treated Jeremiah kindly, allowing him to stay in Judah.
2 KINGS 25:8–20; JEREMIAH 39:9–40:5

## NECO
Egyptian pharaoh who killed Josiah in battle at Megiddo, deposed Jehoahaz, and put Jehoiakim on Judah's throne. He was defeated by Nebuchadnezzar, after which Judah came under Babylonian power.
2 KINGS 23:29–35; 2 CHRONICLES 35:20–36:4

## NEHEMIAH
Cupbearer to the Persian king Artaxerxes. Known for his prayer and action; he returned to Jerusalem and organized the rebuilding of the city walls. He also re-ordered religious life.
NEHEMIAH

## NERO
Roman emperor from AD 54 to 68 to whom Paul appealed. Peter and Paul were probably martyred when Nero was Caesar.
ACTS 25:11

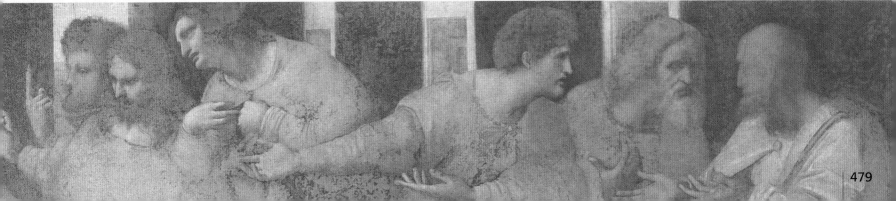

479

## NICODEMUS

Pharisee who came secretly to Jesus, who told Nicodemus that a person could only enter the kingdom of God if he or she is reborn spiritually. Nicodemus later defended Jesus when the Pharisees called for his arrest. He helped Joseph of Arimathea to bury Jesus' body, and brought spices and oils to embalm the body.
JOHN 3:1–21; 7:50–51; 19:39–40

## NIMROD

Grandson of Ham, and known as a great hunter and warrior.
GENESIS 10:8–9

## NOAH

Godly man in a time of great evil, who obeyed God's instructions to build an ark. Noah's ark meant that he was able to save himself, his family, and representatives of the animal species from the flood that destroyed the rest of humanity. After the flood, God promised he would not destroy the Earth again.
GENESIS 6–9; MATTHEW 24:37–39; HEBREWS 11:7; 1 PETER 3:20–21

# O

## OBADIAH

■ Steward from Ahab's household who hid 100 prophets of God to try and save them from Jezebel.
1 KINGS 18:1–16
■ Prophet whose message against Edom is recorded in the book of Obadiah.
OBADIAH

## OBED

Son of Ruth and Boaz, grandfather of David.
RUTH 4:17

## OBED-EDOM

Philistine in whose house the Ark of the Covenant remained after the death of Uzzah.
2 SAMUEL 6:10–12; 1 CHRONICLES 13:12–14

## OG

Amorite king of Bashan, east of the River Jordan. He was conquered by the Israelites and his land was given to the tribes of Reuben and Gad and the half-tribe of Manasseh.
NUMBERS 21:33–35; DEUTERONOMY 3:1–13; NEHEMIAH 9:22

## OMRI

Powerful king of Israel who made Samaria his capital. He was declared king after Zimri had killed Elah. He tolerated the worship of Baal.
1 KINGS 16:15–30

## ONESIMUS

Runaway slave, owned by Philemon, who became a Christian and helped Paul in prison. Paul sent Onesimus back to his owner with a letter asking him to be pardoned, set free, and sent back to Paul.
COLOSSIANS 4:9; PHILEMON 10–18

## OTHNIEL

One of the first judges in Israel, who stopped the Israelites worshipping Baal.
JOSHUA 15:16–17; JUDGES 3:7–11

# P

## PASHHUR

Priest who put Jeremiah in the stocks for saying that Jerusalem would be destroyed.
JEREMIAH 20:1–6

## PAUL

Apostle, previously called Saul. A Roman citizen from Tarsus and a Pharisee who had been taught by Gamaliel, he approved of Stephen's death and persecuted Christians. He experienced a dramatic conversion when he had a vision of Jesus on the road to Damascus. He then spent some years in Arabia, after which he was introduced to the apostles in Jerusalem by Barnabas. Paul zealously spread the Christian message and undertook missionary journeys, with friends such as Barnabas and Silas. He supported himself by tent-making. Paul had a particular calling to share the gospel among Gentiles. He encountered much opposition, including being stoned, but also encountered miracles – he was released from prison and raised Eutychus to life. Paul was arrested, but appealed as a Roman citizen and was brought before the Sanhedrin, Felix, Festus, and Agrippa. He was sent to Rome, was shipwrecked on the way and was then placed under house arrest. Paul wrote many letters, especially to churches he had founded. These letters form part of the New Testament.
ACTS 9–28; ROMANS; 1 CORINTHIANS; 2 CORINTHIANS; GALATIANS; EPHESIANS; PHILIPPIANS; COLOSSIANS; 1 THESSALONIANS; 2 THESSALONIANS; 1 TIMOTHY; 2 TIMOTHY; TITUS; PHILEMON

## PEKAH

Captain in Pekahiah's army who became king of Israel after assassinating his predecessor Pekahiah c.735 BC. He worshipped idols, and was murdered by Hoshea three years after seizing power.
2 KINGS 15:27–31

## PEKAHIAH

King of Israel, assassinated by Pekah.
2 KINGS 15:23–26

## PENINNAH

Elkanah's second wife, who taunted the childless Hannah.
1 SAMUEL 1:2–4

## PETER

Originally called Simon; brother of Andrew, a fisherman, and one of the 12 apostles. With James and John, Peter was part of Jesus' inner circle of disciples. He was present at the raising of Jairus' daughter, at Christ's transfiguration, and in the Garden of Gethsemane. Peter acted as the spokesman for the disciples and tended to be impetuous, sometimes speaking before thinking matters through. He made the significant confession that Jesus was Christ, after which Jesus gave him the name Peter (meaning "rock"). However, when Jesus was arrested Peter denied him three times. After his resurrection, Jesus restored and recommissioned Peter. Peter exercised leadership in the early church, preaching powerfully at Pentecost, and exercising the gift of healing, for which he was imprisoned. One stumbling block for Peter was that he saw Christ's message as limited to the Jews, but God gave him a vision that led him to the Gentile Cornelius, and he came to support the mission to the Gentiles. Later, Peter was criticized by Paul at Antioch. Traditionally regarded as the author of 1 and 2 Peter. Peter is thought to have been martyred in Rome.
MATTHEW 4:18; 16:13–20; 26:33–38, 58, 69–75; MARK 1:16–18; LUKE 5:3–11; 9:28–36; JOHN 1:40–42; 21; ACTS 1:13–15; 2–5; 8:14–25; 10–12; 15:7–11; 1 CORINTHIANS 1:12; 9:5; GALATIANS 2:11–21;1 PETER; 2 PETER

## PHILEMON

Christian owner of the slave Onesimus, to whom Paul wrote his letter.
PHILEMON

## PHILIP

■ One of the 12 apostles, Philip came from Bethsaida in Galilee.
MATTHEW 10:3; JOHN 1:43–48; 6:5–7; 12:21–22; 14:8–9; ACTS 1:13
■ Son of Herod the Great and first husband of Herodias.
MARK 6:17–29
■ Second son of Herod, tetrarch of Iturea.
LUKE 3:1
■ Deacon and evangelist of the early church who spoke to an Ethiopian official. Paul stayed with him in Caesarea.
ACTS 6:5; 8:4–40; 21:8–9

## PHINEHAS

■ Priest and grandson of Aaron, who killed some Israelites when they began worshipping idols instead of God.
EXODUS 6:25; NUMBERS 25:7–13; 31:6; JOSHUA 22:13; JUDGES 20:28
■ Son of Eli, killed by the Philistines when they captured the Ark of the Covenant.
1 SAMUEL 1:3; 2:12–17, 34; 4:11

## PHOEBE

Christian woman deacon known by Paul, who worked in a church in Cenchreae, near Corinth. Benefactor of the early church and probably the person who took Paul's letter to the church in Rome.
ROMANS 16:1–2

## PILATE

Roman procurator of Judea who presided over the trial of Jesus. He interrogated Jesus, was aware of his innocence, but weakly gave way to the crowds, refusing to be responsible for Jesus' death and releasing Barabbas instead. Later, he allowed Joseph to take Jesus' body away, ordering a guard to keep watch over Jesus' tomb.
MATTHEW 27:11–26; MARK 15:1–15; LUKE 3:1; 13:1; 23:1–25; JOHN 18:28–19:16

## POTIPHAR

Egyptian officer in Pharaoh's guard who bought Joseph as a slave. Potiphar's wife wanted Joseph to sleep with her. He refused and was imprisoned, charged with rape.
GENESIS 37:36; 39

**PRISCLLLA** *see Aquila and Priscllla*

**PUL** *see Tiglath–Pileser III*

# Q

## QUEEN OF SHEBA
Queen who visited Solomon in Jerusalem, to verify his riches and wisdom, and who gave him gifts of gold and spices.
**1 KINGS** 10:1–13

## QUIRINIUS
Governor of the province of Syria at the time of the census when Jesus was born.
**LUKE** 2:2

# R

## RACHEL
Laban's daughter who married Jacob. In order to marry her, Jacob had worked for seven years without pay. Rachel was loved more than her older sister Leah, Jacob's first wife. The mother of Joseph and Benjamin, Rachel died giving birth to Benjamin.
**GENESIS** 29:9–31:35; 35:16–20

## RAHAB
Prostitute from Jericho who hid Joshua's two spies. In return, the spies promised that no harm would come to her and her family when Jericho was captured.
**JOSHUA** 2:1–21; 6:22–23; **MATTHEW** 1:5; **HEBREWS** 11:31; **JAMES** 2:25

## REBEKAH
Wife of Isaac, brought to him by Abraham's servant, Eliezer, and mother of twin boys, Esau and Jacob. Jacob (the younger) was her favourite, and she tricked Isaac into blessing him instead of Esau.
**GENESIS** 24; 25:19–26:16; 27

## REHOBOAM
Solomon's son, under whom the Kingdom of Israel was divided. The northern kingdom became known as Israel, and the southern kingdom as Judah. Rehoboam was the first king of Judah.
**1 KINGS** 12:1–24; 14:21–31; **2 CHRONICLES** 10–12

## REUBEN
Eldest of Jacob's sons, who tried to save Joseph when his brothers were plotting to kill him. Ancestor of one of the tribes of Israel.
**GENESIS** 29:32; 37:19–22; 42:22, 37; 49:3–4

## REZIN
Syria's last king, who made a pact with King Pekah of Israel. He was killed by Tiglath–Pileser III of Assyria.
**2 KINGS** 15:37–16:6; **ISAIAH** 7:1–8; 8:3–6

## RHODA
Girl who was so astounded to hear Peter's voice at the door after he had escaped from prison that she forgot to let him in.
**ACTS** 12:13–14

## RIZPAH
Saul's concubine, whose sons David gave to the Gibeonites to put to death.
**2 SAMUEL** 3:7; 21:8–12

## RUTH
Moabite woman whose faithful love for her mother-in-law, Naomi, led her to emigrate to Bethlehem. She met Boaz, becoming his wife, and had a son, Obed, who was the grandfather of King David.
**RUTH** 1–4

# S

## SALOME
■ Daughter of Herodias, but not actually named in the Bible. Her dance in front of Herod Antipas so pleased him that he promised her anything she desired. Herodias, angered by John the Baptist's public criticism of her marriage to Antipas, told her to demand the head of John the Baptist.
**MATTHEW** 14:1–12; **MARK** 6:14–29
■ Mother of James and John; she accompanied Jesus and the disciples from Galilee. She was present at Christ's crucifixion and on the resurrection morning.
**MARK** 15:40–41; 16:1

## SAMSON
Judge and leader of Israel for 20 years. Set apart as a Nazirite from birth, Samson was given great strength for which he became famous. He married a Philistine and avenged himself on the Philistines when his wife was taken away from him. His strength was demonstrated by killing a lion and also killing 1,000 Philistines with a jaw-bone. He fell in love with Delilah but was betrayed by her when she discovered the secret of his strength. He died bringing down the temple of Dagon on himself and the Philistines.
**JUDGES** 13–16

## SAMUEL
Prophet; his mother was Hannah, who promised to set him apart for God. As a child, Samuel was brought up by Eli in the temple, where he heard God's call. He was a leader of Israel and was victorious over the Philistines. The people persisted in asking for a king as other nations had, so Samuel anointed Saul as king, rebuking him later for his disobedience, and later again anointing David as king.
**1 SAMUEL** 1–25

## SANBALLAT
Persistent Samaritan opponent of Nehemiah's attempt to rebuild the walls of Jerusalem.
**NEHEMIAH** 2:10, 19; 4:1–9; 6

## SAPPHIRA
With her husband Ananias, she was guilty of deceiving the church.
**ACTS** 5:1–11

## SARAH
■ Wife of Abraham, who remained childless until old age, when she gave birth to Isaac. Sarah sent her maid Hagar, together with Abraham's son by Hagar, Ishmael, away after Isaac's birth. When she died, Abraham bought a cave near Hebron as her burial chamber.
**GENESIS** 11:29–30; 12:10–20; 16–23; **GALATIANS** 4:21-31; **HEBREWS** 11:11
■ Daughter of Raguel who married Tobias.
**TOBIT** 3–12

## SARGON
Assyrian king; son of Tiglath-Pileser III, who was king when Samaria fell.
**ISAIAH** 20:1

## SAUL
■ First king of united Israel; he was chosen by God and anointed by Samuel. He enjoyed military successes but was rebuked by Samuel for his disobedience and then rejected as king. David, son of Jesse, used music to calm Saul's troubled spirit, and was later sent to fight the giant Goliath. Saul gave his daughter Michal to David as his wife, but became jealous when David became more popular than him, so he plotted to kill David. Saul consulted a medium at Endor and was later defeated by the Philistines at Gilboa. Critically injured, he committed suicide.
**1 SAMUEL** 8– 31; **2 SAMUEL** 1–21
■ *See Paul.*

## SENNACHERIB
King of Assyria whose army besieged Hezekiah in Jerusalem. On Isaiah's advice, Hezekiah refused to surrender, and the Assyrian army came under attack from the Egyptians from the south. Sennacherib returned to Assyria, where he was assassinated by two of his sons.
**2 KINGS** 18:13–19:37; **2 CHRONICLES** 3; **ISAIAH** 36–37

## SETH
Third son of Adam and Eve, who was born after Cain had murdered Abel.
**GENESIS** 4:25

## SHADRACH
One of Daniel's friends who was exiled to Babylon. He was thrown into a furnace on the orders of Nebuchadnezzar but was protected by God and survived the flames.
**DANIEL** 1:3–7; 2:49; 3

## SHALLUM
■ Usurping king of Israel who reigned for only one month *c.*745 BC before being assassinated by Menahem.
**2 KINGS** 15:13–15
■ One of King Josiah's sons.
*See Jehoahaz 2.*

## SHALMANESER V
Assyrian king who succeeded Tiglath-Pileser III of Assyria; ruled *c.*727–722 BC. He captured Samaria and took the Israelites into exile.
**2 KINGS** 17–18

## SHAMGAR
One of Israel's judges.
**JUDGES** 3:31; 5:6

## SHAPHAN
Official of Josiah who reported to him the discovery of the book of God's law.
**2 KINGS** 22:3–14; **2 CHRONICLES** 34:8–18

## SHEBNA
State official under Hezekiah who talked with King Sennacherib's Assyrian delegation.
**2 KINGS** 18–19; **ISAIAH** 22:15–25; 36:2–37:2

## SHECHEM
Son of King Hamor, who raped Jacob's daughter, Dinah.
**GENESIS** 34:1–31

## SHEM
Eldest of Noah's three sons.
**GENESIS** 6–11

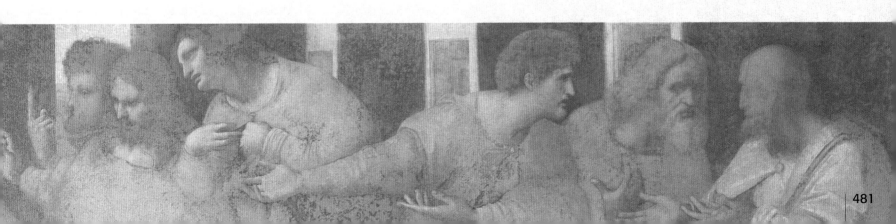

## SHESHBAZZAR

Leader of the exiled Jews, who led the people back to Jerusalem c.537 BC after the Persian King Cyrus allowed them to return. Sheshbazzar laid the foundations for the second Temple in Jerusalem.
EZRA 1:8; 5:14; 1 ESDRAS 2:12

## SHIMEI

Benjamite who cursed David at the time of Absalom's rebellion and accused David of murdering Saul.
2 SAMUEL 16:5; 19:16–23; 1 KINGS 2:8–9

## SHISHAK

Egyptian pharaoh at the time of Solomon and the division of the kingdom between Jeroboam I and Rehoboam. Shishak attacked Jerusalem, carrying off the treasures of the Temple and royal palace.
1 KINGS 11:40; 14:25–26;
2 CHRONICLES 12:2–9

## SIHON

Amorite king east of the River Jordan in the 13th century BC. His land was defeated by the Israelites after he refused to allow Moses and his people to pass through to reach Canaan.
NUMBERS 21:21–35; 32:33; DEUTERONOMY 2:24–35; 1 KINGS 4:19; NEHEMIAH 9:22

## SILAS

Also called Silvanus; leader of the Jerusalem church who accompanied Paul on his second missionary journey and acted as his secretary for some of the letters to the churches.
ACTS 15:22–18:22; 2 CORINTHIANS 1:19; 1 THESSALONIANS 1:1; 2 THESSALONIANS 1:1; 1 PETER 5:12

## SIMEON

■ One of Jacob's 12 sons, ancestor of one of the tribes of Israel, who was left as a hostage with Joseph in Egypt. He and his brother Levi avenged the rape of their sister, Dinah, by the Shechemites. Jacob rebuked them on his deathbed.
GENESIS 29:33; 34–35; 42:24; 49:5–7
■ Devout old man in the New Testament, who gave two prophecies about the baby Jesus. In the temple he held the infant Jesus in his arms and praised God.
LUKE 2:25–35

## SIMON

■ Simon Peter.
*See also Peter.*
■ Simon the Zealot, one of the 12 apostles.
MATTHEW 10:4; ACTS 1:13
■ One of Jesus' brothers or half-brothers.
MATTHEW 13:55
■ Simon the leper, to whose house at Bethany Jesus was invited. While Jesus was there, a woman anointed his head with oil.
MATTHEW 26:6; MARK 14:3
■ Pharisee who invited Jesus to his house where a woman wept at Jesus' feet, then dried them with her hair.
LUKE 7:40–44
■ Simon of Cyrene, who helped Jesus to carry his cross.
MATTHEW 27:32; MARK 15:21–22; LUKE 23:26
■ Simon Magus. Sorcerer who tried to buy the gift of the Spirit from the apostles but was told that God's power could not be gained by money.
ACTS 8:9–24
■ Tanner in whose house at Joppa Peter had his vision.
ACTS 9:43

## SISERA

Canaanite army commander who oppressed the Israelites for many years. He was killed by Jael, who drove a tent nail through his head after he took refuge in her tent, having been defeated by Deborah and Barak.
JUDGES 4; 5:20, 26

## SOLOMON

Son of David and Bathsheba who became the third king of united Israel. He was appointed by David. Solomon was humble enough to ask God for wisdom and he was given wisdom and discernment for settling disputes. Writer of proverbs, a few psalms, and the Song of Songs. He moved Israel from tribal organization to centralized government. Solomon built the temple at Jerusalem, bringing the Ark into it and dedicating it to God. He established a shipping fleet and was known for his great wealth; the Queen of Sheba visited him to verify his wealth and wisdom. However, he did not follow God completely, sacrificing to pagan gods and his many foreign wives turned him away from God: this led to the division of the kingdom shortly after his death.
1 KINGS 1–11; 2 CHRONICLES 1–9

## SOSTHENES

Ruler of the synagogue at Corinth, who was attacked after failing to persuade the Roman governor Gallio to imprison Paul.
ACTS 18:17

## STEPHEN

One of seven deacons chosen to take care of practical matters in the church at Jerusalem. He became the first Christian martyr, killed by stoning for speaking against the temple and against the Law and customs of Moses. Saul (Paul), who was persecuting Christians at this time, was a witness to Stephen's death.
ACTS 6–7

## SUSANNA

Wife of the wealthy Joakim, who was tricked by two elders wishing to have intercourse with her. They said she had been with a younger man, and for this she was condemned to death. But Daniel saved her by questioning the elders, and finding out they were liars when each gave a different answer.
SUSANNA

# T

## TABITHA

Woman from Joppa noted for her good works. She was raised from the dead by Peter. Her Greek name was Dorcas.
ACTS 9:36–43

## TAMAR

■ Daughter-in-law of Judah who was married to Er and, after his death, his younger brother, Onan. Onan refused to continue the family line and so was punished by death. When Judah withheld his third son from marriage with Tamar, believing her to be cursed, Tamar pretended to be a prostitute, and became pregnant by Judah, giving birth to twins, Perez and Zerah. Tamar was an ancestor of David and is mentioned in the genealogy of Jesus.
GENESIS 38; RUTH 4:12; MATTHEW 1:3
■ David's daughter, who was raped by Amnon, her half-brother. She was avenged by her brother Absalom.
2 SAMUEL 13

## TERAH

Father of Abraham. He led the migration from Ur with Abraham, but chose to settle in Haran instead of continuing to Canaan.
GENESIS 11:27–32

## TERTULLUS

Orator who was hired by the high priest Ananias to lay accusations against Paul, claiming that Paul had created a disturbance that was an offence against the Roman government.
ACTS 24:1–8

## THADDEUS

Named as one of the 12 apostles in Matthew and Mark's gospel. Probably the same person as Judas.
*See also Judas 2.*
MATTHEW 10:3; MARK 3:18; LUKE 6:16; ACTS 1:13

## THEOPHILUS

Roman man to whom the Gospel of Luke and the Acts of the Apostles were addressed. He may have been high ranking. The name means "friend [or lover] of God".
LUKE 1:3; ACTS 1:1

## THOMAS

One of Jesus' 12 apostles, known as Didymus, the twin. Absent when the others first saw the risen Christ, he doubted them, refusing to believe in Christ's resurrection, saying that he would have to touch the wounds before he could believe Jesus had risen. Jesus then appeared to him and Thomas believed. According to tradition, Thomas became a missionary to India.
JOHN 11:16; 14:5–7; 20:24–29; 21:1–2; ACTS 1:13

## TIBERIUS

Roman emperor in Jesus' lifetime. He ruled from AD 14 to 37, and was succeeded by Caligula. In the Gospels he is simply referred to as Caesar.
LUKE 3:1; JOHN 19:12

## TIGLATH-PILESER III

Powerful king of Assyria who first invaded Israel while Menahem was king; in Pekah's reign, he deported people to Assyria. Later, Ahaz turned to him for help against Syria and Israel. Also known as Pul.
2 KINGS 15:19–29; 16:7–10;
2 CHRONICLES 28:20

## TIMOTHY

A disciple from Lystra, converted under Paul's ministry, who became Paul's close companion and fellow missionary. Timothy's mother and grandmother nurtured his faith. Having a Gentile father, Timothy was circumcised by Paul to help Paul's mission among Jews. He accompanied Paul on the second missionary journey, went with Paul to Jerusalem and led the church in Ephesus. Known for lacking confidence, he needed encouragement. He is associated with Paul in the letters to the Thessalonians and to Philemon. Paul addresses letters to him which encourage him to stand firm in the faith.
ACTS 16:1–3; 16:2–18:22; 19:22; 20:4; 1 CORINTHIANS 4:17; PHILIPPIANS 2:19–22; 1 TIMOTHY; 2 TIMOTHY; 1 THESSALONIANS 1:1; 3:2; 2 THESSALONIANS 1:1; PHILEMON 1.

## TITUS

Gentile converted under Paul's ministry and his close companion and fellow missionary. Known for his tactfulness, for example in healing the division between Paul and the Corinthian church, he organized financial gifts for other needy believers. Paul entrusted him with strengthening the church at Crete. Paul's letter to Titus provides direction on appointing leaders and teaching different groups within the church, dealing with opposition, and instructions on integrity in living.
2 CORINTHIANS 7:6–15; 8:6–24; TITUS

## TOBIAH

An official in Jerusalem who opposed Nehemiah's attempt to rebuild the city walls.
NEHEMIAH 2:10; 4:3, 7; 6:1–14; 13:4

## TOBIAS

Tobit's son.
TOBIT 1:9–14:15

## TOBIT

A kind and godly Jewish man from the tribe of Naphtali; he helped many Jews during the Assyrian oppression. He was accidentally blinded, but God restored his eyesight, his riches, and his reputation. He taught his son Tobias how he should live; died aged 112 and was buried in Nineveh.
TOBIT 1–14

## TUBAL-CAIN

Lamech's son by his second wife, Zilpah.
GENESIS 4:22

## TYCHICHUS

Christian who went with Paul on his last visit to Jerusalem. He was a messenger for Paul when the apostle was imprisoned in Rome, taking his letters to Colossae and Ephesus.
ACTS 20:4; EPHESIANS 6:21–22; COLOSSIANS 4:7–9; 2 TIMOTHY 4:12; TITUS 3:12

# U

## URIAH

Hittite warrior in David's army, and Bathsheba's husband. He was sent to his death in battle on David's orders, after David had seduced Bathsheba and made her pregnant. David married Bathsheba after Uriah's death.
2 SAMUEL 11

## UZZAH

Israelite in the time of King David who touched the Ark of the Covenant and was struck dead by God as a consequence.
2 SAMUEL 6:3–8

## UZZIAH

Also called Azariah, godly king of Judah who brought peace and prosperity. He was later punished with leprosy after proudly offering incense in the temple, which was the responsibility only of a priest.
2 KINGS 15:1–7; 2 CHRONICLES 26; ISAIAH 6

# V

## VASHTI

Queen whom the Persian king Xerxes deposed after she disobeyed him.
ESTHER 1:9–2:17

# X

## XERXES

The Greek form of an old Persian name of the powerful King of Persia (in Hebrew, Ahasuerus) who deposed Vashti and married Esther. An attempt to assassinate him was uncovered but he later approved Haman's decree to kill the Jews. Esther discovered this plot and the king hanged Haman.
EZRA 4:6; ESTHER

# Z

## ZACCHAEUS

Tax collector who climbed a tree in Jericho to gain a glimpse of Jesus among the crowds. Jesus asked to come to his house, despite the disapproving crowds who maintained that Zacchaeus was a sinner. Zacchaeus was a changed man as a result, and gave half of his property to the poor.
LUKE 19:1–10

## ZADOK

Priest at David's court with Abiathar, who remained loyal to David. After David's death he anointed Solomon as king.
2 SAMUEL 15:24–36; 17:15; 19:11; 1 KINGS 1:8, 32; 2:35

## ZEBEDEE

Father of the apostles James and John, and husband of Salome.
MATTHEW 4:21–22

## ZEBULUN

One of Jacob's 12 sons, who became ancestor of one of the twelve tribes of Israel.
GENESIS 30:19–20; 49:13

## ZECHARIAH

■ Prophet after the Exile who encouraged the rebuilding of the temple.
EZRA 5:1; 6:14; ZECHARIAH

■ King of Israel and son of Jeroboam II; he reigned for six months before he was murdered by Shallum.
2 KINGS 14:29; 15:8–12

■ Father of John the Baptist, struck dumb when he refused to believe the angel Gabriel when he told him that his wife, Elizabeth, was going to give birth to a son.
LUKE 1

## ZEDEKIAH

The last king of Judah. Installed by Nebuchadnezzar, he was in effect a puppet king of the Babylonians after the first Jews had been exiled to Babylon. His ultimate rebellion against the Babylonians led to the destruction of Jerusalem. He was captured and taken away, with his eyes gouged out, as a prisoner to Babylon.
2 KINGS 24:18–25:26; 2 CHRONICLES 36:11–20; JEREMIAH 24:8–10; 32:1–5; 34; 37; 38:14–28; 39

## ZEPHANIAH

Prophet during the reign of Josiah, who described a forthcoming day of the Lord, representing God's judgment against sin but hope and restoration to the faithful.
ZEPHANIAH

## ZERUBBABEL

Leader of the exiles, who returned to Judah and worked with Joshua as governor of Judea; under their leadership the foundations for the new temple in Jerusalem were laid.
EZRA 3:2–4:3; 5:2; HAGGAI 1–2; ZECHARIAH 4

## ZIBA

Saul's servant, who told David that his adopted son Mephibosheth was still alive.
2 SAMUEL 9; 16:1–4; 19:17, 26–29

## ZILPAH

Leah's servant, who bore Jacob two of his 12 sons, Gad and Asher.
GENESIS 19:24; 30:9–13

## ZIMRI

King of Israel who ruled for only one week before being overthrown by Omri.
1 KINGS 16:15–20

## ZIPPORAH

Jethro's daughter, who became the wife of Moses after he had escaped from Egypt. She bore him two sons.
EXODUS 2:21–22; 4:20–26; 18:2

## ZOPHAR

One of Job's three friends who tried to comfort him.
JOB 11; 20

Most people mentioned in the Bible are not acknowledged in other historical documents. However, independent evidence is sometimes found for their existence in sources other than the Bible.

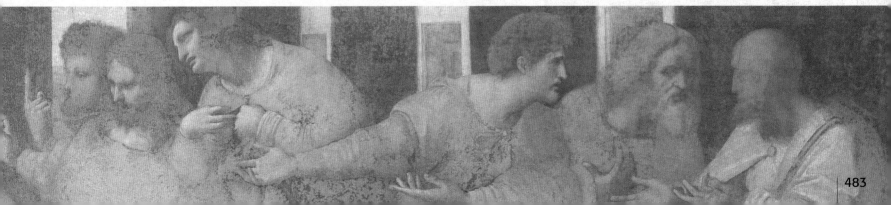

# Places in the Bible

## A

**ABARIM** Mountain range that includes Mount Nebo, located east of the River Jordan and the Dead Sea. Moses viewed the Promised Land from here.
NUMBERS 27:12; DEUTERONOMY 32:49; JEREMIAH 22:20

**ACHAIA** Roman province in southern Greece from 146 BC until Late Antiquity, which was governed from Corinth.
ACTS 18:12; 2 CORINTHIANS 1:1; 9:2

**ACHOR** Valley where Achan, who disobeyed God's command and stole riches in nearby Jericho, was killed along with his family. The Israelites believed his sin brought about their failure to conquer Ai.
JOSHUA 7:24–26; ISAIAH 65:10

**ADULLAM** Cave or fort where David and his men hid while running from Saul.
1 SAMUEL 22:1; 2 SAMUEL 23:13

**AI** Canaanite town in the Promised Land, southeast of Bethel; unsuccessfully attacked by Joshua after he defeated Jericho. "Ai" means "the ruin".
JOSHUA 7–8

**ALEXANDRIA** Port city on the Mediterranean coast of the Nile Delta, founded by Alexander the Great. Capital of Egypt in Graeco–Roman times and a centre of culture, it contained a museum and the Library of Alexandria. It had a large Jewish population, and was the birthplace of Apollos, a distinguished teacher in the early church.
ACTS 6:9; 18:24

**AMMON** State to the east of the River Jordan, with Rabbah (modern Amman) as its capital. The people of Ammon were often in conflict with Israel; David was briefly their king.
2 SAMUEL 12:29–31

**ANATHOTH** Levite town northeast of Jerusalem; birthplace of the prophet Jeremiah.
JOSHUA 21:18; JEREMIAH 1:1; 29:27

**ANTIOCH** (Pisidia) City in southern Asia Minor (modern Turkey) that Paul and Barnabas visited on their first missionary journey. Some Gentiles were converted by Paul's preaching, but he was expelled from the city by his opponents.
ACTS 13:14–51; 14:21; 16:6; 2 TIMOTHY 3:11
■ (Syria) Modern-day Antakya in Turkey, Antioch was the capital of the Roman province of Syria. Persecuted believers fled here from Jerusalem; followers of Jesus were first called "Christians" here; this was the base for Paul's three missionary journeys.
ACTS 6:5; 11:19–26; 13:1; 15:36; 18:23

**ARABAH** The rift valley of the River Jordan, which stretches from the Sea of Tiberias in the north to the Gulf of Aqabah in the south. The Sea of Arabah is an alternative name for the Dead Sea. See Dead Sea.
DEUTERONOMY 1:1; 3:17

**ARAM** Region north of Palestine, from Lebanon to beyond the River Euphrates, which contained a number of smaller regions during the Bronze and Iron Ages. Its capital was Damascus, and Rebekah, Leah, and Rachel came from here. The Israelites served the gods of Aram and suffered at the hands of its army. It was later defeated by the Assyrians. In the New Testament, Aram was a Roman province and Paul travelled through it. The language of this region, Aramaean, became the language spoken by the Judaeans down through Jesus' day.
GENESIS 25:20; 29:16–28; JUDGES 3:8; 10:6; 1 KINGS 11:25; 20–22; 2 KINGS 5–6; ISAIAH 7:1–8; MATTHEW 4:24; ACTS 18–21

**ARARAT** Mountains that extend between the Black Sea and the Caspian Sea; thought to be the place where Noah's ark came to rest. The name is derived from the Iron Age kingdom of Urartu, one of the most powerful enemies of the Assyrians.
GENESIS 8:4; JEREMIAH 51:27

**ARMAGEDDON** see Megiddo

**ARNON** River that runs from the mountains of Gilead into the Dead Sea.

It also formed the southern border dividing the territory of the Amorites from that of the Moabites. Today it is known as the Nahr Mujib, or River Mujib.
NUMBERS 21:13, 25–26; ISAIAH 16:2

**AROER** Amorite city on the north bank of the River Arnon; captured by Israel and given to Reuben and Gad.
DEUTERONOMY 2:36; 3:12
■ Town in south Judah, southeast of Beersheba.
1 SAMUEL 30:28; 1 CHRONICLES 11:44

**ASHDOD** Before the appearance of the Philistines at the end of the Late Bronze Age, Ashdod had a long history as one of the most important port cities on the coast of Canaan. It went on to become one of the five major Philistine cities. The Ark of the Covenant was placed in Dagon's temple here. In the time of Isaiah, Ashdod was captured by King Uzziah of Judah. The city, later known as Azotus, drew the evangelist Deacon Philip, who preached here.
1 SAMUEL 5; NEHEMIAH 4:7–8; ISAIAH 20:1; AMOS 1:8; ACTS 8:40

**ASHER** Territory that extended along the Mediterranean coast of Palestine between Tyre in the north and Carmel in the south; assigned by Joshua to the tribe of this name.
JOSHUA 19:24–31

**ASHKELON** City which had a long and prosperous existence in the Bronze Age before its destruction and reoccupation by the Philistines. It became one of the five main Philistine cities, situated on the coast of Israel between modern Jaffa and Gaza. Samson killed 30 men in Ashkelon to repay a debt. Over the years the city was ruled by Assyria, Babylonia, Tyre, and Persia.
JUDGES 1:18; 14:19; JEREMIAH 25:20

**ASIA** In Roman times, "Asia" was the western part of Asia Minor (modern Turkey), and contained the city of Ephesus. Paul carried out much of his missionary work here.
ACTS 2:9; 19:10; 1 CORINTHIANS 16:19; REVELATION 1:4

**ASSYRIA** A country in north Mesopotamia (modern Iraq) that became a powerful empire. Its king, Tiglath-Pileser III, put down a revolt in Israel and deported the Israelites. Deportation continued under Sargon II. Assyria dominated Judah for over 100 years, but Sargon's successor Sennacherib suffered a humiliating defeat, failing to put down a rebellion in Judah in 701 BC. The Assyrian Empire was defeated in 612 BC by the armies of Babylon and Media.
2 KINGS 15–19; ISAIAH 37:36–37; MICAH 5:4–6

**ATHENS** Capital of modern-day Greece and a cultural centre from the 5th century. In c.AD 50, Paul arrived here on his second missionary journey, and spoke before the Athenian council.
ACTS 17:15–34

## B

**BABEL** City, also known as Babylon and founded in the Early Bronze Age, which was rich and powerful until its abandonment in the Hellenistic period. Its people planned to build a tower that would reach heaven, but God intervened by confusing their language so they could not communicate.
GENESIS 10–11

**BABYLON/BABYLONIA** City on the River Euphrates, 80km (50 miles) south of modern Baghdad. Founded in the 3rd millennium BC, it became the capital of Babylonia. In the Old Testament the name is also used for the Babylonian empire, which was established after the fall of the Assyrians in 612 BC. King Nebuchadnezzar of Babylon conquered Jerusalem in 597 and 586 BC, and the people of Judah (including Ezekiel and Daniel) went into exile. The city was taken over by the Persians under Cyrus in 539 BC. See also Babel.
2 KINGS 24–25; ISAIAH 14; 47; JEREMIAH 50; DANIEL 1–6

**BEERSHEBA** City of the Negev desert in southern Israel, whose name translates as "seven wells" (the most famous of which

was the well dug by Abraham). Site of encounters with God by Hagar, Abraham, Isaac, Jacob, and Elijah. Base for Samuel's sons as judges over Israel.
**GENESIS** 21; 26; 46; **1 SAMUEL** 8:1–2; **1 KINGS** 19:2–3

**BENJAMIN** Territory west of the River Jordan, with Ephraim to the north, Judah to the south, and Dan to the west; assigned by Joshua to the tribe of this name.
**JOSHUA** 18:11–28; **JUDGES** 20–21

**BEREA** Greek city about 80km (50 miles) west of Thessalonica. Paul preached here, and was welcomed by some of the Bereans, but he was forced to leave.
**ACTS** 17:10–15; 20:4

**BETHANY** Village near Jerusalem, on the road to Jericho. Home of Mary, Martha, and Lazarus. Jesus visited often, and it was here that he raised Lazarus from the dead.
**MATTHEW** 26:6–7; **JOHN** 11:1–12:11

**BETHEL** Site near Jerusalem, the exact location of which remains unknown, where Jacob dreamed of a staircase leading up to heaven. God promised to give the land to Jacob's descendants, and Jacob called it "Bethel" (house of God). When the kingdoms of Israel and Judah divided, King Jeroboam I of Israel set up an altar and golden calf at Bethel so that people could worship there instead of at Jerusalem.
**GENESIS** 28:11–22; **JUDGES** 1:22–26; 20:18; **1 KINGS** 12:25–33; **2 KINGS** 23:15

**BETHLEHEM** Village about 8km (5 miles) south of Jerusalem, where Jacob's wife, Rachel, was buried, and Ruth and Naomi settled. The birthplace of David, and where he was anointed king of Israel by prophet Samuel. The prophet Micah foretold that the Messiah would be born in Bethlehem.
**GENESIS** 35:19; 48:17; **RUTH** 1; **1 SAMUEL** 16; **MICAH** 5:2; **MATTHEW** 2; **LUKE** 2

**BETHPHAGE** Village near Bethany, from where Jesus sent two disciples to fetch the colt on which he made his triumphant entry into Jerusalem.
**MATTHEW** 21:1; **MARK** 11:1; **LUKE** 19:29

**BETH SHEMESH** Fortified town west of Jerusalem. The Philistines returned the Ark of the Covenant to Beth Shemesh. Site of the battle between Jehoash and Amaziah.

**JOSHUA** 21:16; **1 SAMUEL** 6:9–21; **1 KINGS** 4:9; **2 KINGS** 14:11–13

**BETHSAIDA** Fishing town thought by many to be on the north shore of Lake Galilee. Home of Jesus' disciples Philip, Andrew, and Peter.
**MATTHEW** 11:21; **MARK** 8:22; **JOHN** 1:44

# C

**CAESAREA** Mediterranean port built by Herod the Great and named after Augustus Caesar. Home of Cornelius. Paul passed through the port many times on his missionary journeys, and was transferred here after his arrest, where he spent two years in prison before being sent to Rome.
**ACTS** 9:30; 10; 11; 18:22; 21:8; 23:23–26:32

**CAESAREA PHILIPPI** Town at the foot of Mount Hermon. Known as Paneas until Philip the Tetrarch renamed it in honour of Caesar Augustus. It was here that Peter declared Jesus to be the Christ.
**MATTHEW** 16:13–16

**CANA** Village in Galilee where Jesus turned water into wine at a wedding. Jesus' disciple, Nathanael, came from Cana.
**JOHN** 2:1–11; 4:46–54

**CANAAN** An area roughly corresponding to the southern Levant, which God promised to Abraham and his descendants. Moses's spies reported on its fruitfulness and Joshua led the people to capture it – it became known as the land of Israel.
**GENESIS** 12:1–7; **NUMBERS** 13; 33; **JOSHUA** 1

**CAPERNAUM** Town on the Sea of Galilee; Jesus' base while teaching in Galilee and home of Levi (Matthew) the tax-collector. Jesus performed many miracles in Capernaum. The people of Capernaum would not listen to Jesus, and he had to warn them of coming judgment. Home to one of the earliest synagogues, and one of the major centres of Judaism after the destruction of the Second Temple in Jerusalem.
**MARK** 1:21–34; 2:1–17; **LUKE** 7:1–10; 10:15

**CARMEL** Mountain range running from Mount Carmel on the Mediterranean coast to the Jordan Valley, and location of two strategic passes, over which the main north–south routes through Israel and Judah passed; site where Elijah

confronted the prophets of Baal.
**1 KINGS** 18:19–46; **2 KINGS** 2:25; 4:25

**CHEBAR** River or canal in Babylonia, where Ezekiel saw visions of God while he was in exile with the Jews.
**EZEKIEL** 1; 3; 10; 43

**CHINNERETH** Old Testament name for the Sea of Galilee.
**NUMBERS** 34:11; **JOSHUA** 11:2

**CILICIA** Region in southern Asia Minor whose capital, Tarsus, was the birthplace of Paul. Cilicia became a Roman province.
**ACTS** 21:39; 22:3

**COLOSSAE** City about 19km (12 miles) east of Laodicea in western Anatolia (modern Turkey). Paul wrote to the church here.
**COLOSSIANS** 1:2

**CORINTH** Located on the strip of land between mainland Greece and the Peloponnese, Corinth was one of the great cities of Mycenaean Greece. After the collapse of the Mycenaean civilization in 1100 BC, the city was revived as a centre of trade and art. It was destroyed and then rebuilt by the Romans. On his second missionary journey, Paul founded a church in the city.
**ACTS** 18; **1 CORINTHIANS** 1:2; **2 CORINTHIANS** 1:1

**CRETE** In the Bronze Age the Mediterranean island of Crete was home to a powerful civilization, known to archaeologists as the Minoans. The island was overrun by the Mycenaeans from mainland Greece, and remained a major centre for trade. En route to Rome, Paul's ship sheltered here; Paul left Titus here to establish a church.
**ACTS** 27:8; **TITUS** 1:5

**CUSH** An area of northeast Africa also known as Nubia, covering approximately northern Sudan and southern Egypt, it was a rival of the kingdom of Egypt during the Bronze Age. Following the fall of the Egyptian Empire, Cushite kings ruled Egypt for a time. Its inhabitants were the supposed descendents of Cush, the grandson of Noah.
**ISAIAH** 11:11; 18:1

**CYPRUS** Mediterranean island, home to some of the most ancient farming communities in the Near East, that had its

own language, script, and civilization. In the Bronze Age it was a major source of copper. It was the home of Barnabas, who came here with Paul on the first missionary journey and returned later with Mark.
**ACTS** 4:36; 13:4–12; 15:39; 27:4

**CYRENE** One of the most important Graeco–Roman cities of North Africa, in modern Libya. Simon from Cyrene helped Jesus carry the cross on Jesus' way to his crucifixion.
**MATTHEW** 27:32; **MARK** 15:21; **ACTS** 2:10

# D

**DAMASCUS** Syrian capital, frequently mentioned in the Hebrew Bible. Said to have been captured by David, but to have regained its independence soon after. Isaiah predicted the destruction of Damascus and after many attacks it fell to the Assyrians in 732 BC. Later, Damascus became a Roman city. It was on the road to Damascus that Saul (Paul) met Jesus in his life-changing encounter. He later had to escape from the city as he was persecuted by the Jewish population.
**GENESIS** 15:2; **2 SAMUEL** 8:5; **1 KINGS** 11:23; **ISAIAH** 17:1; **ACTS** 9

**DAN** Territory on the Mediterranean coast, given to the tribe of this name.
**JOSHUA** 19:40–48
■ One of the most powerful Canaanite cities, located in the far north in Israel, earlier known as Laish and Leshem. When the kingdom was divided, Jeroboam I tried to keep the loyalty of the northern tribes by setting up a golden calf here.
**1 KINGS** 12:25–30

**DEAD SEA** Salty sea in the Jordan Rift Valley, and the lowest point on Earth. Also called Salt Sea, Eastern Sea, and Sea of the Arabah.

**DECAPOLIS** Area south of the Sea of Galilee: a federation of ten Greek towns, mainly populated by non-Jews (Gentiles). Many people joined crowds following Jesus.
**MATTHEW** 4:25; **MARK** 5:20

**DOTHAN** Wealthy and powerful town on the route from Syria to Egypt, where Joseph, son of Jacob, was sold by his brothers to the Ishmaelite traders and

Elisha was rescued from the Syrians.
GENESIS 37:17–28; 2 KINGS 6:13

# E

**EBAL** Mountain facing Mount Gerizim, where Moses commanded Joshua to build an altar and to give the people a choice: to obey God and receive his blessing or to disobey and be punished.
DEUTERONOMY 11:29; 27:4; JOSHUA 8:30

**EDEN** Garden from which Adam and Eve were banished, that enclosed the Tree of Life and the Tree of Knowledge, which were made by God for humanity.
GENESIS 2–3

**EDOM** Region south of the Dead Sea, meaning "red", probably reflecting the area's dark red sandstone. Home of Esau (also called Edom) and his descendants; later the subject of prophetic judgment, after its people plundered Jerusalem.
GENESIS 32:3; NUMBERS 20:14–21;
1 SAMUEL 14:47; ISAIAH 34

**EGYPT** One of the earliest centres of civilization in the world, Egypt had developed writing by 3000 BC and shortly afterwards was a unified kingdom that extended from the Mediterranean Sea along the Nile Valley. It relied on the fertility provided by the Nile, and became a major centre of culture, religion, and civilization. Egypt is the setting of several biblical events, including the Exodus.
GENESIS 12:10; 42:1–3; 45:16–20;
EXODUS 1–11; 1 KINGS 11:40; ISAIAH 19;
MATTHEW 2:13; REVELATION 11:8

**EKRON** Ekron (modern Tel Miqne), an important city in the Bronze Age, became the northernmost of the five Philistine cities, allotted to Judah. The Ark of the Covenant was brought here after its capture.
JOSHUA 15:45–46; 1 SAMUEL 5:10–6:16;
2 KINGS 1:2–6; AMOS 1:8

**ELAM** Country east of Babylonia, located in what is now southern Iran. The Elamites were among the earliest literate people, and, with the rise of the Medes, an ancient Iranian people, were incorporated into the empire of the Persian-speaking peoples. Its capital city was Susa.
GENESIS 14:1–17; ISAIAH 21:2; DANIEL 8:2

**EMMAUS** Village about 11km (7 miles) from Jerusalem. Jesus appeared to two of his followers on the day of his resurrection while they walked on the road to Emmaus.
LUKE 24:13–32

**ENDOR** Town near Mount Tabor; home of the medium that Saul consulted.
1 SAMUEL 28

**EPHESUS** City that achieved great fame and wealth in the Graeco–Roman world as the centre of pilgrimage for the Artemis of Ephesus, whose temple was one of the Seven Wonders of the World. Capital of the Roman province of Asia (western Turkey) and an important port that Paul visited on his second and third missionary journeys. Paul left Timothy, Onesimus, and Tychicus here and wrote to the church.
ACTS 18–20; EPHESIANS 1:1; 1 TIMOTHY 1:3;
REVELATION 2:1–7

**EPHRAIM** Territory west of the River Jordan, assigned by Joshua to the tribe of this name.
JOSHUA 16:1–17

**EUPHRATES** River that rises in east Turkey and flows southeast to the Persian Gulf; one of the great arteries of ancient Near Eastern civilization. The earliest cities in the world grew up along its southern reaches, and in them writing was invented. Mentioned as one of the four rivers of Eden, and in John's vision in the book of Revelation.
GENESIS 2:14; 15:18; EXODUS 23:31;
2 CHRONICLES 35:20–24;
REVELATION 9:14; 16:12

# G

**GAD** Territory east of the River Jordan, given by Joshua to the tribe of this name.
JOSHUA 13:8–28

**GALATIA** Roman province in Asia Minor that Paul passed through on his second and third missionary journeys. Paul wrote to people here. It is widely thought that Galatia was so named after it was invaded and settled by Gauls.
ACTS 16:6; 18:23; 1 CORINTHIANS 16:1;
GALATIANS 1:2; 1 PETER 1:1

**GALILEE** Lake and region of northern Israel and home of Jesus and most of his disciples. A fishing area, with such towns as

Capernaum and Bethsaida mentioned in the Gospels. The Sea of Galilee (the lake), also known as the Sea of Chinneret is a focus of many of the Gospel stories. Galilee became the Jewish heartland following the destruction of Jerusalem and expulsion of Jews from Judaea after the Second Jewish Revolt.
1 KINGS 9:11; 2 KINGS 15:29; ISAIAH 9:1;
MATTHEW 4:12–18; LUKE 5:3; JOHN 21:1–6

**GATH** One of five main Philistine cities, the exact location of which remains uncertain. Home of Goliath and several other giants. David found refuge here from Saul.
JOSHUA 11:22; 1 SAMUEL 1:10–22; 5:8–9; 17:4;
27:2–4; 2 SAMUEL 21:20; 2 KINGS 12:17;
2 CHRONICLES 11:8

**GAZA** Southernmost Philistine city that was captured briefly by Joshua. Gaza was also the place where Samson was imprisoned and died. Philip was on the road to Gaza when he met the Ethiopian official and told him the good news about Jesus.
JOSHUA 10:41; JUDGES 16; 1 SAMUEL 6:17;
JEREMIAH 25:20; ACTS 8:26

**GERAR** Town between Egypt and Philistia, along the Gaza Valley on the southern borders of Canaan, where Abraham stayed. Isaac also stayed here and re-dug the wells that his father, Abraham, had created.
GENESIS 20; 26

**GERIZIM** One of two mountains above Shechem, the most important city in the mountains of Israel in the Middle and Late Bronze Ages. It later became the Samaritans' sacred mountain, where they built their temple.
DEUTERONOMY 11:29; 27:11–12; JOSHUA 8:33;
JOHN 4:20

**GIBEAH** Birthplace of Saul, which was destroyed during the time of the judges because of a crime committed by its people.
JUDGES 19:12–20:48; 1 SAMUEL 10:26

**GIBEON** City north of Jerusalem whose inhabitants tricked Joshua into signing a peace treaty; Saul later broke the treaty. It was the site of the battle between Saul and David's men, and Solomon offered sacrifices here. The people of Gibeon helped to rebuild the walls of Jerusalem after the return from the Babylonian Exile.

JOSHUA 9; 2 SAMUEL 2:12–29; 21:1;
1 KINGS 3:3–5; NEHEMIAH 3:7; 7:25

**GILBOA** Mountain range in north Palestine. Scene of the battle where Saul and his army took their last stand against the Philistines. Saul, Jonathan, and Saul's other two sons were all killed here.
1 SAMUEL 28:4; 31:1, 8; 2 SAMUEL 1:21;
1 CHRONICLES 10:8

**GILEAD** Mountainous area east of the River Jordan, north of the Dead Sea. The tribes of Reuben, Gad, and Manasseh each occupied part of Gilead. Jacob fled here, as did David. Famous for its balm, which is similar to myrrh.
GENESIS 31:21; NUMBERS 32:1;
DEUTERONOMY 3:12–13; 2 SAMUEL 17:22, 26;
JEREMIAH 8:22

**GILGAL** Significant base camp in the Promised Land, between the River Jordan and Jericho. Samuel regularly held court here and it became an important sanctuary. David was welcomed back here after Absalom's rebellion.
JOSHUA 4:19–20; 1 SAMUEL 7:15–16; 10:8;
2 SAMUEL 19:15; 2 KINGS 2:1; 4:38–41;
HOSEA 4:15; AMOS 4:4

**GOMORRAH** One of the five cities of the plain of Jordan, located on the eastern shore of the southern part of the Dea Sea. It is usually linked with Sodom, destroyed by God because of its persistent evil. Often used as an example of human depravity.
GENESIS 14; 18–19; ISAIAH 1:9–10;
MATTHEW 10:15

**GOSHEN** Fertile region in the Nile Delta in Egypt. When Jacob and his family went to join Joseph they settled here. Goshen escaped the plagues suffered by the rest of Egypt. It was a border region to which shepherds, who were religiously impure under Egyptian purity laws, were admitted on a temporary basis.
GENESIS 45:10; EXODUS 8:22; 9:26

**GREECE, GREEK EMPIRE**
Country of southeastern Europe and an eastern-Mediterranean empire under Alexander the Great, with Athens as its captial. In the Bronze Age Greece was home to the Mycenaean Civilization, which had close trading links with the Levant. The influence of Greek civilization and culture was strong in the last centuries before Christ and in New Testament times, when "Greek" meant

"Gentile; non-Jew".
DANIEL 11:2; JOHN 12:20; ACTS 6; 17; 18

# H

**HARAN** Assyrian city and key location in the trade network that included Mesopotamia and the kingdoms of Anatolia. Abraham's father, Terah, settled here after leaving Ur. God spoke to Abram here. Haran was later captured by the Babylonians.
GENESIS 11:31; 12:1–5; 29:4–28; 2 KINGS 19:12; EZEKIEL 27:23

**HEBRON** City high in the Judean hills, originally known as Kiriath Arba. Abraham and his family often camped near Hebron; it was later given to Caleb. David was made king and ruled from here; Absalom's base.
GENESIS 13:18; 23:2; NUMBERS 13:22; JOSHUA 14:12–15; 20:7; 2 SAMUEL 5:1-5; 15:7–12

**HERMON** High mountain on the border between Lebanon and Syria, sometimes called Mount Sirion or Mount Senir. Of great religious significance to Canaanites in the Bronze Age. Close to Caesarea Philippi, it may have been the "high mountain" where Jesus' disciples saw his transfiguration.
DEUTERONOMY 3:9; JOSHUA 12:1; 1 CHRONICLES 5:23; MARK 9:2

**HESHBON** Town east of the northern Dead Sea. First belonged to Moab, then to the Amorites, and later to the tribes of Reuben and Gad.
NUMBERS 21:21–24; 32:37

**HINNOM** Valley south of Jerusalem. Thought by many to be the site of a shrine for the god Molech, where children were offered in sacrifice, although scholarly debate over the authenticity of this has raged for years. Destroyed by Josiah, and denounced as evil by Jeremiah. "Gehenna", meaning "Valley of Hinnom", became a word for hell.
JOSHUA 15:8; 18:16; 2 KINGS 23:10; 2 CHRONICLES 28:3; 33:6; JEREMIAH 7:30–32; 19:2–6; MATTHEW 10:28

**HORMAH** Town in southern Canaan allotted to Simeon after the Conquest.
NUMBERS 14:41–45; JOSHUA 19:14; JUDGES 1:17; 1 CHRONICLES 4:30

# I

**IKONIUM** Ancient city visited by Paul and Barnabas on their first missionary journey, where they met with violent opposition from the inhabitants.
ACTS 13:50–51; 14:1–22; 2 TIMOTHY 3:11

**ISRAEL** Name first given to Jacob and then to the 12 tribes descended from him ("the sons of Israel"). Later became the name for the land occupied by these 12 tribes, which became a kingdom under David and Solomon. After the kingdom divided, Israel referred to the northern kingdom, which fell to Assyria in 722 BC.
GENESIS 34:7; 49:7, 28; DEUTERONOMY 17:4, 20; 18:6; 1 KINGS 11:31, 35; 2 KINGS 17

**ISSACHAR** Territory south of the Sea of Galilee, assigned by Joshua to the tribe of this name.
JOSHUA 19:17–23

# J

**JABBOK** River, known today as the Zarqa, flowing into the Jordan from the east; Jacob wrestled with the angel beside it. Also mentioned as a boundary between the Amorites and the Ammonites.
GENESIS 32:22–30; NUMBERS 21:24; DEUTERONOMY 3:16; JUDGES 11:13, 22

**JABESH GILEAD** Town east of the Jordan. In the period of the Judges, the wives of the Benjaminites were killed and Jabesh Gilead provided replacements. When the town was besieged by the Ammonites, it was rescued by Saul. Men from here risked their lives to remove Saul's body from the Philistines.
JUDGES 21; 1 SAMUEL 11; 31:1–13

**JERICHO** City northwest of the River Jordan, also referred to as the "city of palms". Dating back to 8000 BC, it is the oldest walled settlement yet discovered. Joshua gained his first victory in the Promised Land here, and it became a community of prophets. In the New Testament, Jesus healed blind men here and met Zacchaeus. By New Testament times Jericho contained the winter palace of Herod the Great.
JOSHUA 2; 6; 2 KINGS 2; 2 CHRONICLES 28:15; MATTHEW 20:29; LUKE 19:1–10

**JERUSALEM** Capital of Israel's early kings and later of the southern kingdom of Judah. Probably the "Salem" of which Melchizedek was king in Abraham's time. Before David captured Jerusalem and made it his capital, the city was called Jebus. David brought the Ark of the Covenant to Jerusalem, and his son, Solomon, built the temple here. Jerusalem was destroyed by the Babylonians but rebuilt by Nehemiah after the exile; the temple was rebuilt by Zerubbabel. In the New Testament another temple stood in place of Zerubbabel's. Jesus was brought to the temple in Jerusalem by his parents, at the age of 12. In the last week of his life, he entered the city triumphantly, but was arrested, tried, and killed. Jerusalem continued to be a place for settling controversies, until it was destroyed in AD 70, in fulfilment of Jesus' prophecy.
GENESIS 14:18; JOSHUA 15:63; 2 SAMUEL 5:4–10; 2 KINGS 25:10; EZRA 6; NEHEMIAH 2; LUKE 2:41–42; 19:28, 41–44; 22–24; ACTS 2; 8; 15; REVELATION 21

**JEZREEL** Town in north Israel, where King Ahab of Israel had a palace. Site of Naboth's vineyard, and place where King Joram of Israel went to recover from his wounds. Queen Jezebel was thrown from the palace window and died here.
1 SAMUEL 29:1; 1 KINGS 21:1–16; 2 KINGS 8:29; 9:24–37

**JOPPA** Seaport on the Mediterranean northwest coast of Jerusalem. Jonah set sail for Tarshish (Spain) from Joppa. Dorcas (Tabitha), the woman Peter restored to life, came from Joppa. Peter was in Joppa when he had his vision of the clean and unclean animals. An outcrop of rocks off the coast here were believed to be the site of Perseus' rescue of Andromeda in Greek mythology.
2 CHRONICLES 2:16; JONAH 1:3; ACTS 9:36–43; 10:5–17

**JORDAN** The river that separates the kingdoms of Israel and Judah from Transjordan. Joshua led the people of Israel across the River Jordan from the east, into the Promised Land near Jericho. David escaped across the Jordan at the time of Absalom's rebellion, and Elijah and Elisha crossed it before Elijah was taken up to heaven. Elisha told the Syrian general, Naaman, to wash in the Jordan to heal himself, and John the Baptist baptized people in this river, including Jesus.
JOSHUA 3; 2 SAMUEL 17:21–22; 2 KINGS 2:8–14; 5; MARK 1:9

**JUDAH** Territory in the south of the Promised Land between Jerusalem in the north and Beersheba in the south, assigned by Joshua to the tribe of this name. David was anointed king over this territory. The kingdoms of Israel (north) and Judah (south) split under Rehoboam, and remained in conflict until the Babylonians exiled the people of Judah. By the time of the New Testament, this area had become known as the province of Judea, and was part of Roman Syria, where Jesus was born. The capital of Judah was Jerusalem.
JOSHUA 19:1–9; 2 SAMUEL 2:1–7; 1 KINGS 12–22; 2 KINGS 1–17; 25; MATTHEW 2:1

# K

**KADESH BARNEA** Oasis in northern Sinai, identified with modern Tell el-Gudierat in the Negev, that dates from the late 10th century BC. Kadesh Barnea is mentioned in the campaign of Chedorlaomer and his allies at the time of Abraham, and it was near here that Hagar saw an angel. After the escape from Egypt, the tribe of Israel spent many years wandering in this region. Miriam died here, and Moses brought water out of the rock.
GENESIS 14:7; 16:14; NUMBERS 16:1–3; 20:1–16; 33:36–37; DEUTERONOMY 1:19, 46

**KEBAR** River in Babylonia; exiles lived along its banks and Ezekiel saw visions of God here.
EZEKIEL 1; 3; 10; 43

**KEILAH** Town where David stayed while escaping from Saul. David saved it from a Philistine attack.
JOSHUA 15:44; 1 SAMUEL 23; NEHEMIAH 3:17–18

**KERITH** Tributary east of the River Jordan, beside which Elijah lived during the years of drought and famine.
1 KINGS 17:2–9

**KIDRON** Valley separating Jerusalem and the Temple from the Mount of Olives. David crossed this valley when he left Jerusalem to avoid Absalom's rebellion. The reforming kings Asa, Hezekiah, and Josiah destroyed idols in this valley. Jesus and his disciples crossed it on their way to the Garden of Gethsemane.
2 SAMUEL 15:23; 1 KINGS 15:13; 2 KINGS 23:4–6; 2 CHRONICLES 29:16; JOHN 18:1

**KIRIATH JEARIM** A Gibeonite city originally allotted to Judah. The Ark of the Covenant was kept here for 20 years before David took it to Jerusalem.
JOSHUA 9:17; 15:60; 18:28; 1 SAMUEL 6:21–7:2; JEREMIAH 26:20

**KIRIATHAIM** Town given to Reuben, east of the Dead Sea; later taken over by the Moabites.
JOSHUA 13:19; JEREMIAH 48:1, 23; EZEKIEL 25:9

**KISHON** River flowing across the plain of Esdraelon into the Mediterranean Sea. Site of victory of Deborah and Barak over the Syrians. Elijah had the prophets of Baal killed here.
JUDGES 4:7, 13; 5:21; 1 KINGS 18:40

# L

**LACHISH** Canaanite city southwest of Jerusalem, founded in around 3000 BC. Joshua defeated the king of Lachish and four other Amorite kings here. Rebuilt by Rehoboam; Amaziah fled here but was killed by his enemies, who had followed him. Lachish was captured by Sennacherib of Assyria, and then fell to the Babylonians around the time of the final siege of Jerusalem (589–586 BC)
JOSHUA 10; 2 KINGS 14:19; 18:13–17; 2 CHRONICLES 32:9; ISAIAH 36:1–2; MICAH 1:13

**LAODICEA** City in southwest Phrygia, strategically located on a crossroads in Asia Minor; Paul wrote to the church here; Laodicea was addressed in one of the seven letters in Revelation.
COLOSSIANS 2:1; 4:12–13, 16; REVELATION 3:14–22

**LEBANON** Area north of Israel famous for its forests, especially cedars, which were used to build the Temple and royal palace at Jerusalem. The Bible also mentions its fertile soils in which various fruit and vegetables grew. The name came to be used figuratively to refer to righteousness and glory.
1 KINGS 5; EZRA 3:7; PSALMS 72:16; 92:12; ISAIAH 2:13; 14:8; 60:13; EZEKIEL 31

**LIBNAH** Canaanite town near Lachish. Captured by Joshua; involved in a rebellion against Jehoram. Survived a siege by the Assyrian king Sennacherib.
JOSHUA 10:29–39; 15:42; 21:13; 2 KINGS 8:22; 19:8

**LYSTRA** City in Galatia, which Paul and Barnabas visited on their first missionary journey, and where Paul healed a crippled man. The people believed Paul and Barnabas were gods. Paul was stoned and left for dead. Some of the people became Christians and Paul returned to visit them. Timothy lived here. It was formally made a Roman colony by Augustus in 6 BC.
ACTS 14:6–20; 16:1–5

# M

**MACEDONIA** Region north of Greece. The Macedonians were in conflict with the Greeks for centuries; Philip II of Macedon, father of Alexander the Great, conquered Greece. Rome conquered the region in the 1st century BC. Paul travelled here on his second missionary journey, after he had a vision of a Macedonian man inviting him to help. It was the first stage in taking the Christian message to Europe.
ACTS 16:9–17:15; 19:21; 20:1–6; 2 CORINTHIANS 8:1–5; PHILIPPIANS 4:15–18

**MAHANAIM** Place in Gilead, east of the River Jordan. Angels appeared to Jacob in Mahanaim. Where Ishbosheth reigned and where David took refuge from Absalom.
GENESIS 32:1–2; 2 SAMUEL 2:8–10; 17:24–29; 19:32; 1 KINGS 2:8; 4:14

**MALTA** Mediterranean island south of Sicily that was settled in the Neolithic period and preserved a unique language and culture. Colonized by the Phoenicians in the Iron Age because of its advantageous position on trade routes between Europe and Africa. Paul was shipwrecked here while a prisoner on a voyage to Rome.
ACTS 28:1–11

**MAMRE** Site near Hebron where God promised Abraham a son, and Abraham pleaded with God to spare Sodom.
GENESIS 13:18; 14:13; 18; 23:17; 35:27–29

**MANASSEH** Territory to the west and east of the River Jordan, assigned by Joshua to the tribe of this name.
JOSHUA 13:6–8, 29–31; 17:7–13

**MEDIA** Kingdom of northwest Iran, south of the Caspian Sea, and one of the major powers in the region by the 7th century BC. It was first controlled by the Assyrians, and then, from 612 BC, by the Babylonians, before being brought under the control of Cyrus the Persian in 550 BC. Later, the Medes rebelled under Darius I and II.
2 KINGS 17:6; 18:11; ESTHER 1:3, 14, 19; DANIEL 5:28; 6:8, 12, 15

**MEGIDDO** Ancient city on the edge of the plain of Jezreel, settled in 4000 BC, and strategically located on two trade routes. Also known by its Greek name, Armageddon, because it was the site of countless battles: it was here that Deborah gained a victory over Sisera, and Josiah died fighting the army of the Egyptian Pharaoh Neco. Referred to in the New Testament as the place of God's final victory over evil.
JOSHUA 12:21; JUDGES 1:27–28; 5:19; 1 KINGS 9:15; 2 KINGS 23:29–30; REVELATION 16:16

**MEMPHIS** Egypt's ancient capital, on the Nile south of modern Cairo. The city was important until the time of Alexander the Great. Referred to by the prophets when they condemned Israel's trust in Egypt.
ISAIAH 19:13; JEREMIAH 2:16; 46:14; EZEKIEL 30:13, 16

**MESOPOTAMIA** Meaning land "between the rivers" (Tigris and Euphrates), Mesopotamia included such cities as Babylon, Ur, and Nineveh. The world's first literate civilization was created in southern Mesopotamia by the Sumerians, whose successors, the Akkadians, built the world's first empire. Haran and Paddan Aram, the towns where some of Abraham's family settled, lay here. It was also the home of Balaam, the prophet sent to curse the Israelites. In the New Testament, people from Mesopotamia were in Jerusalem on the day of Pentecost.
GENESIS 24:10; DEUTERONOMY 23:4; JUDGES 3:8; 2 SAMUEL 10:16; ACTS 2:9

**MICHMASH** Town north of Jerusalem. Site of a battle between the Philistines and Israel, when Saul's army fled and Jonathan won; re-occupied after the Exile.
1 SAMUEL 13–14; EZRA 2:27; NEHEMIAH 7:31; 11:31; ISAIAH 10:28

**MIDIAN** Land east of the Gulf of Aqaba, inhabited by Midian's descendants. Moses fled here after killing an Egyptian. Location of the burning bush where God spoke to Moses, sending him back to Egypt to help free the Israelites. At the time of the Judges, Gideon defeated a large force of invaders from Midian.
GENESIS 25:1–6; EXODUS 2:15–21; 3:1–10; JUDGES 6–8

**MILETUS** Port on the west coast of present-day Turkey, where Paul stayed on his way back from his missionary travels. The elders from the church at Ephesus came to meet Paul here, and heard his farewell message.
ACTS 20:15; 2 TIMOTHY 4:20

**MIZPAH** A town in Benjamin, where Samuel presented Saul to the people as their king. After Jerusalem fell to the Babylonians, the governor, Gedaliah, lived at Mizpah.
JOSHUA 18:26; JUDGES 20–21; 1 SAMUEL 7:5–16; 10:17–25; 1 KINGS 15:22; 2 KINGS 25:23–25; JEREMIAH 40–41
■ Town in Gilead, east of the Jordan, where Jacob and Laban made a peace agreement. The home of Jephthah, a judge of Israel who sacrificed his daughter.
GENESIS 31:48–49; JUDGES 10:17; 11

**MOAB** Land east of the Dead Sea, largely captured by the Amorites before being conquered by the Israelites. It was here that Moses explained the law and commandments. Ruth was born here. Often at war with Israel, the country was repeatedly denounced by the prophets.
NUMBERS 21:17–31; 25:1–9; DEUTERONOMY 1:5; RUTH 2:6; 1 SAMUEL 14:47; 22:3–4; 2 SAMUEL 8:2; 2 KINGS 3; ISAIAH 15–16

**MORIAH** Mountain on which Abraham was instructed to sacrifice his son Isaac. Also the name of the site of Solomon's temple in Jerusalem.
GENESIS 22:2; 2 CHRONICLES 3:1

# N

**NAPHTALI** Territory to the west of the Sea of Galilee, assigned by Joshua to the tribe of this name. Its people did not drive out all of the former Canaanite inhabitants. Defeated by Assyria before the fall of Samaria, its people were among the Lost Ten Tribes of Israel deported to Assyria.
JOSHUA 19:32–39; JUDGES 1:33; 2 KINGS 15:29; ISAIAH 9:1; MATTHEW 4:13–16

**NAZARETH** Town in Galilee, southwest of the Sea of Galilee. The home of Mary

and Joseph; Jesus spent his boyhood here but left it to begin his preaching. Jesus was referred to as "Jesus of Nazareth" or "the Nazarene".
**MATTHEW** 2:23; 4:13; 26:71; **MARK** 1:9; **LUKE** 1:26; 2:39, 51; 4:16–30; **JOHN** 1:45–46

**NEBO** Mountain in Moab from which Moses viewed the whole of the Promised Land before he died. Also a city in Transjordan conquered by the Israelites.
**DEUTERONOMY** 32:48–52; 34:1–4

**NEGEV** Area of desert in the far south of Israel. Abraham and Isaac camped here, as did the Israelites before they settled in Canaan. The 12 spies who were sent to scout the Promised Land travelled there from this direction. Negev was an area of dry scrubland and desert, and its name is used in Isaiah to describe hardship.
**GENESIS** 20:1; 24:62; **NUMBERS** 13:17–29; **JOSHUA** 10:40; **ISAIAH** 30:6

**NILE** Egypt's river, which flows northwards into the Mediterranean Sea. It featured in the dreams of Joseph's pharaoh, and at the time of Moses' birth the pharaoh ordered his people to drown all Hebrew baby boys in the Nile. Moses was hidden in a basket in the reeds at the river's edge and survived. The Nile also features in the plagues that were sent by God when the pharaoh refused to free the Israelites. It is often mentioned by the prophets.
**GENESIS** 41:1–36; **EXODUS** 1:22; 2:3–10; 7–8; **ISAIAH** 19:7–8

**NINEVEH** Important city in Assyria, especially in Sennacherib's reign. The city's importance grew as Assyria's power increased, and several Assyrian kings had palaces here. Sennacherib undertook much rebuilding work. Nineveh fell to the Babylonians in 612 BC. Jonah was sent to preach there, and Nahum declared God's judgment against the city.
**GENESIS** 10:11–12; **2 KINGS** 19:36; **JONAH** 1–4; **NAHUM** 1–3; **MATTHEW** 12:41

# O

**OLIVES, MOUNT OF** Hill east of Jerusalem. When David fled from Jerusalem during Absalom's rebellion, he walked up the mount weeping. Zechariah prophesied that on the Day of Judgement

the Lord will stand on the mountain, and it will split in two. On its lower slopes lay the Garden of Gethsemane, where Jesus prayed on the night of his arrest.
**2 SAMUEL** 15:30; **ZECHARIAH** 14:4; **LUKE** 19:29, 37; 21:37; 22:39; **ACTS** 1:12

# P

**PAMPHYLIA** Narrow coastal region on the southwest coast of Asia Minor. Paul visited its capital, Perga.
**ACTS** 2:10; 13:13–14; 14:24–26; 15:36–40

**PAPHOS** Town in southwest Cyprus visited by Paul on his first missionary journey, and whose proconsul believed God's message.
**ACTS** 13:6–13

**PARAN** Desert area in the Sinai Peninsula where Hagar's son, Ishmael, grew up. The Israelites passed through it after the Exodus, and from here spies were sent into Canaan.
**GENESIS** 21:20–21; **NUMBERS** 10:12; 12:16; 13:1–26

**PATMOS** Island in the Aegean Sea where John had the visions recorded in Revelation.
**REVELATION** 1:9

**PENIEL (PENUEL)** Place near the River Jabbok, east of Jordan, where Jacob wrestled with the angel of God.
**GENESIS** 32:22–32

**PERGA** Capital city of Pamphylia, in south Asia Minor. Paul visited here on his arrival from Cyprus on his first missionary journey, and then visited again on his return journey.
**ACTS** 13:13–14; 14:25

**PERGAMUM** First administrative capital of the Roman province of Asia. The city was one of the seven churches to which the letters in Revelation are addressed.
**REVELATION** 1:11; 2:12–16

**PERSIA** Country that conquered Media and overthrew Babylon in the 7th century BC, establishing an empire that continued until Alexander the Great and his conquests in the 4th century BC. Daniel was in Babylon when the city was taken by the army of the Medes and Persians. Cyrus the Persian king

allowed the Jews and other exiles to return to their homelands. The Temple was rebuilt during the reign of Darius, king of Persia. The Jewish girl, Esther, became queen to the Persian king, Xerxes I (Ahasuerus). The Persian empire came to an end at the Battle of Issus (333 BC) when it was defeated by Alexander the Great.
**EZRA** 1:1–19; **ESTHER** 1; **DANIEL** 5:24–28; 6:8–15; 8:20–21;10:1–2; **HAGGAI** 1:1; 2:10

**PHILADELPHIA** City in west Asia Minor to which one of the seven letters in Revelation was addressed. *See Rabbah.*
**REVELATION** 1:11; 3:7–13

**PHILIPPI** City in Macedonia named after Philip of Macedon, the father of Alexander the Great. Paul visited the city after his vision of a man from Macedonia calling for help. Among his converts was a woman named Lydia. The first Christian church in Europe was established here. Paul and Silas were illegally imprisoned here but were later released.
**ACTS** 16:6–40; **PHILIPPIANS** 1:1; **1 THESSALONIANS** 2:2

**PHILISTIA** Land of the Philistines on the coast of Israel, with the main cities of Gaza, Ashdod, Ashkelon, Gath, and Ekron. Seen as Israel's enemy; the giant Goliath was a Philistine.
**EXODUS** 15:14; **JOSHUA** 13:2–3; **1 SAMUEL** 17–18; **PSALM** 60:8; 87:4; 108:9

**PHOENICIA** Small but important trading state on the Mediterranean, north of Israel. Its main towns included Tyre and Sidon.
**MARK** 7:24–30; **ACTS** 11:19; 15:3

**PHRYGIA** Land in Asia Minor, with main cities of "Pisidian" Antioch, Iconium, Laodicea, Colossae, and Hierapolis.
**ACTS** 16:6; 18:23

**PISGAH** One of the peaks of Mount Nebo; Moses viewed the Promised Land from Pisgah.
**NUMBERS** 21:20; 23:14; **DEUTERONOMY** 3:27; 34:1; **JOSHUA** 12:3; 13:2

# R

**RABBAH** Capital city of the Ammonites, whose territory was given to the tribe of Gad but was still occupied by the

Ammonites until Joab captured it. David was helped at Rabbah when he fled from his rebellious son Absalom. The city's wickedness was denounced by the prophets and its destruction was prophesied. Later the city was given the Greek name of Philadelphia.
**DEUTERONOMY** 3:11; **JOSHUA** 13:24–25; **2 SAMUEL** 11:1–15; 12:26–31; **1 CHRONICLES** 20:1–3; **JEREMIAH** 49:2–3; **EZEKIEL** 21:20; 25:5; **AMOS** 1:14

**RAMAH** Town north of Jerusalem, near which Deborah lived. Captured and fortified by Baasha of Israel, and recaptured by Asa of Judah. When Jerusalem fell to the Babylonians, Jeremiah was set free at Ramah. Rachel's tomb was said to be near here.
**JUDGES** 4:5; **1 KINGS** 15:17, 22; **2 CHRONICLES** 16:1–6; **NEHEMIAH** 11:33; **JEREMIAH** 31:15; 40:1
■ The birthplace and home of the prophet Samuel. Later known as Arimathea.
**1 SAMUEL** 7:17; 8:4-6; 19:18; 25:1; **JOHN** 19:38

**RAMESES** Egyptian city on the east side of the Nile Delta. Site of Pharaoh Rameses II's palace. Rameses and Pithom were built by the Israelites as supply centres for the king. The Israelites set out from Rameses on their escape from Egypt.
**EXODUS** 1:11; 12:37

**RAMOTH GILEAD** City east of the River Jordan that was a city of refuge – a centre of assylum for perpetrators of manslaughter. Probably identified as the same place as Mizpah in Gilead, it was the home of Jephthah. One of Solomon's 12 district governors was stationed here. It changed hands several times in the wars between Israel and Syria. King Ahab of Israel was killed in battle here, and Jehu was anointed king.
**JOSHUA** 20:8; **JUDGES** 11:34; **1 KINGS** 4:13; 22:1–38; **2 KINGS** 9:1–24

**RED SEA** Stretch of water separating Egypt and Arabia. The Hebrew *yam suph* translates as "Sea of Reeds". The waters of the Red Sea divided for the Israelites to cross as they followed Moses out of Egypt, but returned to drown the Egyptians who pursued them. The account of the Exodus refers to the area of lakes and marshes between the head of the Gulf of Suez and the Mediterranean Sea (the Suez Canal area).
**EXODUS** 13:17–14:31; **NUMBERS** 33:10; **DEUTERONOMY** 1:40

**REPHAIM** Valley southwest of Jerusalem, where King David fought and defeated the Philistines. Also the name of one of the peoples who lived in Canaan before the Israelite Conquest.
2 SAMUEL 5:18

**REUBEN** Territory east of the Dead Sea, given by Joshua to the tribe of this name.
JOSHUA 13:15–23

**RIBLAH** Town on the River Orontes in Syria, where King Jehoahaz of Judah was taken prisoner by Pharaoh Neco of Egypt. Nebuchadnezzar had his headquarters here. Zedekiah, the last king of Judah, was taken to Nebuchadnezzar at Riblah for sentencing following his rebellion.
2 KINGS 23:33; 25:6, 20–21

**ROME** City on the River Tiber in Italy, capital of the Roman Empire. Jews from Rome were in Jerusalem on the Day of Pentecost and heard Peter's message. There appears to have been an early Christian group in the city. Aquila and Priscilla had come from Rome and had probably been forced to leave when the emperor Claudius expelled all Jews. Paul was a Roman citizen and wanted to preach there. His letter to the Romans names a number of Christians here. Paul eventually came to Rome on the Appian Way after appealing to Caesar; and he was under guard here for two years, when he may have written some of his letters. In Revelation, Rome is pictured as embodying corrupt earthly power. The apostle Peter was associated with Rome and was probably martyred there.
ACTS 2:10; 16:37; 18:2; 19:21; 22:28; 28:14–30; ROMANS 1:7, 15; 15:24; 2 TIMOTHY 1:16–17; REVELATION 17:1–18:24

# S

**SAMARIA** Capital of the northern kingdom of Israel. King Omri began work on building the city, and Ahab, his son, added a new palace. The people of Samaria worshipped pagan gods, so were condemned by many prophets, who warned that their city would be destroyed. Samaria later fell to the Assyrians c.722 BC, and the people were exiled to Syria, Assyria, and Babylonia. With the fall of Samaria, the Kingdom of Israel ceased to exist and the region became known as Samaria. The city was rebuilt by Herod the

Great and renamed Sebaste (or Augusta). The Samaritans, a group of mixed-race Jews, who also worshipped the God of Israel, lived here during this period and were viewed with hostility by the Jews in Judea, but Jesus showed concern for them by travelling through this area. Philip, Peter, and John went to Samaria to preach.
1 KINGS 16:23–29; 2 KINGS 5:3; 6:8–7:20; ISAIAH 8:4; LUKE 17:11; JOHN 4:1–43; ACTS 8:5–25

**SARDIS** City in Asia that was a great trade centre in Roman times; formerly the capital of the kingdom of Lydia under wealthy King Croesus. In Revelation, one of the seven letters to the churches was addressed to the church in Sardis.
REVELATION 1:11; 3:1–6

**SHARON** Israel's coastal plain, extending from Joppa to Mount Carmel. Rich in pasture land and known for its vegetation.
1 CHRONICLES 27:29; ISAIAH 33:9; 35:2; ACTS 9:35

**SHEBA** Wealthy country, probably in southwest Arabia. Its queen travelled to Jerusalem to visit King Solomon and test his wisdom.
1 KINGS 10:1–13; PSALMS 72:10, 15; ISAIAH 60:6

**SHECHEM** Ancient Canaanite town in the hill country of Ephraim, between Mount Ebal and Mount Gerizim. Abraham was told by God that this country would be given to him for his descendants. Jacob also visited Shechem. After the Israelites had conquered Canaan, Joshua gathered the tribes here to renew their promise to worship God; it was also named a city of refuge. Joseph was buried here. In the time of the Judges, Canaanite worship was practised in Shechem. Gideon's son Abimelech was given money by the inhabitants so that he could pay to have his 70 brothers killed. Abimelech made himself king of Shechem, but when the people turned against him he destroyed the town. Solomon's son Rehoboam went to Shechem to be anointed king before the kingdom divided. Jeroboam, the first king of the new northern kingdom, started to rebuild the city. Shechem survived the fall of Israel, becoming the Samaritans' most important city.
GENESIS 12:6–7; 33:18–20; JOSHUA 24; JUDGES 9; 1 KINGS 12; JOHN 4:5–40

**SHILOH** Town in the hills of Ephraim where the Tabernacle was set up, making it the centre of Israel's worship. The tent was replaced by a more permanent building and an annual festival was held. Hannah and Elkanah travelled to Shiloh to worship God. When Hannah prayed for a son, she promised to give him back to serve God. When Samuel was born, Hannah kept her promise and brought him back to Shiloh, where he grew up in the templet. The town was destroyed about 1050 BC, probably by the Philistines. The prophet Jeremiah warned that the temple in Jerusalem would be destroyed, just as the place of worship at Shiloh had been.
JOSHUA 18:1, 8–10; JUDGES 18:31; 21:19; 1 SAMUEL 1–4; 2 SAMUEL 6:2–17; PSALMS 78:59–61; JEREMIAH 7:12–14

**SHITTIM** Site of the Israelites last camp before crossing the Jordan into Canaan. It was likely that they were at Shittim when the king of Moab tried to persuade Balaam to curse them. Here, Joshua was appointed as Moses' successor.
NUMBERS 22–24; 25:1–9; 33:49–50; JOSHUA 2:1; 3:1

**SHUNEM** Town in northern Israel. The Philistines set up camp here before the battle on Mount Gilboa where Saul and Jonathan were killed. Elisha restored a boy to life here.
JOSHUA 19:18; 1 SAMUEL 28:4; 1 KINGS 1:3; 2 KINGS 4:8–37

**SHUR** Desert area in the northwest Sinai Peninsula. Hagar fled here after Sarah treated her unkindly. The Israelites had to travel through this region after escaping from Egypt.
GENESIS 16; EXODUS 15:22–25; 1 SAMUEL 15:7; 27:8

**SIDON** Phoenician port on the coast of modern Lebanon. It was not captured when the Israelites conquered Canaan, and in the time of the Judges its people attacked the Israelites. Gradually the cultures began to merge, and the Israelites were accused of worshipping the gods of Sidon – Baal and Ashtoreth. Jezebel was the daughter of a king of Sidon and promoted the worship of Baal in Israel. The town was opposed to Israel and the worship of God. By New Testament times, most of the people of Sidon were Greek. Many went to hear Jesus preach in Galilee. Jesus visited Sidon and the neighbouring city of Tyre, and Paul stopped here on his way to Rome.

JUDGES 1:31; 10:12; 1 KINGS 16:31; 17:9; ISAIAH 23:1–12; EZEKIEL 28:21–26; MATTHEW 15:21–28; LUKE 6:17; ACTS 27:3

**SILOAM** Underground pool that was one of Jerusalem's main sources of water. When the Assyrians threatened to besiege Jerusalem, Hezekiah realized the city needed its own water supply in order to survive, and had a tunnel cut through the rock to tap the Gihon Spring outside Jerusalem. Jesus cured a blind man by telling him to wash his eyes in this pool. The tower of Siloam probably stood on the slope of Mount Zion, above the pool.
2 KINGS 20:20; LUKE 13:4; JOHN 9:7–11

**SIMEON** Territory in the Negev, southern Israel, assigned by Joshua to the tribe of this name.
JOSHUA 19:1–9

**SIN** Desert area between Elim and Sinai where the Israelites complained to Moses and were supplied with quails and manna.
EXODUS 16; NUMBERS 22:11–12

**SINAI** Mountain in the Sinai peninsula whose exact location is not known. The Israelites set up camp here three months after leaving Egypt. God gave Moses the Ten Commandments on this mountain.
EXODUS 19–34

**SMYRNA** Port town in western Asia Minor. One of the letters in Revelation is addressed to the church here.
REVELATION 1:11; 2:8–11

**SODOM** City usually linked with Gomorrah. Lot settled in this city, which became notorious for its immorality and was destroyed along with Gomorrah. Lot escaped after being warned of the impending disaster.
GENESIS 13:8–13; 14; 18–19; ISAIAH 1:9–10; MATTHEW 10:15

**SUCCOTH** Town in the Jordan valley, part of the territory of Gad. Jacob stayed here after agreeing to part ways with his brother Esau. In the time of the Judges its people refused to supply Gideon and his army.
GENESIS 33:12–17; JUDGES 8:4–16
■ Town where the Israelites first camped on their journey from Egypt.
EXODUS 12:37; 13:20; NUMBERS 33:5–6

**SUSA** Ancient city north of the Persian Gulf, and capital city of the Elamite

empire until it was destroyed in 645 BC by the king of Assyria, Ashurbanipal, who exiled its inhabitants to Samaria. Susa regained importance under the Medes and Persians, being one of the three royal cities of the Persian kings. Darius I built a palace here, and the story of Esther took place in Susa's royal court.
EZRA 4:9–10; NEHEMIAH 1:1; ESTHER; DANIEL 8:2

**SYCHAR** Samaritan town (exact location unknown) where Jesus met and talked to a Samaritan woman. When the inhabitants heard what she said, many believed he was the Messiah. The town was probably built on the site of Shechem.
GENESIS 33:18; JOHN 4:1–42

**SYRIA** *see Aram*

# T

**TAANACH** Canaanite city on the edge of the valley of Jezreel. Barak fought Sisera near Taanach, and it became one of the cities of the Levites.
JOSHUA 12:21; 21:25; JUDGES 1:27; 5:19

**TAHPANHES** Egyptian town in the east of the Nile Delta, where the prophet Jeremiah was taken after the fall of Jerusalem.
JEREMIAH 43:7–13; EZEKIEL 30:18–19

**TARSHISH** Distant place, perhaps in southern Spain, to which Jonah set sail when he disobeyed God's command to go to Nineveh; famous for its ships and valuable cargo.
ISAIAH 23:1, 6; JEREMIAH 10:9; EZEKIEL 27:12; JONAH 1:3

**TARSUS** City on the Cilician plain in Asia Minor. The apostle Paul was born here and returned here shortly after becoming a Christian.
ACTS 9:11, 30; 11:25; 21:39; 22:3

**TEKOA** Town about 10km (6 miles) south of Bethlehem in the Judean hills. A wise woman from Tekoa pleaded with King David to allow his son Absalom to come back to Jerusalem. The town was also the home of the prophet Amos.
2 SAMUEL 14:2–21; AMOS 1:1

**THEBES** City on the River Nile, the ancient capital of upper Egypt. It fell to the Assyrians in 663 BC. Jeremiah and Ezekiel prophesied its destruction by the Babylonians.
JEREMIAH 46:25; EZEKIEL 30:14–16; NAHUM 3:8

**THESSALONICA** Macedonia's principal city and port. Paul visited here on his second missionary journey, but was forced to move to Berea. Paul wrote two letters to the Thessalonian Christians.
ACTS 17:1–15; PHILIPPIANS 4:16; 1 THESSALONIANS; 2 THESSALONIANS

**THYATIRA** City in western Asia Minor. A manufacturing centre for dyeing, fabrics, clothes, pottery, and brasswork; the home of Lydia, the businesswoman who became a Christian when she met Paul at Philippi. One of the seven letters in the book of Revelation was addressed to the church here.
ACTS 16:14–15; REVELATION 1:11; 2:18–29

**TIBERIAS** Town on the west shore of the Sea of Galilee, founded by Herod Antipas and named after the Roman emperor Tiberius.
JOHN 6:23–25

**TIGRIS** Major river in Mesopotamia, second only to the Euphrates. It is mentioned as one of the four great rivers of Eden. The great Assyrian cities of Nineveh, Calah, and Assur were all on the banks of the Tigris.
GENESIS 2:14; DANIEL 10:4

**TIRZAH** Town in north Israel, captured by Joshua. Later the home of Jeroboam I, it became the first capital of the northern kingdom of Israel. King Omri later moved the centre of government to his new city of Samaria.
JOSHUA 12:24; 1 KINGS 14:17; 16:23–28; 2 KINGS 15:14–6; SONG OF SONGS 6:4

**TOPHETH** Place in the valley of Hinnom where children were sacrificed. The shrine was destroyed by King Josiah.
2 KINGS 23:10; JEREMIAH 7:31; 19:6, 10–14

**TROAS** Port in northwest Asia Minor. Here, Paul had a vision of a Macedonian man calling for help, and he sailed from Troas on his missionary travels to Europe.
ACTS 16:8–12; 20:5–12; 2 CORINTHIANS 2:12–13

**TYRE** Large port on the Mediterranean coast, about halfway between Sidon and Acco. Tyre had two harbours, one on the mainland and one on an off-shore island. Tyre became the leading Phoenician port after the Philistines plundered nearby Sidon. It flourished in the time of David and Solomon. King Hiram of Tyre provided the wood and labour to build the Temple in Jerusalem. Tyre is often mentioned in the Psalms and by the prophets, who condemned its pride and luxury. Tyre was captured in succession by the Assyrians, Babylonians, and finally Alexander the Great and his Greek army. It was visited many times by Jesus, who preached to its people.
2 SAMUEL 5:11; 1 KINGS 5; 9:10–14; PSALM 45:12; ISAIAH 23; EZEKIEL 26–28; MATTHEW 15:21; LUKE 6:17; ACTS 21:3

# U

**UR** City in Mesopotamia; Abraham's home before he and his family moved to Haran.
GENESIS 11:28–32

**UZ** Job's home country, probably in the region of Edom.
JOB 1:1

# Z

**ZAREPHATH** Small town belonging to Sidon and later to Tyre. Elijah stayed here with a widow during the time of the drought. Later he restored the widow's dead son to life.
1 KINGS 17:8–24; LUKE 4:26

**ZEBULUN** Territory assigned by Joshua to the tribe of this name; between Asher on the coast and Naphtali in the east.
JOSHUA 19:10–16; ISAIAH 9:1; MATTHEW 4:13–16

**ZIKLAG** Town in south Judah given to David by the king of Gath when he was an outlaw from Saul. David rescued the captives taken by the Amalekites who had raided the town.
1 SAMUEL 27:6; 30

**ZIN** Desert region near Kadesh Barnea in southern Israel, where the Israelites camped after the Exodus.
NUMBERS 13:21; 20:1; 27:14; JOSHUA 15:1, 3

**ZION** Fortified hill that David captured from the Jebusites. The name became synonymous with Jerusalem.
2 SAMUEL 5:6–7

**ZIPH** Hill town southeast of Hebron, belonging to the tribe of Judah. David hid from Saul in the desert near Ziph, and Jonathan came to encourage him there. The people of the town betrayed him to Saul, and he moved to Maon and En Gedi. Later, Ziph was one of the places fortified by King Rehoboam.
1 SAMUEL 23:14–29; 26:1–2; 2 CHRONICLES 11:8

**ZOAN** Ancient Egyptian town northeast of the Nile Delta. Zoan was the capital of Egypt from about 1100 to 660 BC.
NUMBERS 13:22; ISAIAH 19:11

**ZOAR** One of five cities, probably at the southern end of the Dead Sea. Lot fled to Zoar when Sodom and the other cities were destroyed.
GENESIS 13:10; 14:2, 8; 19:18–30

# Bible Lists and Tables

## MONEY AND VALUES

In the Old Testament, coins were measured by weight, which in time became related to value. Weights are listed in more detail in the table below. In the New Testament, more recognisable currencies are present, from a number of different nations. This table shows the relative value of these New Testament coins, and indicates where in the Bible they appear.

### OLD TESTAMENT COINS

Gerah (Hebrew)

Shekel (Hebrew)

Mina (Hebrew)

Talent (Hebrew)

Daric (Persian)

### NEW TESTAMENT COINS

| Roman | Greek | Jewish | Passage in the Bible |
|---|---|---|---|
| | | Lepton (bronze) | Widow's offering (MARK 12:42; LUKE 21:2) |
| Quadrans (bronze) | | 2 lepta | |
| As (bronze) | | 4 lepta | Value of two sparrows (MATTHEW 10:29) |
| Denarius (silver) | Drachma (silver) | | A day's wages for a labourer (MATTHEW 20:2, 9.10) |
| 2 denarii | Didrachma | Half-shekel | The standard annual temple tax (MATTHEW 17:24) |
| 4 denarii | Stater (tetradrachma) (silver) | Shekel | Payment for the temple tax (MATTHEW 17:27) |
| Aureus (gold) | | | |
| 100 denarii | 25 drachmae | | |
| 240 aurei | Mina | 30 shekels | In parable (LUKE 19:11–27) |
| | Talent (amount of value, not coin) | | In parables (MATTHEW 18:24; 25:14–30) |

## WEIGHTS AND MEASURES

A number of unfamiliar weights and measures appear throughout the Bible. This table lists them, compares their value relative to one another, and gives both imperial and metric equivalents. These are approximate equivalents as it is impossible to be precise.

| BIBLICAL UNIT | EQUAL TO | IMPERIAL EQUIVALENT | METRIC EQUIVALENT |
|---|---|---|---|
| **Weights:** | | | |
| Talent | 60 minas | 75 pounds | 34 kilograms |
| Mina | 50 shekels | 1¼ pounds | 600 grams |
| Shekel | 2 bekas | ⅖ ounce | 11 grams |
| Pim | ⅔ shekel | ⅓ ounce | 8 grams |
| Beka | 10 gerahs | ⅕ ounce | 6 grams |
| Gerah | | 1/50 ounce | 0.6 gram |
| **Length:** | | | |
| Mile | | 1,618 yards | 1,478 metres |
| Stadion | | 200 yards | 183 metres |
| Cubit | | 18 inches | 0.5 metre |
| Span | | 9 inches | 23 centimetres |
| Handbreadth | | 3 inches | 8 centimetres |
| **Dry measures:** | | | |
| Cor [homer] | 10 ephahs | 6 bushels | 220 litres |
| Lethek | 5 ephahs | 3 bushels | 110 litres |
| Ephah | 10 omers | ⅗ bushel | 22 litres |
| Seah | ⅓ ephah | 13 pints | 7.5 litres |
| Omer | 1/10 ephah | 4 pints | 2 litres |
| Cab | 1/18 ephah | 2 pints | 1 litre |
| **Liquid measures:** | | | |
| Bath | 1 ephah | 5 gallons [6 US gallons] | 22 litres |
| Hin | ⅙ bath | 7 pints | 4 litres |
| Log | 1/72 bath | ½ pint | 0.3 litre |

## ANCIENT RULERS

The united nation of Israel divided when the northern tribes refused to take Solomon's son Rehoboam as their king. This table shows the rulers of the Kingdom before the divide, and then the rulers of both new kingdoms until their repective falls.

**UNITED ISRAEL**

1050–1010 BC Saul

1010–970 BC David

970–931 BC Solomon

**931 BC The Kingdom divides**

| ISRAEL | JUDAH |
|---|---|
| 931–910 BC Jeroboam I | 931–913 BC Rehoboam |
| 910–909 BC Nadab | 913–911 BC Abijah |
| 909–886 BC Baasha | 911–870 BC Asa |
| 886–885 BC Elah | 873–848 BC Jehoshaphat |
| 885 BC Zimri | 848–841 BC Jehoram |
| 885–880 BC Tibni | 841 BC Ahaziah |
| 880–874 BC Omri | 841–835 BC Queen Athaliah |
| 874–853 BC Ahab | 835–796 BC Joash |
| 853–852 BC Ahaziah | 796–767 BC Amaziah |
| 852–841 BC Jehoram | 792–740 BC Uzziah |
| 841–814 BC Jehu | 740–735 BC Jotham |
| 814–798 BC Jehoahaz | 735–715 BC Ahaz |
| 798–782 BC Jehoash | 715–687 BC Hezekiah |
| 793–753 BC Jeroboam II | 687–642 BC Manasseh |
| 753–752 BC Zechariah | 642–640 BC Amon |
| 752 BC Shallum | 640–609 BC Josiah |
| 752–742 BC Menahem | 609 BC Jehoahaz |
| 742–740 BC Pekahiah | 609–598 BC Jehoiakim |
| 740–732 BC Pekah | 597 BC Jehoiachin |
| 732–722 BC Hoshea | 597–586 BC Zedekiah |
| **722 BC Israel falls** | **586 BC Jerusalem falls** |

## THE BOOKS OF THE BIBLE

The books of both the Old and New Testaments are listed here, first in the order in which they appear, and then alphabetically with page references.

| OLD TESTAMENT | NEW TESTAMENT | IN ALPHABETICAL ORDER |
|---|---|---|
| Genesis | Matthew | Acts (412–59) |
| Exodus | Mark | Amos (222–23) |
| Leviticus | Luke | 1 Chronicles (160–65) |
| Numbers | John | 2 Chronicles (170–75, 226–39) |
| Deuteronomy | Acts | Colossians (449) |
| Joshua | Romans | 1 Corinthians (449) |
| Judges | 1 Corinthians | 2 Corinthians (449) |
| Ruth | 2 Corinthians | Daniel (242–51) |
| 1 Samuel | Galatians | Deuteronomy (108–09, 114–15) |
| 2 Samuel | Ephesians | Ecclesiastes (190–91) |
| 1 Kings | Philippians | Ephesians (447, 449) |
| 2 Kings | Colossians | Esther (256–57) |
| 1 Chronicles | 1 Thessalonians | Exodus (88–113) |
| 2 Chronicles | 2 Thessalonians | Ezekiel (240–41) |
| Ezra | 1 Timothy | Ezra (252–53, 258–59) |
| Nehemiah | 2 Timothy | Galatians (449) |
| Esther | Titus | Genesis (30–87) |
| Job | Philemon | Habakkuk (222–23) |
| Psalms | Hebrews | Haggai (222–23) |
| Proverbs | James | Hebrews (450–51) |
| Ecclesiastes | 1 Peter | Hosea (222–23) |
| Song of Songs | 2 Peter | Isaiah (228–31) |
| Isaiah | 1 John | James (441) |
| Jeremiah | 2 John | Jeremiah (234–35) |
| Lamentations | 3 John | Job (188–89) |
| Ezekiel | Jude | Joel (222–23) |
| Daniel | Revelation | John (306–411) |
| Hosea | | 1 John (460–61) |
| Joel | | 2 John (460–61) |
| Amos | | 3 John (460–61) |
| Obadiah | | Jonah (212–13) |
| Jonah | | Joshua (116–29) |
| Micah | | Jude (440, 461) |
| Nahum | | Judges (130–35) |
| Habakkuk | | 1 Kings (168–75, 192–205) |
| Zephaniah | | 2 Kings (206–39 ) |
| Haggai | | Lamentations (238–39) |
| Zechariah | | Leviticus (110–11) |
| Malachi | | Luke (278–413) |
| | | Malachi (222–23) |
| | | Mark (302–405) |
| | | Matthew (286–413) |
| | | Micah (222–23) |
| | | Nahum (222–23) |
| | | Nehemiah (260–61) |
| | | Numbers (114–15) |
| | | Obadiah (222–23) |
| | | 1 Peter (420–21) |
| | | 2 Peter (420–21) |
| | | Philemon (449) |
| | | Philippians (449) |
| | | Proverbs (190–91) |
| | | Psalms (184–85) |
| | | Revelation (462–65) |
| | | Romans (449, 455) |
| | | Ruth (136–37) |
| | | 1 Samuel (140–59) |
| | | 2 Samuel (160–61, 164–67) |
| | | Song of Songs (190–91) |
| | | 1 Thessalonians (449) |
| | | 2 Thessalonians (449) |
| | | 1 Timothy (443, 449) |
| | | 2 Timothy (443, 449) |
| | | Titus (449) |
| | | Zechariah (222–23) |
| | | Zephaniah (222–23) |

## BIBLICAL SAYINGS

Many biblical quotes have entered into daily use as sayings. Some of them are listed here, along with where you can find them in the Bible.

| SAYING | REFERENCE |
|---|---|
| "A man reaps what he sows." | Galatians 6:7 |
| "all who draw the sword will die by the sword." | Matthew 26:52 |
| "Ask and it will be given to you; seek and you will find; knock and the door will be opened." | Matthew 7:7 |
| "Be joyful in hope, patient in affliction, faithful in prayer." | Romans 12:12 |
| "Blessed are the peacemakers" | Matthew 5:9 |
| "By the rivers of Babylon we sat and wept" | Psalms 137:1 |
| "do not let the sun go down while you are still angry" | Ephesians 4:26 |
| "eye for eye, tooth for tooth" | Deuteronomy 19:21 |
| "for dust you are, and to dust you will return." | Genesis 3:19 |
| "How the mighty have fallen!" | 2 Samuel 1:27 |
| "I am the Alpha and the Omega, the First and the Last, the Beginning and the End. " | Revelation 22:13 |
| "I have fought the good fight." | 2 Timothy 4:7 |
| "I had been like a gentle lamb led to the slaughter" | Jeremiah 11:19 |
| "In the beginning was the Word, and the Word was with God, and the Word was God." | John 1:1 |
| "it is easier for a camel to go through the eye of a needle than for someone who is rich to enter the kingdom of God." | Matthew 19:24 |
| "Let the little children come to me, and do not hinder them, as the kingdom of God belongs to such as these." | Luke 18:16 |
| "Love is patient, love is kind." | 1 Corinthians 13:4 |
| "Man shall not live on bread alone, but on every word that comes from the mouth of God." | Matthew 4:4 |
| "Physician, heal yourself!" | Luke 4:23 |
| "Pride goes before destruction, a haughty spirit before a fall." | Proverbs 16:18 |
| "The Lord gave and the Lord has taken away" | Job 1:21 |
| "The Lord is my shepherd, I lack nothing. He makes me lie down in green pastures, he leads me beside quiet waters, he refreshes my soul." | Psalms 23:1–3 |
| "the love of money is a root of all kinds of evil." | I Timothy 6:10 |
| "The spirit is willing, but the flesh is weak." | Matthew 26:41 |
| "They will beat their swords into ploughshares and their spears into pruning hooks." | Isaiah 2:4 |
| "There is a time for everything, and a season for every activity under the heavens" | Ecclesiastes 3:1 |
| "there is nothing new under the sun." | Ecclesiastes 1:9 |
| "There will be weeping there, and gnashing of teeth" | Luke 13:28 |
| "what God has joined together, let no one separate." | Matthew 19:6 |
| "Where, o death is your sting?" | 1 Corinthians 15:55 |
| "with God all things are possible." | Matthew 19:26 |
| "You are the salt of the earth." | Matthew 5:13 |
| "You of little faith" | Matthew 8:26 |

## PROPHECIES OF THE MESSIAH THAT ARE FULFILLED IN JESUS

The Old Testament contains a number of prophecies about a Messiah, who would save the Jewish people.
In the New Testament, these prophecies are fulfilled by Jesus. This table shows where each prophecy
appears in the Old Testament, and then where it is fulfilled in the New Testament.

| PROPHECY | IN OLD TESTAMENT | FULFILMENT IN NEW TESTAMENT |
|---|---|---|
| To be born in Bethlehem | MICAH 5:2 | MATTHEW 2:1–6; LUKE 2:1–20 |
| To be born of a virgin | ISAIAH 7:14 | MATTHEW 1:18–25; LUKE 1:26–31 |
| To escape to Egypt | HOSEA 11:1 | MATTHEW 2:14–15 |
| To be a prophet like Moses | DEUTERONOMY 18:15, 18, 19 | ACTS 3:20, 22; 7:37 |
| To heal the broken-hearted | ISAIAH 61:1–2 | LUKE 4:18–19 |
| To be rejected by his own people | ISAIAH 53:3 | JOHN 1:11 |
| To be the stone the builders rejected | PSALMS 118:22–23 | LUKE 20:17; ACTS 4:11 |
| To enter Jerusalem as a king | ZECHARIAH 9:9 | MATTHEW 21:1–9; JOHN 12:12–16 |
| To be betrayed by a friend | PSALMS 41:9 | LUKE 22:21–22; JOHN 13:18 |
| To be sold for 30 silver coins | ZECHARIAH 11:12 | MATTHEW 26:14–15; 27:9–10 |
| To be tried and condemned | ISAIAH 53:8 | MATTHEW 26:59–27:26; ACTS 8:32–35 |
| To be silent at his trial | ISAIAH 53:7 | MARK 15:3–5 |
| To be spat on and beaten by his enemies | ISAIAH 50:6 | MATTHEW 26:67 |
| To be hated for no reason | PSALMS 35:19 | JOHN 15:25 |
| To be sacrificed in humanity's place | ISAIAH 53:4–5 | MATTHEW 8:17; ROMANS 4:25; 5:6–8; 1 PETER 2:24 |
| To be crucified with criminals | ISAIAH 53:12 | MARK 15:27–28 |
| To be given vinegar and gall to drink | PSALMS 69:21 | MATTHEW 27:34; JOHN 19:28–30 |
| To be insulted, scorned, and mocked | PSALMS 22:7–8 | LUKE 23:11, 35 |
| Soldiers to gamble for his clothes | PSALMS 22:18 | MATTHEW 27:35–36 |
| To not have one of his bones broken | EXODUS 12:46; PSALMS 34:20 | JOHN 19:36 |
| To have his hands, feet, and side pierced | ZECHARIAH 12:10 | JOHN 19:34, 37; 20:27 |
| To be buried in a rich man's tomb | ISAIAH 53:9 | MATTHEW 27:57–60 |
| To be resurrected from the grave | PSALMS 16:10 | MATTHEW 28:1–10; ACTS 2:22–32; 1 CORINTHIANS 15:4 |
| To ascend to God's right hand | PSALMS 68:18; 110:1 | MATTHEW 26:64; LUKE 24:50–51; ACTS 1:9–11; 2:34; EPHESIANS 4:8 |

## JEWISH CALENDAR

The Hebrew calendar was originally based on the phases of the Moon, with an extra month added
whenever necessary to keep Passover in Spring. Later this system was replaced with mathematical rules,
and now this calendar is mainly used to determine Jewish religious observance (see pp.332–33).

| HEBREW MONTH | ALTERNATIVE NAME | MONTHS IN MODERN (GREGORIAN) CALENDAR | AGRICULTURAL ACTIVITY | RELIGIOUS FESTIVALS AND CEREMONIES |
|---|---|---|---|---|
| Nissan | Abib | March–April | The latter rains | Passover (*Pesach*); Unleavened Bread (*Chag HaMatzot*); Firstfruits (*Bikkurim*) |
| Iyar | Ziv | April–May | Barley harvest begins | Pentecost (*Shavuot*, "Weeks") |
| Sivan | | May–June | Vine-tending; wheat harvesting | |
| Tamuz | | June–July | Grape harvest begins | |
| Ab | | July–August | Full heat of summer | |
| Elul | | August–September | Date and fig harvest | |
| Tishrei | Ethanim | September–October | Former rains; ploughing begins | Trumpets (*Rosh Hashanah*/New Year); Day of Atonement (*Yom Kippur*); Tabernacles (*Sukkot*, "Booths") |
| Marchashian | Bul | October–November | Ploughing, olive harvest | |
| Chislev | | November–December | Wheat and barley sowing | Dedication (*Hanukkah*) |
| Tevet | Tishri, Tebeth | December–January | The main rains | |
| Shebat | | January–February | Almonds blossom | |
| Adar | Marcheshvan | February–March | Citrus harvest; flax harvest | Deliverance (*Purim*) |

## JESUS' PARABLES

Jesus' parables use simple stories to convey important messages. This table shows where the same parables appear in the different gospels. The Gospel of John does not contain "parables" in the same way as the other gospels, though it does convey Jesus' teachings through stories.

| PARABLES | MATTHEW | MARK | LUKE |
|---|---|---|---|
| A lamp on a stand | 5:14–15 | 4:21–22 | 8:16; 11:33 |
| The wise and foolish builders | 7:24–27 | | 6:47–49 |
| New cloth on an old garment | 9:16 | 2:21 | 5:36 |
| New wine in old wineskins | 9:17 | 2:22 | 5:37–38 |
| The sower | 13:3–8 | 4:3–8 | 8:5–8 |
| The mustard seed and the yeast | 13:31–33 | 4:30–32 | 13:18–21 |
| The weeds | 13:24–30 | | |
| The hidden treasure and the pearl | 13:44–46 | | |
| The net | 13:47–48 | | |
| The wandering sheep | 18:12–13 | | 15:4–6 |
| The unmerciful servant | 18:23–34 | | |
| The workers in the vineyard | 20:1–16 | | |
| The two sons | 21:28–31 | | 20:9–16 |
| The tenants | 21:33–41 | 12:1–9 | |
| The wedding banquet | 22:2–14 | | |
| The fig tree as herald of summer | 24:32–33 | 13:28–29 | 21:29–32 |
| Ten virgins | 25:1–13 | | |
| The bags of gold | 25:14–30 | | |
| The sheep and the goats | 25:31–46 | | |
| The growing seed | | 4:26–29 | |
| Creditors and debtors | | | 7:41–43 |
| The good Samaritan | | | 10:30–37 |
| A friend in need | | | 11:5–8 |
| The rich fool | | | 12:16–21 |
| Watchfulness | | | 12:35–48 |
| A fig tree without figs | | | 13:6–9 |
| The great banquet | | | 14:14–24 |
| Counting the cost | | | 14:28–33 |
| The lost coin | | | 15:8–10 |
| The lost son | | | 15:11–32 |
| The shrewd manager | | | 16:1–8 |
| A rich man and Lazarus | | | 16:19–31 |
| A master and his servants | | | 17:7–10 |
| The persistent widow | | | 18:2–5 |
| The Pharisee and the tax collector | | | 18:9–14 |

## JESUS' MIRACLES

Jesus performed a number of miracles as part of his teaching. Here they are listed, grouped by type, with a note of where each is recorded.

| MIRACLE | MATTHEW | MARK | LUKE | JOHN |
|---|---|---|---|---|
| **Healing the sick:** | | | | |
| A man with leprosy | 8:2–3 | 1:40–42 | 5:12–13 | |
| The faith of the centurion | 8:5–13 | | 7:1–10 | |
| Jesus heals many | 8:14–15 | 1:30–31 | 4:38–39 | |
| Two demon-possessed men | 8:28–34 | 5:1–15 | 8:27–35 | |
| A paralyzed man | 9:2–7 | 2:3–12 | 5:18–25 | |
| A dead girl and a sick woman | 9:20–22 | 5:25–29 | 8:43–48 | |
| The blind and the mute | 9:27–33 | | | |
| A man with a shrivelled hand | 12:10–13 | 3:1–5 | 6:6–10 | |
| Jesus and Beelzebul | 12:22 | 7:24–30 | 11:14 | |
| The faith of a Canaanite woman | 5:21–28 | 9:17–29 | | |
| A demon-possessed boy | 17:14–18 | | 9:38–43 | |
| Two blind men receive sight | 20:29–34 | 10:46–52 | 18:35–43 | |
| A man possessed at the synagogue | | 1:23–26 | 4:33–35 | |
| A blind man at Bethsaida | | 8:22–26 | | |
| A crippled woman | | | 13:11–13 | |
| A man with abnormal swelling | | | 14:1–4 | |
| Ten men with leprosy | | | 17:11–19 | |
| Malchus's ear | | | 22:50–51 | |
| An official's son at Capernaum | | | | 4:46–54 |
| The healing at the pool | | | | 5:1–9 |
| A man born blind | | | | 9 |
| **Miracles of nature:** | | | | |
| Calming the storm | 8:23–27 | 4:37–41 | 8:22–25 | 6:19–21 |
| Walking on water | 14:25 | 6:48–51 | | 6:5–13 |
| Feeding the 5,000 | 14:15–21 | 6:35–44 | 9:12–17 | |
| Feeding the 4,000 | 15:32–38 | 8:1–9 | | |
| Coin in a fish's mouth | 17:24–27 | | | |
| The cursed fig tree | 21:18–22 | 11:12–26 | | |
| A catch of fish | | | 5:1–11 | |
| Water turned into wine | | | | 2:1–11 |
| Another catch of fish | | | | 21:1–11 |
| **Raising the dead:** | | | | |
| Jairus's daughter | 9:18–25 | 5:22–42 | 8:41–56 | |
| A widow's son | | | 7:11–15 | |
| Lazarus | | | | 11:1–44 |

# Glossary

**AD/BC** The abbreviation AD stands for *Anno Domini* ("in the year of our Lord"), while BC stands for *before Christ*. The use of BC and AD for numbering years was established by the Christian scholar Dionysius Exiguus in AD 525. He designated 1 BC as the year of Christ's birth; the following year was AD 1 and there was no year 0. However, his dating scheme was later found to carry an error of around five years – when corroborated by other datable events, Christ's birth can be dated to *c.*5–4 BC. Some contemporary texts prefer to use BCE (Before the Common Era) and CE (Common Era) to avoid the Christian implications of BC and AD.

**ALPHA AND OMEGA** "The First and the Last; the Beginning and the End" (Revelation 22:13). The first and last letters of the Greek alphabet respectively. In the book of Revelation, the term is used as a title of Jesus Christ as sovereign over history.

**ALTAR** A raised table or cairn of stones in a holy place, where sacrifices and offerings are made to God. In the Old Testament the altar was usually made of wood, stone, or metal. Both the Tabernacle and Temple had an altar. Pagan altars were also built in ancient Israel.

**AMEN** From a Hebrew verb meaning "to be fixed, firm", hence "trustworthy; surely". It is used to end prayers or religious statements and to express strong acceptance of them.

**ANNUNCIATION** The announcement by the archangel Gabriel to the Virgin Mary that she would conceive her son Jesus as the Son of God by the Holy Spirit.

**ANOINT** To apply oil or ointment to a person or object as a sign of its being dedicated – set apart as special – to God. In the Old Testament, priests, prophets, and kings were anointed. In the New Testament, the sick were anointed and prayed over.

**APOCRYPHA** (or apocryphal – originally meaning "hidden".) Books of the Bible that are recognized as **DEUTEROCANONICAL** (being of secondary canonical rank) by the Catholic and Orthodox churches, but excluded as outside **THE CANON** by Protestant churches. The apocryphal or deuterocanonical books include those recognized by all Catholic and Orthodox churches, those recognized by the Greek and Russian Orthodox churches only, and certain other books.

**APOSTLE** From Greek for "one sent out." The word is used especially to refer to Jesus' 12 disciples whom he appointed as his representatives and to whom he gave his authority. The word is also used to refer to Paul and certain other early Christian missionaries and leaders.

**ARK OF THE COVENANT** A rectangular wooden box, overlaid with gold both inside and out, that God instructed the people of Israel to build. Believed to represent the presence of God, this was the most sacred religious symbol of the Hebrew people and was thought to have contained the stone tablets on which the Ten Commandments were written.

**ARMAGEDDON** The mountain of Meggido (see *Places* section) referred to in Revelation 16:16, either literally or symbolically as the place of God's final victory over evil.

**ASCENSION** Jesus' return from Earth to heaven after his resurrection, when he returned to God the Father after completing his work on Earth.

**BAPTISM** A ceremony using water to symbolize the washing away of sins, and for admission into the church. It symbolizes the believer's death to the old life of sin and resurrection to a new life with God, and the joining in relationship with Jesus Christ.

**BC** See **AD/BC**.

**BEATITUDES, THE** The series of blessings pronounced by Jesus in the Sermon on the Mount on those whose lives are marked by distinctive qualities.

**BIRTHRIGHT** The privilege enjoyed by the firstborn son to inherit a larger share of his father's property. When the estate was divided, the firstborn received a double portion.

**BLASPHEMY** The act of misusing, desecrating, or taking in vain God's name in action, speech, or writing. Blasphemy is strongly prohibited by God because it dishonours his name.

**BURNT OFFERING** A common kind of sacrifice in Patriarchal times and in ancient Israel. An animal was offered completely to God as a gift, to express thanksgiving for his goodness or as an atonement for sin. It also represents the one making the offering dedicating themselves completely to God.

**CANAAN** The land between the River Jordan, Dead Sea, and the Mediterranean Sea (see *Places* section). The Israelites believed that it was promised to them by God after their flight from Egypt, so it is sometimes referred to as the **PROMISED LAND**.

**CANON, THE** From the Greek for "rule". Refers to the list of books accepted as belonging to the Bible. Hence **DEUTEROCANONICAL**, literally "secondary canonical".

**CHERUB** A kind of winged heavenly creature that served God in the tabernacle and the Temple, for example, above the Ark of the Covenant in the Most Holy Place. *Cherub* is singular; *cherubim* plural.

**CHIEF PRIESTS** A group of men with responsibility for the Temple worship in Jerusalem. They were also in charge of discipline in the Temple. As official representatives of the Jewish people, they were afraid of the political effects of Jesus' popularity. They worked with Judas to plot Jesus' death. See also **HIGH PRIEST.**

**CHRIST** From Greek *Christos*, translation of Hebrew *Messiah*, "the anointed one". To be anointed suggested being chosen and commissioned. The term is used in the New Testament as a title for Jesus, the one who fulfils the Old Testament's promises of one who would come as a future anointed leader.

**CIRCUMCISION** The removal of the foreskin. In the Bible, an Israelite (later Jewish) male child was circumcised when he was eight days old (or occasionally when adult) as a sign of membership of God's **COVENANT**.

**CISTERN** An underground reservoir used to store water from springs or rain. Empty cisterns were used for different purposes (for example, Jeremiah was lowered into one). The term is also used in the Bible to refer to well-being.

**CITY-STATE** A city that is also an independent sovereign state. The term is significant in three main ways in the Old Testament: 1. Canaanite territory as organized around city-states, such as Ugarit and Beth Shemesh. 2. The Philistine Pentapolis: Gaza, Ashkelon, Ashdod, Ekron, and Gath were city-states. 3. Phoenician city-states included Tyre and Sidon, Byblos and Beritus.

**CODEX** A manuscript volume in pages with writing on both sides, and so able to be made into books. Examples of such manuscripts include the 4th-century *Codex Sinaiticus*, the 5th-century *Codex Alexandrinus*, and the 4th-century *Codex Vaticanus.*

**COUNCIL OF JERUSALEM** Possibly the first assembly of the Christian church, held about AD 49. The Christians met to consider whether to make Gentiles adopt Jewish customs, such as circumcision, as necessary for their salvation. The Council decided that circumcision was not necessary, but at the same time required Gentiles to behave with consideration towards Jewish Christians.

**COVENANT** A legally binding agreement, based on committed faithful loyalty (Hebrew *chesed*) between those involved. The Hebrew Bible records a series of covenants between God and human beings: for example, with Noah after the Flood; with Abraham; with the people of Israel at Mount Sinai; and with King David. The covenant with Israel is known by Christians as the Old Covenant, renewed and fulfilled in the New Covenant, or Testament, of Jesus Christ, which he established by his death. Such a covenant was prophesied in the Old Testament by prophets including Jeremiah, who wrote that God would "make a new covenant with the people of Israel and... put [the] law in their minds and write it on their hearts" (Jeremiah 31:31–33).

**CUBIT** A distance of about 0.5m (18in). Originally the distance from the fingertips to the elbow, it was used to measure both length and distance.

**CULT** A system of religious worship. In the Hebrew Bible, the Temple cult was the system of sacrifices and rituals at the Temple.

**CUNEIFORM** A writing system that uses wedge-shaped characters. From the Latin *cuneus*, meaning "wedge".

**DENARIUS** A Roman coin which was the standard pay for a day's work; equivalent to the Greek drachma.

**DEUTEROCANONICAL** See **APOCRYPHA.**

**DIASPORA, THE** The dispersal or scattering of large groups of people throughout the world. In the Bible, used to describe the exile of the Jews to Assyria and Babylon in the 6th century BC.

**DISCIPLE** Originally, a learner or pupil. A person called to follow and serve Jesus Christ. In the Gospels, the term is used especially for Christ's inner circle (see **APOSTLE**), the term is applied to Christians in general, highlighting the significance of learning from Christ as teacher.

**DYNASTY** A series of rulers from the same lineage or family, for example, the 18th-dynasty Egyptian pharaohs who included Amenhotep I, Amenhotep II, Amenhotep III, and Tutankhamun.

**ELDER** A traditional local community leader throughout the biblical period. A senior member of a church in New Testament times recognized as having responsibility for leadership, oversight, teaching, service, and church discipline.

**EPISTLE** A letter, in particular one of the letters included in the New Testament, giving greetings, instruction, warnings, advice, encouragement, and news.

**EVANGELIST** One who preaches the **GOSPEL** of Jesus Christ to those who are not believers in him. Their task is to bring people to recognize Jesus as Lord and Messiah by acknowledging their sins and turning back to God, and by having faith (trusting) in God. The word comes from Greek *euangelion*, "gospel, good news". Also, the writers of the four Gospels are known as the four evangelists.

**EXILE, THE** The forced deportation of the inhabitants of Israel and Judah after the conquest by the Assyrians of the northern kingdom of Israel in 722 BC, and the exile to Babylon of the residents of the southern kingdom of Judah. The exile of Judeans took place in three stages: firstly from 605 BC by Babylonian King Nebuchadnezzar; secondly, after the siege of Jerusalem

in 597 BC, which included the prophets Ezekiel and Daniel; finally, the main deportation took place after the fall of Jerusalem in 587 BC. The deportations had been prophesied as judgment for Israel's idolatry, injustice, and worthless religion. The duration and restoration of the exiles were also prophesied.

**EXODUS, THE** From Greek for "way out". The Israelites' departure and release from slavery in Egypt, led by Moses by crossing the Red Sea on their way to the **PROMISED LAND**. The exodus demonstrated the power of God and his provision for his people.

**FALL, THE** The disobedience of Adam and Eve and their fall from God's perfect presence when they disobeyed God's command not to eat the fruit of the tree of the knowledge of good and evil. Because of the fall, sin entered the world and pervaded all humanity, with all human beings being sinners and subject to God's punishment of death. Christians believe that the Bible teaches that only Jesus Christ can set people free from the effects of the fall.

**GENTILE** A translation of the Hebrew word *goy*, which simply means "nation". The term came to refer to those who were not **JEWS**, that is, not Abraham's descendants and therefore excluded from the promise made to him and his descendants. Although Jesus first preached to the people of Israel, his mission quickly spread to the Gentiles, and the Church accepted Gentiles as full members alongside Jews. The apostle Paul had a special mission to the Gentiles.

**GNOSTICISM** From Greek for "knowledge". A general term for 2nd-century sects that sought to escape the body to a purely spiritual life via a special secret knowledge (*gnosis*), known only to them. They included parts of the Christian story in their beliefs and claimed to be the only ones to have the true understanding of it.

**GOSPEL** From the Old English *godspel*, "good news". The teaching that God has redeemed humanity through the salvation Jesus Christ brought by his life, death, and resurrection. Also refers with an initial capital (*Gospel*) to the first four books of the New Testament, which deal with Jesus' life, death, and resurrection.

**GRACE** Abundant and undeserved love, freely given by God to humanity in the salvation offered through his Son, Jesus Christ.

**HANUKKAH** Means "dedication" and refers to the Jewish religious festival lasting eight days that celebrates the victory of the Maccabees and the rededication of the Jerusalem Temple. It is celebrated by the lighting of lamps or candles.

**HEBREW BIBLE** The name by which some non-Jews refer to the Jewish Scriptures. The Jewish term is **TANAKH**.

**HELLENISM** In general, the spirit and characteristics of classical Greek civilization. Also, a movement and approach by the Seleucid Greek rulers, whose empire included Judea; to *hellenize* every country in their empire was to make them Greek in language, culture, and religion. It was broadly welcomed in most of their domain, but most Jews in Palestine were resistant to it on religious grounds.

**HERODIAN** Of or concerning Herod the Great, king of Judea (37–4 BC), or to members of his family.

**HIGH PLACE** A raised place used for religious worship, hence a sanctuary. Especially used with reference to the shrines set up to Canaanite **IDOL** gods.

**HIGH PRIEST** The senior Jewish leader responsible for the nation's spiritual well-being, for example, by teaching and anointing kings. The high priest had the special responsibility for making atonement for the people's sins. Once a year, on the Day of Atonement, he entered the **MOST HOLY PLACE**, which represented the presence of God, to offer sacrifices for the sins of the nation. The New Testament sees Jesus Christ as ultimately fulfilling the role of high priest, making the perfect sacrifice for the sins of his people through his death on the cross.

**HOLY OF HOLIES** See **MOST HOLY PLACE.**

**HOSPITALITY** Showing generosity and friendship to strangers. In the ancient Near East, customs developed that expressed a generous welcome to visitors and strangers. These included greeting with bowing, washing feet, sharing food, providing a place to rest and giving gifts. Hospitality is a quality that God wants in his people as part of their responsibility towards others and to show thanksgiving for their salvation.

**IDOL** An image, often carved and made of wood, metal, or stone, which is worshipped as a god. Hence *idolatry*, meaning such worship.

**INCENSE** A substance usually derived from resin, noted for the fragrant odour it gives off when offered in ritual worship. In the Old Testament, incense was burnt on a special altar in the Tabernacle and Temple.

**ISRAEL AND JUDAH** After the kingdom was divided under Rehoboam, Israel came to refer to the northern kingdom and Judah to the southern kingdom. See also in the *Places* section.

**JEHOVAH** A non-existent name for God derived from an error. Since no vowels were written to accompany the letters YHWH, this name of God cannot be pronounced. The vowels from *Adonai*, "my Lord", were inserted as a signal to pronounce that word instead. Trying to read this mixed word as written produces the impossible Yahowah or Jehovah. See also **YAHWEH**.

**JEWS** A term originally used to refer to the "descendants of the people from the kingdom of Judah" or "Judeans"; the people belonging to one of the tribes of Israel. In the New Testament, it is used more often than Israel to refer to Jewish people generally. The message of the New Testament is equally for Jews and Gentiles. Jesus himself was a Jew, and Jesus and the apostles preached the gospel first to the Jews, and then to **GENTILES** (non-Jews).

**JUDGES** Leaders who ruled among and governed the tribes of Israel from the death of Joshua to the time of Samuel; and the name of the Old Testament book dealing with that period of Israelite history.

**JUDGMENT DAY** All human beings are accountable to God and on the Day of Judgment, which will take place when Jesus returns, he will finally assess every human being by identifying and condemning sin, and vindicating and rewarding the righteous. The basis of God's judgment is his absolute fairness: judgment will be based on a person's deeds, their response to God's revelation in Jesus, and faith in Jesus.

**KINGDOM OF GOD** The teaching that in time the entire world will come to accept the universal and sovereign rule of God. The kingdom of God (or the kingdom of heaven) comes wherever God's authority is recognized. The kingdom of God was realized in Jesus' life: he demonstrated the reality of God's authority by performing miracles, and by declaring the good news of God's forgiveness of sins. The Bible affirms that the reign of salvation that has already come in Jesus Christ will fully come when he returns.

**LAW, THE** An inadequate translation of the Hebrew word **TORAH**, which contains elements of law, teaching, and guidance. It refers to the set of laws and teachings given to the Israelites by God, aimed at creating an ideal society based on their obligations to each other, to the land, and to God under the **COVENANT**. To Jews, the Torah was a gift of God's love that when followed, gave them life in accordance with their covenant relationship with him.

**LEPROSY** An infectious skin disease. In the Bible, the term leprosy covers a wider range of diseases – even including conditions affecting buildings and clothes – other than the one referred to today as Hansen's disease.

**LIVING GOD** A term used throughout the Bible to denote God as a living, active, and powerful deity, often in contrast to the idols of nations opposed to Israel.

**LOTS, CASTING OF** A traditional Israelite way of finding out the will of God in such matters as identifying a guilty person or distributing plunder. Foreign sailors in the Book of Jonah cast lots, suggesting that this was not just an Israelite way of discerning the will of gods. In the New Testament, it was used once, with prayer, before the giving of the Holy Spirit at Pentecost.

**LXX** An abbreviation used for the **SEPTUAGINT**.

**MANNA** Food miraculously provided for the Israelites on their way through the desert from Egypt to the Promised Land. The Hebrew word *manna* means "what is it?"; it had the appearance of coriander seed and the taste of honey.

**MARTYR** From Greek for "witness". Initially used to refer to any who shared the good news of Jesus. Later used to refer specifically to those who die for their faith. Hence *martyrdom*.

**MATRIARCH** The female head of a tribe or family.

**MENORAH** A seven-branched candelabrum used in the Temple. Subsequently an emblem of Israel, and later of Judaism.

**MESOPOTAMIA** Land "between the rivers" (the Tigris and Euphrates), which included such cities as Babylon, Ur, and Nineveh (see *Places* section).

Haran and Paddan Aram, the towns where some of Abraham's family settled, lay here. In the New Testament, people from Mesopotamia were in Jerusalem on the Day of Pentecost.

**MESSIAH** Hebrew for "the anointed one". See **CHRIST.**

**MIDRASH** From Hebrew for "to search". A Jewish commentary on the Hebrew Bible.

**MINISTRY** From Latin for "service". The Old Testament associates the term with the work of the Temple priests. The New Testament describes Jesus as the model for Christian ministry, and ministry is used to refer to all different kinds of Christian service. In a narrower sense, the word refers to the official service of ordained individuals who have been specially set aside by the Church.

**MIRACLE** A spectacular or extraordinary supernatural event. In the Bible, miracles occur at significant moments in the history of God's people and demonstrate his power, authority, and presence. Miracles can add credence to the claims of the person who performs them, but the glory is God's alone.

**MISHNAH** From Hebrew for "instruction". A compilation of Jewish teachings collected together in the late second century. It forms the earlier part of the **TALMUD**.

**MONOTHEISTIC** Of, or concerning the belief that there is only one true God.

**MOST HOLY PLACE** (also **HOLY OF HOLIES**) The most sacred part of the Temple in Jerusalem that represented the presence of God, containing initially the **ARK OF THE COVENANT**. It was curtained off and was entered only once a year on the Day of Atonement by the **HIGH PRIEST**.

**NOMADS** People who had no settled home but moved around from one place to another, often living in tents in the desert. Abraham was a nomad.

**ORDINATION** A ceremony in which someone is appointed into church ministry and leadership when the individual is officially commissioned and given the authority for such a role. In the Old Testament, priests were ordained.

**PAGAN** From Latin *paganus*, meaning rural or of the countryside. The word

came to refer to someone who did not follow the one true God or one who followed a local religion.

**PARABLE** From Greek for "placing beside". A short story that uses events from ordinary everyday life to illustrate, or serve as an analogy of, moral and spiritual truths. Sometimes the parables needed explanation. Jesus used parables extensively in his teaching.

**PARADISE** From Hebrew *pardes*, a Persian word meaning "orchard". In later tradition a blessed place in which the righteous live. Paradise can refer to heaven, or to the Garden of Eden before the expulsion of Adam and Eve.

**PASSOVER** The annual Jewish festival commemorating the Israelites' escape from oppression in Egypt and the **EXODUS.**

**PATRIARCH** The male head of a tribe or family. Used of the Hebrew leaders before the time of Moses, in particular Abraham, Isaac, and Jacob, and also of the 12 sons of Jacob.

**PENTATEUCH** From Greek for "five scrolls". The first five books of the Bible: Genesis, Exodus, Leviticus, Numbers, and Deuteronomy. These books contain, and are also called, the **TORAH**.

**PENTECOST** From Greek for "fiftieth". The Jewish Feast of Weeks on the fiftieth day after **PASSOVER**. On this day, the first fruits of the harvest were presented at the Temple. In the New Testament, the Holy Spirit came on the **APOSTLES** at Pentecost.

**PHARAOH** From an Egyptian word meaning "great house", the title of the ancient Egyptian ruler. The Old Testament mentions several pharaohs, although usually not by name, including the pharaoh of the **EXODUS** (possibly Rameses II); Shishak (Sheshonq I), who attacked Jerusalem during the reign of Rehoboam; and Necho, who killed Josiah.

**PHARISEES** From Hebrew for "separated". One of the main Jewish religious/political groupings of the New Testament period, they were known for their strict adherence to **THE LAW**, to which they added a wealth of oral guidelines in an attempt to help everyday Jews to uphold the Law. Many of them opposed Jesus, whom they regarded as a blasphemer and law-breaker. The apostle Paul was a zealous Pharisee before his conversion to Christ.

**PHILISTINES** The Philistine people descended from the Sea Peoples who had left Crete and infiltrated many places, including Egypt and Syria. They settled in the territory which became known as Philistia along the Mediterranean coast, west of Judea, establishing five cities there. They were the most notorious enemies of the Israelites, as the showdown with their champion Goliath illustrates.

**POLYTHEISTIC** Of, or concerning the belief that there are many gods.

**PRAETORIUM** Originally used to refer to the general's tent in a camp or a military headquarters; the governor's official residence in Jerusalem.

**PREFECT** The title given to government officials appointed to a position of authority. Mentioned in Daniel 3 and 6 among the Babylonian officials during the reign of Nebuchadnezzar's reign.

**PROMISED LAND** See **CANAAN.**

**PROPHECY** The message that is spoken out by a person (**PROPHET**) in the belief that the message is inspired and revealed by God. Prophecy is delivered to an individual, group, or nation, and calls for a response. It addresses the past, present, or future; actions; or attitudes. Much prophecy does not so much predict the future as give exhortation, urging change and turning back to God. Most biblical prophecy is found in the Old Testament. The New Testament refers to this prophecy, indicating it has been fulfilled by Jesus Christ.

**PROPHETS** People who spoke words of **PROPHECY.** Prophets were often called by God to speak his word in times of crisis. The prophets explained to their contemporaries the significance of God's **COVENANT**, both its responsibilities and its privileges. They emphasized that God was concerned about the whole of life. Jesus himself was the supreme prophet, since he not only fully spoke God's word but was himself God's word in the flesh.

**PROVERB** A short popular saying that communicates a lesson about how to live wisely. Proverbs are often based on observations of everyday life. The Book of Proverbs records many such sayings, but they are also found in other books of the Bible.

**PSALM** From Greek for a song accompanied with harp. The 150 sacred songs, poems, and prayers collected as one of the books of the Hebrew Bible.

Often used in worship to express praise, thanksgiving, and prayer.

**PSALTER** Another name for the book of **PSALMS**, or for a book containing all the psalms, often with a musical setting.

**RABBI** From Hebrew for "master" or "teacher". A title of honour given to a qualified Jewish religious teacher. Hence *rabbinic*, relating to a rabbi, their teachings, or writings. In the Gospels, Jesus Christ is called Rabbi by his followers, showing he was considered to be a respected teacher.

**REPENTANCE** A complete change of heart that leads to a change of action. It involves a sincere turning away from sin to God and includes deep regret for, and confession of, **SIN**. The Bible emphasizes the need for individuals and communities to repent from their sin if they are to avoid God's judgment and receive his forgiveness so that they can enjoy full fellowship with God.

**RESURRECTION** The giving of new, eternal life to a dead person, especially referring to the raising of Jesus Christ from the dead by God after his death. Evidence for Christ's resurrection includes his empty grave and his appearances to his disciples. Christ's resurrection is considered by Christians to be the turning point of history, as it affirms his divinity, confirms his words and actions as having God's approval, and opens the way to the future resurrection of believers.

**REVELATION** The disclosure of God's nature, purpose, and will through the Scriptures, his creation of the Universe and life in all its forms, and history. The most significant act of God's revelation is that he has made himself known fully to humankind in Jesus Christ.

**RIGHTEOUS, THE** Especially in the Old Testament, the designation, of people who lead lives that have spiritual and moral integrity according to God's commands.

**SABBATH** The seventh day of the week, the Sabbath was set aside as a day for the worship of God and for rest. It originally began on Friday evening for both Jews and Christians, but as Christ's resurrection took place on Sunday, this displaced the Sabbath for Christians.

**SACRIFICE** An offering made to God, particularly a living animal. In the Hebrew Bible, the people of Israel made sacrifices to express their thanksgiving towards God, obtain forgiveness, or seal a **COVENANT** with God. By the 7th century BC, sacrifice was confined to the Temple in Jerusalem. For Christians, the death of Jesus Christ is the one sacrifice that secures forgiveness by God.

**SADDUCEES** In New Testament Israel, a conservative aristocracy of Jewish priests who dominated both **TEMPLE** worship and also the **SANHEDRIN**. They opposed the **PHARISEES** and Jesus. Unlike the Pharisees, they rejected oral tradition, the resurrection of the dead, and the existence of angels.

**SANHEDRIN** A Jewish council, either local or, in the case of Jerusalem, the supreme council that was directed by the **HIGH PRIEST**. Its members included **ELDERS**, **CHIEF PRIESTS**, and teachers of the law.

**SCRIPTURE** The biblical writings (the Hebrew Bible and/or the New Testament), inspired by the Holy **SPIRIT**, received as the word of God, and to be respected as having his authority. The Scriptures have been given to the church for teaching, guarding against error, and enabling it to grow in faith and maturity.

**SEPTUAGINT** The name given to the Greek translation of the Hebrew Bible, which was probably undertaken in Alexandria. Its name derives from a traditional story that suggested 70 translators worked on this translation. It was the Bible of the Early Church, to which the books of the New Testament were gradually added as they became generally accepted.

**SHEOL** In the Hebrew Bible, used to refer to the grave, the pit, or the tomb; the place where traces of the dead continue.

**SHRINE** A place where worship is offered or devotions are given, often in **PAGAN** worship.

**SIN** A general term that translates a number of Hebrew and Greek words for actions ranging from failure to live up to one's responsibilities, to outright rebellion against God. In the Hebrew Bible such "sins" are regarded as individual acts consequent upon human free will, not a state of being. In Christian thought, sin is seen primarily as a wrong relationship with God, which expresses itself in wrong attitudes or actions towards God, people, or things. The Bible emphasizes that this condition is firmly established in human nature and that only God can break its penalty, power, and presence.

**SPEAKING IN TONGUES** A phenomenon, described in the New Testament as a gift of the Holy Spirit, in which people speak in languages not known to them, or in sounds that do not correspond to any language. The gift of tongues may be used to express praise to God or to declare a message from God, which when accompanied by an interpretation, can encourage other believers.

**SPIRIT** The innermost non-material part of a human being. God is spirit in a unique sense, unconfined by body, space, or time. Also, with an initial capital S (*Spirit*), the third person of the Trinity, the Holy Spirit.

**SYNAGOGUE** From Greek for "gathering". A Jewish place of worship or congregation that meets for worship and religious study.

**SYNOPTIC** From Greek for "seeing things together". The Gospels of Matthew, Mark, and Luke are known as the Synoptic Gospels, because they share much material and have the same basic framework.

**TABERNACLE** The large portable tent that formed the sanctuary in which the Israelites carried the **ARK OF THE COVENANT** during their journey from Egypt to Canaan.

**TALENT** In Old Testament times, a unit of weight equivalent to about 34 kilograms (75 pounds) or 60 minas (a Near Eastern unit of weight and currency). In the New Testament, it was a unit of financial reckoning worth about 20 years' wages of a labourer. Jesus gave the parable of the talents (Matthew 25:14–30), emphasizing the need to use the "talents", also interpreted as abilities by some commentators, one has been given.

**TALMUD** An extensive Jewish religious work containing interpretation of, and commentary on, the **TORAH**, the primary source from which the rest of Jewish religious law has developed. It is made up of the **MISHNAH** and the Gemara, which records debates on the interpretation of the Mishnah.

**TANAKH** An acronym based on the initial letters for the three sections of the Hebrew Bible in the form used by Jews: the **TORAH** (the Teaching/Law – also known as the **PENTATEUCH**),

*Nevi'im* (the Prophets – the books of the Old Testament prophets), and *Kethuvim* (the Writings – the historical books of the Old Testament).

**TEMPLE, THE** In Jerusalem, the Temple was the only place where sacrifices could be made, and the centre of Jewish worship. The First Temple was built by King Solomon (c.1011–931 BC), and was destroyed by the Babylonians (c.587 BC). The Second Temple was built after the exile (c.520 BC), and was extensively rebuilt by Herod the Great. This was the Temple known to Jesus, the first disciples, and the Early Church, but was destroyed by the Romans in AD 70.

**TERAPHIM** Household gods or images venerated by ancient Semitic peoples.

**TORAH** A term meaning "teaching" or "direction", which includes the idea of "law". Originally it applied to the **PENTATEUCH**, the five books of Moses, alone, but in Jewish tradition it came to mean the whole of the Hebrew Bible and teaching derived from it through interpretation.

**TRANSFIGURATION** The revelation of Christ's glory, which happened once during his life on Earth, in which his three closest disciples Peter, James, and John saw him in his full majesty.

**YAHWEH** The most sacred Hebrew name for God, given by God to Moses (Exodus 3:13–14). It is based on YHWH, but because no vowels were written in the letters YHWH, the vowels from *Adonai*, "my Lord", were inserted, leading to the rendering Yahweh. In English Bibles, *Yahweh* is usually written as "the LORD".

**YHWH** See **YAHWEH**.

**ZEALOT** A group of Jewish rebels who fought against the Roman occupation of Judea at the time of Jesus Christ.

**ZIGGURAT** An Assyrian or Babylonian structured tower in the form of a pyramid, in which each successive storey is smaller than the one beneath it. The Tower of Babel is an example of a ziggurat.

**ZION** Originally either the south-eastern hill of Jerusalem, or the earlier fortress built by the Jebusites. It became a synonym for Jerusalem. The Temple was also known as Mount Zion. The word is also used to refer to Israel, the Church, and heaven.

# Index

# Acknowledgments

**Dorling Kindersley** would like to thank the following people for their help in the preparation of this book. For assistance with initial planning: Jemima Dunne, Phil Fitzgerald, Amanda Lunn, Karen Self, and Steve Woosnam-Savage. For editorial assistance: Jamie Ambrose, Lizzie Munsey, Andy Szudek, Laura Wheadon, Alex Whittleton, and Rev Adrian Chatfield.

**cobalt id** would like to thank Dorothy Frame for indexing.

## Picture Credits

The publisher would like to thank the following for their kind permission to reproduce their photographs:

Key: a-above; b-below/bottom; c-centre; f-far; l-left; r-right; t-top

AKG - akg-images; AI - Alamy Images; AA - The Art Archive; BAL - The Bridgeman Art Library; DK - Dorling Kindersley; GI - Getty Images; ZR - Zev Radovan/www.BibleLandPicures.com

**Running head images. 14-25 GI:** Tetra Images. **32-261 Photos8.com. 278-465 Fotalia.com:** Gregor Buir. **470-512 GI:** BAL. **1 AKG. 2-3 Corbis:** Bettmann. **4-5 Corbis:** Frans Lemmens. **6 Corbis:** The Gallery Collection (br). **GI:** Hulton Archive (bl). **7 GI:** Stone / Ed Freeman (bl); Superstock (br). **8 AA:** Gianni Dagli Orti / Musée du Louvre, Paris (br). **GI:** BAL (b). **9 Corbis:** Elio Ciol (br); Dave G. Houser (bl). **10-11 AKG:** Rabatti-Domingie. **14 AKG:** (tr); Gerard Degeorge (c). **AI:** ASP Religion (br). **GI:** BAL (bl). **15 BAL:** Biblioteca Estense Universitaria, Modena. **16 AKG:** Electa (tl). **17 AI:** Lonely Planet Images (tr). **BAL:** Instituto da Biblioteca Nacional, Lisbon (bl). **18 GI:** Stone / Simon McComb (t). **19 AKG:** ZR (bl); Andrea Jemolo (cla). **AA:** Gianni Dagli Orti / Roger Cabal Collection (tr). **20 Corbis:** Historical Picture Archive (tl); JAI / Jon Arnold (bc). **GI:** De Agostini / Pubbli Aer Foto (bl). **21 AKG:** CDA / Guillemot (c). **AI:** INTERFOTO (tr). **AA:** Trinity College, Dublin (l). **22 AKG:** Philippe Maillard (cl). **Corbis:** Richard T. Nowitz (bc). **22-23 Corbis:** Dead Sea Scrolls Foundation / West Semitic Research (tc). **23 Corbis:** Richard T. Nowitz (tr); David Rubinger (br). **24 BAL:** Coram in the care of the Foundling Museum, London (cl). **Corbis:** Burstein Collection (tl). **24-25 DK:** By permission of The British Library (bc). **25 AA:** Bodleian Library, Oxford (br). **Photo Scala, Florence:** White Images (cra). **29 Photo Mendrea:** Radu Mendrea (br). **30 AI:** Timewatch Images (b). **Corbis:** The Gallery Collection (t). **31 GI:** BAL (b). **32 GI:** Stockbyte / Ursula Alter (bl). **ZR:** (clb). **32-33 AA:** Bibliothèque Municipale, Moulins (c). **33 Corbis:** Hoberman Collection (br). **GI:** BAL (tr). **34 AI:** Prisma Bildagentur AG (b). **35 BAL:** Bodleian Library, Oxford (crb). **Corbis:** Arte & Immagini srl (bc); Historical Picture Archive (tc). **36 AI:** Peter Barritt (r, clb). **37 AA:** Bodleian Library, Oxford (tr). **38-39 Corbis:** Araldo de Luca. **40 AKG:** British Library, London (br). **BAL:** Archives Charmet / Bibliothèque Sainte-Genevieve, Paris (bc); Hamburger Kunsthalle, Hamburg (cl). **41 Corbis:** Arte & Immagini srl. **42 AA:** Dagli Orti / Musée du Louvre, Paris (bl). **GI:** Hulton Archive (cra). **42-43 GI:** De Agostini / W. Buss (b). **43 Corbis:** Adam Woolfitt (tc). **GI:** Gallo Images / Danita Delimont (cr). **44 Corbis:** The Gallery Collection (r). **Panos Pictures:** Georg Gerster (bl). **45 Corbis:** Reuters / Ceerwan Aziz (bc). **GI:** BAL (br). **46 AI:** The Art Gallery Collection (t); Timewatch Images (b). **47 Corbis:** Gianni Dagli Orti (bc). **48 AI:** Robert Harding Picture Library / Adam Woolfitt (bc). **Corbis:** (cl). **49 BAL:** Alinari / Collegiata, San Gimignano. **50 T. Credner / AlltheSky.com:** (br). **Photo Mendrea:** Sandu Mendrea (cl). **51 AA:** Dagli Orti / Château de Chambord (tr); Gianni Dagli Orti (br). **Corbis:** Charles & Josette Lenars (bl). **52 AI:** Hanan Isachar (br). **Corbis:** Ricki Rosen (tr). **DK:** Alan Hills and Barbara Winter (c) The British Museum (bl). **52-53 Corbis:** Jose Fuste Raga. **53 Corbis:** David Lees (c). **GI:** DEA / G. Dagli Orti (bl). **54 AKG:** (br). **Corbis:** Dean Conger (cl). **55 AKG:** Erich Lessing (tl). **AA:** Dagli Orti / Collection Antonovich (cr). **GI:** BAL (br). **56 Tyne & Wear Archives & Museums:** Laing Art Gallery. **57 AI:** Sonia Halliday Photographs (tl). **Dreamstime.com:** Sergey Ponomarev (br). **GI:** David Silverman (bc). **58 GI:** Photographer's Choice / Marvin E. Newman (t). **Hanan Isachar:** (cla). **58-59 Corbis:** Elio Ciol (bc). **59 AI:** Mario Mitsis (br); ZR (cr). **60 AKG:** ullstein bild (bl). **AI:** ASP Religion (r). **61 AKG:** (cr). **AI:** The Print Collector (bc). **GI:** BAL (tc). **62 Corbis:** Spaces Images / Noam Armonn (cla). **GI:** Photolibrary / Michel Gunther (b). **63 BAL:** Monasterio de la Vid, Burgos (tr). **GI:** De Agostini / A. de Gregorio (tl). **Hanan Isachar:** (br). **64 AI:** ASAP (t); Eddie Gerald (b). **64-65 Corbis:** Lindsay Hebberd. **65 AI:** Israel images (cr); ZR (tl, tr). **Corbis:** Ricki Rosen (br). **GI:** Tetra Images (bl). **66 AA:** Dagli Orti / Schloss Weissenstein der Grafen von Schänborn, Pommersfelden. **67 Corbis:** Godong / Fred de Noyelle (c); Jeffrey L. Rotman (cl). **GI:** The Image Bank / Remi Benali (br). **68 Corbis:** Francis G. Mayer. **69 Corbis:** JAI / Jane Sweeney (crb); David Turnley (cra); Cory Langley (bc). **Dreamstime.com:** Rostislav Glinsky (tc). **70-71 Corbis:** The Gallery Collection. **72 AKG:** Erich Lessing (c). **AA:** Superstock (cla). **SuperStock:** Photononstop (bl). **73 Corbis:** Elio Ciol (tr); Eldad Rafaeli (b). **74-75 AKG:** A.F. Kersting (b). **75 AA:** Dagli Orti / Musée du Louvre, Paris (tc). **76 GI:** De Agostini / P. Manusardi (r). **ZR:** (cl). **77 BAL:** Wolverhampton Art Gallery, West Midlands (tr). **Corbis:** Richard T. Nowitz (br). **ZR:** (bl). **78 AI:** ZR (bl). **78-79 AI:** First Light (bc). **79 AI:** Hemis (tc). **AA:** Dagli Orti / Klosterneuburg Monastery, Austria (cr). **80 GI:** SuperStock (bl). **81 AKG:** Joseph Martin (tc). **AI:** ZR (cra). **BAL:** The Trustees of the Chester Beatty Library, Dublin (br). **82 AKG:** (br). **BAL:** Collection of the Earl of Leicester, Holkham Hall, Norfolk (cl). **GI:** Photolibrary / ArabianEye / Jochen Tack (bl). **83 Corbis:** Sandro Vannini (tc). **Dreamstime.com:** Georgios Kollidas (cr/ Hebrew Numbers). **GI:** De Agostini / G. Dagli Orti (br). **84 GI:** Robert Harding World Imagery (tr). **84-85 Corbis:** José Fuste Raga (bc). **85 GI:** De Agostini (tc); Photographer's Choice / Peter Phipp (tr). **86 AI:** Hemis (b). **NASA:** Jacques Descloitres, MODIS Land Science Team (cla). **87 AA:** Dagli Orti / San Gennaro Cathedral, Naples (c). **BAL:** Bibliothèque Nationale de Paris (br). **GI:** BAL (tr). **88 AI:** Timewatch Images (b). **BAL:** Zentralbibliothek, Weimar (t). **89 Corbis:** Sandro Vannini (br). **90 AKG:** Erich Lessing (br). **AA:** Dagli Orti / Luxor Museum, Egypt (cla). **Corbis:** Sandro Vannini (cl). **91 AKG:** Tristan Lafranchis (cra). **GI:** DEA / G. Dagli Orti (tl). **92 AKG:** Andrea Jemolo (clb). **Photo Scala, Florence:** Courtesy of the Ministero Beni e Att. Culturali (r). **93 AKG:** Erich Lessing (cr). **AI:** Jon Arnold Images Ltd (bc). **GI:** SuperStock (tc). **94 Dreamstime.com:** Niek. **95 Corbis:** The Gallery Collection (cl); Sandro Vannini (br). **GI:** SuperStock (tc). **96-97 Corbis:** David Lees. **98 AI:** Photoshot Holdings Ltd. **99 BAL:** The Stapleton Collection (tc). **GI:** De Agostini / G. Dagli Orti (br). **100-101 AKG. 102-103 Corbis:** SuperStock / Ron Dahlquist (bc). **102 AI:** Nathan Benn (bl). **Corbis:** Gianni Dagli Orti (tr). **103 Corbis:** Fine Art Photographic Library (br). **104 GI:** Hulton Archive. **105 AKG:** Erich Lessing (cla). **AI:** ASP Religion (bc). **AA:** Dagli Orti / National Museum of Art Mexico (br). **106-107 Corbis:** Alinari Archives. **108 AI:** Eddie Gerald (tr). **AA:** Dagli Orti / Museo del Duomo, Milan (bl). **GI:** Hulton Archive (br). **109 Corbis:** Richard T. Nowitz (c); David H. Wells (br). **110 AA:** Gianni Dagli Orti / Private Collection, Istanbul (c). **111 AKG:** (tr). **AI:** ZR (clb). **Corbis:** Sygma / Jon Jones (br). **112 AKG:** ZR (br). **GI:** Universal Images Group (cl). **113 Corbis:** Hanan Isachar (tl). **GI:** BAL (cr). **Hanan Isachar:** (bc). **114 AA:** Graham Brandon / Victoria & Albert Museum, London (cra). **114-115 GI:** Stone / Ed Freeman (b). **115 GI:** De Agostini / S. Vannini (c); Universal Images Group (tl). **Photo Mendrea:** Radu Mendrea (br). **116 AI:** Timewatch Images (b). **Corbis:** The Gallery Collection (t). **117 BAL:** Delaware Art Museum, Wilmington (bc). **118 DK:** The British Museum, London / Alan Hills and Barbara Winter (c). **Photo Mendrea:** Dinu Mendrea (b). **119 AI:** ZR (br). **BAL:** (tl). **GI:** De Agostini (bc). **120-121 BAL:** Speke Hall, Merseyside / National Trust Photographic Library / John Hammond. **122 AI:** ZR (br). **BAL:** Bibliothèque Nationale de Paris (tr). **123 AKG:** Israel Images. **124 AKG. 125 AA:** Dagli Orti / Musée du Louvre, Paris (bl). **Corbis:** Hans Georg Roth (tc). **126 Corbis:** Annie Belt (b). **126-127 AI:** Chris Hellier. **127 AI:** Hanan Isachar (cb). **128 AI:** ASP Religion (r). **ZR:** (bl). **129 AKG:** (tc). **AI:** ZR (bc). **Hanan Isachar:** (tc). **130 AI:** ZR (tl). **AA:** Bodleian Library, Oxford (r). **131 AKG:** Erich Lessing (tr, br). **Corbis:** Hanan Isachar (bl). **132 AI:** MARKA (r). **ZR:** (cl). **133 AKG:** RIA Novosti (bl). **BAL:** Pierpont Morgan Library, New York (br). **GI:** BAL (tr). **134 AI:** ZR (bl). **GI:** Gallo Images / Danita Delimont (br). **135 AKG:** Erich Lessing (bc). **ZR:** (br). **Photo Scala, Florence:** Art Resource / The Metropolitan Museum of Art, New York (tl). **136 Corbis:** The Gallery Collection (bc). **ZR:** (tr). **137 AI:** ZR (cr, l). **GI:** BAL (br). **138 AKG:** Erich Lessing (b). **Corbis:** Yann Arthus-Bertrand (tr); Reuters (br). **138-139 DK:** Alan Hills and Barbara Winter (c) The British Museum. **139 Corbis:** Hanan Isachar (tl, br). **DK:** Christi Graham and Nick Nicholls (c) The British Museum (c, cr). **140 AI:** Timewatch Images (b). **GI:** SuperStock (t). **141 AKG:** Erich Lessing (bc). **142 BAL:** Mark Gallery, London. **143 AA:** Bodleian Library, Oxford (bl). **Hanan Isachar:** (tc). **144 Corbis:** Charles & Josette Lenars (tl). **144-145 AKG:** (bc). **145 AKG:** Oronoz (crb). **AI:** INTERFOTO (cra). **AA:** Dagli Orti / Agni Cathedral (tl). **146 AI:** INTERFOTO (r). **BAL:** Archives Charmet / Bibliothèque Sainte-Geneviève, Paris (cl). **147 AKG:** ullstein bild (cra). **AI:** ZR (bl). **148 AKG:** ZR (br). **149 AKG:** Erich Lessing (tc). **BAL:** National Gallery, London (br). **150 AKG:** British Library, London (cl). **Corbis:** David Butow (br).

151 AKG: (br); Erich Lessing (c). BAL: ZR (tl). 152 GI: The Image Bank / Marvin E. Newman. 153 AI: Israel Images (clb). AA: Gianni Dagli Orti / Bibliothèque Universitaire de Médecine, Montpellier (br). Corbis: Richard T. Nowitz (tc). 154 Corbis: Richard T. Nowitz (cla); Gianni Dagli Orti (bl). GI: BAL (tr). 155 Corbis: Ali Meyer. 156 AA: Dagli Orti / Szapiro Collection, Paris (cl). 156-157 AA: Dagli Orti / Palazzo Barberini, Rome (bc). 157 BAL: Canterbury Cathedral, Kent (tl). GI: BAL (cr). 158 Corbis: Arte & Immagini srl (cla). ZR: (b). 159 AKG: (tl). Corbis: (br). GI: BAL (bc). 160 AA: Dagli Orti / Bibliothèque Municipale, Arras (tl). GI: Gallo Images / Danita Delimont (bl). 161 AI: ZR (br). AA: Dagli Orti / Bibliothèque Municipale, Valenciennes (l). 162 Corbis: Hanan Isachar (tr). GI: Archive Photos (b). 163 BAL: Chartres Cathedral (cr); Ny Carlsberg Glyptotek, Copenhagen (br). GI: BAL (tc); The Image Bank / Cosmo Condina (bc). 164-165 BAL: Peter Willi / Musée National de la Renaissance, Ecouen. 166 BAL: Staatliche Kunstsammlungen, Dresden (t). 167 AKG: (cl); Erich Lessing (tr). Photo Scala, Florence: (bl). 168 AI: Imagestate Media Partners Ltd / Impact Photos (cb). Library Of Congress, Washington, D.C.: Matson Photograph Collection (tl). 169 GI: (tl). ZR: (tr). 170 Corbis: Alinari Archives. 171 AKG: Israel Images (br). Corbis: Richard T. Nowitz (bl). DK: Jewish Museum, London / Andy Crawford (tr). 172 AKG. 173 AA: Dagli Orti / Bibliothèque Municipale, Valenciennes (br). Corbis: Gianni Dagli Orti (tl, cr). 174 GI: Axiom Photographic Agency / Luke White (bl); Universal Images Group / Leemage (cla). 174-175 naturepl.com: Angelo Gandolfi (b). 175 Corbis: George Steinmetz (tl). GI: Manuel Cohen (br). 176 Corbis: Richard T. Nowitz (b). DK: British Museum (tr). 176-177 AI: Ivy Close Images. 177 DK: Alan Hills and Barbara Winter (c) The British Museum (cl); British Museum (cr, b). 178 AA: Dagli Orti / Palazzo Ducale Urbino. 179 AKG: British Library, London (tc). Corbis: Richard T. Nowitz (bl). ZR: (cra, br). 180 AKG: Erich Lessing (t). AI: Timewatch Images (b). 181 GI: BAL (bc). 182 BAL: Great Malvern Priory, Worcestershire (cra). GI: AFP (b). 183 AI: ZR (tr). Corbis: Hanan Isachar (br); National Geographic Society (bl). 184 BAL: The Royal Collection © 2011 Her Majesty Queen Elizabeth II (b). 185 AKG: Joseph Martin (bl). Corbis: EPA / Anatoly Maltsev (tl); Star Ledger / Aristide Economopoulos (br). 186 Corbis: Richard T. Nowitz (cl). DK: Christi Graham and Nick Nicholls (c) The British Museum (tr). Photo Scala, Florence: Metropolitan Museum of Art, New York (cr). 186-187 Corbis: Brooklyn Museum. 187 AKG: De Agostini Picture Library (ca); Sandro Vannini (ca). DK: Nick Nicholls / The British Museum (cr). 188

AA: Bodleian Library, Oxford (bl); Dagli Orti / Médiathque Francois Mitterand Poitiers (r). 189 AKG: Electa (tl). AI: Ian M. Butterfield (br). GI: BAL (bc). 190 Corbis: Sandro Vannini (tr). 190-191 Hanan Isachar: (bc). 191 BAL: Biblioteca Estense Universitaria, Modena (tr); Musée Condé, Chantilly / Giraudon (br). 192 AKG: Electa (t). AI: Timewatch Images (b). 193 ZR: (bc). 194 AKG: (c). GI: BAL (br). 195 AKG. 196 BAL: Richard and Kailas Icons, London (crb). Corbis: Annie Griffiths Belt (t). 197 AI: ZR (tl, bc). Corbis: Ottochrome / Nathan Benn (r). GI: BAL (br). 198 BAL: Staaliche Kunstsammlungen, Dresden. 199 AI: Peter Schickert (br); ZR (cr). Corbis: Gianni Dagli Orti (cl). 200 GI: SuperStock (bc). www.stpetersbasilica.org: (r). 201 AKG: Erich Lessing (cr). AA: Bibliothèque Municipale, Valenciennes (tl). Corbis: Alinari Archives (bc). GI: BAL (br). 202 AI: The Art Gallery Collection (cla). Photo Scala, Florence: (r). 203 AI: ZR (br). Corbis: Vanni Archive (cra). GI: Stone / Ben Edwards (bl). 204 AI: Israel Images (b). 205 AKG: ZR (tl); Israel Images (tr). AI: ZR (bc). GI: BAL (br). 206 GI: BAL. 207 AKG: (cla). GI: BAL (br). Photo Mendrea: Radu Mendrea (cra). 208 ZR: (b). 209 AKG: ZR (bc). AI: ZR (clb). Corbis: Araldo de Luca (cr). 210 AI: ZR (tl). BAL: Private Collection (b). 211 BAL: Kunsthistorisches Museum, Vienna (bl). GI: SuperStock (br). ZR: (tl). 212-213 AA: Coll. J. Vigne / Bibliothèque Municipale, Amiens / Kharbine-Tapabor. 214 GI: Photolibrary / SuperStock (b). 215 AKG: ZR (ca). DK: The British Museum, London / Alan Hills (bc). GI: De Agostini / G. Dagli Orti (cr). 216 AI: INTERFOTO (br); ZR (t). GI: De Agostini / G. Nimatallah (bl). 217 DK: The British Museum, London (bl). 218 Corbis: Sandro Vannini (bl). 218-219 AI: ZR. 219 AKG: Erich Lessing (br). AI: ZR (cr); Corbis: Roger Wood (c). DK: Alan Hills and Barbara Winter (c) The British Museum (bl). 220-221 AA: Dagli Orti / The British Museum, London. 222 AI: Bildarchiv Monheim GmbH (tl). BAL: ZR (ca). 222-223 Boston Public Library: (b). 223 AKG: Erich Lessing (cr). GI: BAL (tc). 224 AI: Timewatch Images (b). Corbis: Lebrecht Music & Arts (t). 225 AA: Coll. J. Vigne / Bibliothèque Municipale, Amiens / Kharbine-Tapabor (bc). AKG: (tl, clb). Corbis: Godong / P. Deliss (br). 227 Library Of Congress, Washington, D.C.: Matson Photograph Collection (tc). 228 AKG: Joseph Martin (b). AI: ZR (tl). 229 AKG: Israel Images (bc). AI: The Art Gallery Collection (cl); ZR (tr). 230 AA: Dagli Orti / Bibliothèque Municipale, Dijon (r). GI: BAL (bl). 231 AA: Dagli Orti / Museo Civico, Pescia (bl). Corbis: AA / Alfredo Dagli Orti (br); Reuters / Baz Ratner (tc). 232 Art History Images: Holly Hayes (t). 233 AI: ZR (bc). BAL: Photo © Agnew's, London (cra). GI: De Agostini / G. Dagli Orti (br). Hanan Isachar: (tl). 188

234 AI: Mohammed Khaluf (clb); ZR (bl). AA: Scrovegni Chapel Padua / SuperStock (tr). 235 AA: Dagli Orti / Bibliothèque Municipale, Valenciennes (cr). Corbis: The Gallery Collection (l). 236-237 AKG: Erich Lessing. 238 AKG: Erich Lessing (bl). 238-239 AI: AA (bc). 239 AA: Dagli Orti / Bibliothèque Municipale, Moulins (tc). Corbis: Ted Spiegel (cra). 240 Corbis: Arte & Immagini srl (bl). Hanan Isachar: (tr). 241 AKG. 242 AI: AA. 243 AKG: Erich Lessing (cl). BAL: De Agostini Picture Library / C. Sappa (cra). 244 AKG: (br). Photolibrary: Vivienne Sharp (cl). Press Association Images: AP Photo / Bullit Marquez (tr). 244-245 Corbis. 245 AI: AA (cl). Corbis: Gianni Dagli Orti (bl). DK: Alan Hills and Barbara Winter (c) The British Museum (tr, cla, c). 246 BAL: Mark Gallery, London. 247 AKG: (br). BAL: Ancient Art & Architecture Collection (cl). GI: De Agostini (tl). 248-249 GI: Superstock. 250 AA: Ashmolean Museum, Oxford (r). Corbis: The Gallery Collection (l). 251 AI: The Art Gallery Collection (cr); ZR (bc). Corbis: (tc). 252 AA: Gianni Dagli Orti / Archaeological Museum Cividale, Friuli (tl). GI: Axiom Photographic Agency / Chris Bradley (b). 253 BAL: Hamburger Kunsthalle, Hamburg (tl). Corbis: Christophe Boisvieux (tr). ZR: (c). 254 Corbis: Philippe Lissac / GODONG (tr); National Geographic Society / American Colony Photographers (cl); Carl & Ann Purcell (bc). 255 AKG: ZR (c). AI: ZR (bl). Corbis: Christel Gerstenberg (br); Frédéric Soltan / Sygma (bl); Gianni Dagli Orti (bc). DK: Peter Hayman (c) The British Museum (ca). Photo Scala, Florence: BPK, Berlin (tr). 256 AKG: Erich Lessing. 257 AKG: Erich Lessing (bc). Corbis: Christie's Images (cl). Hanan Isachar: (cra). 258 AI: ZR (cl). BAL: ZR (r). 259 AI: ZR (br). Corbis: Gianni Dagli Orti (br). 260 Corbis: Jean-Claude Varga (bl). AA: Dagli Orti / Bibliothèque Municipale, Arras (tl). Corbis: Gianni Dagli Orti (cb). ZR: (ca). 261 AI: Zoo Imaging Photography (b). Corbis: Arte & Immagini srl (tr). 262 AI: Timewatch Images (b). AA: Mudeo del Prado, Madrid (t). 263 Corbis: Richard T. Nowitz (bc). 264 DK: Alan Hills and Barbara Winter (c) The British Museum (tr). GI: Time & Life Pictures (b). 264-265 DK: British Museum. 265 AI: David Parker (b). Corbis: JAI / Julian Love (tl). DK: Nick Nicholls / The British Museum (cr). 266 AI: Print Collector (tr); ZR (cb, bl). 266-267 AKG: Andrea Jemolo. 267 AKG: Erich Lessing (tc). AI: Israel images (cl); ZR (br). 268 DK: Christi Graham and Nick Nicholls (c) The British Museum (tr). 268-269 DK: British Museum. 269 AI: imagebroker (cl). Corbis: JAI / Jon Arnold (bc); Reuters (tr). 270 Courtesy Israel Antiquities Authority: Photo Clara Amit (b). 270-271 Corbis: Jim Hollander. 271 AI: Hemis (tr); Colin Underhill (cl). Corbis: Roger Wood (cr). University of

Cambridge, University Library: (bc). 275 Corbis: Dave G. Houser (br). 276 GI: BAL (t); LOOK / H.&D. Zielske (b). 277 GI: SuperStock (bc). 278 AKG: Electa. 279 DK: The British Museum, London / Alan Hills and Barbara Winter (br). GI: De Agostini / G. Dagli Orti (bl); Robert Harding World Imagery (cl). 280-281 Corbis: The Gallery Collection. 282 AI: Globuss Images (ca). AA: Dagli Orti / Episcopal Museum Vic, Catalonia (cl). 283 AKG: Israel Images (br). AA: Coll. Jean Vigne / Bibliothèque Mazarine, Paris / Kharbine-Tapabor (l). 284 Corbis: Alinari Archives (r). GI: AFP (bl). 285 Corbis: Bettmann (tl); Araldo de Luca (br). ZR: (tr). 286-287 Corbis: Summerfield Press. 288 Corbis: Science Faction / Ctein (cla). 289 Corbis: Arte & Immagini srl (br). GI: BAL (t). 290 GI: SuperStock. 291 AI: Ryan Rodrick Beiler (br). AA: Dagli Orti / San Nicola Basilica, Tolentino (bl). BAL: The Stieglitz Collection (cl). 292 GI: Jonathan Blair (b). GI: BAL (cla). 293 GI: Universal Images Group / Leemage (bl). 294 GI: SuperStock. 295 AI: Horizon International Images (bl). BAL: Library of the Hungarian Academy of Science, Budapest (cl). Corbis: EPA / Oliver Weiken (cra). DK: The British Museum, London / Peter Hayman (br). 296 GI: LOOK / H.&D. Zielske (b); SuperStock / Peter Willi (t). 297 AA: Cleveland Museum of Art / SuperStock (bc). 298 GI: De Agostini / Veneranda Bibliotexa Ambrosiana (l); Flickr / Josef F. Stuefer (cr). 299 AA: Gianni Dagli Orti / Musée du Louvre, Paris (bl). GI: Hulton Archive / Imagno (br); SuperStock / Peter Willi (tc). 300-301 Corbis: Arte & Immagini srl. 302 Corbis: Richard T. Nowitz (br). GI: BAL (bl). 303 BAL: Ashmolean Museum, University of Oxford (br). Corbis: Francis G. Mayer (tr). GI: BAL (tl). 304 GI: National Geographic (bl). 304-305 AI: Steve Cavalier. 305 Corbis: Gianni Dagli Orti (c). DK: Alan Hills and Barbara Winter (c) The British Museum (br). 306 AI: ASP Religion (cla). Corbis: The Gallery Collection (b). 307 Corbis: Hanan Isachar (cr). GI: DEA / G. Dagli Orti (c). Library Of Congress, Washington, D.C.: Detroit Photographic Company (tl). 308 AKG: Erich Lessing (cr). AI: ZR (cl). Hanan Isachar: (br). 309 AI: Megapress. 310 Corbis: Richard T. Nowitz (bl). 310-311 Corbis: Dave G. Houser (bc). 311 AI: ASP Religion (tc). 312 Corbis: (b). 313 AA: Dagli Orti / Cathedral of St Just, Trieste (br). BAL: Vatican Museums and Galleries / Giraudon (tc). Hanan Isachar: (cra). 314 AKG: Erich Lessing (bl). 315 Corbis: Ali Meyer (bl). ZR: (tr). 316 Corbis: Richard T. Nowitz. 317 GI: BAL (bl). 318 DK: St Mungo, Glasgow Museums / Ellen Howdon (cl). 319 Corbis: Andy Aitchison / In Pictures (br); Dave Bartruff (c); Colin McPherson (bl); Reuters (cr). 320 AA: Dagli Orti / Armenian Museum, Isfahan (cla). GI: David Silverman (bc). 321 AKG: Erich

Lessing (cr). **322 Hanan Isachar:** (tr). **322-323 BAL:** Tula Museum of Fine Arts (b). **323 AKG:** (tc). **AA:** Dagli Orti / Sucevita Monastery, Moldavia (cr). **324 AI:** Eitan Simanor (tr). **AA:** Dagli Orti / Museo della Civilta Romana, Rome (bc). **325 The Bridgeman Art Library:** Neil Holmes (clb). **AA:** Dagli Orti / Museo del Bargello, Florence (br). **BAL:** Christchurch, Streatham, London (tr). **326 DK:** Judith Miller (cl). **GI:** Photodisc / Martin Child (cra). **327 Corbis:** Elio Ciol. **328 AKG:** Germanisches Nationalmuseum, Nuremberg (r). **329 AKG:** ullstein blld (br). **AI:** Robert Harding Picture Library (cra). **Corbis:** Gianni Dagli Orti (ca). **330 AI:** Eddie Gerald (tr). **331 AI:** ASP Religion (l). **Corbis:** Burnstein Collection (tr). **332 AKG:** Erich Lessing (bl). **AI:** ZR (cl). **332-333 AI:** Steve Cavalier. **333 AI:** Thornton Cohen (tr); Israel by Blake-Ezra Cole (c); ZR (crb). **DK:** Courtesy of the Museum of London (cl). **334 Corbis:** Images.com (bl). **335 AKG:** (clb). **AI:** Israel Images (cra). **336 AKG:** Oronoz (br). **AI:** ZR (cla). **Corbis:** The Gallery Collection (clb). **337 AA:** Dagli Orti / Musée des Antiquités, St Germain en Laye (cr); Jane Taylor (tl). **338 GI:** SuperStock (bc). **Hanan Isachar:** (tr). **339 AA:** SuperStock (t). **340 AKG:** ZR (br). **BAL:** Galleria degli Uffizi, Florence (tl). **Corbis:** Brooklyn Museum (bl). **341 AKG:** ZR (tc). **342-343 Photo Scala, Florence:** Art Resource / Photo Pierpont Morgan Library, New York. **344 AA:** Dagli Orti / Israel Museum, Jerusalem (tl); SuperStock / National Gallery of Art, Washington (clb); Dagli Orti / Musée des Beaux Arts, Dijon (bc). **345 AI:** Hanan Isachar (t). **BAL:** Musée Municipal, Dunkirk / Giraudon (bc). **346 AKG:** André Held (cra). **AI:** Hanan Isachar (bc). **Hanan Isachar:** (cla). **347 BAL:** National Gallery of Victoria, Melbourne (l). **348 AA:** Dagli Orti / Pharaonic Village, Cairo (cr). **GI:** The Image Bank / Chuck Fishman (cla). **349 AKG:** Erich Lessing (br). **Corbis:** The Gallery Collection (t). **350 AI:** The Art Gallery Collection (bl). **Corbis:** Robert Harding World Imagery / Gavin Hellier (tr). **351 AA:** Dagli Orti / Museo Campano, Capua (br). **GI:** Alinari Archives (bc). **352 AKG:** Erich Lessing (r). **AI:** ASP Religion (cl). **Hanan Isachar:** (bl). **353 AI:** ZR (bc). **GI:** De Agostini / G. Dagli Orti (c). **354 AA:** Dagli Orti / Anagni Cathedral (tl). **Corbis:** David Lees (clb). **Hanan Isachar:** (cra). **355 Corbis:** Summerfield Press. **356 BAL:** Biblioteca Reale, Turin / Alinari (t). **357 Corbis:** Lebrecht Music & Arts / ZR (tc). **ZR:** (bl). **358 AA:** Gianni Dagli Orti / Queretaro Museum, Mexico (bc). **359 AI:** ZR (t). **Corbis:** Michael Maslan Historic Photographs (bl). **Hanan Isachar:** (br). **360 Corbis:** AA / Alfredo Dagli Orti (b). **361 AA:** Dagli Orti / Museo Capitolino, Rome (br). **Hanan Isachar:** (tr). **362 AI:** Bruce Corbett (clb). **363 BAL:** Musée du Louvre, Paris (br). **364 BAL:** Bibliothèque Sainte-

Geneviève, Paris (cl); ZR (bl). **364-365 BAL:** Galleria dell'Accademia, Venice (bc). **365 AI:** The Art Gallery Collection (tl). **366 AI:** Hanan Isachar (tr). **Corbis:** David Lees (b). **366-367 BAL:** ZR. **367 AI:** ZR (bl). **BAL:** ZR (c). **Corbis:** Nathan Benn (br); Bojan Brecelj (cr). **368 AI:** Blickwinkel (b). **369 BAL:** Galleria dell'Accademia, Venica / Cameraphoto Arte Venezia (tl). **Corbis:** TH-Foto (bc). **Hanan Isachar:** (cra). **370 AI:** Bill Forbes (clb). **Corbis:** Richard T. Nowitz (c). **371 AA:** Dagli Orti / National Archaeological Museum, Chieti (c). **Corbis:** Arte & Immagini srl (b). **372 AA:** Alfredo Dagli Orti / Sucevita Monastery, Moldavia (b). **373 AI:** Israel Images (br). **Corbis:** Design Pics / Ron Nickel (bl). **GI:** Workbook Stock / Eitan Simanor (t). **374 AKG:** Erich Lessing (bl). **AA:** Gianni Dagli Orti / Musée du Louvre, Paris (cl); Dagli Orti / Rheinische Landesmuseum, Trier (br). **375 AKG:** Electa (tc); Erich Lessing (b). **376 AI:** Colin Underhill (cra). **AA:** Dagli Orti / Bardo Museum, Tunis (bl). **377 AKG:** Erich Lessing (br). **AI:** ZR (l). **GI:** De Agostini / G. Dagli Orti (tr). **378 Corbis:** Godong / Philippe Lissac (t). **GI:** LOOK / H.&D. Zielske (b). **379 AKG:** (bc). **380 Corbis:** Geoffrey Clements (b). **Library Of Congress, Washington, D.C.:** Detroit Photographic Company (cla). **381 AKG:** Erich Lessing (br). **382 ZR:** (cl, br). **383 AI:** ZR (tl). **BAL:** Musée des Beaux-Arts, Orleans / Giraudon (cr). **Corbis:** Benjamin Rondel (bc). **384 AA:** Dagli Orti / San Apollinare Nuovo, Ravenna (br). **Corbis:** Frank Krahmer (cl). **385 GI:** BAL. **386 DK:** Courtesy of The Museum of London / Dave King (bl). **Br Lawrence Lew, O.P.:** (cl). **386-387 AI:** ZR (bc). **387 Corbis:** Gianni Dagli Orti (br). **Photo Mendrea:** Dinu Mendrea (tl). **388-389 Corbis:** Elio Ciol. **390 AI:** MARKA (b). **DK:** Courtesy of the Ermine Street Guard / Andy Crawford (tl). **391 AI:** The Art Gallery Collection (br). **Corbis:** Richard T. Nowitz (bc). **392 Corbis:** Philadelphia Museum of Art. **393 BAL:** The Israel Museum, Jerusalem / Israel Antiquities Authority (bl). **Photo Mendrea:** Sandu Mendrea (tr). **394 Corbis:** Dave Bartruff (tr); John Nakata (bl); Richard T. Nowitz (br). **395 AKG:** François Guénet. **396 AA:** Dagli Orti / Saint Apollinare Nuovo, Ravenna (bc). **BAL:** The Israel Museum, Jerusalem (cla). **Corbis:** Richard T. Nowitz (cra). **397 Corbis:** EPA / Kobi Gideon (cr). **398 Corbis:** Elio Ciol (cla); National Geographic Society / Hans Hildenbrand (bl). **DK:** Katarzyna and Wojciech Medrzakowie (c). **399 Corbis:** Arte & Immagini srl (bl). **GI:** De Agostini / G. Dagli Orti (br); Gallo Images / Travel Ink (tr). **400-401 AKG:** Erich Lessing. **402 BAL:** National Museums of Scotland (cla). **Corbis:** Burstein Collection (bl); The Gallery Collection (r). **403 Corbis:** EPA / Jim Hollander (ca); Godong / P. Deliss (cr). **404 AA:** Dagli Orti / Bibliothèque Municipale, Abbeville (bl). **Corbis:** Richard T. Nowitz (br). **405 AA:**

Dagli Orti / Klosterneuburg Monastery, Austria (tr). **Corbis:** EPA / Jim Hollander (bc). **406 AI:** ZR (b). **Corbis:** Atlantide Phototravel (tr). **406-407 Corbis.** **407 AI:** Hemis (cl); Lebrecht Music & Arts Photo Library (cr); PhotoStock-Israel (tr); ZR (c). **Corbis:** David Lees (b). **408 Corbis:** AA / Alfredo Dagli Orti (r). **GI:** De Agostini / A. Dagli Orti (cl). **409 AA:** John Webb / National Gallery, London (bl). **Photo Mendrea:** Dinu Mendrea (cra). **410-411 BAL:** Schloss Sanssouci, Potsdam, Brandenburg / Alinari (t). **412 Corbis:** Hanan Isachar. **413 Corbis:** Christophe Boisvieux (clb). **GI:** BAL (cr). **Hanan Isachar:** (c). **414 BAL:** Galleria Doria Pamphilj, Rome / Alinari (t). **GI:** LOOK / H.&D. Zielske (b). **415 Corbis:** Arte & Immagini srl (bc). **416-417 GI:** SuperStock. **418 AI:** Colin Underhill (cl). **BAL:** Christie's Images (tr). **419 AA:** SuperStock / Eglisé Saint Thomas Aquinas, Paris (br). **BAL:** The Israel Museum, Jerusalem (tr). **Koninklijke Bibliotheek, The Hague:** (bl). **420 Corbis:** Sandro Vannini (l). **GI:** Robert Harding World Imagery (bc). **421 AKG:** Cameraphoto (cr). **AI:** Colin Underhill (bc); ZR (tc). **Corbis:** Sylvain Sonnet (cl). **422 AKG:** Erich Lessing (cl). **AI:** ZR (tr). **423 AKG:** Tristan Lafranchis (l). **GI:** Franco Origlia (br). **424-425 AA:** Dagli Orti / Biblioteca Capitolare, Vercelli. **426 AA:** Gianni Dagli Orti / Cava dei Tirreni Abbey, Salerno (tl). **GI:** Hulton Archive (r). **427 Corbis:** Robert Harding World Imagery / Gavin Hellier (r). **GI:** The Image Bank / Keenpress (cl). **428 Corbis:** AA / Alfredo Dagli Orti (br). **GI:** De Agostini / C. Sappa (clb); Photolibrary / Imagebroker / Egmont Strigl (cra). **429 BAL:** Galleria Balbi di Piovera, Genoa / Alinari. **430 AKG:** Erich Lessing (tr). **BAL:** Musée des Beaux-Arts, Arras / Giraudon (cl). **431 AKG:** Erich Lessing (bc). **AI:** Images & Stories (br). **Hanan Isachar:** (tl). **432 AI:** Wild Places Photography / Chris Howes (c). **BAL:** Santa Cecilia in Trastevere, Rome (clb). **433 AKG:** Sotheby's (bl). **AI:** PhotoStock-Israel (tl); ZR (br). **434 AA:** Alfredo Dagli Orti / Musée Archéologique, Naples (bl). **GI:** Photodisc / Steve Allen (br). **435 BAL:** Victoria & Albert Museum, London (tl). **GI:** De Agostini / W. Buss (cr). **436 AI:** Jon Arnold Images Ltd (bl). **437 AKG:** (tl). **GI:** De Agostini / A. de Gregorio (cr). **438 AI:** Images & Stories (br). **438-439 AI:** Rolf Richardson (b). **439 AKG:** Erich Lessing (br). **AA:** Bodleian Library, Oxford (tc). **GI:** SuperStock (cra). **440 Orthodox Church in America (http://oca.org):** (r). **441 AKG:** Erich Lessing (crb). **AA:** Dagli Orti / Abbey of Novacella or Neustift (tc). **ZR:** (bl). **442 AKG:** (cla). **AI:** Greece (clb). **GI:** De Agostini / A. Garozzo (br). **443 BAL:** Archives Charmet (tl); Musée National du Moyen Age et des Thermes de Cluny, Paris (cr). **444 AKG:** Pietro Baguzzi (bl). **Corbis:** Bettmann (t). **445 BAL:** Regional Art Museum,

Uzhgorod (tr). **DK:** ARF / TAP / Joe Cornish (cla). **GI:** Manuel Cohen (bc). **446 Corbis:** JAI / Michele Falzone (ca); Francis G. Mayer (cr). **447 AI:** Peter Horree (tl); INTERFOTO (bc). **GI:** Manuel Cohen (br). **448 AKG:** Leo G. Linder (bl). **AA:** Dagli Orti / Église Saint Sulpice, Paris (r). **449 BAL:** Biblioteca Estense Universitaria, Modena (tc). **Corbis:** Araldo de Luca (bl). **450 Corbis:** Roger Wood (b). **450-451 AI:** Robert Preston. **451 AI:** AA (br). **Evan Bench:** http://www.flickr.com/photos/ austinevan/2506337053 (bc). **Corbis:** Araldo de Luca (tl); Robert Harding World Imagery (bc). **452 DK:** Courtesy of the Ermine Street Guard / Gary Omler (tl). **GI:** BAL (cr). **453 AKG:** Erich Lessing (tl). **GI:** Gallo Images / Danita Delimont (cr). **454 Corbis:** Araldo de Luca (c); Sylvain Sonnet (br). **455 Corbis:** Vanni Archive (t); Araldo de Luca (br). **456 BAL:** Alan Jacobs Gallery, London (b). **457 BAL:** Canterbury Cathedral, Kent (br). **GI:** De Agostini (bl); Gallo Images / Danita Delimont (tr). **458 AA:** Dagli Orti / Ounacoteca Nazionale di Siena (t). **459 AKG:** Erich Lessing (tl). **Corbis:** Alinari Archives (br). **460 Corbis:** Arte & Immagini srl. **461 AKG:** ZR (br). **AI:** ZR (cl). **GI:** De Agostini / G. Dagli Orti (bl). **462 Corbis:** Atlantide Phototravel (cla). **GI:** BAL (b). **463 AI:** Sunpix Travel (bc). **BAL:** Metropolitan Museum of Art, New York (tr). **464 AKG:** (tr). **AA:** Dagli Orti / Accademia, Venice (cr). **465 AKG:** (bc). **AI:** The Art Gallery Collection (tl). **466 Corbis:** Nathan Benn (b); Araldo de Luca (tr). **466-467 AI:** Franck Fotos. **467 AKG:** Erich Lessing (c). **AI:** Yannick Luthy (bl). **Corbis:** Richard T. Nowitz (br). **DK:** Alan Hills and Barbara Winter (c) The British Museum (cl). **470-483 GI:** Universal Images Group / Leemage (b). **484-489 Corbis:** Radius Images (b). **Front Endpapers: Corbis:** The Gallery Collection; **Back Endpapers: GI;** Universal Images Group / Leemage.

All other images © Dorling Kindersley
For further information see:
www.dkimages.com